Human Rights or Religious Rules?

Empirical Research in Religion and Human Rights

VOLUME 1

Human Rights or Religious Rules?

By

Johannes A. van der Ven

BRILL

LEIDEN • BOSTON
2010

This book is printed on acid-free paper.

Library of Congress Cataloging-in-Publication Data

Ven, J.A. van der, 1940–
  Human rights or religious rules? / by Johannes A. van der Ven.
    p. cm. — (Empirical research in religion and human rights ; v. 1)
  Includes bibliographical references (p.   ) and indexes.
  ISBN 978-90-04-18304-9 (hardback : alk. paper)
1. Human rights—Religious aspects. I. Title. II. Series.

  BL65.H78V458 2010
  201'.723—dc22

                                                      2010002262

ISSN 1877-881X
ISBN 978 90 04 18304 9

Copyright 2010 by Koninklijke Brill NV, Leiden, The Netherlands.
Koninklijke Brill NV incorporates the imprints Brill, Hotei Publishing,
IDC Publishers, Martinus Nijhoff Publishers and VSP.

PRINTED IN THE NETHERLANDS

CONTENTS

ACKNOWLEDGEMENTS

My research into religion and human rights dates back to 1993, when what was known as an interim constitution was being negotiated at Kempton Park in South Africa on the eve of its first democratic elections in 1994, when Nelson Mandela became the country's first democratically elected state president. Together with my colleagues Hennie Pieterse and Jaco Dreyer at the University of South Africa, I set a project for a survey among senior secondary school students to explore the relation between religion and human rights. We regarded the students as the future carriers of a human rights culture and were curious whether and to what extent their religious beliefs and participation in religious rites contributed positively to their attitudes towards human rights. The project resulted in many articles and culminated in a book, *Is There a God of Human Rights? The Complex Relationship between Human Rights and Religion: a South African Case*, International Studies in Religion and Society, Volume 2, Brill, Leiden 2004. I thank my two colleagues for our free exchange and stimulating development of ideas, the fruits of which I still cherish and on which I look back gratefully and pleasurably.

Since then the topic of religion and human rights has continued to haunt me. Historical, empirical, and systematic research into it found a fertile matrix in the International Research Programme Human Rights and Religion. The programme has a twofold comparative perspective. The first is a cross-cultural research perspective, implemented by colleagues in some ten European, African, and Asian countries with the aid of an identical questionnaire, translated into eight languages and designed for students at the end of their secondary or the start of their tertiary education. The second comparative perspective concerns the composition of the research population in these countries. It comprises a Christian and a Muslim group, sometimes augmented with a nonreligious group as in European countries or with a Hindu group as in India. Collaboration with colleagues from such diverse parts of the world poses a constant scientific challenge. Regular discussions with colleagues of the Centre for Ethics at Radboud University, Nijmegen, was also a source of ever new ideas. Critical and constructive exchange of opinions with colleagues of the Faculty of Law at Radboud University continually stimulated fresh insights and the reinterpretation and reformulation of previously gained insight. I am very thankful to my academic assistant, Claudia Sarti, because she responsibly took care of the data collection, literature search, footnotes, bibliography and so many other things. I am also very grateful to Marcelle Manley for the professional translation of this book.

The present study is the product of all these forms of collaboration, as well as numerous lectures and papers and the debates about these. In all this oral and written communication there are three key themes: systematic research into religion (chapters 1–3); partly historical, partly systematic research into religion and human rights (chapters 4–6); and finally empirical research into religion and a human rights culture, focusing on religious freedom and the separation of church and state among Christian, Muslim, and nonreligious youths in the Netherlands. Data for this purpose were collected in 2007–2008 (chapters 7–9).

The book forms part of the aforementioned International Research Programme. It comprises the following chapters.

Chapter 1, "Varieties of Religious Weakness and Strength", is based in part on a lecture, entitled 'The Future of Religion', which was given at the University of Groningen on the occasion of the opening of the new building for the Faculty of Theology and Religious Studies in 2002. It also draws on a 2005 lecture for the Conference of the International Academy of Practical Theology (IAPT) at the Catholic University in Brisbane, Australia, entitled "The Multicultural Drama, Religion's Failure and Challenge", and on another lecture given in 2005 to some Dutch universities, entitled "Is Religion out of Date?" (*Is religie achterhaald?*).[1] In part, the chapter is also based on an article entitled, "Where Do Religious Variations Come From?" (*Waar komen verschillen in religie vandaan?*), which was first published in *Tijdschrift voor Theologie*,[2] and later republished, in a somewhat modified form, under the title, "Three Paradigms for the Study of Religion".[3]

---

[1] In J.A. van der Ven (ed.), *Geloof en verlichting* (Faith and Enlightenment), Damon/Soeterbeeck programme, Budel/Nijmegen 2007, 11–44.
[2] In *Tijdschrift voor Theologie* 46(2006)2, 161–180.
[3] In H. Streib (ed.), *Religion Inside and Outside Traditional Institutions*, Empirical Studies in Theology, Volume 15, Brill, Leiden 2007, 7–35.

Chapter 2, "Aspects of Religious Identity", stems from some basic ideas given in my *Formation of the Moral Self*,[4] and from a 2006 lecture to the International Society of Empirical Research in Theology (ISERT) in Bangor, North Wales. It also stems from an article entitled, "Towards a Spirituality of Human Rights" (*Naar een mensenrechtenspiritualiteit*),[5] which was subsequently incorporated into another article: "Religious Identity in Comparative Research".[6]

Chapter 3, "Reflective Comparison in Religious Research", stems from a 2001 lecture given at the 147th anniversary of the Theological University of the Reformed Churches in the Netherlands in Kampen, entitled, "From a Faculty of Theology to a Faculty of Religious Sciences" (*Van een faculteit der theologie naar een faculteit der religiewetenschappen*).[7] This lecture was subsequently revised and published as an article entitled, "Doing Theology in a Faculty of Religious Sciences" (*Theologie beoefenen in een faculteit voor religiewetenschappen*),[8] revised again into "The Relation between Theology and Science of Religion in Comparative Research" (*De relatie van theologie en religiewetenschap in een vergelijkende wetenschapsbeoefening*),[9] and revised yet again for a 2005 lecture at Goethe University, Frankfurt/Main Universiteit. It was eventually published as an article entitled "Reflective Comparativism in Religious Research".[10] Finally, the chapter contains some revised elements from an article entitled, "The Academic Theologian: Believer or Scholar?" (*De universitaire theoloog: gelovige of wetenschapper?*).[11]

Chapter 4, "Human rights: Religious or Nonreligious?", dates back to a 2008 lecture presented to the Institute of Social Studies in The Hague, to a 2009 lecture for the Conference for Eastern Theology at the Institute of Eastern Christianity, Radboud University, and to lectures given in 2009 to some academic institutions in the Philippines,

---

[4] Eerdmans, Grand Rapids 1998.
[5] In *Speling* 59(2007)4, 71–79.
[6] In L. Francis, M. Robbins & J. Astley (eds.), *Empirical Theology in Texts and Tables*, Empirical Studies in Theology, Vol. 17, Brill, Leiden 2009, 41–72.
[7] Kamper Oraties 19, Kampen 2001.
[8] In *Tijdschrift voor Theologie* 42(2002)3, 244–267.
[9] In *Tijdschrift voor Theologie* 45(2005)2, 119–137.
[10] In H.-G. Heimbrock & Chr. Scholz (eds.), *Religion: Immediate Experience and the Mediacy of Research, Interdisciplinary Studies, Concepts and Methodology of Empirical Research in Religion*, Vandenhoeck & Ruprecht, Göttingen 2007, 77–114.
[11] In W. van den Bercken (ed.), *Tussen professie en confessie, Wat geloven theologen?*, Damon, Budel 2008, 156–179.

including Silliman University in Dumaguette City plus three institutions in Manilla: the Institute of Spirituality in Asia, the Institute of Formation and Religious Studies, and De La Salle University.

Chapter 5, "Human rights: Natural or Political", is the outcome of a study into the social doctrine of the Catholic Church, which was conducted at the Centre for Ethics of Radboud University and resulted in the article, "Legitimisation of Human Rights From the Perspective of Nature or Politics?" (*Legitimering van mensenrechten vanuit natuur of politiek?*).[12]

Chapter 6, "Religious Rights for Minorities?", stems from a 2006 lecture given at the University of Aarhus, a 2007 lecture for the Conference of the International Academy of Practical Theology (IAPT) at Humboldt University in Berlin, and a discussion at the Centre for Ethics at Radboud University in 2007 – all of which culminated in an article, "Religious Rights for Minorities?" (*Religieuze rechten voor minderheden?*).[13] This article was later revised into an article entitled, "Religious Rights for Minorities in a Policy of Recognition".[14]

Chapter 7, "Religious Freedom", derives from the following: an article entitled "Religious Freedom and the Public Church",[15] another article entitled "Toward a More Comprehensive Religious Freedom",[16] a discussion of the chapter at the Centre for Ethics at Radboud University in 2009, and yet another article entitled "A Balanced Freedom of Religion" (*Godsdienstvrijheid in balans).*[17]

Chapter 8, "Separation of Church and State", stems from a 2007 lecture given at the University of Copenhagen and a 2008 lecture to the International Society of Empirical Research in Theology (ISERT) at the University of Würzburg. These were later revised into an article entitled "Separation of Church and State and Freedom of Religion: Left to the Gods?[18]

---

[12] In M. Becker (ed.), *Christelijk sociaal denken, traditie, actualiteit, kritiek*, Damon, Budel 2009, 244–278.

[13] In *Tijdschrift voor Theologie* 47(2007)1, 65–84.

[14] *Religion and Human Rights* 3(2008), 155–183.

[15] In R. Osmer & F. Schweitzer (eds.), *Developing a Public Faith*, Chalice Press, St. Louis 2003, 180–202.

[16] In F.M. Shepherd (ed.), *Christianity and Human Rights,* Rowman & Littlefield, New York 2009.

[17] In *Tijdschrift voor Theologie* 49(2009) 4, 346–372.

[18] H.-G. Ziebertz & L.J. Francis (eds.), *The Public Significance of Religion*, Brill, Leiden 2010.

Chapter 9, "Impact of Religion on Attitudes towards Religious Freedom and Separation of Church and State", is based on a paper given at the first conference of the International Programme of Human Rights and Religion at Radboud University in 2008, a lecture to PhD graduates in empirical theology and empirical religious studies at Radboud University in 2009, and a paper given at the University of Oslo in 2009.

LIST OF FIGURES AND TABLES

FIGURES

TABLES

INTRODUCTION

The many problems facing society today often raise the question of where to find ideals, principles, values and norms to deal with them. It starts with marriage and the family: how do we promote equality between husband and wife? What ideals are worth passing on to our children and future generations? How do we strike a balance between protecting our private lives and the social tasks awaiting us in our neighbourhood, suburb, city and region? The latter already takes us from the micro level of emotional security in a small, intimate circle, to the meso level of social groups, communities and institutions. Here too there are umpteen questions. What values and norms protect society against disintegration and ensure an inspiring context that people would like to belong to and from which they derive their identity? Are they the rules of the economy? But which economy? The neo-liberal one or the Rhineland model, which interrelates economic and social life? Or do we use the rules of politics? But which politics? The bureaucratised politics of the state or the politics of a deliberative democracy, rooted in civil society? Do we apply the rules of education? But which education? One in which teachers act as producers and students are their products, or education aimed at human dignity, freedom, equality and solidarity? Are they the rules of the law? But which law? One in which one looks for loopholes to pursue personal profit, or what was traditionally known as 'just law'? Maybe the rules of sport. But which sport? Grinding, exploitive, exhausting sport, or sport aimed at joyous human re-creation? At the macro level of international relations such questions are even more pressing and also greater – well-nigh infinite in their magnitude. I am writing this introduction in 2009, at a time when, starting in 2008, we find ourselves in a global financial, and, concomitantly, economic crisis, the outcome of blind, neo-liberal faith in 'the market'. The real victims are those at the underside of society, especially the millions of large and small groups of people in developing countries. The World Bank estimates that the world's poor that have to get by on less than two dollars a day has grown to one and a half billion as a result of the economic crisis. The Unesco report, *A Matter of Magnitude: the Impact of the Economic Crisis on Women and Children in South Asia* (June 2009), describes the situation in that part of the Asian continent which includes Afghanistan, Bangladesh, India, Nepal, Pakistan and Sri Lanka. Two thirds of the 20% of the world population that live there subsist on less than two dollars a day.

HUMAN RIGHTS AND RELIGION

On the basis of which values and norms should we tackle this overwhelming number of problems? In this book I deal with two approaches to this multitude of problems. The first is a human rights approach, the second a religious approach, which includes religious morality.

The first clear signs of the first – the human rights – approach are evident in the sharp protest by 16th century Spanish groups against the enslavement, exploitation and genocide of the indigenous American population, the Indians, and the fight for their rights. A few centuries later this culminated in the consolidation of these rights in institutions in which human rights were entrenched. The first of these institutions were the democratic constitutions of America and France in 1791.

The second – the religious – approach, including religious morality, is characteristic of all religions that since time immemorial have championed justice, solidarity and love and handed these values down from one generation to the next. Whether it is justice in the codex of Hammurabi, compassion in Asian religions, the duty to help widows, orphans, the poor and strangers in the Jewish Bible, universal solidarity and love in the Second Testament, or righteousness in the Qur'an – they all emphasise the moral duty to care for the indigent, needy other.

Nonreligious people opt for the first approach, that of human rights. They prefer direct, active, subjective rights that are rooted in the dignity of the human person in a democratic legal order in which the people are sovereign, and not an extramundane, sacred order with a divine sovereign at the top, represented, as they see it, by non-elected religious leaders that consider themselves entitled to dispense with any accountability to the people. They are also mistrustful of the moral claims of religions because of the way they easily tend to erase from their collective memory the many forms of bodily and mental violence, inquisition and genocide perpetrated in their name in the course of history.

Adherents of the various religions, on the other hand, tend to opt for the second approach, that of religious morality, not only because it is an extension of their religious beliefs, but also because they may have some objections to human rights. They are said to be products of Western individualism, centring on self-concern and personal profit, with little regard for social relations or commitment to the community. In addition, religious adherents are critical about the foundation of human rights in the absence of a divine order. Is the dignity of the human person not a shaky basis? Does a doctrine of human dignity allow for recognition of historical contingency, human fallibility and evil to be qualified as human guilt? Does it offer sufficient protection in times of disaster caused by dictatorships, wars and terrorism? Do we not need a higher, ultimately supreme, unshakable guarantee of order, justice, reconciliation and, ultimately, love: God?

Choosing between the two – the human rights approach or that of religion and religious morality – is not easy. On the one hand, it should be noted that the aforementioned groups who protested against the cruel treatment of the indigenous population at the time of the 'discovery' of America belonged to the Catholic Dominican order in Spain. And the groups that were a major influence on the foundational documents of America, such as the Virginia Bill of Rights of 1776 and the United States Bill of Rights of 1789, included English dissenters, especially Puritans, Congregationalists, Baptists, Anabaptists, Moravians and Methodists. On the other hand, the most fervent champions of religious freedom were people who had to a greater or lesser extent shaken off the power of religion. It was mainly these people who put an end to the ferocious, bloody, prolonged and constantly recurring religious wars by introducing the separation of church and state, which is an indispensable condition for human rights. And it was they who defended the freedom of religion and selflessly championed the oppressed, marginalised religious minorities in their struggle against the religious majority, who were usually entrenched behind the unassailable walls of a state religion or state church.

HUMAN RIGHTS OR RELIGIOUS RULES?

Against this background it should be clear why I chose *Human Rights or Religious Rules?* as the title for this book on human rights and religion, and why I appended a question mark to it. Is it in fact a choice, or can one find or build a bridge, whether wide or narrow, allowing some sort of traffic between the historically divided banks of human rights and religious morality?

The term 'human rights' in the title refers to what are known as the three generations, even though this term needs some qualifications: the first generation of civic liberties, political and judicial rights; the second generation of economic, social and cultural rights; and the third generation of collective rights, including the rights to development, a healthy environment, peace, co-ownership of the common heritage of humankind, and the right to communicate. One qualification is that the three generations represent a descending order of enforceable juridical rights and an ascending order of non-enforceable moral appeals.

The term 'religious rules' in the title has a long history of various meanings, from which I cite only one salient aspect. Here it is not used in the sense that it has been used for the past millennium and a half or more (!). Its initial meaning was broader than what Tertullian had in mind in the 3rd century. He confined religious rules (*regula fidei*) to rules that governed the dogmatic core of the faith. It also had a polemical connotation against religious monarchianism, which claimed that God was only one person, thus denying the trinity. In later ages, too, religious rules were confined to the dogmatic *proprium* of the faith, especially in the era of Catholic and Protestant confessionalism, when the controversy about the trinity made way for the dispute about the authority of Scripture versus that of tradition and ecclesiastic office. But prior to this dual restriction (to dogmatics and polemical dogmatics), hence pre-Tertullian, the original meaning of religious rules was far broader, all but holistic. Until the middle of the 2nd century, for example, the 'rules of our tradition' referred to the entire corpus of beliefs and practices that one finds in the works of Clement of Rome and others of that period. These are not purely dogmatic rules, but have various other aspects, such as spiritual, moral, disciplinary, sapiential and educational aspects, which in the practical, everyday lives of, one might say, all 'ordinary' believers, constitute a unity and can only be classified in distinct areas on closer analysis and reflection. The term 'religious rules' in the title of this book is used in this original, practical-holistic sense.

Indeed, as noted already, the choice between human rights and religious rules is not easy. The problem becomes even more acute if one does not confine oneself to the past but includes contemporary history as well. On the one hand, one faces the question whether religions genuinely engage with human rights or merely pay them lip service. Are they really moved by the problems of overpopulation, and, at the same time, the carnage that a pandemic like HIV/aids wreaks among the population? How do religious leaders justify the continued invocation of abstract principles like 'natural law' to oppose a concrete approach such as the common sense use of condoms? On the other hand one cannot deny that many religious groups at the grassroots devote great energy to the development of a human rights culture, which is essential for the active application of human rights in society. Without that culture, human rights degenerate into a beautiful but rapidly yellowing parchment in a museum showcase. But does it not suggest hypocrisy, one might add, that religions should vociferously advocate the application of these rights outside their own communities, but sometimes erect a divinely based barrier to their observance within their own walls?

Division into Chapters

These are the sort of complications explored in this book, not in the hope of solving them – that would be presumptuous – but to clarify them through patient historical, empirical and theoretical research.

To this end I confine myself to three themes, dealt with successively in the three parts of this book: religion and religions, religion and human rights, and religion and a human rights culture.

The first part is on religion and religions. It is an important theme, because in many publications on human rights religion not only gets a rough deal, but is often presented in a manner that almost fully identifies it with conservatism, even fundamentalism, or, worse still, terrorism. This part covers variations within religions and the various positions of religions in society: weak and strong, dwindling and growing, and the causes of these (chapter 1). In the midst of these diverse positions there is increasing interest these days, greater than in the past, in the religious identity of majority and minority groups. What is religious identity, what is the relation between continuity and discontinuity in that identity, and what hermeneutic and empirical aspects does it have (chapter 2)? The study of religions in society should take into account its substantial attributes without reducing it to social and psychological phenomena, and should research it both from an empathic inside perspective and the outside perspective of observation. From the combination of both perspectives, the question of 'true religion' (*religio vera*) might be approached in terms of religious 'orthopraxis' in the perspective of human rights (chapter 3).

The conclusion thus reached leads as a matter of course to the second part on religion and human rights. Is the foundation of human rights religious or nonreligious, or does it require an open approach that can be filled from a variety of religious and nonreligious perspectives (chapter 4)? Can human rights be characterised as natural rights inferred from natural law (imbedded in the divine order), or should they be interpreted in terms of the political struggle that oppressed, marginalised groups have fought in the course of history, such as citizens and peasants under the feudal order, workers under the capitalist system, blacks under apartheid, women and homosexuals in the current age of repressive tolerance (chapter 5)? The relevance of human rights is particularly evident in the interaction between majority and minority groups. The majority can take care of itself, and does so in legislation, administration and jurisprudence. This gives rise to the challenging notion that when religious minorities want to deviate from a given social norm, the onus of proof is on the majority (i.e. the state), not on the minority. Does it mean that religious minorities must be able to claim distinctive religious rights, for instance Muslim minorities in the area of personal and family law (chapter 6)?

The key question in the third part is whether, and if so to what extent, human rights are accepted as indicative of the existence of a human rights culture among religious groups as well as nonreligious groups in particular countries, in this case the Netherlands. The part of the Dutch population investigated in the final chapters comprises three groups of Christian, Muslim and nonreligious youths, as will be indicated at the end of this introduction.

The first theme to be examined is religious freedom. Having traced its historical development from oppression via passive tolerance to active tolerance, and, eventually, religious freedom, I try to determine empirically whether, and if so to what extent, the three groups of youths subscribe to religious freedom (chapter 7).

Next I deal with the separation of church and state. First I look at the historical relationship between church and state – from theocracy to church and state union to an autonomous state and eventually separation of church and state. Then I empirically examine whether, and if so to what extent, the three groups of youths endorse this constitutional principle. I focus on two problems in the area where morality affects church and state directly, namely the *res mixtae*, in this case political autonomy in regard to euthanasia and abortion respectively (chapter 8).

Then I examine the empirical question whether, and if so to what extent, religion actually has a positive or negative impact on attitudes towards religious freedom and separation of church and state. This question is important in that the answer can shed light on the contribution of religions to a human rights culture. First, the three groups of youths' religious beliefs and their participation in religious rites are examined empirically. Then follows an empirical analysis of the effects of both beliefs and ritual participation on attitudes towards religious freedom and separation of church and state. Then I reflect on the research findings from the angle of differences between religious beliefs, making distinctions between non-morally laden and morally laden beliefs, and between beliefs relating to the culture of the religion and those relating to its structure. The first two (non-morally laden beliefs and beliefs relating to the culture of the religion) appear to have a slight, ambiguous effect. The second two (morally laden beliefs and beliefs relating to structure) have a rather strong, unambiguous effect on attitudes towards religious freedom and separation of church and state (chapter 9).

These findings relate to the question the title of this book contains: 'Human Rights or Religious Rules?' To some extent religion may contribute to human rights, specifically to human rights culture, which means that in that regard the answer should not be formulated in terms of mutual exclusion but in terms of support: human rights may be supported by religious rules.

Finally, a comment on the three groups of youths I studied empirically: the Christian, Muslim, and nonreligious group. In the empirical study, for which the data were collected in 2007–2008, we chose youths in the Netherlands at the end of their secondary or the start of their tertiary education. The Christian youths represent the Christian culture that forms part of the cradle of Western civilisation in the Netherlands and plays an active role, at varying levels of intensity, in that culture. The Muslim youths represent a qualitatively significant, and in major cities a quantitatively significant minority in Dutch society, which has put the theme of religion high on the political agenda. The nonreligious youths represent the largest part of the Dutch population, which over the past 50 years – like the neighbouring populations of the Netherlands, Belgium and Germany, some Nordic and Baltic countries and other East European countries like the Czech Republic – has seen a drastic decline in religious faith and participation. The first group consisted of 340 Christians, the second of 235 Muslims, and the third of 479 nonreligious youths – together 1054 youths. The three groups are pertinent to a human rights culture, because in the near future they will be the leaders on the micro and meso levels of society. The (continued) support of human rights will largely depend on them.

PART ONE

RELIGION

CHAPTER ONE

VARIETIES OF RELIGIOUS WEAKNESS AND STRENGTH

The religious state of the world today cannot be captured in a single image, if that was ever possible. In the West, particularly in Europe, there are two contrary phenomena. The one is religious weakness caused by decline, especially of the Christian religion; the second is religious strength as a result of resurgence, especially of Muslim religiosity. The long-term outcome of these two developments, whether they will influence each other and what effect that would have, are unpredictable, although there are plenty of opinions. One is that religious weakness will persist in the West and will probably drag Islam down with it. Another is that Muslim strength will persist and will pull the Christian groups upwards. A third view is that the two religions exist independently, and if they continue to develop will do so independently in whatever direction, upwards or downwards, linear or curvilinear.

Irrespective of the predictive value of such opinions, they make religious research in the West a complex but also a fascinating enterprise. The diversity of religious phenomena – that of decline and ascendance – is the feature of the religious landscape that hits one in the eye. I do not fool myself into thinking that I can reduce this variety to a few clear insights, nor is that my intention. All I hope to do is to sketch in broad outline both the religious phenomena themselves and some strategies for researching them.

This chapter first examines religious weakness in the West, more especially in Europe, to demonstrate that this is not a superficial, short-lived phenomenon but the outcome of a far-reaching process stretching over several centuries. It is by no means clear at this stage whether it entails a 'transformation of religion'. Added to that is the problem created by the strength of Islam and its influence on Western society, specifically from the perspective of cultural and religious integration. These two developments make religion in the West a complex and variegated phenomenon (1.1).

Next I propose some strategies that can be used to direct research into the variations of religious weakness and strength. Here I settle for three paradigms: one for researching religious variations between and within countries (macro level), one to study religious variations within countries and intergroup variations (meso level), and one for examining variations between individual group members (micro level). The first strategy I label the secularisation paradigm, the second the economic paradigm, and the third the cognitive paradigm (1.2).

1.1   Complexity of Religious Weakness and Strength

It is sometimes said that religion is back after a period of absence, but the question is whence it has returned and whether it is still the same religion. In Europe, at any rate, there are no signs of a revival of Christianity, and the religion one finds outside it is a different one – Islam. For the time being, the weakness of Christianity continues unabated, simply because the younger generation has dropped out or is dropping out. Islam, by contrast, is conspicuous for its strength. This is largely a result of demographic factors such as the formation or reunion of families and a higher birth rate among Muslim migrants. What is back is religion on the political agenda, the causes being the a-synchronous decline and weakness of Christianity and the ascendance and strength of Islam, and the consequences this has for the multicultural societies that are increasingly manifesting in Western countries.

1.1.1   *Religious Weakness*

Whatever you think of popular TV programmes, to some extent they are a mirror of everyday culture. That applies not only to soaps, but also to talk shows and survival programmes like *Robinson Island*. They bring to light what lives in people's minds, what longings they have, what feelings and ideas they cherish. But they skip things that do not live in their minds, that do not occupy them from day to day, that they disregard. One such thing is religion. In the Netherlands, for instance, religion hardly features in soaps other than by way of conventional marriage and burial services. In talk shows, religion, if it features at all, is mostly an objectionable or ludicrous topic or something one has to put up with: objectionable because society finds it tiresome; ludicrous because some people, it is suggested, still seem to hang on to an outdated illusion; or to be tolerated because there are far more harmful developments in society than religion. In survival programmes, shot on idyllic islands with blue seas and golden beaches, it never enters the heads on those bronzed bodies that they house the image of God. The implicit message of these popular programmes is that the secularised tabernacle we gape at every night is empty.

But not totally empty, there is still a residue: a 'something-ism' (Dutch: *ietsisme*), a sort of 'something-ist' religion among people who do not believe in a personal God but still have faith in 'Something': "There is Something more," these adherents insist. Ronald Plasterk, once an internationally prominent microbiologist, now minister of education, culture, and science in the Netherlands, believed himself to be the originator of the term *'ietsisme'*, unaware of the fact that in his *A Common Faith* the great American philosopher John Dewey wrote about God as *Something more* as far back as the first half of the 20th century. Later Plasterk changed his rather pejorative judgment of *ietsisme*, because he preferred it, he said ironically, to another -ism: fundamentalism.

What has caused the religious decline and weakness in the West in countries where this is the dominant scenario, such as the Netherlands – together with its neighbours Belgium and Germany, some Nordic and Baltic states, and other East European states like the Czech Republic among the religiously weakest countries in Europe? To give some indication of the situation, in the period 1966–2006, the percentage of church members in the Dutch population dropped by 28% from 67% to 39%, and regular church attendance by 34% from 50% to 16%.[1]

To answer the question, I fall back on the theory that sees decline of religion and its resultant weakness as the outcome of a modernisation process that has spread to the rest of the world from its source – the mercantilist capitalism of Northwestern Europe – eventually developing into industrial capitalism. It is not a matter of a changing trend lasting only a few years, nor even a structural change, however many decades it may take, but of what is known as *longue durée*: change over several centuries that radically affects society and thus penetrates religion as well.[2]

According to this theory, modernisation has four aspects. The first is economic modernisation. Put simply, when industrialisation

---

[1] T. Bernts, G. Dekker & J. de Hart, *God in Nederland 1996–2006*, Ten Have, Kampen 2007.

[2] H. McLeod & W. Ustorf (eds.), *The Decline of Christendom in Western Europe 1750–2000*, Cambridge University Press, Cambridge 2003.

supplanted home industries, commercial markets emerged, profit
became the prime consideration and competition replaced cooperation; that was when peaceful family and village communities with the
church at their centre ceased to exist. When farming became an industry, agricultural land and its cultivation came to be expressed in terms
of capital and labour, livestock turned into production units, and small
farmers grew into major entrepreneurs serving markets extending far
beyond national and even continental boundaries – that was when
the heavenly canopy that once spanned harmonious life in the home,
the countryside, and the church collapsed. Whatever one makes of it, the
process of economic modernisation is unstoppable; all one can do is to
channel and counteract the adverse effects on deprived groups that the
process creates. That is what happened in what is known as the Rhineland model, of which the Scandinavian model is a variant form.

The second aspect is political modernisation. Economic liberalisation demanded liberalisation of the governmental structure of society,
from which liberal democracy was born. This democracy replaced the
alliance of king, nobility, and clergy, also known as the alliance of
throne and altar. The contract that citizens entered into with themselves culminated in a constitution characterised by separation of
church and state, civil liberties, later expanded into human rights,
and the checks and balances of separation of powers. Through bodies
of popular representatives citizens impose their will on the government of society. As is evident both in history and in our own day, the
churches – which have always adapted to the prevailing social model,
such as that of the Roman empire, the feudal Middle Ages, and the
absolute monarchy – are still dubious about the separation of church
and state, view democracy ambivalently, and in several respects pay
lip service to human rights, at least inasmuch as they refuse to apply
them within their own walls.

The third aspect is social modernisation. It relates mainly to migration from the countryside to the cities, whereupon the intimate village
communities of yore made way for urban agglomerates in which people consort freely with friends and relatives in their own context and
beyond that interaction is predominantly instrumental and functional.
Thus the bond between family, school, and the church was dissolved.
The family has shed many of its functions; schools concentrate on pre-
paring students for the labour market; and the church has lost it focal
position and finds shelter in obscure neighbourhoods. The upshot of
all this is a loosening of traditional social ties, loss of social cohesion,
and increasing individualisation – at any rate in regard to religion.

The fourth and final aspect is cultural modernisation. This finds expression in the replacement of values from the premodern period, whose validity derived from tradition and authority, with norms that support and direct the modernisation process in the aforementioned three areas. One example is the cultural codes accompanying demographic development. In premodern times, birth control, necessary to maintain a balance between death and birth rates, was governed by codes of taboos, such as the prohibition of premarital sex and the norm of relatively late marriages with a view to responsible conduct of a household. Observation of such norms prevented excessively large families that could not be permitted for economic reasons. In modern times this cultural code of birth control through marriage constraints gradually changed into birth control measures in marriage and alternative forms of cohabitation.[3] This robbed the birth of children as gifts from God of its divine aura, and they became simply humanly planned and loved temporary life partners.

The weakness of religion can be seen as the result of this fourfold modernisation process: economic, political, social, and cultural. Viewed thus, the chances are that God, if he has not yet vanished from the scene, will do so in due course, unless faith in him were to change structurally in a manner compatible with the fourfold process.[4]

Among large groups, at any rate in Western Europe, religious decline can be described in terms of various phases.[5] In the first phase people still live quite contentedly and peacefully in the unquestioned, accustomed 'faith of our fathers', albeit with occasional doubts that can still be resolved with the aid of prevailing dogma. That was typical of the premodern phase, which still has offshoots in our own age. In the second phase, questions about the traditional faith start surfacing, touching not merely the surface but affecting the very core of the inherited doctrine. Such doubts are not easily resolved and persist stubbornly. In Europe this has happened mainly since the Enlightenment. In the third phase, the churches respond to doubts by closing religious ranks and erecting a bulwark, behind which they hide and direct their poisoned arrows at the atheistic outside world. That was

---

[3] Th. Engelen, *Van 2 naar 16 miljoen mensen: Demografie van Nederland, 1800 – nu*, Boom, Amsterdam 2009, 29–56.

[4] J. Casanova, *Public Religions in the Modern World*, University of Chicago Press, Chicago 1994.

[5] Here I am inspired by A. MacIntyre, *Whose Justice? Whose Rationality?*, University of Notre Dame Press, Notre Dame 1988, 349–369.

the period of religious mobilisation from roughly 1850 to 1950. In the fourth phase, believers come out of their strongholds and trigger-happy bunkers, and gradually engage in open dialogue with the outside world. In Catholicism this happened during Vatican II (1962–1965) and the Dutch Pastoral Council (1968–1970). This period is marked by what one could call religious demobilisation. Top of the agenda is dialogue with the modern world.[6] In the fifth phase, such dialogue leads to syncretistic hybrids of traditional belief and new social and cultural circumstances, to the extent that one can now say, 'I am a modern Christian' in much the same way as people in the early centuries identified with Hellenistic Christianity, or, in later times, with feudal Christianity, with Renaissance Christianity, or, in even later ages, with 'enlightened' Christianity. These phases do not proceed identically in all cases, and are certainly not linear. Some revert to an earlier phase from a later phase, such as the leadership in the Catholic church on the macro level that mostly has reverted from the fourth to the third phase. Research shows that the majority have by now started a sixth phase. They have dropped out, bid every form of religion goodbye, and live their lives as pragmatic atheists without needing to fight on the barricades for it. They are found mainly among members of the younger generation that have enjoyed advanced education and live in metropolitan areas.[7]

But modernisation is not the sole source of religious weakness in the West. Another major factor is the individualisation process that is a concomitant of social modernisation. Here we must be wary of facile generalisations such as that 'modern people' are individualised. The change process has been one of decline of rural communities (*Gemeinschaft*) with their accent on the common will (*Wesenswille*) and social controls attuned to it, and their replacement by society (*Gesellschaft*), with its accent on individual, reasonable, free choice (*Kürwille*) based on contractual thinking in terms of long-term, well considered self-interest.[8] The question remains, can one speak of a dissolution of some specific social bonds, or should individualisation be regarded as a comprehensive social process, as many aver? It is rather a transformation

---

[6] Ch. Taylor, *A Secular Age*, Harvard University Press, Cambridge 2007, 465–472.

[7] J. Verweij, *Secularisering tussen feit en fictie*, Tilburg University Press, Tilburg, 143–148.

[8] F. Tönnies, *Gemeinschaft und Gesellschaft*, Wissenschaftliche Buchgesellschaft, Leipzig 1887.

of rural social bonds into those of urban society, which are not based on connection by birth (ascription) but on free choice (achievement). Apart from religion there is a flourishing social middle ground between family and state, in which people form relationships in networks based partly on mutual sympathy and friendship and partly on mutual utility (e.g. among colleagues), pleasure (e.g. sport clubs and other recreational associations), or solidarity (e.g. working for the disadvantaged in the local or wider environment).[9] Individualisation is more of a differential, marginal phenomenon. By differential I mean that it does not apply to all social domains to the same extent; by marginal I mean that it crops up mainly in domains that are considered to have marginal social significance, such as political parties, trade unions, and churches. For the sake of completeness, it should be noted that political parties, trade unions, and especially churches do forge social bonds for a limited group of core members.[10]

At all events, religious individualisation certainly exists. It is accompanied by processes of religious de-institutionalisation and de-traditionalisation, which jointly result in de-standardisation of the religious lifespan and the emergence of a religious religious free choice biography. The symptoms of de-institutionalisation must not be misunderstood. As I indicated earlier, in Northwestern Europe church membership and participation have dropped by scores of percentage points over the past 50 years. The decline has been less dramatic in South-Western Europe, because there church participation has always been lower. There are also clear signs of religious de-traditionalisation. Religious ceremonies at birth, marriage, and death are declining in frequency, albeit less rapidly, and when they do happen they increasingly deviate from standard religious programmes, unless church leaders resist tooth and nail, which in its turn promotes emigration from the church. This is increasingly leading to consumption of selective religious menus (*religion à la carte*), also known as religious *bricolage*. All this is collated in a religious free choice biography.

---

[9] According to T. van der Meer, *States of Freely Associating Citizens, Cross-National Studies into the Impact of State Institutions on Social, Civil, and Political Participation*, ICS Dissertation Series, Groningen, Utrecht, Nijmegen 2009, p. 60, social participation is about twice as high in Southern Europe compared to Northern Europe, whereas Eastern Europe is somewhat in between.

[10] J.A. van der Ven (ed.), *Individualisering en religie*, Ambo, Baarn 1994.

Of course, one can play down these phenomena by pointing to the low level of church involvement in earlier ages. Thus the inhabitants of Hippo in North Africa struck Augustine as ecclesiastically lax, for the vast majority only attended church on feast days.[11] As for the Middle Ages, church participation was no greater than in present-day Republic of Congo – that is, marginal.[12] In early premodern Italy there were many ecclesiastically organised processions, but they did not always reflect genuine religiosity. Thus in 1663, the new Cambridge graduate Skoppon commented on a procession in Genoa, noting that many of the flagellants that joined the procession were dock hands and were actually street people. They appeared to be making some sort of game of it, even though they were hired by the rich to execute the penances on their behalf.[13] In 19th century Italy, a substantial minority appeared not to have attended Easter rituals, the reasons advanced being involvement in non-church folk religiosity, lack of motivation, and laziness.[14] In 1847, Berlin pastor Krummacher stated that only 6% of residents attended church regularly[15] and in the early 20th century religious indifference was increasing steadily, as in Brie, France where by 1903 church attendance had dwindled to 2.4%.[16] Such data lead to the unavoidable insight that full-out church membership and participation are unattainable wishful thinking, and, equally undesirable, a utopia that can only be achieved through spiritual paternalism or even dictatorship. Elements of that are discernible in the programme of church discipline since the Fourth Lateran Council and the concomitant programme of shame, guilt, and penance, which sought to activate the populace ecclesiastically until well into the 20th century.[17]

---

[11] F. van der Meer, *Augustinus de zielzorger: Een studie over de praktijk van een kerkvader*, Spectrum, Utrecht/Antwerpen 1957.

[12] P. Raedts, De christelijke middeleeuwen als mythe, *Tijdschrift voor Theologie* 30(1990)2, 146–158.

[13] P. Burke, *Stadscultuur in Italië tussen Renaissance en Barok*, Contact, Amsterdam 1988, 34.

[14] Burke, *Stadscultuur*, op. cit., 65.

[15] G. de Bertier de Sauvigny, *De kerk in het tijdperk van de Restauratie (1801–1848)*, *Geschiedenis van de kerk. Deel VIII*, Paul Brand, Hilversum/Antwerpen 1965, 203.

[16] R. Aubert, De kerk van de crisis van 1848 tot Vaticanum II, in: *Geschiedenis van de kerk, Deel Xa*, Paul Brand, Bussum 1974.

[17] J. Delumeau, *Le péché et la peur, La culpbilisation en Occident (XIII–XVIII siècles)*, Fayard, Paris 1983; Id., *Le catholicisme entre Luther et Voltaire*, Presses universitaires de France, Paris 1971; Id., *Peur en Occident: une cité assiégé*, Fayard, Paris 1978.

But when such attempts at religious discipline fail, it does not, strictly speaking, lead to the kind of religious de-standardisation that we find in our time. The standard may remain in place, even if not complied with. It is handed down from one generation to the next, even if not applied in practice. The family, together with the church, is – or one should say, was – the religious socialisation context *par excellence*. What is new in our time is that the importance of the family for religious socialisation – which in rural society used to be a key context for religious transmission of what Goethe calls the chain of generations – is very much on the decline. Counter to all sorts of claims, this emerges from empirical panel research measuring changes over time, in which respondents are questioned at intervals about their religious education and church involvement. Thus Vermeer shows through meticulous regression analyses among 184 respondents, first questioned in 1983 and again in 2007, that the influence of religious socialisation in the family on church involvement has declined by roughly three quarters.[18]

There have been many reactions to these phenomena of modernisation and individualisation. Some groups want to revive the policy of religious mobilisation from the third phase at any cost. Some do not even flinch from fundamentalist orientations. Other groups are on the borderline between the third and the fourth phase, maintaining a middle position and espousing a balanced 'middle orthodoxy'. Yet other groups are on the borderline between the fourth and the fifth phase and strive to launch or maintain dialogue with modernity. There are those who have already emigrated inwardly without renouncing external religious membership. Others have tacitly elected to vote with their feet and have vacated the church. When one speaks about religion today, in this case the Christian religion in Europe, one is speaking about a complex diversity of beliefs and rites and community and leadership forms in an ocean of growing agnosticism and pragmatic atheism.

---

[18] P. Vermeer, Religieuze opvoeding in het gezin: doet dat er (nog) toe? In: C. van Halen et al. (eds.), *Religie doen, religieuze praktijken in tijden van individualisering*, KSGV, Tilburg 2009, 42–58, table 3: in 1983: R^2 .58, in 2007: R^2 .15. Id., Religious Socialization and Church Attendance in the Netherlands between 1983 and 2007, A Panel Study, *Social Compass* 2010 (to be published).

1.1.2   *Religious Strength*

While religion is playing, by and large, a far lesser role in our day than in earlier centuries, a new actor has entered the religious landscape – one which, apart from large parts of the Iberian peninsula and the Balkans, was previously unknown and now ensures religious turbulence: Islam. This turbulence is a result of a far-reaching, worldwide process that is having an impact on religion as well, namely globalisation.

Globalisation manifests itself in the economic, political, social, and cultural spheres, resulting in a global economy, a global polity, a global society, and a global culture.[19] The expansion of space and time that it entails paradoxically leads to a compression of space and time, for instance via information and communication technology, which is a major factor in this regard.[20] Social globalisation has led to relatively large-scale migration, comprising guest workers and their descendants, legal and illegal economic refugees, and asylum seekers, resulting in substantial African and Asian populations in many parts of Europe. This has given the European population a sample of what one could call religious globalisation: it has come into contact with a religion, Islam, that, except for a few southern and eastern regions, has hitherto only sporadically penetrated their countries. Gradually it has become clear that a worldwide religion like Islam has to be viewed in terms of its own historical roots, premises, and beliefs and not simply as a non-Christian religion, because then it is not measured from its own assumptions and criteria, but according to what it lacks, what it is not. Neither can it be characterised as a 'world religion' – a Western construct that obscures the variability of multi-centred belief systems typical of this and other religions.[21] In fact, for a long time Islam was denied recognition as a world religion because it was seen as Arabic in origin, deriving from the spurned Semitic race, in contrast to, for example, Buddhism, which is reputed to stem from superior Arian roots.[22]

---

[19] The classification into four dimensions corresponds with the paradigms of Wallerstein, Meyer, Robertson, and Luhmann; see P. Beyer, *Religion and Globalization*, Sage, London 1994.

[20] M. Castells, *The Rise of the Network-Society*, Blackwell, New York 1996.

[21] H. Vroom, *Religies en de waarheid*, Kok, Kampen 1988, 241ff.; C. Ram-Prasad, Teaching South Asian Religions in Britain, *Religious Studies News*, Fall 2001, 3–6.

[22] T. Masuzawa, *The Invention of World Religions*, University of Chicago Press, Chicago 2005.

The influx of numerous highly visible and vocal groups from Muslim countries made European society aware that it is in fact multicultural – a situation that has existed in Europe with its many national minorities for a long time but that had been firmly suppressed since the 19th century because of the ideology of the nation-state. But the strong Muslim presence has heightened this awareness and actually turned it into a problem. It is not only because Muslims manifest a different culture and practise a different faith, but also because they are located on the fringes of society. They have disproportionately high school dropout rates, unemployment rates, levels of unskilled labour, and criminality, and are under-represented in schooling, skilled labour, and leadership professions, also at the micro level. The problem of social inequality that this exposes also raises questions regarding social cohesion, which has already become problematic as a result of the fundamental difference in their culture and religion. After all, social inequality and social cohesion are interrelated.[23] From a demographic perspective, however, this problem is refuted, because it is said to promote adequate generational replacement in Europe, which, through a mismatch of low fertility and mortality and high life expectancy, is in danger of becoming unbalanced.[24] But this demographic opinion is heavily contested.[25] That makes multiculturalism an even hotter issue in the public debate.

The issue is exacerbated by the question whether the new immigrants and their second and third generation descendants will actually want or be able to integrate with what to them is an alien society. To answer the question, we need to distinguish between integration and some relevant but contrasting terms like assimilation, separation, and marginalisation. To this end, I use a matrix of acculturation strategies in religious minorities groups (figure 1).

---

[23] W. Ultee et al., *Sociologie: vragen, uitspraken, bevindingen*, Wolters-Boordhof, Groningen 1992, 640ff.

[24] J. Chamie, World population in the 21st century, *Justitiële Verkenningen* 27(2001)5; E. Guild, *Moving the Borders of Europe*, Inaugural address, Radboud University Nijmegen 2001.

[25] According to Engelen, op. cit., 179, few prognoses are as unreliable as demographic ones. He adds that fertility, which has dropped sharply to below replacement level since 1960, could increase again if, for example, the Netherlands were to implement the Scandinavian policy by properly regulating parental leave and child care.

		maintenance of religious heritage & identity $+ \longleftrightarrow -$	
lasting relationship	+	(1) integration	(2) assimilation
sought with other religious groups and nonreligious groups	(arrow up) (arrow down) −	(3) separation	(4) marginalization

Figure 1. Acculturation strategies in religious minorities. Adapted from J.W. Berry et al., *Cross-Cultural Psychology: Research and Applications*, 2nd edition, Cambridge University Press, Cambridge 2002, 354.

The horizontal dimension refers to the extent to which a religious group engages in maintaining, keeping alive, and developing its own religious heritage, culture, and identity. The vertical dimension relates to the extent to which the group engages in lasting relationship with other religious and nonreligious groups and expands them. Relating these two dimensions yields four ideal types in the Weberian sense: integration, assimilation, separation, and marginalisation.[26] The typology includes scales on both dimensions, ranging from positive (+) to negative (−). Integration in cell 1 refers to the group's striving to keep its own religious heritage, culture, and identity alive and at the same time maintaining lasting relationships with other groups. Assimilation in cell 2 also stands for a group's aspiration to develop such relationships, but without concern for its own religious heritage and identity. In the separation model represented by cell 3, this concern is vitally present, but the desire for enduring relationships is absent. Marginalisation in cell 4 is characterised by the absence of both interest in its own religious identity and interest in relationships.

The meaning of integration can be explored in greater depth by means of two Aristotelian concepts. The first is the dialectic between the one and the many, in terms of which a population constitutes an integrated whole inasmuch as it is one entity, albeit comprising a mul-

---

[26] J. Berry et al., *Cross-Cultural Psychology: Research and Applications*, 2nd edition, Cambridge University Press, Cambridge 2002, 353–357; J. Berry, Contexts of Acculturation, in: D. Sam & J. Berry (eds.), *The Cambridge Handbook of Acculturation Psychology*, Cambridge University Press, Cambridge 2006, 27–42, here 34–35.

tiplicity of mutually differing groups.[27] How does such multiplicity-in-unity come about? The answer lies in the second Aristotelian concept: the dialectic between the part and the whole. An ethnocultural group contributes to the whole of a population insofar as it reflects (i.e. expresses and actualises) the whole in its beliefs and practices. A plurality of ethnocultural groups contributes to the whole of a population insofar as they participate in each other's beliefs and practices while still nurturing their own identity. Such mutual participation is essential, for the whole of a population does not transcend the groups; it is not something that descends on them from a vacuum beyond. Its wholeness in fact consists in their mutual participation. Wholeness is not overarching but consists in interpenetration. It is not a canopy but a network. There is no wholeness without participation, no integration without interpenetration.[28]

Our description of integration from an Aristotelian perspective may sound delightfully idealistic, but is it adequate, or even remotely realistic? Naturally, integration is a worthwhile goal, and an Aristotelian explanation in terms of participation and interpenetration sounds admirable. But it is doubtful if that goal is – even partly – attainable. After all, in which religious and nonreligious beliefs and practices of indigenous European groups can and should a Muslim group participate? Conversely, in which religious beliefs and practices of these Muslim groups can and should indigenous European groups participate? What interpenetration of which religious and nonreligious beliefs and practices is involved?

When one reflects on it, one is faced with a bewildering complexity. As noted already, the indigenous European, in this case the Dutch population, is highly diverse, ranging from religious to nonreligious, and within this overall picture there is an almost infinite range of religious responses to the processes of modernisation and individualisation in Christian communities. They are split into Catholic and Protestant denominations, to whom ecumenism – after the brief euphoria of the 1960s and 1970s – seems more distant than ever.[29] Protestant

---

[27] Aristotle, *The Complete Works of Aristotle. The Revised Oxford Translation*, Edited by Jonathan Barnes, Princeton University Press, Princeton, NJ 1984, 1054a 20ff.

[28] Aristotle, 210a16, 1023b29.

[29] According to A. Felling, J. Peters and P. Scheepers (red.), *Individualisering in Nederland aan het einde van de twintigste eeuw, Empirisch onderzoek naar omstreden hypotheses*, Van Gorcum, Assen 2000, p. 241, the diversity of confessional cultures is still actively present.

churches are themselves divided into rigidly orthodox, moderately orthodox, and liberal communities with almost no dialogue between them. Apart from the Protestant Church in the Netherlands, which, after decades of overtures, was established in 2004 through a fusion of the Dutch Reformed Church, the Reformed Churches in the Nether-lands, and the Evangelical Lutheran Church, there is no Protestant integration.

Among Muslim communities too, one sees no sign of integration. They are no less varied, as Dutch statistics show. With a membership of some 850,000, they are the second largest religion in the Nether-lands, constituting about 5% of the total population.[30] Their adherents are spread over two main persuasions – mainly Sunni focusing on in principle four different schools of law, and Shia, in principle focus-ing on three different schools of law – while each community in its turn is marked by national differences and within those national dif-ferences by ethnic distinctions. In addition there are Alevites, a branch of the Shiite school, and mystical brotherhoods like the Sufi. Of the two biggest minorities in the Netherlands, Turks and Moroccans, 95% consider themselves to be Muslim, although not all of them take part in mosque services. A quarter of the Turks and a third of Moroc-cans attend these services no more than once a year, if at all.[31] Among youths there is a manifest decline in mosque attendance and prayer practices, albeit a heightened sense of Muslim identity. The latter may be seen as a need for cultural identity, all the more desperate as the harshening multicultural climate of the past decade relentlessly drives them into a minority position.[32]

For the time being, the aim of intra-Christian and intra-Islamic integration remains an alluring prospect and an inspiring ideal, but a great deal of water will have to flow into the sea before, on the macro level, the first signs of it, effectively put into practice, become discern-

---

[30] Centraal Bureau van de Statistiek (CBS), The Hague 2007.

[31] J. Dagevos & M. Gijsberts (eds.), *Jaarrapport Integratie 2007*, Sociaal en Cultureel Planbureau, The Hague 2007, 163–191; CBS, *Religie aan het begin van de 21ste eeuw*, Centraal Bureau voor de Statistiek, Den Haag 2009, tabel 13.1, p. 118.

[32] K. Phalet & J. Ter Wal (eds.), Moslim in Nederland. Religie en migratie: soci-aalwetenschappelijke databronnen en literatuur, Sociaal en Cultureel Planbureau, The Hague 2004; Id., Moslim in Nederland. Diversiteit en verandering in religieuze betrokkenheid: Turken en Marokkanen in Nederland 1998–2002, Sociaal en Cultureel Planbureau,The Hague 2004; Dagevos & Gijsberts (eds.), Jaarrapport Integratie 2007, op. cit., 163–191.

ible. Does not the ideal of Christian-Muslim integration in an Aristotelian perspective provoke even greater skepticism – even on the humble scale of a strategy aimed at lasting relations between the two religions (see cell 1 in figure 1)? Participation of religious groups is actually characterised by bonding instead of bridging. It establishes contacts and trust between people within the same group (bonding) and none or little engagement with (people of) other groups (bridging).[33] Integration by participation represents a goal that can only be achieved in the long term, all circumstances being favourable.

In other words, in many European countries, pre-eminently the Netherlands, we are faced with long-term, concrete, actual separation; hence, a variety of religious movements and communities exist more or less in isolation from each other, with no sign of a strategy aimed at forming lasting relations. The picture is further complicated by the fact that Christianity in Europe, again pre-eminently in the Netherlands, is fast becoming a minority in the midst of a secularised majority. As a result of the steady decline, this minority, as noted already, is marked by clearly discernible religious weakness, whereas Islam is so far supplying a growing need for religiously informed cultural identity. In short, this kind of separation characterised by variety appears inescapable at present. What paradigms can we use for research to map such a variety of religious movements and communities so as to form a clear picture of them in order to better understand them? That is the topic of the next section of this chapter.

1.2   Three Paradigms for the Study of Religious Varieties

To study varieties of religion, one can use three research strategies that, in my view, cover the whole field, though I do not profess that they are the only ones. As pointed out in the introduction, I deal with the secularisation, the economic, and the cognitive paradigms. The first is suitable for studying variation in religious weakness and strength at the macro level of differences between and within countries. The second can be used to investigate variations at the meso level of differences within countries and intergroup differences. The third can be

---

[33] CBS, *Religie*, op. cit., pp. 8–9, 139–140.

used to study variations at the micro level of individual differences and then to link these to intergroup differences. Of course, this does not preclude looking for direct relations between the macro, meso, and micro levels.

A few comments are called for. When we speak about paradigms it must be acknowledged that it is not easy to pinpoint what a paradigm is. Thomas Kuhn, originator of modern paradigm thinking, employs 22 different meanings. He also offers a broad definition. A paradigm, he says, is an overall constellation of concepts, values and techniques.[34] Concepts comprise theories, definitions, and models; values include guidelines like consistency, coherence, simplicity, and transparency; and techniques include data collection, data construction, data analysis, et cetera. The debate between schools of thought always centres on concepts, values, and techniques. Often it is unproductive, because in practice researchers tend to opt for an eclectic approach. There is nothing wrong with that, provided the researcher is prepared to account for her eclecticism in what may be called a reflective eclectic approach.

1.2.1   *The Secularisation Paradigm*

I have said that I shall examine the question of the origin of religious differences between countries at macro level in terms of the secularisation paradigm. That paradigm is under great pressure at present. According to Thomas Luckmann, secularisation is a 'modern myth'.[35] Is secularisation a dead duck? In my view, scholars have been over-ambitious, trying to explain too many phenomena by means of this one paradigm; but that does not mean it must be scrapped altogether. It should, however, be critically reappraised.[36]

Apart from secularist phenomena in the distant past, such as Confucianism and Greek philosophy, 'modern' secularisation in Western society may be regarded as a centuries-old process dating back to the struggle between church and state: the Investiture conflict. The histori-

---

[34] Th. Kuhn, *The Structure of Scientific Revolutions*, University of Chicago Press, Chicago 1970.

[35] Th. Luckmann, *Säkularisierung – Ein Moderner Mythos*, in: Th. Luckmann (ed.), *Lebenswelt und Gesellschaft*, Paderborn, Schöningh 1980, 161–172.

[36] D. Pollak, *Säkularisierung – Ein Moderner Mythos?* Mohr Siebeck, Tübingen 2003; P. Norris & R. Inglehart, *Sacred and Secular: Religions and Politics Worldwide*, Cambridge University, Cambridge 2005.

cal date was 1122: that was when, in the Concordat of Worms (following the Concordat of London in 1107), the Roman patriarchate agreed, at least in principle, to put an end to both Caesaro-papism (political power over religion) and hierocracy (religious power over politics). In their place, two separate centres of power were established: the church and the state. In the one text of this concordat, the *Heinricianum*, the emperor, Henry V, guaranteed free election and consecration of bishops, and ceded the right to invest them with sacred authority by presenting them with the episcopal ring and staff; in the other text, the *Calixtinum*, the pope, Calixtus II, granted the emperor the right to attend episcopal elections and give bishops worldly authority by presenting them with the sceptre. In this perspective, the original meaning of the term 'secularisation' was applied, centuries later, to the state's expropriation of economic goods previously owned by the church, especially in France in 1789, when the church may have owned as much as one sixth of the national territory.[37] Paradoxically, whereas the French church suffered from such secularisation, in the 19th century the German church welcomed it as a source of religious renewal.[38]

The emerging separation between church and state, which started with the Concordat of Worms and became ideologically and politically effective in the age of the Enlightenment and the French revolution, was the judicial outcome of a process of functional differentiation that had been at work in Western society for centuries.[39] Functional differentiation means that society is no longer organised in terms of social stratification – that is, estates and classes – but in functional terms. It evolves into functional systems with their own codes, operating according to their own logic, and with their own characteristic actors. Examples are the economic system (money, profit/loss, producer/consumer), the political system (coalition parties, power/opposition, politicians/voters), the health care system (quality of life, sick/healthy, caregiver/patient), the education system (job allocation, literate/illiterate, teacher/student). As a result of functional differentiation, the various systems develop fairly autonomously, albeit with some mutual

---

[37] L.J. Rogier, *De kerk in het tijdperk van Verlichting En Revolutie. Deel VII*, Brand, Hilversum, Antwerpen, 1964, 166.

[38] H. Lübbe, *Modernisierungsgewinner: Religion, Geschichtssinn, direkte Demokratie und Moral*, Fink, Munchen 2004, 35–45; Id., Die Zivilisationsökumene, Globalisierung kulturell, technisch und politisch, Fink, München 2005, 187–188

[39] M. Gauchet, *Le Désenchantement Du Monde: Une Histoire Politique De La Religion*, Gallimard, Paris, 1985.

influencing by what is called interpenetration. In the case of religion there are two possible perspectives. From the other systems' point of view, secularisation means their emancipation from the religious system. From the religious point of view, it means that religion has less influence over these systems. Thus secularisation is a consequence of functional differentiation.[40]

In this age-long process of functional differentiation, the focus of the various systems was no longer on religious or moral issues but on rationality. This rationality was not what Weber called *Wertrationalitat*, but *Zweckrationalität*, characterised by an emphasis on cause-effect and means-ends relations and on efficiency and efficacy. This *Zweckrationalität* found expression in the economy, especially in all kinds of markets like those of land, production, labour, trade, consumption, and money; in politics, especially in contracts like the constitution, coalitions, and contracts with voters; in social life, in aspects like the marriage contract, family life, and the establishment of functional associations; and in culture, in the rationalisation of science with its orientation to rationally controllable hypotheses, efficiency, and effectiveness.

Science enables us to probe the most remote corners of the universe and the innermost depths of molecules, atoms, and electrons. Whereas in the 17th century Pascal still associated both the mystery of the cosmos and the intriguing mystery of atoms with the mystery of God's presence, by the beginning of the 20th century Max Weber was speaking of a disenchanted world (*Entzauberung der welt*). By this he meant that the world had lost its divine lustre, having become a measurable and make-able scientific research object and material for technological control and intervention. This applied (and still applies) not only to the disenchantment of the external world by the natural sciences, but also to that of the social world by the sociological and politico-scientific disciplines and the inner world of human beings by psychological disciplines.

It was not so much a matter of scepticism about religion as a result of scientific explanations, although the effects of Darwin's evolution theory on the doctrine of creation, for instance, should not be underestimated.[41] It was rather that the rational *Zeitgeist* permeated and still

---

[40] N. Luhmann, *Funktion der Religion*, Suhrkamp, Frankfurt am Main, 1977; Id., *Die Gesellschaft der Gesellschaft*, Suhrkamp, Frankfurt am Main, 1998; Id., *Die Religion der Gesellschaft*, Suhrkamp, Frankfurt am Main 2002.

[41] E.J. Browne, *Charles Darwin. Vol. 1: Voyaging. Vol. 2: the Power of Place*, Pimlico, London, 2003.

permeates all culture and thus the whole of social and individual life, which led and still leads to the notion that fundamentally all problems are rationally soluble, at least in principle.[42]

However appealing a hypothesis the secularisation paradigm may be, it is subject to serious doubts. One of these concerns its point of departure: is it correct to relate secularisation to functional differentiation? The cardinal counter example is the USA, which is inarguably characterised by functional differentiation, but (apparently) not (so much) by secularisation. What is true is that traditional denominations are experiencing a decline in the USA, parallel to that in Europe.[43] According to research in 2004, in the last ten years they lost more than 10% of their members, which is more than 1% a year.[44] At the same time, the Catholic Church keeps its membership on par because of the influx of Spanish-speaking Mexicans. And conservative Protestant churches, such as evangelical, charismatic and Pentecostal communities, have a consistent following, and some of them are even experiencing growth. While the outward phenomena in these churches may astound one, at a deeper level the substance of their proclamation and liturgy, Sunday schools and Bible study appears to be subject to inner secularisation. Thus traditional doctrine is said to be adapting to the conventions of the dominant liberal culture, resulting in what is known as 'easy-believism'.[45]

At all events, this (apparently) quite powerful religiosity is explained in terms of extra-religious factors. Firstly, the USA is said to have embarked on the process of functional differentiation and modernisation later than Europe, so that secularisation on that continent lags

---

[42] S. Bruce, *Religion in the Modern World: From Cathedrals to Cults*, Oxford University Press, Oxford, 1996; K. Dobbelaere, Towards an Integrated Perspective of the Processes Related to the Descriptive Concept of Secularization, *Sociology of Religion* 60(1999)3, 229–247; Id., *Secularization: An Analysis at Three Levels (Gods, Humans & Religion)*, P. Lang, New York, 2002; Id., Assessing Secularization Theory, in: P. Antes, A.W. Geertz & R.R. Warne (eds.), *New Approaches to the Study of Religion. Vol. 2: Textual, Comparative, Sociological, and Cognitive Approaches*, De Gruyter, Berlin, 2004, 228–253.

[43] W. Roof, *Religion in the Nineties*, Sage Periodical Press, Newbury Park, Ca. 1993; Id. *Americans and Religions in the Twenty-First Century*, Sage Periodicals Press, Thousand Oaks, CA 1998; W. Roof, W. & M. MacKinney, *American Mainline Religion: Its Changing Shape and Future*, Rutgers University Press, New Brunswick 1987.

[44] http://www-news.uchicago.edu/releases/04/040720.protestant.shtml

[45] S. Bruce, The Curious Case of the Unnecessary Recantation: Berger and Secularization, in: L. Woodhead et al. (eds.), *Peter Berger and the Study of Religion*, Routledge, London/New York 2001, 89–90.

behind. Secondly, the demographic picture is said to be distorted: in absolute figures the Catholic Church as well as the evangelical, charismatic, and Pentecostal churches' religious market share appears to be stable or even growing, but not percentage-wise. In addition, the link between ethnicity and religion is considered an important factor. Religion is said to contribute to ethnic identity, a need felt by American migrant groups that are more numerous and extensive than their European counterparts. The separation of church and state, which is more rigid in the USA than in (many) European countries, appears to be a further factor. As a result, there is fierce competition between American churches, causing them to focus more on their members' needs – an argument we shall encounter again further on when we deal with the economic rational choice paradigm. In addition, the relatively poor development of the social welfare state in the USA compared to Europe means that American churches feature more prominently as centres of social interaction and cohesion and as a social safety net.[46] Finally, the overall American culture, said to be more masculine than the predominantly feminine culture in Europe, allegedly contributes to religiosity: the more masculine, the more religious; the more feminine, the less religious.[47]

But it is not just disparities between Europe and the USA that are at issue. The prominence of religion in non-Western countries and in the interaction between Western and non-Western countries in recent years raises the question whether the secularisation paradigm has not been done to death in the literature. One should also be wary of rash generalisations, as is evident in studies of secularisation in countries on the African continent, which is by no means as 'incurably religious' as it is said to be.[48] Nonetheless, have we not been sadly mistaken ever since the Enlightenment, when "there was the honest conviction that

---

[46] Norris & Inglehart, *Sacred*, op. cit., 106–110.

[47] S. Bruce, *Religion in the Modern World: From Cathedrals to Cults*, Oxford University Press Oxford/New York, 1996; J. Verweij, *Secularisering tussen feit en fictie: Een internationaal vergelijkend onderzoek naar determinanten van religieuze betrokkenheid*, Tilburg University Press, Tilburg, 1998; G. Hofstede & G.J. Hofstede, *Allemaal andersdenkenden: Omgaan met cultuurverschillen*, Contact, Amsterdam, 2005.

[48] E.M. Metogo, *Dieu Peut-Il Mourir En Afrique? Essai Sur L'indifférence Religieuse Et L'incroyance En Afrique Noire*, Éd. Karthala, Paris, 1997; A. Shorter & E. Onyancha, *Secularism in Africa: A Case Study: Nairobi City*, Paulines Publications Africa, Nairobi, Kenya, 1997.

churches must, after all, move with the times"?[49] Is it not a matter of 'exit secularisation' rather than of 'religion R.I.P.'?[50] It is not America that is the exception, as Europeans sometimes think; rather it is Europe that is the global exception.[51] "There is no reason to think," says Peter Berger,[52] "that the world of the 21st century will be less religious than the world of today." Sometimes this carries a rider: there is some hope even for Europe, but then religion would have to make a paradoxical choice. Instead of resisting functional differentiation, it should adapt to it altogether. If it does that, the argument goes, the removal of religion from the public space and its privatisation will be arrested and may well be turned around.[53] Time will tell whether this hypothesis is correct.

That secularisation is not an irreversible, linear, natural process, but a social one, meaning that it is open to varying human preferences and interventions, is evident in the anti-secularisation movements in many countries. To understand these, one needs to consider a number of factors. The first concerns the carriers of social movements and counter movements. By this we mean that social processes like rationalisation of the economic, political, or cultural system do not operate like the ticking of an automatic clock, but are always carried by socially stratified groups. If these groups are influential, the process is facilitated; if they are a minority, society carries on more or less without them. Thus urban groups are more favourably disposed to rationalisation, and rural groups are less so if at all, just as highly educated people are more inclined to support such processes than less educated ones. It depends which groups are dominant in a particular area and in a particular period of time.

The second factor concerns social conflicts. These erupt when the carriers of social development are thwarted by emerging power groups. An example is the struggle between businesspeople and the

---

[49] P. Gay, *The Enlightenment: An Interpretation. Vol. 1: The Rise of Modern Paganism*, Weidenfeld and Nicholson, London, 1966, 343.

[50] R. Stark, Secularization, R.I.P., *Sociology of Religion*, 60(1999)3, 249–274.

[51] G. Davie, Europe: The Exception That Proves the Rule? In: P.L. Berger (ed.), *The Desecularization of the World: Resurgent Religion and World Politics*, Ethics and Public Policy Center, Eerdmans, Washington, D.C./Grand Rapids, MI 1999, 65–84; Id., *Europe, the Exceptional Case: Parameters of Faith in the Modern World*, Sarum Theological Lectures, Darton, Longman & Todd, London 2002.

[52] Berger (ed.), *The Desecularization*, op. cit., 12.

[53] J. Casanova, *Public Religions in the Modern World*, University of Chicago Press, Chicago 1994.

petty bourgeoisie in 19th century Germany. The former favoured economic rationalisation and were sceptical about religion. The latter were fearful of rationalisation in industry and cherished the (ostensibly) religious Middle Ages. The unresolved conflict between these two groups continued until the rise of national socialism.[54] Another example is present-day Iran. Under the last shah there was economic rationalisation, backed by businesspeople, scientists, and technologists, also inasmuch as it included an a-religious cultural policy. With the 1979 revolution, these groups changed sides, since they could no longer contain the rebellion of the lower strata of the population against the shah's rule; today they support the theocracy.[55]

The third factor, known as non-synchronicity, stems from the previous two. It means that each system develops at its own pace. Thus political democratisation may lag behind economic development, leading to social inequality and social unrest, as happened in Iran and is currently threatening to happen in China. Or morality, under the influence of religion, may get bogged down in absolute prescriptions and prohibitions of specific, concrete actions, instead of developing rationally towards an ethics of responsibility.[56] A conservative morality can halt rational development in other systems such as the economy and politics.[57]

The crucial question in this section is this: can religious differences between countries be explained as differences in the degree of secularisation? To answer the question, we need to distinguish between countries with high or low degrees of functional differentiation. The former are far more secularised than the latter. But this does not mean that secularisation is a linear, irreversible, natural evolutionary process. It is a social process, influenced by all sorts of societal – also nonreligious – factors, both conducive and inhibitory, such as demographic development, the relation between ethnicity and religion, separation of church and state, level of social welfare, and the masculine or feminine nature of the culture. One also has to allow for counter movements

---

[54] J.B.L.M. Peeters, *Burgers en Modernisering: Historisch-sociologisch onderzoek naar burgerlijke groeperingen in het moderniseringsproces van de Duitse Bond 1810–1870*, Dissertation Nijmegen University 1984.

[55] Bruce, *The Curious Case*, op. cit., 95.

[56] W. Schluchter, *Die Entwicklung des okzidentalen Rationalismus eine Analyse von Max Webers Gesellschaftsgeschichte*, Mohr, Tübingen 1979.

[57] M. Weber, *Gesammelte Aufsätze zur Religionssoziologie*, Mohr, Tübingen 1920/ 1978, 252.

and the social conflicts they cause, as well as the support they receive from conservative political and religious leaders, in whatever part of the world.

1.2.2   *The Economic Paradigm*

When one views religious density on earth from a helicopter, one is struck by religious differences not only between countries, but also within countries. Where do these come from? The economic rational choice paradigm could help to answer the question. However, this paradigm, too, is disputed, especially by proponents of the secularisation hypothesis. This is not surprising, for rational choice researchers came into the limelight because of their criticism of the secularisation paradigm. Hence they oppose each other fiercely and vociferously.

Yet the two paradigms cannot be viewed in isolation from each other. As noted already, functional differentiation in society led to the collapse of the sacred canopy of one, all-encompassing religion, and its replacement by a plurality of religious and nonreligious worldviews. This pluralism forms the premise of the economic paradigm, since it leads to competition between worldviews, more particularly religious ones. Their rivalry prompts various developments, such as rational adaptation of the religious supply to human needs, application of the principles of efficiency and efficacy, professionalisation of religious staff, and the resultant bureaucratisation of religious institutions – to mention only a few common characteristics among variants of the economic paradigm.[58]

The economic paradigm provides a conceptual framework for the study of these processes. It is based on certain assumptions that culminate in an empirically researchable hypothesis. These assumptions are as follows: (1) All people are driven by a religious need. (2) All societies have a natural, relatively stable set of 'stalls' on the religious market, and there is an unvarying level of at least one potential religious need. (3) Religious organisations are distinguishable by the extent to which they adapt their supply of religious wares to a religious need. (4) This adaptation is promoted by the demolition of religious monopolies, separation of church and state, deregulation of the religious market,

---

[58] S. Chai, *The Many Flavors of Rational Choice and the Fate of Sociology*, Paper presented at the annual meeting of the American Sociological Association, Atlanta, GA, 2003.

and escalation of religious competition. (5) Religious pluralism does not weaken the plausibility of religious institutions but strengthens it, since the constant variation they have to introduce to secure current and potential clients leads to greater religious activity. (6) To the extent that a religious institution's supply differs from that of another, it becomes more attractive and religious consumption increases. This applies particularly to the sect-to-church process, in which the transition from a sect with high doctrinal, ritual, and social thresholds to an established church with low thresholds, is characterised by reduced religious consumption. (7) In such a religious free market, individuals, on the basis of rational cost-benefit analysis, can join the religious institution that offers them the greatest religious benefit at the lowest cost, which satisfies their striving for religious profit maximisation. (8) Since the greatest religious benefits, such as ultimate reconciliation and/or eternal bliss hereafter, are not immediately forthcoming, their attainment has to be deferred, which is made possible by offering compensation: the promise of ultimate reconciliation and/or eternal bliss. This is anticipated in religious experiences, backed up by religious rituals, religious counselling, religious education, and religious community building.[59] Some avoid the term 'compensation',[60] but not the underlying idea: the exchange relationship with God[61] presupposes trust fraught with risks that are insured against by ritual, prayer, and mystical experience.[62]

I have said that these assumptions culminate in an empirically researchable hypothesis. It reads as follows: countries with an open religious market have greater religious participation than countries with closed, monopolistic religious markets. In short, pluralisation and deregulation result in religious revival.

On the basis of this economic paradigm, we would posit that secularisation, particularly in Europe, is not attributable to functional differentiation in society and concomitant rationalisation, but to overly regulated religious markets and the absence of healthy competition. Religious institutions that are protected, subsidised, and accommo-

---

[59] R. Stark & W.S. Bainbridge, *A Theory of Religion*, Toronto Studies in Religion, Vol. 2, P. Lang, New York 1987.

[60] R. Stark & R. Finke, *Acts of Faith: Explaining the Human Side of Religion*, University of California Press, Berkeley 2000, 84.

[61] Stark & Finke, *Acts*, op. cit., 88–96.

[62] Stark & Finke, *Acts*, op. cit., 106–113.

dated by the state lack efficiency and efficacy, hence fail to attract religious clientele. This insight tallies, it is said, with the empirical fact that there is considerable religious faith in Europe but little church involvement. So the hypothesis reads that there is 'believing without belonging'.[63] In the USA, the reasoning goes, people move from one church to another rather than leave the church, because American churches fight for clientele – although this argument overlooks the decline of established denominations.

There have been various objections to this paradigm, both its assumptions and the hypothesis. In regard to assumptions (1) and (2), it is a moot point whether all people are driven by and aware of a religious need. In other words, the proposition which has to be demonstrated is taken for granted. This boils down to a methodological failure, because the hypothesis to be tested turns into an assumption which is taken as a self-evident truth. Besides, as noted already, Europe presents an exception, which makes the question of an innate religious need all the more intense and sharp. All in all, the human brain has no demonstrable area, or set of areas, where a talent for 'religious musicality' is located.[64] Nor can such areas ever be located, for even if they existed, it would still require interpretation of the firing of innumerable neurons and this must perforce derive from culturally determined religious traditions. The point is, firing neurons do not communicate about God, they do not witness, they do not pray. Religion is a cultural rather than a natural phenomenon,[65] and in that sense is not a genuinely universal but a quasi-universal, mainly cultural phenomenon, as will be seen below.[66] There is a further point. Some founding fathers of the economic paradigm define religion as faith in an omnipotent actor, who, in exchange for the offer of eternal peace, demands investment in a religious organisation.[67] This would make religion a barter transaction that merges into barter-oriented institutionalised religion. This idea

---

[63] G. Davie, Believing without Belonging: Is This the Future of Religion in Britain? *Social Compass*, 37(1990)4, 455–469.

[64] P. Thagard, The Emotional Coherence of Religion, *Journal of Cognition and Culture* 5(2005)1/2, 69–72.

[65] J. Feith, *Probing Neurotheology's Brain or Critiquing an Emerging Quasi-Science*, Paper presented at the Critical Theory and Discourse on Religion Section. The American Academy of Religion Convention, Atlanta, Georgia, 2003.

[66] D. Brown, *The MIT encyclopedia of the cognitive sciences*, MIT Press, Cambridge, MA 1999.

[67] Stark & Bainbridge, *A Theory*, op. cit., 39.

overlooks the notion of religion as a gratuitous gift, not to be paid for but freely and gratefully received and wholeheartedly cherished.

If assumption (3) is interpreted strictly, it poses no problem. Religious organisations undeniably distinguish themselves from each other by the extent to which they adapt their supply to the contextually determined religious demands of human beings. This applies not only to differences between churches and denominations, but also to those within churches and denominations. An example may be found in present-day Italian Catholicism, in which the church leadership competes with various religious organisations within this church (associations, congregations, confraternities, religious orders, movements) which focus on expressions of popular religiosity like the veneration of sacred images and relics, pilgrimages, processions, vows, counting the rosary, et cetera.[68] But if one translates this descriptive statement into a prescriptive rule, in the sense that churches have to adapt maximally to human demands, then religion is reduced to a commodity. Businesses get rid of old products because they are not in demand on the market, and replace them with new ones. But churches cannot and must not do that; they are bound by their religious identity, origin and tradition.[69] This realisation is not confined to religious leaders and professionals; it is shared by church members. Hermeneutic continuity with sources and traditions, experienced and valued by both clergy and laity, is intrinsic in religious institutions. It cannot be 'sold out'.

If assumption (4) is read in conjunction with (5), one is caught up in the economic and political debate that has raged ever since Adam Smith and Alexis de Tocqueville. Assumption (4) posits the economic hypothesis that competition on the religious market will lead to religious growth; assumption (5) posits the political hypothesis that the abolition of a state church or an established church is conducive to religious growth. The two hypotheses need to be tested separately. That this does not always happen is evident in research based on the economic paradigm that was conducted in Europe.[70] In this study, testing of the political hypothesis (assumption 5), led to erroneous conclu-

---

[68] F. Zaccaria, *Participation and Beliefs in Popular Religiosity: An Empirical-Theological Exploration among Catholic Parishioners in the Diocese of Conversano-Monopoli in Italy*, Dissertation Radboud University Nijmegen, 2009.

[69] S. Bruce, *Choice and Religion: A Critique of Rational Choice Theory*, Oxford University Press, Oxford/New York 1999, 124–129.

[70] L. Iannaccone, The Consequences of Religious Market Structure: Adam Smith and the Economics of Religion, *Rationality and Society* 3(1991)2, 156–177.

sions about the economic hypothesis (assumption 4), since the abolition of a state church or an established church does not automatically result in religious competition.[71]

Assumption (6), too, is debatable. The sect-to-church theory may hold water for Protestant churches, especially in the USA, but not for the Catholic Church, because its doctrinal, ritual, and social structure does not fit the identity of a sect. It may display certain sectarian features, as when it seeks to manifest itself forcefully from a marginal position in society, for instance in the Netherlands after 1853 (restoration of episcopal hierarchy), and certainly after 1870 (Vatican I), when it displayed sect-related features of high religious consumption, especially from 1879 to 1960;[72] but even then there was no question of a sect in the strict sense of the word.

The objection to assumption (7) concerns the way human beings, hence believers, are reduced to calculators that rationally weigh costs and benefits, settling for profit maximisation. Firstly, one could question whether people in fact make choices when it comes to religion, since in this respect they are motivated by ascription rather than achievement, which means that one is born into a religious community rather than consciously and voluntarily choosing one's religious affiliation. Secondly, if and inasmuch as they do make such choices, are these based mainly or even exclusively on their assessment of costs and benefits? Are they not based more on psychological processes, such as emotional attraction and identification, and social processes like imitation and convention? Besides, if choices are made by weighing costs and benefits, does it not lead to equilibrium between costs and benefits rather than profit maximisation?[73] Finally, if this appraisal is made, is it as rational a process as the economic paradigm would have it? Even in the economic sphere, appraisal occurs mainly unconsciously, driven by emotional motives, incorporated rule systems,

---

[71] M. Chaves & D. Cann, Regulation, Pluralism, and Religious Market Structure, *Rationality and Society* 4(1992)3, 272–290.

[72] E. Sengers, *"Al zijn wij katholiek, wij zijn Nederlanders": Opkomst en verval van katholieke kerk in Nederland sinds 1795 vanuit rational-choice perspectief*, Eburon, Delft 2003; Id., "You Don't Have to Be a Saint or a Practicing Catholic...": Higher Tension and Lower Attachement in the Dutch Catholic Church since 1970, *Antonianum: periodicum trimestre* 78(2003)3, 529–545.

[73] L. Cosmides & J. Tooby, Neurocognitive Adaptations Designed for Social Exchange, in: D.M. Buss (ed.), *The Handbook of Evolutionary Psychology*, Wiley, Hoboken, NJ 2005, 584–627, here 617–619.

social customs, and social desirability, without any rational explication, let alone rational monitoring.[74] On the whole, conscious processes are the exception rather than the rule, as will be seen when we deal with the cognitive paradigm.[75]

Finally, assumption (8) likewise denigrates the value of religion. It is quite bizarre to speak of religious processes like religious experience, counselling, rites, and community building as compensations, as though they merely offer a surrogate for the eschatological promise hidden in the end-time. It disregards the intrinsic value of these religious processes, which represent ends in themselves. The compensation idea also does not do justice to the human existential constitution of time, based on the dialectic between present, past, and future. It separates present, past, and future by ignoring the discontinuous continuity between them. The past is the past of the present, the future is the future of both the past and the present, and the present is the past of the future.[76] This dialectic stems from the polarity between human actions like promise and hope, desire and anticipation. Rational choice theory reduces all that to what is attainable – or rather, for sale – here and now, while what will be attained later rather than here and now must be compensated for. This is religious bookkeeping taken to the nth degree.

That brings us to the hypothesis in which rational choice theory culminates. It posits, as noted already, that deregulation, competition, and pluralisation will result in religious revival. In the early 1980s its validity was tested in countries with a Catholic population of more than 80 percent: Ireland, Spain, Italy, Belgium, Austria, and France. According to the economic paradigm, one would expect them to have low 'religious consumption', but it turned out that they vary greatly:

---

[74] V. Welten, De Surfer Op De Golven: Psychologie Van Cultuur En Gedrag, in: A. Felling & J. Peters (eds.), *Cultuur en sociale wetenschappen. Beschouwingen en empirische studies*, ITS, Nijmegen 1991, 31–50; Id. *Greep op cultuur: Een cultuurpsychologische bijdrage aan het minderhedendebat*, Catholic University (now Radboud University), Nijmegen 1992; J.S. Bruner, *Acts of Meaning*, The Jerusalem-Harvard Lectures, Harvard University Press, Cambridge, MA 1990; J.F. Yates & P.A. Estin, Decision Making, in: W. Bechtel & G. Graham (eds.), *A Companion to Cognitive Science*, Blackwell, Oxford 2002, 186–196.

[75] P. Hagoort, Het zwarte gat tussen brein en bewustzijn, in: N. Korteweg (ed.), *De oorsprong: Over het ontstaan van het leven en alles eromheen*, Boom, Amsterdam 2005, 107–124.

[76] P. Ricoeur, *Time and Narrative. Vol. I–III*, University of Chicago Press, Chicago 1988.

from extremely high (Ireland) to extremely low (France) 'consumption'.[77] Among Protestant countries, too, one finds examples that appear to falsify the hypothesis, namely the USA, Canada, Australia, and in Europe, especially Britain and the Scandinavian countries.[78] An even greater reason for rejecting the hypothesis is the religious density in Islamic countries. On the whole this is not a result of religious pluralism, even though there may be other, socially peripheral religions, and certainly not of serious religious competition. Yet religious density is extremely high. This may be ascribed, however, to mutually advantageous alliances between religious and political leaders in these countries.[79]

Does all this mean that the economic paradigm is totally worthless? No, that would not be true. One can cite countries where it does have limited validity, as in Africa and Latin America where the independent churches are experiencing turbulent growth. Even though the two continents differ greatly – in Africa they are reacting against pagan society, while in Latin America they spring from Christian soil – there are parallels, most notably that their members are living in situations of economic poverty, political oppression, social uprootedness, and cultural alienation. The churches offer a refuge in that they represent a community of fellow sufferers, try to offer a way out of destitution, and above all afford faith and hope, so their members do not drown in total despair.[80] In Brazil, for instance, there are signs of the operation of a religious market, reinforced by competition between the charismatic independent churches and the Catholic Church. While this church tries to adapt itself to the needs of the poor by developing charismatic rituals inside and outside its own official liturgical context, its share in the 'religious market' lags behind because of its links with the traditional church hierarchy. So in this case, the internal hierarchical structure of the church is the issue rather than the religious market. We should be wary of distortion, however, for in Brazil only eight to ten million Catholics belong to the charismatic movement, as opposed

---

[77] Chaves & Cann, *Regulation*, op. cit.
[78] Bruce, *Choice*, op. cit., 58–120.
[79] G. Kepel, *The War for Muslim Minds: Islam and the West*, Belknap Press of Harvard University Press, Cambridge, MA 2004.
[80] Ph. Jenkins, *The Next Christendom: The Coming of Global Christianity*, Oxford University Press, Oxford/New York 2002, 72–78.

to the remaining 122 million Catholics who practise a form of traditional folk Catholicism.[81]

The question in this section, then, is this: should differences between religions, churches, and denominations within countries be seen as differences in (intentional) interventions in the religious market? I am not inclined simply to swallow the economic rational choice paradigm's forceful insistence that pluralism and the concomitant competition lead to religious vitality. Human beings cannot be reduced to organisms driven by profit maximisation and religion to a machine set by default on competitive barter relations between religious production and consumption. Instead of this rather radical position, I would propose a more moderate one: within the framework of their hermeneutically explicable continuity with their origins and traditions, religious institutions indeed differ in their sensitivity to the specific requirements and needs of specific groups, which leads to greater religious engagement, such as among rural and urban communities, youths and the aged, educated and less educated people, the cultural majority and minorities, religious conservatives and liberals. A striking example of the latter two is that hellfire preaching at 'the market of evil and sin' is characterised by higher religious consumption among conservatives than among liberals.[82]

1.2.3   *The Cognitive Paradigm*

At the outset of this section, it should be noted that the question about differences in religion cannot be answered exclusively in terms of macro level secularisation processes or economic rational choice processes at meso level. This does not alter the fact that macro level secularisation has a very real influence on the micro level, for instance individual secularisation as a result of the compartmentalisation of religion in relation to the rest of the personal life world.[83] Deregulation of the religious market at meso level likewise affects the micro

---

[81] M. Vasquez, Book Review of A. Chestnut, 2003, Competitive Spirits: Latin America's New Religious Economy, *Journal of the American Academy of Religion* 73(2005)2, 524–528, here 525.

[82] S. Cameron, *The Economics of Sin: Rational Choice or No Choice at All*, Edward Elgar, Cheltenham 2002.

[83] Dobbelaere, *Secularization*, op. cit., 169–172.

level, as evidenced by the religious revival in Italy.[84] But these explanations are not exhaustive; individual persons are not swallowed up by their environment. The question is: could differences in religion possibly be attributed, in part, to processes in individuals at micro level? If so, which processes, and in what sense do they differ from one person to another? I have said that I shall try to answer these questions in terms of the cognitive paradigm that is peculiar to cognitive religious studies, a discipline that developed from cognitive neuroscience about twenty years ago.

First we must look into the term 'cognitive'. It may be misconstrued as synonymous with such terms as 'conscious', 'knowledge-oriented', 'rational', or 'rationalistic'. In general one could say that the cognitive paradigm relates to information, communication, and meanings generated by the interaction between the brain and lower and higher cognitive functions. The interaction entails processes like sensation, perception, automatic responses, emotion, motivation, frames, scripts, memory, thought, imagination, volition, evaluation, planning, decision making, and action. Studies of this interaction have shown that traditional concepts like experience, thought, and meaning have a neurological basis, so that one may speak of a 'biology of meaning', which statement can gradually be enriched by empirical research.[85] We must reiterate: many of these processes occur unconsciously: "Our brains are constantly processing information that does not penetrate consciousness but does direct our behaviour".[86]

How are these processes coordinated? What agency directs them? The literature gives diverse answers, each more complex than the other. One thing is certain: the brain has no central agency that functions as a director or general, a homunculus, an 'I' that regulates its processes. Neither does rationality fulfil a directive function, as philosophers and theologians have supposed for centuries. Here, especially in view of religious experience that will be our next focus, I fall back on Tooby and Cosmides, who maintain that emotions fulfil a coordinating function. According to them, emotions direct and orchestrate

---

[84] M. Introvigne & R. Stark, Religious Competition and Revival in Italy: Exploring European Exceptionalism, *Interdisciplinary Journal of Research on Religion* 1(2005)1, 3–20.

[85] J.A. den Boer, *Neurofilosofie: Hersenen, Bewustzijn, Vrije Wil*, Boom, Amsterdam 2004, 223–240; A.R. Damasio, *Looking for Spinoza: Joy, Sorrow and the Feeling Brain*, Vintage, London 2004.

[86] Hagoort, Het zwarte, op. cit., 108.

the coordination programme. Through the emotions, the processes of sensation, perception, motivation, cognition, thought, planning, et cetera are assimilated into the human neuropsychological architecture, where they are harmonised.[87]

A much simplified input-throughput-output model would explain the interactions thus. Emotions are stimulated by sensations and perceptions in a given situation that affect the person's ideas, interests, and values (input), on the strength of which these emotions stimulate memory and thought processes and imaginative and interpretive processes (throughput), whereupon planning and decision-making processes are triggered and action is taken (output). In other words, environmental input is regulated by emotional throughput to culminate in a particular action aimed at effecting equilibrium between persons and their environment with a view to survival (Lazarus 1991). I have said that the model is much simplified, and moreover suggests a linear process with, as it were, three separate phases. Nothing could be further from the truth. Not only does environmental input affect throughput; the latter in its turn retroacts on the input, and the relation between throughput and output is similarly interactive. There is no question of a linear process because of these constant feed-forward and feedback interactions.[88] That is why the by now traditional computational models, such as Pinker's,[89] which entail serially linked processes, have been replaced by a connective model that allows for parallel links between mutually influencing processes.[90]

Below I try to clarify religious experience within the cognitive paradigm by making a selection from the diverse processes involved. The selection is confined to sensation, perception, and response processes; feeling and processing of emotions; spiritual experience; and actual religious experience. Although this list suggests that we have empirically validated knowledge at our disposal, we know very little as yet about the interaction between neural and cognitive processes, and

---

[87] Cosmides & Tooby, Neurocognitive, op. cit., 52–61.

[88] A.R. Damasio, *The Feeling of What Happens: Body and Emotion in the Making of Consciousness*, Harcourt Inc., New York 2000, 55.

[89] S. Pinker, *How the Mind Works*, Norton, New York 1999; Id., *The Blank Slate: The Modern Denial of Human Nature*, Viking, New York 2002.

[90] Den Boer, *Neurofilosofie*, op. cit., 123–190.

much of it is speculative. To my mind, however, it presents a promising prospect.[91]

First of all, every religious experience arises from an event in our environment that triggers a particular sensation. Bending over a cradle arouses tingling excitement, sitting by the deathbed of a loved one causes gnawing pain. These sensations stimulate perception, as does looking at a person we feel committed to, listening to the sound of his voice, touching his hand, inhaling his familiar smell, tasting his skin when kissing him. Such perceptions trigger a complex of electrochemical processes that evoke automatic responses, resulting in four possibilities: approach, withdrawal, freezing on the spot, or remaining contentedly where we are. The particular automatic response will depend on the pleasantness or threat ascribed to the perception. Seeing a baby attracts and makes us bend even lower over it. The sight of an exhausted body tends to repel, although we surmount that response through the ensuing emotion.

Emotions are important, especially primary ones like positive emotions of joy and surprise, and negative emotions of fear, revulsion, and grief, all of which are probably universal and innate.[92] Secondary emotions are complex, comprising elements of primary emotions; they include embarrassment, shame, and guilt, which are similar in that they make one blush and try to hide one's face. Guilt entails the realisation that one has harmed the other, and shame is felt when that guilt is discovered by others.[93] Emotions are important because they provide nonverbal information and assign meaning to our situations, which we communicate to others.

In addition, they impart a sense of personal involvement: I am the one feeling these emotions, it is my body in which they are expressed. Even primary emotions are not purely a result of genetic disposition, for they are influenced by culture, particularly as regards the situations

---

[91] P. Hagoort, *De toekomstige eeuw der cognitieve neurowetenschap*, Inaugural address Radboud University Nijmegen 2000.

[92] A.R Damasio, *Descartes' Error: Emotion, Reason, and the Human Brain*, Putnam, New York 1994, 149–164; Id., *The Feeling*, op. cit., 279–295.

[93] Ch. Darwin, *The Expression of the Emotions in Man and Animals*, Introduction, afterword and commentaries by Paul Ekman, HarperCollins, London 1999, 250–277, 310–344; P. Ekman, Afterword, in: Darwin, *The Expression*, op. cit., 363–393.

in which they are felt or repressed and the manner in which they are expressed.[94]

Feeling of emotions is followed by processing of emotions. The difference between the two processes is that the former is largely unconscious and the latter partly conscious, partly unconscious. Perhaps for that reason the latter may be called 'feeling of feeling of emotions'.[95] Once processed, emotions become material for higher processes like attention, cognitive framing, memory, imagining, scripts, and the like. The interplay of attention and framing intensifies them. Interplay with memory deepens and enriches them, and blending them with imagination opens up a broader horizon of fictional conceptions, unsurmised perspectives, and possible, hitherto undreamt of worlds, which broaden one's cognitive and behavioural repertoire.

Spiritual experience may be located in the processing of emotions. This experience could happen in the aforementioned situations – the birth of a child or the death of a loved one – but not only there. It is also triggered by situations of moral self-sacrifice, the grandeur of nature, the tone of music, or scientific wonderment. It leads to partly unconscious, partly conscious reflection that, according to Darwin, distinguishes humans from all other living beings: reflection on life and death, origin and goal, transience and finitude.[96] When we bend over a cradle, we are moved by the vulnerability of the infant, the uncertainty of its future life; when we moisten the lips of a dying loved one, we are aware of the helplessness attending both living and dying. Not that life is living towards death (*sein zum Tode*), but at any rate 'living until death'.[97] At a more abstract level, such spiritual processing of emotions entails the dialectics between contingency and absoluteness, between finitude and infinity.[98]

According to the psychiatrist and geneticist Cloninger, such experiences, which he calls experiences of self-transcendence, have three aspects: absorption, identification, and mysticism. Absorption means

---

[94] Ekman, Afterword, op. cit., 392; R.M.L. Winston, *The Human Mind: And How to Make the Most of It*, Bantam, London/New York 2003, 52–55, 225–227.

[95] Damasio, *The Feeling*, op. cit., 36–37, 279–295.

[96] Ch. Darwin, *The Descent of Man: And Selection in Relation to Sex*, Penguin, London 2004, 105.

[97] P. Ricoeur, *La critique et la conviction*, Calmann-Lévy, Paris 1995, 236; Id., *La memoire, l'histoire, l'oubli*, Seuil, Paris 2000, 459–480.

[98] L. Ferry, *L'homme-Dieu: Ou, le sens de la vie*, B. Grasset, Paris 1996; L. Ferry & M. Gauchet, *Le religieux après la religion*, Bernard Grasset, Paris 2004.

that one is so fascinated by the infant in the cradle that one as it were forgets oneself. Identification implies a strong sense of solidarity, so that one virtually merges with the other, yet without losing oneself as at the bedside of a dying person with whom one has shared one's life. Finally, mysticism means that one is mesmerised by the inexpressible, unfathomable wonder of it all – the wonder that one may experience in the (sometimes tragic) dialectics between identity and difference, dependence and independence, self-regard and other-regard, meaning and meaninglessness of suffering, the beginning and completion of life, the human species and the unique individual human person, the individual and the community. They may be seen as the aporias of human existence which we may wonder about and reflect on, without being able to get to the bottom of them and solve the enigmas.[99] Such experiences happen (irrespective of gender, ethnicity and age, albeit more powerfully after the age of 40) when we are confronted with life's paradoxes.[100]

Spiritual experiences of self-transcendence may be regarded as a necessary, albeit not sufficient condition for religious experience. That implies that they should be distinguished from each other more clearly than usually happens. Following the neuro-geneticist Hamer, the distinction can be described as follows. Spiritual experiences, at any rate when conceived of as experiences of self-transcendence, are neurogenetically determined. That means that they occur throughout our lives, to a greater or lesser extent, more or less intensely and more or less frequently, in many situations or only rarely. At all events, they are inherently part of human life. They may be regarded as universal experiences, even though they are undeniably subject to cultural influence as regards their intensity and expression. But they are primarily innate.[101]

Religious experience builds on spiritual experience but is not confined to experiences of self-transcendence, since it entails experience of the transcendent itself, the Supreme, the Eternal, the Infinite, the deity, God. These experiences are not just a matter of absorption, identification, and mysticism of the kind described above, but go beyond these. They are experiences in the presence of the One and All in Greek

---

[99] P. Ricoeur, *Oneself as Another*, University of Chicago Press, Chicago 1992.

[100] C. Cloninger et al., A Psychological Model of Temperament and Character, *Archive of General Psychiatry* 50(1993), 975–990.

[101] D. Hamer, *The God Gene: How Faith is Hardwired into Our Genes*, Doubleday, New York 2004.

philosophy; the God of Abraham, Isaac, and Jacob as recounted in the Jewish Bible; the God of Jesus the Christ as recounted in the Christian New Testament; and of Allah, the God of his prophet Mohammed, as taught in the Muslim Qur'an. They are not primarily innate, but are the result of knowledge and especially familiarity with a culturally determined religious tradition, of which one is part and in which one lives. Hence they are primarily cultural, even though they presuppose a neuro-genetic foundation. The point is, spiritual experience is something that can happen to anybody but religious experience is not, because inner connectedness with the culture of the relevant religious tradition plays a crucial role. This is not to deny that the disposition to become conversant with a religious culture is traceable to the person's genetic makeup. But actually becoming conversant with a particular religious culture among a host of other religious cultures and getting to understand its language from the inside are not primarily natural but cultural processes. The same distinction applies to the disposition to learn a language and actually learning a particular language among a host of other languages.[102]

The difference between spiritual and religious experience becomes even more apparent when one looks at the specific function of the latter, namely religious attribution – a function not found in spiritual experience. Attribution generally is part of what is known as information processing, which relates to the interpretation of events in everyday life. To this end, people look for information to enable them to put events in a meaningful perspective. Attribution is a special form of information processing, in that the events are ascribed to a particular cause or causes. Thus phenomena in the physical, biological, social, and psychological domains are attributed to physical, biological, social, and psychological causes. But how does attribution work when people are confronted with experience of an existential nature, such as questions concerning the origin and goal, the meaning of existence, of life and death? According to the evolutionary psychologist Bering, this is where attributional-domain thinking ends and meta-attribution takes over, in which the events that triggered these existential experiences are related to God or ascribed to his causation. This divine causation

---

[102] K.R. Popper & J.C. Eccles, *The Self and Its Brain: An Argument for Interactionism*, Routledge, London/New York 2000, 48; H. Schilderman, *Wat is er geestelijk aan de geestelijke zorg?* Inaugural address Radboud University Nijmegen 2009.

may be seen as an efficient cause (*causa efficiens*), a teleological or final cause (*causa finalis*), or an appealing, example-related cause (*causa exemplaris*). That is how religious attribution works.[103]

As I have said, this element is not present in spiritual experience in the sense of self-transcendence, but is the hallmark of religious experience. Some cognitive scholars believe that such religious experience is marked by an 'attribution fallacy' that lures people into a 'cognitive illusion', in which they yield to 'over-belief'.[104] But how will those scholars respond to nonreligious experiences of the meaning of life? People may express that meaning by saying: 'this is my lot, I must bear it', 'that's how it's got to be', 'this is my task in life'. What are 'my lot', 'how it's got to be', 'my task' if not signs that the person is rising above the immanent attributional domain and reaching out for that which transcends it? Is it not an indication of the meta-attribution which I've just mentioned, albeit a nonreligious one? Without it their lives would be void and meaningless, which would be intolerable.[105]

Or does religious meta-attribution make God a 'God of the gaps' (*Lückenbüsser*) who is gradually eclipsed as science forges ahead in the immanent domains? That strikes me as an untenable proposition, however frequently it crops up in the debate, for the simple reason that the existential questions raised in the religious domain can never be answered fully by science. However much science may enable us to intervene in human life, to shift the boundaries of birth and death, even to 'make life', the fundamental questions about 'human' life, its origin and goal, chance and destiny, freedom and conditioning, vocation and destination continually hover round the enigma of human existence in religious terms, the mystery of the human being and his or her God. The significance of religion is that it enables the human person to deal with these questions explicitly in ritual and prayer rather than repress them, however insoluble they may be, as is evident in religious

---

[103] P. Boyer, *Religion Explained: The Evolutionary Origins of Religious Thought*, Basic Books, New York 2001, 196–202.

[104] S. Guthrie, *Faces in the Clouds: A New Theory of Religion*, Oxford University Press, New York 1993; D.J. Slone, *Theological Incorrectness: Why Religious People Believe What They Shouldn't*, Oxford University Press, Oxford/New York 2004, 58.

[105] J.M. Bering, The Evolutionary History of an Illusion: Religious Causal Beliefs in Children and Adults, in: J.E. Bruce & D.F. Bjorklund (eds.), *Origins of the Social Mind: Evolutionary Psychology and Child Development*, Guilford Press, New York 2005, 411–437; J. Bering & D. Johnson, "O Lord...You Perceive My Thoughts from Afar": Recursiveness and the Evolution of Supernatural Agency, *Journal of Cognition and Culture*, 5(2005)1/2, 118–142.

people's tales about bereavement. When they complain that God has forsaken them and express it in lament or even accusations against God, they bring it into their relationship with God.[106]

Once again, I give a global answer to the question of where religious differences come from, this time between individuals at the micro level. To this end, I mention three conditions for people's varying religious experience. The first concerns emotions that play a major role in religious experience, for instance joy, sorrow, gratitude, shame, and guilt. People differ not only in the way they feel their emotions, but also in their processing and expression of emotions. It is a result of both genetic disposition and cultural influences. Some cultures encourage the experience and expression of emotion, others repress it. Anyway, the differences between individual people depend on the extent to which they are predisposed to the feeling and processing of emotions. Some people are good at it, others less good.

The second condition concerns spiritual experience as an experience of self-transcendence, which is a necessary condition for religious experience. The three processes involved – absorption, identification, and mysticism – should be seen as three scales. One pole of the continuum is a low degree of intensity, the other a high degree. People vary on these three scales: the experience of self-transcendence happens more easily for some, less easily for others. In other words, the difference between peoples' religious experience depends partly on the extent to which they are predisposed to absorption, identification, and mysticism.

The third condition concerns the extent to which people have appropriated the religious culture of a particular tradition and are conversant with it, for there can be no religious experience unless the narratives, images, ideas, and concepts of a religious tradition have been internalised. Here, too, individuals differ. It is said that the decline in religious knowledge is responsible for the fact that the younger generation has fewer religious experiences and that these leave them indifferent: "They don't even know what Christmas and Easter are about." What they lack is not so much knowledge, although such knowledge may well be necessary, but familiarity with a religious tradition, and this is precisely where people differ. Some genuinely base their lives on their

---

[106] P. Zuidgeest, *The Absence of God: Exploring the Christian Tradition in a Situation of Mourning*, Brill, Leiden/Boston 2001.

religious tradition, others are lukewarm, yet others more or less indifferent. In secularised countries the last category is, of course, growing. At all events, differences in people's religious experience depend on familiarity with their religious tradition.

In the foregoing discussion, I have taken a theoretical decision that warrants separate mention, since it is based on a fundamental choice. It concerns the perspective from which one should approach the operation of (some of) the higher cognitive functions, which include religious experience. Theoretically, there are three possible points of departure: (a) the area of the brain; (b) the interaction between brain and mind; or (c) the interaction between brain, mind, and the surrounding culture. Applied to religious experience, these perspectives raise the question: does religious experience occur in the area of the brain, in the interaction between brain and mind, or in the interaction between brain, mind, and the surrounding religious culture? The problem in choosing between the alternatives is that it is not clear what is meant by 'mind'.

Some cognitive neuro-scientists settle for the first option, but keep silent when they are unable to describe and explain certain higher functions, such as faith, hope, and love, or more mundane matters like goal setting and planning, in terms of brain functioning. It also applies to complex problem solving, writing a book, making a sculpture, composing a fugue – even delivering an inspired sermon. This is not to deny the need for the infrastructure of brain processes in these sublime areas. On the contrary, there can be no faith, no hope, no love, no recital, no sermon without the brain.[107] This condition, although necessary, is not sufficient. Yet these scientists prefer to close their eyes to the problem, hoping that research will advance to a point where it is possible to provide the required explanations for, say, faith, hope, love.

Other cognitive neuro-scientists choose the second alternative. They believe that mind should be seen as the conversion of third-person perceptions involved in brain research into first-person experiences of people executing the aforementioned creative artistic and religious activities. These activities are said to 'emerge' from brain processes – hence the term 'emergentism'. But how does one understand this emergence of first-person experiences from third-person perceptions in the

---

[107] Hagoort, *De Toekomstige*, op. cit., 5.

brain, and how do the experiences, once they have surfaced, influence the brain in their turn? Another term used is 'supervenience', but again one must ask whether this means more than the metaphor that first-person experience builds on – hence the term 'supervenience' – neurological processes without explaining what such 'building on' actually entails. At this stage, one cannot prove more than that the processes (i.e. third-person perceptions and first-person experiences) correlate. Certainly there is no variation in religious experience without variation in neural processes, but co-variance is not the same as causality. Other scientists introduce the concept of self-organisation. But what exactly does it mean if one argues that the connectivity of neural-perception processes results in a system of higher cognitive functions that is self-organising and not reducible to individual neurological functions? It sounds tempting, but the empirical meaning of this sheer speculation remains hidden for now.[108]

The reader will have noticed that I have provisionally chosen the third option – albeit not blindly and dogmatically, for as yet there are insufficient research results to make a final choice, if that is ever possible. But at this stage I would say that without the culture of a religious tradition, in which the person concerned participates more or less intensely, it is not possible to have a religious experience, defined as an experience of transcendence, and distinct from spiritual experience, defined as self-transcendence. I base this on the view that religious experiences, like many other higher cognitive processes, are not merely embodied in people, but are also embedded in cultural wholes. Some researchers believe that cognitive processes occur wholly in the mind and that culture is simply an extension of these, a kind of dependent variable. But in a connectivist approach, culture also contributes input to these processes in the form of stimuli, examples, models and strategies, inspiration and challenges – a kind of independent variable. After all, are higher cognitive processes such as imagination, creative thought, composing music and poetry, as well as religious experience, not expressed specifically in culture and language? In other words, do

---

[108] J. Kim, *Mind in a Physical World: An Essay on the Mind-Body Problem and Mental Causation*, MIT Press, Cambridge, MA 1998; A. Stephan, *Emergenz: Von der Unvorhersagbarkeit zur Selbstorganisation*, Dresden University Press, Dresden 1999; S. Pihlström, A Pragmatic Critique of Three Kinds of Religious Naturalism, *Method and Theory in the Study of Religion* 17(2005)3, 177–218.

they not emerge from brain processes in interaction with mind and culture?

These questions are not gratuitous. In cognitive science of religion, for instance in the work of McCauley and Lawson, two leading scholars of ritual, one encounters a cognitivist limitation, albeit in the guise of a naturalistic form of religion among non-literate peoples, which they consider to be a model for all religion. By stressing the function of the brain, they set up their naturalistic approach in opposition to a culturalist approach.[109] McCauley[110] goes so far as to claim that religion antedates history and culture. But surely religion cannot exist without prescribed rituals, conducted in pre-existent communities, by pre-existent leadership, in designated social venues, at socially set times, which exert the necessary influence on the participants' intra-psychic experience.[111] The problem, clearly, is how to theoretically balance (neural) nature, mind, and culture – probably by alternately treating them as independent and dependent variables. This is the significance of Popper's 'three worlds', the material (neural), cognitive, and cultural worlds, and his notion of a 'self anchored in world 3', to which I would add a 'religious self anchored in world 3'.[112]

Again, I conclude the section by asking whether interpersonal differences in religion can be explained in terms of differences in cognitive functioning. In view of the foregoing debate on whether and in what sense one can confine oneself to neural processes when it comes to religion, or whether one should view them as interactive with mind and culture, some caution is called for. My answer, therefore, is

---

[109] R. McCauley & E. Lawson, *Bringing Ritual to Mind: Psychological Foundations of Cultural Forms*, Cambridge University Press, Cambridge, UK/New York 2002, 38–88.

[110] R. McCauley, The Naturalness of Religion and the Unnaturalness of Science, in: R.A. Wilson & F.C. Keil (eds.), *Explanation and Cognition*, MIT, Cambridge, MA/London 2000, 61–86, here 80.

[111] G. Flood, Reflections on Tradition and Inquiry in the Study of Religions, *Journal of the American Academy of Religion* 74(2006)1, 47–58, here 49–51.

[112] Popper & Eccles, *The Self*, op. cit., 36–50, 144–147; cf. T.W. Deacon, *The Symbolic Species: The Co-Evolution of Language and the Brain*, W.W. Norton, New York 1997, 409–410; J.S. Jensen, *The Study of Religion in a New Key: Theoretical and Philosophical Soundings in the Comparative and General Study of Religion*, Aarhus University Press, Aarhus/Oxford 2003, 258, 273; M. Day, The Ins and Outs of Religious Cognition, *Method and Theory in the Study of Religion* 16(2004), 241–255; W.E. Paden, Comparative Religion and the Whitehouse Project: Connections and Compatibilities? *Method and Theory in the Study of Religion* 16(2004)3, 256–265; Schilderman, *Wat is er geestelijk*, op. cit.

conditional. If and inasmuch as religious experience is in part culturally determined – which is my assumption at this stage – interpersonal
differences in religion, here religious experience, are not dependent
solely on their disposition to all kinds of perceptions, feeling, and processing of emotion, and spiritual experience (defined as an experience
of self-transcendence), but also on the extent to which people participate in and are conversant with the culture of a particular religious
tradition.

Conclusion

I have tried to clarify the varieties of religious decline and ascendance
between and within countries in terms of secularisation at macro level,
with due regard to nonreligious factors influencing their range, pro-
fundity, and rate, as well as to the counter movements and conflicts
to which they give rise. Secondly, I tried to explain the differences
within countries and between groups in terms of the economic rational choice model at meso level. However, since its strong thesis of
religion as a compensatory barter relationship with God aimed at religious profit maximisation contradicts the essential nature of religion, I
defended the more modest position in which differences between religious institutions may be confined to differences in sensitivity to the
'religious market' within the hermeneutically reconstructible continuity with the origins and traditions of religions. Next, I tried to account
for the varieties at micro level in terms of the cognitive paradigm,
and traced them to differences in disposition to perception, feeling,
and processing of emotions and spiritual experience, and participation
in and familiarity with the culture of a particular religious tradition.
Finally, I pointed out the interaction between phenomena at macro,
meso, and micro levels as they condition one another. In so doing I
provided three broad outlines for future research projects.

   Three strategies may be used to trace, study, and interpret the
varieties of religious weaknesses and religious strengths in terms of
differences between and within countries, and between and within
groups. This can help to clarify the influence that the a-synchronicity
of religious strength and religious weakness exerts on a society that is
increasingly characterised by multiculturalism and multi-religiosity. It
can also facilitate interpretation and evaluation of the variety of religious phenomena that feature on the political agenda.

CHAPTER TWO

RELIGIOUS IDENTITY

Identity is a term frequently heard in public debate nowadays. It makes one surmise that there is some sort of identity crisis. One reason for it is the process of functional differentiation that divides Western society, and increasingly non-Western societies as well, into a variety of relatively autonomous systems, in which the individual person fulfils a multiplicity of different roles. This could obstruct a unified picture of the individual person, the group to which she belongs, the nation of which she is a member. Another reason is the globalisation process, as a result of which individuals, groups, and communities from diverse, previously alien cultures enter into permanent contact and mingle, making one ask what distinguishes them from each other and what one's own identity is. Identity and difference are interrelated, which makes it a relational concept as in classical ontology. Identity may be defined as continuous awareness that individuals, groups, and communities, despite all discontinuity, remain 'the same', remain 'themselves' over time. The tension between continuity and discontinuity is essential. Identity cannot be grasped exclusively in terms of permanence, for that would imply stasis and ignore ongoing historical change. Identity means that, although transformation takes place in the course of the vicissitudes of time and history, in that transformation the individual person or the group still manifest as 'the same', as 'himself' or 'itself'. But the temporal dimension expressed in discontinuous continuity between past and present is not the only relevant one. There is another temporal dimension extending from the past and the present towards the future. Part of identity is that one not only views the past from a vantage point in the present, but also that the reflection of events that possibly will occur in an unpredictable future is assimilated into the identity of the person, of the group one belongs to, of the community one is engaged in, without ignoring these events or forfeiting identity.

Against this background, religious identity acquires more precise meaning. The process of increasing functional differentiation undoubtedly militates against a conception of religious identity encompassed by the sacred canopy that once extended over the whole of society.

A collective and individual identity that accords with such a stabilising universality no longer exists. The religious identity of individuals, groups, and communities has become one among many identities,
such as economic identity as a wage earner, political identity as a party
member, social identity as a spouse and parent, and professional identity as, for example, a teacher or doctor. In view of functional differentiation, then, the only valid question is whether, in what way, and to
what extent religious identity influences the other identities in a framework of interpenetrating functional systems. The most basic question
is whether such an influence exists, for it could be zero. The nature
of the influence is likewise not predetermined, for it could be positive or negative, just as the influence of other systems and their corresponding identities on religious identity could be positive or negative.
The extent of the influence is equally relevant, for it could range from
extremely weak to extremely strong. In addition to functional differentiation, globalisation also creates a religious identity crisis. Ongoing
contact with members, groups, and communities of other religions
not only puts one's own religion's claims to uniqueness, universality,
and absoluteness at risk, but also raises questions about what religious
truth and authority still mean in a religiously pluralistic context. Is
religious identity more than a sense of religious incoherent coherence
in one's particular relationship with a particular religion that one has
grown up with and that one expects to adhere to, more or less, for the
rest of one's life?

This chapter seeks to answer two questions: what does the religious
identity of individuals and communities consist in, and how can we
research it? The concept of religious identity comprises two terms:
religion and identity. In this chapter the term 'religion' refers to individuals and communities dealing with the dialectical relation between
autonomy and contingency, especially in existentially meaningful situations and experiences, in a perspective of divine transcendence. For
the term 'identity' there is no better source to start with than book ten
of Aristotle's *Metaphysics*, in which identity is viewed in terms of a
dialectic relation between 'same' and 'other'.[1] 'Same' in religious identity is expressed in permanence over time (2.1), and 'other' in the rela-

---

[1] Aristotle, Topics, in: *The Complete Works of Aristotle*, The Revised Oxford Translation, edited by Jonathan Barnes, Princeton University Press, Princeton, NJ 1984,
1054a30–1059a14.

tion between identity and alterity (2.2). Finally, I analyse the relation in comparative research into religious identity by way of two methods (qualitative and quantitative) and from two perspectives (insider and outsider) (2.3).

2.1 IDENTITY: PERMANENCE OVER TIME

In this section, I discuss the following themes in identity as permanence over time. The first is that permanence of identity over time can be described in terms of the dialectics between sameness and self. Even though identity may appear to be homogeneous, it is characterised by multiplicity and hybridity and may comprise any number of aspects. Like all forms of identity, religious identity is marked by the dialectics of ascription and achievement. But is achieved identity a free choice based on personal intentionality, or is it conditioned by extraneous, structural factors? And finally, is that choice mediated by religious representations (ideological identity), religious rites (ritual identity), and religious institutions (institutional identity), or by some or all of these?

2.1.1 *Sameness and Self*

A hallmark of identity, whether individual or communal, is that it remains the same over time. It survives the 'ravages of time'. But the fact that it is not affected by time does not make it an invariable constant. Because of temporal change, identity undergoes necessary transformation, evidenced by individual human development. That does not imply that it changes its form while the essence remains untouched. Such essentialism should yield to the following argument. Just as individuals or communities used to relate to historical circumstances in a bygone era (T1), so they relate, analogously, to current historical circumstances (T2). Thus permanence of identity lies in continuity of relations to time, for example T1 and T2.

This leads to an important insight. Identity does not precede time, is not above or buried in the depths of time, but is embodied in time. It is not a reified process independent of its carriers, be they individuals or communities. It is actualised in the interaction between these carriers and the surrounding culture in time. It is grounded in the way individuals and communities, in interaction with culture, see themselves as 'the same' in varying circumstances throughout history up to the present. That determines its hermeneutic character.[2]

That tells us something about the past and the present, but what about the future? Permanence in the past and the present can be reconstructed hermeneutically after the event. But reconstructing future permanence in retrospect is a contradiction in terms. It negates the very nature of future time. Future permanence cannot be reconstructed hermeneutically; it can only be expressed, attested, proclaimed hermeneutically as a promise. One can only promise that one will be 'the same' in the future – that one will remain loyal, engaged, committed.[3] In so doing, one promises to keep one's word and puts oneself under a certain obligation to do what one says. Stating that one will keep one's promise entails a risk, for who can foretell the future, who foresees the long- and short-term consequences of one's own and other people's actions? All the other party can look to is the trustworthiness of the person making the promise. The only 'guarantee' offered is that person's reliability. The underside is betrayal: the suspicion of a trap can always rear its head; any promise can be broken.[4] This applies to the collective self as much as to individual selves. The permanence of a community's future identity, too, resides in a promise, whose sole basis is trustworthiness and reliability: a promise to keep to the social contract, the rule of law, within that community, or to adhere to contractual treaties between communities. The essential difference between groups of animals and groups of human beings is that the latter are able to make and keep promises.[5]

Needless to say, such future-oriented identity is also enacted in a continuity of relations. Just as individuals and communities related to the historical circumstances of a bygone era (T1) and relate to present circumstances in terms of their current self-understanding (T2), so they promise to relate to the unknown historical circumstances that will befall them in the future (T3). Permanence over time is based on

---

[2] Cf. J.A. van der Ven, De relatie van theologie en religiewetenschap in een vergelijkende wetenschaps-beoefening, *Tijdschrift voor Theologie* 45(2005)2, 119–137, here 120–123.

[3] P. Ricoeur, *Oneself as Another*, University of Chicago Press, Chicago 1992, 115–125.

[4] P. Ricoeur, *The Course of Recognition*, Harvard University Press, Cambridge, MA 2005, 127–134.

[5] E. Cassirer, Vom Wesen und Werden des Naturrechts, *Zeitschrift für Rechtsphilosophie in Lehre und Praxis* 6(1932)1, 1–27.

hermeneutic self-understanding, for the past and the present in the mode of reconstruction, for the future in the mode of promise.

2.1.2 Multiplicity and Hybridity

While identity does imply permanence, it does not mean oneness. According to Aristotelian dialectics, we have to distinguish between sameness and self on the one hand, and on the other between one and many. In other words, individuals and communities have not just one but several identities. Thus, apart from religious identity, they have a social, an economic, a political, and a cultural identity. People are not just members (or non-members) of religious communities, but also have – probably stronger – ties with their partners, parents, children, siblings, friends (social identity), teachers, pupils, colleagues, bosses and underlings (professional identity), adherents or members of political parties (political identity), and active or passive practitioners of folk or classical art (cultural identity). In other words, the dialectics between sameness and self is not enacted only in the area where ultimate questions about autonomy and contingence are symbolised and ritualised in a transcendent perspective (religious identity). It also functions in areas pertaining to primary relations and the life world (social identity), careers (professional identity), the exercise of political power (political identity), and the symbolisation of all these domains (cultural identity). People perceive their identity not merely in terms of religious sameness and self, but also of social, economic, political, and cultural sameness and self. This is expressed in taking responsibility and fulfilling duties.[6] It does not concern self-evident undertakings but life plans entailing long- and short term goals, in which desirability and feasibility compete with each other, as well as means and resources that are scarce and have to be distributed equitably.[7] It is important, because it gives their history 'life coherence', to which they attest in their 'narrative coherence'.[8]

But that does not mean that these identities necessarily constitute an integral whole. Euphoric speculations can too easily lead to talk

---

[6] A. Sen, *Identity and Violence: The Illusion of Destiny*, W.W. Norton & Co., New York 2006.

[7] J. Rawls, *A Theory of Justice*, Belknap Press of Harvard University Press, Cambridge, MA 1971, 399–433.

[8] P. Ricoeur, *La Memoire, l'histoire, l'oubli*, Seuil, Paris 2000, 484, n. 41.

of a 'polyphonic identity'. Usually there is a hybrid combination of diverse identities without any optimal harmony between them. This may take more or less pathological forms like dissociation, levelling and elimination of areas of identity, as well as a double bind when two or more areas conflict.[9] Max Weber realised long ago that religious identity can conflict with economic identity because of the opposing principles of religion (solidarity) and economics (competition); with political identity because of the differing authority claims of revelation and democracy; with sexual identity because of different values and norms about sex and sexual orientation; or with intellectual identity because of the conflicting demands of academic freedom versus intellectual sacrifice (*sacrificum intellectus*).[10] There are three possible ways out of this kind of conflictive, hybrid identity construct:[11] tolerating cognitive dissonance if one does not want to give up any of the identities (conflicting loyalties), critically championing changes in one of these areas (critical voice), or deciding to quit (exit).

2.1.3 *Ascription and Achievement*

Against the background of such multiple identities one could ask to what extent they are ascribed or achieved.[12] The question also pertains to religious identity. It is often said that one is born into a particular religious community because one's parents (and other relatives) belong to it. This argument based on kinship can be further explicated with reference to the helplessness and need for security of (young) children, their emotional dependence on, and the emotional influence of, the family, which include internalisation of family values and identification mechanisms. That would explain religious ascription in terms of religious kinship relations.

In non-Western countries religious ascription cannot be underestimated, but even there phenomena are emerging that are typical of religious identity in Western countries: a decline in religious ascription and growing religious (or nonreligious) achievement at an increas-

---

[9] H.J.M. Hermans, *Waardengebieden en hun ontwikkeling*, Swets & Zeitlinger, Amsterdam 1974, 239–276.

[10] Cf. M. Weber, *Gesammelte Aufsätze zur Religionssoziologie*, Mohr, Tübingen 1920/1978, 542–571.

[11] A. Hirschman, *Exit, Voice, and Loyalty: Responses to Decline in Firms, Organizations, and States*, Harvard University Press, Cambridge, MA 1970.

[12] T. Parsons et al., *Theories of Society*, Free Press, New York 1965.

ingly early age. Religious choice can be differentiated into acceptance or rejection of one or more religious representations, rituals and/or forms of participation in a religious institution, including total rejection of the latter ('believing without belonging'). People may also opt for multiple religious belonging, and not only in Africa, where some groups take part in African traditional rituals as well as those of Christian churches and Islamic mosques,[13] or Japan, where Shinto rituals are performed at the beginning of life, Buddhist rituals at the end of life, and Christian rituals for marriage,[14] but also in Western countries where Christian and Zen rituals or Christian and Taoist wisdom are sometimes combined. In other words, religious identity in itself is complex, quite apart from its interaction with economic, political, social, and cultural identities.

A choice based on reflective achievement offers a better chance of tolerance of other religions than a choice based on convention. That is because in weighing one's options one discovers similarities as well as differences, and that differences between religions are often much smaller than those within religions. Another reason is that one considers not just the pros and cons of one's own religion but also those of other religions. In addition, such a choice is an ongoing, dynamic process, which means that tolerance is constantly nurtured. During the Renaissance, that was not considered an evil, since faith in God and differences between religions were seen as manifestations of the relation between the one and the many (e.g. Pico della Mirandola), and truth about God as the totality of viewpoints about God (e.g. Nicholas of Cusa).[15]

In the so-called radical Enlightenment, however, Christian denominations regarded tolerance as an evil, because it threatened the absolute, universal, and 'exclusive' truth claims of these churches. Tolerance might trigger a reflective choice process, leading to a liberal interpretation of the trinity and Christology, which in its turn could foster

---

[13] J.A. van der Ven, J.S. Dreyer & H.J.C. Pieterse, *Is There a God of Human Rights? The Complex Relationship between Human Rights and Religion: A South African Case*, Brill, Leiden/Boston 2004, 350–355; F.-V. Anthony, Churches of African Origin: Forging Religio-Cultural Identity of a Third Kind, *Kristu Jyoti* 19(2003)1, 61–90.

[14] P. Valkenberg, *Sharing Lights on the Way to God: Muslim-Christian Dialogue and Theology in the Context of Abrahamic Partnership*, Rodopi, Amsterdam 2006, 130.

[15] D. Coskun, *Law as Symbolic Form: Ernst Cassirer and the Anthropocentric View of Law*, Dissertation Radboud University Nijmegen, Wolf Legal Publishers, 2006, 62–63.

deism, agnosticism, and atheism. These fears were rife, not only in the Christian world but also in Judaism and Islam. There, too, reflective religion was considered hazardous.[16] This makes the relation between ascription and achievement a less innocuous issue than it seems at first glance. Does the heavier emphasis on religious achievement that characterises present-day, mainly Western culture indeed result in a sliding scale of tolerance, religious liberalism, deism, agnosticism, and atheism?

2.1.4   *Intentionality and Structure*

What I have said about deliberative reflection in religious choice could create the impression that it is entirely an outcome of the individual or community's own intentions. That is by no means true. There are two dimensions to religious choice: one's own intention, and structural factors. The latter are factors that surpass the individual or community and condition them by way of supra-cyclical economic, political, judicial, social, and cultural trends.

Thus, the principle of the separation of church and state, so intrinsic to the democratic state, conditions attitudes towards religious representations, rituals, and institutions. It makes quite a difference whether that principle is interpreted from a cooperative, an accommodative, or a laicist angle.[17] A cooperative interpretation sees state and church as two independent entities, but with the state subsidising the church by way of funding its clergy and schools, maintaining its buildings, and/ or exempting it from taxes. An accommodative interpretation does not allow for such subsidies. Instead the church is viewed as part of the national culture, and conditions are created for preserving it by recognising the religious calendar and granting financial exemptions. A laicist interpretation erects a wall of separation between state and church, and the latter is cordoned off to prevent it from playing any role in the public domain.

There is also reverse conditioning of society by religious identity in the form of religious influence on certain economic factors, such

---

[16] J. Israel, *Enlightenment Contested: Philosophy, Modernity, and the Emancipation of Man*, 1670–1752, Oxford University Press, Oxford/New York 2006, 97.
[17] W. Durnham, Perspectives on Religious Liberty, in: J. Witte & J.D. van der Vyver (eds.), *Religious Human Rights in Global Perspective: Legal Perspectives*, Nijhoff, The Hague/Boston 1996.

as the selective affinity (*Wahlverwandschaft*) between Calvinism and capitalism (Weber) or the traditional role division between males and females, justified by a conservative interpretation of divine creation. Religion, moreover, influences civil society, for instance through charitable, diaconal and voluntary work, mutual solidarity, integration and cohesion, and the impact of religious culture on the legal culture, hence on legislative, administrative, and judicial decisions.

In short, the interaction between religion and society is characterised by antecedent and consequential relations. Society influences religion (antecedent relations), while religion influences society (consequential relations), which in its turn feeds back into the antecedent relations. This results in a dynamic, ongoing spiral process, which can be frozen at any point and subjected to research. The process does not have a linear upward or downward movement, for from which angle would it be seen as moving either upward or downward? According to a one-sided secularisation hypothesis, the growing influence of society on religion could be regarded as an upward movement, but critics of that hypothesis would view it the other way round. It seems more likely that the process is curvilinear. At all events, the relative strength of antecedent and/or consequential relations can only be determined by careful empirical research into religious representations (about God, Jesus, Muhammad, creation, salvation), religious rituals (weekly and annual, as well as rites of passage), and religious institutions (mono-cratic, democratic, congregationalist). One also has to allow for the possibility that relations can range from positive, negative, or ambivalent, to zero.

At a theoretical level, one might ask whether intentionality and structural causes are not mutually exclusive. The answer is negative, because there is no such thing as total intentionality or total causality, at least not in the human sciences. Total intentionality would mean that everything people do is a product of their own initiative without any influence from the contributions of earlier generations, including the institutions they shaped. That is inconceivable, since human beings are woven into synchronic and diachronic networks and the institutions embodying these. People do take the initiative, but it is their initiative *in* the world, not the initiative *of* the world. In other words, it is never more than an intervention.[18] But total causality does not exist either. If

---

[18] I. Kant, *Critique of Pure Reason*, St. Martin's Press, New York 1965, 410ff.

it did, the primary experience of 'mine-ness' would be an illusion, for instance that the actions I perform are *my* actions, the body I have and am is *my* body, the memory storing my knowledge is *my* memory, the thoughts I think are *my* thoughts, and the imagination I use to plan my future is *my* imagination designing *my* future.[19] These experiences cannot be reduced to *qualia* (the quality of 'mine-ness'), explicable exclusively in terms of our physiological hardware, in this case the brain.[20] That would be to negate the structural interaction between body and mind, as well as the interaction between mind and culture, in which the manifold symbolisations of 'mine-ness' are accumulated in love, art, morality, religion, and (scientific) 'aha'-experiences. In fact, it would reduce human life to its material substratum.

2.1.5   Religious Representations, Rituals and Institutions

I have now distinguished between different substantial aspects of religion: religious representations, rituals, and institutions. They may be regarded as three possible carriers of religious identity, namely ideological, ritual, and institutional identity. After all, some individuals and communities experience their religious identity as primarily ideological, others as mainly ritual, and yet others as institutional. But is this trichotomy correct? There are other possible classifications, such as those of Glock[21] and Stark and Glock.[22] They discern five substantial aspects, of which the first two are an ideological aspect (belief), corresponding with what I call religious representations, and a ritualistic aspect. Their other three aspects are an experiential aspect (feeling), an intellectual aspect (knowledge), and a consequential aspect, which refers to the influence of religion on daily life (effects). It is noteworthy that this classification does not include the aspect of religious institutions, even though notions about the essential characteristics of such institutions, as well as their structure and function, could determine the religious identity of individuals and communities.

---

[19] Ricoeur, *Oneself*, op. cit., 104–112.

[20] J.A. den Boer, *Neurofilosofie: hersenen, bewustzijn, vrije wil*, Boom, Amsterdam 2004, 68–69.

[21] Ch.Y. Glock, On the Study of Religious Commitment, *Religious Education* 57(1962)4, 98–110.

[22] R. Stark & Ch.Y. Glock, *American Piety: The Nature of Religious Commitment*, University of California Press, Berkeley 1968.

In empirical research, there seems to be some uncertainty about the adequacy of the classifications. Glock and Stark eventually removed the consequential aspect from their list, since it refers to a consequence rather than a component of religion. In some empirical studies three of the remaining four aspects – the ideological, ritualistic, and experiential aspects – appear to cluster together, the ideological aspect being the dominant one. Other studies yield two dimensions, one comprising the ideological plus the experiential aspect, the other comprising the ritualistic aspect. In yet other research, the aspects appear to form a single factor, the ideological aspect again being dominant. This raises a question: is religion in fact controlled by acceptance of religious truths, the ideological aspect, or is it because the measuring instrument is such that the other aspects are heavily tinctured by the ideological aspect and are therefore not properly differentiated? The polemical question has been asked whether Glock and Stark's list does not constitute a sacred artefact.[23] Certainly the last word has not been said, even though the literature tends to treat Glock and Stark's list as axiomatic, despite the fact that it really calls for critical study and conceptual reflection.[24] The crucial question is: does the crux of religion lie in religious representations (ideological aspect), or in a combination of religious representations and rituals, as Pals[25] concludes from his study of the literature. If we focus on religious identity the question reads: does religious identity primarily comprise an ideological identity (religious representations) and/or a ritual identity?

In present-day cognitive religious studies, Glock and Stark's list has been superseded by the dichotomy that Pals found in the literature. He sees religion as comprising mainly religious representations and religious rituals, without devoting any substantial attention to my third aspect, that of religious institutions. But quite apart from that, the view that religion consists of religious representations and religious rituals tells us very little unless the relation between these two aspects is clarified, for that relation is the real issue when we look for the core of religion and religious identity.

---

[23] A. Felling, J. Peters & O. Schreuder, *Religion im Vergleich: Bundesrepublik Deutschland und Niederlande*, Lang, Frankfurt am Main 1987, 40.

[24] D.M. Wulff, *Psychology of Religion: Classic and Contemporary Views*, Wiley, New York 1997, 208–219.

[25] D.L. Pals, *Seven Theories of Religion*, Oxford University Press, New York 1996, 270, 282–283.

Although cognitive religious studies does recognise the relation of religious representations to religious rituals, it barely looks at the converse relation of religious rituals to religious representations. But before dealing with this converse relation, let me first examine the relation of religious representations to religious rituals.

Cognitive religious studies speculates on the functioning of religious representations in ritual in a specific way. This specificity refers to ritual participants' notions about God's role in such celebrations. These notions can be divided into two categories: representations of direct divine acts, and representations of indirect divine acts. The Catholic mass is said to be an example of representations of direct divine acts. After all, during the Catholic mass, in the minds of Catholics, God intervenes directly by way of a transubstantiation of bread and wine into the body and blood of Jesus. An instance of representations of indirect divine acts is the baptismal rite. In the minds of participants, according to this view, God intervenes indirectly, for the direct actor in this ritual is the ordained priest: he is the one who baptises, not God. In this view, the baptismal act is traceable to the ordination act by an ordained bishop, whose legitimacy in turn derives from the acts of the apostles, whose legitimacy derives from Jesus' acts, whose legitimacy stems from God's sending of Jesus, his son. The message, then, is this: in transubstantiation God acts directly, in baptism he acts indirectly.[26]

My objection concerns the conceptual shakiness of this speculation, arising from the distinction made between the two sacraments, baptism and the eucharist. After all, in both instances the ritual act is performed by an ordained priest in communication with the religious community: in that respect there is no difference between the two sacraments. But that is not all. The question is how to interpret the relation between the human act of the priest and the community on the one hand and the divine act on the other. The answer is not to assume indirect divine action in baptism and direct action in the eucharist. In both instances God's active presence is both direct and indirect. The solution lies in replacing the causal, mechanistic operation that is said to characterise

[26] E. Lawson & R. McCauley, *Rethinking Religion: Connecting Cognition and Culture*, Cambridge University Press, Cambridge 1990; P. Boyer, *Religion Explained: The Evolutionary Origins of Religious Thought*, Basic Books, New York 2001, 258ff.; R. McCauley & E. Lawson. *Bringing Ritual to Mind: Psychological Foundations of Cultural Forms*, Cambridge University Press, Cambridge/New York 2002; T. Vial, How Does the Cognitive Science of Religion Stack up as a Big Theory, a La Hume? *Method and Theory in the Study of Religion* 18(2006)4, 351–371.

the indirect divine act in baptism, including the purely instrumental chain of causes and effects, with a dialectic relation between divine act and human act. This dialectic entails that God does not act only *via* the acts of the officiating priest (indirectly), artificially mediated though the chain of the bishop's, the apostles', and Jesus' acts, but also *in* those acts (directly). In both baptism and the eucharist, God acts both *via* (indirectly) and *in* human acts (directly). As Schillebeeckxs[27] puts it, God's activity is that of mediated immediacy, in which 'mediated' refers to the 'via' in indirect acts and 'immediacy' refers to the 'in' in direct acts. One could see it as a typical example of Catholic sacramentology,[28] deriving from underlying conceptions of creation and grace.[29] This sacramentology is applicable to our instances, since they concern both eucharist and baptism.

But the relation between religious representations and rituals should not be seen only in terms of representations relating to rituals, but also, as noted already, the other way round, rituals relating to representations. According to Catholic sacramentology, that relation could be described as follows. People's religious experience during ritual celebrations is translated into the symbolic language of religious representations that have crystallised in many age-old religious traditions. The rituals activate memory and open up the archives of these traditions, broadening and deepening people's experience of the celebrations, thus enhancing their emotional saliency, promoting their interiorisation, reinforcing personal identification with them, and rendering them fruitful for the non-ritual side of their lives.

In other words, the relation between religious representations and rituals is dialectical. On the one hand, religious representations (about God's indirect and direct action) are effectively operative in religious rituals, implying that religious representations influence them. On the other hand, religious rituals help to enrich those representations, broadening and deepening them by opening up religious archives, which are embedded in religious traditions as they are preserved, treasured, and kept alive in religious institutions. According to this perspective, religious institutions may not and should not be ignored in the study of religions.

---

[27] E. Schillebeeckx, Stilte Gevuld Met Parabels, in: *Politiek of mystiek?* Emmaus/Desclée De Brouwer, Brugge 1973, 69–81.

[28] E. Schillebeeckx, *De Sacramentele heilseconomie*, Nelissen, Bilthoven 1952; Id., *Christus, Sacrament van de godsontmoeting*, Nelissen, Bilthoven 1963.

[29] P. Schoonenberg, *The Christ: A Study of the God-Man Relationship in the Whole of Creation and in Jesus Christ*, Herder and Herder, New York 1971.

2.2   IDENTITY AND ALTERITY

However important the identity of individuals and communities in terms of permanence over time, it cannot be isolated from other individuals and communities. It is only in the interaction and communication with other individuals and communities that one's own identity and that of one's community are developed. To explain this point, I first explore the reciprocity of the identity of self and other. Then I outline a critical condition for that reciprocity: taking the other's perspective. Finally I relate the five themes examined in the first section to the identity of the other – both an individual and a collective other.

2.2.1   Self and Other

The identity of self is constituted by active pursuit of recognition by the other and passive longing for such recognition. Such recognition is fundamental. It is a necessary condition for human flourishing, whereas non-recognition or mis-recognition damages it. Recognition can be explained with the aid of the analysis by Honneth[30] of the young Hegel's concept of recognition (*Anerkennung*) in his *Jenaer Schriften*, augmented by notes from Ricoeur.[31] Honneth describes three models of recognition by illustrating the reciprocity of the identities of self and other: love, respect, and esteem. Violations of recognition correspond with these three models of reciprocity.

The first model is family love. Here one already sees that the development of identity is marked by a polarity between active striving to earn recognition and passive striving to be recognised. Both poles are actualised in the security, trust, care, and love offered by the family. They are expressed in a striving to lose oneself in the other and separate oneself from the other, the need for attachment and detachment, the longing to be together and to be alone, the desire to be present and absent. This dialectic gives rise to identity. But there are also violations of this striving: non-recognition or mis-recognition rather than recognition, humiliation rather than care. That happens when a child

---

[30] A. Honneth, *Kampf um Anerkennung: Zur moralischen Grammatik sozialer Konflikte*, Suhrkamp, Frankfurt am Main 1994.
[31] P. Ricoeur, *The Course of Recognition*, Harvard University Press, Cambridge, MA 2005.

is either ensnared in a symbiotic relationship,[32] treated with dubious love,[33] or abandoned to its fate. In both instances it feels misunderstood, either sucked in or declared nonexistent.

The second model is respect (*Achtung*) in a democratic state. Again mutual recognition is crucial. In fact, the rule of law is based on it, as is evident in the social contract that citizens have with each other in a reconstructive rather than a genetic, historical sense. The legal system, especially human rights, is based on the notion that every citizen deserves to be recognised on the basis of her intrinsic human dignity. That is why everybody is equal before the law and has equal freedom. Violations of this principle assume two forms. One is discrimination on the grounds of attributes like gender, sexual orientation, race, colour, language, culture, or religion, which violates the dignity of individuals and drives them to all kinds of struggle – economic, political, cultural, and religious.[34] They rebel against the way the upper classes are recognised, whereas they, the underclass, who are seen as second rate people, *Untermenschen*, are not.[35] Following Hegel, and Rousseau, who strongly influenced Hegel in this regard, one might say: "The struggle for recognition can find only one satisfactory solution, and that is a regime of reciprocal recognition among equals".[36] The other violation of the principle of equal freedom is crime, which infringes mutual recognition, the bedrock of the legal system. It is a breach of the social contract, to which the state's only proper response is coercion. The accent is not on the alienation of property but on the person who is injured, wounded by the crime – "my honour, not the thing".[37]

---

[32] M. Jacoby, *Individuation and Narcissism: The Psychology of the Self in Jung and Kohut*, Routledge, London/New York 1990.

[33] J. van den Berg, *Dubieuze liefde in de omgang met het kind: Over de late gevolgen van te veel of te weinig moederlijke toewijding tijdens de jeugd*, Callenbach, Nijkerk 1958.

[34] A. Margalit, *The Decent Society*, Harvard University Press, Cambridge, MA 1999.

[35] A. Honneth, *Unsichtbarkeit: Stationen einer Theorie der Intersubjektivität*, Suhrkamp, Frankfurt am Main 2003; N. Fraser & A. Honneth, *Umverteilung oder Anerkennung? Eine politisch-philosophische Kontroverse*, translated by Wolfgang Burckhardt, Suhrkamp, Frankfurt 2003.

[36] Ch. Taylor, The Politics of Recognition, in: A. Gutmann (ed.), *Multiculturalism: Examining the Politics of Recognition*, Princeton University Press, Princeton, NJ 1994, 25–74, here 50.

[37] Ricoeur, *The Course*, op. cit., 184.

For that reason the penalty transcends vengeance in pursuit of justice, for the aim is to restore "my injured self [as] recognized".[38]

The third model is social esteem. Ideally society should be structured so that every person enjoys the social esteem he merits by virtue of his contribution to the good life from diverse social positions in the various sectors, with due regard to differences in responsibilities, burdens, and contributions. But this presupposes a homogeneous community with homogeneous values, norms, and criteria for measuring each person's contribution. Such a society does not exist (at any rate, no longer exists), marked as it is by axiological diversity. Appraisals within and between sectors differ, and the very functions performed in these are assessed differently. This has implications for mutual recognition in society. When individuals and groups disagree, the only solution is to agree on the requisite assessment through reasoned legitimisation. If the parties fail to reach agreement, and agreeing to disagree does not resolve the deadlock, it needs something other than discourse ethics in Habermas's sense, namely a culture of readiness to compromise. Such a culture not only accords with the present state of society, as is evident in the empirical study by Boltanski and Thévenot.[39] It is also the only way to express the human dignity of the parties to the conflict.[40]

The relevance of these three models to religious identity is easy to see. In the first model, that of love and care in a religious home, the child's religious identity flourishes, whereas neglect and lovelessness stunt the growth not just of its identity in general but also of its religious identity. In the second model, democratic principles such as freedom of conscience and religion are basic to the development of individuals' and communities' religious identity. It grows from their experience of respect and recognition on an equal footing with other – religious and nonreligious – individuals and communities. This is inimical to either religious privilege or religious discrimination. The third model, in which social esteem is based on reasoned legitimisation and mutual readiness to compromise, also applies to religious individuals and communities. Inasmuch as the latter learn to give up their absolute claims and participate in consultation and negotiation

---

[38] Ricoeur, *The Course*, op. cit., 184; Cf. J.A. van der Ven, Theologie beoefenen in een faculteit van religiewetenschappen, *Tijdschrift voor Theologie* 42(2002)3, 244–267.

[39] L. Boltanski & L. Thévenot, *De la justification: Les economies de la grandeur*, Gallimard, Paris 1991.

[40] Ricoeur, *The Course*, op. cit., 206.

with due regard to the principle of give and take, they will get the social esteem they are entitled to – a form of recognition that is essential for their identity.

2.2.2   Taking the Other's Perspective

Development of mutual recognition hinges on an ability to take the other's perspective. That raises two questions. First, who *is* the other and what does the relation between self and other entail? Secondly, is it really possible to take the other's perspective?

There are several answers to the first question: who is the other? They can be subsumed under the concepts of anteriority, posteriority, exteriority, interiority, and superiority. Anteriority means that the phenomenon of the self is preceded by that of the other and is constituted by it. Levinas says that the pleas, 'do not kill me', 'do me justice', 'love me', that the other addresses to the self, constitute the self when it responds to them. In posteriority the phenomenon of self is followed by that of the other, as in Husserl's phenomenology, and understanding of the other is preceded and influenced by self-understanding. In exteriority, as in Sartre's thinking, the other threatens the self, because by looking at the self from outside the other freezes, objectifies, and reifies the self. In interiority, as conceptualised by Buber, constitution of self and other lies in the depth of the interpersonal relationship: in their encounter they become I and Thou.[41] Postmodernism has added a fifth approach. It sees the other as an enigma. The other does not belong to the category of *différence* but represents a separate, irreducible category, *différance* – certainly for Derrida, who deconstructs the other into 'unnameable not-being'.[42] That puts the other on a level that transcends, in an absolute sense, the level at which the self knows itself and its world, and thus is superior to self. But it does not end there, for the self is likewise an irreducible category, *différance*: the self is always 'another' to himself. To complicate matters further, what does this twofold superiority of other and self imply for the one who is studying the other? She studies 'another' that enigmatically eludes her, at the same time eluding herself as 'another'. And who is the 'real

---

[41] M. Theunissen, *Der Andere: Studien zur Sozialontologie der Gegenwart*, De Gruyter, Berlin 1965.

[42] H. de Vries, *Philosophy and the Turn to Religion*, Johns Hopkins University Press, Baltimore, MD 1999.

other' in such a study – the one who is studied or the one studying the other and penetrating the latter's world as 'another'?[43]

It is not easy to choose between these approaches. From a strong conceptualist perspective, they are contradictory and contrasting. From the perspective of weak conceptualism, they do not refer to the relation between self and other as such, but to varying aspects of that relationship in varying circumstances: sometimes the other emerges as anterior, sometimes as posterior, sometimes as exterior, sometimes as interior, sometimes as superior, sometimes as equally superior.

Weak conceptualism brings me to the second question: is it at all possible to take the other's perspective? Here a brief reference to developmental-psychological research into empathy is helpful.[44] In the five developmental phases, different aspects feature in differing circumstances. In phase 1, the infant develops automatic, non-voluntary responses to stimuli received from others, such as crying (infants, adults). No distinction is made between self and other at this stage (global empathy). In phase 2, when the infant is about a year old, it is capable of realising that the person in distress is someone else, not the self, but that person's inner state is as yet unknown to the infant, who assumes it to be same as its own (egocentric empathy). In phase 3, at about two or three years, the child develops empathy for the distinctiveness of the other's feelings and knows that they differ from its own (altruistic empathy). Phase 4, in late childhood, sees the development of an empathy with the other's feelings that transcends the situation here and now, and the child shows understanding for the other's life conditions and history, even for those of an entire group. This empathy can develop into a feeling of compassion, accompanied by a desire to help the other because the child feels sorry for him. Thus it is not (only) a matter of assuaging the sorrow of the child who empathises with the other, but (also) of alleviating the other's need (sympathy). In phase 5, causal attribution processes emerge, in which the child looks for the causes of the other's feelings of distress. If it concludes that the other is to blame for these feelings, empathy may decline and

---

[43] J.Z. Smith, *Relating Religion: Essays in the Study of Religion*, University of Chicago Press, Chicago 2004, 260.

[44] M.L. Hoffman, Empathy, Social Cognition, and Moral Education, in: A. Garrod (ed.), *Approaches to Moral Development: New Research and Emerging Themes*, Teachers College Press, New York 1993, 157–179; J.A. van der Ven, *Formation of the Moral Self*, Eerdmans, Grand Rapids, MI 1998, 313–315.

even cease. If it concludes that it is attributable to causes beyond the other's control, moral feelings may develop, such as empathic anger, a sense of injustice, or guilt, be it guilt because of inaction or guilt by association.

More generally, as development progresses, the self forms a theory of mind, that is, a set of notions in its own mind about what goes on in others' minds – in other words, what experiences, emotions, beliefs, arguments, conclusions, plans and the like are operating in the other's mind. Research has shown that the theory of mind is not a solid, massive constant, but comprises numerous, varying aspects. I mention three: proximity, motivation, and levels of understanding. Firstly, understanding other people depends on how well people know each other, although some are better at understanding others and some people are easier to understand. Here proximity is a factor. Reading others' minds depends on the size of the group to which the other belongs, from the most intimate to the most tenuous, entailing groups of 5, 12, 150, 500 – up to 2000 individuals.[45] The second aspect concerns the strength of the motivation to understand the other. Thus, research indicates that couples who have been together for brief lengths of time show more mutual empathy than couples who have been together for lengthy periods, probably because they are more motivated to understand one another. Paradoxically, often the 'radically other' is the proximate rather than the remote other.[46] The third aspect concerns levels of understanding. The first level is the ability to read the other's mind separately from one's own. The second is to read the other's mind inasmuch as the other has certain ideas or wishes relating to the self and the self perceives these. The third level is to read the other's mind, including her ideas and wishes relating to oneself, so as to anticipate these by either accepting or rejecting them, or by simulating acceptance while actually rejecting them. The latter is a much researched form of (conscious or unconscious) deception, which is why the theory of mind has been called 'Machiavellian intelligence'.[47]

Remarkably, the theory of mind, on which taking the other's perspective is based, plays a minor role in religious literature. Religious

---

[45] R.I.M. Dunbar, The Social Brain Hypothesis, *Evolutionary Anthropology* 6(1998)5, 178–190, here 187.

[46] Smith, *Relating*, op. cit., 253.

[47] T. Givón, *Context as Other Minds: The Pragmatics of Sociality, Cognition, and Communication*, John Benjamins Pub., Amsterdam/Philadelphia, PA 2005.

individuals and communities have a lot to say about dialogue with the other, either religious or interreligious, but often that is overshadowed and dominated by their own vision and mission. This is justified by arguing that one cannot have dialogue without introducing one's own views and that dialogue complements mission[48] or even serves the purpose of mission.[49] But how should the dialogue be conducted when each partner takes his own convictions to be absolute and absolutely unique? Or, as John Locke put it, when "every church is orthodox to itself"? Can it mean anything other than that not only one's own religion deserves recognition, especially respect and esteem, but also the other's religion?

Let me take the declaration of the Congregation for the Doctrine of the Faith of the Catholic Church, *Dominus Jesus* (2000), by then cardinal Ratzinger, and find out how this document says interreligious dialogue should be conducted. The document may be characterised as predominantly exclusivist, even though some inclusive aspects are discernible. The accent on exclusiveness is evident in the emphasis on God's unique, universal, complete, absolute revelation to its fullest extent in Jesus Christ, which precludes an approach that regards this revelation as limited, incomplete, imperfect, or even complementary to revelations in other religions (number 6 and 15). At the same time, various paragraphs radiate some inclusiveness by mentioning positive elements and participated mediations (*mediationes participatae*) of this revelation in other religions (nos. 8 and 14). The declaration moreover specifies that interreligious dialogue should be conducted in freedom and from a perspective of equality (no. 22). With regard to freedom, it cites the declaration on religious freedom of Vatican II, stating that it must be respected. Equality, however, is qualified more precisely: "Equality, which is a presupposition of inter-religious dialogue, refers to the equal personal dignity of the parties in dialogue, not to doctrinal content, nor even less to the position of Jesus Christ – who is God himself made man – in relation to the founders of the other religions." The fact that 'equal personal dignity' occupies a focal position in the text should be seen as positive sign for authentic interreligious dialogue.

---

[48] E. Chia, *Towards a Theology of Dialogue: Schillebeeckx's Method as Bridge between Vatican's Dominus Iesus and Asia's FABC Theology*, Dissertation Radboud University Nijmegen, 2003, 188ff.
[49] D.J. Bosch, *Transforming Mission: Paradigm Shifts in Theology of Mission*, Orbis Books, Maryknoll, NY 1991, 483–489.

But it is noteworthy that personal dignity is disjoined from the beliefs people cherish and the ritual practices they enact on the basis of these beliefs, even when these religious beliefs and ritual practices concern the very meaning of human existence. This contradicts the anthropological insight that the core of personal identity and the concomitant core of personal dignity consist in the interaction of existential beliefs and ritual practices, and cannot exist outside these. Personal identity and personal dignity can only exist in this interaction between existential beliefs and ritual practices.[50] To conduct interreligious dialogue on the presupposition of equal personal dignity, but without due regard to the existential beliefs and ritual practices that the dialogue partners hold 'sacred', is contrary to the principle of personal dignity that underlies, inspires, and orients the principles of freedom and equality. In other words, anyone who proceeds on the principle of personal dignity cannot conduct dialogue with other religions based on an attitude of exclusiveness or inclusiveness. It is simply not possible to conduct such dialogue without an attitude of mutual hospitality, in which one is prepared to be informed and transformed by one's guest – and this entails not just ethical hospitality but also dogmatic hospitality and genuinely engaged ritual hospitality. Speaking from his Jewish background, Derrida[51] observes: "[T]his is indeed really about the Messiah as *hôte*, about the messianic as hospitality."

Is it surprising if adherents of other religions react suspiciously when Christians invite them to interreligious dialogue, since they, the Christians, have the concept of mission in mind, focussing on conversion and church growth?[52] What chance has the other's religious identity of being recognised if we "demand that they can and should shed the narratives and practices they take to be necessary to their lives"?[53]

---

[50] P. Ricoeur, *Oneself as Another*, University of Chicago Press, Chicago 1992; Id., *Figuring the Sacred: Religion, Narrative, and Imagination*, Fortress Press, Minneapolis 1995.

[51] J. Derrida, *Acts of Religion*, Routledge, New York 2002, 362.

[52] M. Thangaraj, Evangelism Sans Proselytism, in: J. Witte & R.C. Martin (eds.), *Sharing the Book: Religious Perspectives on the Rights and Wrongs of Proselytism*, Orbis Books, Maryknoll, NY 1999; C. Hasselmann, De wereldethiek-Verklaring Van Chicago, *Concilium* 37(2001)4, 24–37, here 31.

[53] T. Asad, *Formation of the Secular: Christianity, Islam, Modernity*, Stanford University Press, Stanford 2003, 75.

2.2.3   *The Other's Identity*

The ability to take the other's perspective implies reading the other's life through the other's eyes. This could involve all five of the themes mentioned in section 1. The first is the hermeneutic dialectics of sameness and self in the course of time, which applies not only to the identity of the self but also to that of the other. Continuity of relations means that the self is absorbed in the way the other understood herself at various points in time and still understands herself as 'the same'. This 'hermeneutics of the other' also applies to the other's self-understanding as remaining 'the same' in the future and attesting it in a promise of loyalty, which is made both individually and collectively.

The second theme is the multiplicity and hybridity of identity. Particularly in a time like ours, in which religion functions in a global scene, there is a risk that the collective and individual identity of the other will be seen as exclusively religious. History has shown that even when religion is at its most powerful, identity is still shaped by other factors as well. The clash of civilisations, in terms of which Churchill – not a conventionally religious man – interpreted the war with Nazi Germany, and in which he claimed the survival of Christian civilisation was at stake, was not dominated by the desire to maintain a Christian identity but by a will to save Western economic, political, and social identity from collapse. Only if it is clear that this latter identity can be preserved for future generations "men will still say, 'This was their finest hour'", as Churchill put it.[54]

The third theme concerns the dialectics between achieved and ascribed religious identity. By and large, identity in Western cultures is characterised by personal, reflective decisions more than in non-Western cultures, where authority, tradition, community, and convention are more influential. Taking the other's perspective is impaired when encounters with non-Western individuals and groups are dominated by the researcher's expectation that notions about individual self-determination are wholeheartedly shared by non-Western people. He should observe the insights of research ethics.[55]

---

[54] M. Burleigh, *Sacred Causes: Religion and Politics from the European Dictators to Al Qaeda*, HarperPress, London 2006, 214–215.
[55] M.A. Mentzel, A.J.F. Köbben et al. (eds.), *Ethische vragen bij sociaal-wetenschappelijk onderzoek*, Van Gorcum, Assen 1995.

The fourth theme is even more complex. It concerns the extent to which religious choices are indeed based on personal considerations, or are unconsciously based on the influence of pre-existing institutional structures. This presents the researcher with the ethical dilemma of deciding whether to stick to the other's insider notions, in which she sees her identity as self-chosen, or whether to expose that self-chosen identity in terms of 'false consciousness' from an outsider perspective. This is a common problem in research into religious sects, whose members make much of the 'new life' which, from their insider perspective, they claim to have chosen without seeing through the pious jiggery-pokery of religious control, manipulation, and indoctrination. The same phenomenon is observable in established religions, inasmuch as unbridled power and deprivation of mental freedom feature in these as well. The problem looms large when human rights like freedom of conscience, religion, expression, association, and assembly are curtailed, and adherents of the religion magnanimously take it for granted. It has to be resolved on the basis of human dignity by prudently complementing an insider perspective with an outsider perspective, but without declaring the latter superior to the former as some scholars tend to do,[56] for that too would undermine the requisite freedom.

The fifth and last theme is the substantial aspects of the other's religious identity, individual and collective, that need to be taken into account: the religious representations, rituals, and institutions. More particularly, to what extent are these representations, rituals, and institutions really characteristic, distinctive, even unique features of the religion concerned? From the insider perspective of the other they are, but does that hold if they are compared with other religions? What is meant by characteristic, distinctive, unique? People often refer to a canon of texts, on which their 'unique' beliefs and 'characteristic' practices are based. But that does not solve the problem, for there are different kinds of canonical texts: normative texts that are binding, such as creeds; socio-religious texts that provide a shared vocabulary at the time and create socio-religious identity; and exemplary texts that serve as religious models for daily life. Besides, the traditions

---

[56] R.T. McCutcheon, "It's a Lie. There's No Truth in It! It's a Sin!" On the Limits of the Humanistic Study of Religion and the Costs of Saving Others from Themselves, *Journal of the American Academy of Religion* 74(2006)3, 720–750.

that grew from these texts are equally diverse, as are their authoritative pronouncements on conflicting interpretations of texts. From the perspective of the other, the need for 'uniqueness' is understandable, since it draws a line between orthodox and heterodox groups, between that religion and other religions, and also impedes religious mobility in the form of 'conversion' from that religion to another. Yet the emphasis on uniqueness makes one lose sight of common roots, mutual influencing, and plain similarities between religions. Again, we face the dilemma of insider perspective and outsider perspective, for religious overlapping is only discernible from an outsider perspective. Here, too, the solution lies in complementary use of both perspectives. In so doing, one should not lose sight of the necessary dialectics in such complementation, for anything taken from other religions is interpreted in terms of the self-understanding of one's own religion and is assimilated discursively into that tradition, like 'the image of God' from Egyptian religion into the Jewish Bible or Stoicism into the New Testament. Only by deciphering this discursive tradition can we trace the nature of the other's 'unique' religion.[57]

2.3 Religious Identity in Qualitative and Quantitative Comparative Research

What we have said so far could give rise to the misconception that the best approach to comparative research into religious identity is the qualitative method, because it does more justice to the insider perspective, and that quantitative methods merely serve to complement the outsider perspective. But the distinction between qualitative and quantitative methods is not the same as that between insider perspective and outsider perspective. That is to say, both a qualitative method in respect of non-numerical, mainly verbal data, and a quantitative method in respect of numerical data offer scope for the use of both the insider and the outsider perspective, as is evident in the following figure: cells 2 and 3 are as relevant as cells 1 and 4.

---

[57] M.L. Satlow, Defining Judaism: Accounting for "Religions" in the Study of Religion, *Journal of the American Academy of Religion* 74(2006)4, 837–860.

	qualitative method	quantitative method
insider perspective	(1)	(2)
outsider perspective	(3)	(4)

Figure 2. Perspectives and methods.

The relevance of all four cells also applies to comparative cross-cultural research, which, like cross-sectional research, makes use of both qualitative and quantitative methods. Both types of research seek to trace and analyse similarities and differences. In cross-sectional research, one examines similarities and differences in the relation between two or more variables among two or more culturally homogeneous groups in a given population. In cross-cultural research, one examines similarities and differences in the relation between two or more variables among two or more culturally heterogeneous populations or two or more different ethnic groups in the same country. In other words, cross-cultural research can employ both qualitative and quantitative methods, and both methods can be used from an insider and an outsider perspective. This is counter to Ragin's view[58] that qualitative, quantitative, and comparative research are respectively aimed at commonalities, covariation, and diversity.

To substantiate this view, I deal with the following themes: the interaction between theory and data in both methods; the level of abstraction in theory formation; synchronicity and diachronicity; the relationship between individuals, groups, and contexts; and cultural and linguistic equivalence.

2.3.1   Interaction between Theory and Data

All scientific research proceeds from a problem, as we know from theory of science since Dewey in the first half of the 20th century.[59] The problem could stem from contradictions between theory and data, between different data, or between different theories. In order to get a

---

[58] Ch.C. Ragin, *Constructing Social Research: The Unity and Diversity of Method,* Pine Forge Press, Thousand Oaks, CA 1994, 77–154.

[59] J. Dewey, *Logic: The Theory of Inquiry,* The Later Works of John Dewey, Vol. 12, Southern Illinois University Press, Carbondale 1986; J.A. van der Ven, The Qualitative Inhaltsanalyse, in: J.A. van der Ven & H.-G. Ziebertz (eds.), *Paradigmenentwicklung in der Praktischen Theologie,* Deutscher Studien Verlag, Weinheim 1993, 113–164, here 124–128.

grip on the problem, the researcher analyses it in order to break it up into several questions. This activity of analysing the problem consists of two dimensions: one bases the analysis on theoretical insights, the other conducts the analysis in such a way that an answer to the problem emerges from the data to be collected. Hence at the very outset of the study there is an inchoate interaction between data and theory. As a general rule, there can be no theory without data and no data without theory. Naturally this calls for qualification, for there is enough speculative theory in which data are sorely lacking. But theory without data is inconceivable if that theory is to make reliable, valid reference to the relevant domain in the empirical world. Conversely, there are plenty of descriptions of so-called facts, such as anecdotes, stories, and journalistic reports, in which theory is lacking. It does not make these descriptions trivial, but they only acquire the connotation of data when they are presented in organised fashion and qualify for analysis and interpretation.

The idea that all research is characterised by an interaction between data and theory is sometimes overlooked in debates on the relation between qualitative and quantitative methods. The qualitative researcher is assumed to be interested mainly or exclusively in data, undirected by theory, and only arrives at relevant insights on the basis of these data. The quantitative researcher is assumed to be interested only in her own theory, which she imposes on the data by manipulating control variables, dependent and/or independent variables, or by reconceptualising the key concepts to confirm her theory-generated hypotheses.[60] Of course, these are caricatures, but I have been around the scientific world long enough to know that such assumptions hold sway when controversies reach boiling point. The false assumption is that the less theory you have, the better for the insider perspective, and the more theory, the better for the outsider perspective.

But scientific insight does not happen without interaction between data and theory – an observation first explicated by August Comte. If it is true that every theory must be based upon observed facts, it is equally true that facts can not be observed without the guidance of some theories. Without such guidance, our facts would be desultory and fruitless; we could not retain them: for the most part we could

---

[60] Ch.C. Ragin, *The Comparative Method: Moving Beyond Qualitative and Quantitative Strategies*, University of California Press, Berkeley 1989, 67.

not even perceive them. In quantitative and qualitative research alike, there is theory formation both before and after data collection. Let me explain in more detail.

In qualitative research, prior theory formation can assume various forms: a system of categories in terms of which the data are approached, as in basic content analysis; an open series of categories, as in the template method; a conceptual framework, as in the researcher's map of territory; or an open questionnaire, as in ethnographic content analysis. Without this theory formation one fumbles in the dark when deciding which data to research and what aspects of these data are relevant. Theory formation after data collection is no less important in qualitative research. It comprises several steps: systematic data description; selection and reduction of data through classification; construction of typologies, for instance by crossing two categories from one class with those of another class; and pattern construction.[61] In research into religious identity, for example, it may turn out that religious burial rites deal more in transcendent-God images than religious birth rituals, which are characterised by immanent-transcendent or simply immanent God images.

In quantitative research, prior theory formation consists in a structure of concepts, resulting in a conceptual model. Here the rule is parsimony: the fewer the concepts and the more they are conceptually interrelated, the better. The concepts are rendered observable and measurable by operationalising them with a view to data collection. Data collection is followed by subsequent theory formation. This takes the form of systematic data description; reduction of data through, for example, factor analysis, also applying the criterion of interpretability, which is not possible without theoretical scrutiny;[62] empirical exploration or testing of the conceptual model; considering the empirical reliability and validity of the model; and possibly suggestions for modifying the model. In this way one could explore the question why it is that more people in the USA define their identity in religious terms

---

[61] A.R.J. Pleijter, *Typen en logica: Van kwalitatieve inhoudsanalyse in de communicatiewetenschap*, Dissertation Radboud University Nijmegen, 2006.
[62] J. Kim & C. Mueller, *Factor Analysis: Statistical Methods and Practical Issues*, Sage Publications, Beverly Hills 1984.

than in Europe, which could disclose differences in regard to the welfare state and/or religious mobility because of religious competition.[63]

So the difference between qualitative and quantitative research does
not lie in mutually exclusive attention given to data or theory. The
emphasis on data or theory may differ, but that applies as much to
projects within qualitative and quantitative research as between qualitative and quantitative research. Moreover, the notion that qualitative
research is more amenable to an insider perspective *because* it puts
greater emphasis on data, and that quantitative research is more amenable to an outsider perspective *because* of its greater emphasis on
theory conflicts with (methodo)logical thought.

2.3.2   Level of Abstraction in Theory Formation

Even if there is consensus that research stands or falls by the interaction between data and theory, the difference between qualitative and
quantitative methods is still sought in different levels of abstraction.
The level is said to be lower in the qualitative approach than in the
quantitative approach. It is associated with the notion that the lower
the level of abstraction, the better for the insider perspective, and
the higher that level, the better for the outsider perspective. But is
that true?

The focus can be narrowed down to an element that is a precondition for any theory formation at whatever level of abstraction: classification. Classification occurs in both the insider and the outsider
perspective. By way of example we can look at the images religious
leaders in the Catholic Church have of themselves, like priest, father,
friend, spiritual leader, helper, prophet, mother, guide, therapist, sister,
brother. In his quantitative survey research, Schilderman[64] interprets
these images with the help of concepts from these religious leaders'
insider perspective. He does so rightly and convincingly, because
they function as these leaders' self-images. Some of these images, like
father, mother, brother, sister, and friend are undeniably concepts at
a low level of abstraction. But, I would add, since these concepts are
used analogously, one can legitimately ask what they mean to both the

---

[63] J. Verweij, *Secularisering tussen feit en fictie: Een internationaal vergelijkend
onderzoek naar determinanten van religieuze betrokkenheid*, Tilburg University Press,
Tilburg 1998.

[64] H. Schilderman, *Religion as a Profession*, Brill, Leiden/Boston 2005, 190–199.

religious leaders themselves and to members of their religious institutions. Does the concept 'friend' refer, for both leaders and members, to
one or more of the forms of friendship identified by Aristotle – mutual
profit, recreational pleasure, and mutual intimacy? Does the concept
of kinship, from which father/mother and brother/sister derive, indeed
colour their relationship by way of sharing life, sacrificial love, and
kin altruism (versus reciprocal altruism)? Asking these simple questions, which is necessary for getting further analytical insight into the
meaning of these images, immediately raises the level of abstraction.
In addition, from an outsider perspective, one has to ask what these
images mean in the framework of the typically hierarchic structure of
religious institutions. More particularly, how do these images of kinship and friendship relate to the typology of authority, such as charismatic, traditional, legal, and professional authority?[65] What do they
mean in a traditional, legalistic, professional institution such as the
Catholic Church, where research has shown this typology applies?[66]
Both kinds of concepts – kinship-related and authority-related – are
necessary in order to deepen the meanings of the insiders' images
concerned. When it comes to level of abstraction they might be seen
as equal.

The idea that religious people proceeding from an insider perspective use only concrete concepts or ones at a low level of abstraction is
illusory. What does one make of a homemade, so to speak, centrifugal
classification of Christian denominations by the Catholic church, in
which the first on the list is considered closest and the last on the list
the most distant, i.e., Eastern Christianity, Anglicanism, Lutheranism,
Calvinism and the Free Churches?[67] The question is what this classification is based on. Explicating the reasons why Eastern Christian
identity is considered closer to the Catholic Church than that of the
Free Churches will necessarily entail a high level of abstraction in relation to concepts like 'priesthood', 'ordination', 'sacrament', 'eucharist',
'apostolic succession'. And what about the taxonomic classification

---

[65] M. Weber, *Wirtschaft und Geselschaft*, Mohr, Tübingen 1980.

[66] Kl. Sonnberger, *Die Leitung der Pfarrgemeinde: Eine empirisch-theologische Studie unter niederländischen und deutschen Katholiken*, Kok/Deutscher Studienverlag,
Kampen/Weinheim 1996.

[67] See, for example, the rapprochement with the 'Nestorian' tradition in the *Déclaration christologique commune entre l'Église catholique et l'Église assyrienne de l'Orient*
(1994), in: H. Teule, *Les Assyro-Chaldéens: chrétiens d'Irak, d'Iran et de Turquie*, Brepols, Turnhout 2008, 103–106.

of the relation with other religions by members of various Christian denominations, when they define their religious identity in terms of exclusiveness, inclusiveness, pluralistic inclusiveness, inclusive pluralism,[68] or pure pluralism?[69] To expound this classification, one needs an explicit theology of religion on a rather high level of abstraction.[70] At all events, differences in level of abstraction are not essentially linked with the difference between insider and outsider perspectives. Both have low and high levels of abstraction.

Even if the levels of abstraction of the insider and the outsider perspective are not essentially different, is it not better to keep the level of abstraction as low as possible in studies of religion and religious identity? Is there not a danger that by raising that level the focus will be on similarities between individuals and groups rather than on differences? Does it not obscure the uniqueness of the religious identity of certain individuals and groups in comparison with others? I do not think so. An optic metaphor may be helpful. When one constructs more abstract concepts, one's eye may travel upwards from below and downwards from above. When looking upward from below, that is from concrete phenomena to a more overarching category, one notices the similarities. If one looks down from that category at the concrete phenomena, the differences become apparent. The rule is probably – I say 'probably' because empirical study of classification is still in its infancy – that raising the level of abstraction and looking down from that level at concrete phenomena increases the chance of identifying differences.[71] This parallels Aristotle's insight in his *Topics* that the genus concept, in terms of which two or more phenomena are regarded as a species, highlights difference: "A genus is what is predicated in what a thing is of a number of things exhibiting differences in kind".[72]

---

[68] J. Dupuis, The Truth Will Make You Free, *Louvain Studies* 24(1999)3, 211–263.

[69] J. Hick, *An Interpretation of Religion: Human Responses to the Transcendent*, Yale University Press, New Haven 1989.

[70] P. Valkenberg, *Sharing Lights on the Way to God: Muslim-Christian Dialogue and Theology in the Context of Abrahamic Partnership*, Rodopi, Amsterdam 2006, 97–98.

[71] D. Medin & S. Waxman, Conceptual Organization, in: W. Bechtel & G. Graham (eds.), *A Companion to Cognitive Science*, Blackwell, Oxford 2002, 167–175.

[72] Aristotle, Topics, in: *The Complete Works of Aristotle*, The Revised Oxford Translation, edited by Jonathan Barnes, Princeton University Press, Princeton, NJ 1984, 102^{a}31–32.

2.3.3 *Diachronicity and Synchronicity*

One objection to quantitative methods is that they focus on population attributes here and now without regard to their history. Their focus is synchronic. From the aforementioned hermeneutic point of view that religious identity is actualised in past, present, and future, this is a serious objection. If the so-called analogy of relations in time and the promise for the future play no role, it would curtail an essential dimension of that identity.

Qualitative methods, on the other hand, offer ample scope for the diachronicity of religious identity. The moment one starts a dialogue with religious individuals and communities, it almost automatically activates their religious memory and everything stored in it since early childhood. It offers unique access to the religious archive in which individuals and communities preserve their representations and experience, their codes and scripts from one generation to the next. Interviewing individuals and groups from different generations reveals the historical layers in that archive.[73] In the process of interviewing them, one can also ask them how they relate to the future, not only as regards their hopes and desires, but also their commitment and engagement – in effect their promises.

It would be facile, however, to claim that quantitative methods offer no scope for diachronicity. The so-called multi-moment approach could be used more often than has been the case hitherto. In this approach, respondents may be asked retrospectively about such matters as the following: family history (including relations with partner(s), parents, grandparents, children and relocations); school career; professional career; roles as voluntary workers and members of associations in past and present; history of their dealings with colleagues; and relations with bosses. In conjunction with this, one can also look into issues with a more direct bearing on religious identity: history of the respondents' interpretation of religious representations and participation in religious rituals; history of their membership in religious communities and institutions; history of their orientations to ethical issues like abortion, euthanasia, and same-sex marriage.[74] The multi-moment approach breaks through the supposedly essential difference between

---

[73] D. Hervieu-Léger, *La Religion pour mémoire*, Cerf, Paris 1993.
[74] W.C. Ultee, *De Nijmeegse sociologie de laatste tien jaar en nu*, available at: http://www.socsci.kun.nl/maw/sociologie/ultee/

qualitative and quantitative methods in connection with diachronicity and synchronicity. It also severs the supposedly exclusive link of
the former with an insider perspective and the latter with an outsider
perspective.

2.3.4   *Relationship between Individuals, Interactions and Contexts*

Another respect in which qualitative and quantitative methods are said
to differ is that the former allows for the unrepeatable uniqueness of
the individual, whereas the latter views her as merely a specimen from
a particular category. Another alleged difference is that qualitative
methods view individuals in their interactions with other individuals
and communities, whereas quantitative methods ignore these interactions. A third difference is that the qualitative approach is said to place
individuals in their broad context, while the quantitative approach disregards context and treats individuals like atomised monads and communities like islands in an otherwise empty ocean.

These assumptions exaggerate the differences. In the case of individuals, qualitative methods do enable us to highlight their uniqueness,
but when analysing qualitative data we still have to look for categories that will accommodate similar individual traits, which once again
obscures their uniqueness. Quantitative methods, on the other hand,
include not just closed questions but can also entail open questions,
thus affording scope for personal experience and representations; but
here, too, these are slotted into categories during analysis. In the case
of interactions with other individuals and communities it is just as
easy to exaggerate the differences. When researching these interactions,
respondents may be questioned about their interactions with grandparents, parents, partner(s), children, siblings, and friends (e.g. friends
for profit, recreation, and/or personal concern).[75] The same applies to
their interactions with groups and communities (e.g. in the economic,
political, social, cultural, and religious spheres). As for context, official
administrative data on suburb, municipality, province and country
can be incorporated into the study, and in regard to the specifically
religious context there are often survey and/or ecclesiastic data on
membership, participation and voluntary activities available from different denominations and religions, like the studies into religiosity,

---

[75] R. Eisinga et al., *Religion in Dutch Society 2000*, Steinmetz Archive, Amsterdam
2002.

national context and voluntary work in 53 countries by Ruiter and De Graaf.[76]

This refutes the notion that qualitative methods are actor-oriented and quantitative methods purely variable-oriented.[77] As noted already, quantitative methods are enriched, not only by a multi-moment approach, but also by a multi-actor and a multi-context approach.[78] Given such a 3Mac approach (multi-moment, multi-actor, multi-context), there are no essential differences between the two methods on this score. The exclusive link between qualitative methods and an insider perspective on the one hand, and quantitative methods and an outsider perspective on the other, is also severed.

2.3.5   Cultural and Linguistic Equivalence

Comparative research rightly concerns itself with the problem of cultural and linguistic equivalence in relation to the populations or countries concerned. The problem is differentiated into construct equivalence, method equivalence, and item equivalence.[79] Construct equivalence concerns the definition of the concepts under investigation in a manner that corresponds with their purport in the relevant populations. That does not always happen, as when the identical definition of religious shame and guilt is used among West European and Asian populations. They refer to different connotations and meanings in different countries and continents. Is this an essential difference between qualitative and quantitative methods? In both methods, researchers, whether from an insider or an outsider perspective, have to use techniques that reduce the danger of cultural construct bias in their open questions to informants and the closed questions submitted to them.

An example of a quantitative technique in relation to construct equivalence is the factor analysis in three steps used by Hermans[80] and

---

[76] S. Ruiter & N. de Graaf, National Context, Relgiosity and Volunteering: Results from 53 Countries, *American Sociological Review* 71(2006), 191–210.

[77] Ch.C. Ragin, *Issues and Alternatives in Comparative Social Research*, Brill, Leiden 1991.

[78] Ultee, *De Nijmeegse*, op. cit.

[79] F. van de Vyver & K. Leung, *Methods and Data Analysis for Cross Cultural Research*, Sage, London 1997.

[80] C.A.M. Hermans, *Empirische theologie vanuit praktisch rationaliteit in religieuze praktijken: Epistemologische reflecties op de ontwikkeling van een academische discipline*, Inaugural address Radboud University Nijmegen, 2004.

Anthony, Hermans and Sterkens[81] in their study of Christian, Islamic, and Hindu students in India. First, they conducted a factor analysis of the combined items scores of all three populations, which resulted in an adequately interpretable factor pattern. Next, they conducted a factor analysis of the individual items scores of each population separately. Third, having removed items in the second step that appeared to deviate from the factor pattern discovered in the first step, they conducted a factor analysis of the combined scores of all populations again, but now on the remaining items only. This procedure not only yielded a general pattern of items for the three populations in the third step, but also a differential pattern for each population in the second step, which might be seen as indicative of the 'otherness' of each. Thus in the third step all three populations appeared to refer to the idea of *commonality pluralism*, expressed as follows "different religions reveal different aspects of the same ultimate truth". In the second step the Hindu population alone appeared to refer to the idea of a *universal religion*, expressed as follows: "the similarities among the religions are a basis for building up a universal religion".

The second form of equivalence, that of method equivalence, pertains to the problem whether in questioning informants sufficient allowance is made for differences in, for example, social desirability, response styles (e.g. extremity scoring and acquiescence), stimulus familiarity, and interviewer/tester effects. This problem, too, arises in both qualitative and quantitative methods. In both instances, researchers should use techniques to reduce the risk of method bias; these can be found in various handbooks.

Finally, item equivalence requires that the questions in both qualitative and quantitative studies represent an accurate cultural and linguistic operationalisation of the concept under investigation. Here the method used by Leslie Francis and his co-workers is commendable. They developed specific religiosity scales for Judaism, Christianity, Islam, and Hinduism.[82] They did not use the application technique (i.e. implementing the same instrument among different populations), but

---

[81] F.-V. Anthony, C. Hermans & C. Sterkens, Interpreting Religious Pluralism: Comparative Research among Christian, Muslim and Hindu Students in Tamil Nadu, *Journal of Empirical Theology* 18(2005)2, 154–186.

[82] L.J. Francis & Y.J. Katz, Measuring Attitude toward Judaism: The Internal Consistency Reliability of the Katz-Francis Scale of Attitude toward Judaism, *Mental Health Religion and Culture* 10(2007)4, 309–324.

opted for an adaptation and assembly technique, which enabled them to achieve a sort of indigenisation that contributed to the appropriateness of the instrument for each specific religion.[83] In addition, they used the translation/back-translation procedure, which may entail a risk of setting too much store by literal translations,[84] but may also be seen as a first step in the TRAPD procedure, which implies translation, review, adjudication, pretesting, and documentation.[85] Again, there is no essential difference between the qualitative and quantitative methods, since both need special techniques to reduce item bias.

CONCLUSION

The message of this chapter is twofold. The first is that comparative research into religious identity falls short if we content ourselves with answers to one or a few questions by two or more populations. It is a complex task, since it is structured by a dialectic between two dimensions: identity as permanence over time and the relation between identity and alterity. Both dimensions are hermeneutic; imply multiplicity and hybridity; contain ascribed and achieved religiosity; are determined by both personal choice and structural factors; and are conditioned by religious representations, religious rituals and religious institutions. The second message is that the research should cut across certain traditional dichotomies, such as those between qualitative and quantitative methods and between an insider and an outsider perspective. Both methods and both perspectives are characterised by interaction between theory and data; similar levels of abstraction; tension between diachronicity and synchronicity; interplay between individuals, interactions, and contexts; and lastly, similar challenges of cultural and linguistic equivalence.

---

[83] Van de Vyver & Leung, *Methods*, op. cit., 36–37.
[84] Van de Vyver & Leung, *Methods*, op. cit., 39.
[85] J. Harkness et al., *Cross-Cultural Survey Methods*, Wiley, Hoboken 2003, 38–43.

CHAPTER THREE

REFLECTIVE COMPARISON IN RELIGIOUS RESEARCH

If one were to have advocated comparative studies in the human sciences, especially in religious research, at a scientific congress a decade or more ago, one would have run a real risk of speedy or slightly slower scientific suicide. Anything that smacked of looking for common characteristics, corresponding regularities, general mechanisms, structures and processes, let alone universal rules and laws, was dismissed as an inappropriate, anachronistic offering to the god of modernity. That was the heyday of postmodernism, with its emphasis on the absolute otherness of the other. Comparative methods were written off as imperialistic, colonialist, evolutionist, and anti-contextual, and in the case of religion, as religiously biased, proselytising, and ideological.

At the start of the 21st century, however, the tide appeared to be turning. That did not imply an uncritical return to (ostensibly) a-theoretical comparative research in the history of religions, nor to (ostensibly) a-historical and a-contextual patterns in the comparative religion of yore, however highly we acclaim the work of Mircea Eliade and his school for its grand vision and approach.[1] Indeed, the objections to comparative study of religion are not groundless and call for serious reflection. But that is not the same as dismissing comparative research out of hand. To put it boldly, all research is implicitly or explicitly comparative. There is always some background, frame of reference, model, yardstick, or criterion that is used to describe the phenomenon under investigation, categorise or classify it, place it in a taxonomy, interpret and evaluate it. Research is never a-conceptual or a-theoretical, a-cultural or a-contextual, hence it can never be neutral or value-free. There are always criteria by which the research object is described and measured. Hence comparative research may be regarded as an explication of that which characterises all research, from (comparative) biology and (comparative) psychology to (comparative) literary theory: the researcher seeks to describe and explain differences and

---

[1] J.Z. Smith, *Relating Religion: Essays in the Study of Religion*, University of Chicago Press, Chicago 2004.

similarities between phenomena and the patterns within these. Nonetheless the objections levelled at comparative research in the past compel us to examine the principle of comparison reflectively – hence the title of this chapter.

What is meant by the second term in the title, 'religious research'? I take it to mean the development of theories and investigations in the field of religions, including their theology (or, as in the case of Buddhism, philosophy). In so doing, I am consciously breaking with the partitioning of the field that has prevailed at universities ever since the emergence of religious studies (*Religionswissenschaft*) in the mid-19th century, whereby theology was confined exclusively to the Christian religion, and religious studies focused on non-Christian religions.[2]

One reason is that in secularised, especially West European countries, Christianity is no longer considered relevant just from a purely participant perspective but rather from an observer perspective, as it contributes to the underlying suppositions, paradigms, values, and norms of modern society and culture. Secularised people are less inclined to look for Christianity's self-interpretation and self-evaluation than for its functions, structures, and meanings in comparison with those of other religious and nonreligious worldviews. This does not mean that the participant perspective is no longer relevant or necessary, because it is impossible to study religions, including Christianity, if the participant perspective is neglected. A second reason is that, as a result of increasing migration and globalisation, there are no longer any isolated, independent cultures and religions such as 'the' Christian religion and 'the' non-Christian religions – if they ever existed at all. The traditional partitioning of the field between theology and religious studies no longer fits the mosaic of group and individualised forms of religion, the elements of which derive from various religious traditions, classical and non-classical, ancient and recent. We are living in an age of moving cultures and moving religions.[3] There

---

[2] Cf. J.G. Platvoet, Pillars, Pluralism and Secularization: A Social History of Dutch Science of Religions, in: L. Leertouwer, G.A. Wiegers & J.G. Platvoet (eds.), *Modern Societies & the Science of Religions: Studies in Honour of Lammert Leertouwer*, Brill, Leiden/Boston 2002.

[3] J. Janssen, De jeugd, de toekomst en de religie, *Jeugd en samenleving* 18(1988)7/8, 407–426; H.J.M. Hermans & H.J.G. Kempen, Moving Cultures: The Perilous Problems of Cultural Dichotomies in a Globalizing Society, *American Psychologist* 53(1998)10, 1111–1120.

are no 'pure' religions anymore, if there ever were, only 'interpenetrating religions'.[4]

In the approach I am advocating, Christianity is a religion alongside other religions, and theology is a collective noun for their various theologies, such as Judaic, Christian, Islamic, and Hindu theology and Buddhist philosophy. In this approach, both the participant and the observer perspective are necessary, as will be clarified further on in this chapter.

Nowadays, one can discern two distinct approaches to religious research: a narrow and a broad one. The former focuses exclusively on acquisition of knowledge about religions in keeping with the goal of all scientific research, which is the production of new knowledge. The broad approach likewise aims at producing knowledge about religions, but in addition it seeks to clarify and promote the contribution of these religions to 'a good life' for individuals and communities in the societies of which the religions form a part. According to this approach, scholars of religion not only have the role of researchers in the narrow sense, accountable only in their own scientific terms, but also that of public intellectuals, accountable not only to their own scientific forum but to three others as well: academia, society, and the religion or religions they study.[5] This threefold accountability resembles the functions of a Humboldt type of university, which aims at communicative unity between these functions.[6] To this I would add that while scholars of religion are scientifically accountable for their statements about the religions they study, they are not responsible for the religions themselves.

In this chapter, I adopt the second, broader approach, the dominant one in the American Academy of Religion,[7] and I do so from a cognitive paradigm. By this I mean that I draw on theoretical insights and empirical findings of the cognitive approach, which is the orientation of a growing number of academic disciplines, from linguistics, psychology, sociology, anthropology, education, and law, to philosophy.

---

[4] H. Nicholson, A Correlational Model of Comparative Theology, *The Journal of Religion* 85(2005)2, 191–213.

[5] D. Tracy, *The Analogical Imagination: Christian Theology and the Culture of Pluralism*, Crossroad, New York 1986.

[6] J. Habermas, *Zeitdiagnosen: Zwölf Essays 1980–2001*, Suhrkamp, Frankfurt 2003, 78 104; Cf. P. Bourdieu, *Science of Science and Reflexivity*, Polity Press, Cambridge 2004.

[7] D. Wiebe, Promise and Disappointment: Recent Developments in the Academic Study of Religion in the USA, in: Leertouwer et al. (eds.), *Modern Societies*, op. cit.

It also influences the study of religion (cognitive religious studies). In all science, including comparative science, one can only arrive at new knowledge if one embraces a particular paradigm and structures one's research accordingly. From the entire arsenal of phenomenological, hermeneutic, linguistic, semiotic, cultural, narrative, and cognitive paradigms used to reveal diverse aspects of the phenomenon of religion, I opt for the last, the cognitive paradigm, albeit not uncritically. Broadly, this paradigm aims at studying human attribution of meaning in terms of the interaction between brain, mind, behaviour, and cultural environment. Among non-initiates, there is a misconception that cognitive science focuses exclusively on conscious, intellectual, or rational processes. Nothing can be further from the truth. Its focus is the neural architecture and processes that constitute the infrastructure of human functions such as sensations, perceptions, automatic responses, feeling emotions, processing emotions, memory, imagination, conceptualisation, reasoning, decision making, planning and acting, which for the most part function unconsciously. Religious experience, religious knowledge and religious reasoning, too, happen for the most part unconsciously, as they are imbedded in a perceptual and emotional infrastructure from which they cannot be divorced and which constantly influences them.[8] Evidence of this is the growing literature on cognitive religious studies over the past 20 years, notably in book series, monographs, edited volumes, and journals.[9]

Against this background, the chapter deals with the following themes: goals of religious research (3.1), object of religious research – general aspects (3.2) and specific aspects (3.3) – relation between insider and outsider perspectives in which religious research is conducted (3.4), the principle of comparison (3.5), and finally, the normative implications at issue, especially human rights (3.6).

3.1   GOALS

I do not regard the study of religion as a science *sui generis*, even though its history – especially in Eliade's school – abounds in such

---

[8] L.W. Barsalou, et al., Embodiment in Religious Knowledge, *Journal of Cognition and Culture* 5(2005)1/2, 14–57; P. Thagard, The Emotional Coherence of Religion, *Journal of Cognition and Culture* 5(2005)1/2, 58–74.

[9] U. Schjoedt, The Religious Brain: A General Introduction to the Experimental Neuroscience of Religion. *Method and Theory in the Study of Religion* 21(2009)3, 310–339.

claims. In its broadest sense, religion needs to be studied with due regard to the full spectrum of both conventional and critical notions in the humanities and the sciences, in unrestricted academic freedom at a comprehensive, broad university – what Derrida calls a university without conditions (*université sans conditions*).[10]

To this university without conditions belongs the principle of academic freedom. Academic freedom derives from freedom of expression, one of the most fundamental rights in a constitutional democracy. Freedom of expression includes the right to cherish views without external influencing, as well as the right to look for information and ideas of whatever kind, to receive these and communicate them orally, in writing or in print, in the form of art or via any other medium of one's choice, including artistic or scientific publications. By extension, academic freedom can be defined as the freedom of lecturers, students and academic institutions to obtain, produce and publish knowledge without outside interference from the state or any non-academic group or organisation. The last category includes business, professional organisations, trade unions, as well as moral and cultural institutions like religions and other worldviews. Academic freedom pertains to all phases of scientific research and every aspect of these. It applies to the phenomenon being researched (the object), the research problem, choice of paradigms and theories employed (thus also in opposition to established paradigms and theories), how the research is conducted (methods and techniques), what results are envisaged, evaluation of the research and its termination, as well as publishing in any medium of one's choice. A fundamental premise is that human knowledge is a process of looking for truth that never ends and can never be concluded, and that every truth claim, whoever or whatever makes it, is in principle open to amplification, correction and review. This implies unconditional acknowledgment of scientific pluralism and its importance in every domain of knowledge and every discipline. An important condition is that students are consciously introduced to this pluralism, familiarised with it, and learn to appreciate its value. That is the only way to break down conventions and taboos regarding notions that traditionally passed for knowledge, to continually shift the boundaries of knowledge, and to fairly settle disputes about knowledge claims before a forum of scientists by means of logically and empirically based

---

[10] J. Derrida, *L'université sans condition*, Galilée, Paris 2001.

arguments. After all, truth can only be approximated if there is freedom of research and free exchange of conflicting views.

Seen thus, the goal of comparative study of religion does not differ fundamentally from that of any other scientific discipline, namely the production of new knowledge. Having said that, cognitive theory of science specifies four research goals for every academic discipline, including, to my mind, the academic study of religion.[11]

The first goal is descriptive research, which entails optimally accurate recording of phenomena as well as of the differences and similarities between them, and, on that basis, developing classifications, typologies and taxonomies. Thus one can describe the similarities and differences between religious practices, including their experiential, emotional, and representational aspects.

The second goal is explanatory research, which examines the intentional, functional, and structural relations between phenomena, including their similarities and differences. This goal, too, is relevant to research into religious phenomena. It refers to the intentions of religious actors, which may be regarded as the authors of religious plans and practices. After all, actors think of the consequences of their actions, both consciously and (mostly) unconsciously.[12] Because there is always interaction between a plurality of actors' intentions and a plurality of contextual variables, one may speak of a quasi-causal rather than a purely causal relation between intentions and actions.[13] But the goal of explanatory research is not confined to the relation between intentions and practices. It also entails functional explanations, so-called part/whole explanations, of religious intentions and practices by placing them in a larger religious or cultural framework. This framework may be seen as the independent variable which influences religious intentions and actions, the dependent variables. Conversely, the intentions and practices may be considered independent variables – in the sense of necessary conditions – for the larger religious and cultural framework, which may be interpreted as the dependent variable. The human sciences are not concerned with 'strictly causal

---

[11] T.A.F. Kuipers, *Structures in Science: Heuristic Patterns Based on Cognitive Structures: An Advanced Textbook in Neo-Classical Philosophy of Science*, Kluwer Academic Publishers, Dordrecht/Boston 2001, 73–130.

[12] G. Lakoff & M. Johnson, *Metaphores We Live By*, The University of Chicago Press, Chicago 1980, 54–55.

[13] P. Ricoeur, *Oneself as Another*, University of Chicago Press, Chicago 1992, 110.

explanations' in the sense of sufficient conditions, but, as Max Weber showed, with 'causally adequate explanations' in the sense of conducive and necessary conditions.[14] Finally, structural phenomena are also relevant enough to be studied cautiously, that is, the institutional forms religious phenomena take, like economic resources, power distribution configurations, leadership patterns, and participatory strategies. All these may influence religious intentions and functions, and, conversely, be influenced by them.

The third goal is to design research emanating from descriptive and explanatory research. There are two varieties: theoretical and practical design projects. The former entails designing new (always partial) theories in response to reformulated or (relatively) new theoretical problems. The second focuses on designing, describing, and evaluating methodical intervention in practices so as to discover what factors influence their processes, effects and results by determining the underlying mechanisms. Here one thinks of experimental research in laboratory situations or quasi-experimental research in situ, 'in the field', in order to investigate actual processes in religious rituals, counselling, community building or education. In addition, it should be noted that design research not only emanates from descriptive and explanatory research, but also influences it inasmuch as it involves the finding and formulation of new hypotheses.

The fourth and last goal relates to explicative research aimed at defining concepts in accordance with epistemological criteria like logical discrimination, extension, intension, consistency, and coherence. Such concepts are necessary so as to get beyond intuitive impressionism and to describe and explain religious phenomena in terms of the degree of resemblance and difference between them. In the broad framework of constructive realism, which is implied in the cognitive paradigm, explicative research does not refer to the traditional claim of so-called correspondence truth, but to that of fallible, probabilistic truth marked by degrees of approximating truth, as will be seen in the conclusion to this chapter.

What I have said so far may create the impression that the goal of scientific research is couched on rationalistic rather than cognitive

---

[14] M. Weber, *Wirtschaft und Geselschaft*, Mohr, Tübingen 1980, 5. S. Kalberg, *Einführung in die historisch-vergleichende Soziologie Max Webers*, Westdeutscher Verlag, Wiesbaden 2001, 202ff.

lines. It is important to distinguish clearly between the two. The rationalist approach rests on the assumption that science is the product
of a purely rational mind, whereas the cognitive approach proceeds
on the premise that science is the product of an embodied, imbedded
mind: the human mind is influenced in innumerable ways by the body,
including its emotions and unconscious reasoning, just as it in its turn
influences the body, all the while imbedded in and nourished by the
cultural context in which it is shaped and which it also shapes.[15] This
distinction has major implications. The rationalist approach swears
by universal, hard and fast premises, clear-cut concepts, strait and
narrow theories and universal, irrefutable test results. The cognitive
approach introduces all sorts of qualifications, which are particularly
important for comparative research. Thus one should realise that some
premises may be considered universal, for instance general statements
about perceptions and feeling emotions in religious rituals, but others
are determined by the cultural context, for instance statements about
processing emotions, experiences of self-transcendence or of transcendence itself, which does not alter the fact that those cultural aspects of
religion are channelled and limited by the infrastructure of the brain.[16]
Furthermore, whereas the rationalist approach to science defines concepts in terms of dichotomies and even antinomies, proponents of
the cognitive paradigm stress the emotion-driven, metaphor-driven
and praxis-driven nature of concepts and hence continuity between
concepts. Besides, rules and theories do not stem purely from the
researcher's brain, but are characterised by cultural contexts and cultural maps in the society of which they are part. Finally, there is no
such thing as universally irrefutable empirical outcomes, since they
always have to be proved anew in each new context and may moreover forfeit their alleged self-evidence in the light of rival paradigms.
This does not mean that all scientific practice is up in the air, and/or
that we should not keep striving for optimally accurate conceptualisation and theorising and the acquisition of precise test results in the
interest of descriptive and explanatory research. But it does mean
that we must take cognisance of all relevant perceptual, emotional,

---

[15] G. Lakoff, *Women, Fire, and Dangerous Things: What Categories Reveal About the Mind*, University of Chicago Press, Chicago 1987; Lakoff & Johnson, *Metaphores*, op. cit.
[16] J. Bulbulia, Are There Any Religions? An Evolutionary Exploration, *Method and Theory in the Study of Religion* 17(2005)2, 71–100.

pragmatic and cultural factors in which human cognition is embodied and imbedded.

3.2 OBJECT: GENERAL ASPECTS OF RELIGION

I have indicated that the object of comparative study of religion is the field of religions. In this section, I give a general, and in the next a specific, definition of religion as a study object.

To look for a general definition of religion is to open a veritable can of worms, the more so since the literature yields more than a hundred definitions.[17] The knottiest problem is certainly that religion as such does not exist, because it is a scientific construct. What exists in real life is 'sacred' spaces and times, 'sacred' objects and behaviour, connected with rituals, beliefs, emotions, gatherings, priests, and prophets. The term 'religion' is an abstraction, the product, not of 'lived religions' like Judaism, Christianity, Islam or Hinduism, but of scientists,[18] even scientists of the modern era.[19] At least three kinds of definitions of this scientific construct are in circulation, with all their implicit problems.[20]

The first is what is known as substantive definitions, which see religion as a set of practices before and about an 'ultimate reality'. The latter is referred to by such terms as the 'absolute', the 'transcendent', the 'holy', the 'divine', the 'deity' or 'God' – terms which moreover connote various cultural and religious contexts, as well as diverse approaches and theories about 'ultimate reality' within these contexts. Scientific terminology is by no means a-theoretical, and that goes for scientific study of religion as well.[21]

---

[17] J.G. Platvoet, Contexts, Concepts and Contests: Towards a Pragmatics of Defining 'Religion', in: J.G. Platvoet & A.L. Molendijk (eds.), *The Pragmatics of Defining Religion: Contexts, Concepts and Contests*, Brill, Leiden 1999, 463–516, here 505.

[18] J.Z. Smith, Religion, Religions, Religious, in: M.C. Taylor (ed.), *Critical Terms for Religious Studies*, University of Chicago Press, Chicago 1998, 269–284: Id., *Relating Religion: Essays in the Study of Religion*, University of Chicago Press, Chicago 2004.

[19] T. Asad, *Formation of the Secular: Christianity, Islam, Modernity*, Stanford University Press, Stanford 2003.

[20] Platvoet & Molendijk, *The Pragmatics*, op. cit.

[21] I. Dalferth, Theologie im Kontext der Religionswissenschaft, *Theologische Literaturzeitung* 126(2001)1, 4–20; Id., *Die Wirklichkeit des Möglichen*, Mohr, Tübingen 2003.

The second type comprises functional definitions. These do not centre on practices performed before and about God, but on those practices that function as 'ultimate reality' as religion does, fulfilling similar functions and arousing similar emotions. The standard example is football, which functions as an ultimate end in itself; but one can cite several others, such a pop music, liquor or sex, or serious activities like caring for a family or climbing the professional ladder: these too can function as ultimate reality. The drawback of this approach is that the research object becomes so broad that it comprehends literally everything (everything can function as a religion), hence it lacks the clear demarcation that every science requires. A study of religion that purports to be a science-of-everything leads everywhere, hence ends up leading nowhere. Consequently religion as a distinctive, more or less precisely definable domain of phenomena ceases to exist.

The third type of definition is reductive. At the macro level it sees religion purely as a social factor, be it an aspect of the relation between equality and inequality, social order and cohesion, social and political power and/or as their legitimisation and ideology, or it considers religion more specifically as a factor of social or political violence, instigating this violence, conditioning or accompanying it, and/or as its justification. At the micro level, it studies religion purely in terms of pathology, such as emotional repression, rationalisation, projection, compensation, or narcissism. I call these definitions reductive because they explain away religion as a relatively independent domain and reduce it to sociological, political, and/or psychological factors.

To determine the object of the study of religion, I settle for the first type of definition, the substantive variety, because the other two strip religion of its distinctive character and render it meaningless and vacuous. Substantive religion has, as noted already, two aspects: practices performed before an 'ultimate reality' and practices performed about an 'ultimate reality' or, more succinctly, practices before and about God. Practices performed before God are prayer, meditation, liturgy, and religiously informed moral activities, traditionally termed *coram Deo*. Practices about God are religious reflection, dialogue, counselling, care, education and instruction, community building, and the like.

In these religious practices, 'God' can be viewed in terms of the dialectical relation between transcendence and immanence. This relation could, but should not, be seen as a dichotomy. Rather it is a continuum between two extremes: in religious practice one can discern forms of transcendence in which the aspect of immanence cannot, or

can hardly, be detected (absolute transcendence), or, conversely, forms
of immanence in which the transcendent aspect cannot, or can hardly,
be seen (absolute immanence). There are also practices – the majority –
which display intermediate forms. In immanent transcendence, the
emphasis is on transcendence manifesting itself in immanent reality,
whereas in transcendent immanence the emphasis is on immanence
taking on transcendent height and depth.[22]

A possible objection to such a definition is that, whereas it covers
the Christian religion and major aspects of the other two monotheistic
religions, Judaism and Islam, it may marginalise a polytheistic religion
like Hinduism and an atheistic one like Buddhism. Here prudence is
called for, because the study of the history of religions reminds us
of the variety of academic inclusions and exclusions of non-Western
religions, which originally Christianity also was. For example, in the
second half of the 19th century, Buddhism – a Western construction –
was valued positively, because it was seen as a universal religion,
although some doubts were expressed whether it was a religion at all,
whereas the other religions, even Islam, were seen as national religions
only. In the last decades of the 19th century Hinduism – no less a
Western construction – was added to the list of preferential religions,
because it was positively valued for its Aryan roots, which Christianity shared, whereas the other religions, especially Judaism and Islam,
were deprecated because of their Semitic roots.[23] Be this as it may, we
now realise that Hindu polytheism is underpinned by a monotheistic
structure. We also realise that the atheism of Theravada Buddhism is
actually a form of non-theism, which does contain beliefs about the
Buddha as a superhuman being, endowed with soteriological talent to
help humans to attain supermundane goals. We see, moreover, that
folk Buddhism has manifestly theistic features.[24]

But there is a further point. Underlying the aforementioned objection that religions differ too widely to be lumped together under the
proposed definition (religious practices performed before and about

---

[22] J.A. van der Ven, *God Reinvented? A Theological Search in Texts and Tables*, Brill,
Leiden 1998.

[23] T. Masuzawa, *The Invention of World Religions: Or, How European Universalism
Was Preserved in the Language of Pluralism*, University of Chicago Press, Chicago
2005.

[24] M. Spiro, Religion: Problems of Definition and Explanation, in: M. Banton (ed.),
Anthropological Approaches to the Study of Religion, Tavistock, London 1978, 85–126,
here 87–96.

God) is an implicit striving for an all-encompassing, universal definition of religion. Because of the diachronic and synchronic pluralism of religious practices, however, that aspiration is a fallacy. The reason is that one cannot avoid a definition of religion based on cultural familiarity with one's 'home' religion. It cannot be otherwise if one uses a cognitive paradigm, in which the embodied and culturally imbedded mind is focal. Concepts, definitions, and rules in whatever field or cultural science are based on families of resemblances, in their turn based on prototypes.[25] In any definition of religion, one's 'home' religion fulfils this prototypical function, which indicates the focal purport of the concept of family resemblance: the closer a member of the family corresponds with the prototype, the more typical it is.[26] Scientifically, it is better to reflect critically on this prototypical structure than to act as if it does not or did not exist and strive blindly for universal concepts, definitions, and rules.[27] That means that one must constantly consider whether a definition needs to be adjusted, or even fundamentally modified, when one moves from one culture to another in order to study its religion or religions in situ. Opting for a prototypical approach to the concept of religion amounts to opting for a pluralistic contextuality of this concept.

From the history of the study of religion, especially traditional Christian theology, the question may be raised whether the substantive definition of religion that I propose (religious practices performed before and about God) amounts to the notion propounded in ancient documents of theological tradition, to the effect that the object of

---

[25] P.M. Churchland, *The Engine of Reason, the Seat of the Soul: A Philosophical Journey into the Brain*, MIT Press, Cambridge, MA 1995; W.F.G. Haselager, *Cognitive Science and Folk Psychology: The Right Frame of Mind*, Sage Publications, London/ Thousand Oaks, CA 1997.

[26] R.B. Edwards, *Reason and Religion: An Introduction to the Philosophy of Religion*, Hartcourt Brace Jovanovich, New York 1972, compiled a matrix, whose horizontal axis comprises a selection of members of the 'religious family', such as: (1) Christianity, Judaism, Islam; (2) Vedanta, Hinduism; (3) early Buddhism and Hinayana Buddhism; (4) early Greek Olympian polytheism, et cetera. The vertical axis comprises a selection of prominent characteristics of this family, such as: (1) belief in a supernatural intelligent being or beings; (2) belief in a superior intelligent being or beings; (3) complex worldview interpreting the significance of human life; (4) belief in experience after death; (5) moral code; et cetera. The more attributes a 'family member' scores on, the closer it comes to the nucleus of the religious family, the prototype, in the case of Edwards's example the monotheism of Christianity, Judaism and Islam. The fewer attributes a 'family member' scores on, the more it is seen as a borderline case.

[27] Platvoet, Contexts, op. cit.; M. Day, The Undiscovered and Undiscoverable Essence: Species and Religion after Darwin, *The Journal of Religion* 85(2005)1, 58.

study is just: 'God'. On this point there is a parting of ways. Liberal Protestantism gave up the notion of theology as the science of God at the time of the Enlightenment – even though semantically that is the meaning of the word 'theo-logy' – and instead described it as the scientific study of religion or of religious practices.[28] But of course a semantic approach to what constitutes the object of theology – God or religious practices – does not offer a conceptual solution.

What arguments are advanced for God as the object of theology? They range from biblical and historico-theological arguments to theory of science. I cite what strikes me as the most important of this latter variety. It maintains that all sciences are invariably based on certain explicit and implicit historical, cultural, and worldview-related presuppositions: there is no science without these (*Es gibt keine voraussetzungslose Wissenschaft*). A science without presuppositions would even be impossible, as Troeltsch rightly observes, for it would imply an infinite regression.[29] That applies to theology as well, hence – the argument goes – this discipline can legitimately proceed from God's existence as one of its presuppositions, even its cardinal presupposition, without denying its scientific character.

I have some objections to this view. The first is that it is peculiar to every science that its presuppositions, whatever they may be, are subject to criticism and could be reviewed or even rejected, and that no non-scientific agency can or may stifle that criticism. Spranger rightly pointed out that the true character of science does not consist in being free from presuppositions but in self-criticism of these.[30] Pannenberg supports this view.[31] In regard to theology, he says, its presuppositions likewise call for critical scrutiny, although he does not consider reviewing or rejecting them.

My second objection concerns the manner in which theological presuppositions ought to be critically tested. According to Pannenberg, once they have been explicated they have the status of hypotheses,

---

[28] V. Drehsen, *Neuzeitliche Konstitutionsbedingungen der praktischen Theologie: Aspekte der theologischen Wende zur sozialkulturellen Lebenswelt christlicher Religion*, Gütersloher Verlagshaus G. Mohn, Gütersloh 1988, 72–96.

[29] E. Troeltsch, *Gesammelte Schriften*, Vol. I–IV, Mohr, Tübingen 1912–1925, Vol. II, 183–192.

[30] E. Spranger, *Der Sinn der Voraussetzungslosigkeit in den Geisteswissenschaften*, Quelle & Meyer, Heidelberg 1964.

[31] W. Pannenberg, *Wissenschaftstheorie und Theologie*, Suhrkamp, Frankfurt 1973, 299–303.

which in his view also applies to God's existence. To him, 'God' is a hypothesis, and, like all hypotheses, must be verifiable, c.q. falsifiable – a statement endorsed by Kuitert[32] at that time and with which I then agreed.[33]

But the fundamental, obvious question is whether God can actually be researched as a hypothesis. Can he in fact be subjected to scientific research, for instance in the four forms I described above – scientific description, explanation, design research, and conceptual explication? It is hard to see how statements about God can be falsified, since they cannot be controlled intersubjectively. His typical form of presence consists in his constant coordination of his own absence, as Ricoeur aptly puts it.[34] He eludes every descriptive or explicatory image, concept or theory. He is an ever receding horizon.

But, one may continue, is God really a falsifiable hypothesis? Does he function as a hypothesis in theology, or as an assumption? The distinction between an assumption and a hypothesis is crucial. In theory of science the two terms have a totally different status. In science an assumption is taken as assumed, as the word indicates, as read, without systematically making it an object of critical study. Thus the biological sciences assume that there is life, the social sciences that humans are social beings and psychology that people have an inner world. The relation between assumptions and hypotheses is indirect, because theories intervene – theories whose reference to some part of reality one wants to explore. The steps of scientific research are, briefly, the following: (a) the researcher proceeds from a particular assumption, (b) decides to investigate some part of the relevant scientific domain more closely, (c) formulates a research question, (d) develops a theory in the sense of a network of concepts that is imposed on the part of reality under investigation, (e) infers one or more hypotheses from it, (f) exposes these hypotheses to the most rigorous falsification procedures, and (g) concludes whether the hypotheses have stood up to these procedures. If they do, the hypothesis does not become a thesis but is considered a corroborated hypothesis.

---

[32] H. Kuitert, Waarheid en verificatie in de dogmatiek, *Rondom het woord* 14(1972)2, 97–130; Id., *Wat heet geloven. Structuur en herkomst van de christelijke geloofsuitspraken*, Ten Have, Baarn 1977.

[33] J.A. van der Ven, *Practical Theology: An Empirical Approach*, Peeters, Leuven 1993, 102–106.

[34] P. Ricoeur, *Figuring the Sacred: Religion, Narrative, and Imagination*, Fortress Press, Minneapolis 1995, 217–235.

Hence assumptions are not hypotheses, nor are hypotheses directly inferred from them. In the biological sciences, the hypothesis is not life, but its evolution – anyway a very strong hypothesis at that. In the social sciences the hypothesis is not people as social beings but, for example, certain factors that influence group formation in terms of equality and inequality. In psychology, the hypothesis is not people's inner world but, for instance, certain brain mechanisms that play a role in the feeling of emotions and the perception of those emotions in other people. If one were to change the status of a particular science's assumption into that of a hypothesis, falsification of the hypothesis would mean the end of that science. In other words, if God were the hypothesis rather than the assumption of theology and his existence were to be falsified through critical research – which to my mind is as impossible as scientific verification of his existence – it would be the end of theology. Theology would have abolished itself. Hence the distinction between an assumption and a hypothesis is crucial. This leads to the conclusion that science produces knowledge that is domain-specific, perspectival, approximate and hypothetical. Science is not about 'the' truth but about truth claims regarding parts of real-life domains. Science does not pertain to reality as a whole: it is not a science of everything.

Now for a third and final objection. Supposing God were the hypothesis of theology – which, as I have indicated, is absurd – what would the process of verification/falsification look like? Let me go back to Pannenberg and critically examine his notion of theological verification, as he calls it (note: not falsification!). The way he sets about it defies everything that is intrinsic to scientific work. What he does is to abandon the actual academic arena and shift it to the area of Christian belief in divine revelation in salvation history and its consummation at the end of time. According to Pannenberg, God will be fully verified in his future, final self-revelation, in which he will be seen as the all in all. No matter how fervently this eschatological statement may be believed, the theological proposition leads to a religious statement and as such falls outside the vocabulary of science. More precisely, this is an unwarranted switch from one keyboard to another, from a scientific to a religious keyboard, however melodious the composition.

In short, in Pannenberg's work and that of other theologians displaying a similar approach, the reasoning, viewed schematically, is threefold: (1) God is the basic assumption of theology; (2) God is declared a hypothesis; (3) to verify the hypothesis God is then turned into an argument – 'because' God revealed himself in salvation history, which self-revelation will be consummated at the end of time. In terms of theory of science this cannot but be seen as a Wittgensteinian category blunder. In effect one and the same 'datum' – here 'God' – functions in one and the same explication in three different capacities: those of an assumption, a hypothesis and an argument.

To clarify the issue two distinctions are needed. The first is between God and religion, the second between religion and religious studies or theology. In regard to distinction one, the direct object of theology or religious studies is not God but religion. In itself this is not remarkable. The sober fact is that theologians and scholars of religion always work – day by day, year by year – with religious texts, archives, documents, ecclesiastic doctrines, theories of colleagues, and empirical data collected from informants and respondents. That is what they study and research – not God himself. They deal in experiences about God, ritual prayers to him, rites involved with him, sermons about him, historical and academic texts about him – they are not directly dealing with God himself. God can only be seen as the indirect (never the direct) object of theology and religious studies, since he is the direct object of religion – a notion that does derive from Pannenberg.[35]

The second distinction is that between religion and religious studies or theology. Religion is the object of religious studies or theology, which engages in the study of this object. It is important to distinguish between the two domains, the object domain and the scientific domain, otherwise one inadvertently switches from the second to the first and performs a composition, as Pannenberg does, on two different keyboards. In the object domain, one performs religious actions, namely practices before God; in the scientific domain one performs scientific actions, not religious ones.[36] One finds an analogous distinction in ethics, between virtue and virtue ethics. The former has to do with a virtuous attitude and virtuous action, the latter is the study of these, as Thomas Aquinas indicated.[37] Purely by the way, it should be noted that whilst I here cite Aquinas in a positive sense, my previous discussion contradicts him, for he insisted that God is the object of

---

[35] Van der Ven, *Practical*, op. cit., 102–106.
[36] E. Schillebeeckx, s.v. Theologie, *Theologisch Woordenboek*, deel III, 1958, 4485–4542; Id., *Openbaring en theologie*, H. Nelissen, Bilthoven 1964, 80–81.
[37] Thomas Aquinas, *Summa Theologica*, (Abbr.: STh), I, 1, 6, ad 3.

theology;[38] but that is because of his deductive, Aristotelian concept of science, which conflicts with present-day theory of science.[39]

3.3   OBJECT: SPECIFIC ASPECTS OF RELIGION

So far I have defined the object of the study of religion in the general terms of a substantive concept of religion (i.e. practices before and about God). Now I want to look at some specific aspects of religion, which, depending on one's sources, may range from three to fifteen.[40] To avoid the randomness of a mere list of aspects, I classify them into three levels: the micro level of religious individuals, the meso level of religious communities and institutions, and the macro level of the relation between religion and society. At the micro level, the following aspects may be distinguished: experiential, emotional, narrative, representational, reflective, ritual, and moral aspects, which respectively relate to religious experiences, emotions, story telling, beliefs, reasoned inquiry, ritual participation, and moral commitments. At the meso level, the following aspects may be distinguished: communitarian aspects, which refer to building groups and communities, and institutional aspects, which relate to doctrinal rules, organisational, and leadership structures. At the macro level, all kinds of societal factors influence religious practices and even determine their economic, political, social, and cultural aspects – for example their financial infrastructure, juridical basis, social scope and cohesive strength, and cultural plausibility and accessibility. This classification must be seen as analytical rather than ontological, in the sense that the aspects never occur separately but always in conjunction with each other.

Let me comment on this threefold distinction. First, by listing those aspects, I am taking a stance in some of the debates in this field. For

---

[38] STh, I, 1,7.

[39] M.-D. Chenu, La théologie comme une science au XIIItième siècle, Vrin, Paris 1943; Id., La théologie au douzième siècle, Vrin, Paris 1957; A.C. Crombie, *Styles of Scientific Thinking in the European Tradition: The History of Argument and Explanation Especially in the Mathematical and Biomedical Sciences and Arts*, Vol. I–III, Duckworth, London 1994.

[40] N. Smart, *Dimensions of the Sacred: An Anatomy of the World's Beliefs*, University of California Press, Berkeley 1996; D.S. Cannon, *Six Ways of Being Religious: A Framework for Comparative Studies of Religion*, Wadsworth Pub., Belmont, CA 1996; J.B. Carman & S.P. Hopkins, *Tracing Common Themes: Comparative Courses in the Study of Religion*, Scholars Press, Atlanta, GA 1991.

instance, I do not consider Asad's arguments about whether religion is practice or belief relevant, for the simple reason that there is no such thing as religious practice without beliefs, nor can there be – at any rate not in terms of the cognitive paradigm.[41] I also think the two aspects (practice and belief), to which Daniel Pals[42] confines himself in the consensus he reaches in his *Seven theories of religion*, should be expanded to include the aspects listed above: religion is more complex than just practice or behaviour and belief.

But there is yet another distinction that I want to underscore, even though it complicates the debate further. It has to be noted, since it will prevent unnecessary controversy. I am speaking about the difference between on-line and off-line religious practice. Both are forms of religious practice. On-line religious practice happens when people are actively occupied with religion and engage with it actively – what could be described as religious performance. Off-line religious practice indicates reflection on the personal decision underlying participation in a religious performance, for without such a reflective decision religious performances would no longer happen in present-day individualised and secularised Western culture, either in (for instance) Christian or Muslim groups.[43] On-line and off-line religion are related, in that participation and reflection are dialectically linked: the one is a condition for the other and, conversely, each has an effect on the other. Boyer, a leading proponent of cognitive religious studies, makes a clear distinction between the two.[44] Others, like Ilkka Pyysiäinen, observe the way each implies the other and the transitions between them.[45] Pyysiäinen is right, I think, for off-line religious practice can be seen as an extension of the aforementioned aspect of reflection on on-line religious practice. Moreover, in both on-line and off-line religious practice there are reasoning processes at work, probably more

---

[41] T. Asad, *Genealogies of Religion: Discipline and Reasons of Power in Christianity and Islam*, Johns Hopkins University Press, Baltimore 1993, 27–54; K. Schilbrack, Religion, Models of, and Reality: Are We through with Geertz? *Journal of the American Academy of Religion* 73(2005)2, 429–452.

[42] D.L. Pals, *Seven Theories of Religion*, Oxford University Press, New York 1996.

[43] O. Roy, *Globalized Islam: The Search for a New Ummah*, Columbia University Press, New York 2004, 148–200.

[44] P. Boyer, *Religion Explained: The Evolutionary Origins of Religious Thought*, Basic Books, New York 2001, 277–285.

[45] I. Pyysiäinen, Intuitive and Explicit in Religious Thought, *Journal of Cognition and Culture* 4(2004)1, 123–150.

reflexive in the case of participation and more reflective in the case of thoughtful decision making.

Lastly, one could ask whether the trichotomy which relates to religious aspects at the micro level, at the meso level, and at the macro level, adequately accounts for the shifts in 'modern religiosity', such as current processes of religious de-communitarisation, de-institutionalisation, de-traditionalisation, and individualisation. Does it take account of the modern phenomenon encapsulated in the slogan, 'believing without belonging' that refers to these processes, especially in Europe? More pertinently, is there any point in noting communitarian, institutional, and societal aspects? It depends on one's definition of these aspects. Communitarian aspects refer to patterns of social relation in religions, however short-lived and loose. Institutional aspects have to do with phenomena like admission criteria, however low the thresholds, and with structures of formal and informal leadership, whether they are broad or narrow in scope and autocratic or democratic in nature. Doctrinal rules, too, fall under institutional aspects. These are not confined to *ex cathedra* pronouncements, but include beliefs that a given religious group considers 'true' or 'valuable', whose observance and maintenance are watched over, in which regard members are protected, with gentle insistence or firm coercion, against backsliding or apostasy. Communitarian and institutional aspects are found in all forms of religious practices, not only in the established churches and denominations but also in sects and cults. Societal aspects are no less important, for there is no form of religious practice that is not conditioned by economic, political, social, or cultural factors, even though they are not always mentioned in a phenomenological description.

Let me dwell briefly on doctrinal rules, since they give rise to many misconceptions. Three aspects must be clearly distinguished: scriptures containing religious rules considered foundational for religious groups, the extent of reflection on these rules, and the degree of enforceability of and obedience to them. Note that each aspect represents a continuum: it is a matter of how foundational they are, how much they are reflected upon and how enforceable they are. This may vary from very low to very high. In some denominations and sects they are very low, in others very high, with all sorts of levels in between. Let me elaborate on these three aspects shortly.

Scriptures consist in source texts such as the Hindu Vedas, the Pali canon of Theravada Buddhism, the Mahayana sutras and the vinaya of Mahayana Buddhism, the Jewish Bible, the New Testament of

Christianity, and the Qur'an of Islam. They are the enduring point of reference and norm for that religious group or community's faith. But the moment its members become aware of inconsistencies in these texts or there are conflicting interpretations, a second agency steps in, namely the tradition of the religious community. It resolves the conflict by invoking some historical statement by a prominent leader or teacher, a group of leaders or teachers, or a school or several schools. If this authoritative statement fails to resolve the conflict or new conflicts arise, a third actor intervenes, namely the person or group currently leading the community. Such current doctrinal statements may have authority over a small group or community but may also hold good for all affiliated communities in a region, a country, a continent, or even, as in the case of the Catholic Church, all over the world. It varies from place to place and from one era to another.[46]

The measure of reflection on which the interpretation of texts, tradition and current doctrinal rules are based likewise varies from one place and era to another. In Christianity alone there are substantial differences between denominations and sects. Thus fundamentalist and charismatic groups are marked by reflection at a fairly low level of abstraction, whereas reflection in the traditional denominations often assumes the form of consistent, coherent arguments, with due regard to their relation to society at large. In that case, reflection turns into doctrine proper, in which theology plays a major role. A distinction should be made, however, between the doctrine and the theology of a religious community. The author of doctrine is the religious community or its leaders, the author of theology is an individual theologian. Because the two are continually interacting, they are easily confused, so much so that even the religious community's leadership may see theology as the apology for – or any rate a reasonable exposition of – doctrine, and proceeds to identify the two. As a result, theology may be regarded as an extension of the official doctrine, not only by members and leaders of the religious community but also by some theologians themselves and even outsiders – which confuses the distinction between doctrine and theology altogether.[47]

Finally, the enforceability of and obedience to the more or less strict doctrines of religious community leaders likewise vary from one place

---

[46] Weber, *Wirtschaft*, op. cit., 279–285.
[47] Boyer, *Religion*, op. cit., 277–285.

and era to the next. There are 'liberal' religious groups that have no enforceable obedience at all and where ongoing dialogue between members plays a greater role than consensus of whatever kind. By participating in the religious practices of these groups, members indicate their engagement, while taking the doctrines imbedded in these practices to be 'true', albeit according to their own insight and belief – that is sufficient. Here free religious communication is the way to approach religious truth. In other religious communities, there are not only beliefs that are considered 'true', but they are also associated with ostensibly unshakable truth claims that are never subject to hypothesising and falsification, and are even entrenched in truth regimes, complete with sanctions such as suspension from participation in religious practices or even total exclusion through excommunication. Here the distinction between truth, truth claims, and truth regimes is pivotal. In severe cases, freedom and truth conflict and, in order to prevent or resolve it, 'the' truth is given priority over freedom; in extreme cases freedom is wiped out in order to protect truth.[48]

3.4   Insider and Outsider Perspectives

I have now outlined the goals and the object of the study of religion. The goals are to describe, explain, design, and define religious practices. The object comprises aspects of substantive religious practice in general and specific aspects of this practice at the micro, meso, and macro levels in particular. But that is just a general framework. I still have to show that these aspects of religious practice can and should be viewed from both an insider and an outsider perspective.

Let me start by saying what the two terms do *not* imply. They are not substantive, in that they have no substance in their own right, even though they can be given substance; they are purely formal. In this respect there are all sorts of misconceptions, associated with the goals and objects of research and the person of the researcher.

The first misconception concerns goals. It is that studies from an insider perspective are identified with descriptive research and those from an outsider perspective with explanatory research. Yet both

---

[48] B. Lincoln, Theses on Method, *Method and Theory in the Study of Religion* 8(1996)3, 225–228; E. Poulat, *Notre laïcité publique, La France est une République laïque*, Berg, Paris 2003, 25, 67.

perspectives can and should be adopted in both kinds of research. In this view, members of a religious community may present descriptions and explanations of processes going on in their communities from their own insider perspective, and non-members may come with different descriptions and explanations from their outsider perspective.

The second misconception concerns the object. From an insider perspective, it is said, the object of study is God; from an outsider perspective it is religion or religious practices. But I have already argued that God can never be the object of either descriptive or explanatory research, because his presence in fact consists in coordinating his own absence. He cannot be posited as a descriptive or explanatory hypothesis, since his existence cannot be falsified. So the only possible object for the study of religion is human beings' relation to God, as expressed in religious practices in which people address themselves to God or communicate about him, with all the aspects at the three levels I mentioned. This applies to Christian and non-Christian religions alike. They can all be studied from an insider and an outsider perspective.

The third misconception regards the researcher personally. In an insider perspective, it is said, researchers have to be believers themselves, whereas in an outsider perspective they are non-believers, outsiders operating on a methodologically agnostic basis. As will be seen below, the insider perspective is not per se determined by people who belong to a particular religious group or community and/or participate in the community's religious ceremonies out of personal commitment. The insider perspective is not per se that of people who *are* on the inside but those who *adopt* the perspective of the insider. Nor is an outsider perspective per se that of non-members or those who do not join in ceremonies out of personal engagement. They *are* not outsiders but merely *adopt* that perspective. Thus, believers can adopt both an insider and an outsider perspective on their own religion, and so can non-believers.

The fourth and last misconception is that researchers who adopt an insider perspective are wholly, even exhaustively, determined by the cultural and religious context in which they conduct their study, and those who adopt an outsider perspective are free from such contexts. This misconception is encountered not only in secularist approaches to the study of religion, but also in a particular phenomenological school that insists that researchers should 'bracket' or suspend themselves, their ideas, situation, and context entirely. This shows a sad disregard for the insight that the researcher is always a positioned subject, a situated observer, an embodied agent, an imbedded investigator. Some researchers nevertheless try to be methodologically agnostic so as to ensure objectivity and neutrality,[49] but fail to realise that objectivity and neutrality do not and cannot exist in cultural studies, especially religious studies. The only possibility is to strive for impartiality.[50] I want to underline *strive*, because impartiality is not a descriptive concept but, in Kantian terms, a regulative idea. In contrast to neutrality, impartiality is an ideal, because it is founded on, again in Kantian terms, the categorical imperative that one has to treat human beings never simply as a means, but always at the same time as ends, an intrinsic value, especially in moral and religious affairs.[51] This means that religion has to be studied as independently as possible of one's own beliefs and interests, wants and needs, convictions and biases. Rawls says of a rational and impartial sympathetic spectator: "His own interests do not thwart his natural sympathy for the aspirations of others and he has a perfect knowledge of these endeavours and what they mean for those who have them."[52] His sympathetic impartiality stems from 'purity of heart'.[53] Those who embrace the idea of neutrality rather than impartiality do not realise that in so doing they are themselves adopting a stance, even a worldview, albeit a nonreligious one typical of Western secularised society. In other words, detached objectivity is impossible; there is no such things as a view from nowhere.[54]

In short, the twin concepts 'insider and outsider perspective' are not identical with such pairs as descriptive and explanatory research, God-oriented or religion-oriented research, committed and non-committed research, and religious and secular research.

Having indicated what the two terms do not mean, let us examine what they do mean. The best way to clarify them is with reference to

---

[49] G. Wiegers, Afscheid van het methodologisch agnosticisme? *Tijdschrift voor Theologie* 45(2005)2, 153–167.

[50] P. Ricoeur, *La Memoire, l'histoire, l'oubli*, Seuil, Paris 2000, 413–436.

[51] I. Kant, *Groundwork of the Metaphysic of Morals*, Harper & Row, New York 1964, 96; M.C. Nussbaum, *Frontiers of Justice: Disability, Nationality, Species Membership*, The Belknap Press of Harvard University Press, Cambridge, MA 2006, 12.

[52] J. Rawls, *A Theory of Justice*, The Belknap Press of Harvard University Press, Cambridge, MA 1971, 186.

[53] Nussbaum, *Frontiers*, op. cit., 409.

[54] G.D. Flood, *Beyond Phenomenology: Rethinking the Study of Religion*, Cassell, London/New York 1999, 143–168; J. Habermas, *Zwischen Naturalismus und Religion: Philosophische Aufsätze*, Suhrkamp, Frankfurt am Main 2005, 119–154.

what is known in phonology as emic and etic analysis, '-emic' and '-etic' functioning as suffixes of 'phoneme': *phonemic* and *phonetic*. According to Pike, who coined the two terms as far back as 1954, the former pertains to the study of speech sounds in a given language according to the native usage of her informants; the latter refers to the same speech sounds in more general terms, independently of this native usage. From phonology, via cultural semantics, the two terms penetrated the social sciences – especially anthropology and comparative psychology – during the 1980s, whereupon they found their way into religious studies. The multiplicity of meanings covered by the two concepts in cultural semantics and the social sciences is also found in religious studies.[55]

The most common meaning of emic and etic in religious studies is that of researchers who adopt either an insider or an outsider perspective. 'Emic' refers to the study of religions from an insider perspective on the relevant religious practices, and 'etic' to studies from a more general meta-perspective, in which emic descriptions can be transformed, compared and analysed at a higher level of abstraction.[56] More specifically, they mean that in an insider perspective one would use the semantics, grammar, and pragmatics used in that religion, and in an outsider perspective those semantics, grammar, and pragmatics are translated into general categories transcending the particular religion so as to permit comparative study of several religions in terms of these broader categories.

Naturally, there is constant cross-pollination between research from an insider, emic or first-order perspective and an outsider, etic or second-order perspective. For one thing, through their schooling and programmes on the media, members of a particular religion are gradually influenced by the results of research from an outsider perspective. They come to adopt the terminology of that research – terms like 'religious fiction', 'myth', 'ideology', 'taboo', 'performance' – and thus in a sense broaden their own insider perspective. At the same time, many terms used from an outsider perspective derive from studies in

---

[55] Th.N. Headland, Introduction: A Dialogue between Kenneth Pike and Marvin Harris on Emics and Etics, in: Th.N. Headland, K.L. Pike & M. Harris (eds.), *Emics and Etics: The Insider/Outsider Debate*, Sage Publications, Newbury Park, CA 1990, 20–24.

[56] J.S. Jensen, On a Semantic Definition of Religion, in: J.G. Platvoet & A.L. Molendijk (eds.), *The Pragmatics of Defining Religion: Contexts, Concepts and Contests*, Brill, Leiden 1999, 422.

an insider perspective, albeit with different loadings, for instance terms like 'faith', 'belief', 'experience', 'image', 'sacrifice', and 'ritual'.[57]

Besides, the deciding factor in the case of emic and etic is not the source of knowledge but its aim. Hence it does not matter whether emic categories derive from etic categories, or vice versa. The important thing is what is envisaged: gathering knowledge from the perspective of either the inside or the outside.[58] In the case of the insider perspective, the 'new' terms are associated with 'old' terms and believers incorporate them into their understanding of their own religion, while the researcher tries to grasp that self-understanding, including the new terms, from the believer's perspective. In the case of the outsider perspective, it is a matter of translating 'old' and 'new' native testimonies into more general categories that permit comparison between religions, thus turning them into comparative categories.

Having clarified the difference between insider and outsider perspectives, we need to consider their interrelationship. Here there are two approaches. The first interprets the two terms as dichotomous, the second puts them on a continuum. First let me explain what the term 'dichotomy' means in this context. It refers to two areas separated by a boundary: an inside and an outside. If one is inside a particular religion, one adopts an insider perspective; if one is outside it, one adopts an outsider perspective. It is a choice which is dichotomous in coordinate fashion: one must adopt either one perspective or the other.

According to the second approach, which I shall follow below, one has to realise that the term 'perspective' is a spatial metaphor, comprising a longitudinal, latitudinal, and vertical dimension. The first dimension refers to the length of the historical period that the religious practices one studies are located in, the second relates to the width of the class or classes of religious practices under investigation, and the third (height) concerns the level of abstraction of the study. The difference between insider and outsider perspective can be seen in terms of gradually extending the historical period and/or broadening the number of classes and/or raising the level of abstraction. If we do that, we find that the relation between insider and outsider perspective is not a matter of two dichotomous positions, between which we

---

[57] Cf. M.C. Taylor, *Critical Terms for Religious Studies*, University of Chicago Press, Chicago 1998.

[58] J. Lett, Emics and Etics: Notes on the Epistemology of Anthropology, in: Headland et al. (eds.), *Emics and Etics*, op. cit., 127–142, here 137.

have to choose, but of ordinal, expanding positions on a continuum. Put differently, from an insider perspective one both describes and explains religious practices in terms of the semantics, grammar, and pragmatics of its participants, that is in terms of their experience, motivations, beliefs, thought processes, and reasoning. If one adopts an outsider approach, one expands the diachronic scope, broadens the synchronic range, and ascends to a higher level of abstraction so as to make comparisons. Let me illustrate it with reference to two religious practices from Christianity and Hinduism in which I have taken part myself.[59]

In Catholic liturgy, the Palm Sunday ritual is a performance with many bodily, experiential, cognitive, and social aspects, imitating Jesus' entry into Jerusalem. In the Hindu bedroom procession in the Hindu temple in Madurai, a statue of the goddess Minaksi, accompanied by elephants, is followed by a train of worshippers on its way to the bedroom of her consort, the god Siva – also a ritual performance.[60] From the insider perspective of both Christianity and Hinduism, the two rituals can be studied independently. The first ritual may be interpreted in terms of the paradox of Jesus being hailed as the Messiah while riding on the humblest of animals, a donkey, which anticipates the kenosis of his impending suffering and death. The second may be understood in terms of the care Hindus show for their beloved Gods and expressing their wonderment and thanks in return for the care they receive from them. But they can also be compared by studying the similarities and differences from an outsider perspective at a higher level of abstraction. In that case, the comparative category could be 'procession', with various aspects. In the cognitive paradigm such a procession is characterised by three semiotic aspects, which Peirce analysed in his linguistics and Deacon applied to rituals: iconicity (both processions depict a religious incident), indexicality (both processions put participants in touch with the incident, resulting in religious engagement), and symbolism (both processions function as a 'journey to God').[61]

---

[59] J.A. van der Ven, *Religie tussen Oost en West: Een reis door India*, Ambo, Baarn 1987, 23–40.

[60] For a parallel with ancient Egypt, see E.M. Curtis, *Man as the Image of God in Genesis in the Light of Ancient near Eastern Parallels*, Dissertation University of Pennsylvania, 1984, and for a parallel with ancient Mesopotamia see J.Z. Smith, *Relating Religion: Essays in the Study of Religion*, University of Chicago Press, Chicago 2004.

[61] T. Deacon, *The Symbolic Species. The Co-Evolution of Language and the Brain*, Norton, New York 1997, chapter 3.

Against this background, the religious doctrines implied in those practices can be studied from both an insider perspective and a comparative outsider perspective. From an insider perspective, the Palm Sunday procession may be interpreted as a 'performative revelation' occurring in the ritual, and within that framework as a 'personal revelation' of the compassionate God in Jesus' compassionate ministry. From an insider perspective, the Hindu procession to the bedroom in Madurai may be regarded as an example of how the term '*avatara*' is used in some Hindu traditions to express the physical concreteness of God, who is ritually put to bed. From an outsider perspective, the similarity of the two religious doctrines can be encapsulated in the term 'incarnation'[62] or, even better, 'manifestation', in view of both Christian and Hindu theology's objections – albeit on different grounds – to the term 'incarnation'.[63] The manifestation at issue is a manifestation of God, who appears in ritual activities of worship. Such a divine manifestation correlates with a religious experience among the faithful who perform this ritual, in which positive emotions of thankfulness, goodness, joy, and infinity, and negative emotions of dread, disappointment, suffering, and finitude are integrated and reconciled in a kind of *coincidentia oppositorum*.[64]

In another language game, an emic approach to the study of religion can be called a first-order analysis, and an etic approach a second-order analysis. Sometimes the former is associated with what is known as 'thick descriptions' of religious phenomena in their native context, approximating Eliade's programme of 'reliving' native experience, like Bellah's *Habits of the heart*.[65] In contrast to such 'thick description', the etic approach can be called 'thin description', because it abstracts from the freshness and richness of the various concrete aspects implied in the emic approach by entering them into analytical categories.

At the same time, terms like 'thick description' and 'thin description' could lead to the misconception that the difference between the

---

[62] F.X. Clooney, *Hindu God, Christian God: How Reason Helps Break Down the Boundaries between Religions*, Oxford University Press, Oxford/New York 2001, 101–123.

[63] Cf. Th. Ryba, s.v. Manifestation, in: W. Braun & R.T. McCutcheon (eds.), *Guide to the Study of Religion*, Cassell, London/New York 2000, 168–189.

[64] H.M. Vroom, *Religions and the Truth: Philosophical Reflections and Perspectives*, Eerdmans, Grand Rapids, MI 1989.

[65] R. N. Bellah, *Habits of the Heart: Individualism and Commitment in American Life*, University of California Press, Berkeley 1985.

two merely concerns the descriptive versus the explanatory goal of the study of religion. That is far from true, as should be evident from the first part of this chapter. More than that, the four goals I have mentioned (descriptive, explanatory, design-related, and explicative research) are important in both approaches, and both approaches entail comparative analyses at high levels of abstraction.[66] Hence, rising to a high level of abstraction is not peculiar to etic or second-order analysis, as is sometimes wrongly averred, but is also characteristic of emic or first-order analysis, for conceptualisation and classification, reflection and comparison occur in participant approaches as well.[67] There are plenty of examples, like the comparative classification in the theology of God, particularly absolute transcendence, immanent transcendence, transcendent immanence, and absolute immanence (Hartshorne 1976), or the comparative classification in New Testament christology, particularly *maranatha, theios aner*, wisdom, and *pascha* christology,[68] or the comparative classification of truths in the *hierarchia veritatum*, particularly God, Jesus, and the Spirit at the highest level, church and sacraments at the second level, and statements on morality, which fall outside any infallibility claim at the third level.[69]

But there is a further point. The study of religion from an insider perspective and that from an outsider perspective are not separate enterprises. I have already mentioned the constant cross-pollination between the terminology used in the two perspectives. Along with that there is also constant cross-pollination between the theories they use. One could even say that both are characterised by a combination of theoretical insights deriving from insider and outsider research. The difference is that when the insider perspective has priority, theories from an outsider perspective are *ultimately* integrated with the insider perspective, and conversely, when the outsider perspective is given

---

[66] M.L. Satlow, Disappearing Categories: Using Categories in the Study of Religion, *Method and Theory in the Study of Religion* 17(2005)4, 287–298.

[67] F. Vosman, Het 'samenwonen' van katholieke theologie en godsdienstwetenschap, *Tijdschrift voor Theologie* 46(2006)2, 101–112, here 105–106.

[68] E. Schillebeeckx, *Jesus: An Experiment in Christology*, The Seabury Press, New York 1979, 404–438.

[69] E. Schillebeeckx, Breuken in de christelijke dogma's, in: E. Schillebeeckx et al. (eds.), Breuklijnen: grenservaringen en zoektochten. 14 essays voor Ted Schoof bij zijn afscheid van de theologische faculteit Nijmegen, H. Nelissen, Baarn 1994, 15–50, here 39–48.

priority, those from the insider perspective are *ultimately* integrated with the outsider perspective.

Yet mutual integration of insider and outsider theories is by no means the rule. In many instances, such integration is not only unfeasible but also undesirable from the angle of academic freedom. That happens when description and/or explication of insider and outsider data reveals contradictory differences. There are plenty of examples, as when religious leaders interpret their unconditional condemnations in regard to sex and sexual orientation as 'service to humanity' in terms of their insider perspective, whereas religious researchers from their outsider perspective see it as a violation of human rights, especially the prohibition of discrimination on grounds of sex and sexual orientation and the right to privacy; or when fundamentalists see apostasy as warranting the death penalty, whereas religious researchers regard that as a violation of the fundamental right to life; or when citizens of a sovereign state prepare for genocide against infidels, while religious researchers interpret it as grounds for international humanitarian intervention.[70] In all these instances, mutual integration of insider and outsider perspectives is not only unfeasible but also scientifically unacceptable. All that can be done then is to describe the differences between the two perspectives accurately and contrast them.[71]

3.5   REFLECTIVE COMPARISON

From what we have said so far it is evident that the distinction between insider and outsider perspective brings us to the attribute of religious research that is the focus of this chapter: comparative research. Put simply, if we study two religious phenomena in two different religions from each one's insider perspective, we may (note: not *must*) conclude that they relate to each other as two species of the same genus. That may be an oversimplification, for this conclusion is fraught with all kinds of problems that could easily lead to misunderstanding. I cannot dwell on all the problems, but let me mention just four of them.

---

[70] A. Ferrara, *The Force of Example: Explorations in the Paradigm of Judgment*, Columbia University press, New York 2008, 147–163.

[71] R.T. McCutcheon, "It's a Lie. There's No Truth in It! It's a Sin!" On the Limits of the Humanistic Study of Religion and the Costs of Saving Others from Themselves, *Journal of the American Academy of Religion* 74(2006)3, 720–750.

First, when making a comparison one employs categories, as is evident in the foregoing example where I suggested the comparative category 'procession'. In a sense this category is self-evident, but it becomes less so when we ask ourselves what we actually do when we fit religious phenomena such as the Palm Sunday ritual and the Hindu bedroom ritual into a category. The use of categories is commonplace. In our everyday lives we categorise not only things but also abstractions like events, actions, emotions, spatial relations, social relations, forms of power and authority and, of course, all sorts of cultural phenomena, including religious ones. It should be noted that such categories are often applied unconsciously, as in the case of 'furniture', 'kitchenware', 'profit and loss', 'democracy' and 'abstract art', and in the religious sphere 'rituals', 'prayers', 'sermons', and 'God concepts'. In science it is different: here categories are chosen consciously, reasons are advanced for them, and it is debated whether this or that category should be chosen to cover the phenomena under investigation. It may even lead to major scientific conflicts between different traditions and schools, for instance on the question of what is 'practice', what is 'religious practice', and even whether there is such a thing as 'religious practice', or rather 'practice in religion'. This illustrates that categorisation is not a natural imperative, as it were inherent in the phenomena themselves, but the outcome of scientific allocation. The Palm Sunday and the Hindu bedroom happenings are not processions in themselves, but phenomena to which a scientist attributes the nature of a procession. Thus, Smith observes that the application of categories to phenomena causes them to be 're-visioned', 're-described' by the researcher.[72] They are judged to be similar on the basis of some point of view, framework, or model that the researcher considers apposite. Hence categorisation is not dyadic, as if it were confined to the two phenomena, but triadic. A third element, albeit of a different order, is added to the two phenomena, namely the respect in which they are considered to be similar: "there is always a 'with respect to'", as Smith rightly says. Hence the categorisation of similar phenomena is a result of the researcher's intellectual operations.[73]

---

[72] J.Z. Smith, *Drudgery Divine: On the Comparison of Early Christianities and the Religions of Late Antiquity*, School of Oriental and African Studies, University of London, London 1990, 42; Id., *Imagining Religion: From Babylon to Jonestown*, University of Chicago Press, Chicago 1982, 37.

[73] Smith, *Drudgery Divine*, op. cit., 51.

Secondly, the use of the term 'similar phenomena' poses a knotty problem in comparative research. What does it mean when we consider phenomena to be similar? One objection to this kind of research is that it disregards the unique character of the research object to the extent of destroying it altogether. But 'unique' is a complex concept. It can be used in a numeric sense, as when one says that there is no other specimen of a particular phenomenon. Or it may be used in an aesthetic, rhetorical sense, as when one calls a particular phenomenon beautiful, superb, or outstanding. It can also be used ontologically. Then it indicates that a given phenomenon is absolutely new, absolutely original, and, in an epistemological sense, totally incomparable with anything else. This last usage is sometimes encountered in objections to comparative religious research. They may be seen as a defensive strategy to legitimise religious claims to the absoluteness and universality of one's own religion, its founder, scriptures, tradition, and authority. That means that any comparability with, and, more than that, any influencing by other cultures and religions, are ruled out. That, too, should be seen as a defensive strategy. It should be noted that the antonym of uniqueness is sameness. But that is an equally complex concept: like uniqueness, it can be conceived of numerically ('the same specimen'), aesthetically, and rhetorically ('conventional, mediocre'), but also ontologically with the accent on identity when two phenomena are said to be identical. So the question is what it means when religious phenomena are said to be unique or not the same.

To avoid any misconception, comparative research is conducted not in the area between uniqueness (absolute originality) and sameness (identity), but in the area between difference and similarity, whereby the emphasis is on difference.[74] So if a comparative researcher posits that two phenomena relate to each other as two species of the same genus, she is not referring to the antonyms 'uniqueness' and 'identity' but to the antonyms 'difference' and 'similarity'. The concept of genus highlights difference, as in Aristotle's definition: "A genus is what is predicated in what a thing is of a number of things exhibiting differences in kind".[75] This implies that the hypothesis to be tested relates to the presence of difference or the absence of similarity. In figure 3 we

---

[74] Smith, *Drudgery Divine*, op. cit., 47–53.
[75] Aristotle, Topics, in: *The Complete Works of Aristotle* The Revised Oxford Translation, Edited by Jonathan Barnes, Princeton University Press, Princeton, NJ 1984, 102^{a}31–32.

see what this means for the hypotheses, null hypotheses, and the falsification process. The hypothesis may be formulated in terms of the presence of difference or the absence of similarity, and the null hypothesis,
in a reversed way, in that of the absence of difference or the presence
of similarity. When difference is actually present or similarity absent,
the null hypothesis is falsified, and when difference is actually absent
or similarity present the null hypothesis is not falsified.

Thirdly, we have to distinguish between two types of similarities:
strong and weak. The former refers to relations between genus and
species according to classical epistemology. That is to say, different
species have a clearly delineated common characteristic, and both
genus and species are demarcated by clear dividing lines. This does
not apply to weak similarities, because there are no common characteristics indisputably shared by all species. The lines dividing genus
from species, and one species from another, are likewise not sharply
defined. This is because there are all sorts of hybrid forms midway
between genera, between genera and species, and between species. It
is also caused by new or newly discovered instances that are classified
under a given genus but necessitate expanding the boundaries of that
genus.[76] Even in such an (ostensibly) exact conceptual science as law,
this is common practice if one wants to keep abreast, judicially, of
changing concepts and circumstances.[77]

What characterises all these similarities is not that they can be
decisively, unambiguously, and almost eternally classified in a single
category, nor that they all display the same attributes, but that they
belong to the same family in varying degrees of closeness and remoteness. The question is, close or remote according to what criterion? The

	difference	similarity
hypothesis	+	−
null hypothesis	−	+
falsification of null hypothesis	+	−
no falsification of null hypothesis	−	+

Figure 3. Hypothesis testing regarding difference and similarity.

---

[76] Day, The Undiscovered, op. cit.
[77] S.L. Winter, *A Clearing in the Forest: Law, Life, and Mind*, University of Chicago
Press, Chicago 2001, 254–256.

benchmark is the family member(s) taken to be the best example or better examples of that family. The term 'better examples' reveals the flaw: these are no clear-cut definitions of attributes, only intuitive, indicative orientations. In other words, weak similarities are based on what Wittgenstein calls family resemblances, in which the prototype plays the key role, and the other family members display countless gradations. This relates to the embodied and imbedded, metaphorical and pragmatic nature of (the use of) categories that derive from everyday life and thence find their way into science.[78]

Finally, having distinguished between strong and weak similarities, one could ask in what order these similarities should be classified. What types of order are there? Smith proposes four types: encyclopaedic, morphological, evolutionary, and ethnographic – a typology many authors recommend for the study of religion, despite some theoretical weaknesses.[79] Jensen, following Shweder and Bourne, opts for three types of order: universalistic, with the emphasis on homogeneity; relativist, with the accent on diversity; and evolutionary, marked by ranked diversity – a typology which is not free from conceptual weakness either.[80] An insight from the history of science in the European tradition may help to solve the classificatory problem. In this history one can discern six styles of scientific thinking, three of which are comparative: taxonomic, probabilistic, and evolutionary. In the taxonomic type, phenomena are systematically classified on a ladder (*scala naturae*); in the probabilistic type, phenomena are grouped on the basis of statistical characteristics like frequencies and correlations; in the evolutionary type, they are classed on the basis of genetic similarities.[81] To my mind, the study of religion has so far confined itself mainly to the taxonomic type; the probabilistic type might be used in empirical branches of the discipline and the evolutionary type in evolution-related cognitive religious studies, which may open up a perspective for future classifications.

---

[78] Lakoff & Johnson, *Metaphores*, op. cit.; Lakoff, *Women*, op. cit.

[79] Smith, *Imagining*, op. cit., 22–24.

[80] J.S. Jensen, *The Study of Religion in a New Key: Theoretical and Philosophical Soundings in the Comparative and General Study of Religion*, Oxford, Aarhus University Press, Aarhus 2003, 113–127.

[81] Crombie, *Styles*, op. cit., Vol. II, 1245–1443, Vol. III, 1547 1765; C. Kwa, *De ontdekking van het weten: Een andere geschiedenis van de wetenschap*, Boom, Amsterdam 2005, 223ff.

What we can conclude from all this is, firstly, that the categories used in comparative research are triadic. That is to say, classifying phenomena in these categories depends on a third factor, namely in which respect the researcher compares them with each other. Secondly, in the comparison the accent is on differences, similarities being the object of a null hypothesis to be falsified. Thirdly, there are strong and weak similarities. The former function according to the principles of classical logic (induction, deduction, and abduction), the latter according to those of family resemblances and prototypes. Finally, much conceptual work remains to be done in order to complement the taxonomic classification type with the probabilistic and evolutionary types.

3.6   Comparative Normativeness

In a reflection on comparative religious research, one cannot avoid the question of normativeness, at least, not if one adopts the second approach to religious research mentioned at the beginning as one's point of departure. The first approach only aims at producing religious knowledge, whereas the second not only seeks to produce knowledge but tries to justify newly gained insights in relation to the good life to three forums: academia, society, and the religions it studies.

The problem is that the relation between religion and the good life is extremely ambiguous. Of course, one may be awed by the love and justice religions preach and teach, their solidarity with people who suffer from evil, both contingency-related and guilt-related, their fellowship with the weak, the compassion they show, and the comfort and consolation they offer. One may feel inspired by their commitment to the struggle for liberation in order to improve the life of the masses in underdeveloped countries, to set them free and make them owners of their own lives. One may admire the Afro-American civil rights movement led by religious figures like the Baptist minister Martin Luther King and respond emotionally to his exquisitely filmed "I have a dream" in the Civil Rights Institute in Birmingham in the United States. One may feel grateful for the struggle against apartheid in South Africa under the leadership of religious leaders like the Anglican archbishop Desmond Tutu and the Dutch Reformed minister C.F. Beyers Naudé, the process of reconciliation they helped to instigate and their ceaseless proclamation of hope so as not to lapse into cynicism.[82]

But both history and our own time present other images as well. I confine myself to just a few historical events: the compulsory conversion to Christianity of entire groups and nations, the crusades, the Inquisition, pogroms, and finally, Auschwitz. Our own times, too, are dominated by religious phenomena that one cannot simply ignore as a detached observer, as if it does not matter that Jewish settlers deprive Palestinians of their prosperity and well-being by invoking their status as God's chosen people; American television preachers who call for God's blessing on the tanks in Iraq and Afghanistan to support the 'crusade' in those countries; and Saudi Arabian imams' prayers to end the 'crusade' through victory in the jihad. Does the study of religion stop short at this point, because it marks the boundary between descriptive and explanatory research on the one hand and evaluative, normative research on the other?

My reaction is that a university should be a *université sans conditions*, but not without normative commitments. It would be wrong to ban normativeness from research for the sake of so-called neutrality. Neutrality does not exist; it never exists. Theory of science offers two important insights, one cognitive, the other social. According to cognitive theory of science, descriptive and explanatory research culminates in evaluative design-related research, both theoretical and practical, which in its turn contributes to description and explanation.[83] According to social theory of science, research is always a product of social interest regimes and always contributes to these.[84] Hence finding criteria for normative evaluation is a serious concern.

There are three ways to solve the problem. The first is to investigate the relevant sources of the religion one studies – particularly its scriptures, traditions and doctrinal statements – and then evaluate the

---

[82] J.A. van der Ven, The Moral and Religious Self as a Process, in: H.J.C. Pieterse (ed.), *Desmond Tutu's message*, Brill, Leiden 2001, 74–95; H.J.C. Pieterse, Prophetic preaching in context, in: Pieterse (ed.), *Desmond*, op. cit., 96–111; J.A. van der Ven, "Laat mij toch nog een klein beetje langer leven", Utopie en ideologiekritiek in het leven van C.F. Beyers Naudé, in: *Praktische Theologie* 26(1999)4, 418–437.

[83] Kuipers, *Structures*, op. cit.

[84] Th. Kuhn, *The Structure of Scientific Revolutions*, 2nd edition, enlarged, University of Chicago Press, Chicago 1970; P. Bourdieu, *Science of Science and Reflexivity*, Polity Press, Cambridge 2004.

actual religious practices in terms of these sources. One could say that in principle every religion has a self-purificatory capacity in that it can invoke its own sources. But what if the sources are ambivalent, contradict each other, maybe even engage in a battle of (veiled) comments on each other? And what if the sources refer to (events and) narrations in which unjust punishments, unlawful killings, ethnic cleansing, and aggressive armed conflict are praised instead of rejected? Anyone familiar with the scriptures of Judaism, Christianity, and Islam will know that one cannot get anywhere without interpreting such narrations with due regard to the constantly changing cultural contexts in which they originated and in whose terms they have to be understood and explained. But we also know that each interpretation will always evoke new, supplementary, corrective, conflicting reinterpretations. In short, one can neither ignore narrations of unjust and cruel actions, nor avoid conflicting interpretations.[85] If ultimately one nonetheless takes some sort of stance, however provisional, it always entails, willy-nilly, a normative choice, even if one adds with full scientific candour that one would be prepared to abandon that judgment for a better one if hitherto un-researched or new data were to cast fresh light on the issue. One could call this a normative approach from the insider perspective of the religion one studies.

The second route to criteria for normative evaluative research in whatever religion is to consult one's own religion and relate their insider perspectives. That is the way favoured by Clooney and Ward in their respective projects of comparative theology.[86] They assess the religious practices of other religions, including legitimisations of these practices, according to the extent to which they correspond with those of the Christian religion. Other religions are not just compared with but are actually judged by Christian standards. They are positively judged insofar as they contain elements and traces that correspond with particular characteristics belonging to the very core of the Christian religion. This is called the inclusive approach in Christian theology of religions, whether based on the trinitarian doctrine,

---

[85] P. Ricoeur, *The Conflict of Interpretations: Essays in Hermeneutics*, Northwestern University Press, Evanston 1974.
[86] Clooney, *Hindu*, op. cit., 7–12; K. Ward, A Guide for the Perplexed, in: T.W. Bartel (ed.), *Comparative Theology: Essays for Keith Ward*, Society for Promoting Christian Knowledge, London 2003, 190–198.

christology, pneumatology or soteriology,[87] even if 'inclusive' is preceded by the term 'pluralist', as in 'pluralistic inclusiveness',[88] or the other way round, as in 'inclusive pluralism',[89] and even if it is labelled dynamic as opposed to static inclusiveness, meaning that it entails a mutual learning process.[90] Naturally, I do not dispute the right of this kind of theology, nor the right of other religions, to devise their own forms of inclusive theology, such as a Muslim theology that evaluates Christianity according to Islamic criteria.[91] The ideal might even be to have two (or more) inclusive theologies engage in dialogue, for instance an inclusive Christian theology entailing a comparative evaluation of Islam and an inclusive Muslim theology entailing a comparative evaluation of Christianity. It could contribute significantly to a Christian or Islamic theology of interreligious dialogue. That would require an exchange of perspectives, in which two approaches from two insider perspectives – Christian and Muslim – interact in dialogue, like in the *Groupe de Recherches Islamo-Chrétiens*.[92]

The third route – which I shall describe briefly and which I advocate, without disqualifying the other routes – stems from the question whether the study of religion cannot and ought not to do more than it is doing. Apart from an approach from the insider perspective of the religion concerned (first route) and an exchange of insider perspectives of two religions (second route), these routes can be augmented with an approach from a combination of insider and outsider perspectives. That is the third route, propounded by Neville in what he calls his 'comparative religious ideas project'.[93] The difference between this route and the previous one is immediately apparent from the two designations: 'comparative theology' (Clooney, Ward, and many

---

[87] P. Valkenberg, God ademt overal: Mogelijkheden en grenzen van een trinitaire theologie van de godsdiensten, *Tijdschrift voor Theologie* 43(2003)2, 166–190; Id., *Sharing Lights on the Way to God: Muslim-Christian Dialogue and Theology in the Context of Abrahamic Partnership*, Rodopi, Amsterdam 2006.

[88] S.M. Ogden, *Is There Only One True Religion or Are There Many?* Southern Methodist University Press, Dallas 1992.

[89] J. Dupuis, The Truth Will Make You Free, *Louvain Studies* 24(1999)3, 211–263.

[90] H. Nicholson, A Correlational Model of Comparative Theology, *The Journal of Religion* 85(2005)2, 191–213.

[91] Ward, A Guide, op. cit., 195; H. Kim, *Prolegomena to a Christian Theology of Religions*, University Press of America, Lanham, MD 2000.

[92] Valkenberg, *Sharing*, op. cit., 202–203.

[93] R.C. Neville, *The Truth of Broken Symbols*, State University of New York Press, Albany, NY 1996; Id., *Religion in Late Modernity*, State University of New York Press, Albany, NY 2002.

others) and 'comparative religious ideas project' (Neville). Since its inception in the second half of the 19th century, comparative theology has been mostly Christian theology with a theologically inclusive if not missionary orientation, in which the Christian insider perspective clearly dominates.[94] The other approach, 'comparative religion', aims or should aim at combining insider and outsider perspectives, although not all projects with this or similar names achieve this aim, as we know from Eliade's work. Inspired by Neville's project, but more or less independently of it, I shall elaborate on it below in order to clarify its normative nature. It entails devising normative criteria that incorporate but at the same time transcend the insider perspectives of the two religions involved.

A key premise here is what is known as the golden rule, however formulated, found in many cultures, religions, and worldviews.[95] The literature contains long lists of versions of this rule. They range from those of ancient Egyptian religions to those of West Asia (Judaism, Christianity, Islam), South Asia (Hinduism and Buddhism) and East Asia (Confucianism). They can also be found in nonreligious worldviews such as those of the Council for Secular Humanism and the British Humanist Association.

The golden rule occurs at various levels of abstraction. Its most concrete version is: "anyone who kills a person must be killed". Note that its meaning is phrased negatively and is tied to a specific instance: you should not murder. At an intermediate level of abstraction it reads: "counter kindness with kindness and injury with injury". At this level there is some generalisation, not just by combining a negative and a positive element, but especially because it is no longer tied to specific instances like killing. It only speaks of kindness and injury in the abstract. At the highest level of abstraction, its negative form reads: "don't do to others what you would not have them do to you". The positive version is: "treat others as you would be treated yourself".[96]

At this last level there is not just a combination of a negative and a positive element and no link with specific instances, but, more

---

[94] Masuzawa, *The Invention*, op. cit., 72–104; Valkenberg, *Sharing*, op. cit., 193–210; An illustrative example of the relation between comparative theology and missiology is A. Exeler, Vergleichende Theologie statt Missionswissenschaft? In: H. Waldenfels (ed.), "...*denn Ich bin bei Euch*", Zürich 1978, 199–212.

[95] A.D. Renteln, *International Human Rights: Universalism Versus Relativism*, Sage Publications, London 1990.

[96] A. Dihle, *Die Goldene Regel*, Vandenhoeck & Ruprecht, Göttingen 1962, 80–82.

importantly, an exchange of perspectives, particularly an exchange of insider perspectives. 'I' am called to adopt 'your' perspective, and vice versa. That explains why the golden rule occurs in many religions and worldviews. It responds to the universal human capacity to take the other's perspective, and in so doing not merely to understand that person's feelings, intentions, ideas, and decisions in his own terms, but also to 'reason' in these terms and predict the other's feelings and thoughts. People can 'read' each other's emotions, thoughts, and actions and, through reading, anticipate them. This propensity is not peripheral to what makes us human but belongs to the core of it, as is evident in the latest development in cognitive science, which regards the human mind as a social mind. Put differently, it constitutes humans as social beings, which does not detract from – indeed, is manifest in – the fact that its roots can be traced to the evolution of the higher animal species which, in analogous fashion, appear to have a 'feeling' for each other.[97]

Why is this golden rule so important? One answer may be found in the aforementioned alternating positive and negative formulations encountered in many religions and worldviews. It has to do with the fact that people can do both good and harm to each other, can treat each other both symmetrically and asymmetrically. Symmetry stems from the fundamental equality and reciprocity between people, asymmetry from the inequality between them, the disparities in power and the threat of violence these entail. Human life is always frail, vulnerable, and wounded, simply because one person's activity implies the other's passivity. The golden rule should be seen as one which elevates the exchange of perspectives to an ethical plane that puts an end to asymmetry. It reads: adopt each other's perspective. It refers to the double insider approach which is characteristic of the second route I mentioned.

But in Kant's categorical imperative, which may be regarded as a conceptual elaboration of the golden rule, something changes. The difference is that Kant's categorical imperative decentres and universalises the golden rule. It reads: "Act in such a way that you always treat humanity, whether in your own person or in the person of any

---

[97] Ch. Darwin, *The Descent of Man: And Selection in Relation to Sex*, Penguin, London, 2004, 119–151; Cf. W.E. Ritter, *Charles Darwin and the Golden Rule*, Compiled and edited by E.W. Bailey, Storm Publishers, New York 1954.

other, never simply as a means, but always at the same time as an end.[98] This statement has a decentring effect, because it no longer says "treat others as *you* would be treated", but "treat *neither* yourself *nor* the other simply as a means". The reason for this is not egocentric, as if one should treat the other well so as to be treated well *oneself* (*do ut des*). The reason explicitly stated is that ill treatment of *both* self *and* other is counter to our humanity. Those who obey this categorical imperative no longer act egocentrically but engage in decentring.[99] In addition, the exchange of perspectives is not between an 'I' and a 'you', as is implied in the golden rule, but between an 'I' ('your own person') and a 'he/she' ('the person of any other'). Both, 'your own person' and 'the person of any other', are regarded as manifestations of the abstraction, 'humanity'. This rules out selective versions of the golden rule that limit it to one's fellow citizens, co-religionists, or one's neighbour (Lev. 19:18). The categorical imperative not only decentres the golden rule but also universalises it: it applies to all people in all ages everywhere.[100]

From this perspective of decentring and universalisation, the golden rule has been a major source of inspiration for moral philosophy, human rights law, and jurisprudence. An example is the work of the moral and legal philosopher Alan Gewirth, who relates the golden rule to human rights by reformulating the rule as follows: "Act in accord with the generic rights of your recipients as well as of yourself." The universal orientation of this statement is implied in the term 'generic rights', which refer to the generic features of human beings and human action, that is freedom and well being. Human rights should be seen as such generic rights.[101] The term 'generic' is important here, because it might prevent the golden rule from permitting a subversion of the principle of justice when people consent to be treated in a way that violates their rights and/or treat others in that way.[102]

One could ask why it is so important to convert the golden rule, which is found in many religions and worldviews, into Kant's categorical

---

[98] Kant, *Groundwork*, op. cit., 96.
[99] Ricoeur, *Oneself*, op. cit., 218–227.
[100] Ricoeur, *Oneself*, op. cit., 222.
[101] A. Gewirth, *Human Rights: Essays on Justification and Applications*, University of Chicago Press, Chicago 1982, 3, 135; Cf. C. Hübenthal, *Grundlegung der christlichen Sozialethik Versuch eines freiheitsanalytisch-handlungsreflexiven Ansatzes*, Forum Sozialethik, Bd. 3, Aschendorff, Münster 2006, 222–285.
[102] Gewirth, *Human*, op. cit., 128–132.

imperative and Gewirth's imperative of generic human rights. Is it not in order if each religion posits and propagates its own formulation of the golden rule and leaves it at that? Does that not have the advantage that adherents of the various religions find it easier to embrace and practise the golden rule, because it is organically linked with the myths and rites in which they engage and by which they live? The answer must be negative. The religious ideas and practices in which the golden rule is imbedded in different religions may deter adherents of other faiths and nonbelievers from accepting and applying it. This applies particularly in democratic societies characterised by the separation of church and state. It would be counter to the nature of a democratic state to make the golden rule, and concomitantly the religious beliefs and practices attached to it, the basis of the state. Because they are defined in abstract terms, the categorical imperative and human rights provide a means of unifying and structuring the modern state, and can at the same time be spelled out and actualised in every religion in the way it finds appropriate in its own religious semantics and behaviour. It would be structurally wrong to elevate a particular religion, or any religion at all, to the status of a privileged religion or even an established religion by favouring its golden rule and its particular mythical and ritual interpretation of that rule. Hence, neither the first route (insider perspective of the religion concerned) nor the second route – that of interreligious dialogue (insider perspectives of two religions) – will do. We need a third route – one which respects the religious impartiality of the state and its public rules and at the time same offers the various religions opportunities to concretise these rules in terms of their own traditions. In this route, a two-way translation process can happen: from the golden rule within the various religious traditions to human rights, and from human rights back to the religious traditions.[103]

Or is all such speaking in terms of human rights just show? Anyone who is conversant with the debate on human rights will know that their universality is disputed. Are they not a Western instrument to maintain hegemony over non-Western countries – and non-Western religions?[104] Do they not put too much emphasis on rights and not

---

[103] J. Habermas, *Zwischen Naturalismus und Religion: Philosophische Aufsätze*, Suhrkamp, Frankfurt am Main 2005, 106–154; G. Brune, *Menschenrechte und Menschenrechtsethos: Zur Debatte um eine Ergänzung der Menschenrechte durch Menschenpflichten*, Kohlhammer, Stuttgart 2006.

[104] Nussbaum, *Frontiers*, op. cit.

enough on duties – duties which religions in particular underscore? Do they not put an excessive accent on the individual rather than the community and the value of community engagement? Do the claims of the autonomous *ego* not override care for the *alter* – which is what religions emphasise?[105] I will deal with these questions in chapter 4 and explain that human rights require what may be called a 'foundation-open' approach, including a 'foundation-open' interpretation of human dignity, which can be substantiated in terms of various religious and nonreligious worldviews, as well as by the ongoing debate on the contextualised interpretations and applications of human rights.

All this does not lead to some form of endless relativism. Article 4 of the International Covenant on Civil and Political Rights (1966), which gives a partial, detailed exposition of the Universal Declaration of Human Rights (1948), describes some specified human rights as non-derogable rights that cannot be suspended under any circumstances, not even a national state of emergency. They include the prohibition of discrimination solely on grounds of race, colour, sex, language, religion, or social origin (art. 4); the right to life and the prohibition of genocide (art. 6); the prohibition of torture, or cruel, inhuman or degrading treatment or punishment (art. 7); the prohibition of slavery and servitude (art. 8, 1–2); the principle that there is neither crime nor punishment without previous law (*nulla poena* principle – art. 15); everyone's right to recognition everywhere as a person before the law (art. 16); and lastly the freedom of thought, conscience, and religion (art. 18).

CONCLUSION

What does the discussion of this chapter imply for a normative evaluation of religions? Let me answer the question in terms of 'true religion' (*vera religio*). But before doing so, the term 'true' has to be qualified in terms of five characteristics: constructivist, probabilistic, exemplary, approximate, and practical. *Constructivist* truth means that it is imbedded in implicit and explicit theoretical presuppositions by those making the truth claim. Put differently, a 'true' proposition is always a version of reality whose truth value can only be tested by comparing it

---

[105] Brune, *Menschenrechte*, op. cit.

with other versions, but not by testing it directly with reality, for reality never presents itself other than in our versions of it. Here truth and comparative research correlate.[106] *Probabilistic* in this context means that truth is not based on truth claims considered infallible, but claims resting on estimates.[107] *Exemplary* means that the regulative idea of universalism that in principle inheres in every truth claim manifests itself in a contextualised manner in a concrete case in situ. It does so in such a way that the reflective judgment, which results in a truth claim, anticipates its trans-contextual validity by demanding that the case be followed in other, analogous cases. The aim of this reflective judgment is the advancement of humanity, that is human flourishing.[108] *Approximation* implies that there is no absolute truth, only approximations of it that vary in their degree of closeness to or remoteness from the truth.[109] *Practical* means that truth claims primarily refer to concrete practices and thence to the underlying ideas and theories implied in those practices and dialectically regulating them.[110]

What, then, is the relevance of human rights to true religion? Let me answer the question with the help of some probabilistic, exemplary, approximate, and practical aspects of truth claims, both negative and positive ones, based on some constructivist presuppositions regarding religion. An example of a negative truth claim might be: "Religious community A, which rationally justifies capital punishment, yields a lower estimation of its proximity to 'true religion' than religious community B, which abstains from any justification, and even more so than religious community C, which criticises capital punishment, and consequently community A is not seen as an example that reasonably demands to be followed." A positive truth claim might be: "Religious community A, which requires pariahs living on the fringes of society to be treated in practice as free and equal in dignity, yields a higher estimation of its proximity to 'true religion' than religious community B, which ignores their poverty, and even more so than community C,

---

[106] N. Goodman, *Ways of Worldmaking*, Hackett Pub. Co., Indianapolis 1978.

[107] J. Wentzel van Huyssteen, *The Shaping of Rationality: Toward Interdisciplinarity in Theology and Science*, Eerdmans, Grand Rapids, MI 1999.

[108] Ferrara, *The Force*, op. cit.

[109] Kuipers, *Structures*, op. cit.

[110] According to B.A. Holdrege, *Veda and Torah: Transcending the Textuality of Scripture*, State University of New York Press, Albany, NY 1996, Hinduism and Judaism emphasise orthopraxis rather than orthodoxy and Buddhism, Christianity and Islam do the reverse.

which reinforces their economic and social alienation by legitimising the status quo, and as a result community A is seen as a model that reasonably demands to be imitated." From the perspective of human flourishing, human rights can be seen as an exemplary universal criterion in situ for the normative evaluation of religious practices, including the underlying religious beliefs which are dialectically related to those practices.

PART TWO

RELIGION AND HUMAN RIGHTS

CHAPTER FOUR

HUMAN RIGHTS: RELIGIOUS OR NONRELIGIOUS?

It is easy to forget that human rights are by no means a new invention. Even though the Universal Declaration of Human Rights of 1948 is rightly acclaimed for its well-established, lucid formulation of the dignity, freedom, and equality to which every person is born, the roots of these rights go much further back. One finds significant elements of them in all the major religions, from the Mesopotamian heritage among which the Epic of Gilgamesh and the Code of Hammurabi, the earliest Hindu and Buddhist texts, Confucian doctrine, the Jewish Bible, the New Testament and the Qur'an to Christian patristics and scholasticism, which were deeply influenced by Greek and Roman philosophy.[1]

This chapter cannot cover the entire history, so I confine myself to some milestones in more recent Western history (4.1). I then turn to the Universal Declaration of Human Rights (4.2). Thereafter I explore the problem of the foundation of human rights, which reads as follows: which religious or nonreligious worldview offers a theory that will underpin all human rights? Do we have such a theory to which all countries that endorse the Declaration will assent? Or does each religious and nonreligious worldview have its own conception, so that we have not just one universal foundation, but a plurality of particular foundations? (4.3.)

4.1 Milestones in the History of Human Rights

The development in human rights I will describe here is characterised by interrelatedness of political and juridical praxis and political and juridical theory. I divide this short survey into premodernity, including

---

[1] J. Yacoub, The Dignity of the Individual and of Peoples: The Contribution of Mesopotamia and of Syriac Heritage, Diogenes 54(2007) 3, 19–37; M. Ishay, The History of Human Rights: From Ancient Times to the Globalization Era, Longman, New Delhi 2008; M. Haas, International Human Rights, A Comprehensive Introduction, Routledge, London 2008, 10–71.

High Scholasticism and Late Scholasticism, Early Modernity, and Modernity.

4.1.1   *Premodernity*

High Scholasticism

A first milestone in human rights thinking is the work of Thomas Aquinas in the 13th century. Even though he does not use any terms that can be rendered literally as 'human rights', he is eloquently clear about the way one should behave towards others and what is due to every human being without exception. From this one can logically infer what rights the other person has. Thomas's aim is to clarify how one should conduct oneself towards others, for justice always relates to the other party (*iustitia est ad alterum*). It means giving others what is theirs (*quod suum est*) and what is their right (*ius suum*). Thomas lists violations of the rights to which all people are entitled. These include the right not to be deliberately killed by a private person and not to be subjected to deliberately inflicted physical harm. The right not to have one's property stolen nor to suffer damage at the hands of others is also cited. Yet another is the right not to be falsely accused. Thomas also mentions adultery, which could refer to the rights of various others who may be harmed by it in different ways.[2] On close scrutiny, these are all duties that we owe other people rather than rights they possess. Their rights are actually indirect and passive: they are implicit in our duties.[3]

When were others' direct rights first highlighted – direct rights not originating from my duty towards others but inherent in their own capacities, like claim-rights, privileges, powers or immunities?[4] In short, when did the indirect, passive concept of a right residing in objective obligations to others make way for a direct, active, and subjective concept residing in the person of the other, and, what is more, in the person of every human being?

The question has given rise to an interesting debate.[5] The traditional view still found in many publications is that it was the outcome of early modernist legal theories from the 17th and 18th centuries, four

---

[2] Thomas Aquinas, *Summa Theologica* (Abbr.: STh), II-II 122, 6, ad 2.
[3] J. Finnis, *Aquinas, Moral, Political, and Legal Theory*, Oxford University Press, Oxford 1998, 137–138.
[4] W. Hohfeld, *Fundamental Legal Conceptions as Applied in Juridical Reasoning*, ed. by W. Cook, Greenwood, Westport 1978.
[5] H. Syse, *Natural Law, Religion, and Rights*, St. Augustine's Press, South Bend 2007.

to five centuries after Thomas. But more recent historical research has shown that the notion of people's own rights dates back to the early 13th century. Jurisprudence from that time onwards indicates that canon lawyers worked on the principle of active, subjective rights rather than obligations to another person.[6] They treated these rights as capacities or competences (*potestas*) that the person has. By no longer putting the accent on obligation towards the other, as was the case in various community codes, jurisprudence moved in the direction of direct rights, thus responding to the individualising trend inherent in emerging urban mercantile capitalism. In a way, community and obligation are interrelated concepts, just as individual and right are. The community imposes obligations that, as already noted, imply others' rights; individuals have rights, which entail an obligation to respect the rights of others.

The philosophical and theological elaboration and justification of these changes are to be found in William of Ockham's voluntarism in the 14th century. His voluntarism centres on God's omnipotent free will, which is not subject to anything or anybody and is not determined by any outside influence. To get rid of the Greek notion that God created the world and human beings out of necessity or pressure, Ockham claimed that in his absolute omnipotence (*potentia absoluta*), God, from the plenitude of possibilities, could have created the world and humans differently from the way he did. But once he had created them as they are, he did not change his mind about the existing created order (*potentia ordinata*) and simply maintained it.[7] In this order, each creaturely component is directly dependent for its existence on God's actual will. Relations between people and things do not stem from some mutual connection residing in the people and things, but solely from God's actual, contingent will. That is why, viewed in themselves, people and things are contingent, individual beings that exist

---

[6] For literature on the influence of canon law on Western legal history generally, such as the relation between accusatorial and inquisitorial procedure, imprisonment instead of mutilation and social exclusion, the doctrine of intent and guilt, as well as the public-law distinction between rule *by* law (execution of political policy by way of legislation) and rule *of* law (politicians are bound by the law themselves), see P. Nève, *Driewerf Rome. Enkele opmerkingen over de (voor)geschiedenis van de grond- of mensenrechten*, Inaugural address Catholic University of Brabant (now University of Tilburg), Tilburg 1992, 21–27. For *lex regia*, a concomitant of rule by law and rule of law, see E. Kantorowicz, *The King's Two Bodies: A Study in Mediaeval Political Theology*, Princeton University Press, Princeton 1997, passim.

[7] William of Ockham here refers to the traditional distinction between '*potentia absoluta*' and '*potentia ordinata*' in Thomas Aquinas' *Summa* (I, 25, 5 and 1).

only in isolation from one another. Their relations are contingent and do not emanate from themselves but from relations that God their creator has with every one of them. This means that the rights people have do not reside in any mutual connectedness between them which would result in mutual obligations, but in the separate individuals they are, contingently created by God.[8]

Late Scholasticism
A further political step in the legal transition from an indirect, passive, and objective to a direct, active, subjective concept of rights and their political importance was taken by the 16th century Spanish theologians Francisco de Vitoria and Bartolome de las Casas at the time of the Spanish conquest of America. The question raised was whether one could annex the property of the indigenous population, the 'Indians', and take up arms against them if they resisted and enslave them. If so, on what account? Because they were sinners prone to intrinsically evil deeds that are counter to natural law such as cannibalism, murder, sodomy, and theft, hence were in need of punishment? Because they were heathen? Because they were irrational beings? Or did the members of these indigenous nations, like all human beings, have personal, subjective rights that have to be unconditionally respected and protected, whether they were sinful, Christian, irrational or not?[9] The theologian Albertus Magnus had referred to them previously, using a term borrowed from Aristotle, as 'natural slaves', who could be hunted

---

[8] The nominalism in William of Ockham's epistemology corresponds to this voluntarism. Inasmuch as humans and things owe their individual existence and survival to God's will and his created order, their knowledge does not extend beyond this individuality. Knowledge is knowledge of individual people and things, and, like the people and things themselves, it is contingent. The notion of individual, contingent knowledge conflicts with the traditional doctrine of universal ideas. Nominalism rejects the notion that these universal ideas are adequate representations of and vehicles of access to a reality which exists of its own or are a reality themselves that exist of their own. They are seen as names (*nomina*) used conventionally to indicate groups of people, animals and things, which – according to Ockham – have a semiological function in relation to reality. Cf. F. Oakley, *Natural Law, Laws of Nature, Natural Rights*, Continuum, New York 2005; J. Beckmann, s.v. Nominalismus, *Lexikon für Theologie und Kirche* 7, Herder, Freiburg 1998, 894–896; Id., s.v. Wilhelm von Ockham, *Lexikon für Theologie und Kirche* 10, Herder, Freiburg 2001, 1186–1191; J. Kreuzer, s.v. Nominalismus, *Religion in Geschichte und Gegenwart* 6, 356–359.

[9] F. de Vitoria, *Political Writings*, Cambridge University Press, Cambridge 1991, 231–251; see G. Steunebrink, Natural Law and Human Rights in an Intercultural Context, *Reader*, Radboud University Nijmegen 2004–2005.

like animals.[10] But there were others who said that such things were not permitted, because, as Thomas Aquinas argued, they were people who had not yet received the Christian faith, hence could not be punished as sinners or heretics.[11] To this was added that, being unbelievers, they did not fall under the jurisdiction of the church or the pope, hence were outside the temporal jurisdiction of 'Christian princes' in the Iberian peninsula as well.[12] There was an ecclesiastic political factor at work here, for the statement that these people did not fall under the jurisdiction of the church had an anti-papist connotation. It gave the Spanish court an argument to refute the Vatican's claim to power, to the effect that the pope, as self-appointed lord and master (*dominus*) of the world (*dominium terrae*), had the authority to decree which parts of the new world – such as North and South America – fell under the jurisdiction of which part of the old world, such as Spain and Portugal. Repudiating this claim to power required a non-ecclesiastic, non-Christian, nonreligious solution to a tricky secular problem that aroused vehement feelings.

Two groups emerged. The first, to which Gerson belonged and which Suárez later joined for his own reasons, maintained that humans are not only free to dispose over their property by buying and selling, but also over their freedom, their bodies and their lives, for these formed part of their property. It meant that people could sell their bodies and freedom into slavery and that buyers and sellers could legitimately collaborate in the transactions.[13] For his part, Suárez added that what applies to individuals also applied to an entire nation. In other words, an entire nation can subjugate itself collectively to a master through a commercial transaction and can also subjugate itself to an absolute ruler through political agreement.[14] Here the ideology of mercantile capitalism went hand in hand with that of political absolutism. The second group, to which De Vitoria belonged, although recognising the right to ownership, claimed that it had to be limited by God-given, objective natural law. He held that slavery conflicted with natural law,

---

[10] Aristotle, Politics, in: *The complete works of Aristotle*, Princeton University Press, Princeton 1984, 1993–1994, 1256^{b}20–25.

[11] STh, II 12,2.

[12] R. Tuck, *The Rights of War and Peace: Political Thought and the International Order from Grotius to Kant*, Oxford University Press, Oxford 1999, 65–72.

[13] Fr. Suárez, *Selections from Three Works*, Clarendon Press, Oxford 1944, 278–279.

[14] R. Tuck, *Natural Rights Theories, Their Origin and Development*, Cambridge University Press, Cambridge 2002, 54–57.

but added a further qualification: when life was at stake, as when indigenous people are in danger of being slaughtered if they refused to submit to enslavement, life takes priority over freedom. In that case it was permissible to submit to the coloniser by selling themselves into slavery. After all, life is more precious than all the gold in the world.[15]

4.1.2　Early Modernity

The political significance of rights in the sense of direct, subjective, individual rights, which, counter to Suarez's view, can be invoked to legitimise rebellion against an absolute monarch, featured prominently in the Republic of the United Provinces of the Netherlands at the time of the Union of Utrecht (*Unie van Utrecht* 1579). This document may be seen as the founding charter of the Republic, which lasted until 1795 when the Netherlands, in the wake of the French revolution, was 'liberated' by France. In the text of the treaty, signed in Utrecht cathedral, the predominantly Protestant provinces decided to join forces against outside domination, more particularly against the Catholic Spanish king, while retaining their separate internal arrangements. For purposes of joint action against foreign powers a common army was established, with conscription, and a system of taxation was organised. The provinces of Holland and Zeeland introduced personal religious freedom (article XIII).[16] In a second document, the Declaration of Independence (*Plakkaat van Verlatinghe* 1581), a number of

---

[15] Tuck, *Natural Rights*, op. cit., 49, n. 42.

[16] The interpretation of this article led to a debate on the main motive of the struggle against Spain between those who saw it as total emancipation from Spanish rule, including religious freedom, and those who felt it was principally a question of religious freedom from the Catholic yoke that Spain had imposed. The former were magnanimous in their tolerance towards Catholics, the latter espoused a more stringent interpretation of the article against Catholics in the Republic. Politically this put the stadtholder Johan van Oldenbarnevelt at loggerheads with Maurits, prince of Orange, and religiously the moderates (followers of Arminius, the Arminians or Remonstrants) clashed with the strict Calvinists (followers of Gomarus, the Gomarists or counter-Remonstrants). At the national synod of Dordrecht (1618–1619), which laid down the Rules of Dordt (*Dordtse regels*) that, along with the Dutch confession (1561) and the Heidelberg Catechism (1563), constitute the three Formularies of Unanimity (*Drie Formulieren van Enigheid*), the former lost to the latter, leading to the decapitation of Van Oldenbarnevelt in 1619 and the imprisonment of Hugo Grotius at Loevestein castle; see H. Nellen, *Hugo de Groot: Een leven in strijd om de vrede 1583–1645*, Balans, Amsterdam 2007, 226–262; L. Wessels, De beste aller werelden? Politiek, religie en een weerbarstige samenleving, Nederland 1650–1850, in: E. van der Wall & L. Wessels (eds.), *Een veelzijdige verstandhouding: Religie en verlichting in Nederland 1650–1850*, Vantilt, Nijmegen 2008, 36–72.

provinces declared their independence from the Spanish king Philip II, whom they deposed as their monarch.[17]

Elsewhere there had been a much earlier mention of rights in the context of rebellion against a royal sovereign, in the British Magna Carta of 1215. That was not a rebellion of ordinary citizens, however, but of the nobility, the barons, who demanded special privileges from the British king. The rights were not founded on human nature, but were meant for those who had to share powers. Among the nobility, the archbishops, bishops, and abbots occupied a special place: the salutation addresses them first, before the counts, barons, judges, and the rest. Hence the first article of the text deals with the freedom of the English church, whose rights and freedoms, it is stated, remain intact. For the rest it deals with areas known today as law of succession, fiscal law, and criminal law. The latter proclaims, for the first time in the history of criminal law, the rule of habeas corpus, which gives an arrested person the right to a prompt verdict by a judge on the legitimacy of the arrest. Popular revolutions in Britain did not happen until the 17th century, when the aim of both the English Revolution of 1640 and the Glorious Revolution of 1688 was to secure political, fiscal, legal, and religious rights, culminating in the British Bill of Rights of 1689. These rights were not based on human nature as such, as they were rights of Englishmen.[18]

At this time, some noteworthy theoretical treatises on human rights appeared. On the European continent, they were mainly the writings of Hugo Grotius in the Netherlands, Samuel Pufendorf in Germany, and Jean Barbeyrac and Jean-Jacques Burlamaqui in France.[19] Grotius is considered the founder of modern law and his international significance is recognised to this day. The influence of Pufendorf, who shared Grotius' theory despite deviations on some sensitive issues, extended to France and England already during his lifetime. Jean

---

[17] These two documents were not the first manifestations of human rights in the Netherlands, since the 'privileges of Brabant' in the inthronisation document which regulated relations between the Duke of Brabant and his subjects (*Blijde Incomste*), were instituted as far back as 1356 by Johanna of Brabant and her husband Wenceslas. This document contains rules on taxation and jurisdiction and the right to rebel when the monarch infringes the privileges; for the text, see swww.republikanisme .nl/brabant.html; cf. Nève, *Driewerf Rome*, op. cit., 2–4.

[18] J. Griffin, *On Human Rights*, Oxford University Press, Oxford 2009, 13.

[19] B. Bernardi, *Le principe d'obligation: Sur une aporie de la modernité politique*, Vrin, Paris 2007.

Barbeyrac tried to synthesise the doctrines of Grotius and Pufendorf. He was Jean-Jacques Burlamaqui's teacher during their years together in Groningen.[20] Burlamaqui was among the first to work out and theoretically substantiate the development of objective and passive rights into subjective, active, individual rights. Partly for that reason, he was very influential in England and Germany, and thus came to influence the founding fathers of the United States.[21] In England there was Thomas Hobbes, who has exercised a gigantic influence on the rest of the Western world right up to the present, as well as thinkers like John Milton and John Locke. It is impossible to trace the connecting lines between the ideas of all these scholars without disregarding major differences on main and side issues.[22] Any attempt at striking a balance is bound to fail, since even a very general outline is bound to favour some author or other.[23]

At all events, the aforementioned authors all base themselves on a natural state in which human beings have subjective, active, individual, inalienable, or otherwise, 'natural' rights. These, whether starting with a 'horizontal' contract with all other people or not, are transferred to the sovereign by way of a 'vertical' contract with a view to forming a state, be it monarchic, aristocratic, or democratic. The aim of the transfer is to prevent a war of all against all, or at least to ameliorate the hardships that people suffer in their natural state and enhance their position in it. According to some scholars, including Hobbes, contractual transfer of 'natural' rights entails alienation from them. But according to others, like Grotius, Pufendorf, Barbeyrac, and Burlamaqui, they continue to possess them, for together all people constitute the body of the state of which the sovereign is the head. Some theorists see contracts of this nature as real entities in a historical or empirical sense; others, like Milton, regard them as metaphoric con-

---

[20] D. Williams (ed.), *The Enlightenment*, Cambridge University Press, Cambridge 1999, 85.

[21] Bernardi, *Principe*, op. cit., 102–103, 227, 321.

[22] Thus I cannot deal with the question of which of these scholars, who are all categorised as contract theorists, see the contract as an ancillary concept in realising the objective, moral principle of justice, or use it as an ancillary concept in applying the utilitarian principle of mutual advantage in favour of the contracting parties. See M.C. Nussbaum, *Frontiers of Justice, Disability, Nationality, Species Membership*, Harvard University Press, Cambridge 2006, 54–68.

[23] Bernardi, *Le principe*, op. cit.; Tuck, *Natural Rights*, op. cit., offers a different list: the Middle Ages (Thomas Aquinas, Scotus and Ockham), the Renaissance, Hugo Grotius, John Selden, Selden's followers, Thomas Hobbes.

tracts, or, like Burlamaqui, as conjectures.[24] Either way, the contract functions as a real or fictional instrument to make the organisation of the state comprehensible and plausible, and especially to highlight human rights. The latter concern mainly civil freedoms (e.g. those of conscience, religion, expression, the press, assembly, and association), political rights (e.g. to petition and to have free elections), marital and family rights (e.g. privacy, equal rights of husband and wife in entering into a marriage or in case of divorce, parents' right to raise their children, and the right to education), legal rights, and, last but not least, separation of church and state.[25] The contract model is still very influential in political and legal philosophy, as can be seen in the work of John Rawls. He works on the assumption that the parties to the contract are free participants in a symmetric relationship. Without being able to account for their factual position (they find themselves 'behind a veil of ignorance'), their freedom and symmetry result in fair distribution of primary goods, more particularly liberties and rights, powers and opportunities, as well as income and wealth.[26] Among politicians and jurists, too, the contract model remains attractive. This is evident from the following characterisation of the South African constitution of 1996, which is considered the most modern and progressive constitution in the world: it is the "founding charter of our nation and (...) an expression of the nation's compact with itself".[27]

4.1.3 Modernity

In America, 18th century developments in political science and philosophy of law, partly under the influence of English Protestant dissenters, led to the compilation of the Virginia Bill of Rights of 1776 and the United States Bill of Rights of 1789. Dutch dissenters also had a hand in these documents, so much so that the second president of the

---

[24] D. Armitage et al. (eds.), *Milton and Republicanism*, Cambridge University Press, Cambridge 1995; J.-J. Burlamaqui, The Principles of Political Law, in: *The Principles of Natural and Political Law*, Liberty Fund, Indianapolis 2006, 277, 279.

[25] E.g. John Milton championed these rights (including the right to divorce) in many political tracts. See J. Witte, Prophets, Priests, and Kings: John Milton and the Reformation of Rights and Liberties in England, *Emory Law Journal* 57(2008)6, 1527–1604.

[26] J. Rawls, *A Theory of Justice*, Harvard University Press, Cambridge 1971.

[27] According to Edwin Cameron, judge of the Supreme Court of Appeal in South Africa, cited in G. Devenish, *A Commentary on the South African Bill of Rights*, Butterworth, Durban 1999, 16.

United States, John Adams, was to comment that the American rebellion against England was a copy of the Dutch uprising again Spain and that the two countries shared the same spirit.[28]

The first document, the Virginia Bill of Rights, lists the rights that all people have by virtue of their nature. Focal among these are the rights to life, liberty, and the pursuit of happiness. The equality of all humans is also accentuated, entailing the abolition of all privileges. Sovereignty of the people and separation of powers are highlighted. The same applies to the right to reform, change, or terminate the rule of a government that, in the view of the popular majority, is counter to their will. Freedom of the press and religious freedom are also mentioned as rights.

This array of rights greatly influenced the United States Bill of Rights of 1789, which was appended to the constitution of the United States of 1791 in the form of the first ten amendments. Among these, in addition to freedom of expression, the press, association, petition, privacy, and certain judicial rights, are religious freedom and separation of church and state. Freedom of religion means that religious communities are autonomous in relation to the state, which may not interfere with them. The definition of this freedom is known as the free exercise clause. Separation of church and state implies the state's autonomy in relation to religious communities, which may not interfere with the state. It means that the state cannot establish a state church or any religious community whatsoever. The definition of the separation of church and state is known as the no establishment clause.

The French *Déclaration des droits de l'homme et du citoyen* of 1789 probably was largely inspired by the Virginia Bill of Rights, but there are important differences. These stem from the different historical situations of the United States and France. Firstly, they have different histories. The United States was a product of a British political tradition dating back several centuries, in which economic liberalism gradually gained ground. In the process, more and more privileges, eventually civil liberties, were gradually won from the once absolute monarch in order to promote free market trade. The focus was preeminently economic, and the sphere involved was the private sector. The right to political participation was only tentatively broached, as

---

[28] J. Witte, *Religion and the American Constitutional Experiment: Essential Rights and Liberties*, Westview, Boulder 2000, 18.

evidenced, for example, by John Locke's idea of government by consent, according to which the monarch retains the initiative. France did not have this long tradition, and, when the revolution erupted in 1789, it had to go beyond Britain's economic liberalism and entailed not just the market and civil economic liberties but also a democratic state and political liberties. Thus French – and continental – liberalism was politically creative, in the sense that it centred on replacing the absolute sovereignty of the monarch with the absolute sovereignty of the people. This also meant replacing the private sphere of feudal society, in which public offices could be bought, with the public sphere centring on public interest. The state was to play a vital role in establishing a socio-political order in which political rights fulfil an essential function. To this end, the citizenry, the third estate, had to free itself from the patronage and power of aristocratic and clerical interest groups in feudal rural society. Notwithstanding these differences between the two countries, they shared a *Zeitgeist* in which natural rights, contract thinking, liberalism, and republicanism were focal.[29]

More than a century later, after the end of World War I – the war to end all wars, it was thought – the League of Nations was established. In 1919, it proclaimed the Covenant of the League of Nations, which bristled with rules for international cooperation to prevent future wars. The intention was to include individual human rights and collective minority rights as well, but that did not happen. Later, in 1929, the Institute of International Law, a private body of jurists in Europe, North and South America, and Asia, incorporated individual rights in the Declaration of the Rights of Man. Minority rights ended up in a system of minority treaties between kin states and states where these minorities were found. But the treaty ensuring League of Nations supervision of the system only lasted until the rise of Nazism in 1933 and Poland's withdrawal in 1934.[30] The charter of the League of Nations contains, besides numerous international arrangements, an article (no. 23) that could be seen as a pallid forerunner of the Universal Declaration of Human Rights of 1948, nearly three decades later. It mentions the importance of international organisations for humane labour conditions for men, women, and children (!). Working

---

[29] K. Hilpert, *Menschenrechte und Theologie: Forschungsbeiträge zur ethischen Dimension der Menschenrechte*, Herder, Freiburg 2001.

[30] M. Evans, *Religious Liberty and International Law in Europe*, Cambridge University Press, Cambridge 1997, 145–171.

conditions were in fact greatly improved by the International Labour Organisation and national labour organisations. The same cannot be said of the other problems mentioned in article 23 – women and child trafficking and the trafficking of opium and other dangerous drugs. Over the past 90 years all these abuses have escalated. Progress in the field of international treaties and the creation of institutions to implement them has yet to be made in the world we live in today.

4.2　Universal Declaration of Human Rights

Nonetheless, at the end of World War II, which brought about the final collapse of the League of Nations, world leaders had the courage to meet on 24 October, 1945, and establish the United Nations. It was accomplished through ratification of the Charter of the United Nations by the five permanent members of the Security Council (China, France, the Soviet Union, the United Kingdom, and the United States), and many other members. Just as national constitutions often start with the words, "We, the people", so the charter opens with the words, "We, the peoples of the United Nations".[31] The preamble gives the reasons for the establishment of the United Nations. Future generations have to be preserved from the scourge of war that had twice inflicted unspeakable suffering on a global scale. The nations joined forces, swearing to promote human rights: the dignity and value of the human person, equal rights for men and women and for all nations, big or small. It was firmly resolved to uphold international treaties and other sources of international law. It was also resolved to promote social progress and improve standards of living in greater freedom. Apart from the preamble, human rights are mentioned six times in the actual text of the charter. Article 1 includes respect for and observance of human rights among the goals of the United Nations. Article 55 lists

---

[31] The opening words, "We, the people", are not (purely) constative but (also and especially) performative. In terms of the classification by J. Austin (*How to Do Things With Words*, Harvard University Press, Cambridge 1975) into five kinds of performative speech acts (verdictives, exercitives, commissives, behabitives and expositives) the phrase "We, the people" may be seen as a commissive: through the declaration the members of the United Nations commit themselves to each other and thus constitute themselves as "peoples of the United Nations". In terms of the distinction between locutionary, illocutionary, and perlocutionary speech acts of J. Searle (*Speech Acts: An Essay in the Philosophy of Language*, Harvard University Press, Cambridge 1969), one would call it a perlocutionary speech act.

observance of human rights among the components of international economic and social cooperation. According to article 56, all members commit themselves to take joint and separate action to ensure this. Article 62 assigns the socio-economic council the task of making recommendations on how to promote respect for and observance of human rights, and article 68 authorises the appointment of commissions for human rights. Finally, chapter XII and XIII lay down special rules for the international trusteeship system for the administration and supervision of special mandate territories, among which number some parts of the defunct Ottoman empire and German colonies, especially Iraq and Palestine (British mandates), Syria and Lebanon (French mandates), and South West Africa, now Namibia (South African mandate). It stipulates that respect for human rights should be encouraged in these territories without discrimination on grounds of race, sex, language, or religion (article 76 c).

The Universal Declaration of Human Rights of 1948 is the outcome of the advocacy of human rights in the charter.[32] When it came to the vote, 48 countries were in favour of it and none opposed it. Eight countries refrained from voting, however: countries of the former Soviet bloc, Saudi Arabia, and South Africa. The declaration is not a legally valid document, but, partly because it incorporates general legal rules, it is such an authoritative guideline that it has considerable indirect legal force. In the Preamble there is only one passing reference to the two world wars, which, it points out, led to barbarous deeds that outraged the conscience of humankind. The text then switches to a positive approach. It says that the advent of a world in which people enjoy their liberties is among the supreme aspirations of all human beings. Following the four freedoms (two freedoms of and two freedoms from) that the American president Roosevelt listed in his State of the Union address in 1941, these are: freedom of speech and of belief, and freedom from fear and from want.

The Declaration spells out the four freedoms in 30 articles, each dealing with one or more human rights, without any further classification, although they are frequently grouped in two categories, also known as generations. The first comprises three sub-categories: civil

---

[32] J. Morsink, *The Universal Declaration of Human Rights: Origins, Drafting and Intent*, University of Pennsylvania Press, Philadelphia 1999. Haas, *International Human Rights*, op. cit., 72–99.

rights like freedom of expression, political rights like active and passive franchise, and judicial rights like the right to due process. These are called blue rights, because they pertain to the rights and liberties of citizens. The second category comprises socio-economic rights such as housing, food, clothing, education, and social security. They are called red rights, because they emanate from workers' struggle for a decent life. The two categories belong together, for human rights constitute an indivisible, interdependent, and interlinked whole, as is often stated in the literature as well as in the official Vienna Declaration and Programme of Action by the World Conference on Human Rights of 1993 (article 5).[33]

But that also poses a knotty problem. In the first place, the first category – that is civil, political, and legal rights – is in principle enforceable. These right are dichotomous: freedom of expression either exists or it does not; active and passive franchise either exists or it does not; one either has a right to judicial support by a lawyer in a criminal trial or not – even though in some cases these rights are limited. But the second category rights are not dichotomous; they are always a matter of degree. Thus the right to housing implies that everybody is entitled to a house to shelter them against natural forces like cold, rain, wind, and sun, and to afford necessary privacy. But how big and of what quality must such a house be? The cardboard and corrugated iron roofs in squatter areas surrounding major cities cry out for a policy on provision of decent housing, but the scale of such a policy ranges from nothing to minimal to adequate to realised. The question is what these scale values mean: when is housing minimal, adequate or realised, and for what percentage of residents?[34] Partly for this reason, rights in this category are basically unenforceable.

The fact that the indivisibility, interdependence, and interrelationship of civil, political, and socio-economic rights are far from being realised was evident in the debate surrounding the compilation of the Declaration. It was decided to abandon the initial plan to accompany

---

[33] R. Drinan, *The Mobilization of Shame: A World View of Human Rights*, Yale University Press, New Haven 2001.

[34] A distinction is made between minimal core content on the one hand, that is the essence of a particular right (what is the minimal core content of 'housing'?), which concerns quality, and on the other the minimal threshold of that right, which concerns quantity (what is a minimal percentage of houses in terms of total population?). See D. Brand & S. Russel (eds.), *Exploring the Core Content of Socio-Economic Rights: South African and International Perspectives*, Protea, Pretoria 2002.

the Declaration with a legally binding treaty. Instead, the proclamation of the Declaration would be followed by two separate covenants, each to be signed and ratified separately: one for civil, political, and judicial rights, the other for socio-economic rights. After intensive negotiations, these covenants were finally proclaimed nearly 20 years later, in 1966. The United States, while it had played a leading role in the creation of the Universal Declaration, ratified the International Covenant on Civil and Political Rights, but not the International Covenant on Economic, Social, and Cultural Rights.

The indivisibility, interdependence, and interrelationship of human rights have proved equally recalcitrant when it comes to concrete political policy. Thus many Western countries maintain substantial relations with foreign governments for the benefit of their own economies, at the same time tolerating gross violations of civil, political, and judicial rights by those same governments.[35] The latter have always argued that they are 'deferring' civil, political, and judicial rights in order to prioritise – rightly or wrongly – the socio-economic rights. Rightly or wrongly indeed. In many developing countries governments have no option but to prioritise socio-economic rights – which is not the same as 'deferring' civil and political rights, but all the same it provides dictatorial regimes with a front for nakedly political considerations, while neglecting civil, political, and judicial rights all together.[36] Proper priorities are vitally important. Thus it is said that the first priority should go to a level of basic security that will guarantee a life free from constant fear of murder, serious injury, or robbery. A second priority is a level of basic provision of primary socio-economic needs. The third and last priority concerns good governance that provides stability and ensures civil, political, and judicial rights.[37]

Apart from the diptych of 'blue' and 'red' rights, one comes across other classifications. An important instance is the European Union

---

[35] W. Safran, Civil Liberties in Democracies: Constitutional Norms, Practices, and Problems of Comparison, in: V.P. Nanda et al., *Global Human Rights: Public Policies, Comparative Measures, and NGO Strategies*, Westview Press, Boulder 1981, 195–210.

[36] J. Habermas, *Die postnationale Konstellation: Politische Essays*, Suhrkamp, Frankfurt 1998.

[37] A. Etzioni, Stel je prioriteiten goed: veiligheid komt vóór democratie, *NRC Handelsblad*, 16 June 2008, 17, see http://archief.nrc.nl/?modus=l&text=etzioni&hit=4&set=2; S. Kinzer, *A Thousand Hills: Rwanda's Rebirth and the Man Who Dreamed It*, Wiley, Hoboken 2008; Id., Mensenrechten staan niet op de eerste plaats, *NRC Handelsblad*, July 12, 2008, 7.

Charter of Fundamental Rights (Nice, 2000), which is an amplification of the 1948 Declaration. *Inter alia* it synthesises the European Convention for the Protection of Human Rights and Fundamental Freedoms (1950), which is based on the Universal Declaration, the European Social Charter (1961, revised in 1996), and other international treaties to which the European Union or its member states are party. The Treaty of Nice forms part of the draft European constitution of 2004, which was rejected by referendums in France and the Netherlands. In the Treaty of Lisbon, which replaced it, the charter is explicitly acknowledged but without including the actual text.

The Charter of 2000 divides human rights into six, as opposed to the original two, groups: dignity, freedoms, equality, solidarity, citizens' rights, and justice.[38]

4.2.1   *Dignity*

This includes the inviolability of human dignity, the right to life, prohibition of the death penalty, right to the integrity of the person, the prohibition of torture and inhuman or degrading treatment or punishment, and prohibiton of slavery and forced labour (articles 1–5).

4.2.2   *Freedoms*

These include the right to liberty and security; the right to respect for private and family life; the right to protection of personal data; the right to marry; and the right to found a family; the right to freedom of thought, conscience, and religion; the right to freedom of expression and information; the right to freedom of assembly and association; freedom of the arts and sciences; the right to education; the freedom to choose an occupation and the right to engage in work; the freedom to conduct a business; the right to property; the right to asylum; and protection in the event of removal, expulsion, or extradition (articles 6–19).

4.2.3   *Equality*

It includes equality before the law; prohibition of discrimination; respect for cultural, religious, and linguistic diversity; equality of men

---

[38] For the problem of classification of human rights see: M. Haas, *International Human Rights, A Comprehensive Introduction*, Routledge, London 2008.

and women; the rights of the child; the rights of the elderly; and the right of persons with disablties to integration (articles 20–26).

4.2.4   Solidarity

It includes workers' rights to information and consultation within the undertaking; the right of collective bargaining and action; the right of access to placement services; protection in the event of unjustified dismissal; the right to fair and just working conditions; prohibition of child labour and protection of young people at work; protection of family life, especially connected with maternity and parental leave; respect for the entitlement to social security and social assistance; the right of access to health; respect for access to services of general economic interest; environmental protection and consumer protection (articles 27–38).

4.2.5   Citizens' Rights

These include active and passive franchise for the European parliament and municipal councils, the right to good administration, the right of access to documents, the right to refer to the ombudsman, right to petition the European Parliament, freedom of movement and residence, and protection by diplomatic and consular authorities (articles 39–46).

4.2.6   Justice

This includes the right to effective remedy and to a fair trial, presumption of innocence and right of defence, principles of legality and proportionality of criminal offences and penalties, and the right not to be tried and punished twice in criminal proceedings for the same criminal offence (articles 47–50).

Classification into these six categories is not arbitrary. According to the preamble to the charter, they represent the indivisible, universal values of human dignity, freedom, equality, and solidarity. They are based on the principles of democracy and the rule of law. In addition, the European Union assigns human beings a key position by instituting citizenship of the Union and creating an area of freedom, security, and justice.

4.3   Foundations of Human Rights

However fine the aforementioned values may sound, one must ask whether they provide a foundation for human rights. By foundation we mean a worldview that offers a theory that underpins the totality of human rights. Is there such a theory that provides a basis to which all countries that subscribe to the Universal Declaration of Human Rights can assent? I answer this question in a number of stages. The first is historical, indicating how human rights arose from religious considerations in the course of history and on that basis found their way into historical documents. These in fact provided a universal foundation: a religious one, viz. a plurality of Christian ones (4.3.1). The second stage pertains to the flaw – a felicitous one – in the Universal Declaration of Human Rights in that respect: it contains no religious reference at all. As a basic document it is a pragmatic text, which is not foundational but deliberately leaves the establishment of such a foundation open; it is a 'foundation-open' text (a *begründungsoffen* text) (4.3.2). In the third and last stage I show that such an open text does not permit just one universal foundation, but allows for particular foundations in terms of different worldviews, including religious and nonreligious ones (4.3.3).

4.3.1   *Religious Foundations in the Course of History*

Human rights are often described as secular religion. Thus Elie Wiesel calls them a worldwide secular religion, and Nobel Prize winner Nadine Gordimer speaks of "the creed of humanity".[39] Michael Ignatieff explicitly rejects such qualifications, because they run the risk of setting up human rights as an object of idolatrous veneration. Instead, he insists that they should be seen as a historico-political instrument to fulfil human needs: protection against unjust laws and forms of unlawful state action, the power to enter the lists and resist these, and *in extremis* to appeal to other peoples, nations and international organisations.[40] But quite apart from that, claims that human rights are a 'new, modern religion' tend to contradistinguish traditional religions and human rights, so that the latter are seen as superseding

---

[39] Y. Daniel et al., *Fifty Years and Beyond*, Baywood, Amityville 1999, 3 and vii.
[40] M. Ignatieff, *Human Rights as Politics and Idolatry*, Princeton University Press, Princeton 2001, 54–55.

the former. The Enlightenment, the era when human rights were described, worked out and defended on a grand scale against the interests of the monarchy and the church, is especially regarded as the cradle of a-religious or even anti-religious conflict.

Historically, this view is open to correction. Undoubtedly, institutionalised religion was subjected to all kinds of criticism ever since the early Enlightenment in the 17th century, which steadily intensified in the 18th century to the point of total rejection of all religion. One should be careful, however, not to create a biased picture of the Enlightenment as a uniform, undifferentiated, monolithic bloc. It cannot be understood without taking into account how deeply imbedded its roots are in the values and norms of the Christian tradition in Scholastic and late-Scholastic times, as well as in the values and norms that emerged from the discussions between and within Christian denominations since the Reformation.[41] Recent historical research shows that the entire period was marked by three different trends.[42] The first, known as radical Enlightenment, is in fact characterised by a-religious, even anti-religious tendencies. The second, on the other hand, known as moderate or providential Enlightenment, was the mainstream and sought to synthesise the principal themes of the Enlightenment with traditional religions. This school is called providential because of its deistic God concept, centring on the Calvinist divine of providence.[43] Major proponents of providential deism were Locke, Shaftesbury, and Huchtenson.[44] Finally, the third trend saw the Enlightenment as the avowed enemy of religion and went all out to combat it. It constituted a counter-Enlightenment.

A possible explanation of the blind spot for the religious aspect of the Enlightenment often encountered in the literature is the

---

[41] L. Dupré, *Religion and the Rise of Modern Culture*, University of Notre Dame Press, Notre Dame 2008; C. Mervaud & J.-M. Seillan (eds.), *Philosophie des Lumiéres et valeurs chrétiennes*, L'Harmattan, Paris 2008.

[42] J. Israel, *Enlightenment Contested*, Oxford University Press, Oxford 2006, 3–60; D. Sorkin, *The Religious Enlightenment, Protestants, Jews, and Catholics from London to Vienna*, Princeton University Press, Princeton 2008, 1–21, 311–314.

[43] This providence has certain necessary variations: a *providentia generalis* for creation as a whole, a *providentia specialis* for individual micro histories interwoven with macro history, and a *providentia specialissima* in the case of individual supplications in the church community; see H. Oberman, *The Two Reformations: The Journey from the Last Days to the New World*, Yale University Press, New Haven 2003, 130–131.

[44] Ch. Taylor, *Sources of the Self: The Making of the Modern Identity*, Harvard University Press, Cambridge 1989, 245–274.

cultural-territorial evaluation of the phenomenon, evidenced by the notion that France was the hub of the Enlightenment.[45] Certainly that country, with its absolutist *ancien régime*, saw the fiercest conflict between enlightened reason and traditional religion, manifested in virulent anti-clerical and anti-church invective. This is understandable in view of the transition from a religiously dominated, rural, feudal society, to a tolerant, bourgeois, urban society, as well as of the gradual transition from mercantilist to industrial capitalism. But then one ignores the origin of Protestant Enlightenment in the Dutch republic, which at that time was a refuge for thinkers from countries like England, France, and Portugal. More especially, one ignores the cradle of enlightened thought in England, where, under the influence of the moderate Enlightenment, tolerance gradually triumphed. Following Voltaire's importation of enlightened ideas from England, France played a propagandistic rather than a substantive role.[46] From this perspective, some scholars actually consider France the most backward of the enlightened countries.[47] Finally, one ignores the spread of the Enlightenment to northern countries in Germany and the Catholic Enlightenment in Austria, and, to a lesser extent, Italy, Spain, and Portugal. Hence, it is historically imperative to get rid of the biased, uniform picture of the Enlightenment.

Naturally, the second trend was particularly important for developing a religious foundation of human rights, since it tried to establish a religious basis for the Enlightenment that could adapt traditional religions to the new era.[48] The adaptation was not to be wholly pragmatic. The intention was to gain a fundamental victory in the religious warfare between the various Christian denominations that had brought Europe to the brink of a precipice during the 16th and 17th

---

[45] J. Yolton et al. (eds.), *The Blackwell Companion to the Enlightenment*, Blackwell, London 1995, 1–10; W. Cisło, *Die Religionskritik der französischen Enzyklopädisten*, Lang, Frankfurt 2000.

[46] There are references to 'anglomania' in the Enlightenment; see J. Israel, *Radical Enlightenment: Philosophy and the Making of Modernity*, Oxford University Press, Oxford 2001, 445–563, especially 515–527.

[47] A. Macintryre, *After Virtue: A Study in Moral Theory*, Duckworth, London 1985, 17.

[48] According to E. van der Wall, *The Enemy Within: Religion, Science, and Modernism*, NIAS, Wassenaar 2007, pp. 18–19, the theology or 'neology' devised by scholars of the moderate Enlightenment is called 'adaptation theology' by the German historian Schoeps. This formed the basis of 19th century theological modernism, called 'the modernist within' by reactionary critics, but which was in fact 'the Enlightenment within' (p. 47).

centuries. By devising a 'natural' religion, a natural law accessible to all people, along with its corollary, a 'natural' morality, it wanted to find a form of religion that would as far as possible transcend the differences between Christian denominations, even between different religions, so as to prevent future conflicts. The aim was to combat and transcend confessionalism in society and the state.[49] Viewed thus, the Enlightenment may be regarded as a product of religious discourse rather than just a rebellion against religion.

The first traces of the religious Enlightenment are discernible in the Republic of the Netherlands.[50] Here Hugo Grotius (Hugo de Goot) and Dirck Volckertszoon Coornhert, both of them Arminians, led the way. Grotius is often counted among agnostics or atheists because of one sentence that threatens to colour the interpretation of his entire corpus: "What we have been saying would have [a degree of – added since the 1631 edition] validity even if we should concede [*etiamsi daremus*] that which cannot be conceded without the utmost wickedness, that there is no God, or that the affairs of men are of no concern to Him."[51] This comment is almost always interpreted metaphysically, leading to the view that Grotius repudiates the existence of God.[52] But that is to disregard not only the sentence that immediately follows, in which it is said that "the very opposite of this view has been implanted in us partly by reason, partly by unbroken tradition (...). Hence it follows that we must without exception render obedience to God, our Creator, to whom we owe all that we are and have." It also disregards the multitude of religious references and disputes that characterise all the rest of *De jure belli ac pacis* as well as his *Commentary on the law of prize and booty* (*De jure praedae* – 1604) and *Introduction to Dutch jurisprudence* (*Inleidinghe tot de Hollandse Rechts-gheleertheid* – 1631). The sentence cited above should be interpreted epistemologically rather than metaphysically. It concerns the epistemic relation between

---

[49] The confessionalism hypothesis claims that the transition from church to state control in the late 16th and 17th centuries occurred simultaneously in Lutheran, Catholic, and Calvinist territories after the Peace of Augsburg (1555), which increasingly underscored the separation between the three traditions throughout Europe. It is questionable, however, whether this hypothesis sufficiently acknowledges the differences in the church's position and in its relation to the state in different countries and regions (see Oberman, *Two Reformations*, op. cit., 101–105).

[50] Van der Wall & Wessels, op. cit., *Verstandhouding*, passim.

[51] H. Grotius, *De jure belli ac pacis*, 1625, Prolegomena 11.

[52] R. Wokler, s.v. Rights, in: Yolton et al. (eds.), *The Blackwell Companion*, op. cit., 458–459.

God and natural law and the natural rights inherent in the latter. Any reader of Grotius cannot doubt that he sees God as the author of natural law and his will as the source of all rules that the latter entails. In this sense, he is a voluntarist in the tradition of Ockham. But in his *De jure belli ac pacis* the voluntarism is that of divine *potestas ordinata* rather than *potestas absoluta*, to which we refered earlier. Having accomplished his creation, God cannot undo it, and the same applies to natural law. In terms of *potetas ordinata*, God's commandments and prohibitions are not good or bad because he dictates them, but he dictates them because they are good or bad in themselves by virtue of their nature.[53] Epistemologically, that means that God's will need not be revealed for us to know and understand natural law: sound human reason (*ratio recta*) is sufficient for that. Here Grotius concurs with the scholastic tenet that natural law, albeit divinely instituted, can be known by every human being, irrespective of faith. In this sense, Grotius espouses a reasonable – as opposed to a rationalist – approach.[54] Overall, Grotius is an excellent example of how a uniform picture of the Enlightenment, centring on an a-religious and anti-religious approach, can result in distortion, even denial of its pluriform character, which included both religious and nonreligious trends.[55]

Because of the Arminians' defeat, moderate or providential Enlightenment was first fully realised in England, not in the Netherlands.[56] Previously, Dutch and English philosophers were in close contact, because many of the latter had to flee from persecution to the still more tolerant Amsterdam. Among them, John Milton and John Locke, to whom I return in chapter 7, were particularly prominent. On religious grounds, both of them zealously advocated democratisation of the state, separation of church and state, religious freedom, and other rights. Mil-

---

[53] Grotius, *De jure*, op. cit. I, I, X, 1–2, 5; cf. Oakley, *Natural Law*, op. cit., 66–67.

[54] For the distinction between rationalism and reasonableness, see Sorkin, *Religious Enlightenment*, op. cit., 11–14.

[55] A different interpretation of the '*etiamsi*' sentence may be found in C. Larrère, Droit naturel et scepticisme, in: P.-F. Moreau (ed.), *De scepticisme au XVᵉ et au XVIIᵉ siècle*, Tome II, Albin Michel, Paris 2001, 293–308; it is based on the conflict between Gomarists and Arminians, whose side Grotius supported. Yet another interpretation proceeds from the struggle against the scepticism of the day; see R. Tuck, The 'Modern' Theory of Natural Law, in: A. Pagden (ed.), *The Languages of Political Theory in Early-Modern Europe*, Cambridge University Press, Cambridge 1987, 99–119, here 115ff.; Id., *The Rights of War and Peace*, op. cit., 97.

[56] R. Porter, *Enlightenment, Britain and the Creation of the Modern World*, Penguin, London 2000.

ton argued that humans' creation in the image of God was a decisive argument for the freedom and equality of all citizens, including the sovereign and magistrates, and that in cases of severe abuse of power it entailed the right to rebel and depose the wielders of such power. He also felt that the divine vocation of ordinary people in Christian communities to the offices of king, priest, and prophet was basic to a congregationalist concept of the church, which consisted in a union of those who freely joined forces for the sake of their faith. Like Milton, Locke considered human conscience inviolable, because it stood face to face with God without the mediation of priest or church and was accountable to him alone. Consequently freedom of conscience, and thus of religion, were inalienable human rights. To this Milton added freedom of expression and the press, counter to the traditional prerogatives of state and church.

Both Milton and Locke greatly influenced American human rights thought, even its official documents. Let me cite some examples. Historically, the first important document on human rights was the one briefly discussed above: the American Declaration of Independence of 1776 containing the famous text on the three inalienable rights: life, liberty, and the pursuit of happiness. The document starts with a reference to the Laws and the God of Nature (capital letters in the original), which, it averred, gave the people of the thirteen states that constituted the United States of America at that time the right to secede from England. The text continues to state that the following truths are self-evident: all people are created equal and are endowed with certain inalienable rights by their Creator, including the aforementioned rights to life, liberty, and the pursuit of happiness. The document concludes by appealing to the Supreme Judge of the World to assess the genuineness of the signatories' intentions, and by pledging solidarity with one another under the protection of Divine Providence.[57] This text,

---

[57] "When in the Course of human Events, it becomes necessary for one People to dissolve the Political Bonds which have connected them with another, and to assume among the Powers of the Earth, the separate and equal Station to which the Laws of Nature and of Nature's God entitle them, a decent Respect to the Opinions of Mankind requires that they should declare the causes which impel them to the Separation. (…) We hold these Truths to be self-evident, that all Men are created equal, that they are endowed by their Creator with certain inalienable Rights, that among these are Life, Liberty and the Pursuit of Happiness (…). We, (…), appealing to the Supreme Judge of the world for the rectitude of our intentions (…) solemnly publish and declare, That these united Colonies are, and of Right ought to be Free and Independent States, (…). And for the support of this Declaration, with a firm reliance on

one of the building blocks of present-day human rights documents, is full of devotion to the creator God, the dispenser of providence and the supreme judge, and appeals to him to endorse the aforementioned inalienable rights and the lawfulness of secession from England. The God concept it reflects lacks the peculiar attributes of the God of the liberation (*exodus*) from Egypt, the covenant, and the prophets, also those of the God and Father of Jesus, and the Spirit of God and Jesus. It contains all the themes of the deism that characterised the enlightened elite of that time: creation, providence, and judgment of good and evil. To them these religious beliefs were the motive for crediting the substance of the document, respecting it, recognising it, and acting in accordance with it. It is a true example of a religious foundation.

The text of the aforementioned Virginia Bill of Rights of the same year, 1776, depicts a more restricted scenario. It refers to God only once in the context of religious freedom. It stipulates that the religion or duty owing to the creator and the manner in which it is discharged can be regulated only by reason and conviction, not by violence or force. Consequently, all people have a right to exercise their religion freely according to their own conscience before God. That was the origin of the aforementioned free exercise clause. To this the text adds parliament's obligation to maintain the separation of church and state, which gave rise to the aforementioned no establishment clause.[58] The influence of Milton and Locke is discernible in this motivation with its emphasis on religion as a duty, rooted in conscience, that humans

---

the protection of Divine Providence, we mutually pledge to each other our Lives, our Fortunes, and our sacred Honor."

[58] "That religion or the duty which we owe our Creator, and the manner of discharging it, can be directed only by reason and conviction, not by force or violence; and, therefore, all men are equally entitled to the free exercise of religion, according to the dictates of conscience; and that it is the mutual duty of all to practice Christian forbearance, love, and charity towards each other. No man shall be compelled to frequent or support any religious worship, place, or ministry whatsoever, nor shall be enforced, restrained, molested, or burthened in his body or goods, nor shall otherwise suffer on account of his religious opinions or belief; but all men shall be free to profess and by argument to maintain their opinions in matters of religion, and the same shall in no wise diminish, enlarge, or affect their civil capacities. And the General Assembly shall not prescribe any religious test whatever, or confer any peculiar privileges or advantages on any sect or denomination, or pass any law requiring authorizing any religious society, or the people of any district within this Commonwealth, to levy on themselves or others, any tax for the erection or repair of any house of public worship, or for the support of any church or ministry; but it shall be left free to every person to select his religious instructor, and to make for his support such private contract as he shall please" (article 16).

owe God. They held that nothing or nobody may interfere with this conscientious religious relationship and that individual humans are accountable for it to God and to God alone.[59] Thus the text also provides a religious foundation for recognising and upholding a right, here the right to religious freedom.

An intriguing text is the Virginia Statute for Religious Freedom, compiled ten years later in 1786, by one of the founding fathers, Thomas Jefferson. In lucid terms, it defines religious freedom on the basis of four propositions. The first is that God created humans with free minds. He could have created them differently, for instance by imposing faith forcibly by dint of his absolute power (*potestas absoluta*). But what the "Holy Author of our religion" (*potestas ordinata*) had in mind was not to burden people with coercion and not to propagate faith through fear of sanctions. The second proposition is that those who exercise or wish to exercise such coercion, be they civil or ecclesiastic law-givers, are themselves fallible humans who want to impose their own fallible insight on others. This is reminiscent of an idea previously defined by Milton and Locke, to the effect that other people simply do not have access to what happens between God and the individual human conscience, hence have no knowledge of it, and if they think they have, it is merely fallible knowledge.[60] Proposition three states that our civil rights, which include the right to religious freedom, do not depend on our religious opinions any more than they depend on our opinions about physics or mathematics. Opinions are totally irrelevant; what matters is the rules that the creator laid down in the order of creation (natural law). The fourth proposition is that religious freedom is the 'natural right' of every human being and any violation of it must be seen as a violation of 'natural rights'.[61] These

---

[59] Also see chapter 7.

[60] See chapter 7.

[61] "Well aware that Almighty God has created the mind free; that all attemps to influence it by temporal punishments or burdens (…) are a departure from the plan of the Holy Author of our religion, who, being Lord both of body and mind, yet chose not to propagate it by coercions on either, as was his Almighty power to do so; that the impious presumption of legislators and rulers, civil as well as ecclesiastical, who being themselves but fallible and uninspired men, have assumed dominion over the faith of others, setting up their own opinions and modes of thinking as the only true and infallible, and as such endeavouring to impose them on others, hath established and maintained false religions over the greatest part of the world, and through all time; (…) that our civil rights have no dependence on our religious opinions any more than [on] our opinions in physics or geometry; (…) we are free to declare, and do declare,

four propositions provide a chain of arguments that combine to form the religious foundation of this Statute.

The American constitution of 1787, which, as noted already, starts with "we, the people of the United States", contains no reference to either God, natural law, or natural rights. The American Bill of Rights, compiled by one of the founding fathers, James Madison, in 1789, and appended to the constitution in the form of ten amendments in 1791, likewise contains no reference to God, natural law, or natural rights. This is remarkable. The Virginia Bill of Rights of 1776 still linked the free exercise clause and the no establishment clause with God and with conscience, in which people stand face to face with God. The ten amendments of the America constitution, which contain the American Bill of Rights and the first of which explicitly mentions the two clauses, completely omit these religious references. They provide no religious foundation at all.

The French *Déclaration des droits de l'homme et du citoyen* of 1789, which, as noted already, was probably inspired by the Virginia Bill of Rights of 1776, does include a religious reference. The preamble, for example, says that this declaration contains the natural, inalienable and sacred rights of human beings. These are the rights to freedom, property, security, and resistance to oppression. It also claims to have been compiled in the presence and under the protection of the Supreme Being.[62] The same religious passage appears in the interesting, albeit unofficial, *Déclaration des droits de la femme et de la citoyenne*, compiled by Marie Gouse in 1791. It lists the same rights as the *Déclaration* of 1789 – freedom, property, security, and resistance to oppression – with just one difference: the insertion of the word '*surtout*' (above all): "above all resistance to oppression" (*surtout la résistance à l'oppression*").[63] In the epilogue, women are called to claim their

---

that the rights hereby asserted are the natural rights of mankind, and that if any act shall hereafter be passed to repeal the present one or to narrow its operation, such act will be an infringement of natural right."

[62] "Les représentants du people français, constitués en Assemblée nationale, (...) ont résolu d'exposer, dans une déclaration solennelle, les droits naturels, inaliénables et sacrés de l'homme (...). En conséquence, l'Assemblée nationale reconnaît et déclare, en présence et sous les auspices de l'Etre Suprême, les droits suivants de l'homme et du citoyen".

[63] "*Ces droits sont la liberté, la propriété, la sûreté, et surtout la résistance à l'oppression*" (article 2); cf. T. Beattie, "Justice Enacted Not These Human Laws" (Antigone): Religion, Natural Law and Women's Rights, *Religion and human rights* 3(2008)3, 249–267.

inheritance grounded in the wise decrees of nature and to take pride in sharing in the precious treasures bestowed on them by the Supreme Being. Whereas the religious reference in the previously cited official documents already show signs of a deistic God concept, the bare mention of the 'Supreme Being' in the two French declarations could be seen as a pale shadow of deism. Nonetheless, it does represent a type of religious foundation. Some people feel that the texts of these and similar documents, despite an archaic religious reference, are thoroughly secular and as such reflect French society between 1789 and 1848.[64]

4.3.2   *The Universal Declaration of Human Rights:*
A 'Foundation-Open' Text

The Universal Declaration of Human Rights of 1948 broke with this tradition of religious foundations, however watered down the references to God, natural law, or natural rights may have become over the years. The 1948 declaration contains no reference to God whatever, nor to natural law or natural rights, nor to any worldview or even philosophy. It is a 'foundation-open' text (a *begründungsoffen* text). The main reason was the altered scale on which this document was designed. A universal religious foundation of human rights could still be laid for 18th century nation-states, the more so because the vast majority of the population was Christian, be it Catholic, Lutheran, Calvinist, Anglican, or Congregationalist in whatever variant form (conservative or liberal). But even at that time religious minorities like Jews and Muslims posed a problem, if only because – bar the odd group here and there – they were unfamiliar with natural law and the natural rights imbedded in it. For the Universal Declaration, the national scale had to be expanded to encompass the whole world, so religious pluralism inevitably became an obstacle to a universal foundation. Besides, the growing number of groups that had turned their backs on religion of any kind, including the elite of the aforementioned radical Enlightenment, made a universal religious foundation problematic.

All this was already apparent at the start of the activities of the commission headed by Eleanore Roosevelt, which prepared the text of the Declaration between 1945 and 1948. In working through the diverse proposals and amendments, totalling some 900 pages, and discussing

---

[64] See E.J. Hobsbawm, *The Age of Revolution*, New American Library, New York 1962.

them in seven drafting stages, one concluded that any attempt to compile a foundational text was bound to fail.[65] Two members of the commission, the Chinese vice chairman P.C. Chang (Zhang Pengjun) and the Lebanese Charles Habib Malik, could not reach agreement on such a text. The former was a Confucian, the latter an Eastern Orthodox Christian and a proponent of natural law and natural rights. They were unable to find each other, with natural law – it is unknown as such in Eastern philosophy – acting as a further impediment. There are also substantial differences and disputes in this area between and within Christian and Islamic traditions. In Christianity, there are conflicting interpretations between scholastic, late scholastic, and neo-scholastic schools in Catholicism, and between Lutheran, Calvinist, and Anglican schools in Protestantism.[66] In Islam, there are essential disparities in Sunni theology, for instance between the Maturidi school that accepts natural law and the Ashari school that is said to repudiate it.[67] When the German Lutherans got wind of a possible grounding of human rights in natural law during the preliminary activities, they threatened to use their influence on diplomats associated with the commission not only to put a stop to it, but to replace natural law with basic notions from the Christian creed – in effect that of the Lutheran tradition.[68]

On account of such developments, the commission decided to work out a text that, whilst open to any foundation, would contain no religious or worldview-related foundation. It presented the international, multicultural, and multireligious world with a metaphysically open text to fill as various communities see fit: "Christians, Muslims, atheists, Buddhists, Marxists, liberals, and so on, may from their own normative heartland come up with full-fledged justificatory doctrines of globally binding human rights, none of which need be compatible with any of the others, if only each of them provides the proper kind of support to the principle of inherent freedom and equal dignity for every human being".[69]

---

[65] Morsink, *Universal Declaration*, op. cit. 4–12.

[66] See chapter 5.

[67] A. Ezzati, *Islam and Natural Law*, Icas Press, London 2002, 60–92; cf. K.A. El Fadl, Islam and the Challenge of Democratic Commitment, in: E. Bucar & B. Barnett (eds.), *Does Human Rights Need God?* Eerdmans, Grand Rapids 2005, 58–103, here 93–97.

[68] W. Vögele, *Menschenwürde zwischen Recht und Theologie*, Kaiser, Gütersloh 2000, 250–253.

[69] T. Lindholm, Prospects for Research on Cultural Legitimacy of Human Rights: The Cases of Liberalism and Marxism, in: A.A. An-Na'im (ed.), *Human Rights in*

In this regard the consistency of the text is evident in its treatment of the aforementioned four freedoms of president Roosevelt, whose wife chaired the commission. Roosevelt formulated the second freedom thus: "The second is freedom of every person to worship God in his own way – everywhere in the world." The preamble to the Universal Declaration eliminates freedom to worship God, reducing it to freedom of belief. Later in the Declaration, freedom of religion is discussed in greater detail in a concretisation of this reduced interpretation: "Everyone has the right to freedom of thought, conscience and religion; this right includes freedom to change his religion or belief" (article 18). Here thought, conscience, and religion are put on a par. In other words, the article refers not merely to religious thought, conscience, and belief, but also to nonreligious thought, conscience and belief. Religious people may find this offensive, in that it seems to equate the significance and value of nonreligious beliefs with those of religious ones. But why should it be offensive? After all, it does not equate the intrinsic value of religious and nonreligious views but merely declares them equal before the law. The sole aim was to keep the foundation of the Declaration open to any belief.

That does not mean that the document contains no values whatever, for an open foundation does not make the Declaration value-free. Values and the debates about them are evident in the discussions and decisions about the text of the document.[70] Thus socio-economic rights were advocated mainly by Latin American countries and less by countries from the former Soviet bloc, even though the latter were reputed to have fiercely supported these rights. The delegates of India, the Dominican Republic, and Denmark were adamant about inclusive language. The Polish delegate stressed the prohibition of women trafficking, which crystallised in a prohibition of slavery in whatever form (article 4). A young delegate from Pakistan spoke out fervently against child marriages, which in the eventual Declaration culminated in the following article: "(1) Men and women of full age, without any limitation due to race, nationality or religion, have the right to marry and to found a family. They are entitled to equal rights as to marriage, during marriage and its dissolution. (2) Marriage shall be entered into only

---

Cross-Cultural Perspective: A Quest for Consensus, University of Pennsylvania Press, Philadelphia 1991, 400.

[70] Who Wrote the Universal Declaration of Human Rights? See: http://www.america.gov/st/hr-english/2008/November/20081119135247xjyrrep6.023806e-02.html.

with the free and full consent of the intending spouses. (3) The family
is the natural and fundamental group unity of society and is entitled
to protection by society and the State" (article 16). The Philippine delegate championed the prohibition of torture (article 5). And the aforementioned P.C. Chang had a separate article appended to the list of
rights at the end of the declaration on a person's duty to other people
and to the community (article 29).

Proposed amendments also disclosed values that were strongly
coloured by the delegates' background and context and (for that reason) were not accepted. Thus the Saudi Arabian delegate, while he
could reconcile himself with religious freedom, could not accept the
right to change one's religion. The reason he gave was the suffering
inflicted in the Middle East during the Crusades and recent experience of missionary proselytism. The latter was stressed by the Egyptian
delegate, who had much to say about the machinations of certain missions.[71] Finally, an attempt to include minority rights in the text failed
because of the complexity of the issue, especially from the perspective
of both the colonial powers and the Soviet Union.[72]

A further objection to the Declaration was that its underlying
anthropology was steeped in Western thinking, more especially the
accent on the individual person and individuals' rights as opposed to
their duties. Thus the Saudi Arabian delegate stated that the Declaration was grafted onto a Western cultural pattern that differed from
that of Eastern states, adding that it did not mean the Declaration
was counter to the cultures of those countries, even though not the
same. There were also appeals for the inclusion of a religious foundation, or at any rate regret about its omission. Thus the Brazilian
and Dutch delegates among others regretted that the divine origin
of humankind were not mentioned, as well as the origin of human
rights – 'the Supreme Being'. Here these diplomats were on tricky ter-
rain, for such a religious foundation could have led to more detailed
religious concretisations that might have given rise to all manner of
further disputes or conflicts. For that reason a proposal to start article
1 as follows: *"Created in the image and likeness of God* [all human
beings] are endowed with reason and conscience" was rejected, as well

---

[71] *United Nations Yearbook Summary 1948*, (2) Discussion by the General Assembly in plenary meeting, (a) Views expressed by representatives.
[72] Morsink, *Universal Declaration*, op. cit. 269–280.

as a proposal to qualify 'endowed' with: "endowed by nature", because some delegates considered God and nature as opposites and others saw nature as being too narrowly connected with (Catholic) natural law thought.[73] Referring to 'virtually all other Muslim countries', the Egyptian delegate mentioned restrictions on the marriage of Muslim women to adherents of another religion, which, being a religious stricture, could not be ignored. But the commission stood by the 'open foundation' character of the Declaration. Even the stipulation about marriage and raising a family, which was said to have been introduced mainly through the agency of the Christian Democratic movement, has no Christian or other religious basis whatever (article 16), after a proposal by Malik was rejected in which it was said that the "family is endowed by the Creator with inalienable rights antecedent to all positive law".[74]

Despite these objections the Declaration was, as noted already, accepted unaninmously with 48 votes. The Soviet bloc abstained from voting, since it had ideological objections to various articles and to the document as a whole. Saudi Arabia abstained because of religious reservations. Finally South Africa abstained on account of its apartheid regime.[75] Thus the 'open foundation' character of the Declaration was accepted, unfettered by any religious or nonreligious convictions. The plurality of worldviews on a global scale permitted no other option.

In response to surprise that countries with opposing ideologies all signed the Declaration, Jacques Maritain, one of the trailblazers of the document, explained in some detail in his speech at the second international Unesco conference shortly after it was proclaimed: "Yes, they said, we agree about the rights *but on condition that no one asks us why*." He continued: "Because, as I said at the beginning of my speech, the goal of UNESCO is a practical goal, agreement between minds can be reached spontaneously, not on the basis of common speculative ideas, but on common practical ideas, not on the affirmation of one and the same conception of the world, of man and of knowledge,

---

[73] Morsink, *Universal Declaration*, op. cit., 284–290.

[74] Morsink, *Universal Declaration*, op. cit., 254–257; *Howard Center for Family, Religion, Society*: http://www.profam.org/docs/acc/thc.acc.globalizing.040112.htm.

[75] *United Nations Yearbook Summary 1948*, (c) Adoption of the Declaration; Morsink, *Universal Declaration*, op. cit., 21–28.

but upon the affirmation of a single body of beliefs for guidance in action."[76]

Here we have an explicit admission that the Universal Declaration is a document open to a multiplicity of foundations, including religious ones. Hence it is not characterised by Western-style secularism, as many critics in the West but more especially in non-Western societies have claimed, but by a pragmatic common denominator: to reach agreement so as to do what needed to be done.[77]

This pragmatism emerged and still emerges from imagined empathy for the experiences innocent, suffering people went through and still go through, the pain they feel, the angst they live in. This sense of what needs to be done came and still comes from sympathy, in the broad eighteen century meaning of a moral faculty in which one imaginatively identifies with fellow people who are victims of cruel, inhuman or degrading treatment, torture, killings, even genocide.[78] Thus human rights have helped to (further) emancipate slaves, blacks, workers, Jews, minorities, foreigners, women, children, homosexuals – even though some of these groups still have a long way to go.[79]

Furthermore, even though the Declaration was compiled under predominantly Western influence, the notion that the values legally defined in the text are superior to values elsewhere in the world is foreign to it. It was written, as stated in the preambles to both the United Nations charter and the Declaration itself, in full awareness of the horrors of Auschwitz, hence of the barbarous deeds that have outraged the conscience of humankind. It should rather be seen as the West's warning to itself and the rest of the world not to repeat those crimes, but instead to devise a mechanism that can help to prevent them: human rights as an effective tool in the overall body of international public

---

[76] J. Maritain, Inaugural Address to the Second International Conference of Unesco, in J. Witte & Fr. Alexander (eds.), *The Teaching of Modern Christianity on Law, Politics, and Human Nature*, Vol. 2, Columbia University Press, New York 2006, 36.

[77] Ignatieff, *Human Rights*, op. cit., 64.

[78] F. Hutcheson, *A Short Introduction to Moral Philosophy, in Three Books, Containing the Elements of Ethics and the Laws of Nature*, 2nd edition, Robert & Andrew Foulis, Glasgouw 1753, 12–16; A. Smith, *The Theory of Moral Sentiments*, 3rd edition, London 1767; I. Kant, *Metaphysische Anfangsgründe der Tugendlehre, Metaphysik der Sitten, Zweiter Teil*, Meiner, Hamburg 1990, 103–104; L. Hunt, *Inventing Human Rights, A History*, Norton, New York 2007.

[79] Ishay, *The History of Human Rights*, op. cit., passim.

law.[80] The objective is to promote those values of which human rights are the legal articulation: human dignity, freedom, equality, solidarity, citizenship, and justice.[81]

4.3.3   Particular Foundations

All this does not mean that each and every foundation would be irrelevant. It is simply that universal foundations, religious or nonreligious, that claim to hold good for all groups and communities of every nation had become impossible in view of the manifest plurality of worldviews worldwide. This also applies to such pluralism within individual nations. That does not detract from the right of individual (religious or nonreligious) communities, including global ones, to endeavour – as they in fact do – to ground human rights in a view or concept that, from that community's perspective, grounds and substantiates them. One could call these particular foundations. I cite some examples pertinent to present-day (Western) society: a Christian, an Islamic, and a nonreligious, philosophical foundation. I start with the last one.

4.3.4   Human Dignity

The key concept that perhaps could underlie a philosophical foundation is human dignity. In the 1948 Declaration it occupies a preferential position. It appears in the very first sentence of the preamble, qualified by the word 'inherent': inherent dignity. 'Dignity' features a second time in the preamble, as well as in two international covenants that elaborate on the Universal Declaration – the International Covenant on Civil and Political rights and the International Covenant on Economic, Social and Cultural rights, both of 1966. In addition, it occurs in article 1 of the Universal Declaration.[82]

Despite the central role the concept of human dignity plays in official human rights documents and human rights thought, its very

---

[80] Ignatieff, *Human Rights*, op. cit., 65; A. Nollkaemper, *Kern van het internationaal publiek recht*, Boom, The Hague 2007, 255–290.

[81] As noted already, these values provide the structure for the European Charter of Fundamental Rights (Nice 2000).

[82] Human dignity features in numerous documents, especially constitutions; see J.A. van der Ven, J.S. Dreyer & H.J.C. Pieterse, *Is There a God of Human Rights?* Brill, Leiden 2004, 276–280.

meaning is everything but clear.[83] Here it makes sense to distinguish between *concept* and *conception*. A concept can be said to be a semantic entity covering a plurality of metaphorical connotations and denotations, whereas a conception entails a specific interpretation of one of its denotative meanings.[84] From the western tradition, I pass some conceptions of human dignity in review.[85]

The concept of human dignity originated in the work of the classic texts of the Stoics, notably Cicero and Seneca. There it has two aspects. One is the dignity of those who hold public office, hence are vested with public dignity.[86] The other is that human beings, whether or not they hold public office, are imbued with a human spirit that elevates them above all other beings and which constitutes their excellence.[87] The notice and reputation that a person acquires no longer pertains to the sphere of public office, but is transferred to personal awareness of her human dignity and self-esteem.[88] That gives the person 'stoical' serenity to endure life's vicissitudes with equanimity. It makes people sovereigns to themselves.[89] This spiritual character implies the inviolability of other people and human solidarity.[90] Thus nature and humankind, natural law and human dignity are grounded in each other.

Another important development was the interpretation of human dignity by Pico della Mirandola, who was not influenced by the classical texts of the Stoics but stood on the borderline between the Middle Ages and the Renaissance and was affected by scepticism.[91] He, too,

---

[83] Chr. McCrudden, Human Dignity and Judicial Interpretation of Human Rights, *The European Journal of International Law*, 19(2008)4, 655–724; G. Hottois, *Dignité et diversité des homes*, Vrin, Paris 2009.

[84] U. Eco, *A Theory of Semiotics*, Indiana University Press, Bloomington 1979, 54–57; R. Dworkin, *Taking Rights Seriously*, Harvard University Press, Cambridge 1978, 134–137.

[85] J.-P. Wils, s.v. Würde, in: M. Düwell et al. (eds.), *Handbuch Ethik*, Metzler, Stuttgart 2006, 558–563.

[86] Cicero, *De inventione*, II.

[87] Cicero, *De officiis*, I.

[88] Taylor, *Sources of the Self*, op. cit., 152.

[89] M.C. Nussbaum, *The Therapy of Desire: Theory and Practice in Hellenistic Ethics*, Princeton University Press, Princeton 1996, 316–358.

[90] Cicero, *De officiis*, III.

[91] G. Pico della Mirandola, *Over de menselijke waardigheid*, Dutch translation of *De hominis dignitate*, van Loghum Slaterus, Arnhem 1968; L. Valcke & R. Galibois, *Le périple intellectuel de Jean Pic de la Mirandole*, Presses de l'Université Laval, Centre d'études de la Renaissance, Sainte-Foy 1994; for the subsequent influence of the Stoics on the Renaissance, see P.-F. Moreau, Les trois étappes du stoïcisme, in: P.-F. Moreau (ed.), *Le stoïcisme au XVIᵉ et XVIIᵉ siècle: Le retour des philosophies antiques á l'âge classique. Tome I*. Albin, Paris 1999, 11–28. For the influence of scepticism, see

located the peculiar excellence of human beings in their spirit, but what was remarkable was that he saw rationality in the human spirit as the possession of free choice and living according to it, more especially in executing a personal life project. Human beings are sovereign, free artists, who design, sculpt, and model themselves in a form of their own choice.[92] Pico was a champion of life as a freely chosen project (*liberum arbitrium*).[93]

A further important step is to be found in German idealism, especially in the work of Kant. Kant introduced the classical distinction between price and value. Exchangeable things are bought at a price; a value cannot be reduced to anything else.[94] The value underlying human dignity lies in autonomy, which consists in the human being designing a law which he imposes upon himself, with the proviso that it is valid for all people (universalisable). Human self-esteem derives from this autonomy. The criterion is that one should treat every person, including oneself, as an intrinsic end with intrinsic value, and never as a means only.[95] This is a brilliant definition. Nobody can avoid seeing others and themselves as means to be used, but to use (i.e. abuse) oneself and others purely and exclusively as instruments to achieve some useful end is a violation of human dignity.[96] On the basis of the distinction between individual and political autonomy, the Kantian concept is commonly cited as an interpretation of human dignity and is also used as a foundation for human rights.[97] It is a key concept, for example, in the South African constitution of 1996.[98] A judge of the South African constitutional court, L. Ackerman, stated, following

---

M. Granada, Apologétique platonicienne et apologétique sceptique: Ficin, Savonarole, Jean-Francois Pic de la Mirandole, in: P.-F. Moreau (ed.), *Le scepticisme au XVIᵉ et XVIIᵉ siècle: Le retour des philosophes antiques á l'âge classique. Tome II*, Albin, Paris 2001, 11–47.

[92] G. Pico della Mirandola, *De hominis dignitate*.

[93] H. de Lubac, *Pic de la Mirandole: Études et discussions*, Aubier Montaigne, Paris 1974.

[94] I. Kant, *Grundlegung zur Metaphysik der Sitten*, Hamburg 1965, 59; Id., *Metaphysische Anfangsgründe*, op. cit. 110.

[95] Ibid., 52; Van der Ven et al., *Is There a God*, op. cit., 268–271.

[96] It is not enough to behave according to the duty implied in the law, one should behave out of duty; see: J. Rawls, *A Theory of Justice*, Harvard University Press, Cambridge 1971, 177–180.

[97] A. Ingram, *A Political Theory of Rights*, Clarendon Press, New York 1994.

[98] Both G. Devenish, *A Commentary on the South African Bill of Rights*, Butterworth, Durban 1999, 81, and J. de Waal et al., *The Bill of Rights Handbook*, Juta, Lansdowne 2002, 231, use the Kantian concept of human dignity with reference to the South African constitution.

from the Kantian concept of human dignity, that blacks are treated as means to an end only and hardly ever as ends in themselves also. He called it a total inversion of the Kantian imperative of the priceless, intrinsic value and dignity of human beings.[99]

Lastly, Hegel's view may be seen as a critical note on this approach. Human dignity does not lie in the fact that the human being is autonomous, but that he acquires that dignity. It is a product of a life lived under conditions that permit a dignified existence.[100] In this perspective, dignity, contemporary scholars say, is not a metaphysical concept about what a human being is, but a moral, relational and at the same time developmental concept. It refers to the extent to which a human being is, negatively speaking, prevented from being humiliated and, positively, respected and recognised and on that basis develops self-esteem. Kant one-sidedly put emphasis on the legal and rational aspects of autonomy. He modelled morality on legislation and pure practical reason while ignoring all natural development and inclination, while even suppressing and combating inclination as an 'inner enemy'.[101] This resulted into a dichotomous conception of autonomy, instead of a gradual, scalar conception, in which becoming plays a central role, including its transitional stages and its dialectics between continuity and discontinuity.[102]

It is frequently questioned whether human rights, including human dignity, are not a thoroughly Western conception of humanness, and for that reason alone cannot possibly provide a universal code. And indeed, historically they were first lucidly defined and analysed predominantly in Western countries. But logically a distinction should be made between historical origin and substantial validity. History does not decide a concept's validity, only its substantial content does.

Apart from that, human rights' Western background does not mean that they have no links with the norms and values of non-Western traditions. An example is the African Charter on Human and Peoples'

---

[99] S. Cowen, Can 'Dignity' Guide South Africa's Equality Jurisprudence?, *South African Journal on Human Rights* 17(2001), 34–58.

[100] G.W.F. Hegel, *Vorlesungen über die Philosophie der Religion*, Sämtliche Werke, Bd. 15, Stuttgart 1959, 323; Wils, s.v. *Würde*, art. cit., 561.

[101] I. Kant, *Metaphysische Anfangsgründe*, op. cit., 16, 40, 127.

[102] G. Harris, *Dignity and Vulnerability*, University of California Press, Berkeley 1997, 53–84; Id., Agent-Centered Morality, *An Aristotelian Alternative to Kantian Internalism*, University of California Press, Berkeley 1999; D. Luban, *Legal Ethics and Human Dignity*, Cambridge University Press, Cambridge 2008, 65–95.

Rights (1981), in which human dignity features explicitly in the preamble. The first part of the document deals with individual rights in a way that clearly overlaps, even resembles Western documents (articles 2–18). In the second part, the rights of peoples are added (articles 19–24), and in the third part duties towards members of communities and the communities themselves (articles 27–29). The concept of human dignity, moreover, features in other African documents, such as the African Charter on the Rights and Welfare of the Child (1990), the Protocol to the African Charter on Human and People's Rights on the Establishment of an African Court for Human and Peoples' Rights (1998), and the Protocol on the rights of women in Africa (2003).

In addition to these African examples, there are Asian documents like the Asian Human Rights Charter (1998), in which human dignity is mentioned several times, for instance in a general sense in the preamble, as well as in articles 1.7 and 2.2. It is dealt with in more detail in article 2.4, which says that human dignity cannot possibly be achieved in impoverished circumstances; in article 3.2, where it is associated with the right to life; in article 6, where it is related to cultural identity; and in article 11, which pertains to respect for the dignity of handicapped people. The Bangkok Declaration on Human Rights (1993) is another example. The document was compiled preparatory to the world conference on human rights in Vienna (1993), so as to underscore the contribution of Asian traditions in the debate. Human dignity is cited to substantiate children's rights. For the rest it is mainly an appeal by non-Western countries to be taken seriously by rich Western countries, more especially by stressing the indivisibility of first- and second-generation human rights, and a plea not to use human rights as a condition for developmental cooperation.

In view of these African and Asian examples, one could well ask why human dignity cannot apply universally as a foundation for human rights. It ranks among the cardinal concepts, possibly the key concept, in the international codification of human rights and in the constitutions of the vast majority of countries worldwide.[103] It is certainly the basic medium of international judicial matters. But judicial matters is one thing, fundamental legal theory is another. And the latter is where problems arise.

---

[103] Not, however, in the Dutch constitution, which is conspicuously lacking in values that transcend constitutional norms.

History already reveals, as we have seen, a diversity of interpretative conceptions of human dignity, which, while displaying some overlap, are also mutually critical and even mutually exclusive. Thus there is no consensus on human uniqueness arising from the human spirit, because that would be evidence of 'specieism' (humans as the highest species and the centre of nature).[104] Nor is there agreement on what this spirit consists in – Stoic sovereign dignity as in Cicero or dignified project planning as Pico would have it. The difference between Kant and Hegel, too, cannot be denied, since the former posits an absolutely dichotomous concept – human dignity is either there or it is not – whereas the latter propounds a relative, continuous, gradual development of acquired human dignity. Succinctly, is human dignity official (Cicero), sovereign (Cicero again), expressed by way of a project (Pico della Mirandola), intrinsic (Kant), or acquired (Hegel)?

Apart from these philosophers, there are various religions, notably Christianity (see below), which are ready to accept the idea of human dignity – at any rate at a highly abstract level – and incorporate it into their own conceptual framework, but do so with the qualification that it does not afford a sufficiently firm basis and must be critically augmented, for instance by a Christian view on creation, human failure and salvation, or an Islamic view on *shari'a*. As a result, the meaning of the concept is not only given different slants, but its actual content is differently valued. In fact, to these religions, human dignity is or could be a necessary but certainly not a sufficient condition for the presentation and development of the moral and religious convictions from which they look at human dignity. Thus it remains an exemplary key element of a particular foundation, albeit perhaps the most prominent one. At a high level of abstraction – hence without detailed interpretative conceptions such as those of Cicero, Pico, Kant, and Hegel, and without critical detailed augmentation entailing conceptual modification by diverse religions – it could count on broad, but not sufficient, all-encompassing agreement. Human dignity is a key concept, but not a universally foundational one.

---

[104] A. Fiala, Theocentrism and Human Rights: A Critical Argument, *Religion & Human Rights* 3(2008)3, 217–234; see P. Singer, *Animal Liberation*, Random, New York 1990.

4.3.5 *Image of God*

In Christian thought, human dignity, as mentioned already, plays a prominent role – in Catholicism even before the proclamation of the Universal Declaration of Human Rights of 1948. The term featured, albeit marginally, as far back as the social encyclicals of popes Leo XIII and Pius XI respectively: *Rerum novarum* (1891) and *Quadragesimo anno* (1931). In a lengthy radio broadcast in the middle of World War II, on Christmas Eve, 1942, Pius XII explained that human dignity is one of the five basic requirements of social organisation.[105] Since then, the concept has taken root, as evidenced by the encyclicals *Mater et Magistra* (1961) and *Pacem in Terris* (1963) of pope John XXIII. In the documents of Vatican II (1962–1965), especially the constitution *Gaudium et Spes* and the declaration on religious freedom, *Dignitatis Humanae* – as the very title indicates! – it fulfils a key function, specifically in relation to human rights.[106] The former devotes seven sections in the first chapter to human dignity (nos. 12–17) and the latter starts off as follows: "A sense of the dignity of the human person has been impressing itself more and more deeply on the consciousness of contemporary man" (no. 1), while further on it says "that the right to religious freedom has its foundation in the very dignity of the human person as this dignity is known through the revealed word of God and by reason itself" (no. 2).[107]

One could ask whether this does not mean that human dignity provides an adequate foundation for human rights, also and especially for the Catholic Church, and whether that does not make it a candidate for the role of a truly universal foundation. However, human dignity may be considered essential but not sufficient, for what is the basis of its very quality? Disregard of this question opens the door to arbitrary interpretations of its content. Certainly if one uses an idiosyncratic version of relative, continuous, gradual interpretation, there is a danger that the limits of the inviolability of human dignity will

---

[105] A.-F. Utz & J.-F. Groner, *Aufbau und Entfaltung des gesellschaftlichen Lebens, Soziale Summe Pius XII*, Paulusverlag, Freiburg 1954, no. 252.

[106] See chapter 5.

[107] In the other documents of Vatican II, human dignity plays a lesser role, for instance in the declaration on the church's attitude towards non-Christian religions (*Nostra Aetate*) and the declaration on Christian education (*Gravissimum Educationis Momentum*). In the dogmatic constitution on the church, *Lumen Gentium*, it features prominently, but always imbedded in a religious and ecclesiastic frame of reference.

be exceeded. This might lead to severe and even insuperable scruples of conscience about the moral quality of human interventions at the beginning of life and at the end of life.

These agonies of doubt may be overcome by taking notice of the way in which the Catholic Church set the concept of human dignity in a religious framework – that of the creation of human beings in the likeness of God. The narrative metaphor of creation expresses the religious vocation and destiny of humans as being the image of God in and through their dignity. Thus, by virtue of their creation in God's image, life is to be seen as a gratuitous gift of God in which He participates in the life of human beings and allows human beings to participate in His life. This mutual participation is the very meaning of human existence all together. It gives human life its origin and aim, source and destiny, nature and purpose. From this perspective, life should be celebrated in gratitude and cherished in tender loving care. Because life is God's gift, human beings cannot autonomously dispose of it and decide for themselves whether to receive or terminate it. From this perspective, interventions like abortion, assisted suicide, and euthanasia can only be considered as a violation of the gift of and the right to life, which is based in God's creative act.[108] Although this might be in the face of public and political appeals for a pro choice policy for pregnant women in desperate situations, and of public and political appeals for euthanasia as a form of letting people die with dignity, the Catholic Church has no other choice, she says, than to comply with the very first fundamental tenets the book of Genesis opens with: God's creation of human beings by forming them from the dust of the ground and breathing into their nostrils the breath of life (Genesis 2) and by shaping them by His very word in His image: male and female He created them (Genesis 1). In the same vein, the Catholic Church can only comply, she says, with the tenets in God's creative, life-giving act which are inscribed in natural law, and thus denounce same-sex marriage and any same-sex activity because they contradict and violate the intergenerational creativity in human dignity. Again she has no other choice, she says, although this flies in the face of growing

---

[108] Encyclical *Evangelium Vitae* (1995) of pope John Paul II; for Protestant theology, see: C. Schwöbel, Recovering human dignity, in: R. Kendall Soulen & L. Woodhead (eds.), *God and human dignity*, Eerdmans, Grand Rapids 2006, 44–58, here 57.

public and political support for gay movements like...'Dignity'.[109] Even though dignity is manifold, the Catholic church holds on to the insight that human dignity is to be regarded with absolute respect in every phase of life and in every sphere, without taking any mitigating circumstances into consideration. Anyone who infringes that respect, so she teaches, is guilty, she says, of intrinsic evil.[110]

Apart from this orthodox view, which may be critically reflected upon from a developmental ontology as opposed to a substantialist ontology, as Paul Ricoeur suggested,[111] it is quite remarkable that a Christian foundation should put the accent on the theme of the creation of humans in God's image.[112] In the entire Bible, the theme of the creation of humans in God's image is found only in the Jewish Bible, and then in only one book, and only thrice in that book (Gen 1:27; 5:1; 9:6). In addition, the exegetical history of these verses teems with divergent interpretations, not only in the New Testament but also in patristic and scholastic times right up to contemporary liberation theology, often altogether unrelated and sometimes contradictory to their meaning in Genesis, which, of course, is pre-Christian. Thus the

---

[109] Declaration of the Pontifical Council for the Family regarding the Resolution of the European Parliament, *Making de facto unions, including same-sex unions, equal to the family* (17 March 2000).

[110] A tragic case that evoked intense international discussion in the Catholic Church and the media in 2009 was that of a Brazilian girl, who was given the name 'Carmen'. She was raped repeatedly by her stepfather, was already fertile at the age of nine, became pregnant with twins and was given an abortion in the fourth month of gestation, which according to the Code of Canon Law automatically lead to the excommunication of all who cooperated in conducting this abortion. This case took place in the midst of the heavy turmoil of pro-life and pro-choice campaigns by church and state in Brazil, The question was whether this abortion is to be considered intrinsic evil or maybe justifiable in terms of saving Carmen's physical, psychological and social life; see: www.chiesa.espressonline.it on March 23, July 3 and July 10, 2009.

[111] P. Ricoeur, *Oneself as another*, University of Chicago Press, Chicago 1992, explicitly refers to the doubts and scruples of conscience people may go through about the beginning and end of life (p. 285). He underscores the importance of a developmental ontology as opposed to a substantialist ontology (p. 271) in order to allow for the tension between personal uniqueness and a unitaristic concept of 'the human being' (p. 285) and for the intrinsic interrelationship between being (*esse*), action (*actus*) and the capacity to act (*potestas*) (pp. 302–317); cf. Id., *Réflexion faite. Autobiographie intellectuelle*, Esprit, Paris 1995, 83–115. G. Hottois, Dignité et diversité des homes, Vrin, Paris 2009, argues for an ontology of becoming, in which the dialectics of time (past, present, future) and the relation between continuity and discontinuity are taken into account (81–84 94–96), and for an ethical approach in which dignity plays a role in complementarity with other values and moral qualities, like liberty, justice, solidarity, vulnerability (65, n. 1).

[112] Van der Ven et al., *Is There a God*, op. cit., 285–294.

New Testament does not see all of humankind as God's image but only Christian humans, only Christian males – or even only Christ, *the* human, *the* man. Patristic writers narrow it down even further. The significance of Christ as the image of God is worked out not only christologically (who Christ is) but also soteriologically (salvation through Christ) and eschatologically (perfection through Christ at the end of time). In scholasticism, the meaning of the image of God is worked out in trinitarian terms. Christians are the image of God in that God's trinity is located in them – in their recognition, knowledge, and love of God. Liberation theology adds an ecclesiological interpretation. The (Christian) community of human beings as the image of God should mould itself on the prototypical communion between Father, Son, and Holy Spirit. Finally there is a spiritual, mystical interpretation, according to which Christ's disciples come closer to the image of God the more they purify their hearts and embark on a mystical transformation process.[113]

Given this rich interpretive background, we return to the Jewish Bible and try to determine the significance of the theme 'image of God' in that context. Modern scholarship has established that it is not a theme that belongs to the Jewish *proprium*, but ended up in the Jewish Bible under the influence, either directly, of Egypt in the 12th or 11th century BCE, or indirectly from Egypt via Assyria, or directly from Assyria round the time of the exile in the 8th century BCE.[114] From the 14th century BCE onwards, it became customary in Egypt to erect statues of gods, so they could manifest themselves in these and be ritually served and worshipped. Statues of kings were also erected and functioned as centres of the royal cult. The convergence of the two cults, in which the king was seen as the image of God, dates back to that time. Thus the god Amon-re told pharaoh Amenophis: "You are my beloved son who came forth from my body, my image whom

---

[113] For these meanings, see W. Seibel, De mens als beeld Gods, in: J. Feiner & M. Löhrer (eds.), *Mysterium Salutis, Dogmatiek in heilshistorisch perspectief 7*, Paul Brand, Hilversum 1968, 266–281; K. Krämer, *Imago Trinitatis: Die Gottebenbildlichkeit des Menschen in der Theologie des Thomas von Aquin*, Herder, Freiburg 2000; K. Waaijman, *Spiritualiteit: Vormen, grondslagen, methoden*, Carmelitana/Kok, Gent/Kampen 2000, 444–451, 507–510; Van der Ven et al., op. cit., *Is There a God*, 291–293; Soulen & Woodhead, *God and Human Dignity*, op. cit., passim.

[114] F. Curtis, *Man as the Image of God in Genesis in the Light of Ancient Near Eastern Parallels*, University Microfilms International, Ann Arbor 1984; K. Koch, *Imago Dei: Die Würde des Menschen im biblischen Text*, Ruprecht, Göttingen 2000.

I have set up on earth."[115] This is probably a kind of relational analogy: just as the god was king of the other gods, so the pharaoh was king of the people.[116] According to some texts, priests, too, were designated images of God. In fact, they sometimes said it about themselves, like one late Ptolemaic priest: "I am your image who originated from you."[117] An exception is the instruction to king Merikare, probably from 2150–2050 BCE, in which ordinary people are called images of God, without any reference to king or priest: "They are his image, who came from his body."[118] This last text indicates that even at that time there were traces of democratisation of the image of God, indicating that it did not happen only at the time of the Jewish Bible, as some exegetes point out. At any rate, in the first book of that Bible, Genesis, the image of God clearly applies to all people without any reference to kings or priests.[119] Neither is there any reference to Jewish individuals or the Jewish people, for the relevant verses are part of the pre-Abrahamite narrative complex of Genesis 1–11, which precedes the calling of Abraham in Genesis 12 and, even more importantly, the institution of circumcision, the prime covenantal attribute of the Jewish people, in Genesis 17.[120]

What, then, is the significance of the image of God? Modern scholars agree that it does not indicate the divine nature of human beings, nor their ontological nature, nor the anthropological quality of the human condition. The term should be regarded as a critical mirror to help combat the absolutist politics of Eastern despotism. It reflects the trinitarian interrelationship between God, king, and *ma'at*. The last term has two dimensions: the proper cultic relationship between humans and God, and proper, lawful relations among human beings. The king is responsible for maintaing *ma'at*, acting as mediator in both relationships. Thus he officiates in both a priestly and a political capacity, so that the 'image of God', transferred from kings and priests to ordinary human beings and applied to them, has a morally functional connotation.

---

[115] See: Curtis, *Man as the Image*, op. cit., 87.
[116] J. Assmann, *Herrschaft und Heil: Politische Theologie in Altägypten, Israel und Europa*, Carl Hanser, München 2000.
[117] See Curtis, *Man as the Image*, op. cit., 92.
[118] See Curtis, *Man as the Image*, op. cit., 91.
[119] E. Zenger, s.v. Priesterschrift, *Lexikon für Theologie und Kirche* 8, Herder, Freiburg 1999, 578–580; Id., s.v. Schöpfung, Ibid. 9, 2000, 217–220; W. Gross, s.v. Gottebenbildlichkeit, Ibid. 4, 1995, 871–873.
[120] Van der Ven et al., *Is There a God*, op. cit., 171–175.

It means that as images of God human beings must ensure right, appropriate, just relations, both vertically between themselves and God, and horizontally among people on earth. This implies special concern for those who profit least by these relations and even suffer as a result of them: the *personae miserae*, specifically widows, orphans, the poor and aliens.[121] Proper treatment of deprived groups is spelled out in the lawbooks of the Jewish Bible, especially the book of covenantal laws (Ex 20:22–23:33), the social lawbook in Deuteronomy (Deut 12–28), and the more pragmatic holiness laws (Lev 17–26).[122]

From this we conclude that human dignity, according to the exegesis of the image of God metaphor in Genesis, has a meaning other than the one commonly attributed to it. It is not official (Cicero), sovereign (Cicero again), project-based (Pico della Mirandola), intrinsic (Kant), or acquired (Hegel), but is based on justice and charity shown to *personae miserae*. Respect for their dignity shows concern for the dignity of 'the least of my brethren', and in that concern God manifests himself, he who heard the cry of his people and reveals himself in the comfort extended to them (Mt 25: 31–46).

4.3.6 *Shari'a*

Having looked at nonreligious and Christian foundations of human rights, we devote some attention to Islamic documents. Some attention indeed, since Muslim reflection on human rights and their foundation in religious concepts is a recent phenomenon. At the same time, that relatively short period has seen some kind of watershed, despite the persistence of some intractable problems. This can be inferred from differences between the Cairo Declaration on Human Rights in Islam (1990), the Arab Charter on Human Rights (1994), the [Revised] Arab Charter on Human Rights (2004), and the Charter of the Organisation of the Islamic Conference (2008). Let me cite some examples of this development to show how the way Islamic documents have incorporated human dignity into their tradition resembles the procedure in the Christian, more especially the Catholic, tradition. Again it is imbedded in a religious network, which prevents exceeding the boundaries of that dignity, this time seen through Islamic eyes.

---

[121] Assmann, *Herrschaft*, op. cit., 63–69; A. Groenewald, *Psalm 69: Its Structure, Redaction and Composition*, Lit, Münster 2003.

[122] Van der Ven et al., *Is There a God*, op. cit., 184–193.

The Cairo declaration mentions human dignity three times: in the preamble, in article 1 as the basis of the equality of all people, and in article 6 of men and women. But the framework in which both the term and the concomitant rights occur is governed entirely by human subjugation to God, the *shari'a*, and the *ummah*. Thus the preamble underscores the importance of human rights and the right to human dignity in accordance with the Islamic *shari'a*, considered to be an integral part of Islam. Article 1 states that all people are members of the same family through subjugation to God and their descent from Adam, and that all humans are subject to God. Life is seen as a gift from God, which can only be infringed if prescribed by the *shari'a* (article 2). Upbringing and education should likewise conform to the *shari'a* (articles 7 and 9). It is forbidden to exercise force or exploit people's poverty or ignorance in order to convert them to a different religion or to atheism (article 10). Slavery, humiliation, oppression, and exploitation are forbidden, for humans are subject to God alone (article 11). Everyone has a right to enjoy scientific, literary, or technical creations, provided these do not contravene the principles of the *shari'a* (article 16). The same applies to freedom of expression (article 22). Crimes are culpable and punishable only in accordance with the *shari'a* (article 19). Blasphemy is forbidden, in the broadest sense, against the prophet and sacred persons or things (sanctities), the faith and moral and ethical values. Corrupting or harming society is likewise prohibited (article 22). Anybody can hold public office in accordance with the *shari'a* (article 23). All rights and liberties are subject to the *shari'a* (article 24), which is the sole source for interpreting every article in the declaration (article 25).

Comparison between the Arab Charter on Human Rights of 2004 and the Cairo declaration reveals what amounts to a watershed. Human dignity is mentioned far more frequently in the charter than in the Cairo declaration, not only in the preamble but also in the description of racism and Zionism as an assault on that dignity (article 2). The term is also used with reference to the equality of men and women (article 3), the treatment of children in the administration of justice (article 17) and that of all other persons (article 19), children's education (article 33), and treatment of handicapped people (article 40). But the cardinal difference is that references to a religious foundation are kept to a minimum. The preamble mentions the creation of humans by God only once, and the articles contain only one reference to the *shari'a*, namely to the equality of men and women in article 3.

The latter uses a terminology that, if not intended ironically (which it is not), suggests a serious problem. The text reads: "Men and women are equal in respect of human dignity, rights and obligations within the framework of the positive discrimination established in favour of women by the Islamic Shariah, other divine laws and by applicable laws and legal instruments" (article 3, 3). Here one discerns a theme that makes the *shari'a* different from the Universal Declaration of Human Rights of 1948, to which the charter, according to the preamble, otherwise adheres. If there is one fundamental disparity, it is the position of women in Muslim personal and family law. It contradicts the prohibition of discrimination that implies equal treatment of all people, irrespective of race, colour, language, religion, or social position and, specifically, sex (article 4). In a sense, this puts the spotlight on the crux of Islamic, personal, and family law. After all, the *shari'a*, that essentially comprises the Qur'an and the *sunna*, the normative example of the Prophet, pertains mainly to personal and family law rather than to contract law and still less to criminal, fiscal or constitutional law.[123] The problem cannot be solved simply by invoking the legal principle of margin of appreciation. That is the competence of countries to interpret and concretise international treaties on human rights in terms of their own context and laws, which is what the reference to the laws in force in different countries is aimed at (article 33). This would not further equality between men and women and would in fact entrench inequality.

The article contains a further problem. Article 33 states that the family is the natural, fundamental social group, based on marriage between a man and a woman. It fails to mention polygamy and is also not easily reconciled with article 23 of the International Covenant on Civil and Political rights, which contains no definition of marriage.[124] The latter merely mentions the right of men and women to marry at a marriageable age and found a family. Comment 28 of the Human Rights Committee says that article 23 should be taken to imply acceptance of different forms of family life, like unmarried couples with children and single-parent families. It could also include same-sex marriages and adoptive parents. Again one observes that the problem

---

[123] A.A. An-Na'im, *Toward an Islamic Reformation: Civil Liberties, Human Rights, and International Law*, Syracuse University Press, New York 1996, 32.

[124] The same applies to article 10 of the international covenant on socio economic rights.

cannot be solved with reference to the margin of appreciation.[125] In any case it offers no solution to the plight of women, quite apart from the aforementioned 'alternative' forms of marriage and family life.

The preamble to the Charter of the Organisation of the Islamic Conference (2008) refers to human dignity – as well as peace, charity, tolerance, equality, and justice – as an Islamic value without mentioning the *shari'a* at all. It maintains that women's rights have to be respected and secured, as well as their participation in all spheres of life, but with the rider that it must be done in accordance with the laws and legislation of member states. Article 1 again refers to women's rights, in conjunction with the rights of children, youths, the aged, and people with special needs, but in the same breath it adds that Muslim family values need to be protected. At the beginning of this section I spoke about a kind of watershed between earlier and more recent documents. It consists in a gradual decrease in references to the *shari'a*. But I also mentioned an intractable problem. It is glaring: in Muslim countries personal and family law, in which the inequality of women and homosexuals persist, are a real obstacle.

How long will real change take? Those who favour human rights without any restriction by the *shari'a* probably have the advantage, if one considers popular opinion. Research shows that in most countries only a minority regard the *shari'a* as the sole source of law, and assign religious leaders a substantial role in determining the constitution.[126] The majority see the *shari'a* as one of the sources.[127] On the other hand, the majority of jurists and other Islamic scholars defend the status quo, in which the *shari'a* remains the only or dominant source of legislation. This means that not only discrimination against women and homosexuals will continue, but also the oppression of religious minorities. Moreover, the emphasis laid on God's rule, and by implication the *shari'a*, means that leading politicians consider themselves absolved from the obligation to account for their policies to the public. Their power is legitimised not by the sovereignty of the

---

[125] Cf. M. Baderin, *International Human Rights and Islamic Law*, Oxford University Press, Oxford 2005, passim.

[126] *Muslim World*, Special Report, Gallup Poll, World Poll, Gallup Center Muslims Studies 2008; D. Price, *Islamic Political Culture, Democracy and Human Rights: A comparative Study*, Praeger, Westport 1999.

[127] J. Esposito & D. Mogahed, *Who Speaks for Islam? What a Billion Muslims Really Think*, Gallup, New York 2007, 48.

people, but by the sovereignty of God.[128] What is more, in contrast to secularising developments in Islamic law since the 19th century, there has been a re-islamisation in recent decades, especially in the area of personal, marriage and family law, law of succession and parts of criminal law.[129]

4.3.7 Interfoundational Discourse

From the foregoing it should be evident that there is not just one foundation of human rights but a diversity of several particular foundations. Yet this poses a problem. It is not merely that adherents of every religious or nonreligious worldview hold theirs to be the only true 'orthodox' one and reject, (mildly) criticise, or ignore any similar claims by adherents of other worldviews.[130] In fact, logically there cannot be two orthodoxies. But the real problem is how such claims by religious and nonreligious worldviews, made for good reasons from their insider perspective, should be interpreted in a globalising world that is becoming increasingly aware of the plurality of religious and nonreligious worldviews. There are three approaches to the problem.

The first is that, while the existence of pluralism is acknowledged as a fact, it is not recognised and respected as such. This can assume two forms: exclusiveness and inclusiveness. The former regards other religious and nonreligious worldviews as false or heretical, the latter sees them as containing only rudiments, elements, traces of the truth of one's own worldview. Both forms are found in all worldviews – including nonreligious ones, Christianity, and Islam. In both forms the starting point is a participant perspective from one's own worldview, which remains focal. It means sticking to a mono-centric worldview, a mono-religious approach, albeit with some nuances.

The second approach is that of worldview-related liberalism, especially 20th century Protestant liberalism. What it boils down to is that adherents of a given worldview believe that, according to their individual and/or collective subjective belief, hence from their own participant perspective, it is a unique, absolute, universal belief system, but

---

[128] M. Rohe, *Das Islamische Recht: Geschichte und Gegenwart*, Beck, München 2009, 242–254.

[129] Rohe, *Das Islamische Recht*, op. cit., 395–400.

[130] J. Locke, *Epistola de tolerantia (A Letter on Toleration)*, Edited by Raymond Klibansky, translated by J.W. Gough, Clarendon, Oxford 1968, 83.

believe so not dogmatically and without passing any negative judgment on the meaning and value of any other worldview. In addition they try to observe, describe, and interpret every worldview, including their own, as impartially as possible from an observer perspective – certainly not neutrally, but as impartially as possible. Hence there is an alternation of participant and observer perspectives in a more or less compartmentalised way, in various capacities and functions and at different times: as a preacher in the pulpit and an impartial educator at a podium, as officiant at an altar and unprejudiced lecturer of a course, as a pastor in a counselling situation and an open-minded researcher in a library.[131]

The third approach does not consist in compartmentalised alternation of the two perspectives, but in complementary use of both – what one might call a critically reflective style. One's commitment, from a participant perspective, to one's own worldview, which makes its historical claim to uniqueness, absoluteness, and universality understandable, is broadened by self-critical reflection on it based on recognition of, and discourse with, other worldviews. In so doing, one views one's own belief system not only in terms of personal engagement with it, but also through the eyes of outsiders, and so one changes from a 'unilingual' to a 'bilingual' or 'multilingual' believer, one who does not put herself and her own worldview at the centre of the world but is a 'de-centred' believer. This is counter to a conception of truth as a jealously guarded, fiercely defended treasure house (*depositum fidei*). It presupposes an uninhibited relation between freedom and truth, in which the truth claims of one's own worldview and that of others are freely explored. It entails more than just adopting a tolerant attitude, however important that may be. It means that truths that are taken for granted are explicitly contradicted in a fiery interaction between statement and refutation, in order to purge and refine them, perhaps partly reconciling them, which could mean provisionally reconciling them – provisionally, because Truth with a capital T continually eludes the dialogue partners. John Stuart Mill pointed out that in this context it is fitting to be genuinely convinced of one's beliefs and to say so outright. But it would be wrong to assume a certain infallibility by defending this belief by arguing that it is infallible – for that is obviously not

---

[131] T. Masuzawa, *The Invention of World Religions*, University of Chicago Press, Chicago 2005, 107–119.

an argument. One assumes infallibility if one professes to others that it is infallible for them as well, without giving them an opportunity to voice their criticism of it or even listening to their objections.[132] What is needed is what one could call agonistic respect: respect for the views expressed and the participants in the discourse in which the matter is critically disputed.[133] Sound appraisal of any belief requires flexible perspectivism. This implies both a continuous exchange of participant perspectives from the I/we position and the you position, and a continuous exchange of the participant perspective from the I/we position and the observer perspective from the he/she/they position.[134]

For the conduct of such a discourse, we may learn something from the way a court operates. Let us picture an imaginary judge dealing with two opposing parties: their lawyers and witnesses in a lawsuit.[135] What does this imaginary judge do? Let me subdivide the process of judgment, somewhat artificially, into three stages. First, the judge takes the parties and their lawyers seriously, treats them as equals, and assumes their authenticity and sincerity. He hears the parties as well as their lawyers out as fully as possible and takes note of the information provided by their witnesses and expert witnesses. In addition the judge takes into account the specific situations of the two parties, especially factors that determine their singularity, uniqueness, precariousness, and vulnerability. Second, before passing judgment he weighs the arguments for and against the claims pressed by the parties and their lawyers, and tries to determine the pros and cons, effects and side effects of these. Finally, he pronounces a judgment, advancing a concise argument for it. In so doing he passes what Kant would call – in a different context – a reflective judgment.[136] Ricoeur for his part would

---

[132] J.S. Mill, *On Liberty*, University of Toronto Press, Toronto 1977.

[133] W. Connolly, *Identity/Difference: Democratic Negotiations of Political Paradox*, University of Minnesota Press, Minneapolis 1991.

[134] J.A. van der Ven, A Chapter in Public Theology from the Perspective of Human Rights: Interreligious Interaction and Dialogue in an Intercivilizational Context, *Journal of Religion* 86(2006)3, 412–441.

[135] P. Ricoeur, *La mémoire, l'histoire, l'oubli*, Seuil, Paris 2000, 413–436; G. Lohmann, Unparteilichkeit in der Moral, in: L. Wingert & K. Günther, *Die Öffentlichkeit der Vernunft and die Vernunft der Öffentlichkeit*. Festschrift für Jürgen Habermas, Suhrkamp, Frankfurt 2001, 434–455.

[136] Here one can draw on ideas on the development of reflective judgment in I. Kant, *Kritische Urteilskraft*, English translation, *Critique of Judgment*, Hafner, New York 1951; A. Ferrara, *The Force of the Example: Explorations in the Paradigm of Judgment (New Directions in Critical Theory)*, Columbia University Press, New York 2008.

call it an 'attestatory judgment', that is to say, a judgment that is frag-
ile, albeit carefully considered, based not on mathematical proof but
on reasonable insight, and on prudential rather than logical decision;
a judgment not intended to stand for all eternity, but based on current
data and insight, which may come up for review if new information or
insight is ever presented.[137]

What judgments could result from our imaginary judge's operations
in an interfoundational discourse between nonreligious and religious
parties? Let us suppose he passes two different judgments. In the first,
he may judge that the emphasis on absolute human autonomy by the
nonreligious parties has to be relativized when it comes to birth and
death: we did not choose life and we shall not choose not to die. Maybe
he will add that the nonreligious parties do not show sufficient awareness of the fundamental contingency in the vicissitudes of human life.
He may also point out the dialectics between situation and freedom
and between situation and guilt, from which it dialectically follow that
we are guilty of causing evil in situations where we encounter evil –
what Augustinian Christianity has disputably designated 'original sin'
with all the sexual connotations of the term.[138] In the second judgment,
he might criticise the religious parties for not being sufficiently aware
of the violence that their beliefs and actions provoke, accompany, and/
or legitimise. He may point out that their accent on the ideal of harmony and peace is blind to individual and collective forces in society
and those in their own ranks which combat this ideal, and even may
transform it into its opposite. He may decide that they apply double
standards when they prohibit discrimination against women, homosexuals, and religious minorities in the outside world, but permit it in
their own ranks and even explicitly legitimise it.

Conclusion

In other words, interfoundational discourse under the leadership of
our imaginary judge will ideally purify the notions and convictions

---

[137] P. Ricoeur, *Oneself*, op. cit., 21–23, 129, 297–356; Id., *Le Juste*, Seuil, Paris 1995,
185–192; Id, *La mémoire*, op. cit., 413–336; J. Searle, *Rationality in Action*, MIT, Cambridge 2001, 61–96.

[138] P. Ricoeur, *The Conflict of Interpretations*, Northwest University Press, Evanston
1974, 269–286.

that the nonreligious and religious parties consider to be a necessary foundation for human rights. But such purification will not put an end to the plurality of particular foundations. These will remain, only they will – ideally speaking – be seen as less incompatible. Recognition of pluralism is a great good, one of the basic principles of democracy. The alternative is oppression and dictatorship. Hence the choice of an open foundation for the Universal Declaration of Human Rights taken by Mrs Roosevelt's commission and, on its advice, the United Nations in 1948 was a wise one.

CHAPTER FIVE

HUMAN RIGHTS: NATURAL OR POLITICAL?

According to the German historian Wolfgang Schmale, natural law ended up on the guillotine along with the *ancien régime*.[1] Here and there one still finds jurists, ethicists, and theologians trying to legitimise human rights in terms of natural law, but by and large it is pretty well a dead duck. There is, however, one exception: the Catholic Church. To put it somewhat generally, pope Leo XIII started the legitimisation of human rights in terms of natural law in 1891, and pope Benedict XVI became the most recent proponent in 2008.[2] What happened in the interim is the theme of this chapter. To that end, I give a historical account of the legitimisation of human rights in terms of natural law in ecclesiastic documents from Leo XIII to Benedict XVI (5.1), and then highlight political aspects of natural law in these, especially with regard to the relation between church and state (5.2). I proceed to reconstruct the development of the legitimisation of human rights in terms of nature and politics (5.3). That is followed by a conclusion.

5.1 Legitimisation of Human Rights in Terms of Nature

Natural law as a basis for the organisation of individual and social life dates back to Greek and Roman antiquity, and was perpetuated in the patristic and scholastic periods. But the heavy emphasis in official ecclesiastic documents first surfaced in the debate on the socio-economic problems of workers in the course of the 19th century.[3] Since then, natural law has been embraced by church leadership and

---

[1] W. Schmale, Das Naturrecht in Frankreich zwischen Prärevolution und Terror, in: O. Dann & D. Klippel (eds.), *Naturrecht, Spätaufklärung, Revolution*, Meiner, Berlin 1995, 5–22, here 22.

[2] Benedict XVI, *Meeting with the Members of the General Assembly of the United Nations Organization*, New York, Friday 18 April 2008.

[3] J. Fuchs, *Lex naturae, zur Theologie des Naturrechts*, Patmos, Düsseldorf 1955; F.-X. Kaufmann, Wissenssoziologische Überlegungen zu Renaissance und Niedergang des katholischen Naturrechtsdenken im 19. und 20. Jahrhundert, in: F. Böckle & E.-W. Böckenförde (eds.), *Naturrecht in der Kritik*, Grünewald, Mainz 1973, 126–164.

its rejection branded heretical.[4] In my view, however, it is no more than a spatio-temporal, conceptual theological tool (*theologoumenon*), with a historical rise and a historical decline, even though the recent Compendium of the Social Doctrine of the Church glosses that over.[5] Below I analyse the rise of natural law (5.1.1) and its fall (5.1.2), in the course of which I allow myself some sorties into history.

5.1.1   Rise of Natural Law

I have pointed out that natural law made its debut in official ecclesiastic documents fairly recently, when it was accorded prominence in the first two social encyclicals, Leo XIII's *Rerum Novarum* (1891), and Pius XI's *Quadragesimo Anno* (1931).[6] Because of the neo-scholastic spirit prevailing in the church at the time, there are frequent, more or less apposite references to Thomas Aquinas. Hence I note some pertinent aspects of his thinking on natural law.

Society in Thomas's day had three estates: the clergy for spiritual tasks, the feudal nobility for military functions, and innumerable agricultural vassals for material tasks. In the worldview of the intellectual elite – in this case the clergy – these estates and everything around them were conjoined in an objective, cosmological order. That order was eternal, independent of humans, and all-encompassing. Everything and everybody had a fixed position in it. This view obstructed every

---

[4] *Syllabus Errorum* (1864) of pope Pius IX: H. Denzinger, *Kompendium der Glaubensbekenntnisse und kirchliche Lehrentscheidungen*, P. Hünermann, Herder, Freiburg, 2005, 2956.

[5] *Compendium of the Social Doctrine of the Church*, Libreria Editrice Vaticana, United States Conference of Catholic Bishops, Washington 2005.

[6] The encyclical *Rerum Novarum* only appeared in 1891, even though many Catholic individuals and groups had been concerned about the workers ever since the early 19th century with the transition from mercantile to industrial capitalism. There was some dissension on the course to be adopted to ameliorate their lot. The Catholic Romantic school wanted to revert to the feudal structure and the *ancien régime*. The *L'Avenir* school advocated liberal, civil, and political freedoms, at the same time attacking exploitation of workers and seeking to combat it by modifying the capitalist system. The Christian socialists wanted to put an end to two-class society, not through a class struggle but by restoring equality by way of production cooperatives. Alongside and cutting across these differences, the Liège school fought for state interventionism, while the Angers school looked to private initiative and the revival of charity for a solution. To remedy the lack of consensus Leo XIII appointed a commission of inquiry in 1882, the 'intimate committee', which expanded into the Union of Freiburg after 1884 and whose ideas provided the raw material for *Rerum Novarum* (C. van Gestel, *Kerk en sociale orde*, Universitas, Leuven 1956, 19–62; J. Racine, *Rerum Novarum* en zijn ontstaansgeschiedenis, *Communio* 6(1981), 127–138).

attempt to intervene actively in society, the more so because all energy
was absorbed by the sheer struggle for survival in the midst of natural
disasters, famines, epidemics, insurrections, and wars.[7]

God was seen as the acme and basis of the objective cosmological
order. In his bounteous goodness, he brought into existence an
immeasurable universe of creatures, which he governed in his wisdom. These creatures all shared in divine goodness at their own levels:
angels, human souls, human bodies, animals, plants, and things, each
according to its own degree. They did so inasmuch as they portrayed
and imitated God's goodness. They thus returned to their creator. That
made the order teleological. Even creatures at the bottom of the scale
shared in God's goodness, be it ever so marginally, and even though
they barely escaped non-existence. However low they were on the
scale, they were indispensable elements of the hierarchy. In such an
order it was fitting for lower beings to suffer at the hands of higher
ones, even to be destroyed by them. But without them there could be
no all-encompassing order: it would annihilate the principle of wholeness. The order formed a Great Chain of Being, a huge, many-tiered,
interrelated universe.[8]

According to Thomas, this objective order was subject to four kinds
of laws.[9] The first was eternal law (*lex aeterna*), consisting in God's
eternal, all-embracing wisdom that governed the cosmos in regulated,
measured fashion, with God as its origin and goal.

The second is natural law (*lex natura*) that shares in Eternal Reason
and God's wise governance, of which it is a reflection.[10] Its origin and
goal is God, just as nature has God as its origin and goal and shares

---

[7] J. Le Goff, *La civilization de l'Occident médiéval*, Arthaud, Paris 1984, Dutch
translation: *De cultuur van middeleeuws Europa*, Wereldbibliotheek, Amsterdam
1987, 166–405.

[8] This cosmological order offers a 'solution' to the problem of giving chance a teleologically oriented grounding, and of tragedy and suffering that are seen as divinely
willed, permitted, or accommodated. Hence, as Leibniz was to aver later, the existing
world is the best world possible. A. Lovejoy, *The Great Chain of Being: A Study of the
History of an Idea*, Harvard University Press, Cambridge 1978, 24–98; Ch. Taylor, *A
Secular Age*, Harvard University Press, Cambridge 2007, passim. The cosmological
order still features in Locke and Hutcheson (Ch. Taylor, *Sources of the Self*, Harvard University Press, Cambridge 1989, 259–265, 275). This Great Chain of Being
still determines today's conception of progress in evolution theory, see: Chr. Buskes,
Evolutionair denken: De invloed van Darwin op ons wereldbeeld. Nieuwezijds, Amsterdam 2006, 407–410.

[9] Thomas Aquinas, *Summa Theologica* (Abbr.: STh), I–II, 91.

[10] STh, I–II, 94.

in his Eternal Reason. It is knowable to human reason. A fundamental
rule in natural law is that one must do good and refrain from evil. All
other rules are based on that. For example: nobody must be harmed,
there must be no killing, anyone who commits a crime must be punished. These rules apply always and everywhere. There are also rules
for natural human inclinations. The first of these humans share with
all beings: the tendency to self-preservation. The second they share
with animals, mainly concern for progeny, including sexual relations
and nurture. The third inclination is specifically human: an inclination to goodness in accordance with human reason. An example of
the latter is the natural inclination to gain knowledge of God and live
in a community. Whichever inclination is at issue, it only forms part
of natural law inasmuch as its is governed by reason. Hence 'nature'
in natural law is ultimately not nature in the broad sense, but human
nature, more especially the rational nature of human beings.[11]

The third law is human law (*lex humana*). This is positive law which
governments infer from natural law. Here there are two qualifications.
The precepts in these inferences become less valid the more they go
into particulars.[12] The more detailed determinations (*determinationes*)
that act as concrete instances of the inference are not part of natural law but of human law, deriving their validity exclusively from the
latter.[13] An example is determining the kind and severity of punishment to be administered. A human law that contravenes natural law is
not binding, is not law but a perversion of the law. This applies even
when such a law is based on common consent.[14] For the rest, consent
is not irrelevant. When not just one but many laws meet with consistent unanimous resistance, Thomas maintains, rebellion against the
tyrant is warranted, provided it does not lead to greater harm. In such
a situation the tyrant himself is the rebel.[15]

---

[11] J. Arntz, Die Entwicklung des naturrechtlichen Denkens innerhalb des Thomis-
mus, F. Böckle (ed.), *Das Naturrecht im Disput*, Patmos, Düsseldorf 1966, 97–100; J.-P.
Wils, *Nachsicht, Studiën zu einer ethisch-hermeneutischen Basiskategorie*, Schöningh,
Paderborn 2006, passim.

[12] STh, I–II 94, 4.

[13] STh, I–II 95, 2.

[14] STh, II–II 57, 2.

[15] STh, II–II 42, 2, ad 3; see: B. Delfgaauw, *Thomas van Aquino: Een kritische benadering van zijn filosofie*, Wereldvenster, Bussum 1980, 164–173.

The fourth law is divine law (*lex divina*), viz. the law of the Old Testament (*lex vetus*) and the law of the New Testament (*lex nova*), the latter exceeding the first.[16]

To Thomas, natural law does not consist in reading nature, but in actions based on practical reason with the aim of ordering nature. Nature is a pre-moral substrate. It does not determine the moral quality of actions, for that consists in practical reason ordering nature for a moral purpose.

This interpretation of Thomas with its accent on ordering nature through practical reason is not uncontested. After all, it depends on whether the emphasis in natural law is on nature or on practical reason that is used to order nature. Thus some scholars focus on nature, concentrating on the links between human nature and that of animals (*animalia*).[17] Here they cite a particular Thomist tenet, to the effect that not only – rational – human nature shares in Eternal Reason, but nature generally, which includes non-rational beings.[18] Here we need not decide whether or not this interpretation is correct. For the purpose of our argument below, we proceed from our first interpretation: nature is ordered by practical reason.

To what extent do the aforementioned encyclicals on the social issue, *Rerum Novarum* and *Quadragesimo Anno*, correspond with the Thomist conception outlined above?[19] I mention some points of agreement and three relevant differences.

Both in Thomas's writings and the two encyclicals, the term 'order' refers to an objective collective of creatures that together constitute a whole, independent of any human intervention. It is a hierarchically ranked whole, structured teleologically with God as its origin and goal. Finally, via practical reason it is the guideline for action.

But there are also differences. They relate to the following three aspects: the concept of order, the methodical approach and natural rights. Let me shortly elaborate on these aspects.

The objective order that is basic to Thomist thought is cosmological and metaphysical. The moral order forms part of it. In the two

---

[16] STh I–II 91, 5, ad 2.

[17] P. Westerman, *The Disintegration of Natural Law Theory: Aquinas to Finnis*, Brill, Leiden 1997, 21–47; cf. R. George (ed.), *Natural Law*, Ashgate, Dartmouth 2002.

[18] STh, I–II 91, 2, ad 3.

[19] These encyclicals, as well as other documents cited below, are referred to by initial letters only, for instance RN (*Rerum Novarum*) and QA (*Quadragesimo Anno*); numerals refer to section numbers in the documents.

encyclicals, on the other hand, the objective order is almost totally moral. It is almost entirely confined to the sphere of action, approached from a moral perspective. While it may have occasional metaphysical overtones, its predominant character is moral. One could almost say that the encyclicals conform to the modern notion that morality can exist without a cosmological, metaphysical grounding.[20] In the two encyclicals the moral order comprises a three-tiered hierarchy.[21] The first tier is economic values. These are instrumental for the second tier, which includes health, civilisation, culture, human development, and community. These in their turn are subservient to values at the top level, consisting of religion and worship of God (RN 18–21; QA 41–43; 75).

There is a second difference. Whereas Thomas, as noted already, recognises nature as a moral substrate, for the ordering of this nature in terms of practical reason he adopts a specific methodical approach, viz. a deductive one. Lower rules are deduced from higher ones and higher ones from the supreme rule, namely doing good and refraining from evil. The same deductive approach is used when applying the rules to concrete instances. In so doing, the method becomes less valid as it descends to the concrete level. As a result, the more detailed determinations belong to human law, not to natural law.

The two encyclicals, by contrast, combine an inductive and deductive method. That is nothing new. Hugo de Groot did the same. According to him, the deductive method consists in inferring and applying rules from natural law to concrete situations, while the inductive proceeds from pertinent real-life situations.[22] De Groot observes that analysis of concrete situations does not yield the incontrovertible certainty that the deductive method offers, but simply a proximately certain probability.[23] The concrete situations that De Groot considers relevant are taken from international law; in other words, they are rules applicable in all morally higher principled (*moratiores*) nations, including 'wild'

---

[20] P. Ricoeur, *Réflexion faite*, Esprit, Paris 1995, 83–115; Id., *Oneself as Another*, University of Chicago Press, Chicago 1990; A. Saberschinsky, *Die Begründung universeller Menschenrechte*, Schönigh, Paderborn 2002.

[21] N. Monzel, *Die Katholische Kirche in der Sozialgeschichte*, Olzog Verlag, München 1980, 241.

[22] H. Grotius, *De jure belli ac pacis*, II, XXIII, l; C. Larrère, Droit naturel et scepticisme, P.-F. Moreau, *Le scepticisme au XVe et au XVIIe siècle*, Tome II, Albin Michel, Paris 2001, 293–308.

[23] Grotius, *De jure*, op. cit. I, XII.

and 'inhumane' ones.[24] This international law is not the law governing relations between nations (*jus inter gentes*), but the communal law of nations (*jus omnium gentium commune*).[25] It reinforces the precepts of natural law, because it overlaps it in major respects without being identical with it.

As noted already, the two encyclicals differ from Thomas in that they combine a deductive and an inductive method, but they also differ from De Groot's combination. Firstly, they lack the differentiation that the inductive method offers only proximately certain probabilities. As a result, their pronouncements on the rules of natural law sound as if they are beyond all doubt, whereas they are (partly) based purely on relevant concrete situations. This leads to a logical is/ought fallacy, because the reasoning proceeds from facts to normative pronouncements. Secondly, in their inductive method the encyclicals do not take their relevant facts from global and trans-historical law of nations, as De Groot did, but from the spatio-temporally defined situation of workers in Western society at the time of the transition from mercantile to industrial capitalism. From this they infer natural rights. That highlights the aforementioned logical error all the more.

The third and final difference concerns the two natural rights that are centre stage in the encyclicals: the rights to fair wages and to property. The right to fair wages is 'natural', because without it people cannot take care of themselves and cannot survive. Thus the right derives from an even more fundamental natural right, the right to life (RN 44; QA 63–75).

The right to property relates to the right to fair wages, the reason being that people work for wages in order to acquire property (RN 5). They have the right to convert their wages into property (RN 9). Two arguments are presented. The first is anthropological. It maintains that humans are not beings whose consciousness focuses exclusively on the here and now: it includes past and future as well. They are able to make provision for the future and to assure this by accumulating property (RN 7). The second argument is institutional. Human beings –

---

[24] Grotius, *De jure*, op. cit. I, I, XII, 2. I render De Groot's *moratiores* with 'morally higher principled' rather than the 'more civilised' (*meer beschaafd*) in A. Eyffmger & B. Vermeulen's translation, *Hugo de Groot. Denken over oorlog en vrede*, Ambo, Baarn 1991, 65. After all, 'wild and inhumane' peoples, counter to Renaissance ideas, could ultimately be morally superior; see R. Tuck, *Natural rights theories: their origin and development*, Cambridge University Press, Cambridge 1998, 32–81.

[25] B. Bernardi, *Le principe d'obligation*, Vrin, Paris 2007, 109.

that is, man (!) – have a duty to provide for their families. They can do so only by accumulating property and leaving it as a legacy for their children (RN 13). This duty derives from marriage which, besides being a natural law, is also a divine one (RN 12). *Quadragesimo Anno* calls the right to property both a divine and a natural law (QA 45).

Are these two rights consonant with earlier – especially Thomist – tradition? According to that tradition, a fair wage must cover at least the worker's sustenance, and, according to some scholastic scholars, that of the family as well.[26] But as far as I know there is no natural law justification for such a right. The encyclicals base it on the factual situation of workers as proletarians, thus creating a new natural right.

The question of the consonance of the right to property with earlier tradition is even more complex. On the strength of a long tradition, Thomas rejects private property as a natural right, because he regards common property and its use (*ususfructus*) as a natural right. He only recognises property as a positive human right, citing three advantages: it makes people more prudent so as to secure it, work harder for it, and have less conflict about it.[27]

After Thomas, the debate on the natural-law status of property became more focused, concentrating in a struggle between the Dominicans and the Franciscans. It centred on the question whether the vow of evangelical poverty was compatible with property, either individual or collective, as a natural right, or only with usufruct. The Dominicans sided against Thomas, a member of their order, in favour of property as a natural right; the Franciscans settled for usufruct only. Pope Innocent IV concurred with the Dominicans in 1250, but in 1279 pope Nicholas II sided with the Franciscans. In 1329 John XXII finally opted for the Dominican position. Indirectly that conferred natural law legitimacy on burgeoning mercantile capitalism.[28]

In other words, the encyclicals disregard Thomas and concur with John XXII's decision of 1329. They recognise not only usufruct but the right to property as a natural right. It is probably an exaggeration to call the combination of usufruct, which is aimed at general welfare, and the right to individual property contradictory. But it certainly

---

[26] Van Gestel, *Kerk*, op. cit., 188.
[27] STh, II–II, 66.
[28] R. Tuck, Tuck, *The Rights of War and Peace: Political Thought and the International Order from Grotius to Kant*, Oxford University Press, Oxford 1999, 17–24.

creates an awkward tension. It is by no means clear how the two are to be reconciled, if that is at all possible.[29]

5.1.2   Decline of Natural Law

As in our discussion of the rise of natural law in the social encyclicals, we can explain the decline of natural law in terms of the three aspects mentioned in the previous section: the concept of order, the methodical approach, and rights.

Order
Regarding the concept of order, it is noteworthy that natural law gradually shifted from a metaphysical cosmological order, via a moral order, to a hierarchy of values, and via these to human dignity, as we will see in a moment. What vestiges of natural law remained fulfilled an ornamental and ideological rather than a conceptual, substantive function. While that highlights what is called "the eternal truth of the social teaching of the Catholic Church" that penetrates and permeates new circumstances, as the *Compendium* would have it, it obscures the discontinuity.[30]

Whereas *Rerum Novarum* and *Quadragesimo Anno* devote some attention to human dignity, they do so more or less in passing.[31] A new feature in Pius XII's speeches – to which he confined himself, since his predecessors had already dealt with the essentials in their encyclicals – is that he put the spotlight on the dignity of the human person. He based it on the creation of humans in the image of God, as well as on the relation between humans and God as a reciprocal 'you' and 'I'.[32] These tenets form the basis for a series of individual rights that are innovations on the earlier encyclicals, which mention only the rights to wages and property. The new rights include the right to preserve and develop bodily, moral, spiritual, and religious life; private and public worship; charity; marital and family life; work; free occupational choice and practice; and free choice regarding civil state.[33]

---

[29] G. Teeple, *The Riddle of Human Rights*, Garamond, Aurora 2005, 34–35.
[30] *Compendium*, op. cit., 38–39.
[31] *Rerum Novarum*, no. 20, 36, 40; *Quadragesimo Anno*, no. 23, 28, 50, 83, 101, 119, 136; cf. Saberschinsky, *Begründung*, op. cit., 66–67.
[32] A.-F. Utz & J.-F. Groner, *Aufbau und Entfaltung des gesellschaftlichen Lebens: Soziale Summe Pius XII*, Paulusverlag, Freiburg 1954, nos. 27–30 and 152.
[33] Utz & Groner, *Aufbau*, op. cit., nos. 252 and 515.

Human dignity is basic to societal institutions, which are seen as a network of individual persons. Besides being the premise, the human person is also the goal of society.[34]

In his encyclical *Mater et Magistra* (1961), pope John XXIII pursues this track and puts personal dignity at the centre (MM 114). The concern is not with 'the' (ontologically determined) person but with actual human persons (plural: *singuli homines* – MM 219). More concretely than in Pius XII's version, they constitute the basis, origin, and goal of all social institutions (MM 219). It is as individual persons that they have human dignity, actually referred to as 'sacred' human dignity (MM 220).[35]

In *Pacem in Terris* (1963) John XXIII again puts the spotlight on human dignity. That emerges even in the introduction, which describes humans as created in God's image and likeness, endowed with reason and freedom (PT 3). The human person, bearer of this dignity, has to order relations among people, between people and the state, and between the state and the world community (PT 4–7). In this order, human persons, by virtue of their dignity, have rights and obligations (PT 8–10).

Methodical Approach
That is not the only innovation. Another is the evolution of Thomas's deductive approach, via the deductive-inductive combination of the first social encyclicals, to an ever greater emphasis on the inductive approach, notably in *Pacem in Terris* and the constitution of Vatican II on the church and the world in our day, *Gaudium et Spes* (1965). A clear indicator is the concept 'signs of the times'. The substance of this concept features throughout the encyclical *Pacem in Terris*, for instance in the 'characteristics of our time' at the end of part 1 on the description of the striving for equality by workers, women, and underdeveloped nations (PT 39–45); at the end of part 2 on the individual and the state, the constitution and human rights (PT 75–79); at the end of part 3 on order between states (PT 126–129); and elsewhere in the growing realisation that international conflicts should be resolved through negotiation rather than by force of arms (PT 126–129).

---

[34] Saberschinsly, *Begründung*, op. cit., 189, 286–287.
[35] Also see MM 21, 83, 84, 179, 191, 192, 215, 216, 255, 259.

In *Gaudium et Spes* the term 'signs of the times' is expounded as a scrutiny of present-day trends so as to interpret them in the light of the gospel (GS 4; 11). This is done by way of a methodical approach with three phases, evident in the discussion of society (23–39), culture (53–62), economics (63–72), and politics (73–76). The first phase consists in socio-scientifically based description, the second in moral-anthropological analysis of what they mean in terms of human dignity, and the third in an evaluative interpretation in terms of traces of divine grace.[36] Hence these ecclesiastic documents not only use the social sciences and switch from a deductive to a concomitant inductive moral method, but also ground these in a new religious self-understanding. This is rooted in the basic concept of the church, which Vatican II refers to as a sacrament. Calling the church a sacrament means that what salvation occurs in society is interpreted and perfected in the church in the light of divine salvation.[37]

Rights

Finally, when it comes to rights, it is noteworthy that, like Pius XII, the documents mention not only fair wages and property, but a whole string of rights. These are no longer linked with natural law, for the term hardly features in *Pacem in Terris* and *Gaudium et Spes*, certainly not in a conceptual, substantive sense.[38] Instead of natural law (singular), the term 'rights' occupies an important place in the two documents. In *Pacem in terris*, some rights are called natural rights; in *Gaudium et Spes*, rights are presented just as rights, without the qualification 'natural'.

The presentation in *Pacem in Terris* is rather confusing (PT nos. 11–27). It mentions a number of natural rights, like respect, culture, education, freedom of religion, work and decent working conditions, fair wages, property, and freedom of association and assembly. Other

---

[36] The second moral/anthropological phase deals with questions like the following: What is a human being? What is the meaning of suffering, evil, death – which persist in the face of all progress? What is the point of these victories gained at such a huge price? What can humans do for society and what can they expect from it? What comes after earthly life? (GS 10; cf. 12–22).

[37] *Lumen Gentium*, Dogmatic constitution on the church, Vatican II, no. 1.

[38] *Pacem in Terris* refers to natural law only in nos. 28 and 30 to indicate the reciprocity of rights and obligations (in that order!), in no. 81 in which natural law and natural dignity are mentioned in the same breath, and in nos. 124, 133 and 160 in relation to the connection between natural and international law, without any conceptual elaboration. The same applies to *Gaudium et Spes*, nos. 74, 79 and 89.

rights, like the right of founding a family, are not called natural rights, but are connected with something that appears similar, in this case 'the family as the natural, primary cell of human society', whereas a right that is closely connected with it, like the freedom to choose one's civil state, lacks any legitimisation. Yet other rights are legitimised exclusively in terms of human dignity, like economic and political rights and the right to legal protection of rights. Finally, other rights are presented without any legitimisation at all, such as the right to life, which covers a broad range: bodily integrity and proper human development, especially in terms of nutrition; clothing; shelter; medical care, rest, and social benefits in the event of sickness, disability as a result of work, widowhood, old age, and enforced unemployment. One might ask whether these latter rights are so self-evident that they require no legitimisation. A special case is the right to migration, which also lacks legitimisation. A precursor may be found in the appeal of Pius XII, predecessor of John XXIII, to take emigration and immigration problems seriously, since human dignity is at issue.[39] But Pius XII's appeal does not amount to a right, in the sense of being referred to as such in *Pacem in Terris* (no. 25), and the later encyclical of Paul VI, *Octogesimo anno* (no. 17). The 1948 Universal Declaration of Human Rights of the United Nations does recognise individuals' right to leave their countries and return to them (article 13) as well as the right to asylum in the case of political persecution (article 14), but there is no mention of a right to immigration in a general sense. This raises the question of what legitimisation the Vatican connects with the right to immigration. Is there any?[40]

Gaudium et Spes displays a more consistent image than *Pacem in Terris*. It does not legitimise rights as natural rights, but only in connection with human dignity. The entire first part of chapter I deals with the theological and christological aspects of the dignity of the

---

[39] Utz & Groner, *Aufbau*, op. cit., nos. 4023–4026.

[40] Interestingly, *Gaudium et Spes* (no. 65) can be considered a transition from the right of immigration in *Pacem in Terris* to a moral appeal regarding immigration, as it refers to the right of immigration as an aside enclosed between dashes in a section on economic development. In his speech at the World Day of Peace 2001 John Paul II, successor to John XXIII, confined himself to the remark that immigration should be regulated according to criteria of fairness and balance (*Compendium*, op. cit., 297–298). In his message on the 93rd World Day of Migrants and Refugees on 14 January 2007 John Paul II's successor, Benedict XVI, likewise ignored the right to immigration, merely calling for humane treatment of migrants and their families (www.zenit.org/english/visualizza).

human person, who is created in God's image.[41] All subsequent chapters that deal with the church in the modern world present various types of rights, embedded in social-scientific, philosophical, and theological thought and reasoning. They can be classified into the six categories of rights according to the European charter of fundamental rights mentioned in the previous chapter. The six categories and some examples are the following: (a) human dignity: the right to life; (b) freedoms: civil freedoms, the right to work and property; (c) equality: equal treatment irrespective of sex, race, language, religion; (d) solidarity: proper, humane working conditions, membership of trade unions, information and participation within the undertaking; (e) citizens' rights: democratic rights; (f) administration of justice, which is not clearly outlined in *Gaudium et Spes*. Some rights mentioned in *Gaudium et Spes* have no parallel in the European charter, like the right to enjoy culture (GS 60) and minority rights (GS 73).

Rights and Obligations
Another difference between *Pacem in Terris* and *Gaudium et Spes* concerns the relation between obligations and rights, or rights and obligations. In the past, there was a long tradition that saw rights as implications of obligations, hence as indirect, passive rights embedded in objective natural law. As a result, obligations took priority over rights. This still applies to the main representatives of the three generations of the 17th and 18th century doctrine on natural law, such as Samuel Pufendorf and Jean-Jacques Burlamaqui, while Hugo de Groot assigns rights independent status.[42]

Pacem in Terris adopts a different approach. The encyclical starts by discussing rights and proceeds to declare that they entail obligations, just as obligations imply rights. This underscores the reciprocity of rights and obligations (28–30). After this harmonious balance, the exposition in *Gaudium et Spes* is striking. In the vast majority of instances, this council document, following modern legal theory,

---

[41] This first chapter (nos. 12–22) also has a remarkable insertion on atheism (nos. 19–21). The three lines on atheism in the first draft text were expanded to three whole sections in the final document (19–21): Ph. Delhaye, De waardigheid van de menselijke persoon, G. Baraúna (ed.), *De kerk in de wereld van nu: Commentaren op de pastorale constitutie 'Gaudium et Spes'*, Nelissen, Bilthoven 1968, 211–234.

[42] Bernardi, *Le principe*, op. cit., passim, distinguishes between four generations, slotting Barbeyrac in between Pufendorf and Burlamaqui as representing a separate generation.

mentions rights without the addition of obligations, and the few times that the two are mentioned together rights take precedence. This is understandable. Logically rights do take precedence over obligations. Rights can only be realised through the obligations of others; the other way round that does not necessarily follow.[43]

In short, in *Gaudium et Spes*, natural law does not feature. Rights are discussed independently of natural law. They are not passive rights implicit in obligations to others in terms of an objective order, but active, subjective rights residing in the actual person.[44] *Gaudium et Spes* is, *inter alia*, a rights document, grounded in human dignity.

Does this detract from the notion expressed in *Gaudium et Spes* that, from a religious perspective, human dignity stems from the creation of humans in the image of God? On the contrary. The notion of human beings as the image and likeness of God is based on the freedom of God, and on that of human beings, who resemble God by virtue of their freedom (GS 12–18). There is no question of divine heteronomy, according to this interpretation of the council constitution, but of human autonomy, in which humans through their freedom as images of God share in his freedom. Put differently, the secular aspects of human freedom do not detract from the religious aspects but are legitimised by them, as is also evident in the council declaration on religious freedom, *Dignitatis Humanae* (1 and 9).

Some years later pope Paul VI wrote his apostolic letter, *Octogesima Adveniens* (1971) for the 80th anniversary of *Rerum Novarum*.[45] In it he abandons the deductive method in favour of a historical inductive approach. He disregards natural law completely. In the terminology of the philosopher of law Dworkin, he replaces the natural model with a constructive model, in which one does not deduce concrete judgments from fixed principles. Instead one determines which principles

---

[43] N. Brieskorn, s.v. Rechte, in: M. Düwell, C. Hübenthal & M. Werner (eds.), *Handbuch Ethik*, Metzler, Stuttgart 2006, 493–498.

[44] T. Asad, *Formations of the Secular*, Stanford University Press, Stanford 2003, 130–135, associates passive rights with obligation, dependence, and reprimanding individuals when they shirk an obligation, and active rights with the sovereignty of individuals, who claim these rights from the sovereign state, thus establishing a legal concept of the person. The paradox here is that the sovereign state has the task of protecting sovereign individuals from the violation of their rights by the state itself. To a certain extent this paradox can be resolved by separating the three state's powers.

[45] Ch. Curran, *Catholic Social Teaching 1891–Present*, Georgetown University Press, Georgetown 2002, 60–66.

are suitable to legitimise concrete judgments based on intuition and experience.[46] Paul VI no longer uses even the term 'social doctrine'.[47]

A Return to the Past?

John Paul II ushers in a different climate. In his encyclical on the church's social care, *Sollicitudo Rei Socialis* (1987), he scrupulously, albeit suavely, distances himself from Paul VI, speaking about the dynamics between continuity and innovation (SRS 3). He uses the term 'social doctrine' eleven times but the term 'natural law' only rarely. The same may be said of his other two social encyclicals, *Laborem Exercens* (1981) and *Centesimus Annus* (1991).[48] He tends to exchange natural law for theological approaches to social issues, such as the doctrines of creation and incarnation, soteriology and eschatology. Yet throughout he reverts to terms like 'divine law' – not 'natural law' – and 'order of creation', putting these in a metaphysical framework.[49]

But John Paul II's general Christian doctrine does not throw natural law overboard. On the contrary, it features quite explicitly in his encyclical on truth, *Veritatis Splendor* (1993). Here the pope invokes natural law to demonstrate what intrinsically evil acts are: acts that by virtue of their object are and remain evil, in whatever circumstances, with whatever intentions and with whatever consequences they are perpetrated. Thus he excludes developments in moral philosophy like proportionalism, teleology, and consequentialism, and autonomous morality (VS 75). Evil acts are 'incurably' evil, for instance murder, genocide, abortion, euthanasia, suicide, mutilation, torture, and contraceptive practices (VS 80).[50]

---

[46] R. Dworkin, *Taking Rights Seriously*, Harvard University Press, Cambridge 1978, 160ff.

[47] M.-D. Chenu, *La 'doctrine sociale' de l'église comme idéologie*, Cerf, Paris 1979, 79–96.

[48] Curran, *Catholic Social Teaching*, op. cit., 60–66.

[49] According to U. Nothelle-Wildfeuer, *Duplex Ordo Cognitionis, Zur systematischen Grundlegung einer katholieken Soziallehre im Anspruch von Philosophie und Theologie*, Schöningh, Paderborn 1991, 784ff, this is in no way an *Umfundierung* of traditional social teaching.

[50] Cf. M. Vidal, Die Enzyklika 'Veritatis Splendor' und der Weltkatechismus, Die Restauration des Neuthomismus in der katholischen Morallehre, in D. Mieth (Hg.), *Moraltheologie im Abseits? Antwort auf die Enzyklika 'Veritatis Splendor'*, Questiones Disputatae 153, Herder, Freiburg 1994, 244–270; J. Wissink, Hanteert *Veritatis Splendor* een neothomisme? In H. Rikhof & F. Vosman (Red.), *De schittering van de waarheid, Theologische reflecties bij de encycliek Veritatis Splendor*, Meinema, Zoetermeer 1994, 78–95; J. Selling, The context and the arguments of *Veritatis Splendor*, in:

During the Second Vatican Council (1962–1965), the theology professor Joseph Ratzinger, who was elected pope in 2005, showed himself to be no less hesitant than Paul VI to invoke natural law, especially in social doctrine. In the theological debate of those years he lamented the fact that natural law contained numerous ideological elements and is increasingly used to legitimise new rules in ever more new situations.[51]

In discussion with Jürgen Habermas in 2004, only one year before his election to the papacy, Ratzinger, then prefect of the Congregation for the Doctrine of the Faith, again expressed reservations about natural law. Whereas, remarkably, he does not mention Thomas's view of natural law, he praises the 17th century Protestant theorists of natural law Hugo de Groot and Samuel Pufendorf, because their invocation of nature and rationality transcended confessional boundaries and opened the door to dialogue with other religions and secular society. Since then, however, he said, it has become a crude, blunt instrument. He cites two reasons for this: evolution theory has shown that nature is not rational, and more particularly that what humans have in common with animals is not rational. Hence in that discussion, which dealt with reason and religion, he chose not to invoke natural law.[52]

In his first encyclical, *Deus caritas est* (2005), once he had been elected to the supreme office as pope Benedict XVI, he abandoned all reservations, explicitly and positively referring to natural law as basic for the formation of human conscience in political life (no. 28). In his second encyclical, *Spe salvi* (2007), he kept silent about natural law. But in his address to the United Nations in 2008, he stated that human rights are based on natural law that is inscribed on the hearts of human beings in diverse cultures and civilisations. He added that

---

J. Selling & J. Jans (eds.), *The Splendor of Accuracy*, Kok, Kampen 1994, 11–70. The notion of natural law in the encyclical shows resemblances to the New Natural Law of the Finnis-Grisez school, as in J. Finnis, *Natural Law and Natural Rights*, Clarendon, Oxford 1980; Id., *Fundamentals of Ethics*, Clarendon, Oxford 1983, especially 80–108; Id., *Aquinas, Moral, Political, and Legal Theory*, Oxford University Press, Oxford 1998; Id., *The Rights and Wrongs of Abortion*, Princeton University Press, Princeton 1974; cf. N. Bamforth & D. Richards, *Patriarchal Religion, Sexuality and Gender: A Critique of New Natural Law*, Cambridge University Press, Boston 2008; P. Westerman, *The Disintegration of Natural Law Theory: Aquinas to Finnis*, Brill, Leiden 1997.

[51] J. Ratzinger, Naturrecht, Evangelium und Ideologie in der katholische Soziallehre: Katholische Erwägungen zum Thema, in: KI. von Bismarck & W. Dirks (eds.), *Christlicher Glaube und Ideologie*, Kreuz, Stuttgart 1964, 24–30.

[52] J. Ratzinger & J. Habermas, *Dialectics of Secularisation: On Reason and Religion*, Ignatius Press, San Francisco 2006, 67–71.

any attempt to detach human rights from this context entails a risk of yielding to cultural, political, social, and even religious relativism, which jeopardises their universality.[53] He did not stop at that. At the end of the same year he issued another warning, again citing natural law as a fruit of the divine order of creation, against the attempt to undermine the marriage of men and women, by which he condemned same-sex marriage.[54] In 2009, in terms of the same natural law doctrine, he condemned the use of condoms as a measure against the spread of aids in Africa, which triggered widespread criticism.[55] In the same year he wrote his third encyclical, *Caritas in Veritate* (2009), in which he referred three times to natural law, now in the macro context of the international relations between cultures, countries, and peoples, especially the rich and the poor, which are to be governed by natural law, which is 'etched on human hearts', in order to prevent technological and economic excesses (no. 59, 68, 75).[56] Quite apart from all interpretations and applications of natural law, the point is that by invoking natural law to support his argument, Benedict XVI is contradicting his statements in his earlier career, reverting to the era before *Pacem in Terris* by John XXIII and *Gaudium et Spes* by the Second Vatican Council.

5.2   Political Aspects of the Legitimisation of Human Rights

Having described the history of natural law in the legitimisation of human rights in ecclesiastic documents, I now turn to political aspects of the rise of natural law (5.2.1), followed by those of its decline (5.2.2).

---

[53] Benedict XVI, *Meeting*, op. cit., p. 3.

[54] Benedict XVI, *"Veni Creator Spiritus", For an Ecology of Man, A pre-Christmas Address to the Roman Curia*, Rome 22 December 2008. [links to run on] http://www.katholieknederland.nl/actualiteit/2008/detail_objectID681655_FJaar2008.html; http://chiesa.espresso.repubblica.it/articolo/213106?eng=y.

[55] These criticisms were from the Global Fund to Fight Aids in Geneva, the European Commission, the French foreign minister Bernard Kouchner, the former prime minister of France, Alain Juppé, the ministers of foreign affairs of Germany, Belgium, the Netherlands, Italy and Spain, the last of whom symbolically decided to send a million of condoms to Africa; see: www.RKK.nl. d.d. 17.03.09, 18.03.09, 19.03.09.

[56] In note 140 of this encyclical Benedict XVI refers to both his Address to the Participants in the International Congress on natural law, February 12, 2007, and his Address to the Members of the International Theological Commission, October 5, 2007.

5.2.1 *Political Aspects of the Rise of Natural Law*

Before dealing with the 'social issue', Leo XIII had dwelt at length on what is now called the state. Actually, he did not make or recognise a distinction between state and society: the state is a societal state.[57] It consists of two legal corporations: church and state. These are conceived of organistically: like a body, each corporation has a head and members. The head of the ecclesiastic body is the bishop, the head of the political body is the monarch.[58] In his encyclical on the origin of political power, *Diuturnum Illud* (1881), he defends two propositions on the divine origin of that power. The first is that God instituted political power in order to prevent chaos and anarchy. The second is that God bestowed political office on those that hold it. The argument is that political office holders should be able to limit the will of individuals. They cannot do so if they are regarded as equals whose power is not granted by God, the creator and law-giver of all that exists. Although the people elect the ruler, it merely entails designating the person (*designatio*). It does not mean that the people in their own right confer power they possess on the ruler (not *translatio*). The office holder is not a delegate of the people but rules by the grace of God (Dl H-12).[59] This implies that the people obey the ruler not out of fear but out of reverence, thus preventing unrest and insurrection (Dl 13). The ruler should regard this as the church's gift to society, for it maintains the divinely established order. Hence the church should be given complete freedom and the monarch should defend it (Dl 25). It is wrong to assign sovereignty to the people rather than to God and proclaim laws as if God does not exist, which amounts to rejecting Hugo de Groot's view, albeit mistakenly interpreted as mentioned in the previous chapter. Assigning sovereignty to the people is 'counter to nature', Leo XIII avers in his encyclical on human freedom, *Libertas Praestantissimum* (1888). Towards the end, the pope moderates his tone by conceding to American bishops, who had been living in a constitutional democratic state for more than a century, that democracy

---

[57] Curran, *Catholic Social Teaching*, op. cit., 73.
[58] This political notion has medieval credentials: E. Kantorowicz, *The King's Two Bodies: A Study in Mediaeval Political Theology*, Princeton University Press, Princeton 1997, 193ff, 204ff.
[59] Cf. Monzel, *Kirche*, op. cit., 292.

is not wrong, provided it is based on Catholic doctrine on the origin of political power (LP 44).

Thus Leo XIII rejects the contract principle of the aforementioned three generations of 17th and 18th century natural-law jurists and seeks to restore the *ancien régime*. The contract dominating the entire debate was that of Thomas Hobbes, according to which individuals transferred their freedom and power to the sovereign and submit to him totally in order to prevent war by everyone against everyone.[60] Before that, De Groot had posited two pacts: that of association, whereby people joined forces with each other, and that of submission to the sovereign without forfeiting their right to self-determination. Samuel Pufendorf distinguished between three pacts: that of association; that of determining the form of government, such as monarchy, aristocracy, or democracy (or irregular hybrid forms); and thirdly, the pact of choosing a government and transferring sovereignty.[61] The third pact does not entail total rejection of divine power, Pufendorf maintains, but functions on a second plane. Divine right is not direct, as if divinely injected into the sovereign like some sort of physical substance, but indirect. It means that the human striving for order fits into God's plan, but not that the sovereignty of the monarch derives from God. The people not only designate the sovereign, but confer their sovereignty on him.[62]

Naturally, Leo XIII repudiated developments since the Treaty of Munster (1648), which, following the protracted, bloody religious wars of the 16th and 17th centuries, subjugated the church to the authority of the state (*cuius regio illius religio*). But the American and French constitutions of the late 18th century, which promulgated the

---

[60] Th. Hobbes, *Leviathan*, 39,5.

[61] Pufendorf, *De jure naturae et gentium*, VII, II, 7–12, with which Jean-Jacques Burlamaqui, *Les principes de droit politique*, I, IV, XV, concurs. These three pacts – says Pufendorf, *De Jure* VII, II, 13, citing Seneca – make the state a composite moral person, whose will, intertwined with the pacts, is considered the will of all – a will which J.-J. Rousseau, *Du Contrat social*, II, III, insists on calling, not the will of all as the sum of all individual wills, but the common will. Aristotle (1279ª 22–1279ᵇ10) discerned three forms (monarchy, aristocracy, and *politeia*, i.e. constitution) and three deviations from these (tyranny, oligarchy, and democracy). Thomas (STh I–II 95, 4), in a free adaptation of Aristotle, identified the following forms: monarchy, aristocracy, oligarchy, democracy, and, as an absolutely corrupt form, tyranny, plus composite forms.

[62] Pufendorf, *De jure*, op. cit., VII, III, 2–3, rejects De Groot's notion that God approves the state *ex post facto*: like Burlamaqui, *Droit*, op. cit., I, VI, VIII–XIII, he sees the relation between God and the state as *ex ante*.

separation of church and state, were even more odious to him. In his encyclical on the Christian structure of states, *Immortale Dei* (1885), he rejected the separation of church and state. It is a fatal concept that must lead to anarchy (ID 34), because church and state confront people with different norms (LP 18, 38).

As a counter measure, he advocates a correlative approach, according to which both church and state derive their authority from 'nature', hence from God. God is the 'first cause' of church and state, with church and state as the 'second cause' of law and administration (ID 3–4). Both are subject to the authority of God's eternal law and its reflection, natural law, the one directed to the subjects' – or rather, 'children's' – spiritual salvation, the other to their material well-being (ID 5). The church is a society at least as perfect as the state; its laws have the same authority at those of the state (ID 35). They relate in the same way as soul and body – the church as the soul, the state as the body – and are therefore interdependent (LP 18).[63]

Even though the body-soul metaphor may create a different impression, church and state are on exactly the same plane under God's authority. That refutes what Leo XIII considers the modern heresy that the church is only one association among others in civil society. It entails disregard of the equal validity of the two jurisdictions of church and state, so the state usurps the church's jurisdiction over marriage and education, taking legislative and administrative decisions without reference to the church for the sole purpose of paralysing the latter (ID 27; LP 40). Without faith in God, society teeters on the verge of annihilation. Hence explicit unbelief, atheism, is a public crime (ID 6) – a view that John Locke had upheld two centuries before.[64] In fact, Leo XIII wants to return to the 'sacred canopy' of the romanticised *civitas christiana* – romanticised because, although it perhaps existed in the early Middle Ages, it came under increasing pressure from the 12th

---

[63] The concept of a perfect society (*communitas perfecta*) was already used by Thomas to indicate the orientation of members and parts of a community to the common good (I–II 90, 3). In the period following the French Revolution it was used as a battle cry against state hegemony vis-à-vis the Catholic Church and against the notion that the church is simply one among many social institutions (ID 27). The accent was on the church as an independent entity with its own means of achieving its goals, especially jurisdiction and administration. Also see R. Torfs, The Roman Catholic Church and Secular Legal Culture in the Twentieth Century, *Studia Historiae Ecclesiasticae* 25(1999)1, 1–20.

[64] J. Locke, *A letter Concerning Toleration*, London 1991, 45–48.

century onwards.[65] Then the Christian church ruled supreme, whereas other religions, more especially Islam, were at best tolerated. To the pope the equal status of all religions in modern times was an abomination (ID 21).

Against this background it is understandable that Leo XIII should see the only solution to the 'social issue' as harmonious cooperation between church and state, with the necessary enlistment of workers. Even more importantly, the church should lead the way in this. Ultimately the social issue is a moral, even a religious problem, so the church had to issue proper directives for moral life, especially as regards justice. It mediates between entrepreneurs and workers, as well as between the state and workers (RN 16–19).

Not surprisingly, Leo XIII does not bow to the 'rights of man and the citizen', much vaunted since the French Revolution of 1789. Rights like freedom of religion, education, conscience, opinion, and the press must be rejected if they transgress the confines of the divine legal order. They can only be recognised if they are grounded in 'true' freedom, tested by the truth of the law of God and of nature, and if they contribute to harmony under the divine authority of government (LP 19–35).

Some rights derive directly from God. In the case of religious freedom that is self-evident: the freedom to turn to God comes directly from God (LP 20–22). The same applies to freedom of education, at least insofar as it entails religious truth and morality. Because God conferred this freedom on the church, it is an ecclesiastic rather than an individual, personal right (LP 27 29). Freedom of conscience likewise stems from God, since it pertains to human beings' intimate relationship with their God (LP 30–34). Whether freedom of opinion and the press has its origin in God is not clear, but it would certainly have to be exercised within the parameters of Catholic doctrine to avoid excesses (LP 23, 35–36).

Two rights that we have discussed already occupy a special place: those to fair wages and property. We mentioned that they are connected with God and natural law. But that is not all. They are said to display a pre-state character. And since they precede the state, the

---

[65] The secularisation of the state was partly a result of canonists' secularisation of definitions of the church and ecclesiastic institutions; cf. Kantorowicz, *The King's Two bodies*, op. cit., passim.

latter has to accommodate them (RN 7–8). The argument is that they can be traced to marriage and the family, and that the latter, no less than the state, is a true community with its own authority – the father (!) (RN 14).

A final theme to be noted here is the principle of subsidiarity. It is not mentioned explicitly in *Rerum Novarum*, but only 40 years later in Pius XI's encyclical, *Quadragesimo Anno*.[66] Subsidiarity implies that what an individual or group can do they should do themselves. It should not be taken over by a higher agency. Such an agency can and must take over only when the tasks required are beyond the capacity of the individual or group. That has implications for the state. It has to restrict itself to tasks that cannot be performed at lower levels of society. A state structured on these lines furthers well-being and happiness (QA 79–80).

After stating this general principle, the encyclical proceeds to more particular details. *Rerum Novarum* already spoke out in favour of workers' right to form unions (RN 57). Now the theme is elaborated to include employees' and employers' associations, both referred to as syndicates (QA 81 w.). Problems regarding capital and labour should not be resolved by the state, but by the syndicates along with joint employee and employer organisations called corporations. Such syndicates and corporations constitute a legal person and are regarded as state organs and institutions (QA 9). Together they form a syndical and corporative order that should lead to the reconstruction and promotion of a better social order (QA 95). Such a self-governing system is, if not essential, at least natural to civil society (QA 83), suggesting that it might be considered a reflection of natural law.

The syndicates and corporations have to be cast in an explicitly doctrinal mould: divine law, natural law, and the precepts of natural law (QA 43). This makes the antagonism to socialism (not merely radical socialism but also social democracy) – which also strives for a better social order – irreconcilable. Both forms of socialism are based on an atheistic anthropology (QA 117). Terms like religious or Christian socialism are internally contradictory. One cannot be both a good Catholic and a good socialist (QA 120). Socialists must simply return

---

[66] The *Compendium*, op. cit., no. 185, wrongly asserts that it is one of the most consistent directives of social teaching since the first great encyclical, *Rerum Novarum* (1891).

to the bosom of the church (QA 126). The only solution to the social problem is to establish Catholic syndicates and corporations.[67] Clearly there is a long battle ahead before the *civitas christiana* will be restored (QA 83, 87, 91ff). It demands a heroic effort, because the world today is marked by paganism (QA 141). The polemicist terms are not fortuitous: Catholics have to advance like 'soldiers of Christ' (QA 144), fight in 'Christ's war' (QA 147) with a view to the "longed-for and full restoration of human society in Christ", the "Peace of Christ in the Kingdom of Christ" (QA 138), and the spread of Christ's kingdom everywhere (QA 143). It was in this context that the Feast of Christ the King was instituted in 1925, to be celebrated on the last Sunday of October every year (since 1970, the last Sunday of the ecclesiastical year, before the first Sunday of the Advent).

5.2.2   *Political Aspects of the Decline of Natural Law*

Politically, too, Pius XII was a transitional figure. For all his adherence to his predecessors' ideas, he initiated some new themes. He abandoned Leo XIII's societal state and stressed the importance of the democratic state.[68] In his Christmas message in 1944, he related democracy to natural law, albeit inductively in indirect speech, by saying that many people consider democracy a natural requirement, established by reason itself.[69] He emphasised the freedom and equality in a true democracy. His assertion that it cannot happen without authority appears tautological, since democracy is a form of exercising power, but like Leo XIII he adds the rider that this authority is from God. On this basis he claims a special task for the church, since it teaches and defends God's truth and the order founded in it. That is the guideline for every democracy.[70]

The end of the competitive relation between church and state was ushered in by John XXIII. He abandoned all claims defending the church's traditional prerogatives. In *Mater et Magistra* (1961), he outlined a new economic order, based on human dignity, for all three sectors: agriculture, industry, and services. He focused particularly on

---

[67] This happened on a large scale in the Netherlands and other countries like Germany where necessary alliances might be formed with non-Catholic organisations: Van Gestel, *Kerk*, op. cit., 264–279.

[68] Utz & Groner, *Aufbau*, op. cit., no. 3469–3489 (1773–1781).

[69] Utz & Groner, *Aufbau*, op. cit., no. 3474 (1775).

[70] Utz & Groner, *Aufbau*, op. cit., no. 3481–3482 (1778–1779).

agriculture, especially in developing countries, and probed themes like economic infrastructure, taxation, credit provided by banks, social security, price control, overpopulation, and the world agricultural organisation (MM 123ff). Like his predecessors, he underscored the principle of subsidiarity (MM 53, 117), the autonomy of syndicates and corporations, and private property (MM 17, 30, 108–121) and private enterprise (MM 53, 66). He stressed participation in economic decision making, both national and international (MM 91–99).

Whereas *Mater et Magistra* explores the economy, *Pacem in Terris* (1963) deals with politics, both national and international. As mentioned already, human rights are a focal theme. Their protection is seen as one of the state's fundamental tasks (PT 63–65). According to John XXIII, the state derives its authority from God, but that does not imply any restriction of the democratic, free choice regarding type of government, political offices (Pufendorf's second pact), and office holders (Pufendorf's third pact) (PT 52). The footnotes refer to both Leo XIII's *Diuturnum Illud* on the divine origin of offices and incumbents, and Pius XII's Christmas message of 1944. The last one mentions the divine origin of offices, but not that of incumbents; hence there is no restriction of the people's role to mere designation of office holders (*designatio*). In other words, although John XXIII refers to Leo XIII, he backs Pius XII.[71]

The protection of human rights requires the three powers of the state: legislative, executive, and judicial. This is the first time that they are mentioned in an official ecclesiastic document (PT 67–72) since Montesquieu first posited their necessity two centuries earlier.[72] One of the rights in need of protection is that of political participation. John XXIII replaced Pius XI's inductive comment in terms of natural law – "many people consider democracy a natural requirement, established by reason itself" – with an affirmative statement based on human dignity: "A natural consequence of men's dignity is unquestionably their right to take an active part in government" (PT 73). He advocates incorporating this political right in the state's consti-

---

[71] Pius XII and John XXIII concur with a 13th and 14th century tradition, according to which God establishes the empire, but the people choose the emperor. In this choice the title 'by the grace of God' only functions as a remote cause (*causa remota*); see: Kantorowicz, *The King's Two bodies*, op. cit. 296–297, n. 51–54.

[72] Ch.-L. de Montesquieu, *De l'esprit des lois*, 1748, English translation: *Spirit of the laws*, Cambridge University Press, Cambridge 1990, II, II, 6.

tution, along with other rights, as has happened in many countries, thus giving them constitutional recognition (PT 75–79). He adds that these rights have a pre-state origin, hence are independent of all political laws and regulation (PT 78). They derive from human dignity (PT 145).

When it comes to international cooperation, the encyclical underscores the importance of the United Nations, where the Vatican has observer status, and of the Universal Declaration of Human Rights (1948). This is diametrically opposed to earlier ecclesiastic rejections of the French declaration of human rights in 1789. It does contain the qualification that "we are, of course, aware that some of the points in the declaration did not meet with unqualified approval in some quarters; and there was justification for this. Nevertheless, we think the document should be considered a step in the right direction" (PT 144). Which points does the encyclical have in view, which circles and which arguments? The document contains no answer. But it does evaluate recognition of the dignity of every human being positively, followed by the assurance that everyone has a right to pursue the truth and adhere to moral principles (PT 144).

Finally, there is another difference from the aforementioned social encyclicals. *Pacem in Terris* advocates socio-economic cooperation with non-Catholics, including non-believers (PT 157–158). This means that syndicates and corporations with different worldview-related backgrounds can work together.

Passing from the encyclicals to the documents of Vatican II, it is noteworthy that the pastoral constitution, *Gaudium et Spes*, devotes comparatively little attention to politics. Only four sections in chapter IV of part II deal with the subject (GS 73–76). Only four councillors participated in the discussions in the autumn of 1965, although they dealt with major issues.[73]

The constitution emphasises that the state exists for the common good (*bonum commune* GS 74), defined as the totality of social conditions that permit both groups and individuals to achieve their fulfilment more fully and sooner (GS 26). When it comes to more detailed structures, the constitution appears to apply the idea of a contract (GS 74–75), which – if true – could be regarded as a complete about

---

[73] R. La Valle, Het leven van politiche gemeenschap, in: Baraúna, *De kerk*, op. cit., 434–465.

face.[74] The contract principle implies that people, families, and groups have realised that they do not have the means to achieve the common good, which has to be achieved at a more general level: they join forces (Pufendorf's first pact). These groups decide to establish a political order (Pufendorf's second pact). The council document calls on citizens to elect their own government (Pufendorf's third pact). Such election forms part of political participation, which is said to accord fully with human nature (*cum humana natura plene congruit*) (GS 75). To Leo XIII that would have been a nightmare.[75]

The constitution also differs from Leo XIII on another theme: the relation between church and state. There is no trace of nostalgia for the medieval *civitas christiana*. It honours not merely political pluralism as manifested in political parties (GS 75), but also religious pluralism (GS 76). Democracy, too, is accepted without reservation. A new departure is that Christians play two roles: the role they assume on their own responsibility and the role they fulfil in the church's name under the tutelage of their 'shepherds' (GS 76). There is no mention of possible role conflicts, nor of intra-role conflicts in individual believers, nor of inter-role conflicts in the community of the church. The tricky problem of a plurality of roles is disregarded.

Whereas Leo XIII bases himself on the religious and moral unity of the two bodies – church and state – with their equal jurisdiction, the council text accentuates their respective autonomy and independence. In terms of tradition this is not new, for as early as the 12th and 13th centuries the 'dualists' (including Dante in his *De Monarchia*), following an ancient canonical tradition, propagated the mutual independence of emperor and pope.[76] Here, according to the constitution, the church reserves the right, when necessary, to pass a moral judgment,

---

[74] According to La Valle, Het leven, op. cit., 442, the church accepts the contract concept in a descriptive sense, but bases it on the political community, being the fruit of human beings' social nature. In no. 74 there is a reference to the social nature as the basis of the political community, but at the highest conceivable level of abstraction, for it adds that the further determination of the form of administration and the designation of the officials should be left to the free choice of the people. And that is the crux of the matter.

[75] The *Compendium*, op. cit., is ambivalent: on the one hand it calls the contract reductive (no. 203), on the other it concurs with Pufendorf's third pact: transfer of sovereignty (no. 395).

[76] Kantorowicz, *The King's Two Bodies*, op. cit., 451–464.

also on political issues, especially when the fundamental rights of a person or the salvation of souls require it. The constitution does not make an issue of the separation of church and state, as Leo XIII did, albeit in a negative sense. It maintains that church and state should cooperate in their respective service to the same people (GS 76) – an idea also mooted by Leo XIII. But it does not explore what that entails in a society marked by plurality of worldviews, in which communities may have different opinions on moral issues.

The council's declaration on religious freedom, *Dignitatis Humanae*, which was only adopted after intensive discussion at the last moment on the final day of the council, reveals the core of the church's attitude towards this fundamental right. Part I of the declaration deals with religious freedom in secular, moral, and judicial language (DH 2–8), and part II with religious freedom in the light of revelation (DH 9–15). This structure exemplifies the 'signs of the times' approach in recent documents.

The fundamental theme of the declaration centres on two questions: that of truth, and the institutional question. The question of truth concerns the relation between truth and freedom. The first social encyclicals consistently emphasised 'true' freedom, which implied that freedom was necessarily grounded in and limited by God's eternal law and natural law. The institutional question concerns the church's relationship with other worldview-related, religious and nonreligious communities. Historically, the church had always stipulated very narrow boundaries, based on the 3rd-century axiom of Origen and Cyprian of Carthage: no salvation outside the church (*extra ecclesiam nulla salus*). Obviously the two questions are interrelated: how does one reconcile religious freedom with the belief (*credimus*) that the Christian religion is the only true faith and subsists (*subsistere*) in the Catholic Church (DH 1)? One of Vatican II's key pronouncements, in *Lumen Gentium* (8), is that divine truth subsists in the church. It means that truth is to be found in the Catholic Church, albeit not exclusively, since it also leaves traces in other religions.

Not surprisingly, the notion of 'traces' resulted in two positions in the deliberations of Vatican II. The conservative wing put the accent on the idea that these are merely traces: real truth is to be found only in the Catholic Church. They related it to the traditional belief that only truth can be attributed a right and that heresy has no rights. The progressive wing focused on the rich sources that traces in other religions refer to and stressed the significance of dialogue with non-Catholic and non-Christian traditions in the search for truth.[77]

Nor is it surprising that the clash between the two wings led to an accord in the form of a compromise. Logically the accord can be analysed in several steps. The first is the articulation of the idea that all people (*homines cuncti*) are driven by desire for truth (DH 2). The second step is the conversion of this descriptive insight into the prescriptive dictum that all people have a moral duty to search for truth (DH 2). The third step is a closer definition of this duty: all people have to search for truth, especially religious truth (DH 2).[78] The fourth step is an even closer specification of this statement, namely that all people are bound to search for truth, more especially in what concerns God and his church (DH 1). The fifth and final step is that once the truth about God and his church is recognised, it has to be embraced and adhered to (DH1).[79] In short, the descriptive statement that all people are searching for truth culminates in the prescription to search primarily for the truth about God and his church and, once it has been found, to remain faithful to it. This interpretation of religious freedom, which is directed to everybody, simply cannot apply to non-Catholic Christians, people of other faiths, and nonreligious people. It is conceived unilaterally from the perspective of the Catholic Church. There is almost a funnel effect: it starts in general terms, but culminates in a doctrinal obligation.

Apart from this, the compromise also contains an element that conflicts directly with the Universal Declaration of Human Rights of 1948 (article 18) and the European Convention of Human Rights of 1950 (article 9). According to these documents, everybody has the right not only to have a religion of whatever nature, but also to change their religion or live their lives as atheists. Hence religious freedom implies the right to heresy (from the perspective of one's own religion), apostasy (from the perspective of one's original religion) and conversion

---

[77] J. Murray, The Declaration on Religious Freedom: A Moment in Its Legislative History, in: J. Murray (ed.), *Religious Liberty: An End and a Beginning*, Macmillan, New York 1966, 15–44; Id., *The Problem of Religious Freedom*, Newman, Westminster 1965, 7–17.

[78] "Secundum dignitatem suam hominess cuncti (…) morali tenentur obligatione ad veritatem querendam, illam imprimis quae religionem spcctat".

[79] "Homines vero concti tenentur veritatem, praesertim in iis quae Deum Eiusque Ecclesiam respiciunt, quaerere eamque cognitam amplecti ac servare."

(from the perspective of one's new religion).[80] To the church this not only sounds alien, but also incompatible with the conviction that the only true faith subsists (*subsistit*) in the church. The church/state jurist Ernst-Wolfgang Böckenförde rightly says that a change in the relation between freedom and truth has repercussions for the view on the identity of the church and her mission.[81] The erstwhile theology professor, now cardinal Walter Kasper held that the declaration was probably the most important document of Vatican II. In view of its compromise character this judgment seems somewhat exaggerated.[82]

5.3   RECONSTRUCTION OF THE LEGITIMISATION OF HUMAN RIGHTS
        IN TERMS OF NATURE AND POLITICS

In the previous sections, we dealt with natural law in official documents by the Catholic Church because this church is the only powerful global institution that takes it as one of the basic principles of its social doctrine, especially as far as human rights are concerned. We also clarified the relation between natural law and the political position of the church. This final section is an attempt to reconstruct the legitimisation process of human rights in terms of nature and politics by interrelating the two. What kind of relationships should we look for? According to systems theory, one could proceed from the influence of natural law as a form of moral thought on politics, in our case ecclesiastic politics. This fits into the broader perspective of the influence of culture, of which morality forms a part, on structure, of which politics forms a part. One could also reverse the relationship between culture and structure by proceeding from the influence of structure (politics) on culture (natural law). Both approaches have a

---

[80] V. Bader, *Secularism or Democracy?* Amsterdam University Press, Amsterdam 2007, 132.

[81] E.-W. Böckenförde, *Religionsfreiheit: Die Kirche in der modernen Welt*, Freiburg 1990; J.A. van der Ven, Godsdienstvrijheid als ecclesiologisch paradigma, in: C. Sterkens & J.A. van der Ven (eds.), *De functie van de kerk in de hedendaagse maatschappij*, Altiora, Averbode, 2002,17–64.

[82] W. Kasper, Religionsfreiheit, II. Katholische Kirche, in: *Staatslexikon, Recht, Wirtschaft, Gesellschaft*, Band 4, Freiburg 1988, 825–827. Soon after it ended on 8 December 1965 the entire council was described as a 'compromise council'. See: E. Schillebeeckx, *Theologisch Testament. Notarieel nog niet verleden*, Nelissen, Baarn 1995, 41.

formidable tradition.[83] I opt, however, for a more modest approach, which Max Weber indicated with his metaphor of selective affinity (*Wahlverwandtschaft*). It refers to a selective relation between culture and structure.[84] In concrete terms, when natural law and the church as a 'perfect society' arose in early documents, they chose each other as affined; the same may be said when natural law and the 'perfect society' declined in later documents.

Against this background, the sociology of law offers a more specific approach. This discipline argues that in the past natural law was 'chosen' to justify the church's moral convictions in order to reinforce its political position and convert groups with differing views to its beliefs. To this end it cites the so-called immutable, absolute, universal prescriptions of natural law that apply to everybody, both within and outside the church. An example was the church's new status in the 4th century when, after being regarded as a sect, it was elevated to the official religion of the Roman empire. At that time the church needed a concept to instil its beliefs in non-Christian nations. It did so by way of natural law, to which end it absorbed elements of Stoicism and Roman international law (*ius gentium*) into the divine universe of creation, but without assimilating it into official, ecclesiastical documents otherwise.[85]

From the mid-19th century onwards, a similar process unfolded, culminating in the official ecclesiastic documents on the social doctrine.[86] Natural law was invoked to mobilise the church so as to persuade all groups that had taken up the cause of liberalism or socialism, guide them into the direction of the 'true' social doctrine, and win them back for the church. To that end, the church had to be built up as a social bastion in order to conduct its christianising offensive with the necessary authority. Hence it wanted to link the state closely to the church

---

[83] T. Parsons, An Outline of the Social System, in: T. Parsons (ed.), *Theories of Societies*, Free Press, New York 1965, 30–79; for criticism of Parsons and critical functionalism, see: J.A. van der Ven, *Ecclesiology in Context*, Eerdmans, Grand Rapids 1996, 65–77. See also O. Williamson, The New Institutional Economics: Taking Stock, Looking Ahead, *Journal of Economic Literature* 38(2000), 595–613; M. Sakwa, *Bible and Poverty in Kenya: An Empirical Exploration*, Brill, Leiden 2008, 129–135.

[84] M. Weber, *Wirtschaft und Gesellschaft*, Mohr, Tübingen 1980, passim.

[85] E. Troeltsch, Das stoisch-christlische Naturrecht und das moderne profane Naturrecht, *Historische Zeitschrift* 106(1911), 237–267.

[86] Kaufmann, *Überlegungen*, op. cit., 126–164. G. Vattimo, *Dopo la Christianita*, Dutch translation: *Het woord is geest geworden*, Agora, Kampen 2003, 124, points out the relation between the accent on natural law and claims to political power.

by stressing its divine origin, thus strengthening its own political clout. From that time onwards, the doctrine of the Catholic Church became doctrinal 'Catholicism'. It developed its own social organisations to establish 'social Catholicism', its own political parties and press to establish 'political Catholicism', its own special pastoral care to ensure 'devotional Catholicism'.[87] The process permeated the entire church, from bishops to priests, from regular to secular priests, from priests to the laity, from old people to youths.

What underlying factors caused the church to withstand the modern age in order to find a way back to the *ancien régime* via 'Catholicism'? Naturally, the religious backsliding of large groups in society was its first concern, as well as the loss of social and political power and prestige. But probably the most profound cause was the process of functional differentiation that had been going on in Europe for several centuries. As a result, vertical differentiation into estates and classes gradually made way for horizontal functional differentiation, which in time led to the institutionalisation of these functions into distinct systems with their own codes, organisations, and programmes, for instance an economic, a political, a legal, an educational, a health care, an art, and a scientific system.[88] That meant that the broad canopy that the church had previously offered everybody and everything imploded, and the church became a separate organisation alongside other organisations in a religious system alongside other systems. Formerly the church had a largely unquestioned influence on the doings of society. Now it found itself in a position where it had to look for openings for the religious system to penetrate other systems. In addition, it had to find possible points of connection and present these in the codes and languages of these other systems without requiring the latter to sacrifice their autonomy, which they could not and would not do. This made its position precarious, with the result that, far from being at the centre of society, it was forced to the periphery.

The church's position since the mid-19th century may be seen as an attempt to turn the tide and restore the medieval church through

---

[87] J.A. van der Ven, Katholieke kerk en katholicisme in historisch en empirisch perspectief, in: J. Peters et al., *Kerk op de helling*, Kok, Kampen 1993, 62–92. The Dutch Dominicans offer a beautiful example of 'devotional Catholicism' at that time: M. Monteiro, *Gods predikers: Dominicanen in Nederland (1795–2000)*, Verloren, Hilversum 2008, 144–152.

[88] N. Luhmann, *Die Gesellschaft der Gesellschaft*, Bd 1–2, Suhrkamp, Frankfurt 1998.

a policy of 'doctrinal', 'social', 'political', and 'devotional Catholicism'. To that end it invoked natural law, and not only because it is said to apply to all citizens, both within and outside the church. It could also be used to counteract functional differentiation within the law, since such legal differentiations as property, marriage, family, educational, labour, and public law undermined the umbrella function that the church used to exercise in these areas on the strength of its moral and legal authority.[89]

Since the mid-20th century, however, it became clear that mobilisation by way of 'social', 'political' and 'devotional Catholicism' was not having the expected effect. After diverse, dispersed indications of imminent failure, for example in the Netherlands, in the early decades of that century the first clear signal after World War II was the book *Onrust in de zielzorg* (Troubles in pastoral care) in 1947.[90] It interpreted the frustration prevalent among church leaders, priests, and the laity in terms of a crisis for the church, seen as the decay of Christian ideas and the Christian lifestyle and progressive spiritual atrophy.[91] Steady demobilisation followed, not only in the Netherlands but in many other countries.[92] It could be interpreted as the church's gradual acknowledgment of the far-reaching process of functional differentiation. A significant indication of this was the emphasis on what the Second Vatican Council called the doctrine of 'the autonomy of earthly affairs' or 'the autonomy of earthly values' (GS 36 and 43).[93] This doctrine may be regarded as a philosophical/theological reflection of the age-old change process of social differentiation into vertically, hierarchically tiered estates and classes towards differentiation according to horizontally distinguished functions and systems.

The demobilisation process can be viewed from both a moral and a political vantage point. Morally, it consists in the gradual replacement of natural law by human dignity as a regulatory concept. Since

---

[89] N. Luhmann, *Ausdifferenzierung des Rechts: Beiträge zur Rechtssoziologie und Rechtstheorie*, Suhrkamp, Frankfurt 1999.

[90] For dispersed signs before World War II, see Monteiro, *Gods predikers*, op. cit., 184–362.

[91] H. Boelaars et al., *Onrust in de zielzorg*, Spectrum, Utrecht 1947, 18–19.

[92] Taylor, *A Secular Age*, op. cit., 465–472.

[93] "If by the autonomy of earthly affairs we mean that created things and societies themselves enjoy their own laws and values which must be gradually deciphered, put to use, and regulated by men, then it is entirely right to demand that autonomy" (GS 36). See M.-D. Chenu, De rol van de kerk in de hedendaagse wereld, in: Baraúna (ed.), *De kerk*, op. cit., 282–301, here 288–290.

Pius XII and especially John XXIII, the church has appropriated this concept, which it inherited, without any Christian reference, from the Stoics, and, later, the Kantian tradition. This made it possible to dissociate human rights from natural law. It enabled the church to make the transition from rights as indirect, passive, objective rights implicit in one's obligation towards others to direct, active, subjective rights inherent in the person. It also enabled the church to identify itself with the proliferation of previously hardly acknowledged natural rights, such as fair wages and property, as well as with a string of political rights that have been posited since the Universal Declaration of Human Rights: freedom, civil, political, judicial, socio-economic, and collective rights.[94] In 1984, as an observer at the United Nations, the church found that the declaration consciously eschews any reference to natural law.[95] Natural rights become human rights and human rights become fundamental rights, entrenched in fundamental law within national constitutions.

Historically, it is probably unfair to accuse the church of having always opposed human rights, accepting them only when the barriers it erected against them were no longer defensible, with the result that – according to the sociologist Franz-Xavier Kaufmann – it was always too late.[96] The fact is, however, that Pius XII began to accept democracy 150 years after its introduction in the United States and France, and that the Vatican II council adopted religious freedom only after 170 years – and even then in the form of a compromise, as noted above.

It is also a fact that outwardly the church presents itself as a true advocate of human rights, whereas within its own domain it continues to raise obstacles to such principles as democracy generally and non-discrimination in particular, especially with regard to women and homosexuals. It does permit participation of its members in the life and, to some extent, the governance of the church, but it does not tolerate democracy, any more than it recognises the separation of powers. In the case of women, prevailing admission criteria exclude them from priestly office, and in the case of homosexuals, ecclesiastic doctrine on sexual orientation and gender identity inhibits full recognition of

---

[94] It is noteworthy that the church makes little or no mention of judicial rights in connection with the administration of justice.

[95] W. Vögele, *Menschenwürde zwischen Recht und Theologie: Begründungen von Menschenrechten in der Perspektive öffentlicher Theologie*, Kaiser, Gütersloh, 2000, 250–253.

[96] Kaufmann, *Überlegungen*, op. cit. 142.

their human dignity.[97] The picture becomes even gloomier when one compares the rights in the *Codex Iuris Canonici* (1983) with human rights. The rights in the *Codex* are imbedded in obedience owed to the church, which is something of a contradiction in terms.[98] It is like saying, with reference to right and power: the right of A towards B can

---

[97] A typical example is the Vatican's reaction to documents of and pertaining to the United Nations regarding the principle of non-discrimination on the basis of sexual orientation, such as the *UN Declaration on sexual orientation and gender identity* of 2008. Precursors were the decision of the UN Human Rights Commission in Toonen v. Australia in 1994, the Brazilian delegation's Proposal for a Resolution on Human Rights and Sexual Orientation to the UN Human Rights Commission in 2003, and the Yogyakarta Principles of 2006. Judging by recent reactions the Holy See does condemn all unfair discrimination against homosexuals as well as their judicial criminalisation, practised in about 80 countries, where it affects even the right to life. During a United Nations General Assembly panel that met in December 2009, a statement read by the representative of the Holy See said it "opposes all forms of violence and unjust discrimination against homosexual persons, including discriminatory penal legislation which undermines the inherent dignity of the human person.... [T]he murder and abuse of homosexual persons are to be confronted on all levels, especially when such violence is perpetrated by the State" (see: Human Rights Watch, 11 December 2009). At the same time it shows itself to be an avowed opponent of the aforementioned UN Declaration, introduced by France and the Netherlands and endorsed by 66 of the 192 members of the UN in December 2008, which the United States joined in March 2009. These now include all Western countries and all member countries of the Organisation of American States. In some countries, legislation recognizing same-sex marriage already exists: Argentina, Belgium, Canada, the Netherlands, Norway, South Africa, Spain, Sweden, some states in the U.S., and now, in 2010, Portugal (parliament only accepted it in its first reading). The principal reason for the Vatican's rejection of the Declaration, according to a statement by the Vatican's permanent observer at the UN, Mgr Celestino Migliore, is that endorsing the document could lead to national and international pressure to permit same-sex marriages, which the church rejects (see: *Declaration of the Pontifical Council for the Family regarding the Resolution of the European Parliament dated 16 March 2000, making de facto unions, including same-sex unions, equal to the family*, March 17, 2000). In his 2008 pre-Christmas address to the Roman Curia, pope Benedict XVI stated that the church "must defend not only the earth, water, and air as gifts of creation belonging to all. It must also protect man against his own destruction. Something like an ecology of man is needed, understood in the proper sense. It is not an outdated metaphysics if the Church speaks of the nature of the human being as man and woman, and asks that this order of creation be respected. Yes, the rainforests deserve our protection, but man deserves it no less, as a creature in whom a message is inscribed that does not mean the contradiction of our freedom, but its precondition." http://chiesa.espresso.repubblica.it/articolo/213106?eng=y. In his New Year address of 2010, which is called his state of the world address, Benedict XVI repeated his message in the following way: "Creatures differ from one another and can be protected, or endangered, in different ways, as we know from daily experience. One such attack comes from laws or proposals which, in the name of fighting discrimination, strike at the biological basis of the difference between the sexes. I am thinking, for example, of certain countries in Europe or North and South America." http://chiesa.espresso.repubblica.it/articolo/1341681?eng=y.

[98] *Codex Iuris Canonici*, 1983, canon 208–231; cf. O. Boelens, De 'Lex Ecclesiae Fundamentalis': Een gemiste kans of kansloze misser? Dissertation KTU, Utrecht 2002, 263–274.

only be exercised if B exercises power over A![99] In other words, the vestiges of the *ancien régime* have not yet been cleared away.

This brings me to the church's political stance: its position vis-à-vis the state. Leo XIII and his successors still thought of church and state as two equal, autonomous institutions, each with its own jurisdiction, which should cooperate for the sake of social peace and harmony. In this respect they were opposing the social process of functional differentiation that had characterised Europe for centuries. In that process the church is no longer on an equal footing with the state. The latter is part of the political system, the former of the religious – or, more generally, worldview-related – system, in which it is just one among many religious/worldview-related organisations. The church is not unique in that. Pluralism of worldviews and religions cannot simply be wished away: 'the' church is no longer 'the' partner of the state. Yet this view still features, covertly or overtly, in ecclesiastic documents, such as the Vatican II document *Gaudium et Spes*, that still thinks in terms of the twin autonomy of church and state.

From a different perspective, that of civil society, the church's relation to the state appears in yet another light. According to Habermas, Western society comprises two powerful systems: the economic system (the market) and the political system (the state, state bureaucracy, public administration). The associations of civil society are located in between the two.[100] In this triangle of market, state, and civil society, the church – however reprehensible it may have been to Leo XIII – is an association alongside other associations like social, educative, medical, cultural, artistic, or scientific associations.[101] The church finds that hard to swallow, for implicitly or explicitly it still tends to regard itself and the state as twin autonomies, as I said. It is probably not happy with the 'separation of church and state' – a term not used in *Gaudium et Spes* – because it seems to suggest laicism, which might create an enormous gap between the two and preclude any communication.

Yet that is not necessarily so, not even if the church is regarded as an association. An association of whatever kind needs to have three attributes in relation to the state.[102] The first is autonomy: does the

---

[99] Torfs, The Roman Catholic Church, op. cit., 8.

[100] Following phenomenology, J. Habermas, *Theorie des kommunikativen Handelns*, Band 1–2, Suhrkamp, Frankfurt 1981, often refers to civil society as *Lebenswelt* (life world).

[101] C. Malena, Does Civil Society Exist? In: V. Heinrich & L. Fioramonti (eds.), *Civicus: Global Survey of the State of Civil Society*, Vol. 2, Kumarian, Bloomfield 2008, 187–191.

[102] W. Dörner & C. Suarez, Civil Society and the State: Formal Arrangements and

state control it, and to what extent? The second is communication: is its dialogue with the state regular, marginal, or broad? The third is support: does the state provide financial support, and to what extent? All three attributes are pertinent to the relationship between state and church.[103] Autonomy may be indicated, not pejoratively but positively, by the term 'separation', which applies to all sorts of associations such as the separation of market and state (versus a state economy), family and state (versus state pedagogics), education and state (versus state education), science and state (versus state science), art and state (versus state art), hence church and state (versus state church) as well. Separation always goes hand in hand with the other two attributes, also in relations between church and state: communication with the state and extent of state subsidisation, not despite but within the separation between the two. From this perspective, the canonist Torfs says: "Consequently, modern relationships between the state and religious groups are similar to relationships the state develops with other actors in society with regard to problems in fields they are operating in, such as trade unions, professional corporations, environmental organisations, associations protecting consumers. In that line, also religious groups can be interlocutors to the state".[104] Yet because of its age-old allergy the church shies away from it. This again demonstrates that, consciously or unconsciously, vestiges of the *ancien régime* persist.

This applies to Vatican II's declaration on religious freedom well. The compromise it entails shows that one wing of the council was still caught up in the *ancien régime* and the other had entered the modern age. Tradition does not offer a solution here, for the problem to be solved refers to the relation between truth and freedom in a pluralistic society. From the truth perspective one could ask how a religious community can genuinely recognise other communities if it is convinced that it is the only true faith, or at any rate that divine truth subsists (*subsistit*) in it, leaving only traces in other communities. Can it really take those communities' truth claims seriously? From the perspective of freedom one could ask whether a religious community can really proclaim religious freedom if it refuses to accept or even promote reli-

---

Actual Interactions, in: V.F. Heinrich & L. Fioramonti (eds.), *Civicus: Global Survey*, op. cit., 273–288.

[103] Bader, *Secularism*, op. cit., 49–62; cf. S. van Bijsterveld, *Overheid en godsdienst: Herijking van een onderlinge relatie*, Wolf, Nijmegen 2008.

[104] R. Torfs, Relationship between the State and Religious Groups, in: J.-F. Flauss (ed.), *La protection internationale de la liberté religieuse – International Protection of Religious Freedom*, Bruylant, Brussel 2002, 131–152, 136.

gious freedom among its own members, especially if they want to convert to another religion or proceed to live their lives as atheists. Does
that take these members' freedom seriously? And are the missionary
activities of other communities taken as seriously as its own?

To my mind the only way is to prioritise religious freedom as
entrenched in international treaties, at least sequentially, which means:
freedom at first, truth follows. Proceeding from this recognition, religions and worldviews will, in the long term, have to explore each essential truth claim through dialogue and research, alternating between
participant and observer perspectives. The aim should be to analyse
and appraise each theme, taking human rights as an orthopractical test
without any natural law pretensions.[105] I say each theme, for passing a
comprehensive, final judgment is an eschatological prerogative, which
in concrete terms means that the discipline of scientific suspension of
judgment has to be observed, rooted as it is in awareness of the fallible,
approximate character of the truth we may find.[106]

CONCLUSION

Our study of the legitimisation of human rights in the Catholic
Church's social doctrine has produced some clear results. Natural law
as a legitimisation of human rights arose in the 1890s and declined in
the 1960s. Simultaneously, there was mobilisation in a Weberian selective affinity (*Wahlverwandtschaft*) to restore the church of the *ancien
regime*, in its turn followed by demobilisation. Human rights evolved
from divine rights into natural rights, and from natural rights into
fundamental rights. They are not a product of deductive reasoning in
terms of so-called eternal, immutable, universal natural law, but of a
historico-political struggle for a life of human dignity by – in random
order – citizens, slaves, blacks, peasants, workers, women, children,
homosexuals, people of different faiths and nonreligious people, Jews
and other minorities and their champions.[107] They are not rooted in a

---

[105] According to G. Vattimo, Het tijdperk van de interpretatie, in: S. Zabala (ed.),
De toekomst van de religie (Dutch translation of *Futuro della Religione*), Klement,
Kampen 2006, 54, natural law should be abandoned because its claim to metaphysical
truth obstructs dialogue.

[106] J.A. van der Ven et al., *Is There a God of Human Rights?* Brill, Leiden 2004,
511–550.

[107] M. Ishay, *The History of Human Rights: From Ancient Times to the globalization
Era*, Orient Longman, Dehli 2008.

metaphysical, natural law order elevated above time and space, but in the struggle for a humane constitution of the state, which incorporates human rights as politico-historical rights.[108] In his encyclical *Pacem in Terris*, John XXIII explicitly advocated this. But they are also rooted in international treaties as cogent law (*jus cogens*) for member states, notably in the European Convention for the Protection of Human Rights and Fundamental Freedoms (1950), the International Covenant on Civil and Political Rights (1966), and the International Covenant on Economic, Social, and Cultural Rights (1966).

But is that enough? Do we not still need an organ to guard over human rights, even though they are entrenched in our constitutions? Following a long tradition, John XXIII maintains that human rights have a pre-state origin and are independent of all political laws or regulation. To this the philosopher of law Ernst Cassirer adds that they antedate not only the state but also the church.[109] Not only the state but also the church run the risk of infringing human rights with their rules, and have done so frequently right up to the present, evidenced by discrimination against women and homosexuals. Hence Cassirer believes that natural law remains a necessary touchstone. It can be used as a criterion to distinguish between law and justice, and to iden- tify an unfair law as unjust. But what can an abstraction like poly- interpretable 'natural law' add to the provisions laid down in the order of democratic constitutional states under international treaties? A con- stitutional amendment, including one affecting human rights, requires more than just a straight majority; the division of powers implies that each power is responsible for the just interpretation and application of human rights; laws and rules are tested against fundamental rights by a constitutional court and a separate court for human rights. One could also ask what a poly-interpretable abstraction like natural law adds to the human rights culture that is systematically cultivated by independent institutions like Amnesty International, Human Rights Watch, and other NGOs.

Apart from these pragmatic questions there is a principle at issue. Above I opted for the view that in Aquinas's thinking natural law is

---

[108] M. Ignatieff et al., *Human Rights as Politics and Idolatry*, Edited and introduced by A. Gutman, Princeton University Press, Princeton/Oxford 2001.

[109] E. Cassirer, *Freiheitsidee und Staatsidee, Gesammelte Werke*, Band 7, Meiner, Hamburg 2001, 319–387; Id., *Vom Wesen und Werden des Naturrechts*, ibidem, Band 18, 2004, 203–276; cf. D. Coskun, *Law as Symbolic Form: Ernst Cassirer and the Anthropocentric View of Law*, Dissertation Radboud University Nijmegen 2007.

characterised by an ordering of nature according to practical reason. Because the interpretation and application of poly-interpretable natural law depends on practical reason, natural law – as its history proves – increasingly becomes 'rational law' (*Vernunftrecht*), of which Christian Wolff is an exponent.[110] How does this *Vernunftrecht* differ from the operation of 'public reason' in a democratic constitutional state, which elaborates human rights – articulated in the constitution and international treaties – into rules and laws that are in their turn tested against human rights?[111] This is not primarily meant to exclude the concept of natural law from scientific and political debate out of hand, but the question remains what 'more' it offers – what does it add? Neither do I want to exclude morality from law, certainly not when it comes to human rights, because morality fulfils a regulative function in legislation and policy involving human rights. But in a democratic constitutional state with all its institutions, 'public reason' probably suffices to legitimise and guarantee human rights. And perhaps natural law as *Vernunftrecht* only fulfils a negative function in extremely exceptional situations such as the adjudication of the crimes of the Nazi regime in order to indict, beyond the violation of human rights, the violation of human 'nature' – that 'nature' being human dignity.[112] Human dignity is focal in our constitutions and international treaties. Does that not make natural law redundant after all?

---

[110] In Wolff's work, natural law becomes *Vernunftrecht*, in that he considers a whole range of precepts and concomitant rights to be deducible from human nature, especially in his *Grundsätze des Natur- und Völkerrechts worin alle Verbindlichkeiten und alle Rechte aus de Natur des Menschen in einem beständigen Zusammenhang hergeleitet werden*, Halle 1754. These include the precept of and right to freedom (§78) and equality (§95), security (§95), defence and punishment (§95), forming alliances (§97), food, drink and medical aid (§103), clothing (§115), housing (§116), natural beauty (§117), whatever can contribute to happiness (§118) and a comfortable life and contentment (§119), and work according to capacity and health (§124). In this book Wolff concedes that all these rights can be inferred from natural law, but does not specify what kind of reasoning is used, which is all the more necessary if one compares this long list with the one principle that Thomas Aquinas relates to natural law, namely that one must do good and refrain from evil (STh I–II 94), and with the limited principles that Hugo de Groot infers from nature, namely respect for goods belonging to others, returning goods, reparation for damage, keeping promises and imposition of deserved punishment (Grotius, *De jure*, op. cit., Prolegomena 8).

[111] J. Rawls, The Idea of Public Reasons Revisited. *The University of Chicago Law Review* 64(1997)3, 765–807

[112] Cf. N. Luhmann, *Das Recht der Gesellschaft*, Suhrkamp, Frankfurt 1995, 507–519; Id., Das Paradox der Menschenrechte und drei Formen seiner Entfaltung, in: *Die Soziologie und der Mensch*, Westdeutscher Verlag, Opladen 1995, 229–236; K. Kühl, s.v. Recht und Moral, in: Düwel et al., *Ethik*, op. cit., 486–493, here 490–491.

CHAPTER SIX

RELIGIOUS RIGHTS FOR MINORITIES

In the latter half of the 20th century, religion appeared to be on its way out in Western society. It was predicted that in an 'enlightened' society only a small minority would still find it relevant, if it were not to vanish altogether. Yet since the years around the turn of the century it seems to have made a comeback, albeit that much of the religious drive tends to be channelled into personal lives and worlds rather than expressed in traditional religion.

Apart from this renewed interest at the micro level, religion is asserting itself at the macro level of national and international relations, where it is sowing dissension and violence. Horrendous pictures are indelibly etched on our retinas: demonstrations of Soldiers for Christ against abortion clinics in the United States, Catholic and Protestant marches in Belfast, messianic Zionist attacks in Israel, suicide missions by Islamic martyrs, the ferocity of Sikhs' swords in India, the armageddon in a Tokyo subway by Buddhist apocalypticists.[1]

At the meso level of boroughs, cities, and metropolises, religion manifests in other ways. People from diverse ethnic backgrounds strive to maintain their way of life despite constant friction, rioting, protests, disturbances, even armed clashes between majorities and minorities, among different minorities, and between minorities and the police. In this turbulent, multicultural society, religion also features. Sometimes it is the cause of conflict, at others the result or condition of conflict, often merely a concomitant phenomenon, in other instances an ideology seized to legitimise the conflict. Whatever the configuration, it often seems as if there is no violence without some form of religion and no religion without some form of violence. All this has pushed religion to the top of the agenda of multicultural societies.

The problem is how this multicultural agenda should be handled. Certainly a contextual re-sourcing of the various religions, with the accent on tolerance, respect, and recognition (*Anerkennung*) would

---

[1] M. Juergensmeyer, *Terror in the Mind of God: The Global Rise of Religious Violence*, 3rd revised and updated edition, University of California Press, Berkeley 2003.

contribute to a long-term solution. Interreligious dialogue between leaders, lay people, and scientists, in which the meaning of these three concepts are communicated, will certainly bring us closer to a solution. Here taxonomy of the concepts is pertinent.[2] 'Tolerance' is a start, albeit imperfect in view of its asymmetry, especially in relations between a majority and minorities. The former grants the latter permission, so to speak, to endorse certain principles and practices that it actually condemns but permits for the sake of social peace, while reserving the right to revoke that permission at a later stage. Examples include the case of the Huguenots in the Edict of Nantes (1598) and Edict of Fontainebleau (1685), respectively. 'Respect' goes one step further, since the reprehensible notions and practices are allowed out of compassion with the people belonging to these minorities and consideration of their human dignity. 'Recognition' goes even further, for it acknowledges not only their persons but also their beliefs and practices, realising that these symbolise the minorities' ethnic, linguistic, cultural, and religious identity. Since not all expressions of this identity are evaluated positively by the majority (sometimes they are condemned outright, as in the case of genital mutilation), recognition could be a product of political negotiation and compromise.[3]

To prevent this politics of recognition from remaining at the level of abstract idealism, one has to create economic, political, and social conditions for its realisation, and moreover proceed to grant special rights. This chapter focuses on the granting of religious rights for minorities.[4]

In official documents such as the UN Declaration on the Rights of Persons belonging to National or Ethnic, Religious and Linguistic Minorities (1992) and the Framework Convention for the Protection of National Minorities by the Council of Europe (1995), religious

---

[2] R. Forst, *Toleranz im Konflikt*, Suhrkamp, Frankfurt 2003; P. Zagorin, *How the Idea of Religious Tolerance Came to the West*, Princeton University Press, Princeton 2003.

[3] Ch. Taylor, The Politics of Recognition, in: A. Gutmann (ed.), *Multiculturalism: Examaning the Politics of Recognition*, Princeton University Press, Princeton 1994, 25–74; Ch. Taylor, Modes of secularism, in: R. Bhargava (ed.), *Secularism and its Critics*, Oxford University Press, Delhi 1999, 50.

[4] L. Blum, Recognition, Value, and Equality: A Critique of Charles Taylor's and Nancy Fraser's Accounts of Multiculturalism, in: C. Willett (ed.), *Theorizing Multiculturalism: A Guide to the Current Debate*, Blackwell, Malden 1998, 73–99; N. Fraser & A. Honneth, *Umverteilung oder Anerkennung? Eine politisch-philosophische Kontroverse*, Suhrkamp, Frankfurt 2003.

rights for minorities are seen as the application of general rights in the religious domain. What is lacking is a direct approach, concretely defining minority rights in a way that legally recognises the religious ideas and practices that embody their identity. This raises three problems. First, the literary genre of such documents understandably precludes a concrete definition. Secondly, the term 'religious rights for minorities' poses substantive problems: it is by no means clear what religion has to do with rights, and even less clear whether minorities should be granted collective rights. Finally, granting minorities religious rights raises the spectre of legal pluralism, which jeopardises the unitary nature of the state and the law.

These are the problems I shall be exploring. First I deal with problematic aspects of minority rights (6.1). Then I look at complexities in the relation between these rights and religion, particularly against the background of the autonomous state, the separation of church and state, and religious freedom (6.2). Finally, I turn to legal pluralism, more particularly the possibility of incorporating aspects of religious – especially Islamic – personal law and the problems it entails for gender equality (6.3).

6.1   Minority Rights

In modern times, minorities are concomitants of nation states, which burgeoned in the 19th century following the collapse of Europe's large political empires. These nation states conducted a politics of inclusion and exclusion, apparent in the three synonyms for 'boundaries'. Members of a nation are included and the national territory is demarcated by way of *borders*. Those on the other side of these *frontiers* are excluded. To prevent foreigners from intruding, access is denied by way of *barriers*.[5] Nationals finding themselves on the wrong side of the border could gain access to the nation state by way of irredentist annexation. In the myth of the nation state, there are and can be no minorities. The ethnic and cultural entity – the nation – coincides with the geo-political entity, the state.

---

[5] M. Karskens, Staatsvijanden of nieuwe collega's? Hoe natiestaten en de open samenleving migranten waarderen, in: E. Brugmans, P. Minderhoud & J. van Vught (eds.), *Mythen en misverstanden over migratie*, Valkhof, Nijmegen 2007, 205–236.

If minorities still existed notwithstanding this ideology, the rights applicable to nationals were not extended to them. They represented an exception, stipulated in the traditional minority treaties before and after World War I, which focused on assimilation. Minorities were regarded as second class citizens, and their linguistic, cultural, and religious rights were trampled underfoot, invoking their vengeance. They fell prey to 'totalitarian infection'.[6]

6.1.1   Rights for Traditional Minorities

Could the League of Nations, created in 1919, have prevented this? That brings us to a historical problem whose shadow extends to the United Nations, established in 1945. One issue in the debates on the League was whether religious freedom should be specified in a treaty, and whether it should include minority rights. Both questions were answered negatively because of their interrelationship.[7] Religious freedom was considered an issue for minorities – the majority's religion required no such safeguard – and granting this right along with others was seen as incurring the risk of national and international conflict. Instead, a system of separate treaties was instituted between the Allies and a number of East European countries, including Poland with its large Jewish minority. However, the inconsistency and uneven application of these treaties led to mounting protest, and in 1934 Poland abandoned the system, precipitating its collapse.[8]

At the inception of the United Nations, two decisions were taken. The first was to replace the idea of a collective approach to religious freedom with an individual interpretation. In the Universal Declaration of Human Rights (1948) religious freedom is an individual right, like all human rights: individuals are entitled to practise their religion, either alone or in community with other individuals (art. 18). Secondly, minority rights were not included in the Universal Declaration, because human rights, as mentioned already, are individual.[9] This changed in the UN International Covenant on Civil and Political Rights (1966). It did include minority rights, but in the form of

---

[6] H. Arendt, *The Origins of Totalitarianism*, Harcourt, Brace & World, New York 1966, 278.

[7] F. Wilson, *The Origins of the League Covenant*, Hogarth Press, London 1928, 105–107.

[8] M.D. Evans, *Religious Liberty and International Law in Europe*, Cambridge University Press, Cambridge 1997, 83–171.

[9] Ibidem, 177–183.

individual rights that applied in the areas of language, culture, and religion, either individually or in community with other individuals (art. 27).[10] The twofold individual approach did not come from nowhere. It has its preamble in the so-called radical Enlightenment with its doctrine of religious freedom, which Spinoza grounded in individual freedom of conscience, thought, and expression.[11] This provided the historical backdrop to the victory of liberalism over communitarianism in the compilation of the Universal Declaration: the individual is centre stage, the community is derivative.[12]

This is the historically understandable, albeit not justified, course that the two rights – religious freedom and minority rights – followed. In 1919, the League of Nations repudiated their collective, interrelated character. In 1948, the United Nations recognised religious freedom as an individual right, and in 1966 it recognised minority rights as an individual right. The two rights appeared to be inseparable – a conclusion with weighty implications, as will be seen below.

6.1.2   Rights for Migrant Minorities

In the period between the Covenant of 1966 and the collapse of the Berlin wall in 1989, the debate on minority rights died down. But the disintegration of the Soviet Union and the ensuing conflict in the Balkans put it back on the agenda. At the same time, however, new, related problems arose in Western Europe. They concerned migrant minorities, which, at the invitation of the host countries, had settled there since the 1960s to alleviate labour shortages. Since then they have grown exponentially as a result of economic, family, and humanitarian migration.[13] Initially they were welcomed, eventually tolerated because it was anticipated that their stay would be temporary. When it turned out to be permanent and their communities expanded, people made a virtue of necessity and swathed it in a normative ideology of Canadian

---

[10] P. Weller, *The Rights of Minorities in Europe*, Oxford University Press, Oxford, 2005, 77–96.

[11] J. Israel, *Enlightenment Contested*, Oxford University Press, Oxford 2006, 155–163.

[12] J. Morsink, *The Universal Declaration of Human Rights: Origins, Drafting and Intent*, University of Pennsylvania Press, Philadelphia 1999, 241–252.

[13] OECD (Organisation for Economic Co-operation and Development), *International Migration Outlook*, Paris 2006, 26–48.

origin: that of multicultural society. Thus the mono-cultural nation state was declared obsolete.

But over the past decade it has become increasingly evident that multicultural society was not getting off the ground, at any rate not properly. The signals were impoverished neighbourhoods, poor housing, persistent unemployment, alarming linguistic deprivation, high dropout rates at schools, and frightening crime statistics. Integration was getting nowhere, economically, spatially, politically, socially, linguistically, educationally, legally, and culturally.[14] At the same time, there was growing prejudice and animosity against migrant minorities, especially those from Muslim countries, causing increasing alienation and exclusion and culminating in conflict, even armed clashes.[15] Public debate was marked by increasingly fierce emphasis on a multicultural crisis, sometimes called a multicultural drama.[16] The question was raised whether we should keep our borders closed to ward off violence 'from outside' (barriers), or at least leave them fairly open to political refugees and foreigners with economic potential.[17] Should we not revert to the assimilation policy of the monocultural nation state?

The assimilation enterprise, however, is politically impracticable, judicially objectionable, and morally reprehensible. It is politically impracticable because escalating globalisation is eroding the nation state and migrant minorities are growing proportionally faster than the aging indigenous population. It is judicially objectionable because it is condemned in the aforementioned UN and European documents on minorities, which may be considered expressions of international customary law. It is morally reprehensible because migrant minorities are once more reduced to second-rate citizenship, existing by grace of repressive tolerance on the part of the state and society, instead of

---

[14] The lack of judicial integration is evidenced by the inhumane detention of illegal immigrants (A. van Kalmthout et al., *European Foreign Prisoners Project*, Tilburg University Press, Tilburg 2006) followed by deportation (L. Mathieu, *La double peine*, La dispute, Paris 2006), in contravention of the legal principle that a person cannot be punished twice for the same crime; OECD, *International*, op. cit., 76–101.

[15] EUMC (European Monitoring Centre on Racism and Xenophobia), *Muslims in the European Union. Discrimination and Islamophobia*, FRA (Agency for Fundamental Rights), Vienna 2006.

[16] T. Modood, A. Triandafyllidou & R. Zapata-Barrero (eds.), *Multiculturalism, Muslims and Citizenship: A European Approach*, Routledge, London 2006.

[17] V. Bader, Fairly Open Borders, in: V. Bader (ed.), *Citizenship and Exclusion*, Macmillan, London 1997, 28–60.

being respected for their human dignity, let alone their ethnic, linguistic, cultural, and religious identity.

Instead, there should be a sharply focused, consistent, pertinacious policy, based on meticulous research, to overcome the economic, political, social, and cultural problems of multicultural society. Research shows that reducing unemployment and promoting education are major ameliorative forces.[18] Promoting participation in organisations in civil society and political organs is also conducive to positive change.[19]

6.1.3   Towards a Consociational State

What kind of state is needed for such a policy? Whatever name it is called by – consociational state (Lijphart) or associative democracy (Bader) – it would have to promote and judicially legitimise cooperation between the majority of the population and the minorities, and between the minorities themselves. Judicial legitimisation is needed, because without it the state, consciously or otherwise, will always favour the identity, values, and interests of the majority, and impose them on minorities. That makes nonsense of the separation of ethnicity and state, which lies at the root of the prohibition of discrimination on racial grounds. Kymlicka actually holds that in the event of a minority wanting to deviate from state rules, the onus of proof is on the state, not on the minority, because the state is denying the minority's right to contribute to the common good in terms of its own values and interests. The majority has that right, so why deny it to minorities?[20]

Such a state, in which minorities' right to exist is acknowledged and exchange of views is institutionalised in a deliberative democracy, prevents any hidden majority bias.[21] It is needed in deeply divided societies

---

[18] F. van Tubergen, *The Integration of Immigrants in Cross-National Perspective*, ICS, Utrecht 2004.

[19] L. Bloemraad, *Becoming a Citizen: Incorporating Immigrants and Refugees in the United States and Canada*, University of California Press, Berkeley 2006.

[20] W. Kymlicka, Universal Minority Rights? In: Y. Morigiwa et al. (eds.), *Universal Minority Rights*, Steiner, Stuttgart 2004, 13–57; W. Kymlicka, Replies to Commentaries, in: Morigiwa et al. (eds), *Minority rights*, op. cit., 105–123.

[21] V. Bader, Religious Diversity and Democratic Institutional Pluralism, *Political Theory* 31(2003)2, 265–294; V. Bader, Religions and States: A new Typology and a Plea for Non-Constitutional Pluralism, *Ethical theory and moral practice* 6(2003)1, 55–91.

with minorities comprising more than 15% of the population.[22] It may be characterised by a constitution with a clause stipulating that any amendment requires the assent not just of a qualified majority, be it Christian, Muslim, or secular, but also of minorities. This precludes the establishment of a theocracy.[23] Other features could be a combination of central and decentralised administration; an asymmetrical bicameral system, possibly with separate seats for minorities (cf. the Rumanian constitution, art. 62.2); and proportional representation (as opposed to majority electoral systems in which winner takes all). Such a state would be run by coalition cabinets in consultation with representative minority interest groups. It would have elements of direct democracy that offer minorities a legally stipulated opportunity to initiate or block legislation. It would include special rights for minorities that guarantee their values and interests. Its bureaucracy would be ethnically proportional, along with the allocation of funds.

Although granting minorities special rights may seem a good remedy for the problems of multicultural society, it raises fresh ones. One is the multiplicity of migrant minorities: Finland has 31, Germany 32, Sweden 46, Denmark 47, Belgium 49, the Netherlands 54, the United Kingdom 60, Austria 70, Italy 90, the United States 200.[24] One could see it as a purely practical problem, but should and can every one of them be granted special rights? There are also conceptual problems. Firstly, what is a minority? How big must a group be to constitute a minority, what are the bottom and upper limits; is every group of a given size with ethnic attributes a minority; and what are ethnic attributes? The next problem is qualitative: in how far does a group's sense of its distinctive linguistic, cultural, and/or religious identity, and its desire to retain it, carry weight? Is it a matter of – to put it radically – mere social psychology, or does it extend to social history and social geography? Then there is a political problem: how important is the aspect of power? Must a minority occupy a non-dominant position – in relation to the majority or other minorities – to qualify as such?

---

[22] A. Lijphart, Self-Determination versus Pre-Determination of Ethnic Minorities in Power-Sharing Systems, in: W. Kymlicka (ed.), *The rights of Minority Cultures*, Oxford University Press, Oxford 1995, 275–287; A. Lijphart, Definitions, Evidence, and Policy, *Journal of Theoretical Politics* 12(2000)4, 425–431; A. Lijphart, *Democracy in the Twenty-First Century*, NIAS, Wassenaar 2000.

[23] M. Kleijwegt & M. van Weezel (eds.), *Het land van haat en nijd*, Balans, Amsterdam 2006.

[24] Van Tubergen, *The Integration*, op. cit., 63.

Does it also require that their physical and/or economic survival is threatened?[25] Finally there are questions about principles. First, can any entity other than an individual person (e.g. a group or minority) possess rights? Is 'collective rights' in fact an appropriate concept?[26] In Europe since the collapse of the Soviet Union there appears to be scope for such rights, at any rate for national minorities, as witnessed in the Charter of Paris (1990) and the Copenhagen Criteria (1993); yet less than a decade later the Treaty of Amsterdam (1997) reverted to purely individual rights.[27] Secondly, do collective rights, if they exist at all, not infringe the freedom of individual members?[28] Suppose a Muslim minority is granted the right to regulate their own marriages, will women have to suffer the consequences? To obviate the problem, Kymlicka offers a distinction between *intolerable* restrictions such as torture, women trafficking and polygyny, and *tolerable* restrictions such as limited economic or political competency.[29] Even so, the latter still conflicts with gender equality – a point to which I return below.

One can be paralysed by these problems, or one can try to keep a long-term perspective and doggedly, out of basic conviction, work towards a series of partial solutions through negotiation and compromise. It calls for reasoned utopianism, a combination of utopian vision and an incrementalist approach.[30] Both deontological and consequentialist considerations could act as guidelines.[31] In the case of the former, rights are granted according to the aforementioned politics of recognition of human dignity.[32] The latter is prompted by the insight that minorities are prepared to contribute to the common good if they have equal freedom, reflected in human rights.

---

[25] M. Jovanović, Recognizing Minority Identities Through Collective Rights, *Human Rights Quarterly* 27(2005)2, 625–651.

[26] M. Galenkamp, *Individualism versus Collectivism*, Rotterdamse Filosofische Studies, Rotterdam 1993.

[27] J. Hughes & G. Sasse, Monitoring the Monitors: EU Enlargement Conditionality and Minority Protection, The CEEC's *Journal of Ethnopolitics and Minorty Issues in Europe* 2003, 1–36.

[28] J. Habermas, Struggles for Recognition in the Democratic Constitutional State, in: A. Gutmann (ed.), *Multiculturalism: Examining the Politics of Recognition*, Princeton University Press, Princeton 1994, 107–148.

[29] W. Kymlicka, *Multicultural citizenship*, Clarendon, Oxford 1995.

[30] V. Bader & E. Engelen, Taking Pluralism Seriously: Arguing for an Institutional Turn in Political Philosophy, *Philosophy and Social Criticism* 29(2003)4, 375–406.

[31] A. Sen, *On Ethics and Economics*, Oxford University Press, Oxford 1988.

[32] P. Ricoeur, *The Course of Recognition*, Harvard University Press, Cambridge 2005, 196–201.

6.2   Religious Rights for Minorities

After this general overview of problems regarding the granting of rights to minorities, let us look more specifically at religious rights. In a democracy, as opposed to a theocracy, they cannot be taken for granted. Three principles can be used in refutation: the autonomous state, the separation of church and state, and religious freedom.

6.2.1   *The Autonomous State*

The rise of the autonomous state is part of a broad process of functional differentiation that has been going on in Western society for several centuries.[33] It led to the gradual demolition of the trichotomous medieval worldview. According to this view, earth was *spatially* divided into a religious world (*ecclesia*) and a secular world (*saeculum*), both overarched by heaven. *Politically* it was divided into the church as a religio-political power (papal kingdom) and the city of man (Holy Roman Empire), both covered by the city of God (*civitas Dei*). *Ecclesiologically* it was divided into the visible church (*una, sancta, catholica, apostolica ecclesia*) and secular society, both overarched by the invisible church (*communio sanctorum*). Whatever conflicts raged between church and state, there was always a sense of falling under one sacred canopy: *spatially* under heaven, *politically* under the city of God, and *ecclesiastically* under the invisible church (*communio sanctorum*).[34] The collapse of this system as a result of functional differentiation put an end to the rivalry between church and state for rank, status, and reputation, culminating in two separate institutions, each with its own autonomous function: religion for the church and politics for the state.[35]

Church and theology both contributed to this process, as the following two examples testify. Thomas Aquinas already assigned the non-ecclesiastic world – the economic, social, and administrative spheres – a certain autonomy, as opposed to Augustine, who oriented them to different ends with "a different faith, a different hope, a different love".[36]

---

[33] See chapter 8.

[34] J. Casanova, *Public Religions in the Modern World*, University of Chicago Press, Chicago 1994.

[35] N. Luhmann, *Funktion der Religion*, Suhrkamp, Frankfurt 1982.

[36] Augustine, *De Civitate Dei* XVIII; J. Milbank, *Theology and Social Theory: Beyond Secular Reason*, Blackwell, Oxford 1999, 406–408.

In late medieval theology, nominalism and voluntarism replaced the Christian trinity with the monarchic monotheism of God's absolute power. This theology paved the way for the doctrine of the absolute sovereignty of the human being, created by God in his image and, as his lieutenant, having absolute control over all that exists. It also paved the way for the prince, on whom this legal absolute sovereignty was conferred by a contract between him and his subjects, granting him supreme rule over the state in his own right, independently of the church.[37]

The Peace of Westphalia (1648) translated this notion of the autonomous state into practical politics to put an end to the catastrophic religious wars of the 16th and 17th centuries. The treaty not only confirmed the stipulation in the Peace of Augsburg (1555) that the choice of Catholicism or Lutheranism by the rulers of the various German principalities was binding for their subjects (*cuius regio eius religio*). The rule was extended by imposing a similar arrangement on the Reformed churches and on all European countries that were signatories to the peace. In addition, Christians living in states where their denomination was not that of the sovereign were guaranteed the right to practise their faith publicly at appointed times. Thus the Peace of Westphalia not only recognised religious (in effect Christian) pluralism, albeit still territorially limited, but also instituted religious freedom for minorities.

At the level of the German *Reichstag*, the treaty included another special ruling, again following the Peace of Augsburg. Because representatives of the Catholic classes were in the majority, resulting in ineffective assemblies with Protestants when it came to religious affairs, it was decided to apply a parity rather than majority principle in these debates in the *Reichstag*. Both parties had to manage their respective viewpoints as separate communities (*corpus catholicorum* and *corpus evangelicorum*) outside the *Reichstag* (*ius eundi in partes – itio in partes*) in a manner that permitted them to reach an amicable settlement (*amicabilis compositio*). This ruling amounted to a breach of the territorially determined religious pluralism of the German principalities and recognition of a group-based religious pluralism at the level of the *Reichstag*. The Catholic Church, understandably, objected to this

---

[37] Milbank, *Theology*, op. cit., 12–17; H. Glenn, *Legal Traditions of the World: Sustainable Diversity in Law*, Oxford University Press, Oxford 2000, 129–132.

and declared the treaty invalid, but with little impact.[38] Recognition of group-based religious pluralism may be seen as paving the way for the aforementioned consociational state when it came to granting religious rights to minorities.[39]

6.2.2   Separation of Church and State

It would be anachronistic to attribute meanings from later eras to the autonomous state of 1648. It made no separation between church and state since the monarch controlled religion, whereas this separation is an essential feature of present-day Western societies. What does the modern separation between church and state imply?[40] The answer is by no means simple, as different countries present many variations on this principle, evident in classifications like those of Martin,[41] Bader,[42] and Temperman.[43] These classifications are analytical and insightful, but far too complex for the purpose of this chapter. This section does not offer a comprehensive description of all the variations, but merely probes the implications of the separation for the granting of religious minority rights. To that end I use five models from the ideal-typical classification of Durham.[44] The extremes are the first model – identification of church and state in a theocracy – and the fifth, strict separation between the two in seperationism. The remaining three models range on a continuum between the extremes.

In a theocracy, church and state coincide. The laws of the one officially recognised religion are the laws of the state, and the laws of the state are legitimised by religious laws. This model is found in a number of Muslim countries, where the state is structured on the basis of religious fundamentalism, though they vary in the tolerance they display

---

[38] H. Tüchle, *Geschiedenis van de kerk. Deel VI. De kerk tijdens de Contrareformatie*, Brand, Hilversum/Antwerpen 1966, 58–62.

[39] Cf. G. Lembruch, Consociational Democracy and Corporatism in Switzerland, *Publius* 23(1993)2, 43–60.

[40] See chapter 8.

[41] D. Martin, *A General Theory of Secularization*, Harper & Row, New York 1978.

[42] Bader, Religious Diversity, art. cit.

[43] J. Temperman, The Neutral State: Optional or Necessary? A Triangular Analysis of State-Religion Relationships, Democratisation and Human Rights Compliance, *Religion and Human Rights* 3(2007)1, 269–303.

[44] In Durham's classification I omit the endorsed church, inadvertent insensitivity and hostility; W. Durham, Perspectives on Religious Liberty, in: J. van der Vyver & J. Witte (eds.), *Religious Human Rights in Global Perspective: Legal Perspectives*, Nijhoff, The Hague 1996, 1–44.

towards other religions.[45] The second model is that of an established church, which is found in such European countries as Bulgaria, Croatia, Denmark, England, Greece, Macedonia, Norway, and Scotland. Although this model makes no formal separation between church and state, they are all democratic and confer liberal human rights – including religious ones – on other religions.[46] The third model represents cooperation between the state and religions. It stems from an explicitly recognised benevolence towards religions because of their importance for social cohesion and harmony. The state moreover provides funding for religion-related activities, like the maintenance of church buildings, clerical stipends and/or religious education, and may also assist by waiving contributions like the 'church tax' in Germany. This model does not endorse any specific religion but treats all religions equally, even in countries that have concordats with the Catholic Church, such as Spain, Italy, Poland, and several Latin American countries. The fourth model is accommodationist, inspired by benevolent neutrality towards religions. It differs from the third in that the state, whilst supporting religions, does not translate it into financial subsidies. State aid is confined to exemptions in areas such as tax and national service and accommodations in respect of the weekly and annual calendar (Sunday rest, religious feasts). The fifth and last model is radically separationist. The state refrains from offering the religions any support, even by way of accommodations or exemptions. Thus facilitating religious education at public schools other than as a component of historical or cultural education is taboo. Religions are banished from the public domain and relegated to the private sphere as private associations. In some cases the state exercises some control over religions, for instance by requiring them to establish private religious associations, registering and overseeing these. Sometimes separationism is marked by hostility towards religions because of their (supposed) power and dominance.

This review shows the variety of the relations between church and state. Theocracy is marked by the identification of church and state, because there is no separation whatsoever between church and state, as in the view of political Muslims who support the idea: Islam is both religion and state. In the established church model, the state, despite its

---

[45] M. Rohe, *Das Islamische Recht: Geschichte und Gegenwart*, Beck, München 2009, 243–254.

[46] R. Barro & R. McCleary, *Which Countries Have State Religions?* 2004, available at http://economics.uchicago.edu/download/state_religion_03-03.pdf.

public affiliation with a particular religion, recognises religious pluralism. The cooperationist model is marked by equal treatment, including in the financial sphere, of all religions. In the accommodationist model, the state confines itself to granting equal accommodations and exemptions. In the separationist model, the state banishes religions from the public domain and tolerates them exclusively in the private domain.

Apart from the theocratic model, the other four are marked by mutual non-intervention between church and state. This holds even in the case of an established church, not formally but (largely) in practice. It implies that the church refrains from exercising any direct influence over the state other than by way of public opinion in civil society, and the state refrains from exercising influence over the church, unless democracy, public safety, public order, health and morality, or the rights and freedoms of others are at issue (cf. European Convention for the Protection of Human Rights and Fundamental Freedoms 1950, art. 9,2).

Because the five models are ideal types in the Weberian sense, one finds all sorts of combinations and transitional forms in real life. Thus the Netherlands and Belgium combine features of the third and the fourth model. The history of France, the home of laicity (*laicité*), is marked by interesting transitions. In 1804 the Civil Code (*Code civile*) put an end to the Catholic Church's position as the established church, stressed the positive societal function of religion, and underscored equal treatment, including financial, of all religions – all conforming to aspects of the aforementioned third and fourth models. In 1905 the Separation of Church and State Act (*Loi du 9 décembre 1905 concernant la séparation des Églises et de l'État*) makes no mention at all of the positive function of religions, accentuates religious freedom as a private affair, and terminates all financial subsidisation; but it did not deny religions' contribution to the provision of public humanitarian services. The French model does not conform to the fifth model, but combines elements of models four and five.[47]

In this chapter, we examine which model of separation between church and state is harnessed to either obstruct or promote granting of religious rights to minorities. The answer is brief. The theocratic and separationist models do not allow for religious minority rights at all; the other three models do not have any fundamental objections to it.

---

[47] E. Poulat, *Notre laïcité publique*, Berg, Paris 2003, passim.

But this does not resolve all the issues, since the fifth model, separationism with its 'iron logic', appears to have a certain attraction for non-separationists also. In terms of this logic, the argument is sometimes adduced that nonreligious people (may) experience it as discrimination when religious people are granted rights that they are denied. This implies discrimination in favour of believers against non-believers. As a result, the prohibition of discrimination is expounded in two directions: it has to protect believers against discrimination by nonbelievers, and it has to protect non-believers against discrimination by believers. For the rest it accords with the classical interpretation: nobody should be subjected to discrimination, neither on religious grounds nor on grounds of nonreligiosity. From this 'iron logic' the question "why believers need special rights?" was raised in a motion submitted to the Dutch Lower House in 2006. This held that if believers are granted religious rights then nonbelievers should be given nonreligious rights. Since the latter notion is absurd, it is argued, one has to refuse believers' claim to religious rights as well. However, the notion that granting rights to religious minorities discriminates against nonreligious people is equally absurd, since advantages for the former do not automatically entail disadvantages for the latter. Hence to my mind the objection is refutable.

6.2.3   *Religious Freedom*

In addition to the separation between church and state, religious freedom can also be used to advocate or protest against granting religious rights. An argument for granting such rights may be based on the right to religious freedom and on legislation in many countries that details this right in regard to the self-organisation of religious communities and affiliated associations.[48] Apart from this, case law in these countries shows that courts often (almost invariably) assign religious freedom – including that of self-organisation – priority over other fundamental rights. The argument is that religious freedom obligates the state to refrain from any intervention whatsoever. In that perspective, some argue for granting religious minorities special rights in areas directly linked with their religious beliefs, such as the weekly calendar (a weekly day of rest), annual calendar (religious feasts), dress, and

---

[48] Chapter 7.

aspects of personal law (which includes marriage and family law). I return to this last point below.

Granting freedom of religion and self-organisation is one thing. However, adjudication that often (or almost invariably) gives this right priority over other fundamental right is another. The latter conflicts with the conception of human rights as a totality of equal, inseparable, interrelated, and interdependent rights, as upheld in Article 5 of the Vienna Declaration and Programme of Action Adopted at the World Conference on Human Rights (1993). Religion is no higher in the hierarchy than any other right, for there *is* no hierarchy, also according to the latest declaration of the Dutch Ministry of Foreign Affairs (2004). To this I would add the proviso: with the exception of so-called absolute rights, for which no limit applies, such as the prohibition of torture and slavery.[49] Hence it would be better for the judge not to assign religion priority systematically, but to put it on a par with other basic rights and on that basis arrive at an unbiased, reasonable and fair weighing and assessment of each individual case.

The Dutch People's Party for Freedom and Democracy (*Volkspartij voor Vrijheid en Democratie* - VVD) goes one step further. It holds that in cases of collision between religious freedom and the prohibition of discrimination, the latter merits preference if the relevant interpersonal differences arise from factors beyond the person's control because they are of a physical nature. These include gender differences between men and women and differences in sexual orientation between heterosexuals and homosexuals.[50] Religion does not fall in this category: it is not a natural attribute but a quasi-universal cultural rather than a universal physical phenomenon.[51] Applied to the question of granting religious minorities special rights, it poses problems regarding discrimination against women in the area of personal law, while the position of homosexuals remains wholly taboo.

Others go even further, maintaining that religious freedom should be scrapped from the constitution altogether because it is said to be

---

[49] S. Joseph, J. Schultz & M. Castan, *The International Convenant on Civil and Political Rights: Cases, Materials, and Commentary*, Oxford University Press, Oxford 2005, 31.

[50] VVD, *Om de vrijheid, partijprogramma*, 2005; VVD, *Voor een samenleving met ambitie*, 2006.

[51] J.A. van der Ven, Three Paradigms for the Study of Religion, in: H. Streib (ed.), *Religion Inside and Outside Traditional Institutions*, Brill, Leiden 2007, 7–34; J.A. van der Ven, Religion, Morality and Ritual in Evolutionary Perspective, in: H. Schilderman (ed.), *Discourse in Ritual Studies*, Brill Leiden, 2007, 35–80.

redundant. Prohibition of discrimination, it is argued, covers everything that religious people deem important. After all, what every citizen can claim in terms of that prohibition – the exercise of rights like
freedom of conscience, expression, assembly, association, et cetera –
applies to religious citizens as well. Thus many religious court cases
affecting minorities should not fall under religious freedom, but can
be decided satisfactorily in their favour in terms of the prohibition of
discrimination.[52]

That would rid the law of a thorny problem, namely the definition
of religion. Religious freedom is considered a judicially weak right,
because 'religion' is vague and susceptible to many interpretations.[53] It
has not been defined in a substantive sense, and cannot be so defined
in law.[54] It is conceived of in a purely functional sense, and is mentioned in the same breath as belief. It involves every belief that is of
ultimate concern to an individual.[55] Hence it provides no guidelines
for issues like the following. Is Bible reading in public schools permitted?[56] When does the use of incentives by missionaries exceed the
limits of proper proselytism?[57] When is hate speech about other religions justifiable?[58] Can members of a group that administers utilizes
marijuana in worship and regards it as a 'sacrament' claim it as a right
under religious freedom?[59] The law does not know and cannot know
what religion is in essence, which religious beliefs and observances
are 'orthodox' and which are not, what is 'heretical' and what is not.
As the US Supreme Court puts it: "The law knows no heresy, and
is committed to the support of no dogma, the establishment of no
sect."[60] Thus the word 'religion' may as well be scrapped from legal
dictionaries.[61]

---

[52] P.M. Taylor, *Freedom of Religion*, Cambridge University Press, Cambridge 2005,
197.
[53] Ibidem, 23.
[54] C. Evans, *Freedom of Religion under the European Convention on Human Rights*,
Oxford University Press, Oxford 2005, 51–66.
[55] N. Lerner, *Religion, Secular Beliefs and Human Rights*, Brill, Leiden 2006, 6.
[56] F. Ravitch, *School Prayer and Discrimination*, Northeastern University Press,
Boston 1999.
[57] Taylor, *Freedom of Religion*, op. cit., 67–70; J. Witte & R. Martin, *Sharing the
Book*, Orbis, New York 1999.
[58] Taylor, *Freedom of Religion*, op. cit., 77–84.
[59] Ibidem, 197.
[60] G. Jacobsohn, *The Wheel of Law: India's Secularism in Comparative Constitu
tional Context*, Princeton University Press, Princeton 2003, 61, 100.
[61] W. Sullivan, *The Impossibility of Religious Freedom*, Princeton University Press,
Princeton 2005.

This approach is compatible with the secularisation process in Western society. Human rights are not interpreted in a 'storm-free zone' according to eternal, a-temporal rules. They are influenced by the spirit of the age, if only to prevent social unrest and turbulence.[62] When the spirit of the age is secularised, so is religious freedom.

Against this background, advocating religious minority rights resembles the pursuit of an illusory utopia. Separation between church and state – at any rate in the separationist model, whose adherents are not confined to radical separationists – is adduced as a barrier to these rights, and religious freedom is narrowed down to just one right alongside other human rights, if it is retained as a right at all. That would remove the basis for separate religious rights.

6.2.4   Separation of Church and State and Religious Freedom from a Minority Point of View

But before coming to such an uncompromising decision we would be wise to take a look at the debate in the United States. The opening sentence of the first amendment to the American constitution reads: "Congress shall make no law respecting an establishment of religion, or prohibiting the free exercise thereof." The 'no establishment' clause in this sentence relates to separation between church and state, and the 'free exercise' clause to freedom of worship, teaching, practice and observance. Three interpretations of the relation between the two clauses stand out. The first is that the 'no establishment' clause is subordinate to the 'free exercise' clause, in that the absence of state intervention makes religion flourish via market forces and competition between religions – a notion already propounded by Adam Smith.[63] The second is that the 'free exercise' clause serves to compensate the 'no establishment' clause. Separation between church and state does not entail radical banishment of religion from the public domain, for the state offers many accommodations for the benefit of religious

---

[62] W. Safran, Civil Liberties in Democracies, in: V.P. Nanda et al. (eds.), *Global Human Rights*, Westview Press, Boulder 1981, 195–210.

[63] R. Neunhaus, A New Order of Religious Freedom, in: Feldman, S.M. (ed.), *Law and Religion: A Critical Anthology*, New York University Press, New York 2000, 89–95; R. Stark & W. Bainbridge, *A Theory of Religion*, Lang, New York 1987; R. Stark & R. Finke, *Acts of Faith: Explaining the Human Side of Religion*, University of California Press, Berkely 2000; cf. M. Chaves & D. Cann, Regulation, Pluralism and Religious Market Structure: Explaining Religious Vitality, *Rationality and Society* 4(1992)3, 272–290; Van der Ven, *Three Paradigms*, op. cit.

freedom.[64] The third is that the two religious clauses serve the same purpose. The first protects religious minorities against the dominant religion, the second grants the same accommodations to all religions alike. The objective of the religious clauses is that they protect minority rights.[65]

The third interpretation is an extension of the historical relation between religious freedom and minority rights mentioned in the first section. In the negotiations about the treaty of the League of Nations, the two concepts were linked and for that reason did not feature in the text of the treaty. The Universal Declaration (1948) incorporated religious freedom as an individual right and the UN International Covenant on Civil and Political Rights (1966) did the same in the case of minority rights.

That brings me to the next question: in the link between religious freedom and religious minority rights, which notion takes precedence? Is religious freedom a function of minority rights, or are the latter simply an application of the religious freedom to which every individual is entitled? According to the UN documents, the second answer is correct, not only temporally (since religious freedom was included earlier in these documents than the minority rights), but also substantively, because religious freedom is a universal category: it is for each and every individual human being. Here one discerns the weight carried by liberalism, which pushes communitarianism to the background. On closer and deeper scrutiny, however, historically we find that the reverse applies. Religious freedom was the freedom of minorities, evidenced by the following examples: the aforementioned Peace of Augsburg (1555) and the Peace of Westphalia (1648); the Union of Utrecht (*Unie van Utrecht* 1589) and the Declaration of Independence (*Plakkaat van Verlatinghe* 1591), in which the Protestant Republic of the Netherlands seceded from Catholic Spain but Catholics were granted religious freedom; the aforementioned Edict of Nantes (1598), which granted Protestant Huguenots freedom of religion in Catholic France; and lastly, the French constitution of 1791, which granted religious freedom not only to Protestant but also to Jewish, Islamic, and Chinese

---

[64] A. Greene, The Incommensurability of Religion, in: S. Feldman (ed.), *Law and Religion: A Critical Anthology*, New York University Press, New York 2000, 226–244.

[65] C. Eisgruber & L. Sager, Equal Regard, in: Feldman (ed.), *Law and religion*, op. cit., 200–225.

minorities – in fact, to members of any sect.[66] In short, religious freedom was not needed for the majority but for the minority or minorities – something that the founding father of international law, Hugo Grotius, had always advocated.[67] In a historical hermeneutic perspective, the religious freedom of every human being in the Universal Declaration of 1948 may be regarded as a generalisation, universalisation, and formalisation of religious freedom that started off as a minority right.

6.2.5   Conditions for the Debate on Religious Rights

Suppose we were to launch a debate on religious minority rights. How should we set about it? I want to look at three aspects: the endogenous nature of these rights; the religious nature of this endogenous development; and the combination of religious and public language in the debate.

To start with the first aspect, nothing is so pernicious to identity as is externally imposed emancipation and rights. To be successful, the process has to be endogenous. Does that mean exogenous forces are irrelevant? That would be going too far. But they would have to link up with forces within the minorities themselves. In the case of Muslim minorities, there are points of contact with groups aiming at practical political reform, renewal of Islamic political thinking, and development of Islamic law in support of the democratic state.[68]

In the latter case, the main thing is to clarify the relation between Islamic and 'universal' human rights. The quotation marks around 'universal' are there because the Western origin of this universality is offensive to many non-Westerners: they cannot but see it as legal neo-colonialism, originating from Western imperialism.[69] Obviously one has to keep the context of origin and legitimation separate, since

---

[66] J. Bauberot, Two Thresholds of Laïcization, in: R. Bhargava (ed.), *Secularism and Its Critics*, Oxford University Press, Oxford 1999, 97–98; L. Hunt, *Inventing Human Rights. A History*, Norton, New York 2007, 146–175.

[67] H. Nellen, *Hugo de Groot: Een leven om de strijd van de vrede 1583–1645*, Balans, Amsterdam 2007.

[68] WRR (Wetenschappelijke Raad voor het regeringsbeleid – Scientific Council for Government Policy), *Dynamism in Islamic Activism: Reference Points for Democratization and Human Rights*, Amsterdam University Press, Amsterdam 2006.

[69] B. Tierney, Religious Rights: An Historical Perspective, in: J. Witte & J. van der Vyver (eds.), *Religious Human Rights in Global Perspective: Religious Perspectives*, Nijhoff, The Hague 1996, 43.

the latter cannot logically be reduced to the former.[70] But that does not alter the fact that political dialogues around human rights matters require much skill and patience, not least because the uniformity of human rights in the West too still leaves much to be desired. There are major differences between the interpretations of the former UN Human Rights Commission and the European Court for Human Rights, for example. The former offered more scope for individuals and groups, the latter is narrower because the Court assigns the state greater discretionary powers.[71] The challenge is to find a broader – that is an inclusive, contextual – interpretation of human rights. This would require formulating rights in a manner that includes all people in every country (quantitative aspect), to which end they have to be interpreted flexibly and contextually (qualitative aspect). It entails, for example, not only including collective rights for minorities, but also assigning socio-economic rights the same, or, in some non-Western countries, even greater importance than civil and political rights.[72] The point is that the process has to be directed endogenously, with exogenous actors taking purely facilitative responsibility.[73] Only then will those rights be experienced as 'ours'.

The second aspect is to link up with specifically religious ideas in this endogenous development. This is new to the European Union. In the past, links were formed with nonreligious, secular movements. It was feared that cooperation with religious groups would lead to 'sharia-ising' the law. But such apprehensions are unnecessary if contact is sought with Islamic movements that favour reform.[74] In the long term there in no need for pessimism on this score. In fact, research in 23 Muslim countries shows that Islamic political culture has no influence on people's attitudes towards democracy and civil rights.[75]

That brings me to the third aspect: to what extent should the debate on religious rights be couched in religious language? Two extremes

---

[70] J.A. Van der Ven, J.S. Dreyer & H.J.C. Pieterse, *Is There a God of Human Rights?* Brill, Leiden 2004, 141–151.

[71] Taylor, *Freedom of Religion*, op. cit., 343–347.

[72] E. Brems, Universaliteit en diversiteit in de internationale mensenrechten, in: P. Cliteur & V. van den Eeckhout (eds.), *Multiculturalisme, cultuurrelativisme en sociale cohesie*, Boom, The Hague, 2001, 65–78.

[73] WRR, *Islamic Activism*, op. cit., 162–169.

[74] Ibidem, 172–175.

[75] D. Price, *Islamic Political Culture, Democracy, and Human Rights*, Westport, Praeger 1999.

should be avoided. The one is to formulate only religious beliefs; the other is to use exclusively nonreligious, public language. The first is typical of the theocratic model, the second of the separationist model. Both models tend to ignore the pluralism that characterises multicultural societies. Theocracies recognise only their own religion, seperationism only its own secularism. Genuinely free political communication means that all religions and worldviews should be able to convey their beliefs in the public debate, including their philosophical and theological premises, at any rate inasmuch as it is required. The idea of public reason advocated by Rawls in its earlier version does not allow for that.[76] It limits the discussion to political convictions, whereas philosophical and theological premises – so-called 'comprehensive doctrines' – must be reserved for the private sphere. It cuts multicultural pluralism short at the very point where religions and worldviews get serious, and thus impairs the very deliberative democracy in the consociational state that I advocate above. Besides, this politics is ineffective, since people cannot but interpret and evaluate new problems and solutions in terms of the same comprehensive doctrines, as is evident in the public debates on abortion, euthanasia, and same-sex marriage.[77]

For the middle way I espouse, I rely on Rawls's recent version of public reason.[78] This middle way may be explained in terms of the metaphor of bilingualism. The one language is meant to present philosophical and religious beliefs, but adapted to the public debate, hence avoiding any form of proselytising. The other language is meant to translate these beliefs into publicly accessible language, in which their political implications are explicated, also to people of other persuasions and nonreligious people, so that they are enabled to possibly take responsibility for them.[79] Whether such bilingualism can lead to

---

[76] J. Rawls, *Political Liberalism*, Columbia University Press, New York 1993.

[77] Taylor, *Modes of Secularism*, op. cit., 49–50.

[78] J. Rawls, *Political Liberalism*, Expanded edition, Columbia University Press, New York 2005. Part four of the expanded edition consists of: J. Rawls, The Idea of Public Reasons Revisited, *The University of Chicago Law Review* 64(1997)3, 765–807, which does not appear in earlier editions. See chapter 8 below.

[79] R. Audi, The Place of Religious Arguments in a Free and Democratic Society, in: Feldman (ed.), *Law and Religion*, op. cit., 69–88; M. Perry, Liberal Democracy and Religious Morality, in: Feldman (ed.), *Law and Religion*, op. cit., 115–148; A. Greene, The Incommensurability of Religion, in: Feldman (ed.), *Law and religion*, op. cit., 226–244; J. Stout, *Democracy and Tradition*, Princeton University Press, Princeton 2004; J. Habermas, *Zwischen Naturalismus und Religion*, Suhrkamp, Frankfurt 2005.

consensus depends on a politics of recognition in a wholeheartedly
accepted religious pluralism and a wholeheartedly accepted deliberative democracy (also see chapter 8). Another important point is that
authentic persuasion and some measure of negotiation and compromise are not mutually exclusive.[80] Some people object to compromises
because they smack of horse trading. But they can also be seen as a
temporary accord between parties which respect each other's beliefs
and recognise each other's personal dignity while upholding the significance of their own beliefs.[81] The temporary nature of the agreement
is important, because all compromises are fallible and one has to build
in sufficient psychological and legal scope for reviewing them when
circumstances and/or insights change.[82]

6.3   Legal Pluralism for the Benefit of Religious Minorities

Even though the incrementalism of negotiation and compromise may
be worth pursuing, it is a moot point whether its purpose – granting
minorities religious rights – will not upset the legal system in Western
countries. On the one hand, it would be a contextualisation of human
rights in response to the accusation that they are a Western 'imperi-
alist export'. On the other hand, there should be certain checks on
them so as not to impair the rule of law and the rights of individual
members of these minorities.[83] Demarcating limits, however, gives rise
to many problems. Do special rights not lead to legal pluralism, thus
jeopardising the state's legal unity? And does it not perpetuate the
age-old patriarchal yoke that oppressed individual members, especially
women? These questions are too important to be swept under the
carpet.

---

[80] Taylor, *Modes of Secularism*, art. cit., 50.
[81] Ricoeur, *The Course of Recognition*, op. cit., 209–210.
[82] The Dutch churches lost the public debate on euthanasia legislation because they
based their case exclusively on religious arguments like creation, salvation, grace and
what is perceived as premodern religious natural law. They did not translate their case
into a public language such as that of human rights, nor did they leave any opening
for negotiation and compromise.
[83] M. Galenkamp, Culturele diversiteit in het recht: Een kritisch perspectief op
grondrechten, in: Cliteur & Van den Eeckhout (eds.), *Multiculturalisme*, op. cit.,
383–396.

6.3.1 Legal Pluralism and Legal Cultures

Paradoxical as it may seem, legal uniformity is the exception rather than the rule, since legal pluralism characterises all major legal families classified in comparative law such as indigenous, civil, common, Asian, Talmudic, Canon, Islamic, and Hindu law.[84] Even more pertinently, the very term 'legal families' has fallen into discredit because they have become hybridised as a consequence of much mutual influence. Roman law comprised different traditions, partly attached to citizenship of the city-state Rome, and partly to the pluriform customary law of citizens of cities other than Rome who had been granted Roman citizenship.[85] The boundaries between Anglo-Saxon common law and continental civil law, too, are porous because of their common origin in Roman law, even though they developed in different directions subsequently.[86] The existence of exclusively uniform systems is a legal fiction.

One cause of legal pluralism is the pluralism of legal cultures, stemming from the pluralism of the communities in a country or state. The term 'legal culture' has become current in literature, although it is subject to debate, because it can be defined variously in terms of both the demand side and the supply side of legal institutions.[87] In this chapter, I am concerned with the demand side centring on customs held dear by members of the community, which determine their identity and which they want to be considered legally valid so that they may be put into practice.[88]

A well-known example is the millet system in the Ottoman empire. Until the 19th century, beside the Muslim millet, the main millets

---

[84] M. Weber, *Wirtschaft und Gesellschaft*, Mohr, Tübingen 1980, 470–482; H. Glenn, *Legal Traditions of the World: Sustainable Diversity in Law*, Oxford University Press, Oxford 2000.

[85] G. van den Bergh, Legal Pluralism in Roman law, in: C. Varga (ed.), *Comparative Legal Cultures*, Dartmouth, Aldershot 1992.

[86] P. Legrand, The Same and the Different, in: P. Legrand & R. Munday (eds.), *Comparative Legal Studies; Traditions and Transitions*, Cambridge University Press, Cambridge 2003, 242–245.

[87] D. Nelken (ed.), *Comparing Legal Cultures*, Darmouth, Aldershot 1997; E. Blankenburg & F. Bruinsma, *Dutch Legal Culture*, Kluwer, Deventer 1994.

[88] Cf. L. Friedman, The Concept of Legal Culture: A Reply, in: Nelken (ed.), *Comparing Legal Cultures*, op. cit., 33–40; L. Friedman, *The Horizontal Society*, Yale University Press, New Haven 1999, 164–179; L. Friedman, Some Comments on Cotterrell and Legal Transplants, in: D. Nellken, & J. Feest (eds.), *Adapting Legal Cultures*, Hart, Oxford 2001, 93–98.

(a Turkish term for a religious community, from Arabic *millah*) in the Ottoman empire were Greek Orthodoxy, Syrian Orthodoxy, Judaism, and Armenianism, the latter actually comprising three millets: the Armenian Orthodox, Armenian Catholic, and Armenian Protestant churches. These millets have been recognised since the 19th century, along with more than ten other millets. They were authorised to organise their social life according to their own personal law, to which end they could maintain separate legal courts. In some post-Ottoman countries like Jordan, Lebanon, Israel, the Palestine Authority, and Egypt, this system continues, albeit to varying extents and in diverse forms. It is also operative in countries like Iran, Pakistan, and Bangladesh.[89]

Another example is the pluralistic legal systems that Western countries introduced in their colonies in bygone centuries. In areas that were regarded by the West as nobody's territory (*terra nullius*), such as North America and Australia, England imported common law with no restrictions; but in Asia and Africa, local personal law was rarely replaced by common law. Although it was introduced in India, Hindu, Muslim, and customary personal law were also legally recognised. The same applied in countries like Kenya and Israel. The effects of this arrangement are evident to this day.[90] The Netherlands likewise imported Dutch laws in its colonies, specifically in Indonesia and Surinam, but legally acknowledged family law like *adat* law in Indonesia according to the Shāfiʿī law school until 1949, while Surinam had separate marriage law systems for the Asian and Muslim populations until 1975.[91]

Such recognition of personal law indicates a weak rather than a strong form of legal pluralism. Strong legal pluralism is when two or more systems operate fully side by side. Weak pluralism is when a given legal system accommodates a particular community in one or a few legal areas only.[92] Personal law is a good example, but weak legal

---

[89] Millet, 2007, available at http://en.wikipedia.org/wiki/Millet_%28Ottoman_Empire%29.

[90] A. Shachar, *Multicultural Jurisdictions: Cultural Differences and Women's Rights*, Cambridge University Press, Cambridge 2001, 78–85.

[91] A. Vestdijk-van der Hoeven, *Religieus recht en minderheden*, Gouda Quint, Arnhem 1991.

[92] N. van Maanen & A. Hoekema, Gemeenschappen komen tot hun recht: Zeven kernproblemen bij onderzoek naar recht, multiculturaliteit en sociale cohesie, in: Cliteur & Van den Eeckhout (eds.), *Multiculturalisme*, op. cit., 217–260.

pluralism also applies in other areas such as labour law. Here there may be specific rulings regarding the weekly religious calendar (Friday, Saturday or Sunday as the weekly day of rest), the annual calendar (Jewish, Christian and Muslim holidays for example) and freedom of dress. In the latter respect, the only restrictions are those "prescribed by law and are necessary to protect public safety, order, health, or morals or the fundamental rights and freedoms of others",[93] as well as restrictions required by occupation, as in aviation, the caring professions, and the like.[94]

6.3.2 *The Group and the Individual*

At first glance, granting collective religious rights to minorities presents a dilemma. One side of this dilemma is that it may legitimise patriarchal, authoritarian structures in such communities, legally perpetuating and even reinforcing them. That leaves individual members, particularly women, exposed to group pressure with no option but to submit to it permanently.[95] Such oppression may manifest itself in different areas, not only in arranged marriages without the woman's consent, unequal marriage relations, unequal upbringing, and humiliating domestic role patterns, but also in education, occupations, and health care, as well as in economic, political, and social life and in recreational activities. At its most appalling, the oppression of women is manifested in different forms of physical, psychological, and sexual violence, including circumcision that was denounced as 'female genital mutilation' by the World Health Organisation (WHO) in 1991,[96] as well as honour-related violence and killings. Group pressure in the case of such violence can be so great that it is adduced as a cultural defence, and may be used in criminal law as an argument for justifications and excuses, which does not detract from the fact that women are the victims of it.[97]

---

[93] J. Witte, *Religion and the American Constitutional Experiment*, Westview, Boulder 2005, 237.

[94] N. Lerner, *Religion, Secular Beliefs and Human Rights*, Brill, Leiden 2006, 24.

[95] See for example: M. Karayanni, Multiculture Me No More! On Multicultural Qualifications and the Palestinian-Arab Minority of Israel, *Diogenes* 54(2007)3, 39–58.

[96] W. Dekkers, C. Hoffer & J.-P. Wils, *Besnijdenis, lichamelijke integriteit en multiculturalisme: Een empirische en normatief-ethische studie*, Damon, Budel 2006.

[97] C. van Eck, *Door bloed gezuiverd. Eerwraak bij Turken in Nederland*, Dissertation, Amsterdam 2004; M. Siesling, *Multiculturaliteit en verdediging in strafzaken*,

The other side of the dilemma is that the state refuses to grant collective rights and focuses exclusively on the lot of individual members, more particularly women. In so doing, it looks after their individual rights such as the rights to life, equality, liberty, and security of persons; freedom from all forms of discrimination; the highest attainable standard of physical and mental health, just and favourable work conditions; and non-subjection to torture and other cruel, inhuman, or degrading treatments or punishments. The result, however, is that minority rights are regarded as purely individual, as in the aforementioned UN International Covenant on Civil and Political Rights (1966).

How does one escape from the dilemma 'collective versus individual'? If the question is focused on personal law – which, as mentioned already, includes marriage law and family law – we can distinguish between two domains: those of status demarcation and property distribution. The former pertains not only to the actual marriage – that is, the transition from the status of a single or previously married person to that of a married person and member of a new family – but also to the (future) social belonging and education of children. The second domain concerns the rights and duties the spouses have to observe in relation to one another and their respective families, as well as custodial implications and economic consequences if the marital status should change, for instance in the case of divorce or death. On the basis of this distinction, status demarcation may fall under the jurisdiction of religious minorities, provided certain criteria are worked out in a satisfactory manner, such as the safeguarding of human rights. Property distribution falls under the jurisdiction of the state. The administration of justice by courts is arranged according to the same dichotomy.[98] Apart from the distinction between status demarcation and property distribution, every member of the minority must nevertheless have the option of relying entirely on the jurisdiction of the state for both status demarcation and property distribution, should he or she wish it.

Dissertation, Utrecht 2006; J. ten Voorde, *Cultuur als verweer*, Dissertation, Rotterdam 2007.

[98] Shachar, *Jurisdictions*, op. cit., goes further, proposing that individuals have the option not only of status demarcation under the jurisdiction of the religious community and property distribution under that of the state, but also the other way round: status demarcation under the jurisdiction of the state and property distribution under that of the religious community. In addition she wants them to have the option at a later stage, if their needs are not fully satisfied, to freely opt out according to a procedure to be worked out, so as to make a transition from the one model to the other. In the UK, Islamic arbitration which operates as an informal court is being invoked for both divorce and succession cases (NRC 30.12.09).

This is an option that exists in the differentiated personal law system in India, for example, and is also required by the aforementioned UN and European documents. If this option is exercised, the person dissociates herself from the community and adopts an exit strategy. From the community's point of view, this may constitute social death, from her own, a social challenge.[99]

6.3.3   The Position of Women

Settling for this model of personal law with two domains raises all sorts of problems regarding the position of women, particularly in the case of Islam – the main minority in West-European societies. For this reason, I devote special attention to the position of women in Islam, specifically as regards Muslim marriage and polygamous marriages.

The common charge in the media is that Islam oppresses women, but a careful analysis of historical sources yields a more differentiated picture. A study of norms from different places and eras reveals different contexts. The first is that of pre-Islamic Bedouin tribal society, which practised unrestricted polyandry and polygyny, and in which women, once married, were part of the patrilinear inheritance. The second context is the Qur'an's reaction to this: abolishing polyandry and permitting polygyny with at most four wives to protect women and their children against destitution in the event of a post-war surfeit of females, or even prohibiting polygyny in terms of a contextual interpretation based on sura 4:3 in conjunction with sura 4:129, and moreover allowing women to own property and inherit from their husbands.[100] The third context is the period up to the 10th century, in which various law schools emerged – four in Sunni and three in Shiite Islam.[101] This led to differing rules in various legal areas: marriage law (celebration of marriage, bridal gift, marriage contract, rights and duties, including diverse sexual rights and duties for husbands and wives), divorce rights (e.g. the wife's qualified initiation rights), family law (e.g. custody of children in the case of divorce), and law of succession (e.g. differential rights of husband and wife, sons and

---

[99] A. Føllesdal, Minority Rights, in: J. Räikkä (ed.), *Do We Need Minority Rights*, Nijhof, The Hague 1996, 70.

[100] N. Shah, Women's Human Rights in the Koran, *Human Rights Quarterly* 28(2006)4, 868–903.

[101] Rohe, *Das Islamische Recht*, op. cit., 27–34. In Sunni Islam: Hanafiya, Malikiya, Safiiya and Hanabila; in Shi'a Islam: Imamiya or Twelvers, Ismailiya or Severers, and Zaidiya or Fivers.

daughters).[102] The present-day context is characterised by the process of urbanisation, in which divergent interpretations in popular Islamic law emerged in urban as opposed to rural areas. In the latter, norms and rules attributed to Islam are often mixed with regional, ethnic, cultural, and subcultural developments, as well as with rural customary law from the past. Cutting across all these contexts are the distinctive approaches of four different groups in the interpretation of texts from these sources: fundamentalist, conservative, moderate, and liberal groups, which respectively strive for the re-Islamisation of traditional rules and norms, which are in any case permeated with non-Islamic and nonreligious elements; for the retention of these traditional rules and norms; for their moderate adaptation to modernity; or for their radical secularisation.[103]

Studies by Islamic feminist theologians unearthed a variety of rights in the Qur'an itself. These apply equally to men and women, such as the right to life, respect, freedom, equality, education, remunerated employment, property, leaving their country in the event of oppression, and a good life.[104] The Qur'an also contains rules that trample roughshod over equal rights, such as sura 4:34, which offers the following three-phase model for dealing with insubordinate wives: talk to her, shun her in bed and, if that proves unavailing, beat her.[105]

The problem is that subsequent notions and practices eroded gender equality and extended and legitimised inequality. Some commentators maintain that this is associated with a verse in the Qur'an that says women are entitled to that which is 'right and proper' (sura 2:228), which was interpreted variously in different places and times, and variously in cities and in rural areas.[106] As regards the latter distinction, most migrant groups in Europe come from the countryside and therefore associate with its more traditional culture. For instance, the birth of a daughter may be seen as a tribulation, whereas a boy child is

---

[102] Rohe, *Das Islamische Recht*, op. cit., 79–103.

[103] Rohe, *Das Islamische Recht*, op. cit., 395–400.

[104] R. Hassan, *One of Another: Gender Equality and Justice in Islam*, available at http://www.religiousconsultation.org/hassan.htm; Id., *Are Human Rights Compatible with Islam? The Issue of the Rights of Women in Muslim Communities*, available at http://www.religiousconsultation.org/hassan2.htm; Id., *Religious Human Rights in the Qur'an*, available at http://www.webbinternational.org/download/word/articles_riffat/Religious_Human_Rights_in_the_Quran.doc; cf. A. Mashour, Islamic Law and Gender Equality, *Human Rights Quarterly* 27(2005)2, 562–596.

[105] H. Küng, *De Islam*, Kok, Kampen 2006, 683.

[106] P. van Koningsveld, *De Islam*, De Ploeg, Utrecht 1996, 83.

a gift, and the following practices may enjoy support: female circumcision, child marriages, awarding children to the husband in divorce cases, and honour-related violence.[107] One might therefore argue that if women in their actual temporal and spatial circumstances were to be entitled to what is 'right and proper' (sura 2:228), it would require equal treatment for men and women in all countries that have signed the UN conventions and incorporated human rights into their constitutions. What would it imply for Islamic marriage and polygyny?

6.3.4 Islamic Marriage

Muslim marriage is a contract based on an exchange of offer and acceptance by two parties or their representatives in the presence of at least two witnesses. In Sunni Islam, marriage is indissoluble, whereas in Shiite Islam, notably the Imamiya school, marriages of limited duration are recognised.[108] Prevailing impediments to marriage must be observed, including the degree of blood relationship and religious (dis)parity. A Muslim man may marry non-Muslim women; however, a Muslim woman cannot marry a non-Muslim man. The argument here is that a Muslim's marriage with an 'infidel' wife profits the husband and Islam, whereas a Muslim woman who marries an 'infidel' man represents a loss. In such cases, the woman would be unable to practise her religion. The wife's representative is her marriage guardian, who also conveys her consent. According to some Sunni schools and the Shia Ismailiya school, forced marriage was granted by the marriage guardian not only in the case of young girls but also of adult women. Throughout Islam, binding agreement is reached on the bride price that the groom has to pay his bride, which is meant to be social security for the wife in the event of divorce or the death of her husband. There is no community of property, so wives should retain control over their own possessions. She retains the right to earn money and to acquire and inherit property. Divorce may be initiated by either husband or wife, and in the latter case she retains her marriage portion. A husband does not have to provide reasons for the separation; a wife is obliged to do so, and these reasons may be rejected. The argument is that males are more intellectual and practical and women are more

---

[107] UNDP, *Arab Human Development Report 2005: Towards the Rise of Women in the Arab World*, New York, 2006, 113–122, 143–147.

[108] Rohe, *Das Islamische Recht*, op. cit., 82–85.

emotional. Marriage has religious significance inasmuch as it is done under Islamic law, but it has no sacred meaning. The marriage feast, which takes place some time later, may start with a religious service including recitation from the Qur'an and hymn singing, and conclude with a blessing.[109]

Why not follow the Spanish model, in which Muslim marriage is recognised in civil law, especially when officially appointed witnesses take care of the registration?[110] In Western society at large, this would accord with the general decline in government interference and the growing contractual trend in marriages.[111] The answer depends on the (in)equality of husband and wife. The foregoing description of Muslim marriage indicates inequalities in the areas of religion and divorce. A strict interpretation of human rights would make this unacceptable. But is this legal inequality tolerable or intolerable in terms of the distinction made earlier? Would a tolerable legal inequality by way of temporary compromise be acceptable to a woman who freely opts for it with a view to – for her – the higher good of a collective right, which is contracting a marriage according to her own tradition? Or might the inequality be abolished altogether by opting for the distinction between domains mentioned earlier, those of status demarcation and property distribution, with the contracting of marriage falling under the former? Here I leave this question open.

6.3.5   Polygyny

In Muslim countries, polygyny occurs among a very small percentage of relatively wealthy men who can afford more than one wife. Of old it was tolerated in these countries, with the exception of Tunisia, the only Arab country where it is prohibited. Though tolerated, it is the subject of much debate, for example in Palestine and a non-Arab country like Indonesia; and legal conditions apply, for instance in Algeria, Iraq,

---

[109] Vestdijk-van der Hoeven, *Religieus recht*, op. cit.; N. Dessing, *Rituals of Birth, Circumcision, Marriage and Death among Muslims in the Netherlands*, Peeters, Leuven 2001; and Al-Zawaj, Islamic Law, in: C. Rautenbach & N. Goolam (eds.), *Introduction to Legal Pluralism in South Africa*, Butterworth, Durban 2002, 61–76.

[110] M. Rohe, *Muslim Minorities and the Law in Europe*, Global Productions, New Dehli 2007; A. Eide, Cultural Rights and Minorities, in: K. Hastrup (ed.), *Legal Culture and Human Rights: The Challenge of Diversity*, Kluwer, The Hague 2001, 25–42.

[111] A. Vonken, De multiculturele samenleving en de bemiddelende rol van het internationaal privaatrecht en de mensenrechten, in: P. Cliteur, et al. (eds.), *Sociale cohesie en het recht*, Meijers Instituut, Leiden 1998, 97–167, here 120.

Morocco, and Syria.[112] In article 6 of the Maputo Protocol, formally called the Protocol to the African Charter on Human and Peoples' Rights on the Rights of Women in Africa, adopted by the African Union in 2003 and brought into force in 2005, it is stated that monogamy is encouraged as the preferred form of marriage. It continues by stating that the rights of women in marriage and family, including in polygamous marital relationships, are promoted and protected. In Western society, this is not an issue for debate, since the migrant minorities largely belong to the least affluent classes. This does not mean that there are no clandestine polygynous marriages, for instance in The Hague in the Netherlands.[113] But this may increase in the future in the event of large-scale migration from West Africa and sub-Saharan countries, where polygyny occurs among much larger percentages of the population, although in Ghana and Kenya it is in sharp decline,[114] in Kenya probably because of the higher rate of women's education.[115] A further consideration is that certain groups among the migrant minorities are penetrating the more wealthy upper-middle class. Or, one might ask, is polygyny merely an evolutionary phenomenon that declines as modernisation progresses? Research into factors influencing polygyny – demographic, economic, educational, and socio-cultural – does not reveal an overall consistent picture.[116]

What are the objections to legal recognition of polygyny? There are three angles: those of Christian-Western normativity, democracy, and human rights.

The exclusiveness of absolutely monogamous marriage in the West stems from Christian doctrine, which still has an enormous effective history (*Wirkungsgeschichte*) in Western civilisation. It views marriage as an unconditional, total, unshared and indissoluble bond between

---

[112] P. Johnson, Agents for Reform: The Women's Movement, Social Politics and Family Law Reform, in: L. Welchamn (ed.), *Women's Rights and Islamic Family Law*, Zed, London 2004, 144–163; G. Therborn, *Between Sex and Power: Family in the World*, Routledge, London 2004.

[113] According to the then mayor of The Hague, Wim Deetman (*Volkskrant*, 17 February 2007).

[114] I. Timaeus & A. Reynar, Polygynists and their Wives in Sub-Saharan Africa, *Population Studies* 52(1998)2, 145–162.

[115] Y. Hayase & K.-L. Liaw, Factors on Polygamy in Sub-Saharan Africa: Findings Based on the Demographic and Health Surveys, *The Developing Economies* 35(1997)3, 293–327.

[116] P. Bretschneider, *Polygyny: A Cross-Cultural Study*, Acta Universitatis Upsaliensis, Uppsala 1995.

a man and a woman, and the contract between them is religiously legitimised by elevating it to a sacrament, for instance in the Catholic Church and the Eastern churches. In this sacrament, the bond between husband and wife is seen as signifying the intimate bond between Christ and the church, which the sacrament enables the spouses to share. Against this background, the Catholic Church condemned polygyny (*anathema sit*) at the Council of Trent (1545–1563). This was not directed to Arab countries and Africa but only to a few reformers, who considered polygyny permissible by way of exception, subject to strict ecclesiastic regulation, in cases of marital problems. In other words, the Tridentine condemnation did not refer to the large population groups in Arab countries and Africa, which means polygyny in those vast regions might be considered, from the perspective of canon law, a case of *extra ius*.[117] In that respect, why should present-day minorities not defend their right to polygyny, when the Catholic Church in the 19th century, with its emphasis on its sacramental nature of marriage, sought to safeguard its jurisdiction over marriage against the secular state thereby?[118]

In addition to the Christian objection, there is a democratic one. In their legislation, the vast majority of Western states follow Christianity in defining marriage as a contract between just one man and one woman. It is considered that a minority cannot tamper with such democratically enacted laws. However, the counter argument is that these are the laws of a Christian majority and monogamous marriage is an institution of *that* majority. Religious minorities that practise, or at any rate tolerate, polygyny are being forced to adapt to this. Does that amount to a democratic institution, considering that it is being suggested that majority rule is dealing fairly and reasonably with the interests and needs of minorities?

Finally, there are objections to polygyny from the point of view of human rights. An advantage of the connection between the marriage contract and the Catholic sacrament was that husband and wife could enter into it as free, equal partners, and that both this freedom and this equality were legitimised religiously and legally. That could be seen as foreshadowing the right to gender equality, a core human right. In

---

[117] E. Hillman, *Polygamy Reconsidered*, Orbis, New York 1975, 217–240.

[118] U. Bauman, s.v. Ehe, *Historisch-theologisch. Lexikon für Theologie und Kirche. 3 Band*, Herder, Freiburg 1995, 471–474.

polygynous marriage, this equality is trampled underfoot in the case of a second and subsequent wives. It fundamentally violates a woman's self-esteem, self-evaluation, and self-respect. From the perspective of the rule of law, which belongs to the most appreciated value systems in countries like the Netherlands, all of this rules polygyny out of court.[119]

Does this mean that here 'the buck stops' and no further reflection is needed? Why do we not look for a solution in, for example, the Recognition of Customary Marriages Act (section 7(6), 7(7)), that came into force in South Africa in 1998? This permits husbands to marry a second wife provided they legally terminate the property system of the first marriage and effect a new division of property in terms of justice, with due regard to all relevant circumstances of the family groups involved. All parties with an interest in the division must be involved, especially the first wife.[120] This Recognition of Customary Marriages Act may be considered an adequate one from a purely legal point of view, but from empirical research we know that its implementation in practice, especially in rural areas, is fraught with problems, especially where equal property rights for men and women are concerned.[121] This means that some doubts may arise when the question is asked whether an analogous arrangement can be made in the case of polygyny under Islamic law. The issue is fiercely debated in the Muslim community in South Africa. One group wants a form of strong legal pluralism, with the *Sharia* as a separate, all-embracing legal system for personal law, alongside the secular legal system. The other group confines itself to a weak legal pluralism, in which polygyny is recognised, but as an accommodation within – not alongside – the secular legal system. The debate, which also centred on the 2003 Draft Bill on Islamic Marriages and Related Matters by the South African Law Commission, gave rise to so much conflict that the talks were called off.[122]

---

[119] I. Buruma, *Murder in Amsterdam: The Death of Theo Van Gogh and the Limits of Tolerance*, Penguin, New York 2006.

[120] T. Bennett, *Human Rights and African Customary Law Under the South African Constitution*, Juta, Cape Town 1999, 192–204; C. Dlamini, Family Law, in: J. Bekker, J. Labuschagne & L. Vorster (eds.), *Introduction to Legal Pluralism in South Africa*, Butterworth, Durban 2002, 46ff.

[121] M. Mamashela, New Families, New Property, New Laws: The Practical Effects of the Recognition of Customary Marriages Act, *South African Journal of Human Rights* 20(2004), 616–641.

[122] A. Tayob, Race, Ideology and Islam in Contemporary South Africa, in: R. Feener (ed.), *Islam in World Cultures: Comparative Perspectives*, ABC-Clio, Santa Barbara 2004, 253–282.

This draft was thought to go a long way in creating legal certainty regarding Muslim marriages. But because of the objections against this draft in relation to women's right to equality, the Parliamentary Office of the South African Commission for Gender Equality drafted an alternative draft bill in 2005, called the Recognition of Religious Marriages Bill, that provides for the recognition of all religious marriages. It is considered a middle position between the present state of non-recognition of Muslim marriages and the draft bill of 2003.[123]

But apart from that, qualitative empirical research among poor and working-class Muslim women in the Cape with personal experiences in the area of polygyny indicates that they suffer from being financially dependent on their husband, from feelings of rivalry between women, and from emotions of disappointment because this type of marriage does not offer them what they want.[124] If the discussion were to resume from a perspective of weak legal pluralism, certain aspects should be carefully clarified, more specifically that the first wife has the right to consent, that the husband has adequate financial resources, that there is no reason to suppose that he will treat his wives unfairly, and that there are no prejudices against the first wife and no feelings of rivalry between the wives. Nevertheless the serious question is this: are requirements of this kind realistic ones and do they really contribute to just conjugal relationships and satisfying experiences? In the aforementioned domain's division between status demarcation and property distribution, could marriage fall in the first domain and matters pertaining to property law and inheritance, child and youth law, in the second in accordance with secular legal norms? Here again I leave this question open.

Either way, as a serious theme for debate and reflection on a possible political option, it would require patient deliberation with, between, and within religious minorities, accompanied by public debate.[125] Each would have to resist the temptation to put pressure on the other to arrive at a speedy decision. It would require a government that does not merely rush from one election to the next, but that regards the

---

[123] R. Manjoo, The Recognition of Muslim Personal Laws in South Africa: Implications for Women's Human Rights, *Human Rights Program at Harvard Law School Working Paper*, July 2007.

[124] Bangstad, S., *Global Flows, Local Appropriations. Facets of Secularisation and Re-Islamization among Contemporary Cape Muslims*, Diss. Nijmegen, Amsterdam University Press, Amsterdam 2007, 99–128.

[125] A. Eisenberg & J. Spinner-Halev (eds.), *Minorities within Minorities: Equality, Rights and Diversity*, Cambridge University Press, Cambridge 2005.

age-old question of polygyny as a complex, long-term problem with any number of side issues to be dealt with in a process of learning, experimentation, and weighing of pros and cons, in whatever direction the ultimate decision might go.[126]

Conclusion

From what I have said, it is plain that the role of religion in multicultural society is not to be dismissed, especially when it comes to religious rights for minority groups. Granting these rights stems from an endeavour to transcend a politics of tolerance of minorities, even a politics of respect, and to treat them in terms of a politics of recognition. For such politics not to remain idealistic and intangible, a legal framework will have to be created. Granting religious rights means that the interpretations of some political principles that dominate the current public debate need to be critically reflected upon: the individualistic interpretation of minority rights, the separationist interpretation of the separation between church and state, the secularist interpretation of religious freedom, and the uniformistic interpretation of the state's legal unity. In granting minorities religious rights, it should be noted that their personal law, including marriage law and family law, features prominently, since these shape social bonds and determine their identity. To incorporate such personal law into the legal systems of Western society one could apply the distinction between the domains of status demarcation and property distribution. The former refers to entering and belonging to a family and a community, the latter to the rights and duties implicit in these social bonds. The first might be regulated by religious personal law, the latter by secular personal law. This distinction might underpin the incorporation of Muslim marriage and polygyny in the legal system. From the perspective of a politics of recognition this is important, but the question is whether marriage under religious personal law and rights and duties under secular personal law can solve the problems women suffer from. The ultimate question is whether a legal structure of this kind can help to solve one of the most fundamental problems of present-day Western society: gender equality in the multicultural drama.

---

[126] WRR (Wetenschappelijke Raad voor het regeringsbeleid – Scientific Council for Government Policy), *Lerende overheid*, Amsterdam University Press, Amsterdam 2006.

PART THREE

EMPIRICAL RESEARCH IN RELIGION AND
HUMAN RIGHTS CULTURE

CHAPTER SEVEN

RELIGIOUS FREEDOM

In premodern and early modern Western society, religious freedom as we know it was unheard of. At best there was religious tolerance, which meant that religious outsiders were tolerated so as to avoid a greater evil. This is understandable, since the majority of the population was Christian or considered to be either Christians or potential converts to Christianity. Society was a hierarchical Christian whole. From the top it was integrated by God who acted through a vertically structured representation by religious groups and social associations, and from below by a vertically structured participation of all these groups and associations in God. The totality constituted an all-encompassing Christian canopy, unified by a descending and ascending ladder of the Great Chain of Being.[1]

In modern society, this unity was destroyed by the emergence of horizontally rather than vertically structured differentiation.[2] An ongoing process of horizontal diversification of functions created more and more autonomous domains like the economy, politics, the law, and morality, each with its own codes, institutions, and programmes, unassociated with Christianity, which in its turn became a distinct domain with its own codes, organisations, and programmes. The religious freedom that succeeded religious tolerance correlated with this process of horizontal differentiation. Along with the emancipation of social associations from the Christian canopy, individuals and groups freed themselves from it. The emancipation of social associations and of individuals and groups from that canopy was complementary.

Does that mean that in our modern society religious tolerance has vanished and has been completely replaced by religious freedom? Has the politics of tolerating other religious groups, and the concomitant striving for the religious superiority and power of one's own faith, been totally superseded by respect for and recognition of all religious

---

[1] A. Lovejoy, *The great chain of being*, Cambridge 1978, 24–98.
[2] N. Luhmann, *Die Gesellschaft der Gesellschaft*, vols I–II, Suhrkamp, Frankfurt 1998.

groups, including their right to unrestricted practice of their religion? Has asymmetrical tolerance made way for symmetrical religious freedom?[3] Or are there still remnants – maybe even clearly recognisable and influential remnants – of it? That has not happened in law: religious freedom as a human right is entrenched in all pertinent international treaties and virtually all constitutions. But in the broad cultural sphere, the answer is less unambivalent. While human rights, including religious freedom, are basic to constitutional democracies, inasmuch as a human-rights culture backed by all citizens is lacking among current and future generations it remains but a shadowy presence – no more than a yellowing sheet of paper on the wall. Religions cannot escape the problem: their adherents are citizens of the state that has elevated religious freedom to a human right and their communities and organisations are part of society. In other words, have the members of religions exceeded asymmetrical tolerance into the direction of symmetrical religious freedom?

Against this background, the present chapter deals with the extent to which religious freedom, seen in the perspective of the importance of a human-rights culture, is accepted as a crucial value, more specifically by the generation that will lead Dutch society at micro and meso level in the forseeable future – in concrete terms, three groups of youths (Christian, Muslim and nonreligious) at the end of their secondary school and the start of their tertiary education. They are the future representatives of the three religiously most influential population groups that will jointly shape Dutch society.[4]

First I consider the development of tolerance in the premodern and early modern eras, since, as I hope to show, it is still a major force in our time. I start with two eminent writers that already showed signs of tolerance whilst still advocating coercion in respect of certain groups: Augustine and Thomas Aquinas. I then turn to John Locke and John Milton, who advocated full-blown tolerance, albeit with some qualifications. (7.1) When it comes to the modern era I focus on religious freedom as normatively legitimised in international public law after World War II. This offers invaluable insights but also poses knotty problems (7.2). I then explore empirically whether and to what extent the aforementioned three groups of youths accept religious freedom. I do so with reference to two 'thorny' issues raised by religious freedom:

---

[3] R. Forst, *Toleranz im Konflikt*, Suhrkamp, Frankfurt 2003.
[4] See Introduction.

the state's negative obligation not to interfere with religious communities and prayer at public schools. I conduct this empirical research in order to investigate legal culture and human rights culture in relation to religious freedom.[5] (7.3). After this empirical scrutiny I conclude with a reflection leading to a more balanced religious freedom (7.4).

7.1 The Development of Religious Tolerance in Premodern and Early Modern Time

In this section I sketch the views of Augustine in Roman antiquity, Thomas Aquinas in the Middle Ages, and John Locke and John Milton in the early modern era.

7.1.1 *Augustine*

A vivid example of undifferentiated religious, moral, and political unity is found in Augustine's texts on tolerance and coercion. He advocated tolerance of heretics, more specifically Manichaeans, Pelagians, and Donatists, on the basis of religious principles. A key religious theme was divine love and patience with heretics, who are blinded by error or corrupted by evil.[6] In addition the doctrine of two cities – one earthly, the other celestial – or two kingdoms that are still mingled, made it impossible for humans to pass the final judgment, which is God's prerogative.[7] Freedom of the act of belief was also important, in that only those who freely believe have true faith (*credere non potest homo nisi volens*). Then there was the ecclesiastic-political argument: toler ance preserved church unity. In the case of Jews, Augustine advanced another ecclesiastic argument. If they are tolerated, they can offer scriptural grounds for the veracity of the gospels and thus contribute indirectly to the church's mission.[8]

After fierce contention, especially since the conference in Carthago in 411, with the Donatists, who espoused a 'pure' conception of the

---

[5] D. Nelken (ed.), *Comparing Legal Cultures*, Aldershot 1997; D. Nellken & J. Feest (eds.), *Adapting Legal Cultures*, Oxford 2001; K. Hastrup (ed.), *Legal Cultures and Human Rights*, The Hague 2001. In J.A. van der Ven et al., *Is there a God of Human Rights*, Brill, Leiden 2004, 81–96, two conceptions of human rights culture are distinguished: respectful acceptance of human rights and reflection on human rights. Here I use the first conception.

[6] Augustine, *De Civitate Dei*, XVVV, 51.

[7] Augustine, *Civitate*, op. cit., I, 35; XX, 5.

[8] Augustine, *Civitate*, op. cit., XVIII, 46.

church and the sacraments and were critical of relations between church and state whereby the church invoked the strong arm of the state, Augustine revised his view of tolerance and replaced it with coercion, for which he produced religious arguments.[9] According to his letters, he felt that God's love required the evil of heresy to be requited with evil and punished as a sin to save heretics from eternal perdition. That required more detailed justification, in which the free act of faith became a bone of contention. As is evident from Augustine's letter to Boniface, governor of Africa, the Donatists complained of the persecution they had to endure, protesting their freedom to believe or disbelieve. In response, Augustine cited Paul, as he regularly did in his letters, who was literally brought to his knees and struck blind before he embraced the gospel.[10]

Augustine also produced moral arguments. In a letter on free will to a schismatic priest in the diocese of Hippo, Augustine distinguished between a good will and an evil will. He maintained that if we love someone, we may not leave her to her evil will but should exercise gentle pressure on her good will. The evil will has to be chastised and tamed, in which regard Augustine, as he was wont to do, cited Proverbs 23:13–14.[11] In a letter to Vincent, a Rogatist and successor to Rogatus, schismatic bishop of Cartenna in Mauritania, Augustine maintained that faith called for a combination of instruction and intimidation. Fear without instruction is unfair, instruction without fear is ineffectual. After all, coercion which gives rise to fear breaks down evil habits and instruction dispels the darkness of heresy and brings the light of truth.[12] The gospel likewise provided justification. Augustine often cited the parable of the wedding (Lk 14:23). The wedding guests were forced to join the banquet, which is how Augustine interpreted the *compelle intrare* in the Vulgate rendering of the Greek *anagkason eiselthein*.[13] In addition, he advanced a descriptive argument. We know from experience, he said, that it is a blessing to be first driven by fear of bodily pain, then to be taught and thereafter to convert what we

---

[9] J. O'Donnell, *Augustine*, Ecco, New York 2005; P. Zagorin, *How the Idea of Religious Tolerance Came to the West*, Princeton University Press, Princeton 2003, 24–33.

[10] Augustine, *Letters*, Fathers of the church, New York 1951, Vol. 4, letter 185 to Boniface, 163–166.

[11] Augustine, *Letters*, Vol. 4, letter 174 to Donatus, 74.

[12] Augustine, *Letters*, Vol. 2, letter 93 to Vincent, 57–59.

[13] Augustine, *Letters*, Vol. 2, letter 93 to Vincent, 61.

had learnt from those words into action.[14] In evidence he cited the fact that entire cities that used to belong to the Donatists have converted to the church for fear of the sanctions of imperial decrees.[15] Hence it is important to distinguish between just and unjust persecution. The former, according to Augustine, is conducted by the church against evil people, the latter by evil people against the church.[16] Addressing a Catholic judge, Marcellinus, and a Catholic proconsul, Donatus, Augustine justified inspiring fear and the use of the Old Testament rod, but strongly condemned extreme punishment such as putting suspects to the rack, torturing them with knives, or exposing them to fire.[17] He rejected the death penalty outright, since it is imposed out of wrath rather than out of Christian clemency. Ultimately good has to triumph over evil.[18] Finally, his ecclesiastical-political argument in favour of persecution of the Donatists was that it is the emperor's Christian duty to suppress heresy.[19] Thus Augustine swung from bad coercion to good coercion.[20]

Against this background it would seem that tolerance is often legitimised by the same arguments as coercion. In regard to religious arguments, in one case heresy is seen as error that blinds people to the truth but is to be tolerated, in another case it is seen as sin that has to be punished. God's love is cited to legitimise both toleration and force. In regard to moral arguments the two wills and the two coercions are referred to in order to legitimise both toleration and punishment. The ecclesiastic-political argument, too, propounds both tolerance and coercion: tolerance furthers unity, but so does coercion.

7.1.2   Thomas Aquinas

Augustine's religious, moral, and ecclesiastic arguments are also advanced by Thomas, the difference being that Augustine, while advocating punishment of heretics, condemns the death penalty. Thomas, on the other hand, favours the latter, albeit only after two prior

---

[14] Augustine, *Letters*, Vol. 4, letter 185 to Boniface, 161.
[15] Augustine, *Letters*, Vol. 2, letter 93 to Vincent, 73.
[16] Augustine, *Letters*, Vol. 4, letter 185 to Boniface, 152.
[17] Augustine, *Letters*, Vol. 3, letter 133 to Marcellinus, 6–7.
[18] Augustine, *Letters*, Vol. 2, letter 100 to Donatus, 141–142.
[19] Augustine, *Civitate*, op. cit., V, 24–25.
[20] R. Forst, *Toleranz im Konflikt*, Suhrkamp, Frankfurt 2003, 297.

warnings.[21] Like Augustine he regarded unbelief as evil and sinful. That applied to heathen, including Muslims, who had not yet embraced the true faith; to Jews, who had already been given a foretaste of faith; and to heretics, who had accepted the faith but then apostatised.[22] The latter was the worst sin, since one had an absolute duty to stick to the faith once one had embraced it. In such cases Thomas favoured physical punishment, thus extending Augustine's approach of compelling entrance to the Christian faith (*compelle intrare*) into compelling the keeping of this faith.[23] But apart from prescribing coercion and punishment, Thomas, like Augustine, used a descriptive argument. Experience shows, said Thomas, that coercion and punishment have brought heretics and apostates back to the fold. However, he held that unbelievers should not be forced to convert, since that was counter to the free act of belief. There were situations in which unbelievers had to be fought, even in armed warfare, not in order to compel them to believe but merely to prevent them from interfering with the faith of believers in their vicinity and spreading the virus of unbelief and apostasy.[24] In all these views, the religious argument is focal: it concerned the salvation of the groups concerned – not only that of Christians who may be infected by apostasy or heresy, but also that of heretics and unbelievers.

Thomas's doctrine becomes clearer if we view it in the social context of his times. There combating unbelievers and making war on them was a tightrope between safeguarding believers against infection by unbelief or forcibly converting unbelievers. The latter occurred on a massive scale, for instance among the Slavs and Saxons. It may have been a result of the by then close intertwinement of church and state: the secular kingdom (secular sword, *regnum, potestas*) and the spiritual kingdom (spiritual sword, *sacerdotium, auctoritas*). There the perennial question was which kingdom was subordinate to which and at whose command secular force was deployed against unbelievers and heretics – the emperor's or the pope's, the monarch's or the bishop's. In such an event, did emperor or monarch act under the authority of the pope or the bishop because it was a spiritual affair, such as spreading and preserving the true faith, or did the monarch derive his power directly from God, just as the emperor was (also) called the

---

[21] Thomas Aquinas, *Summa Theologica* (Abbr.: STh), II-II 11,3.
[22] STh, II-II 10, 4–6.
[23] Forst, op. cit., 93.
[24] STh, II-II 10, 8.

vicar of Christ or even of God,[25] as well as image of God, a priest, a cleric consecrated at his coronation? These questions culminated in a formal *modus vivendi* in the Edict of Worms in 1122 at the end of the investiture struggle, which nonetheless continued until the 20th century. In the course of the Middle Ages, it led to 'imperialisation' of the pontificate on the one hand and to 'clericalisation' of the imperial and royal thrones on the other.[26] Coercion was always, however obscurely, both ecclesiastic and political, just as tolerance, however confusingly, was both ecclesiastic and political.

Tolerance had paradoxical implications. Unbelievers and heretics were an evil to be tolerated in order to prevent a greater evil. The evil was compounded of crime against the majesty of God, the faith, and the church, and against the majesty of the emperor, prince or monarch, morality, and the state. The greater evil was ecclesiastic and political instability. Consequently, unbelievers and heretics were banished from the ecclesiastic and social community (enforced exclusion). However, in order to earn the 'permission' of tolerance, they were disciplined, as a result of which they would, albeit still on the periphery, conform to society's rules in order to retain their place in the community (enforced inclusion).[27]

In Thomas's thinking and in that of the society in which he lived, we see yet again, but far more pronounced than in Augustine, how closely religion, morality, politics, and law were intertwined. Not only were the religious and moral motives concerned with the evil of heresy that obscured the truth and with sin that had to be punished for the sake of salvation. Freedom of religion also featured, whilst the duty to remain within the Christian religion nullified that freedom. The medieval intertwinement of church and state was clearly discernible, because the church used the strong arm of the state in order to mete out punishment and the death penalty for crimes against both: against the body of the church (*corpus ecclesiae mysticum*) and the profane body (*corpus reipublicae mysticum*).[28]

---

[25] It is interesting to note that since the 8th century the islamic Caliph was called vicar of God; see M. Rohe, *Das Islamische Recht: Geschichte und Gegenwart*, Beck, München 2009, 251.

[26] E. Kantorowicz, *The King's Two Bodies: A Study in Mediaeval Political Theology*, Princeton University Press, Princeton 1997, 42–192.

[27] Forst, *Toleranz*, op. cit., 85–86.

[28] Kantorowicz, *The King's Two Bodies*, op. cit., 193–232.

7.1.3   *John Locke and John Milton*

The struggle about the relation between church and state and its implications for tolerance continued unabated in early modernity, but in
an altered framework. That came about when, following the so-called
dualists, the insight gradually dawned that church and state had different functions based on the Gelasian formula of the mutual independence of pope and emperor.[29] Locke's work displays a similar dualism,
as does that of John Milton, an important precursor and contemporary of Locke who, like him, greatly influenced the founding fathers
of the United States and the French Revolution.[30] In Locke's *Letter on
Toleration*, as in many of the writings of his immediate precursors and
contemporaries, church and commonwealth are seen as "absolutely
separate and distinct".[31] The church's domain is defined as oriented to
the individual's spiritual salvation and to that of the state as geared to
its task under natural law: protection of property, which Locke saw as
life, liberty, and possessions. The superordination of property is not
surprising, considering that humans own their lives, liberty, and material goods, and consider them their property. In an earlier work, *Essay
concerning Toleration*, Locke maintained that the church's domain
was confined to people's inner relationship with God. At that time he
still assigned the state authority over the outward form of that relationship. This was mainly because external conduct that is not clearly
prescribed by religious sources, and hence was considered indifferent,
led to many conflicts. These included determining times and places of
worship and the observance of rites such as genuflecting at the mention of Jesus' name, making the sign of the cross at baptism, wearing a
surplice when preaching, kneeling before the sacrament, and fixing the
prayers.[32] Such neutral, external actions should be under state control
in order to prevent unrest. The unrest was by no means imaginary
as evidenced by the fierce struggle against sabbatarianism, in which
so-called radical Puritans contested mandatory attendance of Sunday

---

[29] Kantorowicz, *The King's Two Bodies*, op. cit., 456.

[30] T. Davies, Borrowed Language: Milton, Jefferson, Mirabeau, in: D. Armitage
et al. (eds.), *Milton and Republicanism*, Cambridge University Press, Cambridge 1995,
260–287.

[31] J. Locke, *Epistola de Tolerantia, A Letter on Toleration*, Raymond Klibansky (ed.),
translated by J.W. Gough, Clarendon, Oxford 1968, 84–85.

[32] J. Locke, *Two Tracts on Government*, Edited by Philip Abrams, Cambridge University Press, Cambridge 1967, 124–127.

communion because according to the Gospels Jesus had abolished it, a view shared by John Milton in his *Christian Doctrine*.[33] In regard to the authority of the state, Locke was inspired by the thinking of his time, such as that of Hobbes and Spinoza, on the contract between citizens and sovereign, which assigned regulation of external behaviour to the powers of the state.[34]

In his *Letter on Toleration*, Locke deviates from this view. Religion in the broadest sense of the word does not fall in the domain of the state but primarily in the sphere of the individual believer. Locke's fundamental argument in this regard is that all religious expressions in word and deed stem from religious conscience, in which the individual is accountable to God and God alone – a task that cannot be delegated to any other person or institution.[35] Before him, Milton had already emphasised the importance of individual conscience in religion, more especially its function in understanding the Bible, to which no-one but the individual can and may lay claim, and for which the latter is not accountable to anyone.[36] That meant that in her relationship with God, the individual takes over the role previously played by the two vicars of Christ and God – the church and the state. This corresponds with Locke's view of the church. The church has no claim to authority; its sole method is persuasion. It is a free, voluntary association of individual believers that find one another in public worship of God, believing that he finds it pleasing for their souls' salvation.[37] In his *A Treatise of Civil Power*, Milton defines the church as a voluntary association of believers of the same faith[38] and in *Christian Doctrine*, he stresses that lay people rather than priests occupy the main position in

---

[33] *Complete Prose Works of John Milton*, Vol. I–VII, Yale University Press, New Haven, 1973, here VI, 708–715. Cf. J. Witte, *The Reformation of Rights*, Cambridge University Press, Cambridge 2007, 209–275; Id., Prophets, Priests, and Kings: John Milton and the Reformation of Rights and Liberties in England, *Emory Law Journal* 57(2008)6, 1527–1604.

[34] Th. Hobbes, *Leviathan*, ch. 42; B. de Spinoza, *Tractatus Theologico-Politicus*, 19, 3.

[35] Locke, *A Letter on Toleration*, op. cit., 90–101; I. Bocken, *John Locke, een brief over tolerantie, vertaling, inleiding en essay*, Damon, Budel 2004, 98–102, shows to what extent Locke was epistemologically influenced by nominalism and theologically by voluntarism.

[36] To Hobbes this was an abomination, since personally oriented Bible exegesis jeopardised the sovereign's absolute authority in religious matters, hence endangered peace and harmony. See D. Wolfe, The Advent of Hobbes, in: J. Milton, *Complete Prose Works* IV, op. cit., 30–37.

[37] Locke, *A Letter on Toleration*, op. cit., 71.

[38] Milton, *Complete Prose Works* VII, op. cit., 245.

the church,[39] for according to 1 Peter 2:9 they are the chosen people, the royal priesthood, the holy nation called by the Lord to fulfil their prophetic, priestly, and royal functions.[40] This ecclesiology underscores congregationalism even more forcefully in that it considers the local church autonomous, calling, appointing, and testing its own ministers, although not excluding consultation between local churches.[41] In Locke's view, nobody is born a member of a church but becomes one through personal choice. If the person later discerns errors in the church's teachings or worship, he has the same freedom to leave it as he originally had to join.[42] For that reason, neither power nor coercion are fitting for the church and religion.[43]

Another significant insight is Locke's epistemological argument. Any coercion the state may want to exercise presupposes that it would know in what direction it should go. To do so, it would have to know what is the right relation to God and what that entails, which Locke considers impossible. Although faith consists in firm knowledge, that knowledge is not demonstrable and is essentially fallible. On what grounds, then, would anyone other than the individual, let alone the state, know what religious road the person has to go? What makes it even more difficult is that the religious relationship is not altogether transparent even to the light of the individual's own reason. In his *Areopagitica*, Milton analyses the relation between truth and freedom by positing that no person can contain, let alone comprehend the truth, hence that nobody is infallible and truth is best served by including as many perspectives as possible in the debate, whereupon true knowledge will surface of its own accord and error will be banished.[44] Milton uses the same argument to defend a free press. If its freedom is fettered, it would hamper the progress of truth. In *Areopagitica*, subtitled *For the Liberty of unlicenc'd Printing*, he graphically says that who destroys a good book, kills reason itself, which means that he kills the image of God, as it were in the middle of the eye.[45]

Finally, there is the argument of reciprocity. It holds that in its own eyes every church or religion is the only true, orthodox faith and is

---

[39] Milton, *Complete Prose Works* VI, op. cit., 572.
[40] Milton, *Complete Prose Works* VI, op. cit., 430–437.
[41] Milton, *Complete Prose Works* VI, op. cit., 600–603.
[42] Locke, *A Letter on Toleration*, op. cit., 70–71.
[43] Locke, *A Letter on Toleration*, op. cit., 100–115.
[44] Milton, *Complete Prose Works* II, op. cit., 567.
[45] Milton, *Complete Prose Works* II, op. cit., 492.

heterodox in the eyes of other religions or churches. If coercion and oppression were permitted, they would apply these to each other. The only proper course, says Locke, is to practise tolerance, that is to say, a debate in which the weight of reasonable argument carries the day, along with humaneness and goodwill.[46]

The tolerance that Locke advocated was aimed at dissenters in England who had turned away from and left the Anglican Church, specifically Presbyterians, Puritans, and Independents, as well as Quakers and Baptists.[47] The pragmatic argument was that tolerance did more to promote peace in the commonwealth than coercion and oppression. The fact that these groups had beliefs that conflicted with Anglican policies did not concern the state. For a political measure like tolerance, it was irrelevant whether one group called bread bread and the other worshipped it as the body of Christ, or whether Jews credited only the Old Testament, or whether pagans attached no value to either Testament. After all, laws are not about error or truth but about the security of the commonwealth and the property of every citizen. Through the light it sheds, truth can look after itself, a display of power and coercion merely undermines it.[48] Neither do laws concern sin and salvation. That means that however strongly Christians may condemn idolatry as evil and sinful, the state should keep aloof and not use its power to combat it.[49] As for morality, it concerns the state only insofar as the outward behaviour it gives rise to must not violate the rights of others.[50] Thus Locke posits two principles: religion cannot prohibit what is legal, hence permissible, and it cannot permit what is illegal.[51]

Tolerance was not meant for Muslims, Catholics, Unitarians, and atheists, not because they were heretical, but because they jeopardised the unity and peace of the commonwealth.[52] Muslims were excluded from tolerance because they were loyal to a foreign head of state, the *mufti* of Constantinople, who in his turn was subject to the emperor of

---

[46] Locke, *A Letter on Toleration*, op. cit., 80–85.

[47] Milton shares some of these groups' polemical aversion to the Anglican state church inasmuch as he considers, as evidenced by his *Considerations touching the likeliest means to remove hirelings out of the church* (*Complete Prose Works* VII, op. cit., 277–321), its priests to be hirelings of the state and, according to his *Of Prelatical Episcopacy*, its bishops to act like hierarchs (*Complete Prose Works* I, op. cit., 618–652).

[48] Locke, *A Letter on Toleration*, op. cit., 120–123.

[49] Locke, *A Letter on Toleration*, op. cit., 114–115.

[50] Locke, *A Letter on Toleration*, op. cit., 122–129.

[51] Locke, *A Letter on Toleration*, op. cit., 110–111.

[52] Locke, *A Letter on Toleration*, op. cit., 132–149.

the Ottoman empire. The same applied to Catholics, who owed obedience to yet another foreign head of state, the pope. The latter posed a special danger, because he not only claimed to appoint and depose emperors and kings by divine right, but was also suspected of heading a Catholic league aiming to overthrow the British – in effect the Anglican – state. In his *Areopagitica*, in which Milton, unlike Locke, advocated tolerance of all Christian denominations and religions, he made an exception of the Catholic Church ('popery'), as did virtually everyone who supported the principle of tolerance at that time. According to Milton, it was because this church exterminated state organs and religions by claiming authority over individuals not only in their civil capacity – which jeopardised national sovereignty – but also over individual believers' faith, right up to their conscience, thus coercing God's own Spirit that dwells in believers.[53] Locke also excluded Unitarians from tolerance. They were predominantly Socianists who denied the trinity and Jesus' divinity, and deists, who denied providence, hence divine intervention in history. The reason was that both groups were suspected of inclining towards atheism, so they were not capable of honouring promises and contracts and taking oaths. In addition, tolerance could not be contemplated for those who were intolerant of religion, such as atheists.

If one compares the representatives of premodernity, Augustine and Thomas, with the two representatives of early modernity, Milton and Locke, the differences are paramount and only one resemblance remains. Whereas the first two authors project the image of a society in which religion, morality, politics, and law constitute a single whole, with religion acting as a sacred canopy under which politics and the law are assigned their proper place, Locke and Milton paint a very different picture. Their exposition reflects functional differentiation between religion and morality on the one hand and politics and the law on the other. They detach political tolerance from religious and moral themes like error/truth and sin/grace. In addition, they transpose the exercise of power necessary to enforce the right to tolerance from the obscure intertwinement – but at the same time rivalry – of church and state to government authority, being the transparent wielder of a monopoly of violence under rule of law. The law has nothing to do with error and truth, sin and grace, hence religious legitimisation of coercive power

---

[53] Milton, *Complete Prose Works* II, op. cit., 565; VII, op. cit., 244.

falls away. Thus the freedom to join a religion – including a dissident Christian denomination – becomes a legal right, but so does the freedom to turn one's back on whatever religion.

Yet there is a similarity between Augustine and Thomas on the one hand and Locke and Milton on the other: the indissoluble link between religion and morality. Whereas Augustine and Thomas extended that link to the whole of personal and societal life, Milton and Locke confined it to a religious relationship with God in the individual's conscience. As we pointed out, this conscientious relation to God meant that the individual now occupied the place formerly held by church and state on the strength of their relation to God. This direct individual relationship and the concomitant freedom from state and church were inalienable and could not be transferred to any other person or institution. The religious relationship was the core of conscience, for that was where the individual accounted to God – and to God alone – for her life. That was also why tolerance was not extended to Unitarians and atheists. They could not be trusted to keep their promises, honour contracts and pledge oaths, because they were considered to lack the moral, conscientious core of religion.

7.2 Religious Freedom in International Public Law in Modern Times

All of that changed in the rules on religious freedom laid down in international declarations and covenants after World War II. During the drafting of the Universal Declaration of Human Rights (1948) it was decided to devote a separate article to religious freedom, but in the process to dispense with any religious foundation altogether. The Declaration as a whole would likewise forego any religious reference, in contrast to the religiously performative language that still graces the constitutions of some countries, such as the invocation of the holy, consubstantial, and indivisible trinity (Greece)[54] or simply of God

---

[54] Some people consider this emphasis on the trinity a disregard of the common religious heritage of the three Abrahamic religions, Judaism, Christianity and Islam (H. Lübbe, *Die Zivilisationsökumene, Globalisierung kulturell, technisch und politisch*, Fink, München 2005, 181). We note, however, that this 'common' heritage is explained in three different ways: Judaism claims to be an heir of Abraham through his son Isaac and Islam through Abraham's eldest son Ishmael, whereas Christianity considers Abraham 'the father of all of us' (Rom 4:16); see: Pim Valkenberg, *Sharing*

(*invocatio Dei*) (Switzerland), the supplication of God's blessing (*bene-dictio Dei*) (South Africa), the mention of God's name (*nominatio Dei*) (Germany), and the juxtaposition of God as the source of morality alongside nonreligious sources (Poland). The Declaration omits the reference to the creator or the God of nature in the American Declaration of Independence of 1776 and even refrains from mentioning 'the supreme being' as the French Declaration of the Rights of Man and of the Citizen of 1789 does. Despite the Vatican's endeavour to include a reference to natural law or natural rights in the Universal Declaration, it was decided not to do even that. This was partly because such a typically Catholic reference would cause bad blood with, for example, German Lutherans, who demanded instead an insertion referring explicitly to the Christian God in terms of Lutheran tradition. But a reference to natural law would also affront other religions, as well as large groups espousing nonreligious worldviews.[55] This approach derives from the notion that morality can and does exist independently of religion and that conscience can serve as a moral forum in which individuals account to themselves for their actions in terms of the continuity of their past, present, and future identity without grounding it in a relationship with God.[56] Thus it was a product of functional differentiation, not only between religion, law, and politics, but also between religion and morality. In this respect, there has been no change in international declarations and treaties since 1948.

The same functional differentiation is apparent in the definition of religious freedom per se, as in article 18 of the Universal Declaration of Human Rights (1948) and article 9 of European Convention for the Protection of Human Rights and Fundamental Freedoms (1950). Both articles mention religion alongside thought and conscience. Thus section 1 of the article in the European convention reads: "Everyone has the right to freedom of thought, conscience and religion; this right includes freedom to change his religion or belief and freedom, either alone or in community with others and in public or private,

---

Lights on the Way to God: Muslim-Christian Dialogue and Theology in the Context of Abrahamic Partnership, Rodopi, Amsterdam/New York 2006, 59.

[55] W. Vögele, *Menschenwürde zwischen Recht und Theologie*, Kaiser, Gütersloh 2000; J. Morsink, *The Universal Declaration of Human Rights: Origins, Drafting and Intent*, University of Pennsylvania Press, Philadelphia 1999, 269–280.

[56] N. Luhmann, *Ausdifferenzierung des Rechts*, Suhrkamp, Frankfurt, 1999, 326–359.

to manifest his religion or belief, in worship, teaching, practice and observance".[57]

In this text one can distinguish between three parts. The first concerns freedom of thought, conscience, and religion in the *forum internum*, the second the freedom to change one's religion or belief, and the third the manifestation of religion or belief in the *forum externum*.[58] The distinction between forums is important. Freedom of thought, conscience, and religion offers no protection for manifestation of thought and conscience, since the former pertains to the *forum internum*. In the *forum externum*, freedom of religion or belief does offer such protection. Protection of these religions and beliefs pertains to their individual and collective as well as their private and public manifestations. In European jurisprudence, religions include Hinduism, Buddhism, Sikhism, Judaism, Christianity, and Islam, as well as Jehovah's Witnesses, scientology, and the Moon sect, while beliefs include atheism, pacifism, and communism.[59] As is just said, the manifestation of religion or belief refers to worship, teaching, practice, and observance.[60] The state has the negative obligation not to interfere in those manifestations.

Self-evident as the right to religious freedom may seem, it has any number of intricacies. These can be encapsulated in three questions: Why is the right necessary and what is its legitimacy? In which affairs is the state not allowed to interfere? And what is the scope of the right – in concrete terms, is there a right to religious organisation?

---

[57] The terms 'worship', 'teaching', 'practice' and 'observance' also occur, in varying order, in the Universal Declaration of Human Rights, art. 18 (1948), the International Covenant of Civil and Political Rights, art. 18 (1966), the European Convention for the Protection of Human Rights and Fundamental Freedoms, art. 9 (1950), and the Charter of Fundamental Rights of the European Union, art. 10 (2000).

[58] M. Evans, The Freedom of Religion or Belief and the Freedom of Expression, *Religion and Human Rights* 4(2009)2–3, 197–235.

[59] M. Evans, *Religious Liberty and International Law in Europe*, Cambridge University Press, Cambridge 1997, 290–291. Because of this list of religions and beliefs the discussion about the essence and relevance of 'religion' in law between L. Sager and J. Webber (in: P. Cane et al. (eds.), *Law and Religion in Theoretical and Historical Context*, Cambridge University Press, Cambridge 2008) may be considered as tentatively concluded.

[60] For religion and belief it is essential that they manifest in (one of) those four forms, judging by the decision of the European Court of Human Rights in Pretty v. United Kingdom (2002); see: S. Millns, Death, Dignity and Discrimination: The Case of Pretty v. United Kingdom, *German Law Journal* 3(2002)10: www.germanlawjournal.com./article.php?id=197.

7.2.1 *Legitimacy*

The first question, that of the need for such a right, has to do with its legitimisation, that is, the reasons why it is needed. Firstly, there are historical reasons, especially opposition to coercive measures of inclusion and exclusion as advocated by Augustine and Thomas. It also opposes negative tolerance, which boils down to tolerating others in order to avoid a greater evil such as social unrest. The same argument is found in Milton and Locke, albeit imbedded in positive tolerance of the believer's conscientious relationship with God that nonetheless excluded Catholics, Muslims, and atheists. Religious freedom is indicative of a more advanced civilisation, in that it applies to everyone – believers, people of other faiths, and non-believers. It ensures, judicially, the prevention of religious war and oppression of religious minorities. Along with the separation of church and state, it restricts unreasonable truth claims to uniqueness, absoluteness, and universality by religions, which may well be interwoven with political identity, power, and usurpation.

Does this warrant a separate right like religious freedom, or would a combination of other rights like the principle of non-discrimination, freedom of expression, and freedom of assembly and association suffice?[61] The reason for a separate right is twofold. Firstly, such a combination can hardly cover the full complexity and diversity of the religious phenomenon in its individual and collective, private and public forms, from silent meditation to rowdy pilgrimages, from reverent rituals to ecclesiastic punishments.[62] The second reason is more fundamental. Philosophically and anthropologically, religion is a special domain of existential questions regarding meaning and purpose at critical events of individual and collective suffering, when it provides a transcendent horizon and offers consolation and prospect. The precariousness of religion, steeped as it is in vulnerable questions arising from the depths of human existence, calls for protection against state interference.

---

[61] S. den Dekker-van Bijsterveld, *De verhouding tussen kerk en staat in het licht van de grondrechten*, Willink, Zwolle 1988, 55 56.
[62] J. Witte, *Religion and the American Constitutional Experiment*, 2nd edition, Westview, Boulder 2005, 176–177.

7.2.2   Non-interference in Worship, Teaching,
Observance and Practice

The answer to the second question – regarding affairs in which the state may not interfere – is simple: in religion. The problem is that there is little or no consensus about what religion is, which means that it is difficult if not impossible to deal with it in law. A striking example of non-interference was the European Court of Human Rights verdict on a decision by the Moldavian government, which intervened in a conflict between the Metropolitan Church of Moldavia and the Metropolitan Church of Bessarabia that had seceded from the former. The government refused to recognise the latter, because from a religious point of view the two churches were said to be identical. However, the European Court upheld the demand of the Metropolitan Church of Bessarabia to establish a separate church, because it saw itself as different from that of Moldavia. The Court argued that the state was not competent to decide whether or not there was a difference between the two.[63] Against the background of such incidents, some jurists want to remove the term 'religion' from the legal dictionary, not only because a jurist qua jurist does not know what religion is, let alone what is 'true' religion, hence what is error, apostasy, heresy or schism. When one defines religion in terms of its 'content', its 'intensional' meaning, inequalities arise, because definitions are always contextual, never without a context. Hence its dominant import is always that of the religious majority, whereas religious minorities lose out.[64] As happens all too often, the law has to deal with conventional, apparently clear but in reality vague concepts with porous boundaries.[65] The same applies to religion and, indeed, to the basic concepts of all disciplines. That does not really matter provided one is critically alert to limitations and distortions.

The question of what affairs the state may not interfere in can also be answered more specifically by using the concepts of an 'extensional' definition of religion. Above I mentioned four of these: worship, teaching, observance and practice. But they, too, raise many questions.

---

[63]   P.M. Taylor, *Freedom of Religion*, Cambridge University Press, Cambridge 2005, 223–224.

[64]   W. Sullivan, *The Impossibility of Religious Freedom*, Princeton University Press, Princeton 2005, 138–159.

[65]   S. Winter, *A Clearing in the Forest, Law, Life and Mind*, University of Chicago Press, Chicago 2001.

Firstly, the state may not interfere with worship, but what does worship include? One might say that as a religious ritual, public worship is a sub-category of the broad category of ritual. But what makes it religious? The question brings up again the 'intensional' meaning of religion. The question is not just academic but also practical. In jurisprudence, for instance, the word 'sacrament' is often used to define 'religious ritual' more closely. Anyone who is familiar with the traditions of Rome, Wittenberg, Geneva, and Canterbury will know that the term can cover a host of meanings. But how should one respond to the Klamath tribe in the Native American Church in Oregon that performs the ritual of eating the hallucinogen peyote plant and refers to it as a sacrament? Since this is a culpable offence, the case ended up in federal Supreme Court of the United States, which judged that the laws that prohibited the consumption of peyote without exempting its religious use are not counter to religious freedom. Thereupon certain states, including Oregon, passed laws that did exempt religious use of the drug.[66]

Secondly, the state may not interfere in religions' teaching: it is free. But what does that freedom entail? An example is missionary activities, in which religions propound their beliefs. The state may not interfere with that, any more than with those of humanistic, atheistic, or anti-theistic associations. The problem is that interaction between such associations readily lead to conflict, for instance between religious and nonreligious groups, among religious groups, between denominations, even between factions within a denomination. These groups could agree on a code of conduct, which could incorporate an enforcement mechanism.[67] But apart from that, mission and propaganda are not clearcut, for where does one draw the line between the right to persuade people of a truth that is foreign to them and their right to protection of their original faith? Such questions require judicious balancing of two rights.[68] Another facet is that mission is often accompanied by educational, medical, and social activities that can have political consequences, thus blurring the line diving religion

---

[66] The case is known as the Employment Division v. Smith (1990), in: Witte, *Religion*, op. cit., 163–176.

[67] R. Torfs, Church and State: Relevant Issues for a Democratic State, *Nederduitse Gereformeerde Teologiese Tydskrif* 42(2001)1&2, 147–157, here 155; Id., Relationship between the State and Religious Groups, in: J.-F. Flauss (ed.), *International Protection of Religious Freedom*, Bruylant, Brussel 2002, 131–152, here 147–148.

[68] M. Evans, *Religious liberty*, op. cit., 284, n. 13.

from politics. Missionary activities may also be accompanied by provision of material or social benefits, such as training, employment, or
psychological care. This can blur the dividing line between proper and
improper, legitimate and illegitimate missionary activities.[69]

In addition, the state may not interfere with religious observance.
Again it raises all sorts of problems, such as labour law prohibiting
the wearing of veils or participation in Friday prayers. Section 2 of
article 9 of the European Convention subjects religious freedom to
legal constraints in the interests of public safety, public order, health
and morality, and to protect the rights of others. Thus there are dress
rules that prohibit the wearing of veils in certain situations and prison
laws that prohibit the wearing of a prayer chain. But there are more
complex issues. Thus Friday prayer in a mosque is indubitably a right
to religious observance. But can an employee refuse to work on Friday afternoons, any more than Jews can refuse to work on Saturdays
and Christians on Sundays? May such employees be fired for refusing
to work? Are they entitled to unemployment benefits? If not, is it
discriminatory?

Finally, the state may not interfere with practices that are manifestations of religion. But what is a manifestation? European jurisprudence uses a narrow definition. Not every activity relating to religion
qualifies as a manifestation. Thus a religiously inspired or motivated
action is not considered a manifestation, neither is one that is religiously influenced, nor an extension, outcome or consequence of religion and certainly not actions that are merely consistent with it. The
criterion is that it must be an actual religious expression, which has
to be applied very sensitively. Thus a European judge ruled that the
British government's conviction of a pacifist, Pat Arrowsmith, who
distributed leaflets calling on soldiers to refuse to serve in Northern
Ireland was not a violation of religious freedom because the leaflets
were not actual expressions of pacifism. To qualify for that they would
have to spell out the principles of pacifism.[70] Others maintain that this
interpretation is too narrow, for the distribution of leaflets is an integral part of pacifism. What else can a pacifist do but protest against
acts of war?[71] According to them, the narrow interpretation favours

---

[69] Taylor, *Freedom*, op. cit., 54–70.
[70] Taylor, *Freedom*, op. cit., 211.
[71] C. Evans, *Freedom of Religion Under the European Convention on Human Rights*,
Oxford University Press, Oxford 2003, 111–115; Evans, *Liberty*, op. cit., 313.

established, mainly Christian denominations with highly developed doctrines and practical rules. They disadvantage minority worldviews that do not make a subtle distinction between manifestation and manifestation-through-expression.[72] In other words, does it not depend on the specific worldviews, practices, and contexts whether something sufficiently qualifies as a manifestation?[73]

7.2.3   Right to Religious Organisation

The third and last question concerns the scope of religious freedom. Since religion is always practised in an organisational context, the question of the right to religious organisation is pertinent. It is not explicitly raised anywhere, neither in the Universal Declaration nor in the European Convention. The section of the Declaration dealing with the elimination of all forms of intolerance and discrimination on grounds of religion or worldview (1981) does mention issues pointing in this direction, such as the freedom to have places of worship and teaching, to run charitable or humanitarian institutions, to edit publications, to collect funds, to train and appoint leaders, to observe days of rest, to celebrate feasts and communicate nationally and internationally (art. 6). These freedoms cannot be realised without an organisation, but the right to religious organisation is not explicitly mentioned.[74] Yet it exists. According to European jurisprudence, it lies in a combination of article 6 (right to due process), article 9 (religious freedom), and article 11 (freedom of association and assembly). If believers establish an association, it can seek protection for itself, its members and property in terms of article 6.[75] According to the United Nations special rapporteur, the problem is that the non-discrimination principle is violated by governments that refuse to recognise religious communities as such by withholding or delaying the necessary registration.[76] They favour the religion(s) of the majority and disadvantage those of minorities because of their geographic origin, relatively small member-

---

[72] Evans, *Freedom*, op. cit., 122–123.
[73] Evans, *Liberty*, op. cit., 314.
[74] *Declaration on the Elimination of All Forms of Intolerance and Discrimination Based on Religion or Belief*, 1981; P. Marshall (ed.), *Religious Freedom in the World*, Roman & Littlefield, New York 2008.
[75] Taylor, *Freedom*, op. cit., 227.
[76] Torfs, *Relationship*, op. cit, 141–145, has a more differentiated view of these features.

ship, relatively short lifespan, ideological views, and avoidance of social unrest.[77] Such discrimination occurs mainly in Eastern Europe.[78]

From this overview of questions and problems, it is abundantly clear that the right to religious freedom is anything but straightforward and is fraught with intricacies. But that is no reason to scrap it from the legal dictionary – on the contrary. The complexity of the right to religious freedom is one thing, the far greater complexity of that freedom in society is another. The legal rules are merely a reflection of it. The more complex rights are and the more they are intertwined with existentially sensitive issues arising from the human condition – as religion is – the more they need protection and sensitive treatment in legislation and jurisprudence.

7.3   ACCEPTANCE OF RELIGIOUS FREEDOM IN AN EMPIRICAL PERSPECTIVE

Having described the development of premodern coercion, premodern and early modern forms of tolerance, and the problems connected with the modern right to religious freedom, we can now inquire into the extent to which the three groups of Christian, Muslim, and nonreligious youths that we investigated subscribe to religious freedom. In 2007–2008, the research group consisted of 1054 Dutch youths at 25 schools, of which eleven are public, six are Catholic, four Protestant, two interconfessional, and two Muslim. Three quarters of the youths have Dutch as their home language, the rest represent 34 different languages. According to their own religious self-attribution, 340 youths may be considered Christian (of whom 61% called themselves Catholic, 10% Protestant, and 29% Christian, including a group of Catholics by birth), 235 Muslim and 479 nonreligious.[79]

---

[77] Taylor, *Freedom*, op. cit., 230–234.

[78] S. Ferrari et al. (eds.), *Law and Religion in Post-Communist Europe*, Peeters, Leuven 2003.

[79] For the scale of self-attribution see Appendix IV. The respective percentages of males and females in the Christian, Islamic and nonreligious group are: 45%/55%, 43%/57% and 48%/52%. On a scale ranging from 1 (totally disagree) to 5 (fully agree) the three groups, in the same order, are: ambivalent about political saliency: 2.8, 3.0, 2.7; attach great value to personal autonomy 3.7, 4.0, 3.9; and manifestly disagree with social criticism: the Christian group is ambivalent, the Muslim group strongly in favour and the nonreligious group negatively ambivalent: 3.0, 3.6, 2.8. The personal

Our research focused on two features of religious freedom that form part of the foregoing discussion: the prohibition of state interference in religious communities and the right to religious manifestation in the public arena, more specifically that part of the area occupied by public schools and, concretely, prayer at public schools.

To that end, we used two items. Item (i) concerns religious freedom inasmuch as it implies religious communities' right to manifest their faith according to their own ideas and rules in the areas of worship, teaching, practice, and observance. The right means that there can be no political interference in these spheres. This is an instance of what is known as the vertical operation of civil liberties, here religious freedom, which protect citizens from state interference. The state has a so-called negative obligation to refrain from the execution of power.[80] The obverse of this vertical operation is horizontal operation, a private law application inferred from the vertical operation. It means that citizens should refrain from interfering with each other, which is not pertinent to this discussion.[81] Thus item (i) reads: "Politicians are not allowed to interfere with religious communities."

Item (ii) concerns a tricky problem, namely whether the right to religious freedom is applicable to public schools. As noted already, this freedom includes the right to religious manifestation, both individual and collective, both private and public. That would include prayer, one of the most poignant manifestations of religion. Our question is whether this right applies to prayer at public schools, which, as we know, are not run by religious or worldview-related organisations but by the state. Thus item (ii) poses the question whether prayer is prohibited at public schools or not. In the questionnaire submitted to the youths, the item was deliberately phrased negatively to prevent so-called response set.[82] In the questionnaire item (ii) reads: "Prayer at public schools should be forbidden." In this kind of empirical research

---

characteristic of psychological stability is pronounced among all three groups: 3.8, 3.5, 3.8. See for the items: appendix V.

[80] P.H. van Kempen, *Repressie door mensenrechten*, Wolf, Nijmegen 2008, 13.

[81] According to L. Besselink, Voetangels en klemmen: de horizontale werking van burger- en politieke rechten, in: C. Flinterman & W. van Genugten (eds.), *Niet-statelijke actoren en de rechten van de mens: Gevestigde waarden, nieuwe wegen*, Boom, The Hague 2003, 3–18, the horizontal operation may be seen as a private law application of the fundamental values contained in human rights, which actually form part of public law.

[82] In the questionnaire, these two items are separated by eight items on Christian rights.

it is methodologically permissible to invert an item both content- and score-wise for the sake of lucid presentation.[83] That is what happened to item (ii). Below it reads, "Prayer at public schools should not be forbidden."[84]

The youths were asked to indicate on a five-point scale to what extent they agree with items (i) and (ii), with 1 indicating 'totally disagree', 2 'disagree', 3 'not sure', 4 'agree', and 5 'fully agree'. Scores of 1 and 2 were combined to indicate non-agreement (–), 3 was left to indicate uncertainty (±), and scores of 4 and 5 were combined to indicate agreement (+). 'N' indicates the number of youths (table 1).

Table 1. Attitudes towards religious freedom (%)

	Christian			Muslim			Nonreligious		
	–	±	+	–	±	+	–	±	+
(i) political interference forbidden	40 N = 338	33	28	13 N = 231	33	55	46 N = 472	37	17
(ii) praying in public schools not forbidden	13 N = 339	27	60	14 N = 228	20	65	21 N = 471	26	54

In the case of item (i) the percentages provide a highly differentiated picture. A good quarter of the Christian group (28%), more than half the Muslim group (55% – almost double the percentage for the Christian group), and about one sixth of the nonreligious group (17% – more than ten percentage points below that of the Christian group) agree that political interference in religious communities is forbidden. However, two fifths of the Christian group (40%) and almost half of the nonreligious group (46%) do not agree with item (i). Just over one tenth of the Muslim youths (13%) do not agree with it either. Remarkably, all three groups contain a relatively large middle group who are uncertain, varying from 33% (Christian and Muslim) to 37% (nonreligious).

---

[83] A. Sen, *The Idea of Justice*, Harvard University Press, Cambridge 2009, 174.

[84] The scores on the five-point scale for item (ii) were recoded accordingly: score 1 into score 5, score 2 into score 4, score 3 remained score 3, score 4 into score 2 and score 5 into score 1.

The responses to item (ii) present a very different picture. A clear majority of the Christian group (60%), almost two thirds of the Muslim group (65%) and more than half the nonreligious group (54%) agree that prayer at public schools should not be forbidden. All three groups contain relatively small minorities who believe that prayer at public schools should be forbidden: the Christian group (13%), the Islamic group (14%) and a somewhat larger nonreligious group (21%). The three ambivalent middle groups are almost equally large: Christian group (27%), Muslim (20%), and nonreligious (26%).

To find out whether the differences between the means of the three groups are statistically significant, we established the means and standard deviations (sd) and conducted variance analyses (eta) and the related Scheffé tests (table 2).

Table 2. Attitudes towards religious freedom (means)

	Christian		Muslim		Nonreligious		
	mean	sd	mean	sd	mean	sd	eta
(i) political interference forbidden	2.9[a] N = 338	1.0	3.7[b] N = 231	1.1	2.6[c] N = 472	1.0	.37*
(ii) praying in public school not forbidden	3.7[a] N = 339	1.0	4.0[b] N = 228	1.3	3.5[a] N = 471	1.2	.16*

[a][b][c] Distinctive indices in the rows indicate statistically significant means: Scheffé p < .05.
* eta p < .01.

The means in this table are noteworthy.[85] The Christian group's mean for item (i), the prohibition of political interference, indicates ambivalence (2.9). The Muslim group agrees with it (3.7). The nonreligious group is on the borderline between negative ambivalence and rejection (2.6). The differences between the three groups' means are significant (eta .37*).

---

[85] The interpretation of the means is: 1.00–1.79: totally disagree; 1.80–2.59: disagree; 2.60–2.99: negative ambivalence; 3.00–3.39: positive ambivalence; 3.40–4.19: agree; 4.20 5.00: fully agree.

The means for the item on prayer at public schools (ii) indicate that both the Christian (3.7) and the Muslim group (4.0), as well as the nonreligious group (3.5), are of the opinion that such prayer should not be forbidden. The differences between the means of the Christian and the Muslim group and those of the Muslim and the nonreligious group are statistically significant. The difference between the means of the Christian and the nonreligious group are not statistically significant (eta .16).

These findings raise the question why the scores on item (i) (political non-interference) and item (ii) (prayer permitted at public schools) differ so markedly. There seems to be no connection between attitudes towards the two items, although logically we might formulate the expectation that item (ii) will correlate with item (i), because permitting prayer at public school (item ii) may be considered a logical concretisation of political non-interference (item i). To answer this question we conducted correlation analyses, one for each group (table 3).

Table 3. Correlations between attitudes towards religious freedom (r)

(i) political interference forbidden	(ii) praying in public schools not forbidden		
	Christian	Islamic	Nonreligious
Christian	−.13* N = 337		
Islamic		.02 N = 226	
Nonreligious			.00 N = 466

* p < .05.

In this table only the attitude of the Christian group towards political non-interference (item i) appears to correlate with the attitude towards permitting prayer at public schools (item ii). But the correlation is negative (r −.13), which means that the more the Christian group agrees with political non-interference, the more they reject prayer at public schools – contrary to the aforementioned logical expectation. The correlation is significant but rather low and not relevant. The correlations between the other two groups (Muslim: r .02; nonreligious: r .00) are not significant. From this we conclude that items (i) and (ii) are independent of each other. Although logically we expected them to be connected, in the minds of the three groups of youths they display no relevant connection whatsoever.

7.4   REFLECTION

How should the empirical research data be interpreted in terms of the asymmetric tolerance and symmetrical religious freedom discussed in sections 1 and 2? I first look at the prohibition of political interference in religious communities (7.4.1), and then at prayer in public schools (7.4.2).

7.4.1   *Political Interference*

A striking finding is that only a minority of Christian youths (28%) and an even smaller minority of nonreligious youths (17%) subscribe to political non-interference. The rest of the youths oppose it, or are ambivalent. In other words, the majority of Christian and nonreligious youths do not accept symmetric religious freedom. They do not accept free manifestation of the religion of every person, alone or in community with others, publicly or in private, in public worship, teaching, practice and observance, as well as that of religious organisations. I take this to indicate asymmetric tolerance.

Among Muslim youths, the position is very different. The majority (55%) accept religious freedom; the mean for the attitude of the group as a whole is manifestly positive (3.7). That is easy to interpret. Research shows that the intensity with which Muslim youths cherish their religious identity is increasing, because they experience growing opposition between native Dutch people and foreigners. This does not mean that their prayer practice or attendance at mosques has increased – on the contrary, it is declining. Their religious ideas, too, have become more open. But the cultural significance of Islam makes them cherish it more intensely. That is why, in my interpretation, they endorse religious freedom.[86]

---

[86] K. Phalet & J. ter Wal (eds), *Moslim in Nederland, diversiteit en verandering in religieuze betrokkenheid: Turken en Marokkanen in Nederland1998–2002*, The Hague 2004, 25–42; Id., Moslim in Nederland, *De publiekediscussie over de islam in Nederland: een analyse van artikelen in deVolkskrant 1998–2002*, The Hague 2004, 29–81; J. Dagevos

How does one interpret the extensive non-acceptance of religious freedom among Christian and nonreligious youths, which I take to be evidence of asymmetric tolerance? I defined an asymmetric attitude as lack of respect for a religious population group in its own right, and as tolerating that group for some extraneous reason, to achieve a greater good such as social harmony or, negatively formulated, the avoidance of overt conflict. We have noted that Augustine favoured tolerance of heretics by invoking church unity, but that he later legitimated coercive measures when church unity and the unity of church and state were no longer attainable by practising tolerance. We have seen that Aquinas regarded not only heretics but also Jews and Muslims as an evil. He even advocated war against them, not in order to convert them but to prevent them from contaminating Christians. In the early modern period there was some change in this regard: the legitimacy of asymmetric tolerance was no longer based on doctrinal differences regarding religious truth, but on the maintenance of public order by the state. However, certain groups were excluded from such tolerance: Catholics in the case of both Locke and Milton, and in Locke's case Muslims, Unitarians, and atheists as well.

The vicissitudes of Muslims in the Netherlands today parallel those of heretics and unbelievers in the premodern age of Augustine and Aquinas, and especially those of Catholics, Muslims, Unitarians, and atheists in Locke's early modern England. Not that the vicissitudes are identical – the social and ecclesiastic contexts differed too greatly for that – but from a comparative perspective there are correspondences in the relation between majority and minority. This applies particularly to early modern England where, as in the Netherlands today, it was a matter of maintaining law and order rather than a conflict about religious truth and ecclesiastic control.

The parallels are not merely unsurprising. They may even be said to be the natural outcome of a certain historical continuity between the premodern and early modern era on the one hand, and the present era on the other. To substantiate this continuity, I venture to surmise that when religious freedom comes under pressure as a result of well

& M. Gijsberts (eds), *Jaarrapportage Integratie 2007*, The Hague 2007; D. Korf et al., *Van vasten tot feesten*, Rotterdam 2007; D. Korf & M. Wouters, *Geloof en geluk*, Guijs, Rotterdam 2008, 32–68; S. Ketner, *Marokkaanse wortels*, Diss.Groningen 2008; H. Entziger & E. Dourleijn, *De lat steeds hoger. Deleefwereld van jongeren in een multiethnische stad*, Van Gorcum, Assen 2008, 38–51.

nigh intolerable tensions and (potential) conflict, symmetrical relations between majority and minority are abandoned and people revert
to asymmetrical tolerance. The latter entails, as we have seen, enforced
exclusion and, in order to avoid this, enforced inclusion – in short,
discipline.

This is not surprising, since asymmetric tolerance is part of the collective memory of Western society, which functions as a persistent
cultural pattern in the mental scripts of Dutch citizens. This surmise
is based on a twofold, synchronic and diachronic insight. The synchronic notion is that cultural patterns exercise a major influence on
individuals' thought and actions. The antithesis that early sociologists
posited between individuals and institutions – either people shaped
their own lives or their lives are determined by institutions – has made
way for the notion of an interaction between individuals and institutions, in which society constructs, reproduces, and transforms itself.
Thus Bourdieu's concept of habitus establishes a connection between
the individual and institutions, while Gidden's idea of structuration
combines the individual with structure.[87] The diachronic notion concerns the distinction between three levels of history: a surface, middle,
and depth level. Changes at the first level consist in fluctuating contemporary events (*événements*), at the second level they comprise variable trends over a period of 50 to 100 years, and the third level consists
in extremely slow evolutionary processes over four or more centuries
(*longue durée*).[88] In these terms, the replacement of asymmetric tolerance by symmetric religious freedom in the Netherlands is, from a
constitutional perspective, barely two centuries old. The first time it
was included in a constitution was the *Staatsregeling voor het Bataafse
Volk (1798)*, article 19. We know that fundamental values like constitutional principles take a long time to be assimilated, via socialisation,
internalisation, and transfer from one generation to the next, into the
plausibility structure of a society's symbolic universe.[89] In other words,
it is by no means impossible that remnants of asymmetric tolerance

---

[87] P. Bourdieu, *Outline of a theory of practice*, Cambridge University Press, Cambridge 1977; A. Giddens, *The constitution of society, Outline of a theory of structuration*, Polity, Cambridge 1984; for empirical research, see T. van der Meer, *States of
freely associating citizens*, diss. Nijmegen 2009.

[88] F. Braudel, *Écrits sur l'histoire*, Flammarion, Paris 1969.

[89] P. Berger & Th. Luckmann, *The social construction of reality*, Anchor, New York
1967, 163ff.

live on in the active memory of the Dutch population and that people revert to them when it comes to the push.

In short, the Muslim youths in our study have an interest in symmetric religious freedom, and the Christian and nonreligious youths show signs of asymmetric tolerance. I assume that the latter two groups do demand their own religious freedom, including the nonreligious group, since religious freedom protects their agnosticism and atheism also. But they do not want adherents of the second major religion in the Netherlands, Islam, to enjoy the same right. In other words, they want political interference in Islam. From the public debate in recent years, one can derive the type of principles that refer to such interference. The two main problems in national and international discussions are: the right to change one's religion, which refers to the interaction of Islam with other religious and nonreligious worldviews, as well as the principle of non-discrimination. In the current debate, Muslims are accused of violating these two principles.[90] Let me briefly describe Muslim and Christian notions in this regard – more particularly those of the Catholic community in view of the high percentage of Catholic youths in our research population – and show how these notions support a reversion to asymmetric tolerance.

The Right to Change One's Religion

With regard to the right to change one's religion, Islam makes a distinction between non-Muslims and Muslims. Officially Islam exercises no coercion on non-Muslims. In terms of sura 2:256 in the Qur'an non-Muslims are free to become Muslims, but coercion is prohibited. Some restrict the prohibition to Jews and Christians, but others, citing sura 10:99, feel that the prohibition also applies to adherents of polytheistic religions. According to the Islamic scholar Mashood Baderin, the only proper way of dealing with adherents of other religions is intellectual argumentation and honest preaching.[91]

The position of Muslims who want to change their religion is different. Counter to religious freedom as defined in the Universal Declaration of Human Rights, converting from Islam to another religion is proscribed and the right to heresy (from a Muslim perspective),

---

[90] A.A. An-Na'im, *Toward an Islamic Reformation, Civil Liberties, Human Rights, and International Law*, Syracuse University Press, New York 1996, 175–181.

[91] M. Baderin, *International human rights and Islamic law*, Oxford 2005, 120.

apostasy (from a Muslim perspective) or conversion (from the perspective of the other religion) is rejected.[92] Apostasy is when a Muslim
rejects the fundamental dogmas of Islam or the validity of the absolute commandments and prohibitions of the Shari'a and acts accordingly. It includes dishonouring the prophet and usury, which number
among the strictest religious taboos.[93] According to suras 2:90–91 and
106:106–109, anyone guilty of violating these must expect punishment, in extremis the death penalty, and in any event eternal suffering. According to progressive thinkers, however, individual apostates
should not be punished, although they no doubt will be hereafter. It
is another matter when (group) apostasy jeopardises public safety and
the survival of the state.[94] In most Muslim countries, apostasy is no
longer punishable, but that does not make it socially acceptable. The
reason for such penalties as are still imposed is not apostasy, but conflictive interaction with believers and/or attempts to persuade them to
apostatise.[95]

All this is abhorrent to people living in modern Western societies.
Religion is free, as is conversion to another religion and the choice
to live without any religion as an agnostic or atheist. Anyone who
impedes another person's freedom of choice when it comes to religion or worldview violates a fundamental principle of constitutional
democracy. Hence it is understandable that in public debate politics
is invoked and there are demands that the state should intervene in
Muslim communities to put an end to such deprivation of religious
freedom.

Where does the Catholic Church stand in this regard? As mentioned
already, Augustine in no way wants to spare the Old Testament rod
when a person apostatises, but he rejects extreme punishment, including the death penalty. To Thomas Aquinas, the latter is permissible.
Whilst freedom to join the faith is respected (free inclusion), heresy
and apostasy are punished by every possible means (enforced permanent inclusion). In our day, the church's sanctions are no longer cruel,
but they have not disappeared. Under the *Codex Iuris Canonici* of
1983, an apostate and a heretic incurs excommunication, as a penalty

---

[92] V. Bader, *Secularism or democracy?* Amsterdam 2007, 132.
[93] Rohe, *Recht*, op. cit., 134–135.
[94] Badarin, *Human Rights*, op. cit. 123–124.
[95] Rohe, *Recht*, op. cit., 2662–2667.

incurred *ipso facto* when the delict is committed (c. 1364), and public apostates and heretics are denied a church burial (c. 1184).

Strange as it may seem, the religious grounds for these punishments are to be found in the Declaration on religious freedom (*Dignitatis Humanae* – DH) of the Second Vatican Council (1962–1965). This document is often held up, to my mind wrongly, as the epitome of religious freedom. Let me explain.

The theme of the declaration centres on the relation between religious truth and religious pluralism. The Second Vatican Council solved this problem by claiming that Christianity is the only true faith and 'subsists' in the Catholic Church (*Dignitatis Humanae* 1; *Lumen Gentium* 8)? The fact that God's truth subsists in the church means that the truth is to be found in the Catholic Church, albeit not exclusively, because it also leaves traces in other religions.

As it is said in chapter 5, the notion of 'traces' led to two disparate positions in the deliberations of Vatican II. The conservative wing stressed that these are no more than traces and that truth in its fullness dwells in the Catholic Church. They relied on the traditional belief that truth alone can be attributed a right and that heresy has no rights – a doctrine proclaimed by Pius XII a mere ten years earlier.[96] The progressive wing, on the other hand, used the notion of 'traces' to justify dialogue with non-Catholic and non-Christian traditions in the search for truth.[97]

No less surprising is the fact that the conflict between the two wings led to a compromise.[98] It can be broken down into a few logical steps as it is said in chapter 5. The first is the postulate that all human beings (*homines cuncti*) are driven to search for truth (DH 2). The second

---

[96] Pius XII, *Allucutiones iuvenibus ex Italiae diocesibus qui annua certamina de doctrina religionis vicerunt, Acta Apostolicae Sedis* 45 (1953), series II, vol. XX, 799: "What contradicts truth or moral norms has not in itself the right to exist neither to be propagated nor to be acted upon". To this the pope added the traditional doctrine on tolerance: "However, not forbidding it through state laws and coercive measures can be justified from a higher and broader good".

[97] J. Murray, The declaration on religious freedom: a moment in its legislative history, in: J. Murray (ed.), *Religious liberty, an end and a beginning*, Macmillan, New York 1966,15–44; Id., *The problem of religious freedom*, Newman, Westminster 1965, 7–17.

[98] Shortly after the council closed on 8 December 1965 Vatican II as a whole was described as a 'compromise council'; see E. Schillebeeckx, *Theologisch testament. Notarieel nog niet verleden*, Baarn 1995, 41.

step is to convert this descriptive insight into the prescriptive statement that people have a moral duty to search for truth (DH 2). The third step is to specify this duty, namely that all people have to search in the first place for the truth regarding religion (DH 2).[99] The fourth step is to further specify this specification, namely that all people are bound to search for truth, more especially (*praesertim*) the truth of God and his church (DH 1). The fifth and final step is that once the truth about God and his church is known and acknowledged, it must be embraced and held fast to (DH1).[100] In a nutshell, the descriptive statement that all people are in search of truth culminates in the prescription to look primarily for the truth about God and his church, and, having found that, to remain faithful to it. This interpretation of religious freedom, to which everyone is entitled, simply cannot apply to non-Catholic Christians, adherents of other religions and nonreligious people. It is conceived of unilaterally from a Catholic perspective. It is something like a funnel, proceeding from a generality to a doctrinal duty.

Besides, when it comes to the right to abandon one's faith, it makes those who have found the truth of God and his church (i.e. Catholics) unfree. They have a duty not only to embrace the truth they have found and to banish doubt – which is branded heresy in canon 751 and according to canon 1364 in the *Codex Iuris Canonici* leads to automatic excommunication – but also to preserve this truth. The erstwhile theology professor, now cardinal Walter Kasper, maintained that this declaration was probably the most important document produced by Vatican II. Considering the deprivation of freedom that it entails, his opinion seems somewhat hyperbolical, if not implausible.[101] The church/state jurist Ernst-Wolfgang Böckenförde rightly points out that changing the relation between freedom and truth has repercussions for the church's vision and mission.[102]

---

[99] "Secundum dignitatem suam hominess cuncti (…) morali tenentur obligatione ad veritatem querendam, illam imprimis quae religionem spectat."

[100] "Homines vero concti tenentur veritatem, praesertim in iis quae Deum Eiusque Ecclesiam respiciunt, quaerere eamque cognitam amplecti ac servare."

[101] W. Kasper, Religionsfreiheit, II. Katholische Kirche, in: *Staatslexikon, Recht, Wirtschaft, Gesellschaft, Band 4*, Freiburg 1988, 825–827.

[102] E.-W. Böckenförde, *Religionsfreiheit, Die Kirche in der modernen Welt*, Freiburg 1990; J.A. van der Ven, Godsdienstvrijheid als ecclesiologisch paradigma, in: C. Sterkens & J. van der Ven (eds), *De functie van de kerk in de hedendaagse maatschappij*, Altiora, Averbode, 2002, 17–64.

Of course, the Catholic doctrine on preserving the truth is no more than a pale shadow of the Islamic doctrine. But it is a striking phenomenon in Western society that, whereas the Muslim duty to cling to one's faith is criticised, that of Catholics is not; also that Islamic sanctions are condemned, whereas nothing is said about those of the Catholic Church. Yet in both cases the doctrine conflicts with the internationally recognised right to change one's religion or to opt for a nonreligious life. What doctrine calls a crime the Universal Declaration calls a right, a human right.[103] This is clearly biased, and it is this bias, as I see it, that forms the basis for Christian – especially Catholic and nonreligious – youths' choice in favour of asymmetrical tolerance of Islam. These youths opt for political interference in Islam rather than symmetric religious freedom.

Non-discrimination
In addition to changing one's religion, another principle at issue in the public debate on religious freedom is non-discrimination against women and homosexuals. Let us take a look at the two categories.

Violation of women's right to equal treatment in the Muslim community is a bone of red hot contention. By and large women are considered inferior to men. While this has no grounds in the Qur'an, traditional religious rules and customary law are intermingled in various contexts. These include female circumcision, honour killing, child marriage, awarding custody of children to the husband in divorce cases, unequal law of succession, unequal marital and household roles, unequal education and schooling, and disciplinary rules in regard to public conduct.[104]

None of this applies to the Catholic Church. It recognises the equality of men and women, but this does not imply equality in a legal sense. The big bone of contention is the ordained priesthood, to which women are not admitted. The argument is based on the historical fact that Jesus chose only men to become 'the twelve'. Substantively this is

---

[103] J. Rawls, *Political liberalism*, expanded edition, Columbia University Press, New York 2005, 468, 476, n. 76. Part IV of the expanded edition consists of: J. Rawls, The idea of public reasons revisited, *The University of Chicago Law Review* 64 (1997)3, 765–807, which does not appear in earlier editions.

[104] *Arab human development report 2005*, New York 2006; B. van Stokkum, Negatieve beeldvorming over moslims; intolerantie of cultuurconflict? *Justitiële Verkenningen: Religie en grondrechten* 33(2007)1, 50–69.

a shaky argument and logically it is no argument at all.[105] Even more importantly, the ecclesiastic authority claims the right to call believers to the priesthood. Although this claim needs to be differentiated in terms of church history, under civil law on religious organisation the church authority cannot be denied this right. But it does conflict with the democratic ethos, according to which every citizen has active and passive franchise and thus in principle has access to every office. In many countries, among which the Netherlands, this exclusiveness is increasingly offensive to many people, men and women alike.

Islam also discriminates against homosexuals. Their sexual identity is repudiated and they face corporal punishment or even the death penalty if their sexual practices are discovered. To the majority of the Dutch population this is abominable, and again many are looking to the state to intervene. It is argued that in a conflict between religious freedom and the principle of non-discrimination in this area the latter has priority over the former, because sex and sexual orientation are part of a persons' nature and not a matter of choice.[106]

Again the situation of homosexuals in the Catholic Church is just a faint shadow of their situation in Islam. Nonetheless there is some discrimination in this church, even though it calls on people to avoid it. The church sees homosexual relations as perverse, intrinsically disorderly, and counter to natural law, a barrier to the gift of life and true affective and sexual complementarity.[107] Same sex marriage is wicked altogether. This view likewise conflicts with the tolerance in this regard in democratic societies.

From a legal point of view, it is argued that women and homosexuals join religious communities voluntarily and are free to leave them

---

[105] *Inter Insigniores* (1976); *Mulieris dignitatem* (1988) and the *Letter of John Paul II to women* (1995).

[106] VVD, *Om de Vrijheid, Partijprogramma VVD* 2005, p. 13; Id, *Voor een samenleving met ambitie, Verkiezingsprogramma* 2006. For the debate on the relation between religious freedom and discrimination, see W. van der Burg, *Het democratisch perspectief*, Arnhem 1991, 201–207.

[107] *Persona Humana* (1975); *Letter to the bishops of the Catholic Church on the pastoral care of homosexual persons* (1986); *Considerations regarding proposals to give legal recognition to unions between homosexual persons* (2003). In the Eros myth in his *Symposium*, Plato describes how people yearn for one another in order to achieve integrity and wholeness. That, according to Plato, is why a man takes a woman and they procreate, and a man takes a man to experience satisfaction and happiness (chapter 15). In his first encyclical, *Deus caritas est* (2005), pope Benedict XVI refers to this myth, but mentions only the union of a man and a woman, ignoring that of two men (chapter 11, note 8).

if some doctrine affronts them. The psychological argument is that there is always some tension between religious ascription (belonging by birth) and religious achievement (free choice).[108] Besides, leaving a religion in which one has grown up can be tantamount to social isolation, even 'social suicide'.[109] Hence it is by no means simple to leave 'the religious nest'. Viewed thus, the prioritisation of religious freedom over discrimination is unjustifiable.

If one compares Islam and the Catholic Church in this regard, it is again evident that opinion in the public debate targets Islam and the Catholic Church is left alone. The state should act against discrimination in Islam – that is what opinion makers demand. The Catholic Church is not called to account. Again one discerns bias, and this bias too, at any rate to my opinion, explains the asymmetric tolerance displayed by Christian (mainly Catholic) and nonreligious youths. They opt for political interference rather than symmetric religious freedom, thus taking issue with wrongs in Islam.

7.4.2   Prayer at Public Schools

Remarkably, the majority of Christian, Muslim and nonreligious youths agree with prayer at public schools (60%, 65%, 54% respectively), while we have seen that only a minority of Christian and nonreligious youths accept the prohibition of political interference. After all, are both these rules not products of religious freedom?! Certainly they are, but what follows logically by no means always does so psychologically. Psychologically they are unconnected in practice, as is evident in table 3.

How should we interpret the agreement with prayer at public schools? There are various aspects.[110] Usually people think that because of the separation of church and state, religion has no place at public schools. The problem is solved by reproducing, so to speak, this separation – relegating the existential, kerygmatic, or religious aspects to confessional schools, while public schools confine themselves to

---

[108] T. Parsons et al. (eds.), *Theories of society*, New York 1965, 239–264.

[109] A. Føllesdal, Minority rights, in: Räikkä, J. (ed.). *Do we need minority rights?* Nijhof, The Hague 1996, 59–84.

[110] F. Ravitch, *School prayer and discrimination*, Boston 1999; Id., A crack in the wall, in: S. Feldman (ed.), *Law and religion*, New York 2000, 296–314.

culture-historical and social aspects. Prayer does not fall in the latter category, for what is more religious than prayer?

That is not all, for we are concerned not only with the separation of church and state but also with religious freedom. Prayer at public schools infringes the rights of nonreligious and anti-religious pupils. Religious freedom, after all, includes the right not to be confronted with religious activities. But that is not the end of the story. Prayer at public schools also infringes the rights of adherents of other religions – in the case of Christian prayer those of Islam, in the case of Muslim prayer those of Christian denominations.

Sometimes a solution is sought in prayer texts that transcend religious differences in a 'unitarian' sense, inclining to 'natural' or 'rational' religion. That, too, can violate the rights of a-religious or anti-religious pupils, as well as those of Christian and Muslim students insofar as these texts might contradict their exclusive or inclusive religious conceptions of truth. They have a right not to be confronted with what strikes them as defective or even mutilated forms of religion.

Do spiritual, meditative texts that transcend both religious and nonreligious worldviews offer a solution in terms of the maxim 'religion: no; spirituality: yes'? Whatever one may think of the slogan, the solution it offers leads to reflection on existential preconditions – love and suffering, contingency and tragedy, fate and destiny – but it is not prayer. Texts of this nature and contemplation of them have no addressee. They are not directed to God, nor are they expressed with a sense of his presence. Even in Buddhist traditions, prayer is often aimed at devotion to an extra-mundane reality realised in a relationship of mutual involvement.[111] Prayer is not purely reflective; it is a performative act that evokes the reciprocal relationship of God and human beings. Psychologically the processes at work in prayer and reflection may be much the same,[112] but in a ritual sense the performative dimension is essential for prayer.[113] Schilderman distinguishes between three dimensions of liturgy: ritualising, believing and belonging.[114] In these terms, prayer is a ritual performative act of believing

---

[111] M. Spiro, Religion: problems and definition and explanation, in: M. Banton (ed.), *Anthropological approaches to the study of religion*, London 1978, 85–126, here 91–96.

[112] S. Bänziger, Still praying strong, diss. Nijmegen 2007.

[113] C. Bell, *Ritual, perspectives and dimensions*, Oxford University Press, Oxford 1997, 72–76.

[114] H. Schilderman, Liturgical studies from a ritual studies perspective, in: Id. (ed.), *Discourse in ritual studies*, Brill, Leiden 2007, 3–34, here 22–26.

in the imaginative sphere of God's presence based on belonging to an imaginative religious community.

Still, the agreement of nonreligious youths with prayer at public schools is remarkable. I can see only one explanation, namely that they make a distinction between prayer as part of the public school curriculum and extra-curricular prayer, which latter they support. But extra-curricular prayer is also problematic. In the USA, the provision of rooms in school buildings without charging rent and with free lighting and heating has triggered debate. Non-provision of these amenities for political, social, and cultural groups is seen as discriminatory. So is the refusal of staff to spend time on guiding such groups, whereas they are prepared to do so in the case of religious groups.[115] In Europe the issue is less contentious. Often schools are left to decide for themselves whether or not to arrange a special room for prayer for Muslim students. On 10 March 2008, for example, the Berlin administrative judge adjudicated the case of Yusuf M, a 14-year-old pupil at Diesterweg Gymnasium in Berlin, who asked for prayer facilities. The judge's provisional decision was that under religious freedom he should be offered a special room for prayer.[116] The *Vereniging van Nederlandse Gemeenten* (VNG – Association of Dutch Municipalities) announced that the provision of premises for prayer in public organisations can be granted, provided it does not infringe the religious freedom of others, the various religions receive equal treatment and there is no excessive substantive interference.[117]

It seems plausible that the three groups of youths for the most part agree with facilitation of extra-curricular prayer.

CONCLUSION

From our findings, it appears that the majority of the youths appreciate a pragmatic approach to the separation of church and state and reject a separationist interpretation of the relation between church and state. This is counter to the supposed French model of *laicité*. I say 'supposed', because in France church-state relations are in fact characterised by a

---

[115] Witte, *Experiment*, op. cit., 301–302.
[116] *Pressemitteilung Senatsverwaltung für Justiz* 11.03.08, Berlin.
[117] VNG (Vereniging van Nederlandse Gemeenten – Association of Dutch Municipalities), *Tweeluik religie en publiek domein*, The Hague 2009.

pragmatic modus vivendi. This pragmatism implies that the church on the one hand is deprived of all power in the public sphere, but on the other hand is entrusted with certain public, humanitarian services and is granted certain public privileges such as the use of churches, funding of religion in public institutions like the army, judicial institutions and hospitals, freedom of internal organisation, freedom of education and the secret of the confessional. Almost all church buildings used by religions are state property.[118] From our empirical research, the three groups of Christians, Muslims, and nonreligious youth appear to opt for a pragmatic interpretation with scope for individual and collective, private and public manifestation of religion.

Contrary to the unanimity of the three groups in regard to praying in public schools, we noted the discrepancy between the majority of Muslim youths who accept religious freedom in the sense of political non-interference and the majority of the Christian and nonreligious youths who do not. If my interpretation is correct, this is evident in the public debate on changing one's religion and discrimination against women and homosexuals. In my interpretation, Christian and nonreligious youths' opposition to the prohibition of changing one's religion and to discrimination against women and homosexuals in Islam means that they favour political intervention. In so doing, they opt for asymmetric tolerance rather than symmetric religious freedom.

How does one resolve the dilemma of asymmetric tolerance and symmetric religious freedom? The only solution I can see is to reconsider the relation between religious freedom and the other fundamental rights, including the right to change one's religion and the principle of non-discrimination. At the moment, the law and public administration mostly prioritises religious freedom in the case of conflicts between religious freedom and the other fundamental rights. Naturally judges will punish honour killing and female circumcision, but here we are referring to oppression of Muslim women on religious grounds,

---

[118] E. Poulat, *Notre laïcité publique*, Paris 2003. The Netherlands has no constitutional clause on the separation of church and state, although this constitutional principle is implicit in non-discrimination (Den Dekker-van Bijsterveld, *Kerk en staat*, op. cit., 91–94). The sole exception is the aforementioned, short-lived *Staatsregeling voor het Bataafse Volk* (1798), adopted by the National Assembly once it had been purged by a coup d'etat. See W. Velema, Revolutie, republiek en constitutie, in: N. van Sas & H. te Velde (eds), *De eeuw van de grondwet*, The Hague 1998, 20–45; E. van der Wall, Geen natie van atheïsten, in *Jaarboek van de Maatschappij der Nederlandse Letterkunde te Leiden*, 1995–1996, 45–62.

discriminatory sermons about homosexuality by imams, and religious pressure to prevent apostasy.

Any number of national and international documents claim that there is no hierarchy in fundamental human rights,[119] which is contradicted by reality on the ground. However, prioritising religious freedom over other fundamental rights is not self-evident in a multicultural society, in which over half the population no longer has any religious affiliation. I feel, therefore, that when they conflict, religious freedom should be accorded the same treatment as (almost) every other fundamental right. That means that in each case or category of cases, the judge should make an unbiased, impartial appraisal of religious freedom vis-à-vis other fundamental rights.[120] The impartiality of the judge, according to this interpretation, will neutralise the bias evident among the Christian (mainly Catholic) and nonreligious youths. That is the only way to create a balance in religious freedom.

---

[119] Ministry of the Interior, *Nota Grondrechten in een pluriforme samenleving*, The Hague 2004; Minister of Foreign Affairs M. Verhagen, address to UN meeting on human rights and sexual orientation. New York 2008; Vienna declaration and programme of action adopted at the World Conference on Human Rights 1993.

[120] The first signs are already apparent in legislation and jurisdiction. Thus article 5, section 2 of the Dutch General Equal Treatment Act (1994) stipulates that religiously based institutions, including confessional schools, can set no requirements that can lead to discrimination exclusively on grounds of, *inter alia*, gender or sexual orientation. Examples in jurisdiction are sentences in the Netherlands and Belgium in which the administration of justice under Catholic canon law is declared liable in some divorce cases. This led to top-level consultations in Rome, resulting in a decision that canon 1680 in the *Codex Iuris Canonici*, which deals with obtaining expert advice on cases of mental illness, should be given an interpretation that precludes any conflict with secular law. See H. Warnink, Ecclesiastical tribunals, procedures, judicial bodies and the state, *Nederduits Gereformeerde Teologiese Tydskrif* 42 (2001), 158–166.

CHAPTER EIGHT

SEPARATION OF CHURCH AND STATE

Like religious freedom, separation of church and state as we know it today was totally unknown in premodern Western societies. Not that church and state were always identified. That only happened when God was seen as the supreme authority of the state (theocracy), or the priesthood represented and/or legitimised that authority (hierocracy), or, conversely, priestly power was wholly subordinated to a secular ruler who claimed complete authority over ecclesiastic affairs (caesaropapism).[1] Paradoxically, the unity of church and state also manifested itself in what is known as the twin autonomy of the two institutions. This meant each had its own jurisdiction with its own interrelated institutions, organisations, and roles but worked in harmony for the sake of a unified society. This unity was symbolised by the 'sacred canopy' spanning both. Under that canopy the church sometimes had the upper hand, sometimes the state.

But all that has changed. In modern society the process of functional differentiation has put an end to any such unity.[2] The ongoing process of splitting up functions has created more and more autonomous domains with ever more institutions and organisations working according to their own codes and programmes. The sacred canopy imploded. The upshot was that the church became a domain in its own right, separate from the economy, politics, education and teaching, welfare, health care, science and technology, art and culture. In relation to the state, it has grown into an independent body with its own codes, institutions, organisations, and programmes, although this does not exclude what Parsons and Luhmann call the interpenetration of

---

[1] M. Weber, *Wirtschaft und Gesellschaft*, Mohr, Tübingen 1980, 688–690.
[2] N. Luhmann, *Die Gesellschaft der Gesellschaft*, Bd I–II, Suhrkamp, Franfurt 1998. Luhmann distinguishes between four forms of social differentiation: segmented differentiation based on kinship and occupied space; differentiation in terms of centre and periphery, such as city and countryside; stratified differentiation based on class or caste; and functional differentiation, the hallmark of modern society.

domains – an interpenetration that was and remains manifest in relations between church and state.[3]

In this chapter, I first look at the developmental process of the separation of church and state in the course of Western history, divided into a premodern and an early modern period. In the case of the former, I look at two outstanding figures who epitomise the numerous conflicts between church and state that took place under the sacred canopy: pope Boniface VIII and his critic Dante. In the case of the second period, I devote attention to Samuel Pufendorf, a model for the emerging functional differentiation of church and state, who greatly influenced his contemporaries and later generations of scholars, including Rousseau (8.1). I then examine how the constitutional principle of the separation of church and state is legitimised in modern times and how it relates to religious freedom.[4] Here I draw on the ideas of, *inter alia*, John Rawls and Jürgen Habermas.[5] Realising that these authors arrive at different conclusions on certain points, I resort to a – I trust justified – eclecticism (8.2).

Next I explore, by means of empirical research, whether and to what extent the separation of church and state is accepted by the citizens of the democratic state who are supposed to be its carriers. I do so with reference to two thorny issues: the autonomy of politics in regard to euthanasia, and the autonomy of politics in regard to abortion. The two issues are thorny, both politically and religiously. It is important check to what extent the autonomy of politics in the area of those *res mixtae* is supported by the citizens in terms of a contribution to the legal culture and human rights culture of a nation.[6] For this empirical study, I use the data collected in 2007–2008 among the same three

---

[3] Luhmann, *Die Gesellschaft*, op. cit., I, 108, 378.

[4] I use the term 'constitutional principle' rather than 'constitutional rule', because it is missing from some constitutions, including the Dutch one; cf. R. Alexy, *Theorie der Grundrechte*, Nomos, Baden-Baden 1985, 71ff.; cf. J. Bruggink, Wat zijn 'Mensenrechten'? In: L. Heyde et al. (eds.), *Begrensde vrijheid*, Willink, Zwolle 1989, 87–99.

[5] J. Rawls, *Political Liberalism*, Expanded edition, Columbia University Press, New York 2005, 147, 458–459. Part four of the expanded edition consists of: J. Rawls, The Idea of Public Reasons Revisited, *The University of Chicago Law Review* 64(1997)3, 765–807, which does not appear in earlier editions; J. Habermas, *Faktizität und Geltung*, Suhrkamp, Frankurt 1993; Id., *Zwischen Naturalismus und Religion, Philosophische Aufsätze*, Suhrkamp, Frankfurt 2005.

[6] D. Nelken (ed.), *Comparing Legal Cultures*, Aldershot 1997; D. Nellken & J. Feest (eds.), *Adapting Legal Cultures*, Oxford 2001; K. Hastrup (ed.), *Legal Cultures and Human Rights*, The Hague 2001.

population groups in the Netherlands, namely Christian, Muslim, and nonreligious youths at the end of secondary and the start of tertiary education, whom I referred to in the previous chapter. According to their own religious self-attribution, 340 youths may be considered Christian (of whom 61% call themselves Catholic, 10% Protestant, and 29% Christian, including a group of Catholics by birth), plus 235 Muslim and 479 nonreligious (8.3).[7]

The results of this empirical research call for some reflection, especially on the similarities between the Christian and the Islamic groups on the one hand and the nonreligious group on the other. The separation of church and state appears to be a knotty problem as far as the issue of the *res mixtae* is concerned, especially in the case of euthanasia and abortion (8.4).

8.1 RELATIONSHIP BETWEEN CHURCH AND STATE IN THE PREMODERN AND EARLY MODERN ERAS

In this section, I explore some ideas of representatives from the history of church-state relations. The first is pope Boniface VIII, who assumes a unity of church and state in which the latter is subordinate to the former. Then I describe the reaction to this conception by Dante, who straddled the Middle Ages and the Renaissance. Next I examine church-state relations in the early modern period with reference to the work of Samuel Pufendorf, and the outcome of this development in the work of Jean-Jacques Rousseau.

8.1.1 *Pope Boniface VIII*

Among the medieval popes who adopted a manifestly hierocratic approach to relations between church and state, and who caused great political turbulence by imperialising the pontificate, pope Boniface VIII must rank first. He is not only blamed, rightly or wrongly, for enticing and/or forcing his predecessor, Celestine V, to retire, but more especially for fanning the investiture struggle, which since the Edict of Worms in 1122 had resulted in some sort of – albeit easily derailed – *modus vivendi*. It started with the bull *Clericis Laicos* of 1296, which protested against taxation of the church by monarchs,

---

[7] See for the religious self-attribution of these three groups: Appendix IV.

especially those of France and England, in order to finance their wars. He repudiated the notion that these sovereigns had any jurisdiction over the church, and threatened to excommunicate them, as well as clergy that collaborated with them, if they persisted. He added that no exemption of this excommunication could be granted, unless those who were excommunicated would end up in their death throes.

The bull *Unam Sanctam* of 1302 topped it all. It declared, following Origen and Cyprian of Carthage, that there was no salvation or forgiveness of sins outside the church. It went on to state that the church is one body with only one head – Christ and his vicar Peter, and the latter's successor, the pope. Thus, according to Boniface, the Greeks were fundamentally erring when they failed to obey Peter's successor in the Great Schism between the Western and the Eastern church in 1054. Furthermore, with reference to the Gospel of Luke 22:38, it says that the church has two swords, one spiritual, the other temporal – that is to say, not one sword within the church and another outside it, but both of them within the church and under its power. The first sword is used by the church, the second is wielded on the church's behalf by monarchs and soldiers when the church so desires, for in terms of divine law the temporal power is subordinate to the spiritual power.[8] Citing Matthew 16:19, the pope postulates that whatever he binds or looses will be bound or loosed in heaven as well. The pope concludes the text by declaring that everybody is necessarily subject to him for their salvation.

8.1.2 *Dante*

The bull evoked fierce opposition, *inter alia* from Dante, who condemned Boniface VIII to hell in the *Inferno* of his *Divina Comedia*.[9] According to the medievalist Kantorowicz, Dante's *De Monarchia* was the first medieval text to lucidly and succinctly spell out the dualism of church and state, pope and profane monarch.[10] Dante asks whether the sovereign's power derives from that of the church and the pope or whether it is conferred directly by God. In answer to this

---

[8] J. Pelikan, *Interpreting the Bible and the Constitution*, Yale University Press, New Haven, 2004, 83, observes that the Declaration on religious freedom by Vatican II revises this violent doctrine in number 11 by inverting it: "Not by force of blows does His rule assert its claims" (cf. Mt 26:51–53; John 18:36).

[9] Dante Alighieri, Divina Comedia VI, 65; XV, 112; XIX, 52.

[10] Dante Alighieri, *De Monarchia*, III, I, VIII–IX.

question he refutes the applicability to the relation between church and state of biblical binary oppositions, such as that of the sun that bestows its light on the moon (Gen 1:16); the firstborn Levi the priest, and the later Judah the king (Gen 29:34–35); the prophet Samuel who dethrones king Saul (1 Kings 15); and the gifts of gold and incense brought to Jesus, referring to his spiritual and worldly power (Mt 2:11).[11] He interprets the Matthean verse on binding and loosing on earth and in heaven differently from Boniface. The pope has no power to declare the power of imperial law void, for Peter's power, hence those of his successors as well, do not extend beyond the context of that verse, which pertains only to guarding the gate to the kingdom of heaven. Dante also presents another reading of the reference to the two swords. He points out the context of the Lukan verse, which is about the sword needed by Jesus' twelve disciples to accomplish the mission of the gospel, be it one, two or twelve swords. Jesus' message is not that there have to be two swords, but – according to Dante's reading of Matthew's Gospel – that he has come to bring the sword, not peace.[12] Having augmented these religious arguments with rational historical ones, Dante concludes that the sovereign's power depends directly on God and not on the pope. In fact, the possession of worldly power conflicts with the essence of the church, says Dante.[13] Church and state must keep to their respective mandates given to them by God's unfathomable decree. The state's task is the pursuit of earthly happiness through the practice of moral virtues like justice, wisdom, courage, and temperance, and the church is charged with the pursuit of spiritual happiness that consists in looking on God's face by practising the theological virtues of faith, hope, and love. Because humans, in Dante's view, resemble wild horses stampeding in unbridled fury – an image taken from Plato's *Phaedrus* – they require two guiding forces in their pursuit of these virtues: the monarch and the pope.[14] One observes that whereas Thomas Aquinas still saw moral and theological virtues as one, Dante separates them.[15] That is no doubt a sign of the extension of the functional differentiation between church and

---

[11] Dante, *De Monarchia*, op. cit., III, I–VII.
[12] Dante, *De Monarchia*, op. cit., III, VIII–IX.
[13] Dante, *De Monarchia*, op. cit., III–XV.
[14] Dante, *De Monarchia*, op. cit., XVI.
[15] Thomas Aquinas, *Summa Theologica* (Abbr.: STh), I–II 61–63; 65; E. Kantorowicz, *The King's Two Bodies: A Study in Mediaeval Political Theology*, Princeton University Press, Princeton 1997, 468–469.

state into the area of virtuous living. It comes as no surprise that *De Monarchia* was publicly burnt in Bologna in 1329 and put on the Index, where it remained until Leo XIII reinstated it in 1881.

All this was not merely a matter of legitimising the separation of powers – ecclesiastic and secular – but also of the state's concrete emancipation from ecclesiastic power. State dependence was most obviously problematic in instances where the continuity of secular power was at issue for lack of ecclesiastic legitimisation. Here the question arose whether the sovereign only acquired power at the time of his consecration in an ecclesiastic coronation ceremony, or, as happened in the case of a hereditary dynasty, the moment a royal incumbent died and his power was immediately passed on to his heir without any ecclesiastic intervention by way of a resounding announcement: "The king is dead, long live the king!" The practical implications may be seen in the Great Interregnum following the death of emperor Frederick II, when the coronation ceremony in Rome was deferred for more than 60 years (1259–1312). The debate culminated in the postulate, motivated partly by anti-hierocratic and anti-clerical sentiments, that on his election to or inheritance of the crown, the sovereign is vested with all power due to him, because these derive directly from God independently of any ecclesiastic ceremony. The latter was regarded simply as a solemn confirmation and was valued for its pomp and circumstance. This conclusion robbed the ecclesiastic coronation ritual of its former constitutional significance, thus contributing to the functional differentiation of church and state and so to the secularisation of profane power.[16]

8.1.3 *Samuel Pufendorf*

The reason for choosing the German jurist Samuel Pufendorf is not simply that, according to the French historian Bruno Bernardi, he decisively influenced political theory on the European continent in the early modern period. What makes him all the more interesting is that he explicitly derived many of his ideas from Hugo de Groot and Thomas Hobbes, whilst being roundly critical of both, and that during the Enlightenment he greatly influenced the *Encyclopédie* (1751–1789).[17]

---

[16] Kantorowicz, *The King's Two Bodies*, op. cit., 317–336.
[17] B. Bernardi, *Le principe d'obligation*, Vrin, Paris 2007.

After Dante, functional differentiation between church and state became a topical theme. He substantiated his case by linking the legitimisation of secular power directly to God and no longer to the church. Pufendorf and many of his Protestant contemporaries concurred with this view, but added some important critical glosses to such a direct divine origin. The first was Pufendorf's distinction between the state in general as a political phenomenon and states in real life. He accepted that God is the author of the state in general but not of actual states. The second qualification was that he interpreted God's authorship as indirect rather than direct, to which end he introduced a concept taken from tradition, namely the natural state and natural law. The natural state does not directly clarify the relation between the state and God; that only happens when it is linked with natural law.

Pufendorf acknowledged that the substance of the natural state (*status naturae*) was controversial. The two extreme approaches were those of the Stoics and of Hobbes. According to the Stoics the state of nature was exemplified by early humans' life in truth, goodness, and beauty, free from corruption and evil and representing a utopian ideal. According to Hobbes, the state of nature entailed humans waging a life-and-death struggle for survival in which they fought each other like wolves.[18] Hugo de Groot and Samuel Pufendorf were midway between these extremes, the former siding more with the Stoics, the latter with Hobbes but without sharing his radical opinion. De Groot rejected the notion that people in their natural state threatened each other with physical violence. Instead he stressed that their linguistic and rational faculties gave them the will and the competence to engage in social intercourse. They had no knowledge of virtue, but neither were they vicious; their qualities were simplicity and innocence.[19] Pufendorf agreed with De Groot about the non-violence of the natural state, but that did not mean it was perfect. Whilst it may have been so before the Fall, it certainly was not perfect after that, when people, although free and equal, lived wretched, primitive, impoverished, almost bestial lives, so there was no such thing as mutual trust and they existed in a state

---

[18] S. Pufendorf, *Samuel Pufendorf's on the Natural State of Men: The 1678 Latin Edition and English Translation*, Translated, annotated, and introduced by Michael Seidler, Mellen, Lewinston 1990, 28–30, 130; Th. Hobbes, *Leviathan* I, XIII.

[19] H. Grotius, *De jure belli ac pacis*, Prolegomena, 6–7.

of labile, precarious peace.[20] They did have their own law but no courts of law, and without courts people will try to devour each other.[21]

Given Pufendorf's conception of the state of nature it is not surprising that he should introduce natural law, in the sense of law that forms part of human nature and that can be rationally deduced from it. From this rational deduction, human sociability emerges, which entails two absolute obligations: the first is that one may not inflict harm on another person, and the second that, when such harm is inflicted, compensation is made. These obligations are absolute because they are prerequisite for the self-preservation, protection, and security of humans among themselves. Here, says Pufendorf, the golden rule applies.[22] It is that anyone who enjoys a right owes others the same right.[23]

In order to ensure observance of these natural laws, the state has to be established. The state, says Hugo de Groot, whom Pufendorf frequently quotes, is based on the intrinsic relation between promise and obligation. Put differently, the state exists by virtue of the fact that people promise to obligate themselves mutually. Hence obligation is the essence rather than the consequence of the promise: the promise is mutual obligation (*obligatio ex promisso*).[24] This relation of promise and obligation finds concrete expression in the obligations entered into by mutual consent when making a contract with a view to creating and protecting positive law in a state (*obligatio ex consensu*). De Groot considers two contracts essential: one to join forces in order to protect one's own rights (*consociatio*), and one to confer these rights on the sovereign, thereby subjecting oneself to the sovereign (*subjectio*) without forfeiting one's personal rights. In other words, the sovereignty residing in the monarch as the head is still vested in the people as the entire body, of which the head is a part.[25] Pufendorf speaks of three contracts, in that he inserts a separate contract between the foregoing two, in terms of which people who have joined forces and before

---

[20] Pufendorf, *On the Natural State of Men*, op. cit., 111–117.

[21] S. Pufendorf, *De jure naturae et gentium* II, 2–3.

[22] Pufendorf, *De jure*, op. cit. III, II, 1.

[23] Pufendorf, *De jure*, op. cit. III, II, 4.

[24] This shows that the pact requires no further socio-anthropological substantiation but is self-substantiating. According to N. Luhmann, Das Paradox der Menschenrechte und drie Formen seiner Entfaltung, in: *Soziologische Aufklärungen 6: Die Soziologie und der Mensch*, Westdeutscher Verlag, Opladen 1995, 229–236, this entails the paradox that the classical rule of *pacta sunt servanda* (pacts that have to be observed) in fact requires a pact.

[25] Grotius, *De jure*, op. cit., II, IX, VIII, 1.

they confer their rights on the sovereign determine the form of government. The form could be a democracy, an aristocracy, a monarchy, or a hybrid of these, which latter – counter to Aristotle[26] – he considers irregular.[27] Pufendorf, citing Seneca, defines the state established by these three pacts as a composite moral person, whose will is law and to which everyone owes obedience, and whose will, interwoven with and unified by the three contracts, is regarded as the will of all[28] – what Rousseau was to call the common will.[29]

What this signifies for God's position is that the relation between God and the state is indirect rather than direct. The indirect relation proceeds via the natural state and natural law. The natural state needs to be ordered by natural law and ensuring that order needs the state. God is not the author of the state, as Dante still held, for the author of the state is the people on the basis of its own sovereignty. But God is the author of natural law, hence only indirectly the source of the state – not as a concrete entity but as a general phenomenon. This approach distances God from the state.

The same approach is evident in Pufendorf's discussion of the relation between God's sovereignty and that of the people. Here he makes a distinction between direct and indirect divine law. If people's sovereignty was based on direct divine law, it would be a negation of this sovereignty (imperium commune). It finds expression in the choice of a sovereign (imperium proprium) without forfeiture of popular sovereignty, which is in fact reflected in the choice of a sovereign. That means that people's sovereignty is based on indirect divine law. At most one can say that people's endeavour to establish order and peace via a state in conformity with natural law accords with God's plan. De Groot stretched the relationship with God even further, arguing that God sanctioned the state as a general phenomenon only ex post facto. Pufendorf does not go that far. He maintains that God regards the

---

[26] Aristotle, Politika, In: The Complete Works of Aristotle. The Revised Oxford Translation, Edited by Jonathan Barnes, Princeton University Press, Princeton, NJ 1984, 1294^{a}30–1294^{b}41.

[27] Pufendorf, De jure, op. cit., VII, V, 3–14.

[28] Pufendorf, De jure, op. cit., VII, II, 13.

[29] J.-J. Rousseau, Du contrat social, ou Principes du droit politique, II, III, distinguishes between the will of all and the common will, the former being the aggregate of the wills of all individuals and the latter the generalisation of these wills aimed at the common good.

state as a general phenomenon in accord with his plan *ex ante*.[30] But, says Pufendorf, this does not detract from the fact that the people dispose over its own sovereignty and confers it on the sovereign.[31] Hence it is false to claim that popular sovereignty is confined to pointing to the sovereign and that his sovereignty actually derives from God.[32] Here, too, one observes that God is put at a distance.

In short, whereas in Dante one observes a functional differentiation between church and state, Pufendorf reveals an incipient differentiation between religion and the state, even between God and the state. One also observes that Pufendorf's God displays marked deistic features. He saw God as creator (creaturely deism) and wielder of providence (providential deism) – not as a specific providence intervening in concrete cases for the benefit of actual people (i.e. not *providentia specialis*), but as a universal providence at a supreme, abstract, macro level in terms of the goal and plan of history (*providentia generalis*). Unlike De Groot, Pufendorf's legal works do not mention any religious criminal procedure for the evil people perpetrate and the sins they commit, thus depriving God of his position as judge. Immanently, evil punishes itself, and, immanently, people injure themselves (hence not a retributive deism). Again in contrast to De Groot, Pufendorf's legal thinking repudiates the 'last judgment' at or after death, because he considers it irreconcilable with natural law and because in his view the 'natural religion' contained in natural law says nothing about life after death (i.e. not a deism of immortality).[33] The upshot is that via the natural state and natural law, God is not only remote from the state, the sovereign, and the administration of justice, but his very being is detached from political life.

8.1.4   *Rousseau*

The sovereignty of the people is the illustration par excellence of functional differentiation between church/religion and the state. That is how Rousseau, in his *Du contrat social*, launches the onslaught on natural law's apparently harmonious balance between association of

---

[30] Pufendorf, *De jure*, op. cit., VII, III, 2; Cf. J.-J. Burlamaqui, *Principes du droit politique*, I, VI, VIII–XIII.

[31] Burlamaqui, *Principes du droit politique*, op. cit., I, VI, VIII–XIII, follows Pufendorf in this regard.

[32] Pufendorf, *De jure*, VII, III, 3.

[33] Pufendorf, *De jure*, op. cit., II, III 19.

the people (*associatio*) and the duty of submission to the sovereign (*subjectio*), whether the latter is seen as father, shepherd, absolute monarch, terrorising ruler, king by the grace of God, or God himself.[34] It is a matter of striking a proper balance between active and passive obligation. Active obligation had always been on the part of the sovereign, who imposed demands on the people, and passive obligation on the part of the people, who owed the sovereign obedience. The only solution was to vest both active and passive obligation in the people – the people's own obligation to itself. Only such self-commitment, as opposed to mandatory commitment, results in freedom. That means that the people imposes self-made laws on itself, which amounts to autonomy in the sense of auto-legislation.[35] Neither God nor natural law imposes laws on the people; the people itself imposes them.

Functional differentiation takes the form of the self-sufficiency of popular sovereignty, without any direct or indirect reference to God via natural law, as in Pufendorf's thinking. But religion is not declared useless and is certainly not rejected. Its usefulness is clarified by what one might call internal functional differentiation, hence not differentiation between religion and the state but differentiation within religion. Following Spinoza and Locke, Rousseau's *Du contrat social* distinguishes between internal and external religion.[36]

But prior to this, Rousseau distinguishes between three forms of religion. The first is the religion of humans and occurs in the *forum internum*, the domain of individuals' private devotions with no temples, churches or rituals. The second is the religion of citizens. It is directed to the God or gods of a particular country, is committed to dogmas peculiar to that country and performs its rituals, and depicts everything else as heathen and barbarous. The third form is the sacerdotal religion typical of the Catholic Church. Here there are always two domains of jurisdiction, two wielders of authority, two sets of rules and obligations, all of them relating to profane and spiritual power with the latter in command. Rousseau rejects this third form out of hand, since it is a perennial source of power struggles. It prejudices secular authority and the legal system, thus making good politics impossible: people do not know whom to obey, the monarch or the priest.[37] He sees the

---

[34] Bernardi, *Le principe*, op. cit., 33–39.
[35] Rousseau, *Du contrat*, op. cit., I, 4.
[36] Rousseau, *Du contrat*, op. cit., IV, 8, 464–466.
[37] Rousseau, *Du contrat*, op. cit., IV, 8, 462.

second form as containing some good elements, because it links God with love of the laws of the land and makes the citizen's mother country an object of reverence. But he is also critical of it, because it is based on error and lies and its rituals easily degenerate into empty ceremony. It is also exclusive, readily assumes tyrannical forms, makes the people intolerant and blood-thirsty towards other peoples who worship different gods, and triggers holy wars. Although Rousseau is sympathetic towards the first form, it has the drawback of being unrelated to society and serving no social purpose, because its adherents, especially those who espouse a pure gospel, obey whatever worldly authority is in power, even if vested in a despot. They are totally submissive and always behave like slaves. It is a religion of slaves.

The religion advocated by Rousseau has two dimensions.[38] The first one can call the internal cult, which corresponds most closely to the first form of religion – that of humans. Rousseau maintains that citizens are not accountable to the sovereign for it. The second is the external cult, which corresponds closely to the second form of religion but minus its drawbacks. The external cult is demonstrably related to society and is socially useful. In terms of the social contract, the sovereign has a right to regulate it and call citizens to account. Hence the external cult is under the authority of the sovereign, not that of the church. The sovereign is concerned about dogma inasmuch as it furthers public morality and duties. He stipulates the articles of faith, albeit not as pure dogmas but in regard to their significance for social sentiments and to promote observance of the law and civic duties. This establishes a purely civil creed with deistic doctrines. It entails faith in a powerful, rational, benevolent deity – qualities already attributed to God by Burlamaqui, a French philosopher of Pufendorf's school, to which Burlamiqui added a fourth attribute: God as the creator.[39] In keeping with his benevolence, the supreme being shows foresight and providence, entailing – counter to Pufendorf's view – life after

---

[38] Rousseau, *Du contrat*, op. cit., IV, 8, 468–469.

[39] J.-J. Burlamaqui, *Principes du droit naturel*, I, IX, VI–VIII, used the four divine attributes to substantiate sovereignty, following Bodin, as the right to issue commands – which obviously conflicts with Rousseau's thinking. Burlamaqui differs from Pufendorf in that he advocates a rationalist orientation in which human reason functions as the power that stimulates, by its analytical reasoning from God's goodness, human surrender to divine sovereignty, whereas Pufendorf shows signs of a voluntarist orientation in that human surrender is an act of the will, prompted by God's benevolence; cf. Bernardi, *Le principe*, op. cit., 243–244.

death and ultimate judgment of good and evil.[40] In Rousseau's *Emile*, these three attributes of the supreme being are again mentioned, adding a fourth attribute that already as I said Burlamaqui posited in conjunction with the first three: the creator, to whom humankind is indebted.[41] In this educational book, Rousseau sees retribution after death as happiness or unhappiness resulting immanently from observance or non-observance of obligations rather than as external reward and punishment by the deity.[42] At all events, in the state the contract and laws made in the name of the Supreme Being are sacred and sacrosanct. There is one negative dogma: intolerance. With manifest reference to pope Boniface VIII, Rousseau "excommunicates" those who claim that there is no salvation outside the church from the state, for such a claim can only be made in a theocracy.[43] Here Boniface VIII's subordination of the state to religion is reversed. Civil religion (*foi purement civile*) subordinates religion to the state.

Rousseau's heritage is apparent today in innumerable studies of civil or public religion in Western countries.[44] Essentially, it consists in beliefs, values, and rites deemed fundamentally important for a given nation. These are connoted with the ever elusive horizon of a deistically coloured, all-embracing supreme being, a supreme "something" ('something-ism'), which is shared – more or less consciously or unconsciously – by church-affiliated, unaffiliated, and even nonreligious compatriots. These notions are associated with a religion considered to exist actually, albeit often 'invisible' or 'hidden', which elevates these beliefs above day-to-day life. They indicate what a particular people considers 'holy'. They include 'ultimate' notions about the history, destiny, and mission of the nation, such as freedom, equality, and solidarity; values cherished, such as rationality, reasonableness, fairness, and tolerance; and rites performed on national feast days and days of commemoration. They are expressed in (annual) addresses by political and government leaders and at public ceremonies. They fulfil

---

[40] Rousseau, *Du contrat*, op. cit., IV, 8, 468.
[41] J.-J. Rousseau, *Émile, ou de l'éducation*, IV.
[42] Rousseau, *Émile*, op. cit., IV.
[43] Rousseau, *Du contrat*, op. cit., IV, 8, 468–469.
[44] R. Bellah, Civil Religion in America, in: R. Richey & D. Jones (eds.), *American Civil Religion*, Harper & Row, New York 1974, 24–41; L. Laeyendecker, Publieke godsdienst: wat moeten we ermee? In: G. ten Berge (ed.), *Voor God en vaderland: Nationalisme en religie*, Kok, Kampen 1992; J. Habermas, *Zwischen Naturalismus und Religion*, Suhrkamp, Frankfurt 2005, 129ff.

many functions, such as preserving and enhancing social cohesion, integrating diverse groups in a nation, psychological integration of individual citizens by expressing their identity, and coping with common national problems and crises. They sustain what the sociologist Bellah and his co-workers call a culture of coherence.[45] Examples of civil religion rituals include the annual State of the Union address in the USA, *le quatorze juillet* in France, and the Day of the Commemoration of the Dead on 4 May in the Netherlands.[46]

8.2   SEPARATION OF CHURCH AND STATE
IN THE MODERN ERA

Of course, civil or public religion is not the only manifestation of religion in present-day society. Far from it. The principal ones are those expressed in Jewish, Christian, Muslim, and numerous other communities in the traditions of South and East Asia, including their doctrines, rites, observances, professionals, organisations, and buildings like temples, churches, mosques, and prayer houses. Their relation to society and the state is beset by many problems. Historically, as appeared from what we have said so far, these proved so complex that Western states gradually came to opt for a separation of church and state.

To trace this development in modern times, I first deal briefly with the Peace of Augsburg (1555) and the Peace of Westphalia (1648), which separated state from church but did not solve the problem of minorities (8.2.1). I then look at the American Bill of Rights of 1789 and, in more detail, at the French Constitution of 1791 and some subsequent French documents, because in the Netherlands, both formerly and today, the *laïcité* in some of these texts is often held up as the ideal model (8.2.2). Next, I try to outline a framework for relations between church and state by basing it on the relation between society and the state (8.2.3). Finally, I use this framework to evaluate the actual relationship between church and state (8.2.4). Here I divide the views of,

---

[45] R. Bellah et al., *Habits of the Heart: Individualism and Commitment in American Life*, Perennial Library, New York 1986, 281–283.

[46] D. Capucao, *Religion and Ethnocentrism: An Empirical-Theological Study of the Effects of Religious Attitudes on Attitudes Towards Minorities Among Catholics in the Netherlands*, Brill, Leiden 2009, chapter 8.1.

especially, Rawls into two separate parts (society and state and church and state) for the sake of lucidity.[47]

8.2.1   Separation of Church and State in the Peace of Augsburg and the Peace of Westphalia

Historically, the separation of church and state was preceded by state emancipation from the church. This resulted in separation of the state from the church, rather than separation between the two, and left the church under absolute state control. The first legal crystallisation of this emancipation was the Peace of Augsburg in 1555 between the Catholic emperor Charles V, represented by his brother Ferdinand I and the Schmalkaldic League of Lutheran princes.[48] The treaty ruled that the German princes could choose between Catholicism and Lutheranism in their domains. That gave them power over the churches in their various territories. The rule was 'whose the territory, his the religion' (*cuius regio eius religio*), in effect 'the prince's religion prevails in that prince's territory'. This division into Catholic and Lutheran principalities put an end to the one, Catholic, Holy Roman Empire. It defused the tension and sealed the peace, at any rate for Catholics in Catholic territories and for Lutherans in Lutheran territories, but not the other way round: not for Catholics in Lutheran territories nor for Lutherans in Catholic territories. They were encouraged to emigrate, without forfeiting their property, while those who elected to stay obtained the right to practise their faith, often publicly, albeit only at set times. In other words, if they stayed, they were tolerated. All types of tolerance

---

[47] Rawls is sometimes considered to be hostile towards religion, which is contradicted by his 'generic theism' in his recently published *On my Religion*; see R. Adams, The Theological Ethics of the Young Rawls and Its Background, in: J. Rawls, *A Brief Inquiry into the Meaning of Sin and Faith: With "On my Religion"*, edited by Th. Nagel, Harvard University Press, Cambridge 2009, 24–101, here 101. As is evident from his *On my Religion* (p. 266), Rawls was fascinated by the conclusion to Jean Bodin's *Colloquium Heptaplomeres de Rerum Sublimium Arcanis Abditis* 1588 (Princeton 1975), which recounts a conversation about religions between a Catholic, a Jew, a philosophical naturalist, a Calvinist, a Lutheran, a sceptic and a Muslim. It ends not in a common homophony or counterpoint, but in divinely modulated harmony, whereafter there is no further conversation about religions and everybody defends his religion through holy commitment to life (471).

[48] The Schmalkaldic League was established after the breakdown of official talks in the Augsburg Reichstag in 1530 between Catholics and Lutherans under the leadership of emperor Charles V; E. Honée, *Witboek historisch onderzoek: Toelichting bij mijn lijst van geschiedkundige publicaties*, Nijmegen 2009, 12.

tactics were used that had been prevalent even in the Middle Ages in the traffic between Christians, Jews, and Muslims. These tactics included tilling the land together, maintaining social contacts, inter-marriage, raising sons in the father's religion and daughters in the mother's, transit rights for other believers en route to their religious gatherings (*Auslauf*), and use of each other's buildings for such gath-erings. This tolerance had a twofold effect. On the one hand, disciplin-ing dissident groups by way of tolerance tactics for the sake of public order furthered political development in the direction of an absolute, unitary state. On the other hand, state curbing of confessionalism that caused the two groups to oppose each other contributed to economic development.[49]

But this did not apply, at least not to the same extent, to Calvin-ists. Article 17 of the Treaty of Augsburg explicitly excluded every-body other than Catholics and Lutherans from the ruling. In 1618 this erupted in the Thirty-Years War, mainly between Catholics and Cal-vinists. The war ended in the Peace of Westphalia in 1648, of which the Peace of Münster in the same year formed part. The treaty extended the effectiveness of the Peace of Augsburg to states outside Germany and broadened it to include Calvinists. It enhanced the plausibility of the emancipation of states vis-à-vis the churches, both in Germany and elsewhere, and further increased state power over the churches. A telling example was the state's removal of science from the church's sphere of influence, evidenced by the emperor's permission, in terms of the treaty of Westphalia, for the Swedish king to establish an acad-emy or university separate from the church,[50] as well as the establish-ment of state academies of sciences unassociated with the churches in London and Paris.[51] In other words, the state's emancipation from the church, inherent in the *cuius regio, eius religio* rule, furthered the development of absolute states and state churches, or at any rate of state-preferred churches.

All this manifested most noticeably in the seaboard powers of North West Europe. That is the area to the west of the west-east axis that

---

[49] B. Kaplan, *Divided by Faith*, Harvard University Press, Cambridge 2007, 127–293.

[50] See article X, 13 in the *Instrumentum Pacis Osnabrugensis* (IPO), part of the *Instrumentum Pacis Monasteriensis* (IPM).

[51] F. Cohen, *De herschepping van de wereld: Het ontstaan van de moderne weten-schap verklaard*, Bakker, Amsterdam 2008, 175–189, here 180.

divided the Europe of that era into a monetary and urban culture and
a rural culture, and to the north of the north-south axis that split it
into Protestant and Catholic halves.[52] Absolute states were not favoured
only by politicians intent on increasing economic and political power,
but also by scholars on both sides of the Channel, such as Hobbes,
Locke, and Hume on the western side and De Groot and Spinoza on
the eastern side, partly to prevent a recurrence of the bloody, brutal
wars that had afflicted Europe in the 16th and 17th centuries. Whenever the confessional struggle worsened, state intervention increased
and tolerance declined, and vice versa: when the struggle abated, state
intervention decreased and tolerance increased.[53]

The flipside was that the churches had to safeguard their identity
as a spiritual power against the state for the sake of their members'
spiritual needs and desires, which did not always accord with state
interests.[54] Because the state imposed increasing social and religious
discipline on the populace, there was constant friction between state
and church. In addition, there was friction between other religious
communities and the state because they were excluded from the peace
treaty of Westphalia. The problem of religious minorities was far from
resolved.

8.2.2   American and French Legislation Regarding
Separation of Church and State

That solution only came 150 years later with the separation of church
and state, in the sense of a mutual separation between the two, when
the 1789 Bill of Rights was appended to the American constitution in
the form of ten amendments in 1791. The first amendment contained
what is known as the 'no establishment clause', which prohibited the
passing by congress of any act pertaining to a religious institution.
In addition, the so-called 'free exercise clause' prohibited the passing
of any act that impeded free religious practice.[55] The interpretation

---

[52] P. Flora et al. (eds.), *State Formation, Nation-Building, and Mass Politics in
Europe: The Theory of Stein Rokkan*, Oxford University Press, Oxford 1999, 141–147.
[53] Kaplan, *Divided by Faith*, op. cit., 15–47.
[54] M. Terpstra, Politieke orde en het alleenrecht op duiding: Het 'rijk van de vrijheid'
in de vroegmoderne filosofie, in: S. van Erp (ed.), *Vrijheid in verdeeldheid: Geschiedenis en actualiteit van religieuze tolerantie*, Valkhof, Nijmegen 2008, 125–151.
[55] The first part of the first amendment reads: "Congress shall make no law respecting an establishment of religion, or prohibiting the free exercise thereof."

of the 'no establishment clause' in terms of separation of church and state, even a wall of separation between them, was that of the erstwhile Anglican, later Puritan and Baptist, Roger Williams, founder of the colony of Rhode Island, when he condemned the state's persecution of things like idolatry, desecration of the sabbath, illegitimate participation in services of worship, and blasphemy.[56] These are matters for the churches to decide, he maintained, in which the state had no business to meddle, for there is 'a wall of separation between church and state'. One of the founding fathers, Thomas Jefferson, adopted this phrase, albeit in his own way.[57] On 1 January 1802 he wrote in a letter to a group that called itself the 'Danbury Baptists':

> Believing with you that religion is a matter which lies solely between Man & his God, that he owes account to none other for his faith or his worship, that the legitimate powers of government reach actions only, & not opinions, I contemplate with sovereign reverence that act of the whole American people which declared that their legislature should 'make no law respecting an establishment of religion, or prohibiting the free exercise thereof', thus building a wall of separation between Church & State.[58]

This separation of church and state enabled dissenters and members of other religious communities to secure equal rights and freedoms. In the absence of such a separation, equal rights and freedoms for religious dissidents from the mainstream and nonreligious people were imperilled.[59]

Following the American Constitution of 1791, the French Constitution of that same year also stipulates separation of church and state.[60] The preamble states that the law does not recognise any religious vows,

---

[56] R. Williams, *The Bloudy Tenent of Persecution for Cause of Conscience*, London 1644.

[57] But Jefferson stands the meaning of the wall of separation on its head. Whereas Williams refers to the 'garden of religion' and the 'wilderness of government', and the 'wall of separation' has to protect the 'garden of religion' against the state, Jefferson envisions the reverse – protecting the state against religion; N. Feldman, *Divided by God: America's Church-State Problem – and What We Should Do about It*, Farrar, New York 2005, 24.

[58] Jefferson's *Letter to the Danbury Baptists*, U.S. Library of Congress.

[59] For the difference between Roger Williams and John Locke, who favours earlier restrictive notions especially in regard to Catholics and atheists, see: M.C. Nussbaum, *Liberty of Conscience: In Defence of America's Tradition of Religious Equality*, Basic, New York 2008, 34–71.

[60] For the relation between the two, see: K. Hilpert, *Menschenrechte und Theologie, Forschungsbeiträge zur ethischen Dimension der Menschenrechte*, Herder, Freiburg 2001.

which meant that Catholic orders and congregations of priests, brothers and sisters lost their official status. The first title, dealing with fundamental freedoms, says that citizens have a right to elect the ministers of their religion (*cultes*), which put an end to the Catholic Church's monopoly. Article 7 of the second title posits that the law regards marriage as a civil contract, thus cancelling the official validity of a church marriage. Marriage is a crucial institution, since it is seen as a cornerstone of the state and society and as the source and matrix of future generations. The purport of this article is said to be that henceforth one no longer had to enter society via the sacristy.[61]

The development of the separation of church and state in subsequent French legislation merits attention, since it is constantly mentioned in debates in the Netherlands especially with reference to the typically French principle of *laïcité*, which, as we shall see, does not feature in the constitution of 1791 nor in subsequent constitutions until the constitution of the Fourth Republic of 1946.[62]

During the first republic (1792–1799), the decree of 1794, composed by Jean-Pierre Cambon who presided over the French convention several times, 'consecrated' the separation of church and state. While the first article declares that the practice of any religion whatever may not be hindered (*troublé*), the ensuing articles stipulate that the state does not recognise any minister of religion (*ne reconnait aucun minister du culte*), does not pay his stipend, does not provide a place for the practice of a religion and will not establish any fund for that purpose. Hence the decree proclaims strict separation of church and state, but also recognises pluralism and religious equality, albeit only as private communities. This recognition of pluralism and equality, with many variations, has remained intact. It is the hallmark of French public law, with only one intermission: the constitution of 6 April 1814, proclaimed when Napoléon, who made himself First Consul and later Emperor of what is now known as the First Empire (1804–1814), was dethroned and the house of Bourbon was restored. Article 5 of that constitution reiterates that everybody has an equal right to practise their religion; article 6 adds the rider: the

---

[61] "Désormais, ce n'est plus par la porte de la sacristie que l'on entrera dans la société"; see E. Poulat, *Notre laïcité publique, la France est une république laïque (Constitution de 1946 et 1958)*, Berg, Paris 2003, 60.

[62] For these and other relevant constitutions, see: L. Duguit & H. Monnier, *Les constitutions et les principales lois politiques de la France*, Librairie générale de droit et du jurisprudence, Paris 1908.

Catholic, apostolic, Roman religion is the state religion.[63] That is not surprising, because the restoration of the *ancien régime* implied the restoration of the Catholic church as a state church. But it did not entail any exclusive privilege for the Catholic Church, for article 7 states that not only Catholic clergy but ministers of other Christian churches as well will be salaried by the state. However, the privileging of Christian clergy abolished the equality before the law of non-Christian religions, more particularly Judaism.[64] A year later, article 1 of the *Projet d'acte constitutionel* of 29 June 1815 stipulated that everyone has the right to confess and practise her religion freely, adding that no religion may ever become exclusive, dominant or privileged.[65] But the constitution of 1830 restores the special position of the Catholic Church and other Christian churches. Article 6 of this constitution again grants ministers of these churches remuneration from state coffers, and the Catholic Church is reinstated in a special position, this time not by legally declaring it the religion of the state but by arguing that it is the faith professed by the majority of French citizens, hence a purely empirical description.[66]

With the Second Republic (1848–1852), the special position of the Catholic and other Christian churches vanished once again. Article 7 of the constitution of 1848 not only reaffirms the freedom of every religion to profess its faith, but also that the ministers of all officially recognised religions, present or future, are entitled to a government salary. Thus the constitutional equality of all religions was fully restored.

After the interregnum of the Second Empire, proclaimed by Louis-Napoléon Bonapart (1852–1870), this remained the case under the act on the separation of church and state of 1905.[67] The first title follows

---

[63] "Cependant la religion catholique, apostolique et romaine, est la religion de l'État."

[64] Between 1789 and 1791 the law granted equal rights not only to the largest minority, the Protestants, but also to Jews. This happened after heated debates, influenced by deep-seated prejudice against Jews – not so much the Sephardic Jews in southern France, who were refugees from Spain and Portugal, but the Ashkenazi Jews in Alsace-Lorraine in eastern France; L. Hunt, *Inventing Human Rights: A History*, Norton, New York 2007, 150–160.

[65] "Les droits suivants sont garantis á tous les Francçais (…) 6⁰ La liberté de professer et d'exercer librement leur culte, sans qu'aucun culte puisse jamais devenir exclusif, dominant ou privilégié."

[66] "Les ministres de la religion catholique, apostolique et romaine, professée par la majorité des Français, et ceux des autres cultes chrétiens, reçoivent des traitements du trésor public."

[67] *Loi du 9 décembre 1905 relative à la séparation des Églises et de l'État.*

the tradition that had been honoured all but consistently, namely that the state – in effect that of the Third Republic (1870–1940) – guarantees free religious practice. But the principles of the First Republic immediately resurface: the state does not recognise, pay salaries for, or subsidise any religion. All sorts of church subsidies that the state had reinstated in recent years lapsed, underscoring yet again the private character of religions. One exception was funding or remuneration for religious services in public institutions with residential facilities, like the army, hospitals, prisons, and schools. The second and third titles stipulate that all fixed and movable property (church buildings, residences for clergy, seminaries) accrue to the state. The fourth title states that all such state property is transferred to ritual associations (*associations cultuelles*) in order to be used for worship. Title 5 lays down practical rules for conducting ceremonies and processions and for erecting religious symbols in public places. In addition, religious education for six- to thirteen-year-olds at public schools is permitted only as an extra-curricular activity.

This act of 1905 is widely regarded as a milestone in the separation of church and state. But according to the French sociologist Émile Poulat, it marks the beginning of a new chapter rather than the end of church-state relations in that it transfers the relationship from public law to private law. In terms of the act, the churches forfeit every public power and function, but are still called upon to render certain services to society and continue to benefit by privileges in the form of accommodations and exemptions. Thus they continue to perform public services in the common interest and general social or humanitarian tasks.[68] In Poulat's view, this and subsequent acts replaces the classical division between the spiritual and temporal domains – God and Caesar – with a modern division between private and public law. It does not deprive the churches of their services to society, but these now fall under private rather than public law.[69]

The 1905 act is also regarded as a milestone in the development of *laïcité*, although, as mentioned already, the term was not used until the constitution of the Fourth Republic (1946–1958), which in its preamble states that France is an indivisible, laic, democratic, and social

---

[68] Poulat, *Notre laïcité publique*, op. cit., 130–131.
[69] Poulat, *Notre laïcité publique*, op. cit., 293. By way of illustration Poulat compiles three lists: one of matters now recognised by the republic, a second of state salaried positions and a third of subsidised or remunerated activities (pp. 131–135).

republic.[70] That is reiterated in the first article of the constitution of the Fifth Republic (1958). In addition, it affirms that all citizens are equal before the law with no discrimination on grounds of origin, race, or religion, and that all religions are respected.[71]

It is evident, then, that French law has no rigid separation of church and state, and even the term '*laïcité*' entails nothing like a separationist model of church-state relations.[72] Neither does it imply a static phenomenon, but is dynamic, flexible, and varied. I cite an example that has roused strong feelings over the past twenty years. In 1989, the wearing of visible religious symbols such as yarmulkes, crucifixes, and veils was permitted in schools by the then minister of education Jospin, even though it caused a stir because of the alleged 'indivisibility' of the republic – a battle cry against the historically loaded term 'two Frances', referring to the *Kulturkampf* between religious France and the secular, laic, anti-clerical France of the 19th and 20th centuries. However, in 2004 the then president Chirac proclaimed a special act on *laïcité*. It prohibited the wearing at school of conspicuously visible symbols designed to be noticed, that is, symbols that not only indicate adherence to a religion but also convey a political message. The prohibition included the Muslim hijab, the Jewish yarmulke, the Sikh turban and large Christian crucifixes, while permitting small crucifixes, stars of David, and 'hands of Fatima', an ornament symbolising the prophet's favourite daughter.[73] Then, in January 2008, the current president Sarkozy declared roundly, following the civilisation politics of the philosopher E. Morin, that French culture is inconceivable without Christianity, which should be given lasting recognition.

---

[70] "La France est une République indivisible, laïque, démocratique et sociale."

[71] "La France est une République indivisible, laïque, démocratique et sociale. Elle assure l'égalité devant la loi de tous les citoyens sans distinction d'origine, de race ou de religion. Elle respecte toutes les croyances. Son organisation est décentralisée."

[72] A separationist interpretation of the separation of church and state may be found on both the political and the religious side. Political examples are mentioned by W. Durham, Perspective on Religious Liberty: A Comparative Framework, in: J. van der Vyver & J. Witte (eds.), *Religious Human Rights in Global Perspective: Legal Perspectives*, Nijhoff, The Hague 1996, 1–44, here 21–23, like the former Stalinist regime and other regimes which persecute religious individuals and groups. An example on the religious side, in which Christianity is considered to be exclusively oriented to the 'other', non-immanent, supernatural world, is D. Hart, *A Secular Faith: Why Christianity Favors the Separation of Church and State*, Dee, Chicago 2006.

[73] "*Loi encadrant, en application du principe de laïcité, le port de signes ou de tenues manifestant une appartenance religieuse dans les écoles, collèges et lycées publics* (2004)."

Whereas president Chirac still advocated a negative *laïcité*, president Sarkozy in his address to pope Benedict XVI in Paris in September 2008 championed a positive *laïcité* with renewed acknowledgment of the Christian roots of French society. He did not confine himself to this cultural historical notion, moreover, but went so far as to venture an explicit pronouncement on God, hence a type of confession: God knows, he said, that our societies are in need of dialogue, tolerance, respect, and calm.[74]

This brief review from the Peace of Augsburg in 1555 and the Peace of Westphalia in 1648, which symbolise absolute state control of the church, to present-day French legislation, which epitomises separation of church and state, contains the following lessons for our time. There is no longer any question of a dichotomous choice between either a state church in an absolute state or a separationist model of strict division in a democratic state. The first did actually exist, the other in its most radical form never did. The former restricted religious freedom and amounted to oppression of religious minorities. The latter, as a conceptual model or (less kindly) a myth, entails distortion and suppression of actual relations that have always existed, with varying frequency and intensity, between church and state, also in France. Hence this dichotomy should be replaced with a more balanced approach that accords with political reality. That would allow scope for diverse forms of cooperation between church and state and/or for state accommodations and exemptions in regard to manifesting religion in public worship, teaching, observance, and practice.[75]

By way of illustration of this variation, the present state churches in Europe – both the powerful state church in Greece and the weaker

---

[74] See: Discours de Nicolas Sarkozy accueillant 'avec respect' le pape Benoît XVI, Vatican.va. The distinction between *laïcité negative* and *laïcité positive* more or less corresponds to the distinction between *laïcité en combat* and *laïcité ouvert*; *see* N. Nathwan, Islamic Headscarves and Human Rights: A Critical Analysis of the Relevant Case Law of the European Court of Human Rights, *Netherlands Quarterly of Human Rights* 25(2007)2, 221–254.

[75] S. den Dekker-van Bijsterveld, *De verhouding tussen kerk en staat in het licht van de grondrechten*, Willink, Zwolle 1988; S. van Bijsterveld, *Overheid en godsdienst, herijking van een onderlinge relatie*, Wolf, Nijmegen 2008; Id., State and Church in the Netherlands, in: G. Robbers (ed.), *State and Church in the European Union*, Nomos, Baden-Baden 1996, 209– 228, here 215–216; S. Ferrari, Islam and the Western European Model of Church and State Relations, in: W. Shadid & S. van Koningsveld (eds.), *Religious Freedom and the Neutrality of the State: The Position of Islam in the European Union*, Peeters, Leuven 2002, 6–19, here 10–11.

ones in England, Scotland, Norway, Denmark, Malta, and Finland (with two state churches, one Lutheran, the other Eastern Orthodox) – all recognise religious pluralism and the equality of religions. They also recognise religious freedom and manifestation, both private and public, individual and collective, in accordance with the European Convention of Human Rights of 1950 (article 9). All these state churches and other, non-state, churches (the vast majority), whether recognised as public law entities (*Körperschaft des öffentlichen Rechts*) as in Germany and Austria or falling under private law, have diverse arrangements with the state in the form of accommodations (religious calendar, burial, religious education at public schools, confessional schools, religious care in the aforementioned residential institutions, social and charitable church institutions, subsidies for maintenance of buildings) and/or exemptions in such areas as fiscal and labour law. The separation of church and state is not uniform but differs in degree from one country to the next.[76]

8.2.3 Separation of Society and State as a Framework for the Separation of Church and State

Since the debate on the separation of church and state often centres on actual and/or desirable national or regional arrangements between the two, hence tends to float in the air of too detailed a discussion, we need to distance ourselves and find a more abstract, conceptual premise. Such a premise is the relationship between society and the state. This relationship is frequently described in terms of 'separation' as well, like separation of society and the state. The reason I like to deal with it here refers to the fact that the church – here the term refers to all religions – is located in society, of which it forms a part along with other communities and institutions. Hence I first examine the separation between society and the state, and in the next section use this as a basis for analyzing the separation of church and state.

Explicating the relation between society and the state, more especially the separation of the two, is typical of the post-feudal period. In feudal times, political life comprised a network of relations between lord and vassal, marked by a pledge of mutual trust: the lord will provide means of subsistence, the vassal will be loyal to the lord. In some

---

[76] V. Bader, *Secularism or Democracy? Associational Governance of Religious Diversity*, Amsterdam University Press, Amsterdam 2007, 47, 63.

rituals associated with this relationship the vassal kneels before the lord and lays his hands in the lord's, whereupon he may kiss him. When fighting as a knight (*miles*) in the lord's army the oath of loyalty meant that he is prepared to die for him, which in medieval sagas is regarded as a sacrificial death out of loyalty (*fidelitas, fides*).[77] He would not be dying for his country (*pro patria*), like soldiers did in Roman times, but for his lord (*pro domino*). He had to defend his lord, even against his own son or father (*etiam contra filium vel patrem*), but not against himself or his country (*non tamen...contra seipsum vel contra patriam*).[78] The complexity of these relations stemmed from the fact that vassals could hold diverse goods in fief from different lords, which could lead to conflicting loyalties.[79] Whereas feudal society comprised interpersonal relations between lord and vassal, implying that political relations were personal and personal relations were political, the post-feudal period saw differentiation between personal relations on the one hand and political and legal relations on the other. Functional relations were not a matter of personal allegiance but were defined in terms of impersonal legal rules, and conflicts were not resolved through violence but through application of such rules by impartial state officials and judges. Gradually this evolved into two domains: society with its voluntary personal relations and voluntary participation in societal institutions, and the state and its state institutions with its imperative power via what gradually emerged as distinct bodies with legislative, administrative, and judicial powers.

But the two domains are not entirely divorced from each other. Their relationship is not separationist but dialectical: they influence one another. Society is characterised by the functioning of groups and institutions with divergent ideas of and interests in the development of that society, seeking to persuade others of their ideas and striving to achieve their interests, often regardless of whether this benefits or impairs the freedom and equality of others. Via democratic channels these divergent ideas and interests in society penetrate the deliberative political communication of the state. Whatever ideas are adopted in that communication and whatever interests are considered legitimate, the ultimate assessment and the democratic majority decision that is

---

[77] Kantorowicz, *The King's Two Bodies*, op. cit., 234.

[78] Kantorowicz, *The King's Two Bodies*, op. cit., 237, n. 133.

[79] W. Blockmans & P. Hoppenbrouwers, *Eeuwen des onderscheids, een geschiedenis van middeleeuws Europa*, Prometheus, Amsterdam 2002, 171.

made are directed, or should be directed, by a twofold criterion: the endeavour to promote freedom and equality for all. This is how the state influences political processes in society, via – ideally – legal structures designed to promote this endeavour and enforce its observance. Thus one could say that politics in the broad sense, which is enacted in political processes in society, affects politics in the narrow sense, which is enacted in the deliberative democracy of the state that in its turn influences politics in the broad sense.[80]

What is required of political communication in a deliberative democracy? The question is important, because the ideas and interests espoused by different social groups and institutions rest on very different premises, are based on different principles and entail different arguments. They represent distinct combinations of visions of the human person and society, moral notions, political convictions and other normative views, as well as beliefs regarding increasing efficiency and effectiveness, emerging from self-interest, well-considered self-interest and/or ideas about the common good. These combinations of normative ideas and interests which direct the private life of individuals and the social life of groups and institutions, are called comprehensive doctrines by the political philosopher John Rawls. How should this plurality of doctrines be handled in a deliberative democracy aimed at promoting equal freedom and free equality for all? I mention some major requirements.[81]

The first is that groups and institutions that state their beliefs publicly and strive to have them realised accept the basic principles of constitutional democracy out of regard for their intrinsic value. These basic principles include freedom and equality reflected in civil liberties and rights, opportunity to realise them, the rule of law and the majority principle. Such recognition goes beyond democracy as a kind of modus vivendi that is accepted because it is inescapably part of

---

[80] D. Held, *Models of Democracy*, Polity Press, Cambridge 1987, 274–289. In Habermas's terms politics in the broad sense concerns opinion formation in society, and politics in the narrow sense refers to will and decision formation in the state; see: J. Habermas, *Faktizität und Geltung: Beiträge zur Diskurstheorie des Rechts und des demokratischen Rechtsstaats*, Suhrkamp, Frankfurt 1993, 226–229, and Id., Popular Sovereignty as Procedure, in: J. Bohman & W. Rehg (eds.), *Deliberative Democracy: Essays on Reason and Politics*, MIT Press, Cambridge 1997, 55–63, here 35–66.

[81] Here I draw eclectically (in I trust a responsible manner) on both Rawls and Habermas.

present-day conventions and/or for the sake of temporary profit, only to be abandoned as soon as it is no longer profitable.[82]

The second requirement pertains to recognition of a plurality of comprehensive doctrines. This relates to the first requirement, because democracy consists in a struggle to realise divergent beliefs and interests, not by force of arms but using the weapon of reason. It entails recognition not only of a diversity of beliefs, but especially of a diversity of mutually conflicting and irreconcilable beliefs based on different ideas and arguments. Such recognition stems from an epistemological consideration that affects the very core of the relation between truth and freedom. No existential belief ever comprehends the whole truth: it only approximates truth, covers some aspects of it and offers a perspective on it. This consideration is associated with the burdens of judgment.[83] These are as follows: up to a point our concepts are vague; our arguments are complex and discordant; their weight is debatable; our judgments are based on interpretation, estimation and appraisal; our normative criteria when making that judgment are selective; and our justification of them lacks the full body of experience that gives rise to them. From this we make two inferences. Firstly, every individual, group, community, or institution has a right to put its comprehensive doctrine, with all its implications, up for political debate. They are all entitled to communicate it and to be heard. In other words, in a sequential sense freedom has priority over truth, since it is seen as an opening for and a way to truth. Secondly, they all have a duty to present their comprehensive doctrine as reasonable as possible, whatever substantive reasons that involves – metaphysical, natural law, moral, political, judicial, aesthetic, empirical, or whatever. Beliefs put up for discussion whose protagonists renounce all reasonableness and rely totally on authority-related arguments have no place in democratic deliberation. This applies to every form of fundamentalism, not only religious but also, for instance, Enlightenment or scientistic fundamentalism.[84]

The third requirement refers to a *proviso* Rawls introduces.[85] Reasonable comprehensive doctrines may be introduced in public political

---

[82] Rawls, *Political Liberalism*, op. cit., 147, 458–459.

[83] Rawls, *Political Liberalism*, op. cit., 56–57.

[84] Rawls, *Political Liberalism*, op. cit., 483; J. Habermas, *Zwischen Naturalismus*, op. cit., 155–186.

[85] Rawls, *Political Liberalism*, op. cit., 462–463.

discussion, provided, he says, that in due course they are translated in terms that are reasonably acceptable to every other citizen. This requirement stems from the fact that modern society depends on cooperation, for without it society disintegrates, yet at the same time it is characterised by a plurality of rational but conflicting comprehensive beliefs. With a view to cooperation, irreconcilable comprehensive beliefs have to be translated in terms of what Rawls calls public reason. Public reason is built on the aforementioned basic principles of constitutional democracy: freedom and equality, including civil liberties and rights, opportunity to realise these, the rule of law, the majority principle and the plurality of comprehensive doctrines.[86] If the relevant doctrines are translated in terms of public reason, even citizens who do not subscribe to these beliefs may be assumed to find them reasonably acceptable.[87] The term 'reasonably acceptable' should be stressed here, because it is different from 'actually accepted'. Political communication from public reason does not require that (the various!) comprehensive doctrines are accepted by all citizens, but that they are considered reasonably understandable and in that sense acceptable, in principle. The underlying principle of this requirement, then, is reciprocity. Without reciprocity, which develops through the capacity of taking one another's perspective, a democracy cannot exist. Otherwise those beliefs, including their implications for political opinion formation and decision formation, could not be understood by people who do not hold them. In other words, if a comprehensive belief is advocated exclusively in its own terms without in due course being interpreted in terms of public reason, it violates the principle of reciprocity.[88]

---

[86] Habermas, *Zwischen Naturalismus*, op. cit., 128, n. 18, notes that Rawls confines such translation to constitutional issues, which he finds unrealistic, since virtually all conflicting themes can be reduced to constitutional issues. Whether one agrees with this depends on the scope one allows for civil liberties as negative or positive obligations; cf. P.H. van Kempen, *Repressie door mensenrechten: Over positieve verplichtingen tot aanwending van strafrecht ter bescherming van fundamentele rechten*, Inaugural address Radboud University Nijmegen 2008.

[87] I prefer not to use Rawls's term 'reasonable overlapping consensus', indicating that such a translation may be assumed to be rationally acceptable to all citizens, since it causes unnecessary confusion, even though Rawls explicitly says that it does not connote some sort of mean of all possible existential beliefs but exists in its own right; Rawls, *Political Liberalism*, op. cit., 39, 385–395.

[88] Rawls, *Political Liberalism*, op. cit., 478–481.

Here the term used – 'in due course' – is deliberately vague. 'In due course' means that it must be possible for the comprehensive beliefs to be presented without any restriction in their own metaphysical or other normative terms, both in society (politics in the broad sense) and in the state (politics in the narrow sense), but that they at some moment in time should be translated in terms of public reason so that they are reasonably understandable and acceptable, in principle, by all citizens, of whatever faith or belief. Surely, 'in due course'; but a specific moment in time cannot and should not be mentioned in advance, because everything depends on the way the communication develops. That is left open. The other aspect that is left open is the person or group that must do the translating.[89] To ease the burden on the party presenting the comprehensive belief, who has the task of translating it in terms of public reason, Habermas proposes that in principle it be spread over all participants in political communication.[90]

The fourth and final requirement is that, after sufficient communication, the state (politics in the narrow sense) takes a decision in terms of public reason without reference to any comprehensive belief – either a legislative decision by parliament or a legal decision by a judge. Such decisions should be taken autonomously without any influencing by society. It should be made as impartially as possible without privileging any group. The intention is not that the state should act neutrally, as if its actions could be value-free, but that it should be as impartial as possible.[91] That means striking a balance between freedom and equality, realising that freedom may result in inequality and equality in unfreedom. Equal freedom and free equality are to be seen as regulative ideas.

8.2.4 Separation of Church and State

Having clarified some requirements of dealing with conflicting beliefs in political communication in the relation between society (politics in a broad sense) and the state (politics in a narrow sense), I now turn to some corresponding requirements of the relation between church and state. Here the key question is how to deal with religious comprehensive doctrines in political debate.

---

[89] Rawls, *Political Liberalism*, op. cit., 462–466.
[90] Habermas, *Zwischen Naturalismus*, op. cit., 135–141.
[91] P. Ricoeur, *La mémoire, l'histoire, l'oubli*, Seuil, Paris 2000.

The first requirement is that the church (here used as an umbrella term for churches and non-Christian religions) recognise the basic principles of democracy as intrinsically valuable and not merely as a *modus vivendi*. That is not easy, as evidenced by the resistance of, for example, the Catholic Church ever since the 18th century to religious freedom, considered liberal, and even to tolerance. Catholic doctrine at that time read that intolerance of non-Catholics was a mandatory, absolute principle (then known as the thesis). Only in concrete historical situations when Catholics did not constitute a majority and/or lacked the power to enforce the principle was tolerance, depending on circumstances, either permitted, commendable, or even mandatory (then known as the hypothesis). In the latter case the Catholic minority benefited by tolerance, which, of course, incurred the reproach of opportunism and bad faith (*mauvaise foi*).[92] This doctrine was only revoked by the Second Vatican Council (1962–1965).[93] The constitution *Gaudium et Spes* (1965) finally embraced democracy and human rights, as had happened a few years earlier in pope John XXIII's encyclical *Pacem in Terris*, which also supported separation of powers. However, the separation of church and state is not mentioned in any of these documents. In his encyclical addressed to the French bishops in 1892, *Au milieu des sollicitudes*, pope Leo XIII, deemed to be pro-reform, still called it absurd, because in his view it severed political law from divine law (nos. 28–29). Post-Vatican II, such objections are no longer made, but neither has there been unequivocal support of separation of church and state in whatever form.

The second requirement is recognition by the church of religious pluralism along with worldview-related, moral and political pluralism. If such recognition is based on intrinsically democratic awareness and not merely in an attempt to maintain a useful *modus videndi*, it entails admission of the perspectival, partial nature of the truth claims of one's own religion as well. It also implies willingness to justify the key tenets of one's religious belief and to review them when they prove untenable in light of historical, empirical, logical or conceptual research. Here it

---

[92] R. Aubert, l'Enseignement du magistère ecclésiastique au XIXe siècle sur le libéralisme, in: R. Aubert et al., *Tolérance et communauté humaine: Chrétiens dans un monde divisé*, Casterman, Tournai 1952, 75–103; A. Dondeyne, *Geloof en wereld*, Patmos, Antwerpen 1962, 221–224; E. Schillebeeckx, *Wereld en kerk*, Nelissen, Bilthoven 1966, 196–199.

[93] J. Murray, Religious Freedom, in W. Abbott (ed.), *Documents of Vatican II*, Chapman, London 1966, 672–696.

is important to make a proper distinction between beliefs and arguments. Propositions based on 'divine revelation', 'God's will', 'divine law', 'natural law', or 'ecclesiastic tradition' fall in the category of beliefs, and when advanced as arguments they are authority-based, hence not arguments in the strict sense of the word, which do not consist of repetitions in sacred language of a belief presented earlier, but of logically independent reasons given for it.[94]

The third requirement concerns the translation of religious existential beliefs in terms of the aforementioned basic principles of public reason (freedom, equality, and the concomitant democratic principles), in such a manner that these existential beliefs may be considered reasonably acceptable to all citizens. Here Rawls's distinction between public and secular reason is important. The term 'secular' connotes, at any rate in Rawls's vocabulary, a clearly defined set of comprehensive beliefs, namely those that are consciously and explicitly based on non-religious or anti-religious convictions and grounds, such as scientistic or naturalistic views. In respect of politics, these are on a par with religious comprehensive beliefs.[95] The term 'public reason', however, falls in a fundamentally different area, namely that of the translation of both religious and nonreligious or anti-religious comprehensive beliefs in terms of the basic principles of constitutional democracy. Thus proponents of nonreligious or anti-religious beliefs face the same

---

[94] P. d'Arcais, *Eleven Theses Against Habermas*, http://www.filosofia.it/pagine/micromega/11ThesesagainstHabermas.pdf. This means that religious beliefs based on forms of religious voluntarism, as in nominalist natural law, face a far more daunting task than religious beliefs based on forms of religious rationalism, as in rational natural law. For the difference between Hugo Grotius and Samuel Pufendorf in this regard see: Bernardi, *Le principe*, op. cit., 99–187; cf. F. Oakley, *Natural Law, Laws of Nature, Natural Rights*, Continuum, New York 2005, 35–86.

[95] R. Audi, Natural Reason, Natural Rights, and Governmental Neutrality Toward Religion, *Religion and Human Rights* 4(2009)2–3, 157–175, uses 'secular reason' in an *epistemic* sense, which means that "a secular reason for action (...) is roughly one whose status as a justifier for action (or belief) does not evidentially depend on – but also does not deny – the existence of God; nor does it depend on theological considerations, or on the pronouncements of a person or institution *as* a religious authority" (p. 158). Nevertheless, with Thomas Aquinas he considers 'natural reason' (that overlaps 'secular reason') in an *ontic* sense a divine gift which "strengthens the intellectual light" (p. 163) and which may lead our intellect on naturally knowable premises to *generic* theism. Does this naturally reasonable *generic* theism justify, Audi asks, the use of *generic* civil religion in public life, like the Pledge of Allegiance to the Flag of the United States 'under God'? His answer seems to be a positive one as far as *generic* theism in civil religion is free from any infiltration by any particular religion and, consequentially, a negative one as far it is used by particular religious institutions in support of their own particular faiths and interests.

task as champions of religious beliefs, namely to rephrase their views in the terminology of public reason in such a manner that they will in principle be seen as reasonably acceptable by all citizens.[96]

This poses two problems. The first is that such translation reduces religions to their normative political stances, which are moreover reduced to public reason. Such a normative political translation in either teleological-ethical or deontological-ethical terms filters out the transcendent aspects of themes like faith in God, creation, sin, forgiveness, salvation and eschatology.[97] The second problem is an extension of the first. It is that such translation reduces the 'truth', even the 'full truth' as interpreted by religions, to a normative political truth claim alongside other, rival truth claims, both religious and nonreligious. Thus the 'full truth' becomes just a partial truth alongside other partial truths.

A solution to both problems is that such translation does not mean that religious and nonreligious views may be barred from political communication 'in due course' and be replaced by public reason, but that it is a matter of bilingualism. Religious comprehensive beliefs can retain their position, but 'in due course' they are *also* rendered in terms of public reason. Rawls mentions by way of example the double language game of religious and public reason played by champions of civil rights for the black population. They use a combination of biblical and public motives in their speeches: the biblical motives inspire their audience and give it some orientation, and the political motives justify their actions as citizens of a democratic state. In other words, they play two roles: that of members of a religious community that provides them with motivation, orientation, and courage of their convictions, and the role of citizens, being an office of the state. In both capacities

---

[96] In Habermas' *Zwischen Naturalismus*, op. cit., 119–154, 'public' (as in *öffentlicher Vernunftgebrauch*) and 'secular' (as in *säkulare Bürger*) wrongly overlap.

[97] Habermas, *Zwischen Naturalismus*, op. cit., 119–154, says that this normative political translation should be couched in deontological moral terms, so that the result may be considered reasonably acceptable by all citizens, but that is countered by the fact that religions use not only deontological but also teleological moral arguments that have no universal pretensions but are in fact contextually and communally determined, as explained by M. Reder, Wie weit können Glaube und Vernunft unterscheiden werden. in: M. Reder & J. Schmidt (eds.), *Ein Bewusstsein von dem, was fehlt: Eine Diskussion mit Jürgen Habermas*, Frankfurt 2008, 51–68; perhaps P. Ricoeur, *Oneself as Another*, Chicago University Press 1992, 169–296, offers a way out with his trichotomous model of contextual teleology, deontological testing and teleological recontextualisation 'in prudentia'.

they fight for social change. In their religious role they interpret the justice of the biblical prophets and are inspired and strengthened by them; in their civic role they interpret justice as a constitutional principle in a democratic state, in which they address all citizens of whatever religious or nonreligious tradition.[98] They used this bilingualism, whether they were aware of it or not.[99]

The fourth and final requirement is that the state, after due communication, must take an autonomous decision, as impartially as possible, in terms of public reason, without reference to any religious or non-religious comprehensive belief whatever. This also applies to decisions in the moral sphere. In the past, morality was regarded as the exclusive territory of the church, or at any rate as part of the *res mixtae* of church and state. However, ever since the insight dawned, notably in the Enlightenment, that morality can exist without religion as well, taking decisions in the moral sphere has become, from a political perspective, a power of the state. Hence it is the state which, after due deliberative political communication in society – including, if necessary, consultations with the church – must take an autonomous, maximally impartial decision, either a legislative decision by parliament or a legal decision by a judge.

What does all this imply for the foundation of constitutional democracy? The basic principles of such a state, we have said, are freedom and equality, civil liberties and rights plus the opportunity to realise these, the rule of law, the majority principle, and a plurality of comprehensive beliefs. The basis on which it rests does not consist in any particular comprehensive belief, for that would put paid to pluralism. What this means may be clarified from three different perspectives. From a political point of view, the basis on which constitutional democracy rests is necessarily indeterminate – more than that, it should even remain indeterminate. From a philosophical phenomenological perspective on truth, however, this indeterminacy evokes not only hesitancy and fear but also awe and reverence. In this indeterminacy, the truth about human beings and society conceals itself and only reveals itself whenever it is 'un-covered' in the most elementary and cautious political speech acts about the destiny and the meaning of individual and collective life; but it vanishes when it is forgotten once more in conventional political talk (in the sense of Heidegger's interpretation of *das*

---

[98] Rawls, *Political Liberalism*, op. cit., 249–250.
[99] Rawls, *Political Liberalism*, op. cit., 464, n. 54.

Gerede) and truth becomes purely appearance and pretence.[100] From a religious perspective, Nicholas of Cusa says in his *Of Learned Ignorance* (*De Docta Ignorantia*) that truth has no fixed centre or periphery, because the world has no fixed centre or periphery. The reason is that the world is in perpetual motion and because the ever shifting position from which it is seen means that centre and periphery, too, are continually shifting. That means that the centre of the world coincides with its periphery. The most profound reason for this, according to Cusa, is that the world as it were has its centre everywhere and its periphery nowhere, because periphery and centre are both God, who is everywhere and nowhere.[101]

8.3   Acceptance of the Separation of Church and State in an Empirical Perspective

Having described the relation between church and state in the premodern, early modern, and modern periods, we look at the extent to which the three groups of Christian, Muslim, and nonreligious youths that we investigated accept the separation of church and state.

Our empirical research focused on the most essential feature of this separation: state autonomy vis-à-vis religious communities and their leaders. Our premise here, as pointed out in the previous section, is that religious existential beliefs, whilst very pertinent to political communication, including that of the state, are not in themselves sufficient. In due course, we said, they have to be translated in terms of public reason also. After that, the state has to take an autonomous, maximally impartial decision whose reasonableness makes it acceptable to all citizens. To highlight the theme of political autonomy, we chose two topics from public debate that illustrate this most vividly: state autonomy in regard to euthanasia and in regard to abortion. After all, from a religious perspective religion and politics may meet in the area of *res mixtae*, morality, but even there the state, being the legislator, has the final say, provided no citizen forfeits her freedom in these areas and is not compelled to act counter to her religion or belief. The items in

---

[100] M. Heidegger, *Sein und Zeit*, Niemeyer Verlag, Tübingen 1993, 219–226.
[101] Dr Inigo Bocken (Radboud University Nijmegen) drew my attention to chapters 11 and 12 of Book II of Nicholas of Cusa's, *De Docta Ignorantia*, translation by J. Hopkins, Banning Press, Minneapolis 2001, here 93; Latin edition, Meiner, Hamburg, 162; Edition by W. & D. Dupré, Herder, Vienna 1966, Vol. I, II, 12, 396.

which the two topics are operationalised do not rule out consultation with religious leaders but put the accent on political autonomy.

Item (i) relates to politicians' autonomy vis-à-vis religious leaders in the case of euthanasia. It reads: "In regard to euthanasia, politicians should decide irrespective of any religious leader's will." Item (ii) relates to politicians' autonomy vis-à-vis religious leaders in the case of abortion. It reads: "In regard to abortion politicians should take decisions independently of religious leaders."[102]

The youths were asked to indicate on a five-point scale to what extent they agreed with items (i) and (ii), with 1 representing 'totally disagree', 2 'disagree', 3 'not sure', 4 'agree' and 5 'fully agree'. In table 4, scores 1 and 2 are combined to indicate disagreement (−), score 3 is retained to indicate ambivalence (±) and scores 4 and 5 are combined to indicate agreement (+).

Table 4 reveals a differentiated picture of scores on item (i). In each group of youths there are three minorities. The minority endorsing state autonomy in regard to euthanasia is largest in the nonreligious group, almost half (49%), followed by the Christian group, six percent lower (43%), and finally the Muslim group, ten percent lower than the Christian and sixteen percent lower than the nonreligious group (33%). There are also three minorities rejecting political autonomy, albeit smaller than those that agree with it. The smallest of these is in the nonreligious group (23%), while those of Christian and Muslim youths are identical (29%, 29%). Finally there are three minorities midway between acceptance and rejection, hence displaying ambiva-

Table 4. Attitudes towards the separation of church and state (%)

	Christian			Muslim			Nonreligious		
	−	±	+	−	±	+	−	±	+
(i) political autonomy regarding euthanasia	29 N = 338	28	43	29 N = 231	37	33	23 N = 477	28	49
(ii) political autonomy regarding abortion	34 N = 340	29	37	29 N = 229	47	24	25 N = 472	27	49

---

[102] In the questionnaire these two items are separated by eight items on human rights.

lence; the largest is that of Muslim youths (37%), while those of Christian and nonreligious youths are identical (28%, 28%).

In the case of item (ii) there are again three minorities. With regard to abortion the sequence of the three minorities that agree with state autonomy is the same as for euthanasia: the biggest is among nonreligious youths, again almost half (49%), followed by Christian youths, twelve percent lower (37%), and finally Muslim youths, thirteen percent lower than Christian youths and less than half the nonreligious minority (24%). Once again there are three minorities opposed to state autonomy. The smallest is again the nonreligious group (25%), followed by the Muslim minority (29%), while the Christian minority is the largest one that rejects political autonomy (34%). Once again there are three minorities displaying ambivalence. Here too the largest is among Muslim youths, almost half (47%), followed by the Christian (29%) and nonreligious minorities (27%).

To determine whether differences between the means of the three groups of youths are statistically significant, we conducted variance analyses (eta) with corresponding Scheffé tests (p < .05). Table 5 reflects the data. The means for political autonomy regarding euthanasia among Christian youths (3.1) and Muslim youths (3.0) are around or in the middle of the five-point scale, indicating ambivalence, while the mean among nonreligious youths indicates agreement (3.4). The means for political autonomy regarding abortion among the Christian group (3.0) and the Muslim group (2.9) are again around or in the middle of the scale, while that of nonreligious youths goes in the direction of agreement (3.3).[103]

It comes as no surprise that the three groups' means for political autonomy in the case of euthanasia differ significantly. But whereas the Christian and Muslim groups' attitudes do not differ significantly, those of Christian and nonreligious youths and those of Muslim and nonreligious youths are significantly different (a, a, b: eta .12). The pattern for abortion is similar. Again the three groups' attitudes differ significantly. Those of Christian and Muslim youths do not differ significantly, but again there are significant differences between the attitudes of the Christian and nonreligious groups and between the Muslim and nonreligious groups (a, a, b; eta .16).

---

[103] In interpreting the means 1.00–1.79 = disagree totally; 1.80–2.59 = disagree; 2.60–2.99 = negative ambivalence; 3.00–3.39 = positive ambivalence; 3.40–4.19 = agree; 4.20–5.00 = agree totally.

Table 5. Attitudes towards the separation of church and state (means)

	Christian		Muslim		Nonreligious		
	mean	sd	mean	sd	mean	sd	eta
(i) political autonomy regarding euthanasia	3.1ᵃ N = 338	1.1	3.0ᵃ N = 231	1.2	3.4ᵇ N = 477	1.2	.12*
(ii) political autonomy regarding abortion	3.0ᵃ N = 340	1.2	2.9ᵃ N = 229	1.1	3.3ᵇ N = 472	1.3	.16*

ᵃᵇ Marked indices in the rows indicate statistically significant differences between means.
* p < .01.

Table 6. Correlations between attitudes towards the separation of church and state (r)

(i) political autonomy regarding euthanasia	(ii) political autonomy regarding abortion		
	Christian	Islamic	Nonreligious
Christian	.61* N = 338		
Islamic		.44* N = 228	
Nonreligious			.61* N = 472

* p < .01.

Because the means for items (i) and (ii) show an analogous sequential pattern among the three groups, we wanted to know to what extent the two items are empirically independent or dependent on one another. To find out, we executed correlation analyses among the three groups (table 6).

This table shows that among the Christian and nonreligious youth, the correlations between item (i) on political autonomy regarding euthanasia and item (ii) on political autonomy regarding abortion are very strong (r .61, .61), but among the Muslim youths they are just strong (r .44). This explains the analogous sequential pattern between the two items.

8.4   Reflection

What causes the disparities between the two religious groups (Christian and Muslim) and the nonreligious group? To answer the question, I refer to the second section on the relation between church and state in the modern period. There I said that religious beliefs can play a significant inspiring and orienting role in political communication in both society and the state, but that in due course these beliefs, whilst retaining their place in the communication, have to be translated into the language of public reason so that all citizens may consider them reasonably acceptable. I also said that once political communication has reached a certain (always provisional) completeness, the state must take an autonomous, maximally impartial decision.

Against the background of this theory on the different roles of church and state, we consider whether the distinction between the political attitudes of the two religious groups and the nonreligious group can be interpreted in terms of role theory.[104] According to this theory, we are dealing with two role senders that touch the area of *res mixtae*, namely the church and the state. Both of them have certain role expectations of the members who belong to their communities and institutions. Role expectations concern things that role senders think their members should or should not do. Religions expect believers to act according to their leaders' precepts. The state expects citizens to concur with public reason and recognise its autonomy. More concretely, we need to ask a further question: do nonreligious youths fulfil the political role of citizens better than religious youths, because the latter's religious communities do not (fully) recognise the state's autonomy and because their role expectations interfere with accepting the separation of church and state associated with that autonomy?

A counter argument could be that for the past half century there has been growing secularisation, and that even among Muslims the new generation is increasingly distancing itself from the mosque.[105] In view of this, can we really expect them to see themselves as role players

---

[104] A. Visser et al. (eds.), *Rollen, persoonlijke en sociale invloeden op het gedrag*, Boom, Meppel 1983.

[105] CBS, *Religie aan het begin van de 21ste eeuw*, Centraal Bureau voor de Statistiek, Den Haag 2009.

who are substantially influenced by the expectations of their religious communities as role senders? It may seem inconceivable, but it is not, at any rate not in terms of Fernand Braudel's distinction between the surface, middle, and deep levels of history.[106] The surface level comprises current events (*événements*) in contemporary history; the middle level consists of trends over 50 to 100 years, and the depth level of the long-term (*longue durée*) structure over a period of up to four centuries. In these terms one can say that over generations religious communities have left such a profound mark on the historical relation between church and state that, consciously and unconsciously, they have influenced their members' affectively loaded thought patterns right down to their roots in the collective memory, and up to a point, if to a lesser extent, they continue to do so. The widely observed institutional dissociation from religious communities does not and cannot mean that these thought patterns, perpetuated from fathers and mothers to their sons and daughters, from one generation to the next, have been whittled down to the point of extinction. After all, dissociation from institutional structures does not mean relinquishing the corresponding mental and cultural patterns. Applied to the point at issue here, it concerns the mental and cultural rather than the institutional-structural aspects of long-term relations between church and state.[107]

Against this background, I first examine church-state relations in Christian communities with the focus on the Catholic Church, for two reasons. The first is that historically the Catholic Church has expressed the most explicit views on the relation between church and state, and continues to do so – more strongly and explicitly than the other Christian churches that have less powerful and extensive administrative machinery and are also more divided on the issue. The second reason is that the majority of the Christian youths in our research group are Catholics: 206 of the 340 Christian youths (61%), while there is probably a sub-group of youths from Catholic homes among others that call themselves Christian (29%). The rest define themselves as Protestant (10%). After describing the Catholic Church's notions of the separation of church and state, I shall look at those of Muslim communities.

---

[106] F. Braudel, *Écrits sur l'histoire*, Flammarion, Paris 1969.
[107] See the previous chapter, section 7.4.

8.4.1 *Catholic Church*

Traditionally the Catholic Church, which has engaged in fiercer and more frequent competitive struggles with the state than any other church, based itself on a society comprising two judicial corporations, church and state, which are conceptualised organistically: each body has a head and members. The church is where the pope, or the bishop acting on his behalf, is the head; the state is where the ruler, emperor, or king is the head.[108] Formerly the two corporations were closely intertwined. In the Middle Ages, for instance, the church was known as *corpus Christi mysticum* and the state as *corpus reipublicae mysticum*; both pope and sovereign were called vicars of Christ (*vicarius Christi*); their respective rings symbolised their bond with their church or their kingdom/principality respectively; and sovereigns had the title of king and priest (*rex et sacerdos*). For the rest, the latter, as human priests (*sacredotes humani*) administering the law, ranked below the divine priests (*sacredotes divini*) administering the sacred.[109]

But since Dante's times, as we have seen, the two gradually disentangled themselves, as Pufendorf clearly indicated. As a result, in most Protestant circles at any rate, the power of the actual king and that of the monarchy were not associated, either directly or indirectly, with any divine law.

In his encyclical *Diuturnum Illud* of 1881, however, pope Leo XIII still assumed not only that the monarchy was divinely instituted, but that the actual king owed his authority to God: after all, he is king by God's grace – a term that still prefixes the title of the Dutch monarch. Hence the monarch had to function according to divine and natural law as well. Because the church, too, was a product of God's will, God was the 'first cause' of both church and state, and both were regarded as mere 'second causes' of legislation and administration, alongside each other and interdependent as soul and body – the church being the soul as the formative principle (*forma*), with the state as the body (*materia*). In his encyclical *Immortale Dei* (1885), Leo XIII calls this the only proper correlative approach, and rejects separation of church and state as counter to God's will and natural law – a fundamental consideration – and because it can only result in anarchy – a utilitarian

---

108 Kantorowicz, *The King's Two Bodies*, op. cit., 193ff., 204ff.
109 Kantorowicz, *The King's Two Bodies*, op. cit., 119–122, 207–212.

consideration. The idea that the church should be regarded as no more than one among many associations in society was abominable to him. In his view, it would mean that the church lost its jurisdiction over all kinds of legal affairs, especially marriage and education, both being crucial in the organisation and development of, and power over, state and society. Without the church there could be no faith, and without faith no morality, while without morality – in the pope's assessment – disaster was imminent. Accordingly, the rights claimed since the revolutions of the late 18th century from both church and state – those of the *ancien régime* – such as freedom of conscience, expression, religion, and education, should be repudiated if they are not anchored in 'true' freedom, tested by the truth of God and natural law, as the pope put it in his encyclical *Libertas Praestantissimum* of 1888. Forty years later, following Leo XIII's encyclical *Rerum Novarum* (1891), Pius XI still tried to resuscitate the medieval notion of the one *societas christiana* in his encyclical *Quadragesimo Anno* (1931). To this end he used terms like '*societas perfecta*', suggesting that the church was no less, if not more, perfect than the state. He did so in an almost polemological spirit, calling on Catholics to fight as Christ's soldiers for the kingdom of Christ the king, but his attempt had no (lasting) impact.[110]

To this day, as noted already, the Catholic Church has refrained from assenting to the separation of church and state. The reasons are not only the deep mark that the belief in the undifferentiated unity of church and state has left over a history of over a thousand years, a belief in which many successive generations were brought up and probably continue to hold. Apart from this historical fact there is a legal consideration. As an ecclesiastic state – Vatican City – the church is on an equal footing with other states. Separation of church and state pertains to national, intrastatal relations, not to international law, which affects international, interstatal relations. The range of the Catholic Church goes beyond national relations. As an ecclesiastic state, Vatican City

---

[110] The development of the concept of a *societas perfecta* is to be seen as a counterweight to the powerful expansion of the state in various countries, where it sought to subordinate the church to its secular authority – as in Gallicanism, a 17th century form of conciliarism in France, Febronianism in Germany and Josephinism in Austria, and again later during the French revolution and even later under the *Kulturkampf*, initiated in Germany by Bismarck (1871–1890), which resulted *inter alia* in the codification of canon law in 1917; cf. R. Torfs, The Roman Catholic Church and Secular Legal Culture in the Twentieth Century, *Studia Historiae Ecclesiasticae* 25(1999)1, 1–20.

is sovereign under international public law. According to article 1 of its constitution, the pope is head of state with full legislative, administrative, and judicial power. Since the 15th century, the ecclesiastic state has maintained diplomatic relations with numerous countries, with whom it has made treaties and concordats right up to our time, for instance in Europe (including Eastern Europe) and Latin America.[111] Separation of church and state simply does not fit into such a framework. Instead the church, because of its structure, institutions, ideas, and interests, lacks the conditions and talent to recognise separation of church and state as an intrinsic value and has merely adapted to it as a pragmatic *modus vivendi*.[112]

The Vatican II constitution *Gaudium et Spes* (no. 76), in keeping with a long tradition, does underscore the interdependence of church and state, but reserves a special prerogative in regard to morality: "It is only right, however, that at all times and in all places, the Church should have true freedom to preach the faith, to teach her social doctrine, to exercise her role freely among men, and also to pass moral judgment in those matters which regard public order when the fundamental rights of a person or the salvation of souls require it." The fifth word in this quotation, 'however',[113] has a defensive ring and is actually misplaced, for the church has always had the right to pass moral judgments, not only as a moral right but also legally in terms of religious freedom as laid down in international public law. The 'however' may be understood as the church's reaction against political totalitarianism that seeks to exercise control over everything in society, including morality.[114] Possibly, like Jacques Maritain, it is defending itself against idolatry of the sovereignty of the state[115] – the state in Hobbes's sense of 'the mortal God': "The multitude so united in one person is called commonwealth, in Latin civitas. This is the generation of that great

---

[111] G. Barberini, Religious Freedom in the Process of Democratization of Central and Eastern European States, in: S. Ferrari, W.C. Durham, Jr. & E.A. Sewell (eds.), *Law and Religion in Post-Communist Europe*, Peters, Leuven 2003, 7–22.

[112] J. Habermas, Ein Bewusstsein von dem was fehlt, in: Reder & Schmidt (eds.), *Ein Bewusstsein*, op. cit., 26–36.

[113] The second word in the Latin text: '*autem*'.

[114] R. la Valle, Het leven van de politieke gemeenschap, in: G. Baraúna (ed.), *De kerk in de wereld van nu: Commentaren op de pastorale constitutie 'Gaudium et Spes'*, Nelissen, Bilthoven 434–465, here 456.

[115] La Valle, Het leven, op. cit., 456.

Leviathan, or rather, to speak more reverently, of that mortal God to which we owe, under the immortal God, our peace and defence."[116] Such a reaction is understandable against the then still all-powerful communist states, but not – either then or now – against a democratic, constitutional state. After all, morality falls under the state's negative obligation not to interfere in the area of conscience, religion, and belief (Universal Declaration of Human Rights, article 18).

The question the Catholic Church has always raised is whether citizens have a right to defend themselves when the state exceeds its powers and oppresses them, which can and in fact does happen in constitutional democracies as well. Naturally they have that right, was the answer as far back as the time of Thomas Aquinas, following a long tradition dating back to Aristotle, when not just one but many laws meet with unanimous opposition from citizens who consider them unjust. Unjust laws are invalid, hence opposition to a despotic government is permissible, at any rate if it does not result in even greater harm.[117] But by what norms should such resistance be regulated and how are they legitimised? *Gaudium et Spes* offers an answer to this question, in which the church once again sets itself up as sole guardian and guarantor of morality, but without at the same time translating "in due time" in terms of public reason. It says that in such cases "it is legitimate for them [citizens] to defend their own rights and the rights of their fellow citizens against the abuse of this authority, while keeping within those limits drawn by the natural law and the Gospels" (no. 74). There is nothing wrong with citizens deriving motivation and strength from natural law and the gospels to oppose abuses by the state – on the contrary, those who struggled and are still struggling against racist oppression of the black population do so, and quite rightly. But it should not stop there, since both natural law, whatever universally human pretensions it may have historically, and the gospels, however much they may be intended for all human beings, are among the particular comprehensive beliefs of the Catholic Church. Natural law has lost

---

[116] La Valle, Het leven, op. cit., 456; Th. Hobbes, *Leviathan*, II, 17; see for the state as 'the mortal God' in relation with the problem of the church's spiritual power as indirect power (*potestas indirecta*): M. Terpstra, De politieke theologie van een *potestas indirecta*, in: M. Becker (red.), Christelijk Sociaal Denken, Traditie, Actualiteit, Kritiek, Damon, Budel 2009, 197–222.

[117] STh II-II 42, 2, ad 3; See: B. Delfgaauw, *Thomas van Aquino: Een kritische benadering van zijn filosofie*, Wereldvenster, Bussum 1980, 164–173.

its universal validity.[118] And the recognition of a plurality of existential beliefs means that, from a political point of view, the same applies to the gospels. Hence religious resistance inspired by natural law and the gospel needs to be translated in terms of public reason that underlies the democratic state, which in its turn is based on international public law. This enables all citizens, Christian and non-Christian alike, to see the defence as reasonably justified.

8.4.2 Islam

As for Islam, here the relation between religion and politics displays various parallels with premodern and early modern Christianity, the difference being that Islam did not and still does not have a religious administrative centre to impose uniformity as the West had at that time. According to Mohammed Ayoob, religion and politics were separated soon after the prophet's death, but where they do converge and overlap, religion is used to legitimise the political dynasty and effectively subordinated to politics, at any rate under the three great Sunni dynasties, the Umayyads, the Abbasids, and the Ottomans. The theocratic model is usually a fiction, even a myth, to hide the fact that Islam is used for political purposes.[119]

The perennial question is whether Islam is compatible with a democratic political structure. This is understandable, because the democracy imported from the West is a new political configuration for Muslim countries, as it is for all postcolonial and non-Western countries. A fair number of these countries have only been experimenting with it since the latter half of the 20th century – a process that took the West several centuries. But however understandable, the question is often asymmetrical, as if democracy is a uniform, immutable phenomenon, and the bureaucratic, elite-directed, individually, and market-oriented Western democracy is above criticism, and, on the other hand, as if Islam is a uniform, invariable phenomenon and the history of its

---

[118] Outside the Catholic Church natural law hardly features in the approach to moral and/or judicial problems. That applies not only to the majority of other Christian churches but also to, for example, present-day Islam; cf. Khaled Abou El Fadl, Islam and the Challenge of Democratic Commitment, in: E. Bucar & B. Barnett (eds.), *Does Human Rights Need God?* Eerdmans, Grand Rapids 2005, 58–103, here 93–97; one exception is A. Ezzati, *Islam and Natural Law*, Icas, London 2002.

[119] M. Ayoob, *The Many Faces of Political Islam: Religion and Politics in the Muslim World*, University of Michigan Press, Ann Arbor 2008, 10–17.

political philosophy contains no elements of consultation, participation and democracy.[120] The asymmetry stems from a kind of essentialist, a-historical thinking based on an antagonistic premise that reads: the more Muslim countries as political structures drift away from the absolutist 'golden age of the caliphs', the less the belief in God's activity in history matters and the greater the chance that a democratic structure may develop.[121]

Whether the imputation of asymmetry is warranted or not depends on the perspective one takes: that of the actual political status quo or of present-day political attitudes among the people. From the perspective of the actual political status quo in many countries, the imputation is understandable. Most Islamic countries regard Islam as both religion and state and entrench it as a state religion. While the accent is on God's sovereignty as a legitimisation of political leaders' actions, it has the (unintended) effect that they are not (necessarily) accountable to the people.[122] Politically, divine sovereignty and the sovereignty of the people are clearly ill-matched if not mutually exclusive, but the solution offered by some scholars is reminiscent of the Catholic thesis-hypothesis doctrine referred to above, although Muslim scholars do not use these terms. According to them, when Muslims represent a majority, the Islamic state is the ideal and obligatory (in the traditional Catholic doctrine, the thesis). Where Muslims are a minority, they have to adapt to the prevailing political system, hence they have to support the democratic state and actively contribute to it (in the traditional Catholic doctrine, the hypothesis). On the other hand, there are scholars that defend the democratic state roundly, a major argument being that Islam is not religion and state, but solely religion, and that the prophet's mission was not political but spiritual. In their view, his political activity was historically bound. The conjunction of Islam

[120] A. Bayat, *Islam and Democracy*, Amsterdam University Press, Amsterdam 2007; M. Leezenberg, *Islamitische filosofie: Een geschiedenis*, Amsterdam University Press, Amsterdam 2002.

[121] S. Zemni, Islam, European Identity and the Limits of Multiculturalism, in: W. Shadid & P. van Koningsveld (eds.), *Religious Freedom and the Neutrality of the State: The position of Islam in the European Union*, Peeters, Leuven 2002, 158–173.

[122] According to M. Slackman, Ayatollah Khomeini based the founding of the Republic of Iran on two contradictory principles: one of public accountability and one of religious authority. From the start this led to intense disagreements, which were muted partly by Ayatollah Khomeini's 'exalted status' and by a unity forged by an eight-year war with Iraq. When the Ayatollah died the conflicts erupted (International Herald Tribune September 9, 2009).

and state, they believe, is deleterious to Islam and harms its essence. Hence it is in Islam's own interest (as well) to separate itself from the state.[123]

From the perspective of present-day political attitudes among the people, research shows no significant disparity between the attitudes of inhabitants of Western and Muslim countries towards democracy and human rights.[124] Large groups of Muslims in countries like Jordan, Indonesia, and Egypt see good prospects for democracy in Muslim countries, while Muslims in Germany, France, the United Kingdom, and Spain are even more convinced on that score.[125] There is also a political movement in some Muslim countries towards democracy and human rights, for instance in two non-Arab countries, Turkey and Indonesia.[126] But that does not mean that most Muslims see an inverse proportional relation between democracy and the shari'a, as if when democracy expands shari'a declines. Research shows that many people in Muslim countries believe that democracy can function perfectly well in their countries and at the same time indicate that Islam plays a major role in politics, for instance in Morocco and Indonesia.[127] From their attitudinal stance, they ignore any asymmetry, if it exist.

Against this background, it is understandable that most Muslims do not consider separation of church and state, as a principle of constitutional democracy, necessary for their quality of life or for further

---

[123] M. Rohe, *Das Islamische Recht: Geschichte und Gegenwart*, Beck, München 2009, 243–254. A.A. An-Na'im, *Islam and the Secular State, Negotiating the Future of Shari'a*, Harvard University Press, Cambridge 2008, 270, argues for an 'inclusive approach', including both a separation between Islam and state and, at the same time, a flexible interactive connectedness between Islam and politics. The first implies the autonomy of the state, i.e. the secular state, which guarantees the freedom of religion, including the freedom to change religion altogether, and protects religious minorities; the second provides for both the nurturing of politics by religion and the regulation of religion by politics.

[124] D. Price, *Islamic Political Culture: Democracy and Human Rights*, Westpoint 1999; P. Norris & R. Inglehart, *Secular and Sacred*, Cambridge University Press, Cambridge 2005, 145, table 6.3; T. Pettersson, Religious Commitment and Socio-Political Orientations: Different Patterns of Compartimentalisation among Muslims and Christians?, in: J. Haynes (ed.), *Routledge Handbook of Religion and Politics*, Routledge, New York 2009, 246–269. But in their research Norris and Inglehart show that Western and Muslim populations differ in their approval of gender equality, homosexuality, abortion, and divorce (150–151, table 6.4).

[125] Pew Global Attitudes Project, *The Great Divide: How Westerners and Muslims View Each Other*, released 22.06.06; www.pewglobal.org/reports

[126] Ayoob, *The Many Faces*, op. cit.

[127] Pew Global Attitudes Project, *Islamic Extremism: Common Concern for Muslim and Western Publics*, released 14.07.05, 2; www.pewglobal.org/reports

development of the Muslim world. They regard the shari'a as just one of the sources of legislation. In most Muslim countries only a minority claims to regard the shari'a as the sole source of legislation or would like to see spiritual leaders play a substantial role in compiling a constitution.[128]

That does not detract from the reality of at least two fundamental obstacles to the introduction of full constitutional democracy. The first is the inequality between men and women.[129] The report of the 2006 United Nations Development Programme (UNDP) states that women, despite equal status under international public law, are not encouraged to develop and use their talents in the same way as men are. In public life there are legal, cultural, social, economic, and political factors that impede their equal access to education, health care, job opportunities, civil rights, and democratic representation. In private life, traditional upbringing and discriminatory family and personal law perpetuate inequality and subordination. At the same time there is a widespread desire for equality.[130] The second obstacle is inequality between religions, specifically the position of religious minorities. They likewise suffer under social and political inequality and oppression. Often the highest attainable ideal is the classical notion of tolerance, which does entail a duty to protect minorities but is a long way from the right to religious freedom, which entitles all citizens, whatever their religion or worldview, to manifest their belief, alone or in community with others, and in public or in private.[131] Nonetheless, there is growing awareness, among minorities and larger parts of the population as well, that there has to be an end to religious discrimination.

One may question the political force of such desires, yet one must not underestimate the influence on such developments exercised by large groups of Muslims living in Europe. These groups, who settled in Europe in different periods, obey the Islamic law that commands Muslims to abide by the laws of the countries where they are living. Since European countries are constitutional democracies, they learn to adapt to democratically enacted laws. Their obedience does not stem only

---

[128] J. Esposito & D. Mogahed, *Who Speaks for Islam? What a Billion Muslims Really Think*, Gallup, New York 2007; Gallup Poll, *Muslim World*, World Poll, Gallup Center Muslim Studies 2008.

[129] Rohe, *Das Islamische Recht*, op. cit., 254–255.

[130] UNDP, *Arab Human Development Report*, December 2008.

[131] Rohe, *Das Islamische Recht*, op. cit., 255–258.

from the fact that they regard their residence as based on a 'sacred' contract that has to be observed, but also from the basic security and protection that the constitutions and laws of Western countries offer them.[132] The vast majority of European Muslims appear to abide by these laws; only a small minority does not respect them. This is evident in research in London, Paris, and Berlin, where Muslims identify with their country of residence just as much as the rest of the population of these cities.[133] A public text like the Muslims of Europe Charter of 2002 goes even further. It not only expresses agreement with human rights, including religious freedom, but also states that Muslims in Europe adhere to the principle of state neutrality in regard to religious matters (art. 18). Their respect for the religious and worldview-related pluralism of the multicultural societies in which they live is emphasised (art. 22). It is not clear whether this expresses a conviction that democracy, including state neutrality and pluralism, is an intrinsic value. Heiner Bielefedt, for example, claims that the vast majority of Muslims merely tolerate the secular state as long as religious freedom is guaranteed.[134] If so, their respect stems from pragmatic, opportunistic considerations suggestive of a certain *modus vivendi* rather than recognition of its intrinsic value. In terms of the aforementioned parallel with the Catholic doctrine of thesis and hypothesis, the view of a scholar like the Tunisian Rachid Ghannouchi is understandable. He maintains that Muslims have a duty to establish a true – democratic – Muslim state, but when they are in the minority they should cooperate with the secular democracy, especially with its power of enforcement in regard to religious freedom.[135]

One infers that both the Catholic Church and Islam reflect acceptance of separation of church and state as a *modus vivendi* rather than out of regard for its intrinsic value. In view of this, is it not surprising that the attitudinal mean scores among Christian and Muslim youths are in or around the middle of the scale, as the research in the previous section shows. They are ambivalent about state autonomy, specifically

---

[132] B. Parekh, *European Liberalism and 'the Muslim Question'*, Amsterdam University Press, Amsterdam 2008.

[133] European Muslims show no conflict between religious and national identities, Gallup Poll, World Poll, *Special Report: Muslims in Europe* 2008.

[134] H. Bielefeldt, Political Secularism and European Islam, in: J. Malik (ed.), *Muslims in Europe*, Lit, Münster 2004, 147–160.

[135] Rohe, *Das Islamische Recht*, op. cit., 245.

in regard to such sensitive *res mixtae* as euthanasia and abortion. The nonreligious group does not share the concerns of the religious communities. They agree with political autonomy (table 5). Of course, not all Christian and Muslim youths are (equally) ambivalent. There are three kinds of minorities in the two groups. Relatively large minorities agree with state autonomy, hence they differ more or less from the ideas of their religious communities, which ignore, gloss over or keep quiet about it. There are smaller minorities whose attitudes do accord with the views of their religious communities in that they reject political autonomy when it comes to euthanasia and abortion. Then there are minorities of varying size that explicitly indicate ambivalence, in that they are somewhere between rejection and acceptance, hence find themselves between the rejection and agreement that their religious communities show. These minorities are largest among Muslim youths (table 4).

Conclusion

Boniface VIII's conception of state subordination to the church and his defence of the church's interests and values are history. In the meantime, the roles have been completely reversed, especially since the Peace of Augsburg in 1555 and that of Westphalia in 1648, to the extent that the church, in terms of the slogan 'whose the territory, his the religion' (*cuius regio eius religio*), was all but totally subordinated to the state. Such subordination one way or another drew to a close in the modern era as a result of functional differentiation in society, which put an end to any form of subordination. This process of functional differentiation led to the emergence of diverse institutions and programmes in various autonomous systems such as the economic, political, social, cultural, and religious systems, each operating according to its own codes and the concomitant norms but without preventing or impeding interpenetration of systems and institutions. The *res mixtae* is a telling example.

Church-state relations are marked by two principles that present a kind of mirror image of each other. Whereas religious freedom entails the state's negative obligation not to meddle in religious affairs, separation of church and state implies that religious communities recognise the state's autonomy. The rationale for the second principle is that the plurality of religious and nonreligious worldviews does not permit state privileging of any one of these. All comprehensive beliefs, whether religious or nonreligious, are equal before the law, including those of religious and nonreligious minorities. The state should act as impartially as possible towards all world views. The only way it can do so is to render legislative and judicial measures in terms of public reason.

The results of our empirical research into the acceptance of the separation of church and state present a picture that anything but corresponds with the idea of impartial public reason and state autonomy. Granted, the issues of euthanasia and abortion are probably the most stringent test conceivable in this area. In all kinds of other areas the youths we researched would have shown far greater agreement with this idea, for example in the area of equal rights for men and women. Euthanasia and abortion affect fundamental values in individual and social life. They also affect the very aims of both state and church. If there is one issue that concerns the state, and primarily the state, it is that of offering security when it comes to the right to life. At the same time, if there is one issue that pertains to the very foundations of comprehensive beliefs, especially religious ones, it is that of birth and death. In the state's case it is a fundamental basic value, for ultimately its supreme goal is to protect life. In the case of religious communities, this value is imbedded in a broad network of profound convictions, both religious and moral, as well as age-old ritual programs conducted in the perspective of a transcendent reality surpassing all other domains, including politics. It is understandable that in an area so fundamental to both the state and religion, religious freedom and state autonomy would show a dialectical, tense relationship. From that perspective the double language game we referred to in the second section of this chapter is needed as a *conditio sine qua non*. It is a fallacy to reduce the double language game to just one side of it, be it the language of religion or that of the state. 'The' language of religion does not suffice, because there is no such thing as religion per se: all we have are religions (plural), along with nonreligious comprehensive beliefs. To do justice to that plurality, we need the state's public reason. But the language of the state is equally inadequate. It lacks the 'compost' of vibrant religious stories, metaphors, and rites that spring from the existential depths of human life, inspiring and orienting the purpose of life and assigning suffering and death a place in a transcendental framework. The languages of religion and the state cannot be reduced to each other. Both need to be maintained in societal and political communication.

Here there are two important insights. The first is that it would be a lethal blow to religions if their beliefs were to be stripped of their religious transcendent aspects, retaining only ethical teleological or even only moral deontological judgments, as Habermas proposes.[136] This misconception was explicitly fostered by the champions of public reason as the vehicle of a pluralistic state.[137] It was and is also influenced by proponents of a separationist interpretation of church-state relations, who rather defended a fictional ideology than supported legitimate historical and actual developments from a balanced view, as we have seen. The second insight is that religious communities for their part may have to learn to view truth from two different perspectives. The first is the religious inside perspective, in terms of which their truth is covered by claims to uniqueness, universality, and absoluteness. The other is the outside perspective of political reason, in terms of which the political implications of these claims need to be translated into language that is reasonably understandable and reasonably acceptable to all believers of every religion and to nonreligious citizens without arguing from a position of authority. The two perspectives are only reconcilable if truth claims are regarded as human approximations of truth that are fallible and in need of constant reassessment, reinterpretation, amplification, and correction, as in the Catholic Church's self-evaluation: it is a church that is both holy and in need of continual purification.[138] Its holiness in fact consists in ongoing reform.[139] This precludes any prohibition of critical communication, discussion, and debate, since they are vital for such 'holy' reform. Such an attitude is prerequisite if religions, above all the Catholic Church, are to participate plausibly in broad societal and political debate. Without such a dialogical attitude, they lose their social legitimacy. It requires a free church in a free state (*Église libre dans l'État libre*), a slogan coined by Montalembert in the mid-19th century and appropriated by the Austrian church in the Mariazeller manifesto in 1952.[140] Such a free

---

[136] Reder, Glaube und Vernunft, art. cit., 58.

[137] This applies particularly to Rawls's earlier publications, among which are the previous editions of his *Political Liberalism*.

[138] Constitution of the Second Vatican Council, *Lumen Gentium*, no. 8.

[139] E. Schillebeeckx, *Zending van de kerk*, Nelissen, Bilthoven 1968, 11–24.

[140] L. Christoffersen, Religion as a Factor in Multi-Layered European Union Legislation, in: R. Mehdi et al. (eds.), *Law and Religion in Multicultural Societies*, Djøf,

church in a free state and – I would add – in a free society can only emerge if religions, more especially the Catholic Church, accept the autonomy of the state not merely pragmatically as a *modus vivendi* but recognise it as an intrinsic value. Until that happens, religious freedom and state autonomy will remain a bone of contention. That means that religious communities still have a long way to go.

Copenhagen 2008, 111–130, here 112; R. Potz, *Freie Kriche in der Freien Gesellschaft – Vor 50 jahren und heute*, Referat bei der Enquete '50 jahre Mariazeller Manifest, 7.10.2002; http://www.laienrat.at/_alte_website/potz.htm

IMPACT OF RELIGION ON ATTITUDES TOWARD RELIGIOUS FREEDOM AND THE SEPARATION OF CHURCH AND STATE

I have dealt with the process of functional differentiation between religion, morality, politics, and law when it comes to religious freedom and the separation of church and state. Over the centuries, this process has left deep marks on society, in the course of which the sacred canopy, where all institutions were interlinked under God as the apex and keystone, was relegated to the past. Modern, differentiated systems fulfil separate functions: economic, political, judicial, social, cultural, moral, religious, and others. They have three cardinal features. Firstly, each has its own codes, media, organisations, and programmes. Secondly, they have criteria of inclusion and exclusion. These no longer consist in membership of estates or classes as grounds for inclusion or exclusion, but in certain requirements regarding education, occupation, and competence. Thirdly, the systems exist independently and reproduce themselves according to their own codes and programmes, but that does not mean that they have no mutual relevance. They interpenetrate each other inasmuch as the information of the one system is intelligible to another system, in the sense that the former transforms its information into terms of the codes of the latter, so that the latter can link up with existing information in its own programmes. If not, the information is unrecognisable, meaningless, and no more than background noise.[1]

While all systems have difficulty establishing such links, it is particularly complicated in the case of religion, for two reasons. The first reason is factual. The various systems are dynamic, not static. They are marked by processes of expansion and limitation in society as a whole. In modern times, the influence of the monetary, economic, political, and judicial systems has increased markedly, while that of the religious system has been curtailed (de-sacralisation). As a result, religion has

---

[1] N. Luhmann, *Die Gesellschaft der Gesellschaft*, Vol. I–II, Suhrkamp, Frankfurt am Main 1998.

lost many of its relations with the other systems and its sphere of influence has shrunk.[2]

The second reason is substantive. It relates to the distinctive and critical character of its code, immanence and transcendence, compared to the codes of the other systems. Its distinctive character may be clarified in the following way.[3] The codes of some other, important systems are profit and loss in the economic system, power and opposition in the political system, legal and illegal in the juridical system, competence and incompetence in the educational system, true and false in the scientific system, and good and evil in the moral system. All these codes comprise a positive value and a negative value, such as profit/loss, power/opposition, legal/ilegal, competence/incompetence, true/false or good/evil. The religious code, too, contains a positive value and a negative counter value. The positive value is immanence, the negative value is transcendence, in terms of which all immanence is considered contingent. In the religious code, however, the two values are not mutually exclusive counter values, as in the other codes, but mutually inclusive counter values. They are implicational in that they paradoxically imply each other. After all, immanence is where the transcendent manifests itself, but also surpasses the immanent without in the process invalidating it. Such an implicational relationship between counter values is not found in the economic, political, judicial, and moral codes. Economic profit is not manifested in bankruptcy, political power in political loss, legal practice in illegal practice, true research in false research, or good actions in evil actions. These counter values are mutually exclusive; they negate each other. Only the religious code is marked by an implicational relationship. Immanence and transcendence are mutually inclusive, because the immanent includes traces of the transcendent, contains references to the transcendent, opens up angles on the transcendent, offers a perspective to it. So religious people testify to the transcendent while enjoying immanent experiences in nature, friendship and love, meditations into their inner self, or actions of solidarity with 'the least of mine'.

---

[2] Luhmann, *Die Gesellschaft*, II, 757.

[3] N. Luhmann, *Die Religion der Gesellschaft*, Suhrkamp, Frankfurt 2002; R. Laermans & G. Verschraegen, The 'Late Niklas Luhmann' on Religion: An Overview, *Social Compass* 48(2001)1,7–20, point out that Luhmann's sociology largely centres on the Christian religion.

This distinctive character of the religious code, which makes it different from the other systems' codes, relates with its critical character. The mutual inclusion of immanence and transcendence prevents the transcendent to be absorbed in the immanent. The transcendent is experientially approachable from the immanent and can be articulated in terms of the immanent, but never exhaustively. There always is a transcendent 'rest', which always surpasses the immanent. To put this otherwise, the transcendent is present in the immanent, but at the same time exceeds it, while giving way into an even receding horizon.[4] In a nutshell, the transcendent is present in the immanent by continuously coordinating its absence from it.[5] From this paradox of being present and absent at the same time, a critical stance towards the immanent emerges, because from the perspective of the transcendent the immanent is considered contingent, incidental, provisional, limited, finite, non-absolute. From there, all immanent phenomena in all other systems, like the economic, political or juridical system, can be relativised, exposed, criticised. In this perspective, religion may criticise, via the moral loading it carries with it, social abuses and evils in other systems, such as greed in finance and economy, corruption in politics, partisanship in law, prejudice in the administration of justice, doping in sport, merchandising in love, and fraudulence in science (more about that later).[6] All of this makes the religious code, immanence and transcendence, both distinctive and critical.

Considering its distinctive and critical nature, is it at all possible for the religious system to connect with other systems? And does it in fact manage to do so? Does religion actually penetrate into the other systems? Finally, the cardinal question in this chapter: how does religion actively influence the other systems, here the legal system and, more particularly, the legal culture, especially the human rights culture as far as this consists of attitudes towards religious freedom and the separation of church and state?

These questions must be approached step by step. First we must determine how religion, via morality, influences the other systems, more particularly the legal-cultural subsystem, and what role its soteriological orientation plays in this regard (9.1). Then the general question is specified: what aspects of religions influence the other systems,

---

[4] Luhmann, *Die Religion*, op. cit., 77–92.
[5] P. Ricoeur, *Figuring the Sacred, Religion, Narrative and Imagination*, Fortress, Minneapolis 1995, 217–235.
[6] See for morality: Luhmann, *Die Gesellschaft*, op. cit., II, 1043.

i.e. the legal-cultural subsystem? The answer of the so-called axial religions, which include Christianity and Islam, is this: religious beliefs and religious rites (9.2). On this basis we formulate certain hypotheses about the influence of religious beliefs and rites on this subsystem, which refers to religious freedom and the separation of church and state in particular (9.3). Then we turn to our empirical study. The first step of our empirical research is to measure the religious beliefs and rites among the three groups of Christian, Muslim, and nonreligious youths (9.4) The second empirical step is to measure the effects of religious beliefs and rites on the youths' attitudes towards religious freedom and the separation of church and state (9.5). Finally we reflect on our findings (9.6).

9.1 Religion, Morality and Law: A Soteriological Orientation

The point at issue concerns the way religion, via morality, links up with the other systems, more particularly the legal-cultural subsystem, and what role its soteriological orientation plays. To this end, we look at three factors: the connection between religion and morality, the connection between morality and law, and finally, the translation of this connection in soteriological terms.

Firstly, the connection between the religious system with its immanent/transcendent code and the other systems, including the generation of religious information and its recognition by the other systems, takes place via the link that religion has established, at any rate in the West, with morality.[7] It entails a combination of the immanent/transcendent code with that of moral good/evil.[8] Transcendence that, from a religious perspective, is manifested in immanence, is revealed

---

[7] See N. Luhmann, Soziale Systeme: Grundriss einer allgemeinen Theorie, Suhrkamp, Frankfurt 1984, 286ff., for the triad *generation of information* by system A, *recognition* of that information by system B, for which that information has to be translated into the terms of system B in order to be understood by system B, and *connection* of that information with the information already present in system B.

[8] Here I do not dwell on Luhmann's claim in *Die Religion*, op. cit., 182–183, that morality does not represent a separate system alongside the economic, political, legal, and religious systems, since, whilst it has its own code (good/evil), it has not reached consensus on its own programme and cannot guarantee its enforceability. Also see N. Luhmann, *Paradigm lost: Über die ethische Reflexion der Moral*, Suhrkamp, Frankfurt 1990.

in people's good actions, while bad actions indicate disregard of transcendence-in-immanence.[9] Morality as such has no need of religion,
but religion needs morality and makes use of it. For the sake of clarity,
this idea conflicts with the history of Judaism, Christianity, and Islam,
whose inside perspective has always intrinsically linked religion with
morality. In their prophetic critique, they have constantly protested
against negligence towards the *personae miserae*: widows, orphans,
aliens, and the poor. But ours is not a historical overview. We are
simply providing an analytical reconstruction of the relation between
religion and morality from a modern perspective. From an analytic
perspective, Luhmann calls the historical symbiosis of religion and
morality an artefact. Symbiosis implies that the two partners need each
other, which, analytically, is not true of religion and morality: religion
needs morality, but not the other way round.[10]

The combination of the religious and moral codes is the interface
with the other systems, including the economy, politics, law and
education. That is where religion may penetrate and influence them,
provided it attunes its information to these systems' information via
morality. In the process, it converts the combination of religious and
moral information into criticism of and protest against things like
greedy accumulation of property and wealth in the financial and economic system, corruption in the political system, partisan legislation
and administration of justice in the juridical system, pedagogic neglect
in the family system, dominance of instrumental and target-related
rationality (*Zweckrationalität*) in the educational system, vulgarisa-
tion in the cultural system, and depletion and pollution in the eco-
logical system. Morality forms the bridge between the religious system
and the other systems, from where the religious system may have an
impact on the other systems.

But is this true in the case of the legal system? A link between religion
and morality is conceivable, but is there a link between morality and
law? Some jurists tend to be – to put it mildly – sceptical about that,
because the debate on the relation between law and morality is fraught
with complex problems. In that debate one discerns two extremes.

---

[9] By using the term 'action' I, following Habermas, disagree with Luhmann's
notion that systems theory and action theory are incompatible. The combination of
religion and morality that Luhmann explicitly proposes is not feasible without the
concept of action.

[10] Luhmann, *Die Gesellschaft*, op. cit., I, 241.

One is that law is subordinate to morality. In this view morality is grounded in divine law and/or sacred law imbedded in natural law. Law is seen as the enforceable legal formalisation of moral rights and duties inferred from these sources. The objection to this approach is that, since the dawn of modernity, the sacred canopy has collapsed and religion's social hegemony has made way for functional differentiation of systems – including the juridical system – with their own codes, institutions, and programmes. The other extreme is that law and morality have nothing to do with each other and are rigidly segregated systems. This is the typical approach of legal positivists, who maintain that law is that which has been positivised as law by the competent authority, the law-giver, ultimately independently of any moral insight or consideration whatsoever. Here the objection is that such a view completely separates law from morality, basing it purely on the decisions by the politicians who positivise laws. That leaves the law entirely dependent on politics, without connecting the latter with the regulatory function of morality. It damages both the legitimacy of the law and the legitimacy of politics.[11]

The middle position between the two extremes is that law and morality complement each other. To grasp this, we need to distinguish between legality and legitimacy.[12] The two are interrelated. Legality must have moral legitimacy, since if laws that are not reasonably acceptable, i.e. morally legitimate, citizens will be unable and unwilling to observe them. Conversely, moral legitimacy requires legality, since moral rights and duties can only have an effective regulatory influence if, having been transformed into legal rights and duties, they become legally enforceable.[13]

Moral legitimacy consists not only in acceptance of the law, but more especially in its reasonable acceptability. This apparently minuscule difference is the grounds for the mutability of the law. A law is valid only until it is repealed, that is while it is (reasonably) accepted. In any case, the justification for a law's existence becomes invalid when other and better reasons are found for it, as a result of which it is augmented, amended, corrected, or even repealed. It runs a similar risk when, because of variation and/or change in the spatiotemporal

[11] J. Habermas, *Faktizität und Geltung*, Suhrkamp, Frankfurt 1993, 587–588.
[12] Habermas, *Faktizität*, op. cit., 45–60.
[13] Habermas, *Faktizität*, op. cit., 135–151.

context, new cases emerge that are no longer (entirely) covered by
the reasons hitherto advanced.[14] Hence the moral reasons given for
the reasonable acceptability of a law can have both a stabilising and a
destabilising effect. It implies that in principle morality not only legiti-
mises the juridical status quo but also subjects it to critical scrutiny.

This critical scrutiny stems not only from the fundamental concept
of law, namely justice and its differentiation into commutative, res-
titutive, distributive, legal, and social justice, as well as the complex
relation between justice and equality. It also derives from the relation between justice and goodness. After all, justice is not concerned
solely with equal distribution of material goods, in which deviations
from equality have to be justified.[15] Ultimately, it is a matter of equal
opportunities that permit the development of people's capacity for
meaningful action with a view to the 'good life', a flourishing life
(*eudaimonia*). But that presupposes a theory of the good, in which
meaningful actions are distinguished from their reverse or from indifferent actions.[16] Whichever way we look at it, the 'good life' is at least
implicit in justice arrived at by way of reasonable analysis, if not its
ultimate criterion. The counter argument is the existing plurality of
notions of the good and the individual latitude to which everybody is
entitled, certainly in this respect.[17] However, this does not contradict
the relevance of the notion of 'the good life', but makes its extension –
'the good life of all', 'the common good life' – more complex.

Apart from basic concepts, there are many areas on which moral
reflection on law focuses and where it contributes to the critical legitimisation of law. Here the key question is, broadly, what law is just?
I cite some examples. In labour law, one discerns a trend towards
developing a flexible, employable work force, in which workers are
required to upgrade their own professional standard of employability.
But does the resultant impermanence of the labour relationship not
impair mutual trust and loyalty between employee and employer?[18]
In property law, the question is whether the growing gap between

---

[14] Habermas, *Faktizität*, op. cit., 53–57.
[15] J. Rawls, *A theory of Justice*, Harvard University Press, Cambridge, 1971.
[16] M.C. Nussbaum, *Frontiers of Justice, Disability, Nationality, Species Membership*,
Harvard University Press, Cambridge 2006, 392–401.
[17] N. Mazouz, s.v. Gerechtigkeit, in: M. Düwell et al. (eds.), *Handbuch Ethik*, Metzler, Stuttgart 2006, 373–376.
[18] D. Pessers, *Liefde, solidariteit and recht, Een interdisciplinair onderzoek naar het
wederkerigheidsbeginsel*, University of Amsterdam Press, Amsterdam 1999, 213–216.

rich and poor is reasonably acceptable, also considering the resultant infringement of human dignity and the danger it poses for social integration.[19] In insurance law, the question arises whether a contractual approach can accommodate unpaid assistance given in a home situation to people unable to look after themselves as a result of a physical or mental handicap. There are those who advocate progressive replacement of the contract principle with a care principle, which accords such home help political recognition irrespective of the existence of any contract, and subsidises it financially more generously than at present.[20] In administrative law 'elephantiasis' of government bureaucracy is rampant. The question is often raised whether participation by citizens cannot be increased without impairing the efficiency of the public service, and to what extent the principles of carefulness and motivation need to be applied to look after their values and interests.[21] These are a few examples of the relation between morality and the law.

The combination of the codes of religion, morality, and other systems may appear to rest entirely on the outside perspective of Luhmann's systems theory,[22] while ignoring the inside perspective which is embedded in age-long, intrinsic religious convictions, but this is far from true. Religions themselves, especially the axial religions (more about these later), show signs of such a combination and even have special names for it, such as salvation, redemption, liberation, and reconciliation. These can be subsumed under the term 'salvation' or the Greek derivative, 'soteriology', which is the name of the theological subdiscipline in this field. Soteriological religions explicitly link their code of immanence/transcendence with the moral code of good/evil. The salvation expected from the extramundane reality, God, is considered to occur via people's good actions in their mundane lives. The overall idea is that God's goodness is embodied in good human activities, but without merging into these and without being absorbed by these. Good human endeavour is a necessary but not a sufficient condition for God's salvific work: without its mediation the gift of divine salvation is not efficacious, or at any rate cannot be experienced.[23]

---

[19] K. Kühl, s.v. Recht und Moral, in: Düwell et al. (eds.), *Handbuch Ethik*, op. cit., 487–493.

[20] Nussbaum, *Frontiers of Justice*, op. cit., 96–223.

[21] Pessers, *Liefde*, op. cit., 219–223.

[22] Luhmann, *Die Religion*, op. cit., 69 refers to a *Kombinatorik* of codes.

[23] Currently soteriology has several paradigms: (1) *Jesus crucifixus pro nobis*, (2) substitution, (3) completion of freedom, (4) *communio*, and (5) reconciliation (H. Wagner,

Such a soteriological orientation always entails a process of 'salvation from' leading to 'salvation-to': a *terminus a quo* marked by suffering and distress, which humans want to escape from, and a *terminus
ad quem*, in which they hope to fully consummate their humanity,
free from suffering and trouble. The *terminus a quo* is characterised by
innumerable forms of want: absence of material conditions for a decent
life, like water, food, housing, and property; absence of interpersonal
conditions like trust, bonding, care, and love; absence of social conditions like education, work, health care, and social security; absence
of political conditions like political participation, democracy, and the
rule of law; finally, lack of a goal in life, destiny, and perspective – in
effect, lack of meaning.[24] The *terminus ad quem* is characterised by a
longing for and expectation of assuagement of all these forms of deprivation and the flourishing of the human person from the values of
recognition, justice, and love in the perspective of the 'common good
life'.[25] From this description, one could infer that we are speaking of

---

s.v. Erlösung, IV. Systematisch-theologisch, *Lexikon für Theologie und Kirche* 3, Herder,
Freiburg 1995, 808–812). Political and liberation theology are noted for aspects of
paradigms 3 and 4, with which my approach concurs in a somewhat more abstract
sense. Here I differ from the Catholic doctrine of satisfaction, which derives from the
Jewish Bible and the Second Testament (for satisfaction and atonement, see E. Schillebeeckx, *Gerechtigheid en liefde, genade en bevrijding*, Nelissen, Bloemendaal 1977,
442–446) and was fully developed by Anselm of Canterbury in the 11th century; since
the 16th century, as a result of subjective appropriation of salvation and under the
influence of Jansenism, it has evolved into the doctrine of purely divine grace. I also
dissociate myself from a purely personalistic soteriology practised since the advent of
nouvelle théologie, in which salvation entails telling others about Jesus' act of salvation
on the cross as a gift of divine love (see B. Willems & R. Weier, Soteriologie: von der
Reformation bis zur Gegenwart, *Handbuch der Dogmengeschichte*, vol. III, 2c, Herder,
Freiburg 1972) and which is still propounded by G. O'Collins, *Jesus Our Redeemer: A
Christian Approach to Salvation*, Oxford University Press, Oxford 2007. My approach
aims at avoiding two soteriological extremes: that of absolutely transcendent salvation
by God alone and that of purely religious self-salvation.

[24] Compare the exposition in M. Weber, *Wirtschaft und Gesellschaft*, Mohr, Tübingen 1980, 285–314, especially 307–308, which analyses soteriological religions in terms
of their association with specific classes and groups: on the one hand the economically
and politically underprivileged groups, on the other the intellectual groups without
economic and political power, whose ideas filter through to the masses, the former
striving for liberation from external need and the latter for that from inner need,
namely 'meaninglessness'.

[25] For recognition and the relation to justice and love, see A. Honneth, *Kampf um
Anerkennung: Zur moralischen Grammatik sozialer Konflikte*, Suhrkamp, Frankfurt
1994; Id., *Das Andere der Gerechtigkeit*, Suhrkamp, Frankfurt 2000; P. Ricoeur, *Figuring the Sacred: Religion, Narrative and Imagination*, Fortress, Minneapolis 1994,
315–330; Id., *The Course of Recognition*, Harvard University Press, Cambridge 2005,
186–218.

personal salvation. But expressions like 'humans' and 'the human person' should be read as abstractions representing individual persons, groups, communities, and collectivities, from where 'salvation' includes social salvation.

How does salvation proceed from its *terminus a quo* to its *terminus ad quem*? One can explain it by introducing the term 'contrast experience', arising from a sense of justice.[26] On the one hand, this experience is marked by feelings of anger, provoked by the lack of decent living conditions, and indignation expressed in exclamations like 'that is not fit for human beings', 'that's unfair' or 'it cannot go on like that'. On the other hand, it is characterised by motivation and the will to change the desperate situation, to join forces with others and to take action – always with a more or less implicit or explicit awareness that such action will not lead to perfection, because it is itself marked by contingence, inherent human frailty, and guilt.

That inevitably raises awareness of time with its structure of past, present, and future.[27] Past actions – both successes and failures – are inscribed in memory and thus influence our actions here and now. Present actions, however (partially) successful they may be, are and will always be accompanied by a sense of human imperfection and fault and directed into an ever receding horizon of future hopes, because our longing will not cease in any foreseeable future, not even if we extend it to the 'end of time'.

---

[26] E. Schillebeeckx, Theologische draagwijdte van het magisteriële spreken over sociaal-politieke kwesties, *Concilium* 4(1968)6, 21–40, especially 29–34; Id., Het nieuwe Godsbeeld, secularisatie en politiek, *Tijdschrift voor Theologie* 8(1968)1, 44–66, especially 55–56; Id., *Jesus, het verhaal van een levende*, Nelissen, Bloemendaal 1974, 509–510; P. Ricoeur, *Oneself as Another*, University of Chicago Press, Chicago 1992, 197–198. See for the philosophical implications of the relation between empathy, sympathy, and self-interest: Ph. Chanial & A. Caillé et al., L'homme est-il un animal sympathique? Le contr'Hobbes, Revue du Mauss (2008) 1, premier semester, no. 31; see for the biological substratum: Ch. Sekhar Sripada, Nativism and Moral Psychology: Three Models of the Innate Structure That Shapes the Contents of Moral Norms, in: W. Sinnott-Armstrong, *Moral Psychology, Volume 1, The Evolution of Morality: Adaptations and Innateness*, MIT, Cambridge 2008, 319–343; for the relation between justice and economy, see for sense of justice and evolution: J. Cacioppo and W. Patrick, *Loneliness, Human Nature, and the Need for Social Connection*, Norton, New York 2008, 195–197; see for the complexity of emotional and rational (costs/benefits-related) aspects: R. Masters, Naturalistic Approaches to Justice in Political Philosophy and the Life Sciences, in: R. Masters & M. Gruter (eds.), *The Sense of Justice, Biological Foundations of Law*, Sage, Newbury Park 1992, 67–92; A. Sen, *The Idea of Justice*, Harvard University Press, Cambridge 2009, 184–193.

[27] P. Ricoeur, *Time and Narrative, Vol. 3*, University of Chicago Press, Chicago 1988.

Eschatological expectation falls within this horizon. It is characterised by tension between what has been accomplished already and what still has to be accomplished, a tension between 'already' and 'not yet' that is peculiar to all soteriology. Here the sense of what still has to be accomplished is coloured by awareness of the receptive activity it entails. Salvation is both a task to be performed and a gift to be received. In eschatological terms, the perfection people strive for and to which they direct their activities is inconceivable without the hope and belief that it will be accomplished beyond their personal endeavours. It is informed by the belief that 'at the end of time' God will finally consummate good human endeavour in a perspective of reconciliatory recognition, justice, and love.

Religions' capacity to focus their soteriological views, via morality, on other systems and thus to stimulate critical thought and action, applies to the juridical system as well, especially to the legal-cultural subsystem which refers to religious freedom and the separation of church and state. Religions carry age-old, insightful, and rich traditions with them, based on imaginative stories, ethically loaded narratives, and moral key concepts, like dignity, freedom, equality, solidarity, justice, and love, which are full of meaning and relevance for both morality and law – for both morality and law indeed, because themes like these need not necessarily be assigned to either morality or law, but can be approached from both a moral and a juridical angle.[28]

9.2   Axial Religions

The soteriological orientation is what distinguishes axial religions from pre-axial religions, here understood as a typological construct rather than a purely historical phenomenon.[29] The two religions that

---

[28] Habermas, *Faktizität*, op. cit., 137.

[29] Historically the axial religions date to the 5th century BCE, with some strands going back to the 8th century and forward to the 3rd century BCE: S. Eisenstadt (ed.), *The Origins and Diversity of Axial Age Civilizations*, State University of New York Press, New York 1986; Id., *Comparative Civilizations & Multiple Modernities*, Vol. I, Brill, Leiden 2003; J. Arnason et al., *Axial Civilizations and World History*, Brill, Leiden 2005; J. Hick, *An Interpretation of Religion*, Yale University Press, New Haven 1989, 21–69; Ch. Taylor, *A Secular Age*, Harvard University Press, Cambridge 2007, passim. For the importance of reflection on religions from the *Achsenzeit*, see *Ein Bewusstsein von dem, was fehlt, eine Diskussion mit Jürgen Habermas*, M. Reder & J. Schmidt (eds.), Suhrkamp, Frankfurt 2008, 26–36. The classification into pre-axial and

we researched, Christianity and Islam, count among these; at any rate, with their reliance on Judaism they form part of a secondary break-through of axial religions. They can be described in terms of religious beliefs and religious rites. Religious beliefs are marked by variations on the continuum of a vertical axis pertaining to immanence and transcendence, a horizontal axis pertaining to inclusion and exclusion, and a longitudinal axis pertaining to time and history.[30] Participation in religious rites is characterised by variations in frequency.

To start with the vertical axis, pre-axial religions do not distinguish between immanence and transcendence as axial religions do, nor do they make a soteriological connection with the moral code of good and evil, since mundane reality is considered to be peopled by spiritual forces and powers: in the air, in heavenly bodies like the sun, moon and stars, in mountains, trees, plants, in animals and humans, in the entire cosmos. A sense of the fundamental contingency of life, chance, chaos, anomie, suffering, and death that govern mundane reality dawned only once a distinction was made between the mundane and the extramundane world, between immanence and transcendence. Immanence is seen as only relatively valuable and meaningful, although axial religions also contain many themes portraying the world as imperfect, deficient, illusory, bad, even sinful. At all events, the transcendent surpasses the immanent and refers to a real, meaningful, perfect, pristine, beautiful world, which was there from the beginning and will or can happen again in the future. Transcendent reality can be seen as metaphysical or cosmic, anthropomorphic or non-anthropomorphic, monotheistic or polytheistic, as emptiness, no-thing, the void or nothingness. The polarity between mundane or immanent and extramundane or transcendent is resolved soteriologically. This means that salvation has already started in the present, that

---

axial religions is only one of many typologies of religions in philosophy and religious studies, such as those of I. Kant, G.W.F. Hegel, R. Bellah, C. Kolpe, N. Luhmann and A. Kött; see A. Kött, *Systemtheorie und Religion, Mit einer Religionstypologie im Anschluss an Niklas Luhmann*, Königshausen & Neumann, Würzburg 2003, 311–431.

[30] The spatial categories of height, breadth, and length are among the primitive concepts underlying the semantic structures of many languages, referring to 'above' and 'below' (vertical), 'nearby' and 'far away' (horizontal) and 'ahead' and 'behind' (longitudinal): A. Wierzbicka, *Semantics, Culture, and Cognition: Universal Human Concepts in Culture-Specific Configurations*, Oxford University Press, New York/ Oxford 1992; Id., *Understanding Cultures through Their Key Words: English, Russian, Polish, German, and Japanese*, Oxford University Press, New York/Oxford 1997.

is the time between past and future (inchoate), and that it proleptically foreshadows consummation in the future.

Salvation does not happen without human activity, or at any rate active receptiveness, by way of human initiative or intervention, whether individual or collective. Because of their capacity to act, (agency) humans are (co-)responsible for action. Salvation comes through engagement in the mundane world in order to improve it from the perspective of the extramundane world.

A case in point is liberation theology in Latin America, Africa, and Asia.[31] It hinges on an option for the poor and the oppressed, which, as a contrast experience, entails a veto of society as it is, stimulates liberating practices, and arouses longing for and hope of a God-given future of justice and peace.[32] The struggle for democracy and human rights features prominently in all this.[33]

On the horizontal axis, there are also manifest differences between pre-axial and axial religions. The former are tribal religions, whose adherents are confined to members of a particular tribe and their neighbours. The latter are religions of major civilisations that cut across tribal or national divisions and are centred in urban environments with more or less sophisticated social, political, and legal structures, from where they exercise attraction for and influence over the periphery. Or they are religions of large, stratified civilisations, whose distinctions between estates and classes cut right across tribes and nations.[34]

---

[31] R. Fournet-Betancourt, *Befreiungstheologie: Kritischer Rückblick und Perspektiven für die Zukunft*, Bd. I, *Bilanz der letzten 25 Jahre (1968–1993)*, Bd. II, *Kritische Auswertung und neue Herausforderungen*, Bd. III, *Die Rezeption im deutschsprachigen Raum*, Grünewald, Mainz 1997; Id., *Befreiungstheologie: Kritischer Rückblick und Perspektiven für die Zukunft*, Grünewald, Mainz 1997.

[32] G. Gutierrez, *A Theology of Liberation: History, Politics, and Salvation*, Orbis, New York 1973; D. Tombs, *Latin American Liberation Theology*, Brill Leiden, 2002; Chr. Bauer & S. van Erp (eds.), *Salvation in Diversity*, Lit, Münster 2004.

[33] J. Segundo, *Faith and Ideologies*, Orbis, New York 1982; J. Sobrino, *The True Church and the Poor*, Orbis, New York 1989; B. Klein Goldewijk, *Praktijk of principe*, Kok, Kampen 1991; J. van Nieuwenhove & B. Klein Goldewijk, Mensenrechten als rechten van God: een profiel van kardinaal Paolo Evaristo Arns, *Tijdschrift voor Theologie* 34(1994)1, 3–23.

[34] Luhmann, *Die Gesellschaft*, op. cit., II, 609–618, distinguishes between four forms of differentiation: segmented, centre-periphery, stratified, and functional differentiation. According to his evolutionary typology of religions, pre-axial, archaic religions are found in tribes and peoples with segmented differentiation, axial religions in societies with centre-periphery or stratified differentiation, and modern religions in societies that are functionally differentiated; see A. Kött, *Systemtheorie*, op. cit., 173–179.

Inclusion and exclusion of participants in axial religions do not depend on tribal or national limits, but are based on varying boundaries of inclusion and exclusion of groups between centre and periphery. In principle, axial religions are structured universally, although historically and empirically there is always a continuum between particularity and universality. The latter implies that by their very nature axial religions address all human beings as individual subjects, since they cut across tribal and national contexts.[35] That does not rule out inclusion and exclusion, but these come in forms that transcend tribe and nation. The limit of inclusion is peripheral groups that are still relevant to the religion, and that of exclusion is groups that are treated with indifference, disregarded, or rejected.[36]

There are many variations. In the Catholic tradition, for instance, the limits of exclusion and inclusion were extremely narrow, based on the 3rd century axiom of Origen and Cyprian of Carthage: no salvation outside the church (*extra ecclesiam nulla salus*). Vatican II replaced the dichotomy this entailed with a system of concentric circles reflecting decreasing inclusion and increasing exclusion of the following religious traditions: Eastern Christianity, Lutheranism, Calvinism, Judaism, Islam, Asian religions and indigenous religions.[37] In the work of Edward Schillebeeckx, the aforementioned dichotomy, 'no salvation outside the church', is replaced by another, which is loaded with substantively absolutely open meaning while encapsulated in a summons to societal orthopraxis: 'no salvation outside society'.[38] These examples show that inclusion and exclusion affect two domains: inclusion and exclusion of both other social groups and other religious groups.[39]

---

[35] The term 'universal religions' cuts across tribal and national contexts and addresses all human beings, regarding them simply as individual subjects, and therefore allowing for doubt and unbelief, see G. Mensching, *Die Religion, Erscheinungsformen, Strukturtypen und Lebensgesetze*, Schwab, Stuttgart 1959, 65–77; cf. Kött, *Systemtheorie*, op. cit., 353–354. These universal religions are also called soteriological religions; see K. Hoheisel, s.v. Religionstypologie, *Religion in Geschichte und Gegenwart*, Mohr Siebeck, Tübingen 2004, 7, 386–388.

[36] Luhmann, *Die Religion*, op. cit., 233.

[37] Decree on the Catholic Churches of the Eastern Rite, *Orientalium Ecclesiarum* (1964); Decree on Ecumenism, *Unitatis Redintegratio* (1964); Declaration on the Relation of the Church to non-Christian Religions, *Nostra Aetate* (1965).

[38] E. Schillebeeckx, *Mensen als verhaal van God*, Nelissen, Baarn 1989, 24–34, speaks of 'outside the world no salvation', of which 'outside society no salvation' forms a part.

[39] Luhmann, *Die Religion*, op. cit., 197.

On the longitudinal axis, too, pre-axial and axial religions differ. This is illustrated by the way they deal with time and history. It is not that pre-axial civilisations have no sense of time, hence no concept of past, present, and future, as is sometimes wrongly thought.[40] The difference is that they do not see time as a scarce commodity. They focus on short- rather than long-term planning.[41] The distinction I have in mind is the sense of time in oral narrative, which is typical of these civilisations, and the change that writing – more specifically religious scriptures – brought in this respect. In oral narratives, stories that are handed down from one generation to the next are considered to be beyond time. 'Since time immemorial' their truth and signifi-cance were taken for granted, something fixed, immutable, eternal. But writing changed the meaning of stories. They are no longer engraved purely in the collective memory of tribesmen and women, but acquire an independent existence in the sense of objects extraneous to human beings that are then subject to interpretation. That creates awareness of the multitude of contexts in which they originated, the function of memory and reception as well as the synchronic and diachronic complexity of texts, which can result in rival interpretations. It means that bygone events recorded in scriptures can be imbued with broader meaning, as in the case of Deutero-Isaiah, which reinterprets the sto-ries of creation and the exodus in terms of the exile.[42]

The increasing awareness of time and history in relation to texts led to the influential doctrine of scriptural meanings of Augustine of Denmark, who, following earlier introductions such as that of Ori-gen, laid down the rule in the 13th century: "The literal meaning informs us about what happened, the allegorical meaning about what to believe, the moral meaning about what to do, and the anagogic meaning about what to hope for."[43] Nowadays hermeneutics distin-guishes between two forms of interpretation of religious texts, based on different conceptions of time and history: literal and contextual interpretation. The latter takes account of the meaning of texts in the

---

[40] J. Mbiti, *Concepts of God in Africa*, SPCK, London 1975.
[41] E. Mpofu et al., Time Management Practices in African Culture: Correlates with College Academic Grades, *Canadian Journal of Behavioral Science* 28(1996), 1–18.
[42] U. Berges, *Das Buch Jesaja, Komposition und Gestalt*, Herder, Freiburg 1998; see also A. Groenewald, *Psalm 69: Its Structure, Redaction, and Composition*, Lit, Münster 2003.
[43] "Littera gesta docet, quid credas allegoria, moralis quid agas, quid speres anago-gia"; see P. Walter, s.v. Schriftsinne, *Lexikon*, op. cit., Vol. 9, 268–269.

interaction between contexts in the past and between these and present-day contexts.

The soteriological connection between immanence and transcendence in the mode of transcendence-in-immanence is expressed not only in religious beliefs but also in rites.[44] Rites in pre-axial religions are pre-eminently magical, marked by an instrumental relation with spirits. They are meant to secure the spirits' favour on the basis of *do ut des*. In axial religions, rites are characterised by a personal, communicative relationship with God or the gods as valuable in itself.[45] The dichotomy is by no means absolute, for axial religions contain many pre-axial elements, for instance Christian popular religiosity in the West[46] and the syncretism of Christianity and African traditional religions.[47]

Framing fulfils a major function in ritual. By that we mean that the code system according to which everything that is done, said, and sung and all the actors and things that play a role in it serve as semiotic references to the immanent presence of transcendence, which coordinates its absence in its presence. The rite does not simply communicate this absent presence, but stages, represents and enacts it performatively in the activities of the participants. This clothes the entire ritual in an aura of ineffable infinitude.[48]

---

[44] E. Goffman, *Interaction Ritual*, Penguin, London 1972; C. Bell, *Ritual: Perspectives and Dimensions*, Oxford University Press, Oxford 1997; R. Rappaport, *Ritual and Religion in the Making of Humanity*, Cambridge University Press, Cambridge 2000; J.Z. Smith, *To Take Place: Towards Theory in Ritual*, University of Chicago Press, Chicago 1987; Id., *Relating Religion*, University of Chicago Press, Chicago 2004. For commentary on Smith: Book Review Symposium on 'To take place', *Journal of the American Academy of Religion* 76(2008)3, 766–805. For the relation between beliefs and rites, see: P. Doreian & Th. Fararo (eds.), *The Problem of Solidarity: Theories and Models*, Gordon & Breach, Amsterdam 1998; D. Marshall, Behavior, Belonging, and Belief: A Theory of Ritual Practice, *Sociological Theory* 20(2002)3, 360–380; R. Collins, *Interaction Ritual Chains*, Princeton University Press, Princeton 2004; H. Schilderman, Liturgical Studies from a Ritual Studies Perspective, in: Id. (ed.), *Discourse in Ritual Studies*, Brill, Leiden 2007, 3–34.

[45] R. Horton, *Patterns of Thought in Africa and the West*, Cambridge University Press, Cambridge 1995; J. Olupona & S. Sulayman (eds.), *Religious Plurality in Africa: Essays in Honour of John S. Mbiti*, Mouton de Gruyter, Berlin 1993.

[46] Ch. Taylor, *A Secular Age*, Harvard University Press, Cambridge 2007, 439.

[47] Mbiti, *Concepts of God*, op. cit., 64; K. Appiah, *In My Father's House: Africa in the Philosophy of Culture*, Oxford University Press, Oxford, 1992; Id., Old Gods, New Worlds, in: P.H. Coetzee & A.P.J. Roux (eds.), *Philosophy From Africa: A Text with Readings*, Thomson, Johannesburg 1998, 245–274.

[48] C. Geertz, Religion as a Cultural System, *The world yearbook of religion. The religious situation I*, London 1969, 639–688.

Ritual also transforms the identity and status of the participants. On the one hand, they performatively enact the absent presence of the transcendent, on the other they do so realising that they are being given this absent presence and are receiving it. In ritual, they construct their own active receptiveness to transcendence, so that they regard that which they are enacting in the rite as something bestowed on them, a gift. This dialectics of active doing and passive receiving is reflected in their standing and kneeling postures and in feelings of independence and dependence, joy and reverence, which give participants a sense of salvation.[49]

Ritual permits a choice between personal and social salvation. In the case of personal salvation, the presence of transcendence-in-immanence gives participants a sense of personal healing and reconciliation. In the case of social salvation, the ritual extends further, in that the beliefs it activates spill over, as it were, into the extra-ritual sphere of interpersonal and social relations. This is known as the consequential aspect of religion, since it seeks to realise the ritually intensified beliefs in critical 'orthopraxis' in society.[50] Often the two dimensions go together, with the accent sometimes on personal salvation and sometimes on social salvation.

9.3   HYPOTHESES

So far I have outlined a theoretical view of the distinctive nature of the religious system in the midst of other systems in our functionally differentiated society today. I have argued that the independence of these systems does not preclude interpenetration and mutual influence. This applies to the religious system as well. Via morality, the religious system, with its beliefs about immanence and transcendence on the vertical axis, inclusion and exclusion on the horizontal axis, and literal and contextual interpretation on the longitudinal axis, in combination with its ritual expression of these beliefs, can have critical and constructive soteriological relevance for the other systems.

To determine the empirical value of this soteriological approach, we need to measure the effects of the beliefs and rites of the religions under investigation – Christianity and Islam – on attitudes towards

---

[49] W. James, *The Varieties of Religious Experience*, Image, New York 1978.

[50] C. Glock, On the Study of Religious Commitments, *Religious Education* 57(1962)4, 98–110; R. Stark & C. Glock, *American Piety: The Nature of Religious Commitment*, University of California Press, Berkeley 1968.

two principles in the legal system: religious freedom and the separation of church and state. We do so among three groups of Christian, Muslim, and nonreligious youths. Such a study of effects entails formulating hypotheses, which are then tested empirically. From the reflection so far, one can infer six main hypotheses. The first pertains to the overall effect of religious beliefs and rites on attitudes towards the two constitutional principles; the other five concern the unique effects of particular beliefs and rites.

Hypothesis 1

The overall effect of religious beliefs and rites on attitudes towards religious freedom and the separation of church and state is weakest among the nonreligious group, strongest among the Muslim group, with the Christian group falling in between. The reason is that the nonreligious group is most highly secularised, the Christian group less so, and the Muslim group least secularised.[51]

Hypothesis 2

Religious beliefs on the vertical axis about God, Jesus, and Muhammad with the accent on transcendence have a negative effect on attitudes towards religious freedom and the separation of church and state, and those with the accent on immanent transcendence or immanence have a positive effect. The reason is that an emphasis on transcendence distracts attention from the importance of religiously informed moral 'orthopraxis' to improve society, and more particularly from human rights that relate to the two constitutional principles. Conversely, an accent on immanent transcendence or immanence allows for such a focus.

Hypothesis 3

Religious beliefs on the horizontal axis about inclusion and exclusion of other social groups with an accent on exclusion have a negative effect on attitudes towards religious freedom and the separation of church and state, and those with the accent on inclusion have a positive effect. The reason is that a religio-centric emphasis on exclusion prevents concern about the challenges faced by other social groups in

---

[51] In terms of Luhmann's theory, *Die Religion*, op. cit., 278–319, secularisation may be seen as the effect of functional differentiation that proceeds differently in different population groups.

society. Conversely, an open style of interaction and inclusion reveals these challenges, which helps to promote the two constitutional principles that are based on the ideals of freedom and equality of all other social groups.

Hypothesis 4
Religious beliefs on the horizontal axis about inclusion and exclusion of other religious groups which focus on exclusion have a negative impact on attitudes towards both legal principles, and those which focus on inclusion have a positive impact. The reason is that a religio-centric, closed-minded orientation on exclusion ignores the challenges, values, and interests of other religions, whereas religious open-mindedness contributes to realising those challenges, values, and interest from the perspective of freedom and equality of all other religious groups.

Hypothesis 5
Religious beliefs on the longitudinal axis about literal or contextual interpretation of source texts with the accent on literal interpretation have a negative effect on attitudes towards religious freedom and the separation of church and state, and those with the accent on contextual interpretation have a positive effect. The reason is that a literal understanding ignores present-day societal problems. Conversely, a contextual interpretation hermeneutically bridges the divide between the original and the current situation, which is necessary for support of the two constitutional principles.

Hypothesis 6
Rites with an accent on personal salvation negatively affect attitudes required for social 'orthopraxis' in support of the two constitutional principles. An accent on social salvation has a positive effect. However, when the accents on personal and social salvation are combined, the two effects cancel each other out. This last aspect conflicts with much literature, including that of liberation theology, which propounds the all too harmonious notion that personal and social salvation are mutually reinforcing.[52]

---

[52] H. Müller, *Leidenschaft: Stärke der Armen, Stärke Gottes, Theologische überlegungen zu Erfahrungen in Brasilien*, Grünewald, Mainz 1998; B. Weber, *Ijob in Lateinamerika, Deutung und Bewältigung von Leid in der Theologie der Befreiung*, Grünewald, Mainz 1999. The reason might be the abstract character of social and political analytical concepts used in liberation theology on the one hand and the missing link

9.4 Religious Beliefs and Rites

Before examining the effects of religious beliefs and rites on attitudes towards religious freedom and the separation of church and state, we need to conduct an empirical investigation into these beliefs and rites among our Christian, Muslim, and nonreligious youths.[53] The beliefs are divided into the three categories described in the previous section with reference to the attributes of axial religions: beliefs on the vertical axis referring to the polarity between immanence and transcendence, beliefs on the horizontal axis referring to the polarity between inclusion and exclusion, and beliefs on the longitudinal axis referring to the polarity between literal and contextual interpretation of source texts. To these we add the frequency of individual and collective rites.[54]

Tables 7 to 12 reflecting five-point scales for religious beliefs and rites provide the necessary data. The scales for religious beliefs indicate decreasing rejection and increasing agreement (table 7 to 11).[55] They are constructed on the basis of three items each, with the exception of scales for beliefs about God that are based on two items each. Scale reliability was analysed for the entire population of Christian, Muslim, and nonreligious youths collectively (alpha > .60). The tables reflect the means and standard deviations (sd) for each sub-population. The scales for the religious rites are single item scales (table 12). The figures in the tables immediately after the scales indicate the questionnaire items (appendix II).

9.4.1 *Religious Beliefs*

In table 7, beliefs about God are divided according to three sets of images: transcendent, immanent-transcendent, and immanent (appendix II, 1).[56] The transcendent group breaks up into anthropomorphic,

---

with indigenous cultural and religious symbolic expressions, actions and rituals on the other (see: M. Brinkman, Nieuwe Latijns-Amerikaanse beelden van Jezus – Een christologische benadering, *Tijdschrift voor Theologie* 49(2009)3, 273–286.

[53] See for the religious self-attribution of these three groups: Appendix IV.

[54] We distinguish between individual and collective rites regarding the form of rites on the one hand, and personal and social salvation regarding the content of the rites on the other. In the matrix emerging from there both individual and collective rites may focus on both personal and social salvation.

[55] Scale: 1 = totally disagree, 2 = disagree, 3 = not sure; 4 = agree, 5 = agree totally.

[56] The interpretation of the means is: 1.00–1.79: totally disagree; 1.80–2.59: disagree; 2.60–2.99: negative ambivalence; 3.00–3.39: positive ambivalence; 3.40–4.19: agree; 4.20–5.00: fully agree.

theistic images (scale i: mean 3.0; 3.8; 1.8) and non-anthropomorphic, deistic images (scale v: mean 2.9; 2.0; 2.3). The immanent-transcendent group comprises only anthropomorphic images. They are split between panentheistic images in individual life (scale ii: mean 3.0; 4.6; l.7), social life (scale iii: mean 2.9; 4.4; 1.7), and nature (scale iv: mean 2.8; 4.3; 1.7). The immanent group comprises only non-anthropomorphic images. They are split between pantheistic images (scale vi: mean 2.6; 2.0; 2.1) and metatheistic images (scale vii: mean 3.1; 1.9; 2.6).

This table shows the following results: Christian youths score around 3.0, the middle of the scale, with the exception of pantheistic images, which they reject. Muslim youths roundly agree with anthropomorphic images and unanimously reject non-anthropomorphic images. Nonreligious youths disagree with all images.

Table 7. Beliefs about God (means)

	Christian mean	sd	Muslim mean	sd	Nonreligious mean	sd
i. God's theistic presence (1,7)	3.0	1.0	3.8	1.1	1.8	0.9
ii. God's panentheistic presence: individual (2,6)	3.0	1.0	4.6	0.6	1.7	0.9
iii. God's panentheistic presence: social (3,5)	2.9	1.0	4.4	0.8	1.7	0.9
iv. God's panentheistic: nature (4,8)	2.8	1.0	4.3	0.9	1.7	0.9
v. God's deistic presence (9,11)	2.9	1.1	2.0	1.5	2.3	1.2
vi. God's pantheistic presence (12,14)	2.6	1.0	2.0	1.4	2.1	1.0
vii. God's metatheistic presence (10,13)	3.1	1.1	1.9	1.3	2.6	1.2

In table 8, the vertical axis also includes beliefs about images of the founding prophets of Christianity and Islam: the eschatological prophet Jesus (appendix II, 2) and the last prophet, Muhammad (appendix II, 3).[57] As the table indicates, there are again different groups of beliefs, three for each prophet: beliefs with transcendent, immanent-transcendent, and immanent images. Beliefs with transcendent images pertain to Jesus as God's incarnate Son (scale i: mean 2.9; l .7; 1.7) and to Muhammad as the prophet sent by God to proclaim his message (scale vi: mean

[57] For the 15 items on Muhammad in the questionnaire, we consulted Abdulkader Tayob, former professor of Islamic Studies in Nijmegen, currently in Cape Town.

2.3; 4.7; 1.8). Beliefs with immanent-transcendent images of Jesus may be termed 'transdescendent' inasmuch as they pertain to Jesus as a human being inspired by the Spirit (scale ii: mean 3.2; 3. 1 ; 1 .9), and 'transascendent' inasmuch as they pertain to Jesus as the epitome of liberation (scale iii: mean 3.2; 3.3; 2.2) and solidarity (scale iv: mean 3.4; 3.4; 2.3). As for beliefs with immanent-transcendent images of Muhammad, some are transdescendent inasmuch as they portray him as a human being with a unique revelation (scale vii: mean 2.3; 4.6; 1.9), and others are transascendent inasmuch as they refer to Muhammad as a mystical (scale viii: mean 2.2; 4.6; 1.8) and a moral teacher (scale ix: mean 2.3; 4.6; 2.0). Beliefs with immanent images refer to the cultural-historical, humanistic significance of Jesus (scale v: 2.8; 2.4; 2.8) and Muhammad (scale x: 2.7; 2.5; 2.6).

Table 8. Beliefs about Jesus and Muhammad (means)

	Christian mean	sd	Muslim mean	sd	Nonreligious mean	sd
i. Jesus, God's incarnate Son (1,5,12)	2.9	1.0	1.7	0.9	1.7	0.8
ii. Jesus, inspired by the Spirit (2,9,13)	3.2	0.9	3.1	1.0	1.9	0.9
iii. Jesus: liberation (3,6,15)	3.2	0.8	3.3	1.0	2.2	1.0
iv. Jesus: solidarity (4,7,11)	3.4	0.9	3.4	1.0	2.3	1.1
v. Jesus: humanistic view (8,10,14)	2.8	0.8	2.4	0.9	2.8	1.0
vi. Muhammad, prophet of God (16,21,26)	2.3	0.9	4.7	0.6	1.8	0.9
vii. Muhammad: uniqueness (17,22,27)	2.3	0.9	4.6	0.7	1.9	0.9
viii. Muhammad: mystical teacher (18,23,28)	2.2	0.9	4.6	0.6	1.8	0.9
ix. Muhammad: moral teacher (19,24,29)	2.3	1.0	4.6	0.6	2.0	1.0
x. Muhammad : humanistic view (20,25,30)	2.7	1.0	2.5	1.3	2.6	1.2

This table reveals the following. Christian youths tend to subscribe to Jesus as a religious figure except for his incarnation image. Muslim youths agree to all religious images of Muhammad. But there is also a clear difference between the two groups. Muslim youths are far more positively inclined towards Jesus than Christian youths are towards Muhammad, whom they reject. For the rest, both groups are dubious about a humanistic view, the Christian group about such a view of

Jesus and the Muslim group about such a view of Muhammad. Finally, nonreligious youths evaluate both Jesus and Muhammad negatively, except for the humanistic image of Jesus, to whom they react with negative ambivalence.

Table 9 reflects the youths' beliefs on the horizontal axis regarding the polarity between inclusion and exclusion of social groups by religious groups (appendix II, 4). The question is whether the youths agree that religious groups should withdraw into themselves and then directly seek to win over public opinion (scale i: mean 2.8; 3.4; 2.2) or are in favour of real dialogue with social groups in society by prophetically championing marginalised people (scale ii: mean 3.3; 3.8; 2.8), opening themselves up to these groups (scale iii: mean 3.3; 3.2; 3.3) and inviting them in (scale iv: mean 3.5; 3.6; 3.4), with professional knowledge in this regard (scale v: mean 3.3; 3.8; 3.0).

Table 9. Beliefs about inclusion and exclusion of social groups by religious groups (means)

	Christian		Muslim		Nonreligious	
	mean	sd	mean	sd	mean	sd
i. religious groups' focus on public opinion (4,9,14)	2.8	0.8	3.4	0.8	2.2	0.9
ii. religious groups' prophetic practice (1,6,11)	3.3	0.7	3.8	0.7	2.8	0.9
iii. religious groups' openness (2,7,12)	3.3	0.8	3.2	0.9	3.3	1.0
iv. religious groups' inviting orientation (3,8,13)	3.5	0.8	3.6	0.8	3.4	1.0
v. religious groups' focus on professionalism (5,10,15)	3.3	0.7	3.8	0.8	3.0	1.0

According to this table, Christian youths are negatively ambivalent towards religious groups that close themselves off from other social groups and directly seek to influence public opinion, whereas nonreligious youth are purely negative about that. Muslim youths agree with such behaviour. However, all three subpopulations – Christian, Muslim, and nonreligious – are more or less positive about an open, inviting, professional approach to social groups in society by religious groups. Christian and Muslim youths support prophetic championing of the underprivileged, while nonreligious youths are negatively ambivalent.

Table 10. Beliefs about inclusion and exclusion by religious groups of other religious groups (means)

	Christian		Muslim		Nonreligious	
	mean	sd	mean	sd	mean	sd
i. Interreligious exclusivism (1,5,9)	2.3	0.9	4.2	0.8	1.5	0.7
ii. Interreligious inclusivism (2,6,10)	2.5	0.8	3.5	0.8	1.7	0.8
iii. Interreligious dialogue (3,7,11)	2.7	0.9	3.2	0.9	2.2	1.1
iv. Interreligious pluralism (4,8,12)	3.0	0.9	2.9	1.1	2.7	1.1

This table reflects the youths' beliefs about the polarity between inclusion and exclusion of other religious groups (appendix II, 5). The cardinal question is to what extent they agree with interreligious exclusiveness (scale i: mean 2.3; 4.2; 1.5) or interreligious inclusiveness, implying recognition of common features in each other's traditions (scale ii: mean 2.5; 3.5; 1.7), favouring open interreligious dialogue (scale iii: mean 2.7; 3.2; 2.2), and respecting other groups by acknowledging interreligious pluralism, in which all religious traditions are seen as equally valid ways to salvation and grace (scale iv: mean 3.0; 2.9; 2.7).

Compared to the attitudes towards other social groups reflected in the previous table, this table reveals a manifestly different picture of attitudes towards other religious groups. Christian youths display a descending line of rejection from exclusiveness to inclusiveness, dialogue and pluralism, while Muslim youths display a descending line of agreement. Nonreligious youths in their turn reveal a descending line of rejection, but from a more negative point of departure than Christian youths.

Table 11 pertains to beliefs on the longitudinal axis regarding the polarity between a literal and a contextual interpretation of the source texts, the Bible and the Qur'an (appencdix II, 6). A literal interpretation evokes varying degrees of approval and rejection in the case of the Bible (scale i: 3.2; 2.5; 1.8) and the Qur'an (scale iii: 1.9; 4.9; 1.6). Contextual interpretation evokes more positive responses in the case of the Bible, particularly among nonreligious youth (scale ii: 3.1; 3.1; 3.5) than that of the Qur'an, which again nonreligious youth value the most (scale iv: 2.8; 2.1; 3.2).

Table 11. Beliefs about the interpretation of source texts (means)

	Christian		Muslim		Nonreligious	
	mean	sd	mean	sd	mean	sd
i. Bible: literal interpretation (1)	3.2	1.2	2.5	1.4	1.8	1.0
ii. Bible: contextual interpretation (2)	3.1	1.1	3.1	1.3	3.5	1.1
iii. Qur'an: literal interpretation (3)	1.9	1.1	4.9	0.4	1.6	0.9
iv. Qur'an: contextual interpretation (4)	2.8	1.3	2.1	1.5	3.2	1.3

The following picture emerges from this table. Christian youths are positively ambivalent about literal interpretation of the Bible, while Muslim youths strongly agree with such interpretation of the Qur'an. Christians are positively ambivalent about contextual interpretation of the Bible, while Muslim youths reject such interpretation of the Qur'an. Nonreligious youths show the strongest rejection of a literal interpretation and agree most strongly with a contextual interpretation.

9.4.2   *Religious Rites*

As we indicated, we added some items about the participation in individual and collective rites. The five-point scales i–iv in table 12 deal with the frequency of participation in these rites (appendix III).[58]

Table 12. Ritual participation (means)

	Christian		Muslim		Nonreligious	
	mean	sd	mean	sd	mean	sd
i. Prayer (1)	2.3	1.4	4.2	1.2	1.2	0.6
ii. Bible: reading (2)	1.7	1.1	1.3	0.6	1.1	0.4
iii. Qur'an: reading (2)	1.0	0.2	3.9	1.1	1.0	0.1
iv. Collective rites (3)	2.5	1.1	3.4	1.3	1.5	0.7

When it comes to prayer, Muslim youths manifestly surpass Christian and nonreligious youths (item i: mean 2.3, 4.2, 1.2). None of the three groups reads the Bible (item ii: mean 1.7, 1.3, 1.1). Only the Muslim

---

[58] Scale i, ii and iii for individual rites: 1 = never, 2 = rarely, 3 = occasionally, 4 = periodically, 5 = regularly; scale iv for collective rites: 1 = never, 2 = on religious feast days, 3 = occasionally, 4 = monthly or a few times each month, 5 = weekly or a few times each week.

group frequently reads the Qur'an (item iii: mean 1.0, 3.9, 1.0). In the case of collective rites, too, Muslim youths outshine the other two groups (item iv: mean 2.5, 3.4, 1.5).

What the table shows is that Muslim youths pray and take part in collective rites far more frequently than Christian youths. The most striking difference is in Christians' Bible reading as opposed to the Muslims' reading of the Qur'an.

9.5   Effects of Beliefs and Rites on Religious Freedom and Separation of Church and State

Having described religious beliefs on the vertical, horizontal, and longitudinal axes as well as the frequencies of participation in individual and collective rites, we can determine what effect such beliefs and rites have on attitudes towards religious freedom and the separation of church and state. To this end we use regression analyses. These are aimed at making predictions which – at least in the case of properly argued hypotheses – may be interpreted as effects, at any rate in the sense of necessary conditions.[59]

Conducting regression analyses entails certain steps. The first relates to the dependent variables, here the attitudes towards religious freedom and the separation of church and state that we explored in earlier chapters. In chapter 7, we measured the youths' attitudes towards religious freedom twice, namely as the prohibition of political interference in religious communities and as the permissibility of prayer at public schools (tables 1 and 2). In chapter 8, we measured their attitudes towards the separation of church and state twice, namely as political autonomy in regard to euthanasia and political autonomy in regard to abortion respectively (tables 4 and 5). That gives us four dependent variables (figure 4). For each dependent variable we planned a separate regression analysis for each youth group – Christian, Muslim, and nonreligious. That came to a total of twelve regression analyses.

The second step entails the selection of independent variables out of the 30 religious beliefs (tables 7 to 11) and the 4 rites (table 12) we investigated in the previous section. This selection is done with the help of the correlation analyses on which the regression analyses are based.

---

[59] H. Blalock, *Social Statistics*, McGraw-Hill, Tokyo 1979; P. Verschuren, *Structurele modellen tussen theorie en praktijk*, Aula, Utrecht 1991, 27–41.

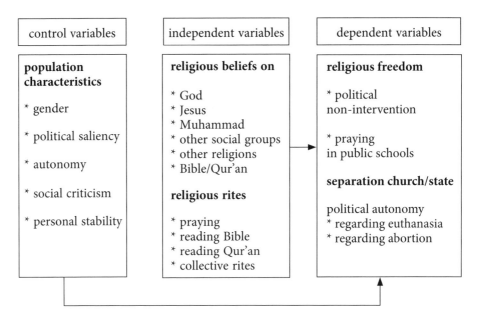

control variables	independent variables	dependent variables

population characteristics

* gender

* political saliency

* autonomy

* social criticism

* personal stability

religious beliefs on

* God
* Jesus
* Muhammad
* other social groups
* other religions
* Bible/Qur'an

religious rites

* praying
* reading Bible
* reading Qur'an
* collective rites

religious freedom

* political non-intervention

* praying in public schools

separation church/state

political autonomy
* regarding euthanasia
* regarding abortion

Figure 4. Conceptual model: effects of religious beliefs and rites on religious freedom and separation church and state.

The correlation analyses between the four dependent variables and all those independent variables were conducted for each of the three youth groups, which came to a total of twelve correlation analyses. If the correlation coefficients are not high enough in that they do not meet a predetermined criterion, there is no point including the independent variables concerned in the regression analyses and they are omitted. As our criterion, we decided that for each of the 30 religious beliefs and 4 rites, there must be two or more relevant correlation coefficients $(r \geq .15)$.[60] Application of this criterion eliminated all 4 religious rites, while only 16 of the 30 religious beliefs remained.

The 16 selected religious beliefs appear in tables 13 and 14: belief in God's panentheistice presence in individual life, his panentheistic presence in social life, and his panentheistice presence in nature; Jesus

---

[60] We chose this criterion of relevance $(r \geq .15)$ because of the findings from the 3rd wave of the European Values Study (EVS 1999–2000) that among the Dutch population the highest correlation coefficient between belief in God (Q30A), importance of God in one's life (Q33), and attending services (Q25) on the one hand and being satisfied with democracy (Q59), confidence in justice system (Q58N), and respect for human rights (Q64) on the other measured r .15.

as God's incarnate Son and the humanistic view of Jesus; the humanistic view of Muhammad; religious groups focused on public opinion, with a prophetic practice, a practice of openness, and an inviting orientation; interreligious exclusiveness, inclusiveness, dialogue, and pluralism; and finally, contextual interpretation of the Bible and of the Qur'an.

The third and final step is the introduction of some population characteristics as control variables in the regression analyses. There are five of these: gender; three social values, namely political saliency, attitudes towards autonomy, and social criticism; and finally personal stability (figure 4 and appendix V). From previous research into the relation between religion, constitutional principles, and human rights, gender appears to be important.[61] Political saliency is crucial, because the principles of religious freedom and the separation of church and state are among the key political arrangements of modern democratic states. Hence political motivation is seen as a major condition for acceptance of the two constitutional principles.[62] The reasons for introducing attitudes towards autonomy and social criticism are analogous to those regarding the degree of political saliency. Ever since the Enlightenment, these have exercised a major influence on the establishment of the rule of law and the underlying human rights. Autonomy, which liberated people from the heteronomous rule of throne and altar, and social criticism as resistance against feudal society and the *ancien régime*, are cornerstones of the modern democratic state.[63] Finally, personal stability is introduced as a control variable in the regression analyses, since the two constitutional principles, religious freedom and the separation of church and state, are objects of often emotional debate, requiring

---

[61] Among the Christian group 45% is male and 55% female, while the percentages for the Muslim group are 43% and 57%, and those for the nonreligious group are 48% and 52%. See for the importance of gender: J.A. van der Ven, J.S. Dreyer, H.J.C. Pieterse, *Is There a God of Human Rights?*, Brill, Leiden 2004, 584, table 14.3.1; J.A. van der Ven, Francis-Vincent Anthony, Impact of Religion on Social Integration from an Empirical Civil Rights Perspective, Part One, *Salesianum* 70(2008) 2, 317–338; Id., Part Two, *Salesianum* 70(2008) 3, 463–489.

[62] The means of political saliency for the Christian, Muslim and nonreligious group are respectively: 2.8, 3.0 and 2.7.

[63] The means of the attitudes towards autonomy for the Christian, Muslim and nonreligious group are 3.7, 4.0 and 3.9, and the means of the attitudes towards social criticism are 3.0, 3.6 and 2.8. See for the relevance of autonomy and social criticism: J. Israel, *Radical Enlightenment: Philosophy and the Making of Modernity 1650-1750*, Oxford University Press, Oxford 2001; Id., *Enlightenment Contested: Philosophy, Modernity, and the Emancipation of Man 1670-1742*, Oxford University Press, Oxford 2006.

a balanced personality structure in order to adopt and maintain an individual stance in such discussions.[64]

The relations between the dependent variables, the independent variables, and the control variables are depicted in the conceptual model in figure 4. The arrow from the independent variables to the dependent variables refers to the effects of the first on the latter. The arrow from the control variables to the dependent variables indicates how the effects concerned are controlled for by the population characteristics in the regression analyses.

We decided on so-called hierarchical regression analyses, conducted with the aid of two models. In the first model, the explained variance (table 13 and 14: R^2 model 1) is calculated only for the impact of the control variables on the dependent variables; in the second model, the independent variables are added to the control variables (tables 13 and 14: R^2 model 2).[65]

9.5.1   The Outcome

For the systematic description of the outcome from the twelve regression analyses (tables 13 and 14), we use the six hypotheses formulated above as a guideline. In relation to hypothesis 1, we first consider the overall effect (R^2 model II).[66] In relation to hypotheses 2 to 6, we then deal with significant unique effects of the respective religious beliefs (significant beta coefficients: $p < .01$; $p < .05$; $p < .10$).

Hypothesis 1 was that the overall effect of religious beliefs and rites on attitudes towards religious freedom and the separation of church and state is strongest among the Muslim group, weakest among the nonreligious group, with the Christian group falling somewhere in between.

As mentioned already, religious rites were not included in the regression analyses because the correlation coefficients were too low. In regard to religious beliefs, the explained variance (R^2 model II) in tables 13 and 14 clearly varies. The religious beliefs among the Muslim group have the strongest overall effect: it varies from moderate to

---

[64] The mean for the personal stability for the Christian group is 3.8, for the Muslim group it is 3.5 and for the nonreligious group it is 3.8.

[65] For the regression analyses we used the enter method, list-wise deletion of missing values and the variance inflation factor (VIF < .10) to test for multicollinearity.

[66] For the interpretation of R^2: $R^2 < .15$: weak effect; $15 \leq R^2 < .25$: moderate effect; $R^2 \geq .25$: strong effect.

Table 13. Effects of religious beliefs on attitudes towards religious freedom (beta), with controls

	No political Interference Christians (N=333)	No political Interference Muslims (N=220)	No political Interference Nonreligious (N=457)	Prayer at publ. schools Christians (N=333)	Prayer at publ. schools Muslims (N=217)	Prayer at publ. schools Nonreligious (N=455)
God's panentheistic presence in the individual	-.10	.01	.04	.00	.00	.03
God's panentheistic presence in social life	.11	.13	.17†	-.01	-.09	-.03
God's panentheistic presence in nature	-.15†	-.02	-.16	.02	-.01	.12
Jesus' incarnation	.01	.14†	-.05	-.02	-.11	-.06
Jesus: humanistic view	.07	-.09	.10	-.11†	-.17*	-.12†
Muhammad: humanistic view	.03	-.15†	-.16*	-.02	-.14†	.20**
Religious groups' focus: public opinion	.12†	-.02	.08	-.17*	.07	-.05
Religious groups' prophetic practice	-.13†	-.10	.15*	.18*	-.17†	.17**
Religious groups' practice of openness	-.04	.08	-.10	-.07	-.02	-.15*
Religious groups' inviting attitude	-.01	.08	.15*	.01	.05	.11†
Interreligious exclusiveness	-.01	.24**	.01	-.08	.14	-.19**
Interreligious inclusiveness	.21*	-.07	-.03	.09	-.04	.05
Interreligious dialogue	-.02	.04	-.07	-.01	-.02	-.02
Interreligious pluralism	.15*	.08	.07	.03	-.17†	.06
Contextual interpretation of the Bible	-.08	.09	.09	-.09	.13†	-.05
Contextual interpretation of the Qur'an	.06	.05	-.05	.13*	.08	.15*
R² Model I: control variables only	.03	.02	.02	.02	.04	.02
R² Model II: control variables + religious beliefs	.13	.16	.11	.09	.28	.15

The dependent variables relate to religious freedom, i.e. (i) prohibition of political interference in religious communities and (ii) prayer permitted at public schools. The effects on both variables are analysed for each of the three groups: Christian, Muslim and nonreligious youth.
Model I controls for gender, political saliency, autonomy, social criticism, and personal stability.
Model II adds the religious beliefs to the control variables.
Significance: ** p < .01; * p < .05; † p < .10 (2-tailed).

Table 14. Effects of religious beliefs on attitudes towards the separation of church and state (beta), with controls

	political autonomy euthanasia Christians (N=333)	political autonomy euthanasia Muslims (N=220)	political autonomy euthanasia Nonreligious (N=459)	political autonomy abortion Christians (N=334)	political autonomy abortion Muslims (N=218)	political Autonomy abortion Nonreligious (N=455)
God's panentheistic presence in the individual	.11	.16	.09	.18†	.00	-.05
God's panentheistic presence in social life	-.19*	-.03	.07	-.23*	-.01	.07
God's panentheistic presence in nature	.05	.13	-.20*	.00	.11	-.08
Jesus' incarnation	-.18*	.10	-.10	-.10	.15†	-.07
Jesus: humanistic view	.13*	-.02	.06	.12†	.05	.05
Muhammad: humanistic view	.02	-.02	.00	.07	-.07	-.02
Religious groups' focus: public opinion	-.08	-.01	-.17**	-.07	-.13	-.22**
Religious groups' prophetic practice	-.01	-.09	.04	.10	.19†	.10
Religious groups' practice of openness	.13†	.13	.20**	.06	-.07	.18**
Religious groups' inviting attitude	.20**	.16†	-.02	.12†	-.06	-.08
Interreligious exclusiveness	.16†	-.05	.03	.02	-.02	-.01
Interreligious inclusiveness	-.05	.08	-.01	-.07	-.03	.08
Interreligious dialogue	.11	-.07	.06	.07	.14	.04
Interreligious pluralism	-.08	.23*	-.03	-.15*	.12	-.01
Contextual interpretation of the Bible	-.04	.01	.13†	.03	.05	.15*
Contextual interpretation of the Qur'an	-.02	.05	-.06	-.03	.00	-.01
R^2 Model I: control variables only	.04	.03	.05	.03	.06	.02
R^2 Model II: control variables + religious beliefs	.15	.22	.18	.13	.17	.16

The dependent variables relate to the separation of church and state, i.e. (i) political autonomy regarding euthanasia and (ii) political autonomy regarding abortion. The effects on both variables are analysed for each of the three groups: Christian, Muslim, and nonreligious youth.
Model I controls for gender, political saliency, autonomy, social criticism and personal stability.
Model II adds the religious beliefs to the control variables.
Significance: ** p < .01; * p < .05; † p < .10 (2-tailed).

strong (table 13. model II: religious freedom: R^2 .16, R^2 .28; table 14, model II: separation of church and state: R^2 .22, R^2 .17). This is followed by the nonreligious – not the Christian – group, with predominantly moderate effects (religious freedom: R^2 .11, R^2 .15; separation of church and state: R^2 .18, R^2 .16). Then follows the Christian group, with predominantly weak effects (religious freedom R^2 .13, R^2 .09; separation of church and state R^2 .15, R^2 .13). In short, hypothesis 1 concerning the Muslim group's dominance in the rank order of the three groups is corroborated, but the one about the positions of the other two groups is falsified.

Hypothesis 2 was that beliefs about God, Jesus, and Muhammad with the accent on transcendence have a negative effect on religious freedom and the separation of church and state, and those with the accent on immanent transcendence or immanence have a positive effect.

As we already indicated, all beliefs about God, Jesus, and Muhammad with the accent on transcendence were eliminated from the regression analyses, except the belief in Jesus as God's incarnated son.

Let us start with the beliefs in God. Belief in God's panentheistic presence in individual life has a positive effect on the separation of church and state among Christian youths (table 14: beta .18). Other beliefs with the same panentheistic emphasis have mixed effects, such as belief in God's presence in social life that has a positive effect on religious freedom among nonreligious youths (table 13: beta .17) but a negative effect on the separation of church and state among Christian youths (table 14: beta –.19, beta –.23). Yet other beliefs, especially belief in God's panentheistic presence in nature, have a negative effect on religious freedom among Christian youths (table 13: beta –.15) and on the separation of church and state among nonreligious youths (table 14: beta –.20).

As for Jesus, belief in Jesus as God's incarnate Son has a positive effect on religious freedom as well as on the separation of church and state among Muslim youths (table 13: beta .14; table 14: beta .15), but a negative effect on the separation of church and state among Christian youths (table 14: beta .–18). Remarkably, a humanistic interpretation of Jesus has a negative effect on religious freedom, particularly praying at public schools, among all three groups of youths (table 13: beta –.11, beta –.17, beta –.12). It has, however, a positive effect on the separation of church and state among Christian youths (table 14: beta .13, beta .12).

A humanistic interpretation of Muhammad has a negative effect on the prohibition on political interference among Muslim and nonreligious youths (table 13: beta –.15, beta –.16), and a negative effect on prayer at public schools among Muslim youths (table 13: beta –.14), but a positive effect among nonreligious youths (table 13: beta .20).

In short, hypothesis 2, that beliefs with the accent on transcendence, like that about Jesus as God's incarnate son, have a negative effect, is partly corroborated, partly falsified. The hypothesis that beliefs with the accent on immanent transcendence and immanence have a positive effect is largely falsified.

Hypothesis 3 was that beliefs that accentuate exclusion of social groups in society by religious communities have a negative effect and those that accentuate inclusion have a positive effect.

Exclusion of other social groups manifesting simply in swaying public opinion in fact has a positive effect on the prohibition of political interference among Christian youths (table 13: beta .12), but a negative effect on permitting prayer at public schools (table 13: beta –.17). It also has a negative effect on the separation –.17, beta –.22).

An inclusive orientation to social groups in society which manifests in a prophetic, open, inviting orientation all have a positive effect on religious freedom and the separation of church and state, with a few exceptions, notably a prophetic orientation among Christian and Muslim youths in the case of religious freedom (table 13: beta –.13, beta –.17) and an open orientation among nonreligious youths (table 13: beta –.15). In short, the hypothesis regarding exclusion and inclusion of social groups is largely corroborated.

Hypothesis 4 was that beliefs that accentuate exclusion of other religious groups by religious communities have a negative effect, and that those that accentuate inclusion have a positive effect.

The empirical picture is different from the previous one about exclusion and inclusion of social groups. Interreligious exclusiveness has a positive effect on religious freedom among Muslim youths (table 13: beta .24), but a negative effect among nonreligious youths (table 13: beta –.19). It has a positive effect on the separation of church and state among Christian youths (table 14: beta .16). Interreligious inclusiveness has a positive effect on religious freedom among the Christian group (table 13: beta .21). Interreligious pluralism has a positive effect on religious freedom and the separation of church and state among the Christian and Muslim groups (table 13: beta .15; table 14: beta .23), but negative effects on prayer at public schools among Muslim youths (table 13: beta −.17) and on the separation of church and state among the Christian group (table 14: beta −.15). In short, the hypothesis regarding exclusion and inclusion of other religions is partly corroborated, partly falsified.

Hypothesis 5 was that literal interpretation of the source texts, Bible and the Qur'an, has a negative effect and contextual interpretation has a positive effect.

As noted above, literal interpretation was not included in the regression analyses because of low correlation coefficients. In the case of contextual interpretation, hypothesis 5 is corroborated in regard to religious freedom among Muslim and nonreligious youth (table 13: beta .13, beta .15) as well as in regard to the separation of church and state among the nonreligious group (table 14: beta .13, beta .15).

Hypothesis 6 was that rites with an accent on personal salvation have a negative effect and rites with an accent on social salvation have a positive effect. As noted above, no rites were included in the regression analyses because of low correlation coefficients, which means that this hypothesis could not be tested.

9.6   REFLECTION

The last two chapters concentrated on the extent to which the three groups, Christians, Muslims and nonreligious youth, support the two constitutional principles of religious freedom and the separation of church and state. This chapter examined the degree to which their religious beliefs and rites influence their attitudes towards the two constitutional principles.

Hypothesis 1 was that the overall effect of their religious beliefs and rites is strongest among Muslims, and weakest among the nonreligious group, with the Christian group falling somewhere in between.

As indicated earlier, this hypothesis could only be tested in relation to the religious beliefs, because the religious rites had to be eliminated from the analyses, as they did not meet the correlation criterion. In regard to the religious beliefs, our research showed, partly contradicting the hypothesis, that the overall effect is moderate to strong among Muslim youths, predominantly moderate among nonreligious youths and predominantly weak among Christian youths. This means that the hypothesis about the Muslim group's dominance in the rank order of the three groups is corroborated, but the ranking of the other two groups is falsified. The middle position of the nonreligious group may be surprising, but it implies that the impact of their religious beliefs on their attitudes towards the two constitutional principles cannot be ignored. They play a relatively important role and deserve to be taken seriously.

The question may be asked what kind of beliefs among the nonreligious group have the greatest impact. One may distinguish between two categories of beliefs: beliefs that are held by religious insiders, and beliefs that are held or may be held by both religious insiders and religious outsiders.[67] The first category refers to beliefs which originate from the essential tenets of religious communities and their religious traditions. The second relates to beliefs which refer to the relation between religion and society as well as religion and culture, more specifically in view of the contribution religion might or should offer to society and culture, for example in terms of freedom, equality, social cohesion, and solidarity. Religious beliefs about God, Jesus, Muhammad – except the humanistic ones – mainly fall in the first category as do those about the interreligious ranking of one's own religion among religious groups generally. Beliefs adopting a humanistic view of Jesus and Muhammad and particularly beliefs about how religious communities should deal with social groups in society, as well as beliefs about the literal or contextual interpretation of source texts, mainly belong to the second category. According to this distinction, the beliefs among the nonreligious group that contribute most to the overall effect on the two constitutional principles fall in the second rather than the first category. This empirical finding invites scholars to pay more scientific attention to beliefs of the second category than usually happens in theology and religious studies.

---

[67] For the difference between 'religious insider' and 'religious outsider' on the one hand and 'taking a religious insider perspective' and 'taking a religious outsider perspective' on the other, see chapter 3. From the matrix which emerges from those distinctions, both religious insiders and outsiders may take both a religious insider perspective and a religious outsider perspective.

Hypotheses 2 to 6 related to the unique effects of religious beliefs and rites on the attitudes towards freedom of religion and the separation of church and state. Hypothesis 2 was that beliefs on the vertical axis about God, Jesus, and Muhammad with the accent on transcendence have a negative effect and those with the accent on immanent transcendence or immanence have a positive effect.

What the findings highlight is the relatively minor effects of beliefs regarding immanence and transcendence on this vertical axis. Let us first pay attention to beliefs about God.

All beliefs that were included in the regression analyses, because they met the aforementioned correlation criterion, pertain to personal God images, more particularly the panentheistic presence of a personal God in individual life, in social life, and in nature. The beliefs that failed to meet this criterion and were therefore excluded from the regression analyses all concern images of a non-personal, transcendent, remote God who is providentially uninvolved, such as the deist belief in 'Something higher' as well as pantheistic and metatheistic God images. That is to say, the God images that exert an influence are the personal ones that are most strongly attested in religious traditions. However, this influence is relatively minor and ambivalent, as evidenced by the slight positive and negative effects.

How should we interpret the relatively minor and ambivalent impact of these beliefs concerning God in both Christianity and Islam? In my view, it is a consequence of the age-old tension between traditional faith in God and the modern 'faith' in human rights. Of course, religions form the moral infrastructure of human rights: from the codex of Hammurabi,[68] Asian religions, the Jewish Bible and the Second Testament, patristics, scholasticism, Spanish late scholasticism, and the English Protestant dissenters in America, to papal addresses to the United Nations. That does not detract from the fact that, apart from some religiously critical groups, human rights were usually wrested from the prevailing powers of throne and altar by liberal citizens (*citoyens*), anti-feudal peasants (*paysants*), socialistically inspired workers (*sansculottes*), slaves (*Cannibals All*),[69] blacks (*niggers*), and to this day

---

[68] See for the Mesopotamian heritage: J. Yacoub, The Dignity of the Individual and of Peoples: The Contribution of Mesopotamia and of Syriac Heritage, *Diogenes* 54(2007)3, 19–37.

[69] Title of the pro-slavery book by George Fitzhugh (1857).

by indefatigable women and militant homosexuals.[70] Human rights came into existence through these groups' gradual emancipation from throne and altar in a society subject to the process of functional differentiation, which furthered emancipation. As a result of the collapse of the sacred canopy under which religion once held all social domains together, 'divine rights', through the de-sacralisation of natural law, became 'natural rights', whereupon the latter, through legal positivisation in fundamental law, i.e. constitutions, became 'fundamental rights' and through international public law in international conventions beyond the constitutional national state became 'human rights'.[71] This heightened the polarity between divine transcendence and human rationality, religious heteronomy and moral autonomy, hierarchy and self-authorisation. The immediate result is a weak, ambivalent influence of religion/religions on human rights, more particularly those of religious freedom, as well as its necessary condition, i.e. the separation of church and state. It would seem that religion has found a pragmatic *modus vivendi* with the two constitutional principles, tolerating them and adapting to them. But this is not heartfelt, in the sense of accepting the two principles as intrinsically valuable.[72]

Does this mean that religions are still more attached to (hybrid forms of) theocracy, clerico-cracy and monocracy than to democracy, which underlies the two principles? That may be going too far, but flatly denying that one still finds substantial remains of such allegiance here and there is likewise exaggerated. The value of championing human rights to the outside world but resisting them inwardly by invoking God, divine revelation, divine law, ecclesiastic doctrine or ecclesiastic tradition, as happens in Christianity, cannot but be regarded as a clear sign of ambivalence. This applies not only to Christianity. In

---

[70] M. Ishay, *The History of Human Rights*, Orient Longman, New Delhi 2008.
[71] See chapters 4 and 5.
[72] J. Habermas, Ein Bewusstsein von dem, was fehlt, in: Reder & Schmidt (eds.), *Bewusstsein*, op. cit., 26–36, here 32. See for the *modus vivendi* also: M. Terpstra, De politieke theologie van een *potestas indirecta*, in: M. Becker (red.), Christelijk Sociaal Denken, Traditie, Actualiteit, Kritiek, Damon, Budel 2009, 197–222. Moreover, T. Pettersson, Religious Commitment and Socio-Political Orientations: Different Patterns of Compartimentalisation among Muslims and Christians?, in: J. Haynes (ed.), *Routledge Handbook of Religion and Politics*, Routledge, New York 2009, 246–269, here 256–257, table 16.1, discovered that the two Catholic countries he investigated, Italy and Spain, show a correlation between religious involvement and a negative-critical evaluation of democracy, which does not apply to the two Protestant countries he also researched, Sweden and Denmark.

Islam, too, one encounters it, as witness the winners of the 2004 Dutch Erasmus prize, F. Mernissi, S. Al-Azm and A. Soroush, respectively from Morocco, Syria and Iran, who describe similar ambivalence arising from tension between divine and popular sovereignty, Islam and humanism, rights and duties.[73] These tensions continue to survive. They are part of the secular age in which religions have found themselves in recent centuries. From the perspective of (the orthodox and mid-orthodox wings in) most religions there are no short-term, clear-cut, convincing solutions in sight.[74]

It is not just beliefs on the vertical axis regarding God's immanence and transcendence that are remarkable; those about Jesus are equally noteworthy. On the basis of the aforementioned correlation criterion, only two of the five beliefs about Jesus were included in the regression analyses, namely the one in Jesus as God's incarnate Son and the humanistic interpretation of Jesus. Both have some influence, albeit – like the beliefs about God – only a slight, ambivalent influence. The point is that these are the two most sharply contrasting beliefs, with the transcendence of the incarnation theme at one extreme and the immanence of a humanistic interpretation at the other. The other three beliefs – those in Jesus' Spirit, his solidarity and liberation – were eliminated from the regression analyses by the correlation coefficient criterion. Clearly the images of Jesus that are relevant because of their impact on the two constitutional themes are structured in the youths' minds according to the two most antithetical coordinates: 'pure' transcendence (incarnation) and 'pure' immanence (humanism). In other words, extremes, invariably, exert the greatest push and pull.[75]

For the sake of completeness, this dichotomy between extremes is not observable in the case of Muhammad, because only the humanistic interpretations of his person and ministry made it to the regression analyses and not, for example, beliefs about him as a prophet or teacher. The latter did not meet the criterion set for correlation coefficients.

---

[73] F. Mernnissi et al., *Religie en moderniteit* De Geus, Zutphen 2004.

[74] Taylor, *A secular Age*, op. cit., passim.

[75] The shades in between only emerge when examined in greater depth through more specialised study. That is, logical: differentiation of attitudes in a particular domain correlates with the measure of differentiated knowledge about that domain (G. Westerhof, *Statements and Stories*, Dissertation Radboud University Nijmegen 1994).

Hypothesis 3 was that beliefs on the horizontal axis that accentuate exclusion of social groups in society by religious communities have a negative effect, and those that accentuate inclusion have a positive effect. Hypotheses 4 was that beliefs on this axis with an emphasis on exclusion of other religious groups have a negative impact, and those with an emphasis on inclusion have a positive impact.

A remarkable finding among all three groups of youth is that beliefs about inclusion and exclusion on the horizontal axis have more effect on attitudes towards freedom of religion and the separation of church and state than those about immanence and transcendence on the vertical axis. The former refer to relations with other groups in this mundane reality, be they social groups or other religious groups. The latter concern relations with religious figures that transcend mundane reality and belong to the extramundane world: God, Jesus, and Muhammad. Hence the former obviously have more impact on the attitudes towards both constitutional themes than the latter. It also explains why the religious beliefs of nonreligious youths – they especially cherish beliefs about open and inviting religious communities – affect their attitudes towards the two constitutional principles.

The difference in impact between the beliefs on the horizontal and the vertical axis may be explained not only from the distinction between the mundane and the extramundane world they refer to, but also in terms of the presence of a moral loading in the former and its absence in the latter. Because of this moral loading, the beliefs about inclusion and exclusion have a manifest effect, those about the transcending extramundane world have hardly any impact. As we said earlier in this chapter about the relation between religion and morality and that between morality and law, morality might be considered the passageway between religious beliefs and the two constitutional themes, or even broader, between religious beliefs and human rights.

When one examines the effects of religious beliefs on the horizontal axis about inclusion and exclusion on both constitutional principles, one observes another striking phenomenon. The effects of beliefs about inclusion and exclusion of social groups in society are greater than those about inclusion and exclusion of other religious groups. Beliefs about a prophetic, social-critical, open-minded, inviting orientation towards social groups have the strongest positive influence on attitudes towards the two constitutional principles. The more prophetic, social-critical, open, and inviting religious communities are for social groups, the more this affects their support for both constitutional principles. One could reverse this finding and broaden it: beliefs which reinforce the unjust and unequal social status quo, leave marginalised groups to their fate, close themselves off from new developments in society and culture, present people with stiff admission requirements, and set high thresholds, have the strongest negative impact on the democratic, constitutional rule of law.

As it is said, beliefs about inclusion and exclusion of other religious groups carry far less weight. Whether religious communities have an interreligiously exclusive, inclusive, or pluralistic orientation does have some effect, but not a great one. An orientation to interreligious dialogue has no effect whatever.

Hypothesis 5 was about beliefs on the longitudinal axis, implying that literal interpretation of the source texts, Bible and the Qur'an, has a negative effect and contextual interpretation has a positive effect.

Because the beliefs about the literal interpretation did not meet the pre-established correlation criterion, only those about the contextual interpretation were entered in the regression analyses. We found that among the Christian and nonreligious groups, beliefs on the longitudinal axis affect attitudes towards the freedom of religion, especially the permission to pray at public schools. They only influence attitudes towards the separation of church and state among the nonreligious group. Among the Christian and Muslim groups, they have no effects in this respect.

Hypothesis 6 was that rites with an accent on personal salvation have a negative effect and rites with an accent on social salvation a positive effect.

As the rites did not meet the correlation criterion, the hypothesis, as said earlier, could not be tested. This could be because many ritual programmes contain a combination of the two aforementioned dimensions (personal and social salvation). More specifically, in many ritual programmes the emphasis is on an individualised type of religiosity, which is understandable in the light of the individualisation process in Western society and religion's withdrawal into the private sphere, but mixed with social and political concerns that are usually couched in abstract moral (and moralistic) terms. From this mix of personal and social salvation, the expected negative correlation of personal salvation with the two constitutional principles and the expected positive correlation of social salvation with these principles cancelled each other out and consequently did not meet the pre-established correlation criterion.

CONCLUSION

From the outset we have referred to the process of functional differentiation which has permeated Western society since early modernity. It replaced the sacred canopy that once covered the whole of society with a number of autonomous systems and subsystems functioning according to their own codes and programs. In that context, religion became a system alongside other systems. The question may be raised whether the functional differentiation of systems is mirrored in a functional differentiation within individual human beings. Is the functional differentiation in society mirrored in a functional differentiation in mind, so that, for instance, there is 'a wall of separation' between people's religious beliefs and their political attitudes? Is there some sort of mental compartimentalisation between religious beliefs and political attitudes? Or does the opposite apply: is the interpenetration between systems on the level of society mirrored in the interpenetration between religious beliefs and political attitudes on the level of the individual? More concretely: do religious beliefs and rites have an impact on attitudes towards constitutional principles, in our case religious freedom and the separation of church and state?[76]

The overall conclusion of our research is that to some extent religious beliefs have an effect on the attitudes towards both constitutional principles and thus contribute to a supportive legal, constitutional, human rights culture. In this sense, the mental compartimentalisation hypothesis cannot be considered to be corroborated.

But some qualifications are needed, one about the relation between religious beliefs and rites, the others about distinctions between religious beliefs.

First, we do not know whether the overall conclusion, just mentioned, also applies to the impact of rites, because, as indicated earlier,

---

[76] K. Dobbelaere, *Secularization: An Analysis at Three Levels*, Lang, Brussels 2002; Pettersson, Religious Commitment, art. cit., 247–252; A. Sjöborg, Religion and Moral Issues – A Private Matter? Young Swedes on the Freedom of Religion and the Freedom of Moral Speech, in: J.A. van der Ven (ed.), *Tensions within and between Religions and Human Rights*, Brill, Leiden 2010 (to be published).

they had to be eliminated from the analyses. Logically, their impact may appear to have three different values: positive, negative, or zero. Future research will have to fill in this gap.

Further, religious beliefs may be distinguished into two categories, beliefs that are held by religious insiders and beliefs that are held or may be held by both religious insiders and religious outsiders. Both kinds of beliefs are important, but the latter are particularly important for nonreligious people who may have strong convictions about the cultural and social functions of religion, especially those of religious communities. From our research, those beliefs appear to have a major impact on attitudes towards the two constitutional principles.

Furthermore, religious belief may be classified into beliefs on the vertical axis, referring to the tension between immanence and transcendence, and beliefs on the horizontal axis, referring to the interaction with other social and religious groups in society. We found that 'horizontal' beliefs about relations with other social groups have a greater impact on attitudes towards freedom of religion and the separation of church and state than 'vertical' beliefs about God and the religious founder figures, Jesus and Muhammad.

Moreover, religious beliefs may be differentiated into beliefs with or without a clear moral loading. We discovered that the greater the mundane, moral quality of religious beliefs, the more impact they have on attitudes towards the two constitutional principles, and the more they are oriented toward a transmundane symbolic universe without carrying an explicit moral meaning, the smaller this impact.

At a higher level of abstraction, this can be understood in terms of the distinction between the identity and mission of religious communities. Beliefs about the cultural and social mission of religious communities have a greater impact on these constitutional attitudes than beliefs about their religious identity.

Finally, at the highest level of abstraction this distinction can be interpreted in terms of culture and structure. Beliefs about policy and action residing in the policy-making structure of these religious communities have a greater effect on these constitutional attitudes than beliefs about their spiritual culture.[77]

---

[77] This was also found in the study of the effects of religion on the peace movement; see R. Jeurissen, *Peace and Religion,* Kok/Deutscher Studiën Verlag, Kampen/ Weinheim 1993.

APPENDIX

The appendix is divided into five parts of measuring instruments:

   I. Religious Freedom and the Separation of Church and State
  II. Religious Beliefs
 III. Religious Rites
 IV. Religious Self-attribution
  V. Population Characteristics

The range of all items and scales is from 1 through 5, unless indicated otherwise:

1 = I totally disagree
2 = I disagree
3 = I am not sure
4 = I agree
5 = I fully agree

I. RELIGIOUS FREEDOM AND THE SEPARATION OF CHURCH AND STATE

[Religious Freedom]

(i) Politicians are not allowed to interfere with religious communities.
(ii) Prayers in public schools should be forbidden.
Reversed into: Prayers in public schools should not be forbidden.

[Separation of Church and State]

(i) In regard to euthanasia politicians should decide irrespective of any religious leader's will.
(ii) In regard to abortion politicians should take decisions independently of religious leaders.

II. RELIGIOUS BELIEFS

1. GOD

The following statements are about God. Would you please indicate to what extent you agree with these statements.

[Theism]

1. God set the world in motion and left it to humans to take care of it
7. God got the world going and left the responsibility for it to humans

[Individual Panentheism]

2. I trust God never to abandon me
6. God knows and understands me

[Social Panentheism]

3. When people are friends that is God's love at work
5. When people live in friendship, God's love is present

[Nature's Panentheism]

4. I experience God's goodness in the peace of nature
8. I experience God's presence in the beauty of nature

The above were all statements about God. However, some people rather speak of 'Something higher' instead of 'God'. What do you think of the following statements about Something higher?

[Deism]

9. There is Something higher, through which the world originated
11. There is Something higher, through which the cosmos and nature came into being

[Pantheism]

12. There is Something higher, with which people and the world form a perfect unity
14. There is Something higher that ties people and the world together in perfect oneness

[Metatheism]

10. There is Something higher, which we cannot name at all
13. There is Something higher that we cannot even imagine

(Source: selection from J.A. van der Ven, *God Reinvented?* Brill, Leiden 1998; J.A. van der Ven, J.S. Dreyer & H.J.C. Pieterse, *Is There a God of Human Rights? The Complex Relationship between Human Rights and Religion: A South African Case*, International Studies in Religion and Society 2, Brill, Leiden/Boston 2004, 588–589)

2. JESUS

The following statements are about Jesus. Would you please indicate to what extent you agree with these statements.

[Incarnation]

1. God sent his son Jesus to earth
5. Jesus is the God-man who existed with the father from the beginning
12. Before Jesus came to earth he had lived with the father from the beginning

[Inspiration]

2. Jesus was a unique prophet, as God's Spirit of mercy directed his work and deeds
9. Jesus was a unique servant, as God's Spirit of compassion animated his life and words
13. Jesus was a unique teacher, as God's Spirit of love was in him

[Liberation]

3. Jesus works among the marginalised in their struggle for liberation
6. Jesus guides the oppressed to the land of justice and peace
15. Jesus supports the poor by liberating them from injustice

[Solidarity]

4. Jesus has shown us how to live in solidarity with others
7. Through his life Jesus showed us what it is like to be a loving human being
11. Jesus was a real example of caring for everybody in need

[Humanist Interpretation]

8. Jesus' only significance is that he started an important historical movement
10. Jesus was a special person, no more
14. Jesus is no more than just one of the great figures in human history

(Source: selection and adaptation from J.A. van der Ven & B. Biemans, *Religie in Fragmenten*, Kok, Kampen 1994, 204–205; J.A. van der Ven et al., *Human Rights*, op. cit., 591–592)

3. MOHAMMAD

The following statements are about Muhammad. Would you please indicate to what extent you agree with these statements?

[Prophet]

16. Muhammad received special revelations which led him to announce God's message.
21. Muhammad was called to preach God's teachings about faith and ethical demands.
26. Muhammad was sent by God as his prophet in order to proclaim his message.

[Uniqueness]

17. Muhammad's journey to, and union with, God is absolutely unique.
22. No one can ever replicate Muhammad's mystical experience.
27. No one can ever copy Muhammad's divine revelations.

[Teacher of Mystic Religion]

18. Muhammad's union with God is the perfect model for everyone's journey to God.
23. Muhammad teaches us how to walk our spiritual path to God.
28. Muhammad's religious experiences inspire and motivate our striving for union with God.

[Teacher of Active Religion]

19. Muhammad motivates us to maintain and strengthen our bond with fellow human beings.
24. Through Muhammad we learn to strive for the common good of society as a whole.
29. Muhammad teaches us to care for everybody in need and distress.

[Humanist Interpretation]

20. Muhammad's only significance is that he started an important historical movement.
25. Muhammad was a special person, no more
30. Muhammad is no more than just one of the great figures in human history.

(Abdulkader Tayob, former professor of Islamic Studies in Nijmegen, The Netherlands, currently in Cape Town, South Africa, has been consulted for the items on Muhammad)

4. INCLUSION AND EXCLUSION OF SOCIAL GROUPS BY RELIGIOUS COMMUNITIES

People have all sorts of ideas about what religious communities should or should not do. Some think they should follow changes in society, others think their task is to preserve the tradition. What do you think of these matters? Would you please indicate the extent of your agreement with the following statements about religious communities?

[Influence on Public Opinion]

4. Religious communities should try to influence public opinion on social problems.
9. Religious communities should exercise their authority over people's thinking about social problems
14. Religious communities should strive to influence people's attitudes towards social issues.

[Public Prophetic Performance]

1. Religious communities should publicly stand up for the underclass
6. Religious communities should publicly discuss social problems people are subjected to.

11. Religious communities should publicly denounce social abuses people suffer.

[Cultural Openness]

2. Religious communities should join in new trends in society as far as possible.
7. Religious communities should go along with changing ideas in society.
12. Religious communities should always keep up with current social trends.

[Inviting Outsiders]

3. Religious communities should never reject people who want to become members.
8. Everyone should be able to join a religious community.
13. Anyone should be able to participate in a religious community without preconditions

[Professionalism]

5. Religious communities should get enough knowledge to speak sensibly about social issues.
10. Religious communities should get enough information to deal with social problems effectively.
15. Religious communities should get sufficiently qualified to speak authoritatively about social problems.

(Source: selection and adaptation from R. Jeurissen, *Peace and Religion*, Kok/Deutscher Studien Verlag, Kampen/Weinheim 1993; K. Sonnberger, *Die Leitung der Pfargemeinde, Eine empirisch-theologische Studie unter niederländischen und deutschen Katholiken*, Kok/Deutscher Studien Verlag, Kampen/Weinheim 1996; J.A. van der Ven et al., *Human Rights*, op. cit., 592–593)

5. Inclusion and Exclusion of Other Religious Groups by Religious Communities

Sometimes people wonder how they should look at the various religions or world views they encounter. Are there essential differences between the various religions or world views? Or do they all hold out the same promise of authentic life?

Authentic life means: an authentic relationship with oneself, other human beings, society, nature, and an ultimate reality, e.g. God or mankind. Please indicate whether you agree or disagree with the following statements.

[Exclusiveness]

1. My religion or world view is the only access to authentic life
5. My religion or world view offers the only path for authentic life.
9. Only in my religion or world view can people receive authentic life.

[Inclusiveness]

2. Compared with my religion or world view, other religions or world views have only elements of authentic life.
6. Compared with my religion or world view, other religions or world views do have some aspects of authentic life, but not the whole of it.
10. Compared with my religion or world view, other religions or world views contain only parts of authentic life.

[Dialogue]

3. Authentic life can only be received through conversation between religions or world Views.
7. Authentic life can only be found when religions or world views communicate with one another.
11. The way to authentic life is only to be found when religions or world views have dialogue with one another.

[Pluralism]

4. Religions or world views are all equal, they are all directed to authentic life.
8. All religions or world views are equally valuable, they represent different ways to authentic life.
12. There is no difference between religions or world views, they all stem from a longing for authentic life.

(Source: selection and adaptation from J.A. van der Ven, Religious Values in the Interreligious Dialogue, *Religion & Theology* 1(1994)3, 244–260; Id., God Reinvented?, op. cit.; J.A. van der Ven et al., *Human Rights*, op. cit., 593–594)

6. BELIEFS ABOUT THE INTERPRETATION OF RELIGIOUS SOURCE
TEXTS, BIBLE AND QURAN

What is the bible for you? Please indicate the extent of your agreement with the statements below.

1. A divine book to be taken literally
2. Just a collection of human, cultural texts

What is the Quran for you? Please indicate the extent of your agreement with the statements below.

3. A divine book to be taken literally
4. Just a collection of human, cultural texts

III. RELIGIOUS RITES

1. PRAYING

Please indicate whether praying forms part of your current life at home and/or at school:

Never	1
Rarely	2
Now and then	3
Occasionally	4
Regularly	5

2. READING RELIGIOUS SOURCE TEXTS

Please indicate if reading the Bible or the Qur'an forms part of your current life.
Please answer this question for the Bible and the Qur'an separately.

	Bible	Quran
Never	1	1
Rarely	2	2
Now and then	3	3
Occasionally	4	4
Regularly	5	5

3. COLLECTIVE RITES

How often do you go to normal religious services in a religious community (church, mosque, synagogue, temple)?

Never	1
On feast days	2
Now and then	3
Monhtly/scrvcral times a month	4
weekly/several times a week	5

IV. RELIGIOUS SELF-ATTRIBUTION

How do you see yourself? Please, make sure that you mark only <u>one</u> answer.

1. Religious
2. Christian
3. Catholic
4. Protestant
5. Anglican
6. Pentecostal
7. Other Christian tradition
8. Islamic
9. Sunite
10. Shiite
11. Other Islamic tradition, namely . . . . . .
12. Jew
13. Buddhist
14. Hindu
15. Other religion
16. Non-religious

(In our empirical study *Christian youth* refers to categories 2–7, *Muslim youth* to categories 8–11, *nonreligious youth* to category 16. The other categories have been eliminated.)

V. POPULATION CHARACTERISTICS

1. GENDER

1. male, 2. female

2. VALUES

Political Saliency

Would you please indicate how important politics is to you?

Politics is

1 = not important at all
2 = not important
3 = I am not sure
4 = important
5 = very important
3. Values

Autonomy

Please indicate what you find important or unimportant in your life by marking one box for each item, according to the following:

1 = not important at all
2 = not important
3 = I am not sure
4 = important
5 = very important

1. Deciding for oneself what is allowed and what is not
2. Not being tied to rules
3. Being independent of anyone

(Source: SOCON, *Religion in Dutch Society, Documentation of national surveys on religious and secular attitudes in 2000*, Steinmetz Archive, Amsterdam 2002)

Social Criticism

1. Contributing to reduction of existing income differences
2. Promoting greater equality in society
3. Breaking through the existing relations of power

(Source: SOCON, *Religion in Dutch Society, Documentation of National Surveys on Religious and Secular Attitudes in 2000*, Steinmetz Archive, Amsterdam 2002)

3. PERSONALITY CHARACTERISTICS

Neuroticism – Reversed into 'Personal Stability'

The next questions refer to some personal experiences. We would like to know if you have ever had experiences like the ones below.

Please answer each question by putting a circle around the 'YES' or the 'NO'.

1 = yes
2 = no

1. Does your mood often go up and down?
2. Do you often feel 'fed-up'?
3. Would you call yourself a nervous person?
4. Are you a worrier?
5. Do you suffer from 'nerves'?
6. Do you often feel lonely?

(*Source*: L. Francis, L. Brown & C. Philip, The Development of an Abbreviated form of the revised Essence Personality Questionnaire (EPQR-A): Its Use among Students in England, Canada, the U.S.A. and Australia, *Personally and Individual Differences* 13(1992)4, 443–449. The title of the instrument 'neuroticism' has been replaced by 'personal stability', the scores have been reversed in the empirical research in this book, and the number of categories of the scale extended from two to five.)

BIBLIOGRAPHY

Human Rights Documents

United Nations Documents

Charter of the United Nations (1945).
Universal Declaration of Human Rights (1948).
International Covenant on Civil and Political Rights (1966).
International Covenant on Economic, Social and Cultural Rights (1966).
Convention on the Elimination of All Forms of Discrimination against Women (1979).
Declaration on the Elimination of All Forms of Intolerance and Discrimination Based on Religion or Belief (1981).
Vienna Declaration and Programme of Action (1993).
Declaration on Sexual Orientation and Gender Identity (2008).

African Documents

African Charter on Human and Peoples' Rights (1980).
Charter on the Rights and Welfare of the Child (1990).
Protocol to the African Charter on Human and People's Rights on the Establishment of an African Court for Human and Peoples' Rights (1998).
Protocol on the Rights of Women in Africa (2003).

Arab and Islamic Documents

Charter of Organization of the Islamic Conference (1972; 2008).
Universal Islamic Declaration of Human Rights (1981).
Cairo Declaration on Human Rights in Islam (1990).
Arab Charter on Human Rights (1994; 2004).

Asian Documents

The Bangkok Declaration on Human Rights (1993).
Asian Human Rights Charter (1998).

European Documents

European Convention for the Protection of Human Rights and Fundamental Freedoms (1950).
European Social Charter (1961; 1996).
Charter of Fundamental Rights of the European Union (2000).

Documents of the Roman-Catholic Church

Vaticanum II

Lumen Gentium (1964).
Orientalium Ecclesiarum (1964).
Unitatis Redintegratio (1964).
Gaudium et Spes (1965).

Nostra Aetate (1965).
Dignitatis Humanae (1965).
Gravissimum Educationis Momentum (1965).

Encyclicals

Quadragesimo Anno (1931).
Rerum Novarum (1891).
Mater et Magistra (1961).
Pacem in Terris (1963).
Evangelium Vitae (1995).

Letters

Letter to the Bishops of the Catholic Church on the Pastoral Care of Homosexual Persons. (1986).
Mulieris Dignitatem (1988).
Letter of John Paul II to Women (1995).

Declarations

Persona Humana (1975).
Inter Insigniores. Declaration on the Question of Admission of Women to the Ministerial Priesthood (1976).
Considerations Regarding Proposals to Give Legal Recognition to Unions between Homosexual Persons (2003).

Publication

Compendium of the Social Doctrine of the Church (2005).

LITERATURE

Abbott, W. (1966). *Documents of Vatican II*. London: Chapman.
Abou El Fadl, K. (2005). Islam and the Challenge of Democratic Commitment. In E. Bucar & B. Barnett (eds.), *Does Human Rights Need God?* (pp. 58–103). Grand Rapids, MI: Eerdmans.
Adams, R. (2009). The Theological Ethics of the Young Rawls and Its Background. In J. Rawls (edited by Th. Nagel), *A Brief Inquiry into the Meaning of Sin and Faith: With "On My Religion"* (pp. 24–101). Cambridge, MA: Harvard University Press.
AIVD (Algemene Inlichtingen- en Veiligheidsdienst or General Intelligence and Security Services) (2004). *Van dawa naar jihad*. The Hague: AIVD.
Alexy, R. (1985). *Theorie der Grundrechte*. Baden-Baden: Nomos.
An-Na'im, A.A. (1996). *Toward an Islamic Reformation: Civil Liberties, Human Rights, and International Law*. New York: Syracuse University Press.
—— (2008). *Islam and the Secular State, Negotiating the Future of Shari'a*. Cambridge, MA: Harvard University Press.
Antes, P., Geertz, A.W. & Warne, R.R. (eds.) (2004). *New Approaches to the Study of Religion. Vol. I. Regional, Critical, and Historical Approaches. Vol. II. Textual, Comparative, Sociological, and Cognitive Approaches*. Berlin/New York: De Gruyter.
Anthony, F.-V. (2003). Churches of African Origin: Forging Religio-Cultural Identity of a Third Kind. *Kristu Jyoti, 19*(1), 61–90.
Anthony, F.-V., Hermans, C.A.M. & Sterkens, C. (2005). Interpreting Religious Pluralism, Comparative Research among Christian, Muslim and Hindu Students in Tamil Nadu. *Journal of Empirical Theology, 18*(2), 154–186.

Appiah, K. (1998). Old Gods, New Worlds. In P.H. Coetzee & A.P.J. Roux (eds.), *Philosophy from Africa: A Text With Readings,* (pp. 245–274). Johannesburg: Thomson.

—— (1992). *In My Father's House: Africa in the Philosophy of Culture.* Oxford: Oxford University Press.

Aquinas, Thomas. *Summa Theologica.*

Arendt, H. (1966). *The Origins of Totalitarism.* New York: Harcourt, Brace & World.

Aristotle. (1984). Topics. In: *The Complete Works of Aristotle* (The revised Oxford translation, edited by J. Barnes). Princeton, NJ: Princeton University Press.

—— (1984). Politics. In: *The Complete Works of Aristotle* (The revised Oxford translation, edited by J. Barnes). Princeton, NJ: Princeton University Press.

Armitage, D. et al. (eds.) (1995). *Milton and Republicanism.* Cambridge: Cambridge University Press.

Arnason, J. et al. (eds.) (2005). *Axial Civilizations and World History.* Leiden: Brill.

Arntz, J. (1966). Die Entwicklung des naturrechtlichen Denkens innerhalb des Thomismus. In F. Böckle (ed.), *Das Naturrecht im Disput* (pp. 97–100). Düsseldorf: Patmos.

Asad, T. (2003). *Formation of the Secular: Christianity, Islam, Modernity.* Stanford: Stanford University Press.

—— (1993). *Genealogies of Religion: Discipline and Reasons of Power in Christianity and Islam.* Baltimore, MD: Johns Hopkins University Press.

Assmann, J. (2000). *Herrschaft und Heil: Politische Theologie in Altägypten, Israel und Europa.* München: Hanser.

Aubert, R. et al. (1952). *Tolérance et communauté humaine: Chrétiens dans un monde divisé.* Tournai: Casterman.

Audi, R. (2000). The Place of Religious Arguments in a Free and Democratic Society. In S.M. Feldman (ed.), *Law and Religion: A Critical Anthology* (pp. 69–88). New York: New York University Press.

—— (2009). Natural Reason, Natural Rights, and Governmental Neutrality Toward Religion. *Religion and Human Rights,* 4(2–3), 157–175.

Augustine. (1951). *Letters.* New York: Fathers of the Church.

Augustinus. *De Civitate Dei.*

Austin, J. (1975). *How to Do Things with Words.* Cambridge, MA: Harvard University Press.

Ayoob, M. (2008). *The Many Faces of Political Islam: Religion and Politics in the Muslim World.* Ann Arbor, MI: University of Michigan Press.

Bader, V. (1997). Fairly Open Borders. In V. Bader (ed.), *Citizenship and Exclusion* (pp. 28–60). London: Macmillan.

—— (2003). Religions and States: A New Typology and a Plea for Non-constitutional Pluralism. *Ethical Theory and Moral Practice,* 6(1), 55–91.

—— (2003). Religious Diversity and Democratic Institutional Pluralism. *Political Theory,* 31(2), 265–294.

—— (2007). *Secularism or Democracy?* Amsterdam: Amsterdam University Press.

—— (ed.) (1997). *Citizenship and Exclusion.* London: Macmillan.

Bader, V. & Engelen, E. (2003). Taking Pluralism Seriously: Arguing for an Institutional Turn in Political Philosophy. *Philosophy and Social Criticism,* 29(4), 375–406.

Baderin, M. (2005). *International Human Rights and Islamic Law.* Oxford: Oxford University Press.

Bamforth, N. & Richards, D. (2008). *Patriarchal Religion, Sexuality and Gender: A Critique of New Natural Law.* Boston, MA: Cambridge University Press.

Bangstad, S. (2007). *Global Flows, Local Appropriations: Facets of Secularisation and Re-Islamization among Contemporary Cape Muslims.* Dissertation Radboud University Nijmegen. Amsterdam: Amsterdam University Press.

Banton, M. (ed.) (1978). *Anthropological Approaches to the Study of Religion*. London: Tavistock.

Bänziger, S. (2007). *Still Praying Strong: An Empirical Study of the Praying Practices in a Secular Society*. Dissertation Radboud University Nijmegen.

Baraúna, G. (ed.) (1968). *De kerk in de wereld van nu: Commentaren op de pastorale constitutie 'Gaudium et Spes'*. Bilthoven: Nelissen.

Barberini, G. (2003). Religious Freedom in the Process of Democratization of Central and Eastern European States. In S. Ferrari & W.C. Durham Jr. (eds.), *Law and Religion in Post-Communist Europe* (pp. 7–22). Leuven: Peters.

Barro, R. & McCleary, R. (2004). *Which Countries Have State Religions?* Available at: http://economics.uchicago.edu/download/state_religion_03-03.pdf.

Barsalou, L.W. et al. (2005). Embodiment in Religious Knowledge. *Journal of Cognition and Culture, 5*(1/2), 14–57.

Bartel, T.W. (ed.) (2003). *Comparative Theology: Essays for Keith Ward*. London: Society for Promoting Christian Knowledge.

Bates, E., et al. (2002). Innateness and Emergentism. In W. Bechtel & G. Graham (eds.), *A Companion to Cognitive Science* (pp. 590–601). Oxford: Blackwell.

Bauberot, J. (1999). The Two Thresholds of Laïcization. In R. Bhargava (ed.), *Secularism and Its Critics*. Delhi: Oxford University Press.

Bauer, C. & Van Erp, S. (eds.) (2004). *Salvation in Diversity*. Münster: Lit.

Bauman, U. (1995). Ehe. In *Historisch-theologisch. Lexikon für Theologie und Kirche. Dritter Band* (pp. 471–474). Freiburg: Herder.

Bayat, A. (2007). *Islam and Democracy*. Amsterdam: Amsterdam University Press.

Beattie, T. (2008). "Justice Enacted not these Human Laws" (Antigone), Religion, Natural Law and Women's Rights. *Religion and Human Rights, 3*(3), 249–267.

Bechtel, W. & Graham, G. (eds.). *A Companion to Cognitive Science*. Oxford: Blackwell.

Becker, M. (ed.) (2009). *Christelijk sociaal denken: Traditie, actualiteit, kritiek*. Budel: Damon.

Beckmann, J. (1998). Nominalismus. In *Lexikon für Theologie und Kirche 7* (pp. 894–896). Freiburg: Herder.

—— (2001). Wilhelm von Ockham. In *Lexikon für Theologie und Kirche 10* (pp. 1186–1191). Freiburg: Herder.

Bekker, J., Labuschagne, J. & Vorster, L. (eds.) (2002). *Introduction to Legal Pluralism in South Africa*. Durban: Butterworth.

Bell, C. (1997). *Ritual: Perspectives and Dimensions*. Oxford: Oxford University Press.

Bellah, R. (1974). Civil Religion in America. In R. Richey & D. Jones (eds.), *American Civil Religion* (pp. 24–41). New York: Harper & Row.

Bellah, R. et al. (eds.) (1986). *Habits of the Heart: Individualism and Commitment in American Life*. New York: Perennial Library.

Bennett, M.R. & Hacker, P.M.S. (2003). *Philosophical Foundations of Neuroscience*. Malden, MA: Blackwell.

Bennett, T. (1999). *Human Rights and African Customary Law under the South African Constitution*. Cape Town: Juta.

Berger, P.L. (1999). The Desecularization of the World: A Global Overview. In P.L. Berger (ed.), *The Desecularization of the World: Resurgent Religion and World Politics* (pp. 1–18). Washington, DC/Grand Rapids, MI: Ethics and Public Policy Center/Eerdmans.

—— (ed.) (1999). *The Desecularization of the World: Resurgent Religion and World Politics*. Washington, DC/Grand Rapids, MI: Ethics and Public Policy Center/Eerdmans.

Berger, P. & Luckmann, T. (1967). *The Social Construction of Reality*. New York: Anchor.

Berges, U. (1998). *Das Buch Jesaja: Komposition und Gestalt*. Freiburg: Herder.

Bering, J.M. (2005). The Evolutionary History of an Illusion: Religious Causal Beliefs in Children and Adults. In B.J. Ellis & D.F. Bjorklund (eds.), *Origins of the Social Mind: Evolutionary Psychology and Child Development* (pp. 411–437). New York: Guilford.

Bering, J.M. & Johnson, D.D.P. (2005). "O Lord…You Perceive my Thoughts from Afar": Recursiveness and the Evolution of Supernatural Agency. *Journal of Cognition and Culture*, 5(1/2), 118–142.

Bernardi, B. (2007). *Le principe d'obligation: Sur une aporie de la modernité politique*. Paris: Vrin.

Besselink, L. (2003). Voetangels en klemmen: De horizontale werking van burger- en politieke rechten. In C. Flinterman & W. van Genugten (eds.), *Niet-statelijke actoren en de rechten van de mens: Gevestigde waarden, nieuwe wegen* (pp. 3–18). The Hague: Boom.

Bhanot, S. & Santosh, R. (eds.) (2001). *The Hindu Youth Research Project 2001*. Oxford: Oxford Centre for Hindu Studies.

Bhargava, R. (ed.) (1999). *Secularism and Its Critics*. Delhi: Oxford University Press.

Bielefeldt, H. (2004). Political Secularism and European Islam. In J. Malik (ed.), *Muslims in Europe* (pp. 147–160). Münster: Lit.

Blalock, H. (1979). *Social Statistics*. Tokyo: McGraw-Hill.

Blankenburg, E. & Bruinsma, F. (1994). *Dutch Legal Culture*. Deventer: Kluwer.

Blockmans, W. & Hoppenbrouwers, P. (2002). *Eeuwen des onderscheids: Een geschiedenis van middeleeuws Europa*. Amsterdam: Prometheus.

Bloemraad, L. (2006). *Becoming a Citizen: Incorporating Immigrants and Refugees in the United States and Canada*. Berkeley, CA: University of California Press.

Blum, L. (1998). Recognition, Value, and Equality: A critique of Charles Taylor's and Nancy Fraser's Accounts of Multiculturalism. In C. Willett (ed.), *Theorizing Multiculturalism: A Guide to the Current Debate* (pp. 73–99). Malden, MA: Blackwell.

Bocken, I. (2004). *John Locke: Een brief over tolerantie, vertaling, inleiding en essay*. Budel: Damon.

Böckenförde, E.-W. (1990). *Religionsfreiheit: Die Kirche in der modernen Welt*. Freiburg: Herder.

Böckle, F. (ed.) (1966). *Das Naturrecht im Disput*. Düsseldorf: Patmos.

Böckle, F. & Böckenförde, E.-W. (eds.) (1973). *Naturrecht in der Kritik*. Mainz: Grünewald.

Bodin, J. (1975). *Colloquium Heptaplomeres de Rerum Sublimium Arcanis Abditis 1588*. Princeton, NJ: Princeton University Press.

Boelaars, H. et al. (1947). *Onrust in de Zielzorg*. Utrecht: Spectrum.

Boelens, O. (2002). *De 'Lex Ecclesiae Fundamentalis' een gemiste kans of kansloze misser?* Dissertation Catholic Theological University Utrecht.

Bohman, J. & Rehg, W. (eds.) (1997). *Deliberative Democracy: Essays on Reason and Politics*. Cambridge, MA: MIT Press.

Boltanski, L. & Thévenot, L. (1991). *De la justification: Les economies de la grandeur*. Paris: Gallimard.

—— (2006). *On Justification: Economies of Worth*. Princeton, NJ: Princeton University Press.

Bosch, D.J. (1991). *Transforming Mission: Paradigm Shifts in Theology of Mission*. Maryknoll, NY: Orbis.

Bourdieu, P. (1977). *Outline of a Theory of Practice*. Cambridge: Cambridge University Press.

—— (2004). *Science of Science and Reflexivity*. Cambridge: Polity Press.

Boyer, P. (1994). *The Naturalness of Religious Ideas: A Cognitive Theory of Religion*. Berkeley, CA: University of California Press.

—— (2001). *Religion Explained: The Evolutionary Origins of Religious Thought*. New York: Basic.

Brand, D. & Russel, S. (2002). *Exploring the Core Content of Socio-Economic Rights: South African and International Perspectives.* Pretoria: Protea.

Braudel, F. (1969). *Écrits sur l'histoire.* Paris: Flammarion.

Braun, W. & McCutcheon, R.T. (eds.) (2000). *Guide to the Study of Religion.* London/ New York: Cassell.

Brems, E. (2001). Universaliteit en diversiteit in de internationale mensenrechten. In P. Cliteur & V. van den Eeckhout (eds.), *Multiculturalisme, cultuurrelativisme en sociale cohesie* (pp. 65–78). The Hague: Boom.

Bretschneider, P. (1995). *Polygyny: A Cross-Cultural Study.* Uppsala: Acta Universitatis Upsaliensis.

Brieskorn, N. (2006). Rechte. In M. Düwell et al. (eds.), *Handbuch Ethik* (pp. 493–498). Stuttgart: Metzler.

Brinkman, M. (2009). Nieuwe Latijns-Amerikaanse beelden van Jezus: Een christologische benadering. *Tijdschrift voor Theologie, 49*(3), 273–286.

Brown, D. (1999). Human Universals. In R.A. Wilson & F.C. Keil (eds.), *The MIT Encyclopedia of the Cognitive Sciences.* Cambridge, MA: MIT Press.

Browne, E.J. (2003). *Charles Darwin. Vol. I. Voyaging; Vol. II. The Power of Place.* London: Pimlico.

Brownlie, I. & Goodwin-Gill, G.S. (eds.) (2002). *Basic Documents on Human Rights.* Oxford/New York: Oxford University Press.

Bruce, S. (1996). *Religion in the Modern World: From Cathedrals to Cults.* Oxford/New York: Oxford University Press.

—— (1999). *Choice and Religion: A Critique of Rational Choice Theory.* Oxford/New York: Oxford University Press.

—— (2001). The Curious Case of the Unnecessary Recantation: Berger and Secularization. In L. Woodhead et al. (eds.), *Peter Berger and the Study of Religion* (pp. 87–100). London/New York: Routledge.

Bruggink, J. (1989). Wat zijn 'Mensenrechten'? In L. Heyde et al. (eds.), *Begrensde Vrijheid* (pp. 87–99). Zwolle: Willink.

Brugmans, E., Minderhoud, P. & Van Vught, J. (eds.) (2007). *Mythen en misverstanden over migratie.* Nijmegen: Valkhof.

Brune, G. (2006). *Menschenrechte und Menschenrechtsethos: Zur Debatte um eine Ergänzung der Menschenrechte durch Menschenpflichten.* Stuttgart: Kohlhammer.

Bruner, J.S. (1986). *Actual Minds: Possible Worlds.* Cambridge, MA: Harvard University Press.

—— (1990). *Acts of Meaning.* Cambridge, MA: Harvard University Press.

Bucar, E. & Barnett, B. (eds.) (2005). *Does Human Rights Need God?* Grand Rapids, MI: Eerdmans.

Bulbulia, J. (2005). Are There Any Religions? An Evolutionary Exploration. *Method and Theory in the Study of Religion, 17*(2), 71–100.

Burlamaqui, J.-J. (2006). The Principles of Political Law. In: *The Principles of Natural and Political Law.* Indianapolis, IN: Liberty Fund.

Burleigh, M. (2006). *Sacred Causes: Religion and Politics from the European Dictators to Al Qaeda.* London: HarperPress.

Buruma, I. (2006). *Murder in Amsterdam: The Death of Theo Van Gogh and the Limits of Tolerance.* New York: Penguin.

Buskes, C. (2007). *Evolutionair denken: De invloed van Darwin op ons wereldbeeld.* Amsterdam: Nieuwezijds.

Buss, D.M. (ed.) (2005). *The Handbook of Evolutionary Psychology.* Hoboken, NJ: Wiley.

Cacioppo J. & Patrick W. (2008). *Loneliness. Human Nature and the Need for Social Connection.* New York: Norton & Company.

Cameron, S. (2002). *The Economics of Sin: Rational Choice or no Choice at all.* Cheltenham: Elgar.

Cane, P. et al. (eds.) (2008). *Law and Religion in Theoretical and Historical Context.* Cambridge: Cambridge University Press.

Cannon, D.S. (1996). *Six Ways of Being Religious: A Framework for Comparative Studies of Religion.* Belmont, CA: Wadsworth.

Capucao, D. (2010). *Religion and Ethnocentrism: An Empirical-Theological Study of the Effects of Religious Attitudes on Attitudes towards Minorities among Catholics in the Netherlands.* Leiden: Brill.

Carman, J.B. & Hopkins, S.P. (eds.) (1991). *Tracing Common Themes: Comparative Courses in the Study of Religion.* Atlanta, GA: Scholars Press.

Casanova, J. (1994). *Public Religions in the Modern World.* Chicago, IL: University of Chicago Press.

Cassirer, E. (1932). Vom Wesen und Werden des Naturrechts. *Zeitschrift für Rechtsphilosophie in Lehre und Praxis, 6*(1), 1–27.

—— (2001). Freiheitsidee und Staatsidee. *In: Gesammelte Werke.* Hamburg: Meiner.

—— (2004). Vom Wesen und Werden des Naturrechts. *In: Gesammelte Werke.* Hamburg: Meiner.

CBS. (Centraal Bureau voor de Statistiek) (2009). *Religie aan het begin van de 21ste eeuw.* Den Haag: CBS.

Chai, S. (2003). *The Many Flavors of Rational Choice and the Fate of Sociology.* Paper presented at the annual meeting of the American Sociological Association Atlanta, GA: Available at: http://www.allacademic.com/meta/p106543_index.html.

Changeux, J.-P. & Ricoeur, P. (2002). *What Makes us Think? A Neuroscientist and a Philosopher Argue about Ethics, Human Nature, and the Brain,* translated by M.B. DeBevoise. Princeton, NJ: Princeton University Press.

Chanial, P. & Caillé, A. et al. (2008). L'homme est-il un animal sympathique? Le contr'Hobbes. *Revue du Mauss, premier semester, no. 31*(1).

Chaves, M. & Cann, D. (1992). Regulation, Pluralism, and Religious Market Structure *Rationality and Society, 4*(3), 272–290.

Chenu, M.-D. (1968). De rol van de kerk in de hedendaagse wereld. In G. Baraúna (ed.), *De kerk in de wereld van nu: Commentaren op de Pastorale Constitutie 'Gaudium Et Spes'* (pp. 282–301). Bilthoven: Nelissen.

—— (1979). *La 'doctrine sociale' de l'église comme idéologie.* Paris: Cerf.

—— *La théologie comme une science au XIIItième siècle.* Paris: Vrin.

—— *La théologie au douzième siècle.* Paris: Vrin.

Chia, E. (2003). *Towards a Theology of Dialogue: Schillebeeckx's Method as Bridge Between Vatican's Dominus Iesus and Asia's FABC Theology.* Dissertation Radboud University Nijmegen.

Christoffersen, L. (2008). Religion as a Factor in Multi-Layered European Union Legislation. In R. Mehdi et al. (eds.), *Law and Religion in Multicultural Societies* (pp. 111–130). Copenhagen: Djøf.

Churchland, P.M. (1995). *The Engine of Reason, the Seat of the Soul: A Philosophical Journey into the Brain.* Cambridge, MA: MIT Press.

Cisło, W. (2000). *Die Religionskritik der französischen Enzyklopädisten.* Frankfurt: Lang.

Cliteur, P. & Van den Eeckhout, V. (eds.) (2001). *Multiculturalisme, cultuurrelativisme en sociale cohesie.* The Hague: Boom.

Cliteur, P. et al. (eds.) (1998). *Sociale cohesie en het recht.* Leiden: Meijers Instituut.

Cloninger, C. et al. (1993). A Psychological Model of Temperament and Character. *Archive of General Psychiatry, 50,* 975–990.

Clooney, F.X. (2001). *Hindu God, Christian God: How Reason Helps Break Down the Boundaries Between Religions.* Oxford/New York: Oxford University Press.

Coetzee, P.H. & Roux, A.P.J. (eds.) (1998). *Philosophy from Africa: A Text With Readings.* Johannesburg: Thomson.

Cohen, F. (2008). *De herschepping van de wereld: Het ontstaan van de moderne wetenschap verklaard.* Amsterdam: Bakker.

Collins, R. (2004). *Interaction Ritual Chains*. Princeton, NJ: Princeton University Press.

Connolly, W. (1991). *Identity/Difference, Democratic Negotiations of Political Paradox*. Minneapolis, MN: University of Minnesota Press.

Coskun, D. (2006). *Law as Symbolic Form: Ernst Cassirer and the Anthropocentric View of Law*. Dissertation Radboud University Nijmegen. Nijmegen: Wolf.

Cosmides, L. & Tooby, J. (2005). Neurocognitive Adaptations Designed for Social Exchange. In D.M. Buss (ed.), *The Handbook of Evolutionary Psychology* (pp. 584–627). Hoboken, NJ: Wiley.

Cowen, S. (2001). Can 'Dignity' Guide South Africa's Equality Jurisprudence? *South African Journal on Human Rights, 17*, 34–58.

Crombie, A.C. (1994). *Styles of Scientific Thinking in the European Tradition: The History of Argument and Explanation Especially in the Mathematical and Biomedical Sciences and Arts. Vol. I–III*. London: Duckworth.

Curran, C. (2002). *Catholic Social Teaching 1891–Present*. Georgetown, DC: Georgetown University Press.

Curtis, E.M. (1984). *Man as the Image of God in Genesis in the Light of Ancient Near Eastern Parallels*. Dissertation University of Pennsylvania. Ann Arbor, MI: University Microfilms International.

D'Arcais, P.F. *Eleven Theses against Habermas*. Available at: http://www.filosofia.it/pagine/micromega/11ThesesagainstHabermas.pdf.

Dagevos, J. & Gijsberts, M. (eds.) (2007). *Jaarrapportage Integratie 2007*. The Hague: Sociaal en Cultureel Planbureau.

Dalferth, I. (2003). *Die Wirklichkeit des Möglichen*. Tübingen: Mohr.

—— (2001). Theologie im Kontext der Religionswissenschaft. *Theologische Literaturzeitung, 126*(1), 4–20.

Damasio, A.R. (2000). *The Feeling of What Happens: Body and Emotion in the Making of Consciousness*. New York: Harcourt.

—— (2004). *Looking for Spinoza: Joy, Sorrow and the Feeling Brain*. London: Vintage.

—— (1994). *Descartes' Error: Emotion, Reason, and the Human Brain*. New York: Putnam.

Daniel, Y. et al. (eds.) (1999). *The Universal Declaration of Human Rights: Fifty Years and Beyond*. Amityville, NY: Baywood.

Dann, O. & Klippel, D. (eds.) (1995). *Naturrecht, Spätaufklarung, Revolution*. Berlin: Meiner.

Dante Alighieri. *Inferno*.

—— *De Monarchia*.

Darwin, C. (2004). *The Descent of Man: And Selection in Relation to Sex*. London: Penguin.

—— (1999). *The Expression of the Emotions in Man and Animals*. Introduction, afterword and commentaries by P. Ekman. London: HarperCollins.

Davidson, D. (2001). *Inquiries into Truth and Interpretation*. Oxford: Clarendon.

Davie, G. (1999). Europe: The Exception That Proves the Rule? In P.L. Berger (ed.), *The Desecularization of the World: Resurgent Religion and World Politics* (pp. 65–84). Washington, DC/Grand Rapids, MI: Ethics and Public Policy Center/Eerdmans.

—— (2002). *Europe, the Exceptional Case: Parameters of Faith in the Modern World*. Sarum Theological Lectures. London: Darton, Longman & Todd.

—— (1990). Believing without Belonging: Is This the Future of Religion in Britain? *Social Compass, 37*(4), 455–469.

Davies, T. (1995). Borrowed Language: Milton, Jefferson, Mirabeau. In D. Armitage et al. (eds.), *Milton and Republicanism* (pp. 260–287). Cambridge: Cambridge University Press.

Dawkins, R. (1998). *Unweaving the Rainbow: Science, Delusion, and the Appetite for Wonder*. Boston, MA: Houghton Mifflin.

Day, M. (2005). The Undiscovered and Undiscoverable Essence: Species and Religion after Darwin. *The Journal of Religion, 85*(1), 58.

—— (2004). The Ins and Outs of Religious Cognition. *Method and Theory in the Study of Religion 16*, 241–255.

De Cusa, N. (2001). *De Docta Ignorantia*, translation by J. Hopkins. Minneapolis, MN: Banning.

—— (1966). *De Docta Ignorantia*, edited by W. & D. Dupré. Vienna: Herder.

De Hert, P. & Meerschaut, K. (eds.) (2007). *Scheiding van kerk staat of actief pluralisme?* Antwerpen: Intersentia.

De Lubac, H. (1974). *Pic de la Mirandole: Études et discussions*. Paris: Aubier Montaigne.

De Montesquieu, C.-L. (1990). *Spirit of the Laws*. Cambridge: Cambridge University Press.

De Spinoza, B. *Tractatus Theologico-Politicus.*

De Vitoria, F. (1991). *Political Writings*. Cambridge: Cambridge University Press.

De Vries, H. (1999). *Philosophy and the Turn to Religion*. Baltimore, MD: Johns Hopkins University Press.

De Waal, F.B.M. (2005). *Our Inner Ape: The Best and Worst of Human Nature*. London: Granta.

De Waal, J. et al. (eds.) (2002). *The Bill of Rights Handbook*. Lansdowne: Juta.

Deacon, T.W. (1997). *The Symbolic Species: The Co-Evolution of Language and the Brain*. New York: Norton.

Dekkers, W., Hoffer, C. & Wils, J.-P. (2006). *Besnijdenis, lichamelijke integriteit en multiculturalisme: Een empirische en normatief-ethische studie*. Budel: Damon.

Delfgaauw, B. (1980). *Thomas van Aquino: Een kritische benadering van zijn filosofie*. Bussum: Wereldvenster.

Delhaye, P. (1968). De waardigheid van de menselijke persoon. In G. Baraúna (ed.), *De kerk in de wereld van nu: Commentaren op de pastorale constitutie 'Gaudium et Spes'* (pp. 211–234). Bilthoven: Nelissen.

Della Mirandola, G.P. *De hominis dignitate.*

Della Mirandola, G.P. (1968). *Over de menselijke waardigheid*. Dutch translation of *De hominis dignitate*. Arnhem: Van Loghum Slaterus.

Den Boer, J.A. (2004). *Neurofilosofie: Hersenen, bewustzijn, vrije wil*. Amsterdam: Boom.

Den Dekker-van Bijsterveld, S. (1988). *De verhouding tussen kerk en staat in het licht van de grondrechten*. Zwolle: Willink.

Denzinger, H. (2005). *Kompendium der Glaubensbekenntnisse und kirchliche Lehrentscheidungen*, edited by P. Hünermann. Freiburg: Herder.

Derrida, J. (2001). *L'université sans condition*. Paris: Galilée.

—— (2002). *Acts of Religion*. New York: Routledge.

Dessing, N. (2001). *Rituals of Birth, Circumcision, Marriage and Death among Muslims in the Netherlands*. Leuven: Peeters.

Devenish, G. (1999). *A Commentary on the South African Bill of Rights*. Durban: Butterworth.

Dewey, J. (1986). *Logic: The Theory of Inquiry*. The Later Works of John Dewey. Vol. XII. Carbondale, IL: Southern Illinois University Press.

Dihle, A. (1962). *Die Goldene Regel*. Göttingen: Vandenhoeck & Ruprecht.

Dlamini, C. (2002). Family Law. In J. Bekker, J. Labuschagne & L. Vorster (eds.), *Introduction to Legal Pluralism in South Africa*. Durban: Butterworth.

Dobbelaere, K. (1999). Towards an Integrated Perspective of the Processes Related to the Descriptive Concept of Secularization. *Sociology of Religion, 60*(3), 229–247.

—— (2002). *Secularization: An Analysis at Three Levels (Gods, Humans & Religion)*. Bruxelles/New York: Lang.

—— (2004). Assessing Secularization Theory. In P. Antes, A.W. Geertz & R.R. Warne (eds.), *New Approaches to the Study of Religion. Vol. II. Textual, Comparative, Sociological, and Cognitive Approaches.* (pp. 228–253). Berlin: De Gruyter.

Dondeyne, A. (1962). *Geloof en wereld*. Antwerpen: Patmos.

Doreian, P. & Fararo, T. (eds.) (1998). *The Problem of Solidarity: Theories and Models*. Amsterdam: Gordon & Breach.

Dörner, W. & Suarez, C. (2008). Civil Society and the State: Formal Arrangements and Actual Interactions. In V. Heinrich & L. Fioramonti (eds.), *Civicus: Global Survey of the State of Civil Society. Vol. II*. (pp. 273–288). Bloomfield: Kumarian.

Drehsen, V. (1988). *Neuzeitliche Konstitutionsbedingungen der praktischen Theologie: Aspekte der theologischen Wende zur sozialkulturellen Lebenswelt christlicher Religion*. Gütersloh: Mohn.

Drinan, R. (2001). *The Mobilization of Shame: A World View of Human Rights*. New Haven, CT: Yale University Press.

Duguit, L. & Monnier, H. (1908). *Les constitutions et les principales lois politiques de la France*. Paris: Librairie générale de droit et du jurisprudence.

Dunbar, R.I.M. (1998). The Social Brain Hypothesis. *Evolutionary Anthropology, 6*(5), 178–190.

Dupré, L. (2008). *Religion and the Rise of Modern Culture*. Notre Dame: University of Notre Dame Press.

Dupuis, J. (1999). The Truth Will Make You Free. *Louvain Studies, 24*(3), 211–263.

Durham, W. (1996). Perspective on Religious Liberty: A Comparative Framework. In J. Witte & J.D. van der Vyver (eds.), *Religious Human Rights in Global Perspective: Legal Perspectives* (pp. 1–44). The Hague: Nijhoff.

Durkheim, E. (1893). *De la division du travail social*. Paris: Presses universitaires de France.

Düwell, M. et al. (eds.) (2006). *Handbuch Ethik*. Stuttgart: Metzler.

Dworkin, R. (1978). *Taking Rights Seriously*. Cambridge, MA: Harvard University Press.

Eco, U. (1979). *A Theory of Semiotics*. Bloomington, IN: Indiana University Press.

Edwards, R.B. (1972). *Reason and Religion: An Introduction to the Philosophy of Religion*. New York: Harcourt Brace Jovanovich.

Eide, A. (2001). Cultural Rights and Minorities. In K. Hastrup (ed.), *Legal Culture and Human Rights: The Challenge of Diversity* (pp. 25–42). The Hague: Kluwer.

Eisenberg, A. & Spinner-Halev, J. (eds.) (2005). *Minorities within Minorities: Equality, Rights and Diversity*. Cambridge: Cambridge University Press.

Eisenstadt, S. (2003). *Comparative Civilizations and Multiple Modernities. Vol. I*. Leiden: Brill.

—— (ed.) (1986). *The Origins and Diversity of Axial Age Civilizations*. New York: State University of New York Press.

Eisgruber, C. & Sager, L. (2000). Equal Regard. In S.M. Feldman (ed.), *Law and Religion: A Critical Anthology* (pp. 200–225). New York: New York University Press.

Eisinga, R. et al. (2002). *Religion in Dutch Society 2000*. Amsterdam: Steinmetz Archive.

Ekman, P. (1999). Afterwoord. In C. Darwin, P. Ekman & P. Prodger (eds.), *The Expression of the Emotions in Man and Animals* (pp. 363–393). London: Harper-Collins.

Ellis, B.J. & Bjorklund, D.F. (eds.) (2005). *Origins of the Social Mind: Evolutionary Psychology and Child Development*. New York: Guilford.

Engelen, Th. (2009). *Van 2 naar 16 miljoen mensen: Demografie van Nederland, 1800–nu*. Amsterdam: Boom.

Entziger, H. & Dourleijn, E. (2008). *De lat steeds hoger: De leefwereld van jongeren in een multi-ethische stad*. Assen: Van Gorcum.

Esposito, J. & Mogahed, D. (2007). *Who Speaks for Islam? What a Billion Muslims Really Think*. New York: Gallup.

Essen, G. (2001). *Die Freiheit Jesu: Der neuchalkedonische Enhypostasiebegriff im Horizont neuzeitlicher Subjekt- und Personphilosophie*. Regensburg: Pustet.

—— (2005). 'Wie observeert religies?' De verhouding van godsdienstwetenschappen en theologie in tijden van terreur. *Tijdschrift voor Theologie, 45*(2), 168–188.

Etzioni, A. (16 June 2008). Stel je prioriteiten goed: Veiligheid komt vóór democratie. *NRC Handelsblad,* 17.

EUMC (European Monitoring Centre on Racism and Xenophobia) (2006). *Muslims in the European Union: Discrimination and Islamophobia.* Vienna: FRA (Agency for Fundamental Rights).

Evans, C. (2005). *Freedom of Religion under the European Convention on Human Rights.* Oxford: Oxford University Press.

Evans, M. (2009). The Freedom of Religion or Belief and the Freedom of Expression. *Religion and Human Rights, 4*(2–3), 197–235.

Evans, M.D. (1997). *Religious Liberty and International Law in Europe.* Cambridge: Cambridge University Press.

Exeler, A. (1978). Vergleichende Theologie statt Missionswissenschaft? In H. Waldenfels (ed.), *... denn Ich bin bei Euch* (pp. 199–212.). Zürich: Benziger.

Ezzati, A. (2002). *Islam and Natural Law.* London: Icas.

Farthing, G.W. (1992). *The Psychology of Consciousness.* Englewood Cliffs, NJ: Prentice Hall.

Feener, R. (ed.) (2004). *Islam in World Cultures: Comparative Perspectives.* Santa Barbara, CA: ABC-Clio.

Feiner, J. & Löhrer, M. (eds.) (1968). *Mysterium Salutis: Dogmatiek in heilshistorisch perspectief 7.* Hilversum: Brand.

Feith, J. (2003). *Probing Neurotheology's Brain or Critiquing an Emerging Quasi-Science.* Paper presented at the Critical Theory and Discourse on Religion Section. The American Academy of Religion.

Feldman, N. (2005). *Divided by God: America's Church-State Problem—and What We Should Do about It.* New York: Farrar.

Feldman, S.M. (ed.) (2000). *Law and Religion: A Critical Anthology.* New York: New York University Press.

Felling, A. & Peters, J. (eds.), *Cultuur en sociale wetenschappen. Beschouwingen en empirische studies.* Nijmegen: ITS.

Felling, A., Peters, J. & Scheepers, P. (eds.) (2000). *Individualisering in Nederland aan het einde van de twintigste eeuw: Empirisch onderzoek naar omstreden hypotheses.* Assen: Van Gorcum.

Felling, A., Peters, J. & Schreuder, O. (1987). *Religion im Vergleich: Bundesrepublik Deutschland und Niederlande.* Frankfurt: Lang.

Ferrara, A. (2008). *The Force of Example: Explorations in the Paradigm of Judgment.* New York: Columbia University Press.

Ferrari, S. & Durham Jr., W.C. (eds.) (2003). *Law and Religion in Post-Communist Europe.* Leuven: Peeters.

Ferrari, S. (2002). Islam and the Western European Model of Church and State Relations. In W. Shadid & S. van Koningsveld (eds.), *Religious Freedom and the Neutrality of the State: The Position of Islam in the European Union* (pp. 6–19). Leuven: Peeters.

Ferry, L. (1996). *L'homme-Dieu: Ou, Le sens de la vie.* Paris: Grasset.

Ferry, L. & Gauchet, M. (2004). *Le religieux après la religion.* Paris: Grasset.

Fiala, A. (2008). Theocentrism and Human Rights: A Critical Argument. *Religion & Human Rights, 3*(3), 217–234.

Finnis, J. (1974). *The Rights and Wrongs of Abortion.* Princeton, NJ: Princeton University Press.

—— (1980). *Natural Law and Natural Rights.* Oxford: Clarendon.

—— (1983). *Fundamentals of Ethics.* Oxford: Clarendon.

—— (1998). *Aquinas: Moral, Political, and Legal Theory.* Oxford: Oxford University Press.

Flauss, J.-F. (ed.) (2002). *International Protection of Religious Freedom*. Brussel: Bruylant.

—— (ed.) (2002). *La protection internationale de la liberté religieuse: International Protection of Religious Freedom*. Brussel: Bruylant.

Flinterman, C. & Van Genugten, W. (eds.) (2003). *Niet-statelijke actoren en de rechten van de mens: Gevestigde waarden, nieuwe wegen*. The Hague: Boom.

Flood, G. (1999). *Beyond Phenomenology: Rethinking the Study of Religion*. London/ New York: Cassell.

—— (2006). Reflections on Tradition and Inquiry in the Study of Religions. *Journal of the American Academy of Religion, 74*(1), 47–58.

Flora, P. et al. (eds.) (1999). *State Formation, Nation Building, and Mass Politics in Europe: The Theory of Stein Rokkan*. Oxford: Oxford University Press.

Føllesdal, A. (1996). Minority Rights. In J. Räikkä (ed.), *Do We Need Minority Rights*. The Hague: Nijhoff.

Forst, R. (2003). *Toleranz im Konflikt*. Frankfurt: Suhrkamp.

Foucault, M. (1989). *Parrèsia: Vrijmoedig spreken en waarheid*. Amsterdam: Boom.

Fournet-Betancourt, R. (1997). *Befreiungstheologie: Kritischer Rückblick und Perspektiven für die Zukunft*. Mainz: Grünewald.

—— (1997). *Befreiungstheologie: Kritischer Rückblick und Perspektiven für die Zukunft. Bd. I. Bilanz der letzten 25 Jahre (1968–1993); Bd. II. Kritische Auswertung und neue Herausforderungen; Bd. III. Die Rezeption im deutschsprachigen Raum*. Mainz: Grünewald.

Francis, L.J. & Katz, Y.J. (2007). Measuring Attitude toward Judaism: The Internal Consistency Reliability of the Katz-Francis Scale of Attitude toward Judaism. *Mental Health Religion and Culture, 10*(4), 309–324.

Francis, L., Brown, L. & Philip, C. (1992). The Development of an Abbreviated Form of the Revised Essence Personality Questionnaire (EPQR-A): Its Use among Students in England, Canada, the U.S.A., and Australia. *Personally and Individual Differences 13*(4), 443–449.

Francis, L. et al. (2008). Assessing Attitude toward Hinduism: The Santosh-Francis Scale. *Mental Health Religion and Culture, 11*(6), 609–621.

Fraser, N. & Honneth, A. (2003). *Umverteilung oder Anerkennung? Eine politisch-philosophische Kontroverse*. Frankfurt: Suhrkamp.

Freidenreich, D.M. (2004). Comparisons Compared: A Methodological Survey of Comparisons of Religion from "A Magic Dwells" to A Magic Still Dwells. *Method and Theory in the Study of Religion, 16*, 80–101.

Friedman, L. (2001). Some Comments on Cotterrell and Legal Transplants. In D. Nelken & J. Feest (eds.), *Adapting Legal Cultures* (pp. 93–98). Oxford: Hart.

—— (1997). The Concept of Legal Culture: A Reply. In D. Nelken (ed.), *Comparing Legal Cultures* (pp. 33–40). Aldershot: Dartmouth.

—— (1999). *The Horizontal Society*. New Haven, CT: Yale University Press.

Fuchs, J. (1955). *Lex naturae: Zur Theologie des Naturrechts*. Düsselfdorf: Patmos.

Galenkamp, M. (1993). *Individualism versus collectivism*. Rotterdam: Rotterdamse Filosofische Studies.

—— (2001). Culturele diversiteit in het recht: Een kritisch perspectief op grondrechten. In P. Cliteur & V. van den Eeckhout (eds.), *Multiculturalisme, cultuurrelativisme en sociale cohesie* (pp. 383–396). The Hague: Boom.

—— (2007). Samenleven van verschillende godsdiensten: Een pleidooi voor een burenrechtelijke benadering van grondrechten. In P. de Hert & K. Meerschaut (eds.), *Scheiding van kerk staat of actief pluralisme?* (pp. 205–222). Antwerpen: Intersentia.

Gallup Poll. (2008). *Muslim World*. Special Report, World Poll. Gallup Center Muslims Studies.

Garrod, A. (ed.) (1993). *Approaches to Moral Development: New Research and Emerging Themes*. New York: Teachers College Press.

Gauchet, M. (1985). *Le désenchantement du monde: Une histoire politique de la religion*. Paris: Gallimard.

Gay, P. (1966). *The Enlightenment: An Interpretation. Vol. I. The Rise of Modern Paganism*. London: Weidenfeld & Nicholson.

Geertz, C. (1969). Religion as a Cultural System. In *The World Yearbook of Religion. The Religious Situation. Vol. I*. London: Evans.

George, R. (ed.) (2003). *Natural Law*. Burlington, VT: Dartmouth/Ashgate.

Gewirth, A. (1982). *Human Rights: Essays on Justification and Applications*. Chicago, IL: University of Chicago Press.

Giddens, A. (1984). *The Constitution of Society: Outline of a Theory of Structuration*. Cambridge: Polity.

Givón, T. (2005). *Context as Other Minds: The Pragmatics of Sociality, Cognition, and Communication*. Amsterdam/Philadelphia, PA: Benjamins.

Glenn, H. (2000). *Legal Traditions of the World: Sustainable Diversity in Law*. Oxford: Oxford University Press.

Glock, C. (1962). On the Study of Religious Commitments. *Religious Education, 57*(4), 98–110.

Goffman, E. (1972). *Interaction Ritual: Essays on Face-to-Face Behavior*. London: Penguin.

Gokul, R. et al. (2002). Islamic Law. In C.R.N. Goolam (ed.), *Introduction to Legal Pluralism in South Africa* (pp. 61–76). Durban: Butterworth.

Goodman, N. (1978). *Ways of Worldmaking*. Indianapolis, IN: Hackett.

Granada, M. (2001). Apologétique platonicienne et apologétique sceptique: Ficin, Savonarole, Jean-Francois Pic de la Mirandole. In P.-F. Moreau (ed.), *Le scepticisme au XVIᵉ et XVIIᵉ siècle. Le retour des philosophes antiques á l'âge classique. Tome II* (pp. 11–47). Paris: Albin Michel.

Greene, A. (2000). The Incommensurability of Religion. In S.M. Feldman (ed.), *Law and Religion: A Critical Anthology* (pp. 226–244). New York: New York University Press.

Griffin, J. (2009). *On Human Rights*. Oxford: Oxford University Press.

Groenewald, A. (2003). *Psalm 69: Its Structure, Redaction and Composition*. Münster: Lit.

Gross, W. (1995). Gottebenbildlichkeit. In *Lexikon für Theologie und Kirche 4* (pp. 871–873). Freiburg: Herder.

Grotius, H. (De Groot, H.). (1991). *Denken over oorlog en vrede*. A. Eyffmger & B. Vermeulen's translation. Baarn: Ambo.

—— (De Groot, H.). (1625). *De Jure belli ac pacis*.

Guthrie, S. (1993). *Faces in the Clouds: A New Theory of Religion*. New York: Oxford University Press.

Gutierrez, G. (1973). *A Theology of Liberation: History, Politics, and Salvation*. New York: Orbis.

Gutmann, A. et al. (eds.) (1994). *Multiculturalism: Examining the Politics of Recognition*. Princeton, NJ: Princeton University Press.

Haarsma, F. et al. (1970). *Kirchliche Lehre: Skepsis der Gläubigen*. Freiburg: Herder.

Haas, M. (2008). *International Human Rights: A Comprehensive Introduction*. London: Routledge.

Habermas, J. (1981). *Theorie des kommunikativen Handelns, Band 1–2*. Frankfurt: Suhrkamp.

—— (1993). *Faktizität und Geltung: Beiträge zur Diskurstheorie des Rechts und des demokratischen Rechtsstaats*. Frankfurt: Suhrkamp.

—— (1994). Struggles for Recognition in the Democratic Constitutional State. In A. Gutmann et al. (eds.), *Multiculturalism: Examining the Politics of Recognition* (pp. 107–148). Princeton, NJ: Princeton University Press.

—— (1997). Popular Sovereignty as Procedure. In J. Bohman & W. Rehg (eds.), *Deliberative Democracy: Essays on Reason and Politics* (pp. 35–66). Cambridge, MA: MIT Press.

—— (1998). *Die postnationale Konstellation: Politische Essays*. Frankfurt: Suhrkamp.

—— (2003). *Zeitdiagnosen: Zwölf Essays 1980–2001*. Frankfurt: Suhrkamp.

—— (2005). *Zwischen Naturalismus und Religion: Philosophische Aufsätze*. Frankfurt: Suhrkamp.

—— (2008). Ein Bewusstsein von dem was fehlt. In M. Reder & J. Schmidt (eds.), *Ein Bewusstsein von dem, was fehlt: Eine Diskussion mit Jürgen Habermas* (pp. 26–36). Frankfurt: Suhrkamp.

Hagoort, P. (2000). *De toekomstige eeuw der cognitieve neurowetenschap*. Nijmegen: Catholic University Nijmegen (now Radboud University).

—— (2005). Het zwarte gat tussen brein en bewustzijn. In N. Korteweg (ed.), *De oorsprong: Over het ontstaan van het leven en alles eromheen* (pp. 107–124). Amsterdam: Boom.

Hamer, D.H. (2004). *The God Gene: How Faith is Hardwired into our Genes*. New York: Doubleday.

Harkness, J. et al. (2003). *Cross-Cultural Survey Methods*. Hoboken, NJ: Wiley.

Harris, G. (1997). *Dignity and Vulnerability*. Berkeley, CA: University of California Press.

—— (1999). *Agent-Centered Morality: An Aristotelian Alternative to Kantian Internalism*. Berkeley, CA: University of California Press.

Hart, D. (2006). *A Secular Faith: Why Christianity Favors the Separation of Church and State*. Chicago, IL: I. Dee.

Haselager, W.F.G. (1997). *Cognitive Science and Folk Psychology: The Right Frame of Mind*. London/Thousand Oaks, CA: Sage.

Hassan, R. *Are Human Rights Compatible with Islam? The Issue of the Rights of Women in Muslim Communities*. Available at: http://www.religiousconsultation .org/hassan2.htm.

—— *One of Another: Gender Equality and Justice in Islam*. Available at http://www .religiousconsultation.org/hassan htm.

Hassan, R. *Religious Human Rights in the Qur'an*. Available at: http://www.webbin-ternational.org/download/word/articles_riffat/Religious_Human_Rights_in_the_ Quran.doc.

Hasselmann, C. (2001). De wereldethiek: Verklaring van Chicago. *Concilium, 37*(4), 24–37.

Hastrup, K. (ed.) (2001). *Legal Cultures and Human Rights: The Challenge of Diversity*. The Hague: Kluwer.

Hayase, Y. & Liaw, K.-L. (1997). Factors on Polygamy in Sub-Saharan Africa: Findings Based on the Demographic and Health Surveys. *The Developing Economies, 35*(3), 293–327.

Haynes, J. (ed.) (2009). *Routledge Handbook of Religion and Politics*. New York: Routledge.

Headland, T.N. (1990). Introduction: A Dialogue Between Kenneth Pike and Marvin Harris on Emics and Etics. In T.N. Headland, K.L. Pike & M. Harris (eds.), *Emics and Etics: The Insider/Outsider Debate*. Newbury Park, CA: Sage.

Headland, T.N., Pike, K.L. & Harris, M. (eds.) (1990). *Emics and Etics: The Insider/ Outsider Debate*. Newbury Park, CA: Sage.

Hegel, G.W.F. (1959). *Vorlesungen über die Philosophie der Religion. Sämtliche Werke. Bd. XV*. Stuttgart: Frommann-Holzboog.

Heidegger, M. (1993). *Sein und Zeit*. Tübingen: Niemeyer.

Heinrich, V. & Fioramonti, L. (eds.) (2008). *Civicus: Global Survey of the State of Civil Society. Vol. II*. Bloomfield, CT: Kumarian.

Held, D. (1987). *Models of Democracy*. Cambridge: Polity Press.

Hermans, C.A.M. (2004). *Empirische theologie vanuit praktische rationaliteit in religieuze praktijken: Epistemologische reflecties op de ontwikkeling van een academische discipline*. Inaugural address at the Radboud University Nijmegen.

Hermans, C.A.M. & Moore, M.E. (eds.) (2004). *Hermeneutics and Empirical Research in Practical Theology: The Contribution of Empirical Theology by Johannes A. van der Ven*. Leiden/Boston, MA: Brill.

Hermans, H.J.M. (1974). *Waardengebieden en hun ontwikkeling*. Amsterdam: Swets & Zeitlinger.

Hermans, H.J.M. & Kempen, H.J.G. (1998). Moving Cultures: The Perilous Problems of Cultural Dichotomies in a Globalizing Society. *American Psychologist, 53*(10), 1111–1120.

Hervieu-Léger, D. (1993). *La Religion pour mémoire*. Paris: Cerf.

Hettema, T.L. & Van der Kooij, A. (eds.) (2000). *Religious Polemics in Context*. Papers presented to the Second International Conference of the Leiden Institute for the Study of Religions (Lisor), Leiden, 27–28 April. Assen: Van Gorcum.

Heyde, L. et al. (eds.) (1989). *Begrensde vrijheid*. Zwolle: Willink.

Hick, J. (1989). *An Interpretation of Religion: Human Responses to the Transcendent*. New Haven, CT: Yale University Press.

Hillman, E. (1975). *Polygamy Reconsidered*. New York: Orbis.

Hilpert, K. (2001). *Menschenrechte und Theologie: Forschungsbeiträge zur ethischen Dimension der Menschenrechte*. Freiburg: Herder.

Hirschman, A. (1970). *Exit, Voice, and Loyalty: Responses to Decline in Firms, Organizations, and States*. Cambridge, MA: Harvard University Press.

Hobbes, T. *Leviathan*.

Hobsbawm, E.J. (1962). *The Age of Revolution*. New York: New American Library.

Hoffman, M.L. (1993). Empathy, Social Cognition, and Moral Education. In A. Garrod (ed.), *Approaches to Moral Development: New Research and Emerging Themes* (pp. 157–179). New York: Teachers College Press.

Hofstede, G. (2005). *Cultures and Organizations: Software of the Mind*. New York: McGraw-Hill.

Hofstede, G. & Hofstede, G.J. (2005). *Allemaal andersdenkenden: Omgaan met cultuurverschillen*. Amsterdam: Contact.

Hoheisel, K. (2004). Religionstypologie. In *Religion in Geschichte und Gegenwart 7* (pp. 386–388). Tübingen: Mohr Siebeck.

Hohfeld, W. (1978). *Fundamental Legal Conceptions as Applied in Juridical Reasoning*. Ed. by W. Cook, Westport, CT: Greenwood.

Holdrege, B.A. (1996). *Veda and Torah: Transcending the Textuality of Scripture*. Albany, NY: State University of New York Press.

Honée, E. (2009). *Witboek historisch onderzoek: Toelichting bij mijn lijst van geschiedkundige publicaties*. Nijmegen.

Honneth, A. (1994). *Kampf um Anerkennung: Zur moralischen Grammatik sozialer Konflikte*. Frankfurt: Suhrkamp.

—— (2000). *Das Andere der Gerechtigkeit*. Frankfurt: Suhrkamp.

—— (2003). *Unsichtbarkeit: Stationen einer Theorie der Intersubjektivität*. Frankfurt: Suhrkamp.

Horton, R. (1995). *Patterns of Thought in Africa and the West*. Cambridge: Cambridge University Press.

Hottois, G. (2009). *Dignité et diversité des homes*. Paris: Vrin.

Howard Center for Family, Religion, Society. Available at: http://www.profam.org/docs/acc/thc.acc.globalizing.040112.htm.

Hübenthal, C. (2006). *Grundlegung der christlichen Sozialethik Versuch eines freiheitsanalytisch-handlungsreflexiven Ansatzes*. Münster: Aschendorff.

Hughes, J. & Sasse, G. (2003). Monitoring the Monitors: EU Enlargement Conditionality and Minority Protection in the CEECs. *Journal of Ethnopolitics and Minorty Issues in Europe, 4* (1), 1–37.

Hunt, L. (2007). *Inventing Human Rights: A History*. New York: Norton.

Hutcheson, F. (1753). *A Short Introduction to Moral Philosophy, in Three Books, Containing the Elements of Ethics and the Laws of Nature, 2nd edition.* Glasgouw: Robert & Andrew Foulis.

Iannaccone, L. (1991). The Consequences of Religious Market Structure: Adam Smith and the Economics of Religion. *Rationality and Society,* 3(2), 156–177.

Ignatieff, M. (ed.) (2001). *Human Rights as Politics and Idolatry.* Princeton, NJ: Princeton University Press.

Ingram, A. (1994). *A Political Theory of Rights.* New York: Clarendon.

Introvigne, M., Stark, R. (2005). Religious Competition and Revival in Italy: Exploring European Exceptionalism. *Interdisciplinary Journal of Research on Religion,* 1(1), 3–20.

Ishay, M. (2008). *The History of Human Rights: From Ancient Times to the Globalization Era.* New Delhi: Longman.

Israel, J. (2001). *Radical Enlightenment: Philosophy and the Making of Modernity.* Oxford: Oxford University Press.

—— (2006). *Enlightenment Contested: Philosophy, Modernity, and the Emancipation of Man, 1670–1752.* Oxford/New York: Oxford University Press.

Izard, C.E. et al. (eds.) (1988). *Emotions, Cognition, and Behavior.* Cambridge/New York: Cambridge University Press.

Jacobsohn, G. (2003). *The Wheel of Law: India's Secularism in Comparative Constitutional Context.* Princeton, NJ: Princeton University Press.

Jacoby, M. (1990). *Individuation and Narcissism: The Psychology of the Self in Jung and Kohut.* London/New York: Routledge.

James, W. (1961). *The Varieties of Religious Experience: A Study in Human Nature.* New York: Macmillan.

—— (1978). *The Varieties of Religious Experience.* New York: Image.

Janssen, J. (1988). De jeugd, de toekomst en de religie. *Jeugd en Samenleving,* 18(7/8), 407–426.

Jefferson, T. *Letter to the Danbury Baptists.* U.S. Library of Congress.

Jenkins, P. (2002). *The Next Christendom: The Coming of Global Christianity.* Oxford/New York: Oxford University Press.

Jensen, J.S. (1999). On a Semantic Definition of Religion. In J.G. Platvoet & A.L. Molendijk (eds.), *The Pragmatics of Defining Religion: Contexts, Concepts and Contests.* Leiden: Brill.

—— (2003). *The Study of Religion in a New Key: Theoretical and Philosophical Soundings in the Comparative and General Study of Religion.* Aarhus/Oxford: Aarhus University Press

Jeurissen, R. (1993). *Peace and Religion.* Kampen/Weinheim: Kok/Deutscher Studien.

Johnson, P. (2004). Agents for Reform: The Women's Movement, Social Politics and Family Law Reform. In L. Welchamn (ed.), *Women's Rights and Islamic Family Law* (pp. 144–163). London: Zed.

Joseph, S., Schultz, J. & Castan, M. (2005). *The International Convenant on Civil and Political Rights: Cases, Materials, and Commentary.* Oxford: Oxford University Press.

Jovanović, M. (2005). Recognizing Minority Identities Through Collective Rights. *Human Rights Quarterly,* 27(2), 625–651.

Juergensmeyer, M. (2003). *Terror in the Mind of God: The Global Rise of Religious Violence.* Third revised and updated edition. Berkeley, CA: University of California Press.

Kalberg, S. (2001). *Einführung in die historisch-vergleichende Soziologie Max Webers.* Wiesbaden: Westdeutscher Verlag.

Kant, I. (1951). *Critique of Judgment.* New York: Hafner.

—— (1964). *Groundwork of the Metaphysic of Morals.* New York: Harper & Row.

—— (1965). *Critique of Pure Reason.* New York: St. Martin's.

—— (1965). *Grundlegung zur Metaphysik der Sitten.* Hamburg: Meiner.
—— (1990). *Metaphysische Anfangsgründe der Tugendlehre, Metaphysik der Sitten, Zweiter Teil.* Hamburg: Meiner.
Kantorowicz, E. (1997). *The King's Two Bodies: A Study in Mediaeval Political Theology.* Princeton, NJ: Princeton University Press.
Kaplan, B. (2007). *Divided by Faith.* Cambridge, MA: Harvard University Press.
Karayanni, M. (2007). Multiculture Me No More! On Multicultural Qualifications and the Palestinian-Arab Minority of Israel. *Diogenes, 54*(3), 39–58.
Karskens, M. (2007). Staatsvijanden of nieuwe collega's? Hoe natiestaten en de open samenleving migranten waarderen. In E. Brugmans, P. Minderhoud & J. van Vught (eds.), *Mythen en misverstanden over migratie* (pp. 205–236). Nijmegen: Valkhof.
Kasper, W. (1988). Religionsfreiheit, II. Katholische Kirche. In *Staatslexikon, Recht, Wirtschaft, Gesellschaft, Band IV* (pp. 825–827). Freiburg: Herder.
Kaufmann, F.-X. (1973). Wissensozio- logische Überlegungen zu Renaissance und Niedergang des katholischen Naturrechtsdenken im 19. und 20. Jahrhundert. In F. Böckle & E.-W. Böckenförde (eds.), *Naturrecht in der Kritik* (pp. 126–164). Mainz: Grünewald.
—— (1989). *Religion und Modernität: Sozialwissenschaftliche Perspektiven.* Tübingen: Mohr Siebeck.
Kepel, G. (2004). *The war for Muslim minds: Islam and the West.* Cambridge, MA: Belknap/Harvard University Press.
Ketner, S. (2008). *Marokkaanse wortels, Nederlandse grond, exploratie, bindingen en identiteitsstrategieën van jongeren van Marokkaanse afkomst.* Dissertation University of Groningen.
Kim, H.-G. (2000). *Prolegomena to a Christian Theology of Religions.* Lanham, MD: University Press of America.
Kim, J. (1998). *Mind in a Physical World: An Essay on the Mind-Body Problem and Mental Causation.* Cambridge, MA: MIT Press.
Kim, J. & Mueller, C. (1984). *Factor Analysis: Statistical Methods and Practical Issues.* Beverly Hills, CA: Sage.
Kinzer, S. (2008). *A Thousand Hills: Rwanda's Rebirth and the Man Who Dreamed It.* Hoboken, NJ: Wiley.
—— (July 12, 2008). Mensenrechten staan niet op de eerste plaats. *NRC Handelsblad,* 7.
Kleijwegt, M. & Van Weezel, M. (eds.) (2006). *Het land van haat en nijd.* Amsterdam: Balans.
Klein Goldewijk, B. (1991). *Praktijk of principe.* Kampen: Kok.
Koch, K. (2000). *Imago Dei: Die Würde des Menschen im biblischen Text.* Göttingen: Ruprecht.
Korf, D. & Wouters, M. (2008). *Geloof en geluk: Traditie en vernieuwing onder jonge moslims.* Rotterdam: Guijs.
Korf, D. et al. (eds.) (2007). *Van vasten tot feesten: Leefstijl, acceptatie en participatie van jonge moslims.* Rotterdam: Guijs.
Korteweg, N. (ed.) (2005). *De oorsprong: Over het ontstaan van het leven en alles eromheen.* Amsterdam: Boom.
Kött, A. (2003). *Systemtheorie und Religion: Mit einer Religionstypologie im Anschluss an Niklas Luhmann.* Würzburg: Königshausen & Neumann.
Krämer, K. (2000). *Imago Trinitatis: Die Gottebenbildlichkeit des Menschen in der Theologie des Thomas von Aquin.* Freiburg: Herder.
Kreuzer, J. (2008). Nominalismus. In *Religion in Geschichte und Gegenwart 6* (pp. 356–359), Tübingen: Mohr Siebeck.
Kühl, K. (2006). Recht und Moral. In M. Düwell et al. (eds.), *Handbuch Ethik* (pp. 487–493). Stuttgart: Metzler.
Kuhn, T. (1970). *The Structure of Scientific Revolutions.* Chicago, IL: University of Chicago Press.

Kuipers, T.A.F. (2001). *Structures in Science: Heuristic Patterns Based on Cognitive Structures: An Advanced Textbook in Neo-Classical Philosophy of Science*. Dordrecht/Boston, MA: Kluwer.

Kuitert, H. (1972). Waarheid en verificatie in de dogmatiek. *Rondom het woord, 14*(2), 97–130.

—— (1977). *Wat heet geloven: Structuur en herkomst van de christelijke geloofsuitspraken*. Baarn: Ten Have.

Küng, H. (2006). *De Islam*. Kampen: Kok.

Kwa, C. (2005). *De ontdekking van het weten: Een andere geschiedenis van de wetenschap*. Amsterdam: Boom.

Kymlicka, W. (2004). Replies to Commentaries. In Y. Morigiwa et al. (eds.), *Universal Minority Rights* (pp. 105–123). Stuttgart: Steiner.

—— (1995). *Multicultural Citizenship*. Oxford: Clarendon.

—— (2004). Universal Minority Rights? In Y. Morigiwa et al. (eds.), *Universal Minority Rights* (pp. 13–57). Stuttgart: Steiner.

—— (ed.) (1995). *The Rights of Minority Cultures*. Oxford: Oxford University Press.

La Valle, R. (1968). Het leven van de politieke gemeenschap. In G. Baraúna (ed.), *De Kerk in de wereld van nu: Commentaren op de pastorale constitutie 'Gaudium et Spes'* (pp. 434–465). Bilthoven: Nelissen.

Laermans, R. & Verschraegen, G. (2001). The 'Late Niklas Luhmann' on Religion: An Overview. *Social Compass, 48*(1), 7–20.

Laeyendecker, L. (1992). Publieke godsdienst: Wat moeten we ermee? In G. ten Berge (ed.), *Voor God en vaderland: Nationalisme en religie*. Kampen: Kok.

Lakoff, G. (1987). *Women, Fire, and Dangerous Things: What Categories Reveal about the Mind*. Chicago, IL: University of Chicago Press.

Lakoff, G. & Johnson, M. (1980). *Metaphores We Live By*. Chicago, IL: University of Chicago Press.

Lamm, J.A. (1996). *The Living God: Schleiermacher's Theological Appropriation of Spinoza*. University Park, PA: Pennsylvania State University Press.

Larrère, C. (2001). Droit naturel et scepticisme. In P.-F. Moreau (ed.), *De scepticisme au XVIe et au XIIe siècle, Tome II* (pp. 293–308). Paris: Albin Michel.

Lawson, E. & McCauley, R. (1990). *Rethinking Religion: Connecting Cognition and Culture*. Cambridge: Cambridge University Press.

Lazarus, R.S. (1991). *Emotion and Adaptation*. New York: Oxford University Press.

Le Goff, J. (1984). *La civilization de l'Occident médiéval*. Paris: Arthaud.

Leezenberg, M. (2002). *Islamitische filosofie: Een geschiedenis*. Amsterdam: Amsterdam University Press.

Legrand, P. (2003). The Same and the Different. In P. Legrand & R. Munday (eds.), *Comparative Legal Studies: Traditions and Transitions*. Cambridge: Cambridge University Press.

Legrand, P. & Munday, R. (eds.) (2003). *Comparative Legal Studies: Traditions and Transitions*. Cambridge: Cambridge University Press.

Lembruch, G. (1993). Consociational Democracy and Corporatism in Switzerland. *Publius, 23*(2), 43–60.

Lerner, N. (2006). *Religion, Secular Beliefs and Human Rights*. Leiden: Brill.

Lett, J. (1990). Emics and Etics: Notes on the Epistemology of Anthropology. In T.N. Headland, K.L. Pike & M. Harris (eds.), *Emics and Etics: The Insider/Outsider Debate* (pp. 127–142). London: Sage.

Lijphart, A. (1995). Self-determination versus Pre-determination of Ethnic Minorities in Power-sharing Systems. In W. Kymlicka (ed.), *The Rights of Minority Cultures* (pp. 275–287). Oxford: Oxford University Press.

—— (2000). Definitions, Evidence, and Policy. *Journal of Theoretical Politics, 12*(4), 425–431.

—— (2000). *Democracy in the Twenty-First Century*. Wassenaar: NIAS.

Lincoln, B. (1996). Theses on Method. *Method and Theory in the Study of Religion, 8*(3), 225–228.
—— (1999). *Theorizing Myth: Narrative, Ideology, and Scholarship*. Chicago, IL: University of Chicago Press.
Lindholm, T. (1991). Prospects for Research on Cultural Legitimacy of Human Rights: The Cases of Liberalism and Marxism. In A.A. An-Na'im (ed.), *Human Rights in Cross-Cultural Perspective: A Quest for Consensus* (pp. 387–426). Philadelphia, PA: University of Pennsylvania Press.
Locke, J. (1967). *Two Tracts on Government*. Cambridge: Cambridge University Press.
—— (1968). *Epistola de Tolerantia (A Letter on Toleration)* (edited by R. Klibansky, translated by J.W. Gough). Oxford: Clarendon.
—— (1991). *A Letter Concerning Toleration*. London.
Lohmann, G. (2001). Unparteilichkeit in der Moral. In L. Wingert & K. Günther (eds.), *Die Öffentlichkeit der Vernunft and die Vernunft der Öffentlichkeit. Festschrift für Jürgen Habermas* (pp. 434–455). Frankfurt: Suhrkamp.
Lovejoy, A. (1978). *The Great Chain of Being: A Study of the History of an Idea*. Cambridge, MA: Harvard University Press.
Luban, D. (2008). *Legal Ethics and Human Dignity*. Cambridge: Cambridge University Press.
Lübbe, H. (2004). *Modernisierungsgewinner: Religion, Geschichtssinn, direkte Demokratie und Moral*. München: Fink.
—— (2005). *Die Zivilisationsökumene: Globalisierung kulturell, technisch und politisch*. München: Fink.
Luckmann, T. (1980). Säkularisierung: Ein moderner Mythos. In T. Luckmann (ed.), *Lebenswelt und Gesellschaft* (pp. 161–172). Paderborn: Schöningh.
—— (ed.) (1980). *Lebenswelt und Gesellschaft*. Paderborn: Schöningh.
Luhmann, N. (1977 and 1982). *Funktion der Religion*. Frankfurt: Suhrkamp.
—— (1984). *Soziale Systeme: Grundriss einer allgemeinen Theorie*. Frankfurt Suhrkamp.
—— (1990). *Paradigm lost: Über die ethische Reflexion der Moral*. Frankfurt: Suhrkamp.
—— (1995). Das Paradox der Menschenrechte und drei Formen seiner Entfaltung. In *Soziologische Aufklärung 6: Die Soziologie und der Mensch* (pp. 229–236). Opladen: Westdeutscher Verlag.
—— (1995). *Das Recht der Gesellschaft*. Frankfurt: Suhrkamp.
—— (1998). *Die Gesellschaft der Gesellschaft*. Frankfurt: Suhrkamp.
—— (1999). *Ausdifferenzierung des Rechts: Beiträge zur Rechtssoziologie und Rechtstheorie*. Frankfurt: Suhrkamp.
—— (2002). *Die Religion der Gesellschaft*. Frankfurt: Suhrkamp.
Macintryre, A. (1985). *After Virtue: A Study in Moral Theory*. London: Duckworth.
Malena, C. (2008). Does Civil Society Exist? In V. Heinrich & L. Fioramonti (eds.), *Civicus: Global Survey of the State of Civil Society. Vol. II.* (pp. 187–191). Bloomfield: Kumarian.
Malik, J. (ed.) (2004). *Muslims in Europe*. Münster: Lit.
Mamashela, M. (2004). New Families, New Property, New Laws: The Practical Effects of the Recognition of Customary Marriages Act. *South African Journal of Human Rights, 20,* 616–641.
Manjoo, R. (July 2007). *The Recognition of Muslim Personal Laws in South Africa: Implications for Women's Human Rights*. Human Rights Program at Harvard Law School. Working Paper.
Margalit, A. (1999). *The Decent Society*. Cambridge, MA: Harvard University Press.
Maritain, J. (2006). Inaugural Address to the Second International Conference of Unesco. In J. Witte & F. Alexander (eds.), *The Teaching of Modern Christianity on Law, Politics, and Human Nature. Vol. II*. New York: Columbia University Press.
Marshall, D. (2002). Behavior, Belonging, and Belief: A Theory of Ritual Practice. *Sociological Theory, 20*(3), 360–380.

Marshall, P. (ed.) (2008). *Religious Freedom in the World*. New York: Roman & Littlefield.

Martin, D. (1978). *A General Theory of Secularization*. New York: Harper & Row.

Mashour, A. (2005). Islamic Law and Gender Equality. *Human Rights Quarterly*, 27(2), 562–596.

Mason, R. (1997). *The God of Spinoza: A Philosophical Study*. Cambridge/New York: Cambridge University Press.

Masters, R. (1992). Naturalistic Approaches to Justice in Political Philosophy and the Life Sciences. In R. Masters & M. Gruter (eds.), *The Sense of Justice: Biological Foundations of Law* (pp. 67–92). Newbury Park, CA: Sage.

Masters, R. & Gruter, M. (eds.) (1992). *The Sense of Justice: Biological Foundations of Law*. Newbury Park, CA: Sage.

Masuzawa, T. (2005). *The Invention of World Religions: Or, How European Universalism was Preserved in the Language of Pluralism*. Chicago, IL: University of Chicago Press.

Mathieu, L. (2006). *La double peine*. Paris: La dispute.

Mazouz, N. (2006). Gerechtigkeit. In M. Düwell et al. (eds.), *Handbuch Ethik* (pp. 373–376). Stuttgart: Metzler.

Mbiti, J. (1975). *Concepts of God in Africa*. London: Society for Promoting Christian Knowledge.

McAllister, J.W. (2002). Historical and Structural Approaches in the Natural and Human Science. In J.W. McAllister & P.A.J. Tindemans (eds.), *The Future of the Sciences and Humanities: Four Analytical Essays and a Critical Debate on the Future of Scholastic Endeavour*. Amsterdam: Amsterdam University Press.

McAllister, J.W. & Tindemans, P.A.J. (eds.) (2002). *The Future of the Sciences and Humanities: Four Analytical Essays and a Critical Debate on the Future of Scholastic Endeavour*. Amsterdam: Amsterdam University Press.

McCauley, R. (2000). The Naturalness of Religion and the Unnaturalness of Science. In R.A. Wilson & F.C. Keil (eds.), *Explanation and Cognition* (pp. 61–86). Cambridge, MA/London: MIT Press.

McCauley, R.N. & Lawson, E.T. (2002). *Bringing Ritual to Mind: Psychological Foundations of Cultural Forms*. Cambridge/New York: Cambridge University Press.

McCrudden, C. (2008). Human Dignity and Judicial Interpretation of Human Rights. *The European Journal of International Law*, 19(4), 655–724.

McCutcheon, R.T. (1997). *Manufacturing Religion: The Discourse on sui generis Religion and the Politics of Nostalgia*. New York/Oxford: Oxford University Press.

McCutcheon, R.T. (2006). "It's a Lie. There's No Truth in It! It's a Sin!" On the Limits of the Humanistic Study of Religion and the Costs of Saving Others from Themselves. *Journal of the American Academy of Religion*, 74(3), 720–750.

Medin, D. & Waxman, S. (2002). Conceptual Organization. In W. Bechtel & G. Graham (eds.), *A Companion to Cognitive Science* (pp. 167–175). Oxford: Blackwell.

Mehdi, R. et al. (eds.) (2008). *Law and Religion in Multicultural Societies*. Copenhagen: Djøf.

Mensching, G. (1959). *Die Religion: Erscheinungsformen, Strukturtypen und Lebensgesetze*. Stuttgart: Schwab.

Mentzel, M.A., Köbben, A.J.F. et al. (eds.) (1995). *Ethische vragen bij sociaal-wetenschappelijk onderzoek*. Assen: Van Gorcum.

Mernnissi, F. et al. (2004). *Religie en moderniteit*. Zutphen: De Geus.

Mervaud, C. & Seillan, J.-M. (eds.) (2008). *Philosophie des Lumiéres et valeurs chrétiennes*. Paris: L'Harmattan.

Metogo, E.M. (1997). *Dieu peut-il mourir en Afrique? Essai sur l'indifférence religieuse et l'incroyance en Afrique noire*. Paris: Karthala.

Mieth, D. (ed.) (1994). *Moraltheologie im Abseits? Antwort auf die Enzyklika 'Veritatis Splendor'*. Questiones Disputatae 153, Freiburg: Herder.

Milbank, J. (1999). *Theology and Social Theory: Beyond Secular Reason.* Oxford: Blackwell.

Mill, J.S. (1977). *On Liberty.* Toronto: University of Toronto Press.

Millns, S. (2002). Death, Dignity and Discrimination: The Case of Pretty v. United Kingdom. *German Law Journal, 3*(10), Available at: www.germanlawjournal.com./article.php?id=197.

Milton, J. (1973). *Complete Prose Works of John Milton. Vol. I–VII.* New Haven, CT: Yale University Press.

Modood, T., Triandafyllidou, A. & Zapata-Barrero, R. (eds.) (2006). *Multiculturalism, Muslims and Citizenship: A European Approach.* London: Routledge.

Monteiro, M. (2008). *Gods Predikers: Dominicanen in Nederland (1795–2000).* Hilversum: Verloren.

Monzel, N. (1980). *Die Katholische Kirche in der Sozialgeschichte.* München: Olzog Verlag.

Moreau, P.-F. (1999). Les trois étappes du stoïcisme. In P.-F. Moreau (ed.), *Le stoïcisme au XVIe et XVIIe siècle. Le retour des philosophies antiques á l'âge classique. Tome I* (pp. 11–28). Paris: Albin Michel.

—— (ed.) (2001). *De scepticisme au XVIe et au XVIIe siècle. Le retour des philosophes antiques á l'âge classique. Tome II.* Paris: Albin Michel.

—— (ed.). *Le stoïcisme au XVIe et XVIIe siècle. Le retour des philosophies antiques á l'âge classique. Tome I.* Paris: Albin Michel.

Morigiwa, Y. et al. (eds.) (2004). *Universal Minority Rights.* Stuttgart: Steiner.

Morsink, J. (1999). *The Universal Declaration of Human Rights: Origins, Drafting and Intent.* Philadelphia, PA: University of Pennsylvania Press.

Mpofu, E. et al. (1996). Time Management Practices in African Culture: Correlates with College Academic Grades. *Canadian Journal of Behavioral Science, 28,* 1–18.

Müller, H. (1998). *Leidenschaft: Stärke der Armen, Stärke Gottes, Theologische überlegungen zu Erfahrungen in Brasilien.* Mainz: Grünewald.

Murray, J. (1965). *The Problem of Religious Freedom.* Westminster: Newman.

—— (1966). Religious Freedom In W. Abbott (ed.), *Documents of Vatican II* (pp. 672–696). London: Chapman.

—— (1966). *Religious Liberty: An End and a Beginning.* New York: Macmillan.

—— (1966). The Declaration on Religious Freedom: A Moment in its Legislative History. In J. Murray (ed.), *Religious Liberty: An End and a Beginning* (pp. 15–44). New York: Macmillan.

Nanda, V.P. et al. (1981). *Global Human Rights: Public Policies, Comparative Measures, and NGO Strategies.* Boulder, CO: Westview.

Nathwan, M. (2007). Islamic Headscarves and Human Rights: A Critical Analysis of the Relevant Case Law of the European Court of Human Rights. *Netherlands Quarterly of Human Rights, 25*(2), 221–254.

Nauer, D. et al. (ed.), *Praktische Theologie.* Stuttgart: Kohlhammer.

Nelken, D. (ed.) (1997). *Comparing Legal Cultures.* Aldershot: Darmouth.

Nelken, D. & Feest, J. (eds.) (2001). *Adapting Legal Cultures.* Oxford: Hart.

Nellen, H. (2007). *Hugo de Groot: Een leven in strijd om de vrede, 1583–1645.* Amsterdam: Balans.

Neunhaus, R. (2000). A New Order of Religious Freedom. In S.M. Feldman (ed.), *Law and Religion: A Critical Anthology* (pp. 89–95). New York: New York University Press.

Nève, P.L. (1992). *Driewerf Rome: Enkele opmerkingen over de (voor)geschiedenis van de grond- of mensenrechten.* Inaugural address at the Catholic University Brabant (now University of Tilburg).

Neville, R.C. (1996). *The Truth of Broken Symbols.* Albany, NY: State University of New York Press.

—— (2002). *Religion in Late Modernity.* Albany, NY: State University of New York Press.

—— (ed.) (2001). *Religious Truth: A Volume in the Comparative Religious Ideas Project*. Albany, NY: State University of New York Press.

Nicholson, H. (2005). A Correlational Model of Comparative Theology. *The Journal of Religion, 85*(2), 191–213.

Nieuwenhuis, A. (2007). Tussen godslastering en bedreiging. *Justitiële Verkenningen: Religie en grondrechten, 33*(1), 95–108.

Nollkaemper, A. (2007). *Kern van het internationaal publiek recht*. The Hague: Boom.

Norris, P. & Inglehart, R. (2005). *Sacred and Secular: Religions and Politics Worldwide*. Cambridge: Cambridge University Press.

Nothelle-Wildfeuer, U. (1991). *Duplex Ordo Cognitionis: Zur systematischen Grundlegung einer katholieken Soziallehre im Anspruch von Philosophie und Theologie*. Paderborn: Schöningh.

Nussbaum, M.C. (1996). *The Therapy of Desire: Theory and Practice in Hellenistic Ethics*. Princeton, NJ: Princeton University Press.

—— (2006). *Frontiers of Justice: Disability, Nationality, Species Membership*. Cambridge, MA: Belknap/Harvard University Press.

—— (2008). *Liberty of Conscience: In Defence of America's Tradition of Religious Equality*. New York: Basic.

O'Collins, G. (2007). *Jesus Our Redeemer: A Christian Approach to Salvation*. Oxford: Oxford University Press.

O'Donnell, J. (2005). *Augustine*. New York: Ecco.

Oakley, F. (2005). *Natural Law, Laws Of Nature, Natural Rights: Continuity And Discontinuity In The History Of Ideas*. London/New York: Continuum.

Oberman, H. (2003). *The Two Reformations: The Journey from the Last Days to the New World*. New Haven, CT: Yale University Press.

OECD (Organisation for Economic Co-Operation and Development) (2006). *International Migration Outlook*. Paris.

Ogden, S.M. (1992). *Is there Only One True Religion or are there Many?* Dallas, TX: Southern Methodist University Press.

Olupona, J. & Sulayman, S. (eds.) (1993). *Religious Plurality in Africa: Essays in Honour of John S. Mbiti*. Berlin: De Gruyter.

Paden, W.E. (2004). Comparative Religion and the Whitehouse Project: Connections and Compatibilities? *Method and Theory in the Study of Religion, 16*(3), 256–265.

Pagden, A. (ed.) (1987). *The Languages of Political Theory in Early-Modern Europe*. Cambridge: Cambridge University Press.

Pals, D.L. (1996). *Seven Theories of Religion*. New York: Oxford University Press.

Pannenberg, W. (1973). *Wissenschaftstheorie und Theologie*. Frankfurt: Suhrkamp.

Parekh, B. (2008). *European Liberalism and 'the Muslim Question'*. Amsterdam: Amsterdam University Press.

Parsons, T. (1959). *Structure and Process in Modern Societies*. New York: Free Press.

—— (1965). An Outline of the Social System. In T. Parsons et al. (eds.), *Theories of Societies* (pp. 30–79). New York: Free Press.

—— (1965). Differentiation and Variation. Introduction. In T. Parsons et al. (eds.), *Theories of Societies*. New York: Free Press.

Parsons, T. et al. (eds.) (1965). *Theories of Societies*. New York: Free Press.

Peeters, J.B.L.M. (1984). *Burgers en modernisering: Historisch-sociologisch onderzoek naar burgerlijke groeperingen in het moderniseringsproces van de Duitse Bond 1810–1870*. Dissertation Catholic University Nijmegen (now Radboud University).

Pelikan, J. (2004). *Interpreting the Bible and the Constitution*. New Haven, CT: Yale University Press.

Perry, M. (2000). Liberal Democracy and Religious Morality. In S.M. Feldman (ed.), *Law and Religion: A Critical Anthology* (pp. 115–148). New York: New York University Press.

Pessers, D. (1999). *Liefde, solidariteit and recht: Een interdisciplinair onderzoek naar het wederkerigheidsbeginsel*. Amsterdam: University of Amsterdam Press.

Peters, J. et al. (eds.) (1993). *Kerk op de helling*. Kampen: Kok.

Pettersson, T. (2009). Religious Commitment and Socio-Political Orientations: Different Patterns of Compartimentalisation among Muslims and Christians? In J. Haynes (ed.), *Routledge Handbook of Religion and Politics* (pp. 246–269). New York: Routledge.

Pew Global Attitudes Project (released July 14, 2005). *Islamic Extremism: Common Concern for Muslim and Western Publics*. Available at: www.pewglobal.org/reports.

Pew Global Attitudes Project. (Released June 22, 2006). *The Great Divide: How Westerners and Muslims View Each Other*. Available at: www.pewglobal.org/reports.

Phalet, K. & Ter Wal, J. (eds.) (2004a). *Moslim in Nederland. De publieke discussie over de islam in Nederland: Een analyse van artikelen in de Volkskrant 1998–2002*. The Hague: SCP.

—— (eds.) (2004b). *Moslim in Nederland. Diversiteit en verandering in religieuze betrokkenheid: Turken en Marokkanen in Nederland 1998–2002*. The Hague: SCP.

Pieterse, H.J.C. (ed.) (2001). *Desmond Tutu's Message*. Leiden: Brill.

Pihlström, S. (2005). A Pragmatic Critique of Three Kinds of Religious Naturalism. *Method and Theory in the Study of Religion 17*(3), 177–218.

Pinker, S. (1999). *How the Mind Works*. New York: Norton.

—— (2002). *The Blank Slate: The Modern Denial of Human Nature*. New York: Viking.

Platvoet, J.G. (1999). Contexts, Concepts and Contests: Towards a Pragmatics of Defining 'Religion'. In J.G. Platvoet & A.L. Molendijk (eds.), *The Pragmatics of Defining Religion: Contexts, Concepts and Contests* (pp. 463–516). Leiden: Brill.

—— (2002). Pillars, Pluralism and Secularization: A Social History of Dutch Science of Religions. In G.A. Wiegers & J.G. Platvoet (eds.), *Modern Societies & the Science of Religions: Studies in Honour of Lammert Leertouwer*. Leiden/Boston, MA: Brill.

Platvoet, J.G. & Molendijk, A.L. (eds.) (1999). *The Pragmatics of Defining Religion: Contexts, Concepts and Contests*. Leiden: Brill.

Pleijter, A.R.J. (2006). *Typen en logica van kwalitatieve inhoudsanalyse in de communicatiewetenschap*. Dissertation Radboud University Nijmegen. Ubbergen: Tandem Felix.

Pollak, D. (2003). *Säkularisierung: Ein moderner Mythos?* Tübingen: Mohr Siebeck.

Popper, K.R. & Eccles, J.C. (2003). *The Self and Its Brain: An Argument for Interactionism*. London/New York: Routledge.

Porter, J. (2009). Does the Natural Law Provide a Universally Valid Morality? In L. Cunningham (ed.), *Intractable Disputes about the Natural Law. Alaisdair MacIntyre and Critics*. Notre Dame: University of Notre Dame Press, 53–95.

Porter, R. (2000). *Enlightenment: Britain and the Creation of the Modern World*. London: Penguin.

Potz, R. (October 7, 2002). *Freie Kriche in der Freien Gesellschaft: Vor 50 jahren und heute: Referat bei der Enquete '50 jahre Mariazeller Manifest*. Available at: http://www.laienrat.at/_alte_website/potz.htm.

Poulat, E. (2003). *Notre laïcité publique: La France est une république laïque (Constitution de 1946 et 1958)*. Paris: Berg.

Pressemitteilung Senatsverwaltung für Justiz. (March 11, 2008). Berlin.

Price, D. (1999). *Islamic Political Culture, Democracy and Human Rights: A Comparative Study*. Westport, CT: Praeger.

Pufendorf, S. (1990). *Samuel Pufendorf's On the natural state of men*. The 1678 Latin edition and English translation. Translated, annotated, and introduced by M. Seidler. Lewinston, NY: Mellen.

—— *De jure naturae et gentium*.

Pyysiäinen, I. (2004). Intuitive and Explicit in Religious Thought. *Journal of Cognition and Culture, 4*(1), 123–150.

Racine, J. (1981). Rerum Novarum en zijn ontstaansgeschiedenis. *Communio, 6,* 127–138.

Ragin, C.C. (1989). *The Comparative Method: Moving Beyond Qualitative and Quantitative Strategies.* Berkeley, CA: University of California Press.

—— (1991). *Issues and alternatives in comparative social research.* Leiden: Brill.

—— (1994). *Constructing Social Research: The Unity and Diversity of Method.* Thousand Oaks, CA: Pine Forge.

Räikkä, J. (ed.) (1996). *Do We Need Minority Rights.* The Hague: Nijhoff.

Rappaport, R. (2000). *Ritual and Religion in the Making of Humanity.* Cambridge: Cambridge University Press.

Ratzinger, J. (1964). Naturrecht, Evangelium und Ideologie in der katholische Soziallehre: Katholische Erwägungen zum Thema. In K. Von Bismarck & W. Dirks (eds.), *Christlicher Glaube Und Ideologie* (pp. 24–30). Stuttgart: Kreuz.

Ratzinger, J. & Habermas, J. (2006). *Dialectics of Secularisation: On Reason and Religion.* San Francisco, CA: Ignatius.

Rautenbach, C. & Goolam, N. (eds.) (2002). *Introduction to Legal Pluralism in South Africa.* Butterworth: Durban.

Ravitch, F. (1999). *School Prayer and Discrimination.* Boston, MA: Northeastern University Press.

—— (2000). A Crack in the Wall: Pluralism, Prayer, and Pain in the Public Schools. In S.M. Feldman (ed.), *Law and Religion: A Critical Anthology* (pp. 296–314). New York: New York University Press.

Rawls, J. (1971). *A Theory of Justice.* Cambridge, MA: Belknap/Harvard University Press.

—— (1993). *Political Liberalism.* New York: Columbia University Press.

—— (1997). The Idea of Public Reasons Revisited. *The University of Chicago Law Review, 64*(3), 765–807.

—— (2005). *Political Liberalism* (expanded edition). New York: Columbia University Press.

—— (2009). *A Brief Inquiry into the Meaning of Sin and Faith: With "On My Religion"* (edited by Th. Nagel). Cambridge, MA: Harvard University Press.

Reder, M. (2008). Wie weit können Glaube und Vernunft unterscheiden werden. In M. Reder & J. Schmidt (eds.), *Ein Bewusstsein von dem, was fehlt: Eine Diskussion mit Jürgen Habermas* (pp. 51–68). Frankfurt: Suhrkamp.

Reder, M. & Schmidt, J. (eds.) (2008). *Ein Bewusstsein von dem, was fehlt: Eine Diskussion mit Jürgen Habermas.* Frankfurt: Suhrkamp.

Renteln, A.D. (1990). *International Human Rights: Universalism versus Relativism.* London: Sage.

Richey, R. & Jones, D. (eds.) (1974). *American Civil Religion.* New York: Harper & Row.

Ricoeur, P. (1974). *The Conflict of Interpretations: Essays in Hermeneutics.* Evanston, IL: Northwestern University Press.

—— (1988). *Time and Narrative 3.* Chicago, IL: University of Chicago Press.

—— (1992). *Oneself as Another.* Chicago, IL: University of Chicago Press.

—— (1994). Entre philosophie et théologie: la Règle d'Or en question. In *Lectures 3: Aux frontières de la philosophie.* Paris: Seuil.

—— (1994). *Lectures 3: Aux frontières de la philosophie.* Paris: Seuil.

—— (1995). *Figuring the Sacred: Religion, Narrative, and Imagination.* Minneapolis, MN: Fortress.

—— (1995). *La critique et la conviction.* Paris: Calmann-Lévy.

—— (1995). *Le Juste.* Paris: Seuil.

—— (1995). *Réflexion faite: Autobiographie intellectuelle.* Paris: Esprit.

—— (2000). *La memoire, l'histoire, l'oubli*. Paris: Seuil.

—— (2005). *The Course of Recognition*. Cambridge, MA: Harvard University Press.

Rikhof, H. & Vosman, F. (eds.) (1994). *De schittering van de waarheid: Theologische reflecties bij de encycliek Veritatis Splendor*. Zoetermeer: Meinema.

Ritter, W.E. (1954). *Charles Darwin and the Golden Rule*. New York: Storm.

Robbers, G. (ed.) (1996). *State and Church in the European Union*. Baden-Baden: Nomos.

Roberts, T. (2005). Rhetorics of Ideology and Criticism in the Study of Religion. *The Journal of Religion, 85*(3), 367–389.

Rogier, L.J. (1964). *De kerk in het tijdperk van Verlichting en Revolutie. Deel VII*. Hilversum/Antwerpen: Brand.

Rogier, L.J., et al. (eds.) (1964). *Geschiedenis van de kerk in tien delen*. Hilversum/Antwerpen: Brand.

Rohe, M. (2007). *Muslim Minorities and the Law in Europe*. New Delhi: Global Productions.

—— (2009). *Das Islamische Recht: Geschichte und Gegenwart*. München: Beck.

Roof, W.C. (1993). *Religion in the Nineties*. Newbury Park, CA: Sage.

—— (1998). *Americans and Religions in the Twenty-First Century*. Thousand Oaks, CA: Sage.

—— (1999). *Spiritual Marketplace: Baby Boomers and the Remaking of American Religion*. Princeton, NJ: Princeton University Press.

Roof, W.C. & MacKinney, M. (1987). *American Mainline Religion: Its Changing Shape and Future*. New Brunswick, NJ: Rutgers University Press.

Rousseau, J.-J. *Du contrat social: Ou Principes du droit politique*.

—— *Emile ou de l'éducation*.

Roy, O. (2004). *Globalized Islam: The Search for a New Ummah*. New York: Columbia University Press.

Ruiter, S. & De Graaf, N. (2006). National Context, Relgiosity and Volunteering: Results from 53 Countries. *American Sociological Review, 71*, 191–210.

Ryba, T. (2000). Manifestation. In W. Braun & R.T. McCutcheon (eds.), *Guide to the Study of Religion* (pp. 168–189). London/New York: Cassell.

Saberschinsky, A. (2002). *Die Begründung universeller Menschenrechte*. Paderborn: Schönigh.

Safran, W. (1981). Civil Liberties in Democracies: Constitutional Norms, Practices, and Problems of Comparison In V.P. Nanda et al. (eds.), *Global Human Rights: Public Policies, Comparative Measures, and Ngo Strategies* (pp. 195–210). Boulder, CO: Westview.

Sakwa, M. (2008). *Bible and Poverty in Kenya: An Emporical Exploration*. Leiden: Brill.

Satlow, M.L. (2005). Disappearing Categories: Using Categories in the Study of Religion. *Method and Theory in the Study of Religion, 17*(4), 287–298.

—— (2006). Defining Judaism: Accounting for "Religions" in the Study of Religion. *Journal of the American Academy of Religion, 74*(4), 837–860.

Scheepers, P., Gijsberts, M. & Hello, E. (2002). Religiosity and Prejudice Against Ethnic Movements in Europe: Cross-National Tests On a Controversial Relationship. *Review of Religious Research, 43*(2), 242–265.

Schilbrack, K. (2005). Religion, Models of, and Reality: Are We Through with Geertz? *Journal of American Academy of Religion, 73*(2), 429–452.

Schilderman, H. (2005). *Religion as a Profession*. Leiden: Brill.

—— (2007). Liturgical Studies from a Ritual Studies Perspective. In H. Schilderman (ed.), *Discourse in Ritual Studies* (pp. 3–34). Leiden: Brill.

—— (2009). *Wat is er geestelijk aan de geestelijke zorg?* Inaugural address at the Radboud University Nijmegen.

—— (ed.) (2007). *Discourse in Ritual Studies*. Leiden: Brill.

Schillebeeckx, E. (1952). *De Sacramentele heilseconomie.* Bilthoven: Nelissen.
—— (1958). Theologie. In *Theologisch Woordenboek. Deel III* (pp. 4485–4542).
—— (1963). *Christus, Sacrament van de godsontmoering.* Bilthoven: Nelissen.
—— (1964). *Openbaring en theologie.* Bilthoven: Nelissen.
—— (1966). *Wereld en kerk.* Bilthoven: Nelissen.
—— (1968). Het nieuwe Godsbeeld, secularisatie en politiek. *Tijdschrift voor Theologie, 8*(1), 44–66.
—— (1968). Theologische draagwijdte van het magisteriële spreken over sociaal-politieke kwesties. *Concilium 4*(6), 21–40.
—— (1968). *Zending van de kerk.* Bilthoven: Nelissen.
—— (1973). *Stilte gevuld met parabels.* Brugge: Emmaus/Desclée De Brouwer.
—— (1974). *Jesus: Het verhaal van een levende.* Bloemendaal: Nelissen.
—— (1977). *Gerechtigheid en liefde, genade en bevrijding.* Bloemendaal: Nelissen.
—— (1979). *Jesus: An Experiment in Christology.* New York: Seabury.
—— (1989). *Mensen als verhaal van God.* Baarn: Nelissen.
—— (1994). Breuken in de christelijke dogma's. In E. Schillebeeckx et al. (eds.), *Breuklijnen: grenservaringen en zoektochten: 14 essays voor Ted Schoof bij zijn afscheid van de theologische faculteit Nijmegen* (pp. 15–50). Baarn: Nelissen.
—— (1994). *Theologisch Testament: Notarieel nog niet verleden.* Baarn: Nelissen.
Schillebeeckx, E. et al. (eds.), *Breuklijnen: grenservaringen en zoektochten: 14 essays voor Ted Schoof bij zijn afscheid van de theologische faculteit Nijmegen.* Baarn: Nelissen.
Schjoedt, U. (2009). The Religious Brain: A General Introduction to the Experimental Neuroscience of Religion. *Method and Theory in the Study of Religion, 21*(3), 310–339.
Schluchter, W. (1979). *Die Entwicklung des okzidentalen Rationalismus eine Analyse von Max Webers Gesellschaftsgeschichte.* Tübingen: Siebeck.
Schmale, W. (1995). Das Naturrecht in Frankreich zwischen Prärevolution und Terror. In O. Dann & D. Klippel (eds.), *Naturrecht, Spätaufklarung, Revolution* (pp. 5–22). Berlin: Meiner.
Schoonenberg, P. (1968). Historiciteit en interpretatie van het dogma. *Tijdschrift voor Theologie, 8*(3), 294–311.
—— (1971). *The Christ: A Study of the God-Man Relationship in the Whole of Creation and in Jesus Christ.* New York: Herder.
Schwöbel, C. (2006). Recovering Human Dignity. In R.K. Soulen & L. Woodhead (eds.), *God and Human Dignity* (pp. 44–58). Grand Rapids, MI: Eerdmans.
Searle, J. (1969). *Speech Acts: An Essay in the Philosophy of Language.* Cambridge, MA: Harvard University Press.
—— (2001). *Rationality in Action.* Cambridge, MA: MIT Press.
Segundo, J. (1982). *Faith and Ideologies.* New York: Orbis.
Seibel, W. (1968). De mens als beeld Gods. In J. Feiner & M. Löhrer (eds.), *Mysterium Salutis: Dogmatiek in Heilshistorisch Perspectief 7* (pp. 266–281). Hilversum: Brand.
Sekhar Sripada, C. (2008). Nativism and Moral Psychology: Three Models of the Innate Structure That Shapes the Contents of Moral Norms. In W. Sinnott-Armstrong (ed.), *Moral Psychology. Vol. I. The Evolution of Morality: Adaptations and Innateness* (pp. 319–343). Cambridge, MA: MIT Press.
Selling, J. (1994). The Context and the Arguments of Veritatis Splendor. In J. Selling & J. Jans (eds.), *The Splendor of Accuracy* (pp. 11–70). Kampen: Kok.
Selling, J. & Jans, J. (eds.) (1994). *The Splendor of Accuracy.* Kampen: Kok.
Sen, A. (1988). *On Ethics and Economics.* Oxford: Oxford University Press.
—— (2006). *Identity and Violence: The Illusion of Destiny.* New York: Norton.
—— (2009). *The Idea of Justice.* Cambridge: Harvard University Press.

Sengers, E. (2003). *"Al zijn wij katholiek wij zijn Nederlanders"*: *Opkomst en verval van katholieke kerk in Nederland sinds 1795 vanuit rational-choice perspectief*. Delft: Eburon.

—— (2003). "You Don't Have To Be a Saint or a Practicing Catholic…" Higher Tension and Lower Attachement in the Dutch Catholic Church since 1970. *Antonianum; periodicum trimestre*. *78*(3), 529–545.

Shachar, A. (2001). *Multicultural Jurisdictions: Cultural Differences and Women's Rights*. Cambridge: Cambridge University Press.

Shadid, W. & Van Koningsveld, S. (eds.) (2002). *Religious Freedom and the Neutrality of the State: The Position of Islam in the European Union*. Leuven: Peeters.

Shah, N. (2006). Women's Human Rights in the Koran. *Human Rights Quaterly*, *28*(4), 868–903.

Shorter, A. & Onyancha, E. (1997). *Secularism in Africa: A Case Study: Nairobi City*. Nairobi, Kenya: Paulines.

Siesling, M. (2006). *Multiculturaliteit en verdediging in strafzaken*. Dissertation University Utrecht.

Simmel, G. (1890). *Über soziale Differentierung*. Leipzig: Dunkcer & Humblot.

Singer, P. (1990). *Animal Liberation*. New York: Random.

Sinnott-Armstrong, W. (ed.) (2008). *Moral Psychology. Vol. I. The Evolution of Morality: Adaptations and Innateness*. Cambridge, MA: MIT Press.

Sjöborg, A. (2010). Religion and Moral Issues – A Private Matter? Young Swedes on the Freedom of Religion and the Freedom of Moral Speech. In J.A. van der Ven (ed.), *Tensions within and between Religions and Human Rights*. Leiden: Brill (to be published).

Slone, D.J. (2004). *Theological Incorrectness: Why Religious People Believe What They Shouldn't*. Oxford/New York: Oxford University Press.

Smart, N. (1996). *Dimensions of the Sacred: An Anatomy of the World's Beliefs*. Berkeley, CA: University of California Press.

Smith, A. (1767). *The Theory of Moral Sentiments*. 3rd edition, London.

Smith, J.Z. (1982). *Imagining Religion: From Babylon to Jonestown*. Chicago, IL: University of Chicago Press.

—— (1987). *To Take Place: Towards Theory in Ritual*. Chicago, IL: University of Chicago Press.

—— (1990). *Drudgery Divine: On the Comparison of Early Christianities and the Religions of Late Antiquity*. London: School of Oriental and African Studies, University of London.

—— (1998). Religion, Religions, Religious. In M.C. Taylor (ed.), *Critical Terms for Religious Studies* (pp. 269–284). Chicago, IL: University of Chicago Press.

—— (2004). *Relating Religion: Essays in the Study of Religion*. Chicago, IL: University of Chicago Press.

Smith, M. (2000). The Polemics of Biblical Monotheism. In T.L. Hettema & A. van der Kooij (eds.), *Religious Polemics in Context: Papers Presented to the Second International Conference of the Leiden Institute for the Study of Religions (Lisor), Leiden, 27–28 April, 2000*. Assen: Van Gorcum.

Sobrino, J. (1989). *The True Church and the Poor*. New York: Orbis.

SOCON. (2002). *Religion in Dutch Society: Documentation of National Surveys on Religious and Secular Attitudes in 2000*. Amsterdam: Steinmetz Archive.

Sonnberger, K. (1996). *Die Leitung der Pfarrgemeinde: Eine empirisch-theologische Studie unter niederländischen und deutschen Katholiken*. Kampen/Weinheim: Kok/ Deutscher Studien.

Sorkin, D. (2008). *The Religious Enlightenment: Protestants, Jews, and Catholics from London to Vienna*. Princeton, NJ: Princeton University Press.

Soulen, R.K. & Woodhead, L. (eds.) (2006). *God and Human Dignity*. Grand Rapids, MI: Eerdmans.

Spiro, M. (1978). Religion: Problems and Definition and Explanation. In M. Banton (ed.), *Anthropological Approaches to the Study of Religion* (pp. 85–126). London: Tavistock.

Spranger, E. (1964). *Der Sinn der Voraussetzungslosigkeit in den Geisteswissenschaften.* Heidelberg: Quelle & Meyer.

Stark, R. (1999). Secularization, R.I.P. *Sociology of Religion, 60*(3), 249–274.

Stark, R. & Bainbridge, W.S. (1987). *A Theory of Religion.* New York: Lang.

Stark, R. & Finke, R. (2000). *Acts of Faith: Explaining the Human Side of Religion.* Berkeley, CA: University of California Press.

Stark, R. & Glock, C. (1968). *American Piety: The Nature of Religious Commitment.* Berkeley, CA: University of California Press.

Stephan, A. (1999). *Emergenz: Von der Unvorhersagbarkeit zur Selbstorganisation.* Dresden: Dresden University Press.

Sterkens, C. & Van der Ven, J.A. (eds.) (2002). *De functie van de kerk in de hedendaagse maatschappij.* Averbode: Altiora.

Steunebrink, G. (2004). *Natural Law and Human Rights in an Intercultural Context.* Reader of the Faculty of Philosophy, 2004–2005, Radboud University Nijmegen.

Stout, J. (2004). *Democracy and Tradition.* Princeton, NJ: Princeton University Press.

Streib, H. (ed.) (2007). *Religion Inside and Outside: Traditional Institutions.* Leiden: Brill.

Suárez, F. (1944). *Selections from Three Works of Francisco Suárez.* Oxford: Clarendon.

Sullivan, W. (2005). *The Impossibility of Religious Freedom.* Princeton, NJ: Princeton University Press.

Syse, H. (2007). *Natural Law, Religion, and Rights.* South Bend, IN: St. Augustine.

Taylor, C. (1989). *Sources of the Self: The Making of the Modern Identity.* Cambridge, MA: Harvard University Press.

—— (1994). The Politics of Recognition. In A. Gutmann et al. (eds.), *Multiculturalism: Examining the Politics of Recognition* (pp. 25–74). Princeton, NJ: Princeton University Press.

—— (1999). Modes of Secularism. In R. Bhargava (ed.), *Secularism and its Critics.* Delhi: Oxford University Press.

—— (2007). *A Secular Age.* Cambridge, MA: Harvard University Press.

Taylor, M.C. (ed.) (1998). *Critical Terms for Religious Studies.* Chicago, IL: University of Chicago Press.

Taylor, P.M. (2005). *Freedom of Religion.* Cambridge: Cambridge University Press.

Tayob, A. (2004). Race, Ideology and Islam in Contemporary South Africa. In R. Feener (ed.), *Islam in World Cultures: Comparative Perspectives* (pp. 253–282). Santa Barbara, CA: ABC-Clio.

Teeple, G. (2005). *The Riddle of Human Rights.* Aurora: Garamond.

Temperman, J. (2007). The Neutral State: Optional or Necessary? A Triangular Analysis of State-Religion Relationships, Democratisation and Human Rights Compliance. *Religion and Human Rights, 3,* 269–303.

Ten Berge, G. (ed.) (1992). *Voor God en vaderland: Nationalisme en religie.* Kampen: Kok.

Ten Voorde, J. (2007). *Cultuur als verweer.* Dissertation Erasmus University Rotterdam.

Terpstra, M. (2008). Politieke orde en het alleenrecht op duiding: Het 'rijk van de vrijheid' in de vroegmoderne filosofie. In S. van Erp (ed.), *Vrijheid in verdeeldheid: Geschiedenis en actualiteit van religieuze tolerantie* (pp. 125–151). Nijmegen: Valkhof.

—— (2009). De politieke theologie van een potestas indirecta. In M. Becker (ed.), *Christelijk Sociaal Denken: Traditie, Actualiteit, Kritiek* (pp. 197–222). Budel: Damon.

Teule, H. (2008). *Les Assyro-Chaldéens: Chrétiens d'Irak, d'Iran et de Turquie.* Turnhout: Brepols.

Thagard, P. (2005). The Emotional Coherence of Religion. *Journal of Cognition and Culture,* 5(1/2), 58–74.

Thangaraj, M. (1999). Evangelism sans Proselytism. In J. Witte & R.C. Martin (eds.), *Sharing the Book: Religious Perspectives on the Rights and Wrongs of Proselytism.* Maryknoll, NY: Orbis.

Therborn, G. (2004). *Between Sex and Power: Family in the World.* London: Routledge.

Theunissen, M. (1965). *Der Andere: Studien zur Sozialontologie der Gegenwart.* Berlin: De Gruyter.

Tierney, B. (1996). Religious Rights: An Historical Perspective. In J. Witte & J.D. van der Vyver (eds.), *Religious Human Rights in Global Perspective: Legal Perspectives.* The Hague: Nijhoff.

Timaeus, I. & Reynar, A. (1998). Polygynists and Their Wives in Sub-Saharan Africa. *Population Studies,* 52(2), 145–162.

Tombs, D. (2002). *Latin American Liberation Theology.* Leiden: Brill.

Tooby, J., Cosmides, L. (2005). Conceptual Foundations of Evolutionary Psychology. In D.M. Buss (ed.), *The Handbook of Evolutionary Psychology.* Hoboken, NJ: Wiley.

Torfs, R. (1999). The Roman Catholic Church and Secular Legal Culture in the Twentieth Century. *Studia Historiae Ecclesiasticae,* 25(1), 1–20.

—— (2001). Church and State: Relevant Issues for a Democratic State. *Nederduitse Gereformeerde Teologiese Tydskrif,* 42(1&2), 147–157.

—— (2002). Relationship between the State and Religious Groups. In J.-F. Flauss (ed.), *La protection internationale de la liberté religieuse: International Protection of Religious Freedom* (pp. 131–152). Brussel: Bruylant.

Tracy, D. (1986). *The Analogical Imagination: Christian Theology and the Culture of Pluralism.* New York: Crossroad.

Troeltsch, E. (1911). Das stoisch-christlische Naturrecht und das moderne profane Naturrecht. *Historische Zeitschrift,* 106, 237–267.

—— (1912–1925). *Gesammelte Schriften.* Vol. I–IV. Tübingen: Mohr.

Tüchle, H. (1966). *Geschiedenis van de kerk. Deel VI. De kerk tijdens de Contrareformati.* Hilversum/Antwerpen: Brand.

Tuck, R. (1987). The 'Modern' Theory of Natural Law In A. Pagden (ed.), *The Languages of Political Theory in Early-Modern Europe* (pp. 99–119). Cambridge: Cambridge University Press.

—— (1999). *The Rights of War and Peace: Political Thought and the International Order from Grotius to Kant.* Oxford: Oxford University Press.

—— (2002). *Natural Rights Theories: Their Origin and Development.* Cambridge: Cambridge University Press.

Ultee, W.C. (2004). *De Nijmeegse sociologie de laatste tien jaar en nu.* Available at: http://www.socsci.kun.nl/maw/sociologie/ultee/.

UN (United Nations) (1948). Adoption of the Declaration(c). *United Nations yearboook summary 1948.*

UNDP (United Nations Development Programme) (2006). *Arab Human Development Report 2005: Towards the Rise of Women in the Arab World.* New York.

—— (December 2008). *Arab Human Development Report.*

Utz, A.-F. & Groner, J.-F. (1954). *Aufbau und Entfaltung des gesellschaftlichen Lebens: Soziale Summe Pius XII.* Freiburg: Paulusverlag.

Valcke, L. & Galibois, R. (1994). *Le périple intellectuel de Jean Pic de la Mirandole.* Sainte-Foy: Presses de l'Université Laval, Centre d'études de la Renaissance.

Valkenberg, P. (2003). God ademt overal: Mogelijkheden en grenzen van een trinitaire theologie van de godsdiensten. *Tijdschrift voor Theologie,* 43(2), 166–190.

—— (2006). *Sharing Lights on the Way to God: Muslim-Christian Dialogue and Theology in the Context of Abrahamic Partnership*. Amsterdam: Rodopi.

Van Bijsterveld, S. (2008). *Overheid en godsdienst: Herijking van een onderlinge relatie*. Nijmegen: Wolf.

—— (1996). State and Church in the Netherlands. In G. Robbers (ed.), *State and Church in the European Union* (pp. 209–228). Baden-Baden: Nomos.

Van de Vyver, F. & Leung, K. (1997). *Methods and Data Analysis for Cross Cultural Research*. London: Sage.

Van den Berg, J. (1958). *Dubieuze liefde in de omgang met het kind: Over de late gevolgen van te veel of te weinig moederlijke toewijding tijdens de jeugd*. Nijkerk: Callenbach.

Van den Bergh, G. (1992). Legal Pluralism in Roman Law. In C. Varga (ed.), *Comparative Legal Cultures*. Aldershot: Dartmouth.

Van der Burg, W. (1991). *Het democratisch perspectief*. Arnhem: Gouda Quint.

Van der Meer, T. (2009). *States of Freely Associating Citizens: Cross-National Studies into the Impact of State Institutions on Social, Civil, and Political Participation*. Groningen/Utrecht/Nijmegen: ICS Dissertation Series.

Van der Ven, J.A. (1987). *Religie tussen oost en west: Een reis door India*. Baarn: Ambo.

—— (1993). Katholieke kerk en katholicisme in historisch en empirisch perspectief. In J. Peters et al. (eds.), *Kerk op de helling* (pp. 62–92). Kampen: Kok.

—— (1993). *Practical Theology: An Empirical Approach*. Leuven: Peeters.

—— (1993). Die Qualitative Inhaltsanalyse. In J.A. van der Ven & H.-G. Ziebertz (eds.), *Paradigmenentwicklung in der praktischen Theologie* (pp. 113–164). Weinheim: Deutscher Studien.

—— (1994). *Entwurf einer empirischen Theologie*. Kampen/Leuven: Kok/Peeters.

—— (1994). Religious Values in the Interreligious Dialogue. *Religion & Theology, 1*(3), 244–260.

—— (1996). *Ecclesiology in Context*. Grand Rapids, MI: Eerdmans.

—— (1998). *Formation of the Moral Self*. Grand Rapids, MI: Eerdmans.

—— (1998). *God Reinvented? A Theological Search in Texts and Tables*. Leiden/Boston, MA: Brill.

—— (2001). The Moral and Religious Self as a Process. In H.J.C.Pieterse (ed.), *Desmond Tutu's Message* (pp. 74–95). Leiden: Brill.

—— (2001). *Van een faculteit der theologie naar een faculteit der religiewetenschappen*. Kampen: Kampen Theological University.

—— (2002). Godsdienstvrijheid als ecclesiologisch paradigma. In C. Sterkens & J.A. van der Ven (eds.), *De functie van de kerk in de hedendaagse maatschappij* (pp. 17–64). Averbode: Altiora.

—— (2002). Theologie beoefenen in een faculteit van religiewetenschappen. *Tijdschrift voor Theologie, 42*(3), 244–267.

—— (2004). An Empirical or an Normative Approach to Practical-Theological Research? A False Dilemma. In J.A. van der Ven & M. Scherer-Rath (eds.), *Normativity and Empirical Research in Theology*. Leiden/Boston, MA: Brill.

—— (2004). Towards a Comparative Empirical Theology of Mindful Action. In C.A.M. Hermans & M.E. Moore (eds.), *Hermeneutics and Empirical Research in Practical Theology: The Contribution of Empirical Theology by Johannes A. van der Ven* (pp. 331–388). Leiden/Boston, MA: Brill.

—— (2005). De relatie van theologie en religiewetenschap in een vergelijkende wetenschapsbeoefening. *Tijdschrift voor Theologie, 45*(2), 119–137.

—— (2005). Unterwegs zu einer vergleichenden empirischen Theologie. In D. Nauer et al. (ed.), *Praktische Theologie* (pp. 244–254). Stuttgart: Kohlhammer.

—— (2006). A Chapter in Public Theology from the Perspective of Human Rights: Interreligious Interaction and Dialogue in an Intercivilizational Context. *Journal of Religion, 86*(3), 412–441.

—— (2007). Religion, Morality and Ritual in Evolutionary Perspective. In H. Schilderman (ed.), *Discourse in Ritual Studies* (pp. 35–80). Leiden: Brill.

—— (2007). Three Paradigms for the Study of Religion. In H. Streib (ed.), *Religion Inside and Outside Traditional Institutions* (pp. 7–34). Leiden: Brill.

—— (2009). Legitimering van mensenrechten vanuit natuur of politiek? In M. Becker (ed.), *Christelijk sociaal denken: Traditie, actualiteit, kritiek* (pp. 244–277). Budel: Damon.

—— (ed.) (2010 in print). *Tensions within and between Religions and Human Rights.* Leiden: Brill.

Van der Ven, J.A. & Anthony, F.-V. (2008). Impact of Religion on Social Integration from an Empirical Civil Rights Perspective. Part One. *Salesianum, 70*(2), 317–338.

—— (2008). Impact of Religion on Social Integration from an Empirical Civil Rights Perspective. Part Two. *Salesianum, 70*(2), 463–489.

Van der Ven, J.A. & Biemans, B. (1994). *Religie in fragmenten.* Kampen: Kok.

Van der Ven, J.A. & Scherer-Rath, M. (eds.) (2004). *Normativity and Empirical Research in Theology.* Leiden/Boston, MA: Brill.

Van der Ven, J.A. & Ziebertz, H.-G. (eds.) (1993). *Paradigmenentwicklung in der praktischen Theologie.* Weinheim: Deutscher Studien.

Van der Ven, J.A., Dreyer, J.S. & Pieterse, H.J.C. (2004). *Is there a God of Human Rights? The Complex Relationship between Human Rights and Religion: A South African Case.* Leiden/Boston, MA: Brill.

Van der Wall, E. (1995–1996). Geen natie van atheïsten: Pieter Paulus (1753–1796) over godsdienst en mensenrechten. *Jaarboek van de Maatschappij der Nederlandse Letterkunde te Leiden,* 45–62.

—— (2007)*The Enemy Within: Religion, Science, and Modernism.* Wassenaar: NIAS.

Van der Wall, E. & Wessels, L. (eds.) (2008). *Een veelzijdige verstandhouding: Religie en Verlichting in Nederland 1650–1850.* Nijmegen: Vantilt.

Van Eck, C. (2004). *Door bloed gezuiverd: Eerwraak bij Turken in Nederland.* Dissertation University of Amsterdam.

Van Erp, S. (ed.) (2008). *Vrijheid in verdeeldheid: Geschiedenis en actualiteit van religieuze tolerantie.* Nijmegen: Valkhof.

Van Gestel, C. (1956). *Kerk en sociale orde.* Leuven: Universitas.

Van Kalmthout, A. et al. (2006). *European Foreign Prisoners Project.* Tilburg: Tilburg University Press.

Van Kempen, P.H. (2008). *Repressie door mensenrechten: Over positieve verplichtingen tot aanwending van strafrecht ter bescherming van fundamentele rechten.* Inaugural address at the Radboud University Nijmegen. Nijmegen: Wolf.

Van Koningsveld, P. (1996). *De Islam.* Utrecht: De Ploeg.

Van Maanen, N. & Hoekema, A. (2001). Gemeenschappen komen tot hun recht: Zeven kernproblemen bij onderzoek naar recht, multiculturaliteit en sociale cohesie. In P. Cliteur & V. van den Eeckhout (eds.), *Multiculturalisme, cultuurrelativisme en sociale cohesie* (pp. 217–260). The Hague: Boom.

Van Nieuwenhove, J. & Klein Goldewijk, B. Mensenrechten als rechten van God: Een profiel van kardinaal Paolo Evaristo Arns. *Tijdschrift voor Theologie, 34*(1), 3–23.

Van Sas, N. & Te Velde, H. (eds.) (1998). *De eeuw van de grondwet: Grondwet en politiek in Nederland, 1798–1917.* Deventer: Kluwer.

Van Stokkum, B. (2007). Negatieve beeldvorming over moslims: Intolerantie of cultuurconflict? *Justitiële Verkenningen: Religie en grondrechten, 33*(1), 50–69.

Van Tubergen, F. (2004). *The Integration of Immigrants in Cross-national Perspective.* Utrecht: ICS.

Varga, C. (ed.) (1992). *Comparative Legal Cultures.* Aldershot: Dartmouth.

Vasquez, M. (2005). Book Review of A. Chestnut's Competitive Spirits: Latin America's New Religious Economy (2003). *Journal of the American Academy of Religion, 73*(2), 524–528.

Vattimo, G. (2003). *Het woord is geest geworden.* Kampen: Agora.
—— (2006). Het tijdperk van de interpretatie. In S. Zabala (ed.), *De toekomst van de religie.* Kampen: Klement.
Velema, W. (1998). Revolutie, republiek en constitutie. In N. van Sas & H. te Velde (eds.), *De eeuw van de grondwet, grondwet en politiek in Nederland, 1798–1917* (pp. 20–45). Deventer: Kluwer.
Vereniging van Nederlandse Gemeenten (The Association of Dutch Municipalities) (2009). *Tweeluik religie en publiek domein.* The Hague.
Vermeer, P. (2010). Religious socialization and church attendance in the Netherlands between 1983 and 2007: A Panel Study. *Social Compass* 2010 (to be published).
Verschuren, P. (1991). *Structurele modellen tussen theorie en praktijk.* Utrecht: Aula.
Verweij, J. (1998). *Secularisering tussen feit en fictie: Een internationaal vergelijkend onderzoek naar determinanten van religieuze betrokkenheid.* Tilburg: Tilburg University Press.
Vestdijk-van der Hoeven, A. (1991). *Religieus recht en minderheden.* Arnhem: Gouda Quint.
Vial, T. (2006). How Does the Cognitive Science of Religion Stack Up as a Big Theory, a La Hume? *Method and Theory in the Study of Religion, 18*(4), 351–371.
Vidal, M. (1994). Die Enzyklika 'Veritatis Splendor' und der Weltkatechismus: Die Restauration des Neuthomismus in der katholischen Morallehre. In D. Mieth (ed.), *Moraltheologie im Abseits? Antwort auf die Enzyklika 'Veritatis Splendor'* (pp. 244–270). Questiones Disputatae 153, Freiburg: Herder.
Visser, A. et al. (eds.) (1983). *Rollen: Persoonlijke en sociale invloeden op het gedrag.* Meppel: Boom.
Vögele, W. (2000). *Menschenwürde zwischen Recht und Theologie: Begründungen von Menschenrechten in der Perspektive öffentblicher Theologie.* Gütersloh: Kaiser.
Von Bismarck, K. & Dirks, W. (eds.) (1964). *Christlicher Glaube und Ideologie.* Stuttgart: Kreuz.
Vonken, A. (1998). De multiculturele samenleving en de bemiddelende rol van het internationaal privaatrecht en de mensenrechten. In P. Cliteur et al. (eds.), *Sociale cohesie en het recht* (pp. 97–167). Leiden: Meijers Instituut.
Vosman, F. (2006). Het 'samenwonen' van katholieke theologie en godsdienstwetenschap. *Tijdschrift voor Theologie, 46*(2), 101–112.
Vroom, H.M. (1989). *Religions and the Truth: Philosophical Reflections and Perspectives.* Grand Rapids, MI: Eerdmans.
VVD. (Volkspartij voor Vrijheid en Democratie or People's Party for Freedom and Democracy) (2005). *Om de Vrijheid: Partijprogramma.*
—— (2006). *Voor een samenleving met ambitie.*
Waaijman, K. (2000). *Spiritualiteit: Vormen, grondslagen, methoden.* Gent/Kampen: Carmelitana/Kok.
Waardenburg, J.J. (1986). *Religionen und Religion: Systematische Einführung in die Religionswissenschaft.* Berlin/New York: De Gruyter.
Wagner, H. (1995). Erlösung, IV. Systematisch-theologisch. In *Lexikon für Theologie und Kirche 3* (pp. 808–812). Freiburg: Herder.
Waldenfels, H. (ed.) (1978). *...denn Ich bin bei Euch.* Zürich: Benziger.
Walter, P. (2000). Schriftsinne. In *Lexikon für Theologie und Kirche 9* (pp. 268–269). Freiburg: Herder.
Waltz, S. *Who wrote the Universal Declaration of Human Rights?* Available at: http://www.america.gov/st/hr-english/2008/November/20081119135247xjyrrep6.023806e-02.html.
Ward, K. (2003). A Guide for the Perplexed. In T.W. Bartel (ed.), *Comparative Theology: Essays for Keith Ward* (pp. 190–198). London: Society for Promoting Christian Knowledge.

Warnink, H. (2001). Ecclesiastical Tribunals, Procedures, Judicial Bodies and the State. *Nederduitse Gereformeerde Teologiese Tydskrif 42*(1&2), 158–166.

Wattles, J. (1996). *The Golden Rule*. New York: Oxford University Press.

Weber, B. (1999). *Ijob in Lateinamerika: Deutung und Bewältigung von Leid in der Theologie der Befreiung*. Mainz: Grünewald.

Weber, M. (1978). *Gesammelte Aufsätze zur Religionssoziologie*. Tübingen: Mohr.

—— (1980). *Wirtschaft und Geselschaft*. Tübingen: Mohr.

Weitzman, S. et al. (2008). Book Review Symposium of J.Z. Smith's To Take Place in the Light of New Historicism. *Journal of the American Academy of Religion 76*(3), 766–805.

Welchamn, L. (ed.) (2004). *Women's Rights and Islamic Family Law*. London: Zed.

Weller, P. (2005). *The Rights of Minorities in Europe*. Oxford: Oxford University Press.

Welten, V. (1991). De surfer op de golven: Psychologie van cultuur en gedrag. In A. Felling & J. Peters (eds.), *Cultuur en sociale wetenschappen. Beschouwingen en empirische studies* (pp. 31–50). Nijmegen: ITS.

—— (1992). *Greep op cultuur: Een cultuurpsychologische bijdrage aan het minderhedendebat*. Nijmegen: Catholic University Nijmegen (now Radboud University).

Wentzel van Huyssteen, J. (1999). *The Shaping of Rationality: Toward Interdisciplinarity in Theology and Science*. Grand Rapids, MI: Eerdmans.

Wessels, L. (2008). De beste aller werelden? Politiek, religie en een weerbarstige samenleving, Nederland 1650–1850. In E. van der Wall & L. Wessels (eds.), *Een veelzijdige verstandhouding: Religie en Verlichting in Nederland 1650–1850*. Nijmegen: Vantilt.

Westerhof, G. (1994). *Statements and Stories*. Dissertation Radboud University Nijmegen.

Westerman, P. (1997). *The Disintegration of Natural Law Theory: Aquinas to Finnis*. Leiden: Brill.

Wiebe, D. (2002). Promise and Disappointment: Recent Developments in the Academic Study of Religion in the USA. In G.A. Wiegers & J.G. Platvoet (eds.), *Modern Societies & the Science of Religions: Studies in Honour of Lammert Leertouwer*. Leiden/Boston, MA: Brill.

Wiegers, G.A. (2005). Afscheid van het methodologisch agnosticisme? *Tijdschrift voor Theologie, 45*(2), 153–167.

Wiegers, G.A. & Platvoet, J.G. (eds.) (2002). *Modern Societies & the Science of Religions: Studies in Honour of Lammert Leertouwer*. Leiden/Boston, MA: Brill.

Wierzbicka, A. (1992). *Semantics, Culture, and Cognition: Universal Human Concepts in Culture-Specific Configurations*. New York/Oxford: Oxford University Press.

—— (1997). *Understanding Cultures through Their Key Words: English, Russian, Polish, German, and Japanese*. New York/Oxford: Oxford University Press.

Willems, B. & Weier, R. (1972). Soteriologie: Von der Reformation bis zur Gegenwart. In *Handbuch der Dogmengeschichte. Vol. III. 2c*. Freiburg: Herder.

Willett, C. (ed.) (1998). *Theorizing Multiculturalism: A Guide to the Current Debate*. Malden, MA: Blackwell.

Williams, D. (ed.) (1999). *The Enlightenment*. Cambridge: Cambridge University Press.

Williams, R. (1644). *The Bloudy Tenent of Persecution for Cause of Conscience*. London.

Williamson, O. (2000). The New Institutional Economics: Taking Stock, Looking Ahead. *Journal of Economic Literature, 38*, 595–613.

Wils, J.-P. (2006). Würde. In M. Düwell et al. (eds.), *Handbuch Ethik* (pp. 558–559). Stuttgart: Metzler.

—— (2006). *Nachsicht: Studien zu einer ethisch-hermeneutischen Basiskategorie*. Paderborn: Schöningh.

Wilson, F. (1928). *The Origins of the League Covenant*. London: Hogarth Press.

Wilson, R.A. & Keil, F.C. (eds.) (1999). *The MIT Encyclopedia of the Cognitive Sciences*. Cambridge, MA: MIT Press.

—— (eds.) (2000). *Explanation and Cognition*. Cambridge, MA: MIT Press.

Wingert, L. & Günther, K. (eds.) (2001). *Die Öffentlichkeit der Vernunft and die Vernunft der Öffentlichkeit. Festschrift für Jürgen Habermas*. Frankfurt: Suhrkamp.

Winston, R.M.L. (2003). *The Human Mind: And how to Make the Most of It*. London/New York: Bantam.

Winter, S.L. (2001). *A Clearing in the Forest: Law, Life, and Mind*. Chicago, IL: University of Chicago Press.

Wissink, J. (1994). Hanteert Veritatis Splendor een neothomisme? In H. Rikhof & F. Vosman (eds.), *De schittering van de waarheid: Theologische reflecties bij de encycliek Veritatis Splendor* (pp. 78–95). Zoetermeer: Meinema.

Witte, J. (2000). *Religion and the American Constitutional Experiment: Essential Rights and Liberties*. Boulder, CO: Westview.

—— (2007). *The Reformation of Rights*. Cambridge: Cambridge University Press.

—— (2008). Prophets, Priests, and Kings: John Milton and the Reformation of Rights and Liberties in England. *Emory Law Journal, 57*(6), 1527–1604.

Witte, J. & Alexander, F. (eds.) (2006). *The Teaching of Modern Christianity on Law, Politics, and Human Nature. Vol. II*. New York: Columbia University Press.

Witte, J. & Martin, R.C. (eds.) (1999). *Sharing the Book: Religious Perspectives on the Rights and Wrongs of Proselytism*. Maryknoll, NY: Orbis.

Witte, J. & Van der Vyver, J.D. (eds.) (1996). *Religious Human Rights in Global Perspective: Legal Perspectives*. The Hague: Nijhoff.

Witteveen, W.J. *Over het retorisch waarheidsstreven van een democratie*. Unpublished article.

Wokler, R. (1995). Rights. In J. Yolton et al. (eds.), *The Blackwell Companion to the Enlightenment*. Oxford: Blackwell.

Wolfe, D. (1973). The advent of Hobbes. In J. Milton (ed.), *Complete Prose Works of John Milton. Vol. IV*. (pp. 30–37). New Haven, CT: Yale University Press.

Wolff, C. (1754). *Grundsätze des Natur: Und Völkerrechts worin alle Verbindlichkeiten und alle Rechte aus de Natur des Menschen in einem beständigen Zusammenhang hergeleitet werden*. Halle.

Woodhead, L. et al. (eds.) (2001). *Peter Berger and the Study of Religion*. London/New York: Routledge.

WRR (Wetenschappelijke Raad voor het regeringsbeleid – Scientific Council for Government Policy) (2006). *Dynamism In Islamic Activism. Reference Points For Democratization And Human Rights, Amsterdam 2006*. Amsterdam: Amsterdam University Press.

—— (2006). *Lerende overheid*. Amsterdam: Amsterdam University Press.

Wulff, D.M. (1997). *Psychology of Religion: Classic and Contemporary Views*. New York: Wiley.

Wuthe, P. (2002). *Für Menschenrechte und Religionsfreiheit in Europa: Die Politik des Heiligen Stuhls in der KSZE/OSZE*. Stuttgart: Kohlhammer.

Yacoub, J. (2007). The Dignity of the Individual and of Peoples: The Contribution of Mesopotamia and of Syriac Heritage. *Diogenes, 54*(3), 19–37.

Yates, J.F. & Estin, P.A. (2002). Decision Making. In W. Bechtel & G. Graham (eds.), *A Companion to Cognitive Science* (pp. 186–196). Oxford: Blackwell.

Yolton, J. et al. (eds.) (1995). *The Blackwell Companion to the Enlightenment*. London: Blackwell.

Zabala, S. (ed.) (2006). *De toekomst van de religie*. Kampen: Klement.

Zaccaria, F. (2009). *Participation and Beliefs in Popular Religiosity: An Empirical-Theological Exploration among Catholic Parishioners in the Diocese of Conversano-Monopoli in Italy*. Dissertation Radboud University Nijmegen.

Zagorin, P. (2003). *How the Idea of Religious Tolerance Came to the West*. Princeton, NJ: Princeton University Press.

Zemni, S. (2002). Islam: European Identity and the Limits of Multiculturalism. In W. Shadid & S. van Koningsveld (eds.), *Religious Freedom and the Neutrality of the State: The Position of Islam in the European Union* (pp. 158–173). Leuven: Peeters.

Zenger, E. (1999). Priesterschrift. In *Lexikon für Theologie und Kirche 8* (pp. 578–580). Freiburg: Herder.

—— (2000). Schöpfung. In *Lexikon für Theologie und Kirche 9* (pp. 217–220). Freiburg: Herder.

Zuidgeest, P. (2001). *The Absence of God: Exploring the Christian Tradition in a Situation of Mourning*. Leiden/Boston, MA: Brill.

INDEX OF SUBJECTS

INDEX OF NAMES